# GUI Programming with Python and Kivy

KAMIL PAKULA

ISBN: 9798774802111

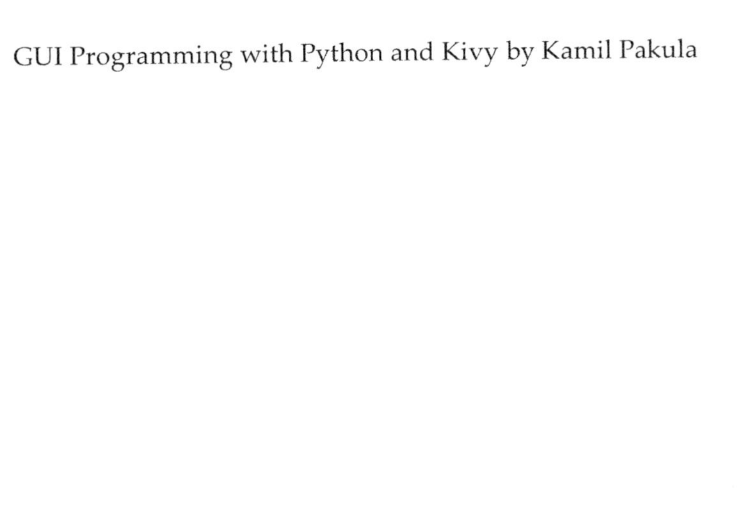

To my beloved wife Barbara and sons Chris and Adam

# CONTENTS

# Preface

This book covers all the basics that you need to start programming GUI applications with Python and Kivy. I assume you have no prior knowledge of the Kivy library, but you should have at least some basic knowledge of the Python programming language, including object-oriented programming with Python because this is the paradigm we'll be using a lot in this book.

After a short introduction to the Kivy library, we'll start by setting up our working environment. Then we'll be talking about some basic stuff like Kivy widgets and Kivy layouts. After we cover the basics, we'll start our Slugrace project - a racing game that we will be developing throughout the whole book. You will find the code and assets that you need for the project (images and sound files) on Github at:

**https://github.com/prospero-apps/python/tree/master/GUI%20Programming%20with%20Python%20and%20Kivy%20BOOK**

The code in the Github repository is arranged by chapter. If you want it to work, don't forget to copy the **assets** folder to your project folder and in the final chapters of the book first copy the **screenshots** folder to the **assets** folder before copying the latter to your project folder.

We'll start the project by building all the screens that we need. After that we'll talk about graphics in Kivy and we'll add graphics to the Slugrace project. Next, we'll introduce Kivy ids and properties and we'll see how particular parts of the project can reference and communicate with one another. With all that in place we'll start programming the game logic. After that we'll add animations, background music and sound effects to the project and finally we'll deploy the app to Windows.

This book is pretty comprehensive and the space available is limited. As I didn't want to give up on any content that I had intended to put into the book, I laid out some of it in two columns to save space. This is also true about some portions of the code, so the portion of the code in the right column should immediately follow the portion in the left column. I used dotted lines there to make it easier for you to see how the code is indented. I also used such lines when the code spans more than one page.

As far as the code is concerned, there's one more convention I'd like you to be aware of. Portions of code that were modified or added are in bold type and highlighted in yellow so that you can immediately see the changes. Portions of code that did not change but I'd like to draw your attention to are also in bold type, but they are highlighted in gray.

I hope you'll have at least as much fun reading the book as I had writing it.

# Part I

# Let's Get Started

In this part of the book we'll set up our working environment and write a basic Kivy app using Python and the Kivy language.

# Chapter 1 - Introduction

In this book we will learn the basics of Kivy, which is a Python library used for GUI applications of any kind, also games. Throughout the book we'll be making a Kivy app, which actually is a game.

Before we start working on the Slugrace project, let's have a look at what it's all about. Slugrace is a game that combines a typical GUI application with animated graphics. This is a game for 1-4 players who put their bets on 4 slugs. Let's have a look at the final version of the app now.

## Settings Screen

When you start the game you first see the Settings screen:

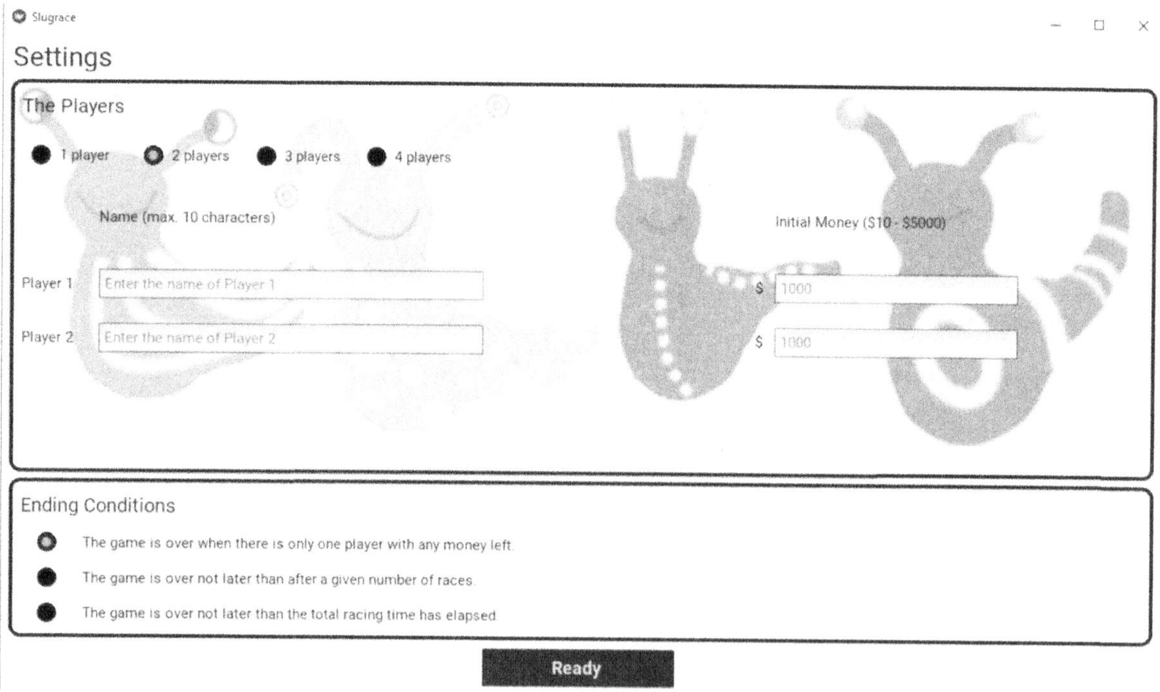


Here you can set the following:

- the number of players (1-4),
- the names of the players (if you don't, the generic names Player 1, Player 2, etc. will be used),
- the initial money each player has when the game begins (there's $1000 by default),
- the ending conditions (when the game should end – there are three options).

## Race Screen

When you press the Ready button, you move on to the main screen of the game, the Race screen:

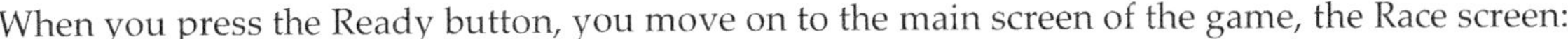

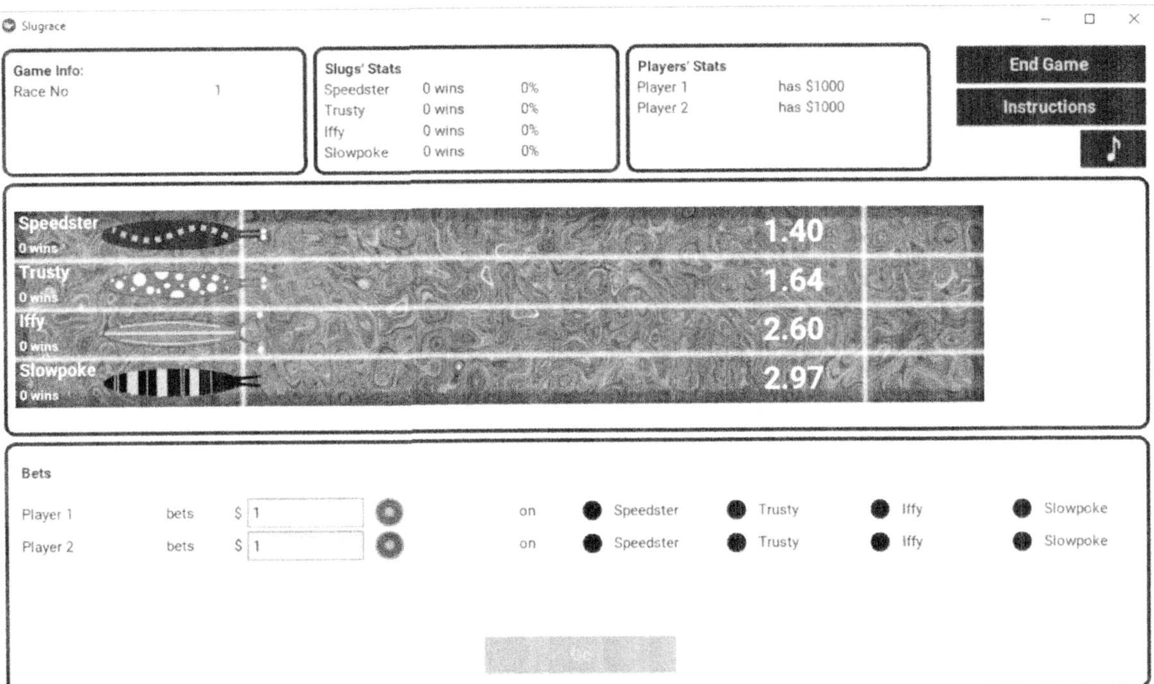


This screen is divided into several panels:

- the Game Info panel where you can see the number of the race, the time of the game, etc.,
- the Slugs' Stats panel where you can see the names of the slugs and their wins (as both absolute values and percentages),
- the Players' Stats panel where you can see the names of the players and their current amount of money,
- the main game panel in the middle with the racetrack where the slugs run (you can also see the odds here, which are updated after each race),
- the Bets panel where you can place your bets by typing them in or using a slider.

## Bets and Results

In the lower part of the Race screen you can see the Bets panel. The Bets panel is actually a separate screen, which we will discuss in due time. When you press the Go button and when the race is over, this panel changes to the Results panel, which also is a separate screen, where you can see the results:

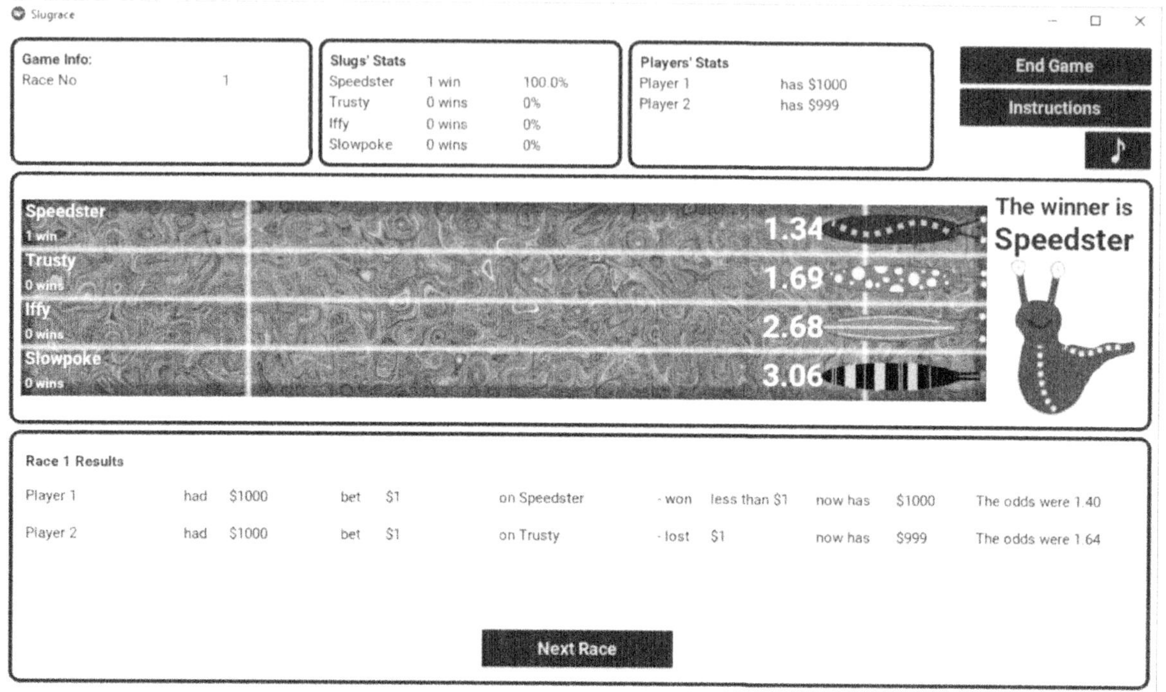


Here you can see how much money each player had before the last race, how much they bet and on which slug and whether they won or lost and how much.

When you press the Next Race button in the Results panel, it'll change back to the Bets panel.

In the upper right corner there are three buttons:

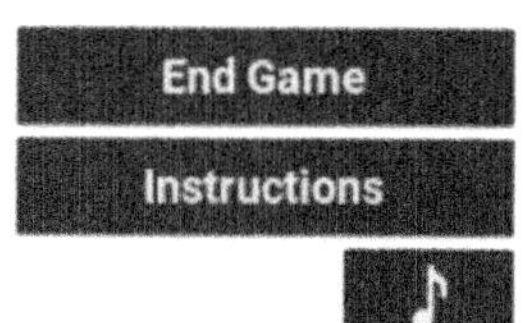


- End Game – this lets you end the game at any time and takes you to the Game Over screen,

- Instructions – this takes you to the Instructions screen,

- Sound – it toggles the sound on or off.

So, this is the application we're going to create using Kivy with Python. But before we start working on our project, in the next couple chapters we'll have a look at the basics of Kivy. We're going to start the project as soon as possible, but first we have to learn what a basic Kivy program looks like. But even before that we have to set up our environment, so in the next chapter I'll show you how to install Kivy (or rather where to find information on how to do it on all possible operating systems) and how to use Visual Studio Code with the Python and Kivy extensions. This is my code editor of choice. If you have other preferences, you can use any editor or IDE you like.

# Chapter 2 – Setting Up the Environment

Now that we know what we want to do, the question is how to do it and what software to use. We will need a minimum of two things: Kivy itself and a text editor or IDE where we can edit our code. This is all we need for our environment setup.

## The Kivy Library

Let's start the environment setup with Kivy. Kivy is an open source Python library for rapid development of applications that make use of innovative user interfaces, such as multi-touch apps. Well, this is what you can read on kivy.org, not my words. So, I suggest you visit the page and read more about Kivy if you're interested and when you are done with that, we can install Kivy.

This may change, but at the time of writing this is what it looks like when you go to the Help tab. Now click on Getting Started with Kivy:

Documentation

- Getting started with Kivy
- API Reference
- Or see the Wiki for a list of projects, snippets and more

Community Support

- Report a bug or request a feature in our issue tracker
- Ask your questions on the Kivy users forums
- Or send an email to kivy-users@googlegroups.com

You can also try to contact us on Discord (online chat), but make sure to read the Discord rules before joining. Connect to Discord

In the sidebar select Installing Kivy. Next, select your platform and installation method for further instructions. There are a couple of options, depending on whether you use Conda or not for example. I wouldn't be able to explain to you how to install Kivy in a better way than you will find it explained on their website. The information you can find there is up-to-date, which is also important. Therefore, I'm going to stop here and you can now take your time to read the instructions and install Kivy on your platform.

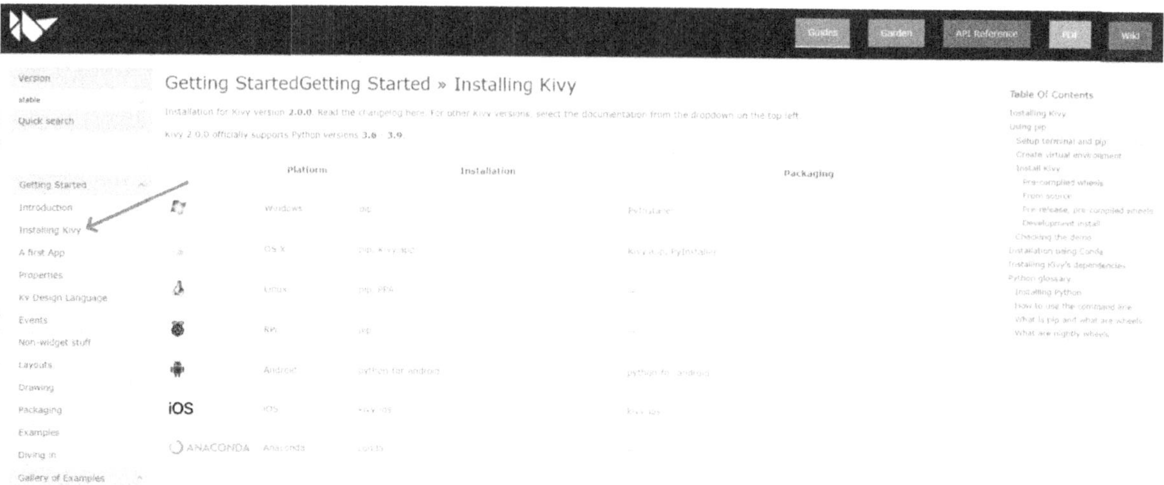


For the next steps I assume you have Kivy installed on your computer.

## The Visual Studio Code Text Editor

The next thing we're going to need for our environment setup is a text editor. I'm going to use Visual Studio Code. You can use any editor or IDE of your choice, but if you want to follow along and use the exact same editor as I do, just feel free to download and install it from their website (code.visualstudio.com). The installation is pretty straightforward.

Now, with Visual Studio Code installed, open it. Your Visual Studio Code editor will probably have a dark theme, with which it comes as a default. I like the light theme better, so I changed it in the settings, but you can choose any theme you like.

## Extensions

In order to use Kivy and Python in Visual Studio Code, we'll need at least the Python extension. Click on Extensions (A) and then type in 'python' in the search box (B). Then install the first extension in the results list by clicking on the Install button (C). You can't see the button here on the screenshot because the extension is already installed on my machine.

Generally, this would be it. You're ready to start coding. But there is one more extension worth installing.

When you work with Kivy you can either write

everything in Python code or you can separate the logic of your application from its graphical interface. Separation of concerns is the way to go in most cases (except for the most trivial ones) and as our application is not going to be extremely trivial, let's go for it. We'll be using Python for the logic and for the layout we'll be using the Kivy language. It's a special language designed for Kivy that makes the separation very clear and simple. Don't be afraid, it's not difficult and you will appreciate going this way very soon.

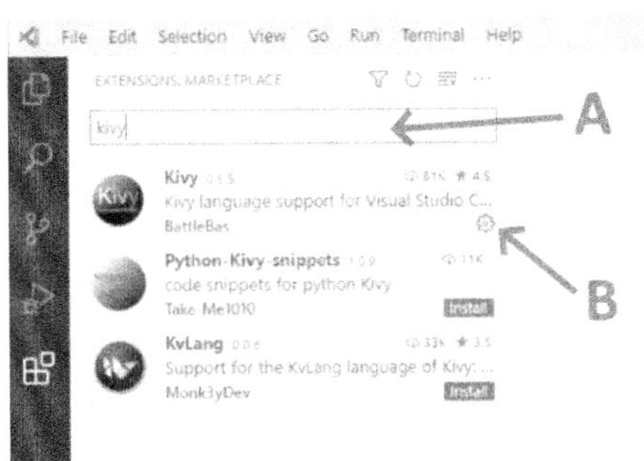


There is an extension in Visual Studio Code that you can install. It will turn on syntax coloring and generally make your work with the Kivy language easier and more pleasurable. Just like before, type in the name of the extension ('kivy') in the search box (A) and install the extension by clicking on the Install button (B). As before, I already have the extension installed on my computer.

Now, with the Kivy library and the text editor installed, along with the two extensions, you're ready to get your feet wet by writing some simple Kivy code. In the next chapter we'll be writing a basic Kivy application.

# Chapter 3 - A Basic Kivy App in Python

Most programming tutorials, regardless of which programming language you're learning, begin with a Hello World program where you can see what a program in that particular language must contain to work at all. Let's do the same here. What does a Hello World program in Kivy look like? Here's our basic Kivy app.

## Hello World - A Basic Kivy App

We're going to write a basic Kivy app that will display the Hello World text. In Kivy, like in many other GUI libraries and frameworks, static text is usually displayed in a label. In Kivy we call simple GUI elements like labels, buttons, sliders, check boxes, etc. widgets, although widgets don't have to be simple at all and you can create your own widgets, which we are going to do later.

## Create a Folder

Anyway, our program is going to display the text Hello World in a label. Before we write the code, let's create a folder where we will save it. I'm going to create a new folder for each chapter in this course so that you can see how far you are in the project at each stage of the course, but you can just create one folder and work on it throughout the whole course.

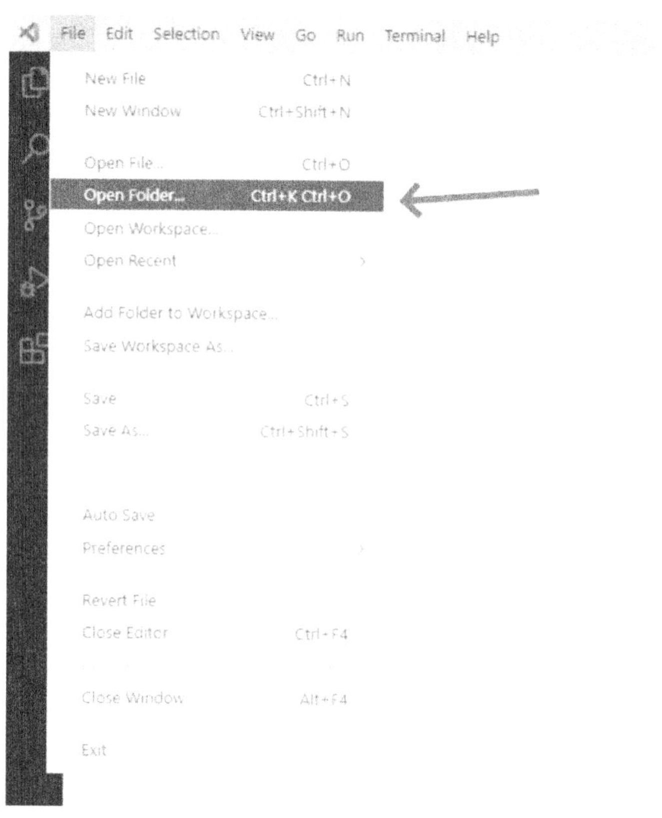


I will name the folders **slugrace3** for chapter 3, **slugrace4** for chapter 4 and so on. So, in **slugrace20** you will find the code as it was at the end of chapter 20 for example.

You can grab the code from Github (**https://github.com/prospero-apps/python**).

So, find a location for your project and create a new folder. You can name your folder whatever you like, but a name like **slugrace** seems fine to me. Whenever we need access to a path with the folder, make sure to use the name you just set. I will name my folder for this chapter **slugrace3**.

Then open the folder in your editor or IDE. In Visual Studio Code you can do it in the File menu.

My text editor of choice is Visual Studio Code and if I explain how to do something in the future, it should be understood as how to do it in Visual Studio Code. If you are using a different editor, you surely know it quite well and will have no problem doing the same stuff in it.

## Create a New File

When you open your folder, you need a file to write the code to. This is going to be a regular Python file, so with the extension **.py**. You can name your file whatever you like, I'll name mine **test.py**. This file is not going to be part of the project, I'll just use it to test stuff, hence the name.

Here's how you can create the file: When you hover your mouse over the name of your folder, a menu with a couple icons will appear. The first icon is the one you should click to create a new file.

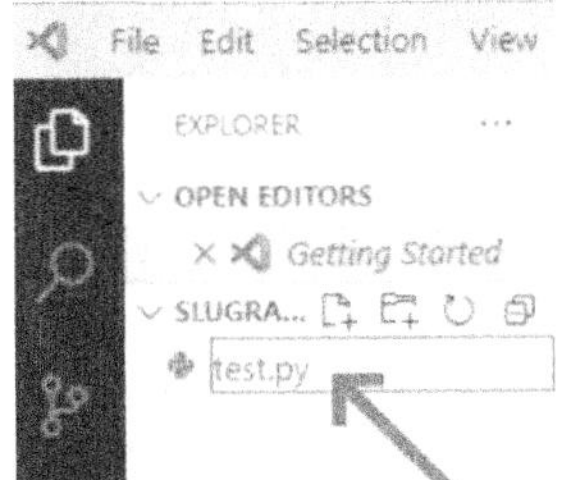


All you have to do is type in the name of the file.

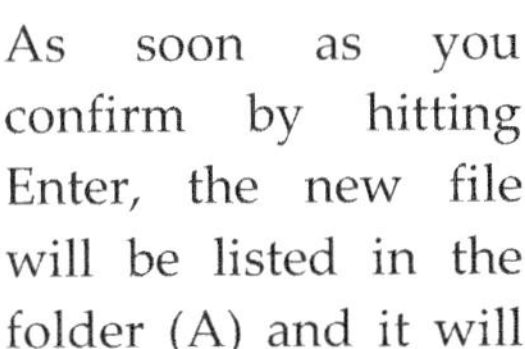

As soon as you confirm by hitting Enter, the new file will be listed in the folder (A) and it will open automatically in a new tab (B). This is how we will be adding new files in the future.

## The Hello World App

Now we are ready to write our code. As there are going to be quite a lot of code files in our project, I will always put the name of the file at the very top. This way it will be much easier for you to keep track of which part of the project you are currently working on.

Also, to make the code more understandable, I will be adding comments, sometimes lots of comments. In the source files most of the comments added in previous chapters will be removed so that the code remains readable. If you forget what a particular piece of code is supposed to do, you can always go back to the previous chapters and see the comments.

Anyway, here's the code:

```
# File name: test.py

# We need the App class. Our application is going to inherit from it.
from kivy.app import App

# We also need the Label widget.
from kivy.uix.label import Label

# Here comes the application class. It inherits from App.
class TestApp(App):
    def build(self):
        # A label is returned.
        return Label(text='Hello World!')

# And this is where we actually run the app.
if __name__ == '__main__':
    TestApp().run()
```

## Run Your Kivy App

This is a basic Kivy application. Now we are ready to run it. There are several ways you can do it. We'll have a look at the most obvious ones in the next chapter. For now, let's just use the Run Python File in Terminal button in the upper right corner (A). Here's what we get when we do that: the application window shows up with our application running in it (B) and a terminal opens at the bottom with the Kivy log (C):

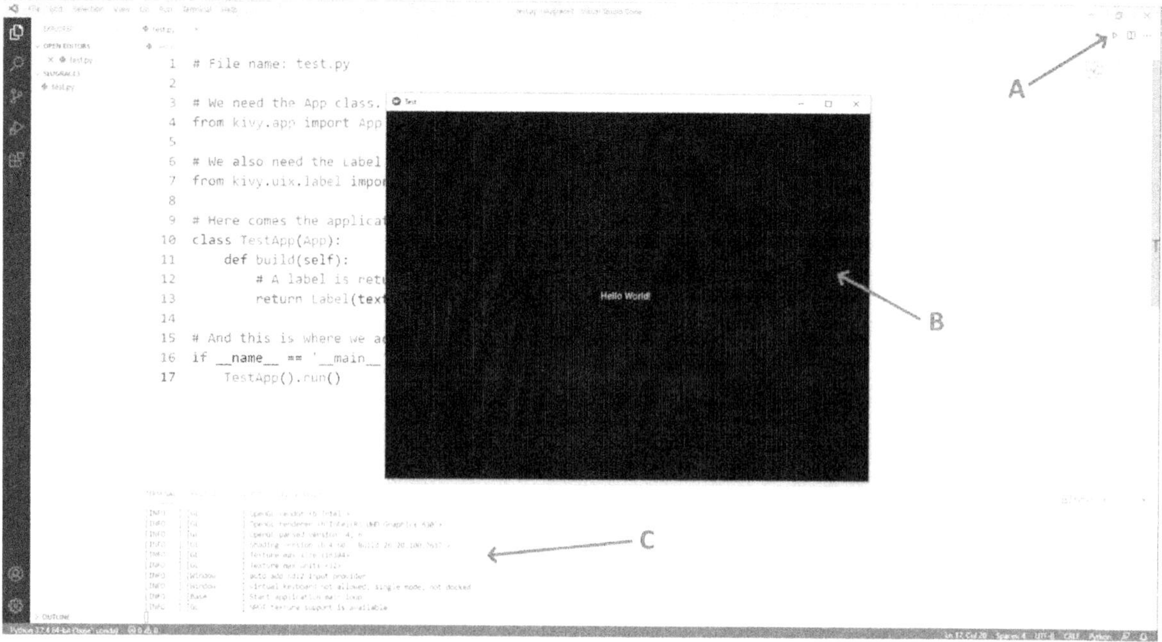

# Chapter 4 - Running Your Kivy App

In the previous chapter we wrote a basic Kivy app, using just Python. Here's the **test.py** file we created, this time without comments so that you can see how long it actually is:

```
# File name: test.py

from kivy.app import App
from kivy.uix.label import Label

class TestApp(App):
    def build(self):
        return Label(text='Hello World!')

if __name__ == '__main__':
    TestApp().run()
```

## How To Run Your App

We used the Run Python File in Terminal button in the upper right corner to run the app. I also mentioned it wasn't the only way to run your app. So, let's see how we can run a Kivy app in Visual Studio Code.

**1) the Run Python File in Terminal button**

The first way to run the app is by pressing the Run Python File in Terminal button in the upper right corner. This is what we already did.

**2) Run the Kivy App Without Debugging in the Run menu**

You can also go to the Run menu and select the second option, Run Without Debugging.

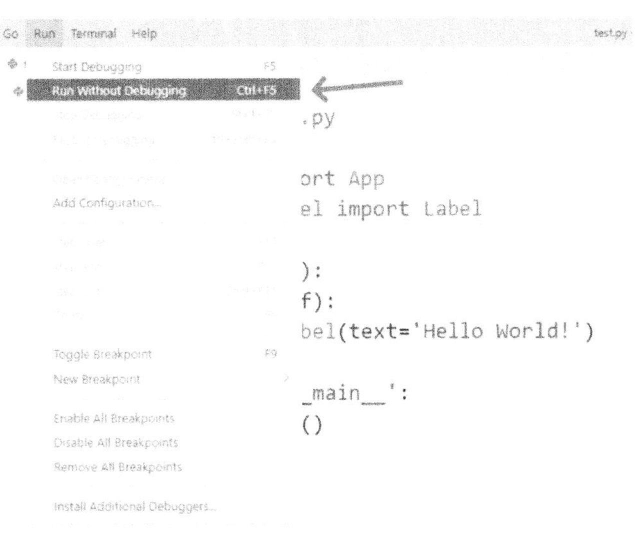

### 3) Start Debugging option in the Run menu

There is also the Start Debugging option in the Run menu. You can choose it and then select a Debug Configuration. Go ahead and select the first option, Python File.

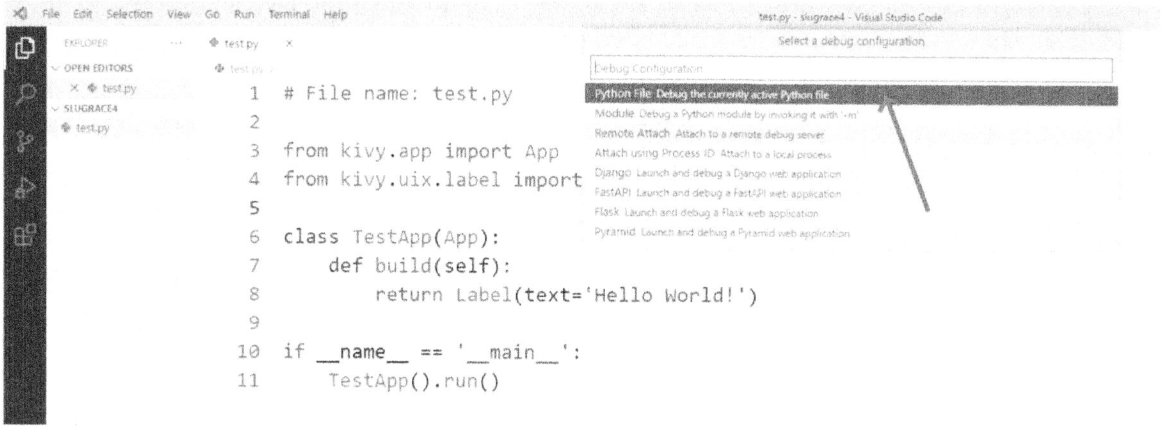

```
# File name: test.py

from kivy.app import App
from kivy.uix.label import

class TestApp(App):
    def build(self):
        return Label(text='Hello World!')

if __name__ == '__main__':
    TestApp().run()
```

### 4) Hotkeys

For the previous two options you can use hotkeys:

- **F5** to start debugging
- **Ctrl + F5** to run without debugging

### 5) Context menu

You can also right-click anywhere in the editor tab where the code of your file is and select Run Python File in Terminal.

```
# File name: test.py

from kivy.app import App
from kivy.uix.label import

class TestApp(App):
    def build(self):
        return Label(text='

if __name__ == '__main__':
    TestApp().run()
```

### 6) External terminal

If you can't or don't want to use the terminal from within Visual Studio Code, you can always use an external terminal, like the Command Prompt on Windows, the Anaconda Prompt or what have you. First you have to go to the directory where the executable file is. In my case, the **test.py** file is in the following location:

`D:\Python\Courses\Kivy Basics Course\book\code\slugrace4`

Then, in order to run the file just type in: `python test.py`

Here's what my Anaconda Prompt terminal looks like when I run the file:

```
(base) C:\Users\PC>d:

(base) D:\>cd D:\Python\Courses\Kivy Basics Course\book\code\slugrace4

(base) D:\Python\Courses\Kivy Basics Course\book\code\slugrace4>python test.py
[INFO   ] [Logger      ] Record log in C:\Users\PC\.kivy\logs\kivy_21-07-06_3.txt
[INFO   ] [deps        ] Successfully imported "kivy_deps.gstreamer" 0.2.0
[INFO   ] [deps        ] Successfully imported "kivy_deps.glew" 0.2.0
[INFO   ] [deps        ] Successfully imported "kivy_deps.sdl2" 0.2.0
[INFO   ] [Kivy        ] v1.11.1
[INFO   ] [Kivy        ] Installed at "C:\Users\PC\Anaconda3\lib\site-packages\kivy\__init__.py"
[INFO   ] [Python      ] v3.7.4 (default, Aug  9 2019, 18:34:13) [MSC v.1915 64 bit (AMD64)]
[INFO   ] [Python      ] Interpreter at "C:\Users\PC\Anaconda3\python.exe"
[INFO   ] [Factory     ] 184 symbols loaded
[INFO   ] [Image       ] Providers: img_tex, img_dds, img_sdl2, img_pil, img_gif (img_ffpyplayer ignored)
[INFO   ] [Text        ] Provider: sdl2
[INFO   ] [Window      ] Provider: sdl2
[INFO   ] [GL          ] Using the "OpenGL" graphics system
[INFO   ] [GL          ] GLEW initialization succeeded
[INFO   ] [GL          ] Backend used <glew>
[INFO   ] [GL          ] OpenGL version <b'4.6.0 - Build 26.20.100.7637'>
[INFO   ] [GL          ] OpenGL vendor <b'Intel'>
[INFO   ] [GL          ] OpenGL renderer <b'Intel(R) UHD Graphics 630'>
[INFO   ] [GL          ] OpenGL parsed version: 4, 6
[INFO   ] [GL          ] Shading version <b'4.60 - Build 26.20.100.7637'>
[INFO   ] [GL          ] Texture max size <16384>
[INFO   ] [GL          ] Texture max units <32>
[INFO   ] [Window      ] auto add sdl2 input provider
[INFO   ] [Window      ] virtual keyboard not allowed, single mode, not docked
[INFO   ] [Base        ] Start application main loop
[INFO   ] [GL          ] NPOT texture support is available
```

So, you know what a basic Kivy app looks like and how to run it. As mentioned before, an application consists of two layers, logic and presentation. Although there isn't any logic in our basic app actually, there is some presentation: you can see a graphical element, the label.

I also mentioned that you can either write the full app in Python or split it into a Python file for logic and a Kivy language file for presentation. In a basic scenario like this, it's overkill to create a Kivy language file to accompany the Python file, but still, I'm going to do that in the next chapter so that you can see how to make a basic Kivy file program using both Python and the Kivy language. We will definitely be using Kivy language files extensively when our GUI becomes more complex and, I promise, it won't be long.

# Chapter 5 - A Basic Kivy App Rewritten with Python and the Kivy Language

Before we rewrite our app using the Kivy language, let's one more time have a look at what we have. We left off with a basic Kivy app written entirely in Python.

Here's the code again:

```
# File name: test.py

from kivy.app import App
from kivy.uix.label import Label

class TestApp(App):
    def build(self):
        return Label(text='Hello World!')

if __name__ == '__main__':
    TestApp().run()
```

I also mentioned that for such a basic program it doesn't make much sense to create two files, one for the logic and one for the presentation. However, let's do it just so that you know how to do it.

Our program contains just one widget, the label. This is all as far as presentation is concerned. We'll move that part to a new file and leave the rest in the **test.py** file.

So, after we remove the presentation part from the **test.py**, this is what we have:

```
# File name: test.py

from kivy.app import App
from kivy.uix.label import Label

class TestApp(App):
    def build(self):
        # Just return a label, but don't
        # specify it in more detail here.
        return Label()

if __name__ == '__main__':
    TestApp().run()
```

As you can see, now we're just telling the app that a label should be used, but it doesn't know anything more about it. In particular, it doesn't know what text the label is supposed to display. This is what the kv file is going to take care of. By the way, I'm going to call the files written in the Kivy language kv files, for the sake of brevity. These files are easily recognizable by the **kv** extension.

## kv Files and the Kivy Language

Now we are ready to create the kv file. Actually, there are two approaches to this. If you have just one kv file, you can go with the simpler approach that I'm going to present as first. But if you have multiple kv files, which will be the case in our program as we proceed, you often have to take the slightly more complicated approach that I'm going to discuss as second.

## Naming Convention

Anyway, first the simpler approach. In this approach we use a naming convention according to which we name the file the same as the app class (the class that inherits from **App**), but without the **-App** part and all lowercase. So, in our example the app class is **TestApp**, so the kv file should be named **test.kv**.

Now, in Visual Studio Code (which I'm going to refer to as VSC from now on, also for brevity's sake), create a new file, just as you did before and name it **test.kv**.

As soon as you hit Enter, the file will open in a new tab. Type the following Kivy language code:

```
# File name: test.kv

<Label>:
    text: 'Hello World!'
```

We're going to talk about the Kivy language in more detail later on, for now it's enough to say that the **<Label>:** part means we're working on the **Label** class, and below we set the **text** property to a string of our choice.

Now save the kv file and go back to the **test.py**. Run the program. You should see exactly the same app window as before with the label that reads 'Hello World!'

## The Builder Class

And now let's have a look at the second approach. This is the one without a naming convention. First of all let's get rid of the kv file we just created by right-clicking it and selecting Delete.

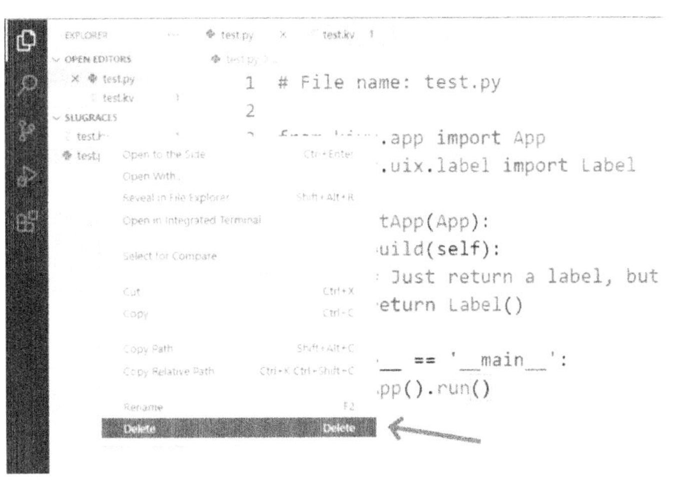


You will be asked to confirm that you want to delete the file. Just confirm and the file will be deleted. Now create a new file and name it **example.kv** or any other arbitrary name except **test.kv**.

Then type the same code as before:

```
# File name: example.kv

<Label>:
    text: 'Hello World!'
```

Save the file, go back to the **test.py** file and run the program. This time you will get a blank window, without the label.

# Linking with a kv File

This is because the **test.py** file doesn't know that it should be linked with the **example.kv** file. It can't figure it out on its own because we can have multiple kv files, so how should it know which one to choose? That's why we have to tell it explicitly that we want it to use the **example.kv** file.

To do that, we'll need the **Builder** class from the **kivy.lang** module. It contains the **load_file** function that we can use to load the file we need.

Now modify your **test.py** file so that it imports the class and loads the file. Here's the full code with comments:

```
# File name: test.py

from kivy.app import App
from kivy.uix.label import Label

# We must import the Builder class from kivy.lang.
from kivy.lang import Builder

# We must explicitly load the kv file that we need.
Builder.load_file('example.kv')

class TestApp(App):
    def build(self):
        return Label()

if __name__ == '__main__':
    TestApp().run()
```

If you now run the program, it will work again. But, as mentioned before, there's no need for importing the **Builder** class and using the **load_file** function in such a basic program like ours. The first approach with the naming convention is the way to go.

Now, you can delete the **example.kv** file because we're not going to need it anymore. Create the **test.kv** file again and type in the same code as before. Make all the necessary changes in the **test.py** file again.

At this moment the two files should look like this:

The Python file:

```
# File name: test.py

from kivy.app import App
from kivy.uix.label import Label

class TestApp(App):
    def build(self):
        return Label()

if __name__ == '__main__':
    TestApp().run()
```

The kv file:

```
# File name: test.kv

<Label>:
    text: 'Hello World!'
```

We've been using just the label widget, with just the **text** property of the **Label** class so far, but there are lots of other widgets and each of them has lots of interesting properties.

In part 2 of the book we'll have a look at some of them. We'll focus on the widgets that we are going to use in our project.

# Part II

# Kivy Widgets

In this part of the book we'll be talking about the basic Kivy widgets like labels, buttons, check boxes, toggle buttons, text inputs and sliders. We'll learn how to define widgets in Python and the Kivy language. We'll also see how to use classes and class rules.

# Chapter 6 - Introduction to Kivy Widgets

Our basic Kivy application is quite simple now. It contains just one widget, a label. Let's have a look at the code again.

Here's the Python file:

```
# File name: test.py

from kivy.app import App
from kivy.uix.label import Label

class TestApp(App):
    def build(self):
        return Label()

if __name__ == '__main__':
    TestApp().run()
```

And here's the kv file:

```
# File name: test.kv

<Label>:
    text: 'Hello World!'
```

If you run the application, which you have to do from the Python file (just a reminder), the application window opens.

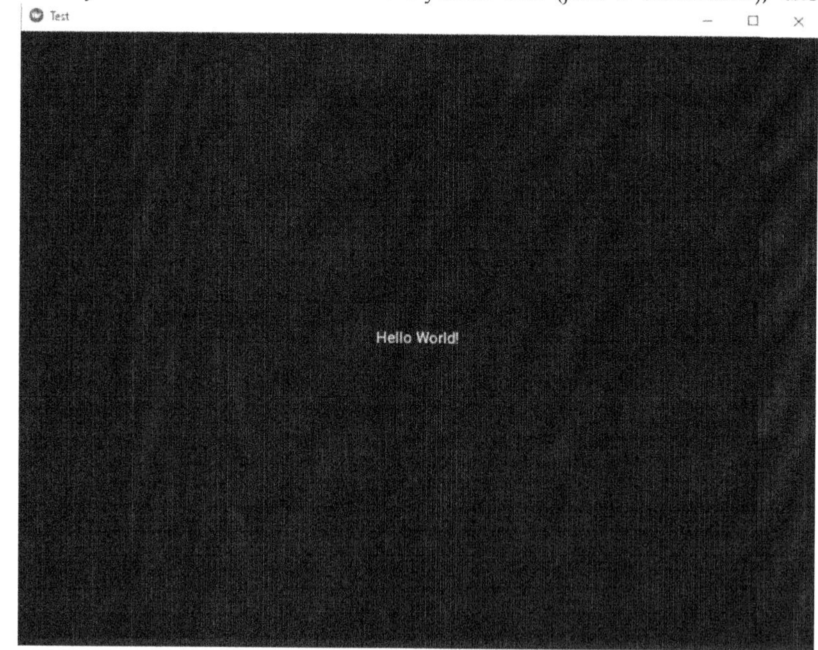


As you can see, there's just the label in the window. And it's a very lightweight label, so to speak. We could change the color of the text or make the text bigger for example. And we will, but first let's talk about Kivy widgets in general.

Now, you may be wondering where exactly the label is: Is it in the center of the window as it seems? No, it's not in the center. As the label is now the only widget in the window, it occupies the whole window. It's positioned at the coordinates (0, 0), which is in the bottom-left corner (unlike many other frameworks where these coordinates indicate the top-left corner) and is the same size as the window. And you will always see such behavior if there is just one widget – it will occupy the whole available space, so the whole window.

On the other hand, if you want to have more widgets, you have to put them in a layout, which we are going to discuss soon. For now let's just stick to one single widget.

# Kivy Built-in Widgets

There are lots of built-in widgets in Kivy. We're only going to use a small selection of them in our project. If you go to the Kivy API documentation (kivy.org/doc/stable/api-kivy.html), you can see (probably you have to scroll down first) what widgets you can use. One of them is the **Label**, which we already used. But there are many others like **Button**, **CheckBox**, **DropDown**, **Image**, **ProgressBar** and lots more. They are all defined in their own modules inside the **kivy.uix** namespace. Let's have a look at some of them. With each widget we will have to make some changes in both Python and kv code, which I will be highlighting here.

## Button

Let's start with the **Button** class.

Here's the Python code:

```
# File name: test.py

from kivy.app import App
from kivy.uix.button import Button

class TestApp(App):
    def build(self):
        return Button()

if __name__ == '__main__':
    TestApp().run()
```

And here's the kv code:

```
# File name: test.kv

<Button>:
    text: 'Click Me!'
```

If you run the program now, you will see a button that fills the whole window. Go ahead and click it. Why not? It's a button after all.

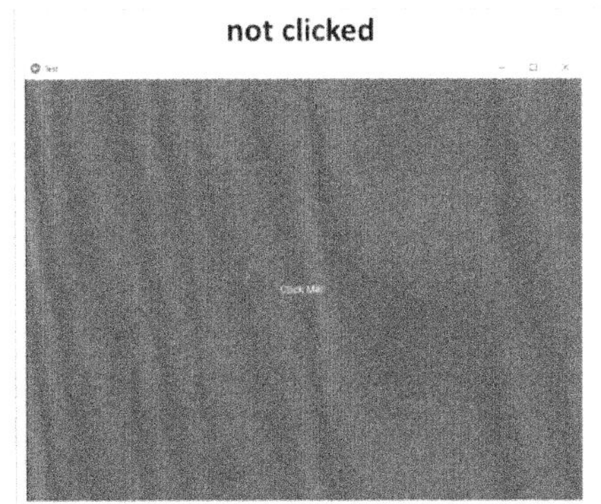


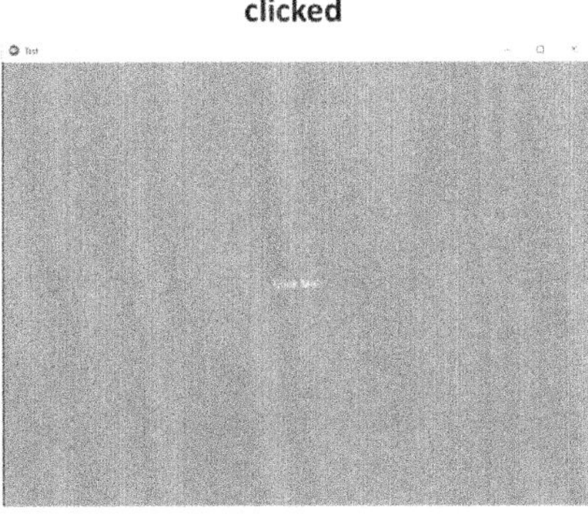


Naturally, nothing is going to happen because we didn't write any code to handle the click event yet, but at least the visual representation of the button will change.

## Carousel

Let's have a look at the **Carousel** now. We're going to use it in the Instructions screen later in the book. Here's our example.

First the Python code:

```
# File name: test.py

from kivy.app import App
from kivy.uix.carousel import Carousel

class TestApp(App):
    def build(self):
        return Carousel()

if __name__ == '__main__':
    TestApp().run()
```

And now the kv file:

```
# File name: test.kv

<Carousel>:
    direction: 'right'
    Label:
        text: 'one'
    Button:
        text: 'two'
    Label:
        text: 'three'
```

The carousel is a widget that may contain an arbitrary number of other widgets, which you can swipe from left to right or from right to left.

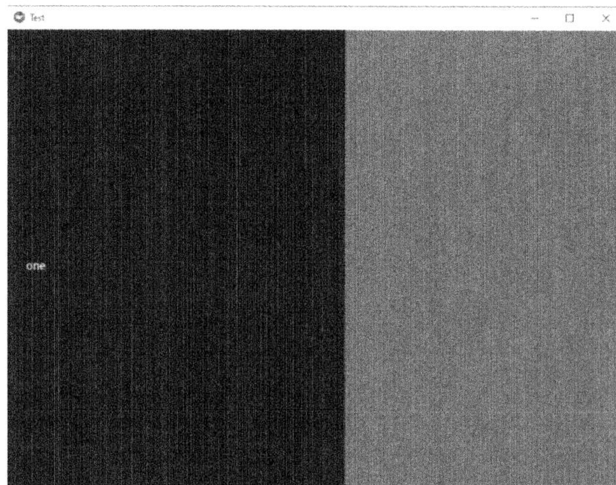


In our example we have three widgets inside the carousel, two labels and a button.

If you run this program, you will see just the first label. In order to see the button, you have to swipe to it from right to left.

The direction in which widgets are placed inside the carousel is set in the **direction** property above.

## Switch

And just one more example, the **Switch**. The name is self-explanatory.

But if you insist on reading the documentation, you will find out that the **Switch** widget may be active or inactive, just like a mechanical light switch.

To change the state of the **Switch**, you have to swipe to the left or right, depending on which of the two states you want to change to.

And here's our simple example with this two-state widget.

Here's the Python code:

```
# File name: test.py

from kivy.app import App
from kivy.uix.switch import Switch

class TestApp(App):
    def build(self):
        return Switch()

if __name__ == '__main__':
    TestApp().run()
```

And the kv file this time is very simple, without any properties:

```
# File name: test.kv

<Switch>:
```

If you run the program now, you will be able to see the switch and toggle it off and on.

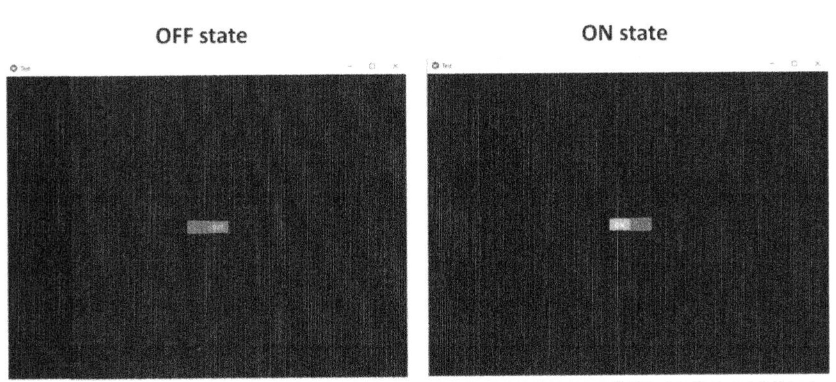


And this would be it for now. There are lots of other widgets, which you can check out in the documentation. Feel free to experiment with them. Some of them may not work as you would expect though, so don't get frustrated if this is the case. They just may need some more code to work.

Anyway, in the following chapters we're going to discuss all the widgets that we need for our project. First we'll have another look at the **`Label`** class and we'll see how to tweak its properties. Then we'll be talking in turn about the **`Button`**, the **`ToggleButton`**, the **`CheckBox`**, the **`TextInput`** and the **`Slider`**. We'll briefly discuss the most important properties of each. Finally we'll create our own custom widgets, which is pretty easy in Kivy.

# Chapter 7 - The Label Widget

In the previous chapter we left off with a basic Kivy app that displays a switch, so let's change it back to a label so that we can discuss the **Label** class in more detail. Your code should now look like this:

The Python file:

```
# File name: test.py

from kivy.app import App
from kivy.uix.label import Label

class TestApp(App):
    def build(self):
        return Label()

if __name__ == '__main__':
    TestApp().run()
```

And the kv file:

```
# File name: test.kv

<Label>:
    text: 'Hello World!'
```

As you can see, the label has a **text** property. This is a special Kivy property, not to be confused with regular Python properties. We're going to use Kivy properties a lot, and even create our own ones, just bear with me.

Anyway, the **Label** class has some more properties. We're going to have a look at the **Label** properties in this chapter and then in the following chapters we'll see how to use the properties of other widgets like buttons, toggle buttons, check boxes, text inputs and sliders, both in Python and in the Kivy language. These are the widgets we'll be making use of in our project.

And now let's have a closer look at the **Label** class and the **Label** properties. You already know the **text** property. It's used to set the actual text you want to display.

By the way, you probably noticed that the name of a property is followed by a colon and then comes the value we want to set the property to. This same syntax is valid for all the other properties.

And now let's have a look at some of the other properties. The next property I'd like to mention is **font_size**.

## The font_size Property

The name is pretty self-explanatory, let me just add that the value is in pixels.

Let's add this property to the code in the **test.kv** file:

```
# File name: test.kv

<Label>:
    text: 'Hello World!'
    font_size: 50
```

If you now run the program, the label text displayed in the window will be much bigger than before.

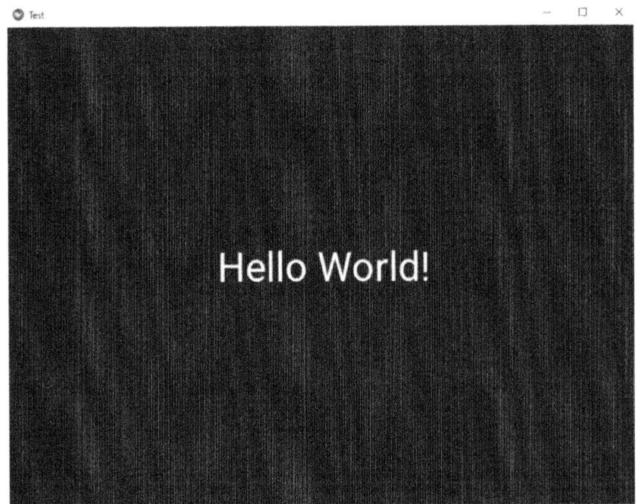


## The color Property

There's another property for the color of the text, called **color** to make things more interesting. What is really interesting about this property, however, is its value, which is a list with four elements: r(ed), g(reen), b(lue) and a(lpha).

The default value is [1, 1, 1, 1], which corresponds to fully opaque white. The values for each component are in the range from 0 to 1, which probably is not exactly what you are used to. In a lot of frameworks the values of **r**, **g**, **b** and **a** are from 0 to 255. Here, it is your task to recalculate the values so that they fit in the 0-1 range. Just keep in mind that 0 is the same in both ranges and 255 in the traditional scale corresponds to 1 in Kivy.

So, if you want the color to be a shade of purple where the values are:

```
r = 126          g = 45          b = 210          a = 255
```

you can either calculate the kv values manually like so:

```
r = 126/255 ≈ 0.56               b = 210/255 ≈ 0.82

g = 45/255 ≈ 0.18                a = 255/255 = 1
```

or type the operations directly in the list. So, in our case you could set the color like so:

```
color: [.56, .18, .82, 1]
```

or like so:

```
color: [126/255, 45/255, 210/255, 1]
```

You can use whichever you like. Go with the second one if you're used to the 0-255 range, but I'm going to use them interchangeably throughout the project so that you get used to both of them. Now the full kv code is:

```
# File name: test.kv

<Label>:
    text: 'Hello World!'
    font_size: 50
    color: [126/255, 45/255, 210/255, 1]
```

And if you run the program, the text will be purple.

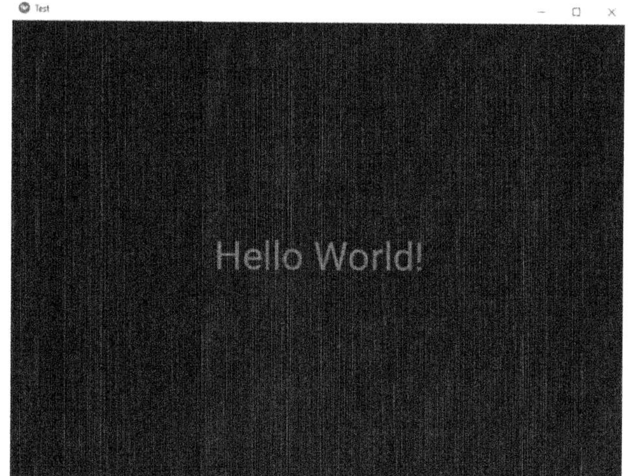


# Text Markup

There are lots of other properties that you can use with the **`Label`** class. Some of them will be used in the project and I'll talk a little more about them when we need them. There is, however, one very interesting property that we are not going to use in the app a lot (only when we implement accidents later in the book), and which is definitely worth mentioning, that's why I'd like to tell you something about it now.

You can style your text using text markup. This is very similar to what you may be familiar with if you know some HTML, however instead of angled brackets (`<>`, `</>`) we use square brackets in kv (`[ ]`, `[/]`). Just like in HTML there's an opening tag and a closing tag, as you can see.

## The Tags

There are lots of tags available. Let's have a look at just a small selection:

**`[b][/b]`** – bold text

**`[i][/i]`** – italic text

**`[u][/u]`** – underlined text

**`[s][/s]`** – strikethrough text

**`[sub][/sub]`** – subscript text

**`[sup][/sup]`** – superscript text

**`[size=<integer>][/size]`** – font size

**`[color=#<color>][/color]`** – text color

## The markup Property

In order to use text markup, you must add one more property, **markup**, and set it to **True**. Let's now change the text to something longer than **'Hello World'** and try the markup tags out. Here's the code:

```
# File name: test.kv

<Label>:
    text: 'normal [b]bold[/b] [i]italic[/i] \n[u]underlined[/u] [s]strikethrough[/s] \n[s
ub]subscript[/sub] [sup]superscript[/sup] [size=100]big[/size] [color=#ff0f]yellow[/color
]'
    font_size: 50
    color: [126/255, 45/255, 210/255, 1]
    markup: True
```

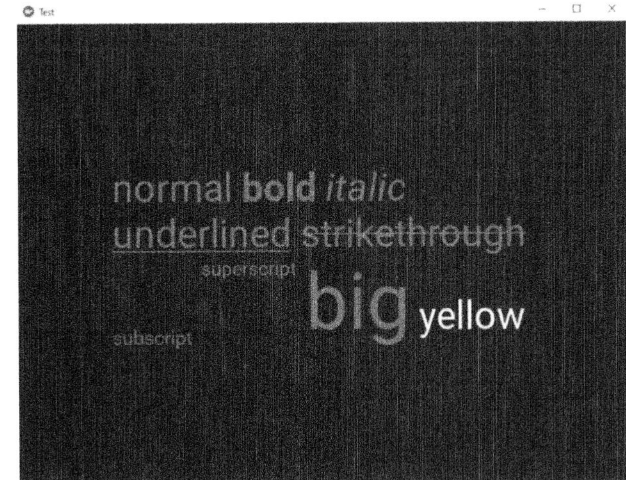


Two things to keep in mind:

First, the value of the **text** property, which is the long string with the markup tags, should be all on a single line.

Second, in text markup we use hex values for colors, so if the rgba for yellow is **(255, 255, 0, 255)** - fully opaque, then its hexadecimal representation is **ff0f**, which you can see in the **color** tag.

Also notice that there are newline characters (**\n**) inside the string.

Now run the app and see the markup in action.

We've been working with just one basic widget so far, the **Label**. But there are lots of other useful widgets, like buttons, toggle buttons, check boxes, text inputs, sliders and many, many more. We're going to use some of them in our application, so in the following chapters I'll show you some of the widgets that we're going to use and some of their most important properties.

But there's one more thing before we're done with this chapter. From now on you will be given exercises to do. They will be related to the topic of the chapter, but sometimes you will have an opportunity to learn something new, beyond what is covered in the chapter. You will find the exercises at the end of each chapter in the **It's Your Turn Now...** section. Don't worry, the solutions are there for you so that you can check your answers, but please try to do the exercises without looking at the solutions first.

When we start working on the project, we'll learn new stuff in each chapter and then implement it in the project. Some of the work will be done by you as an exercise, so you have to do the exercise for the code to be complete. And now, it's time for the first exercises.

## It's Your Turn Now...

### EXERCISE 1

We don't need the markup anymore, so just remove it. The label should display the text **'Test'** using 80-pixel font size.

### SOLUTION

After removing the markup setting the text and the font size, the kv code looks like this:

```
# File name: test.kv

<Label>:
    text: 'Test'
    font_size: 80
    color: [126/255, 45/255, 210/255, 1]
```

If you run the program now, you should see the 80-pixel text displayed.

### EXERCISE 2

You don't even need the markup for simple text formatting. For example you can make your text use bold and italic font styles by setting the properties **bold** and **italic** to **True** directly on the label. This is what you are supposed to do.

### SOLUTION

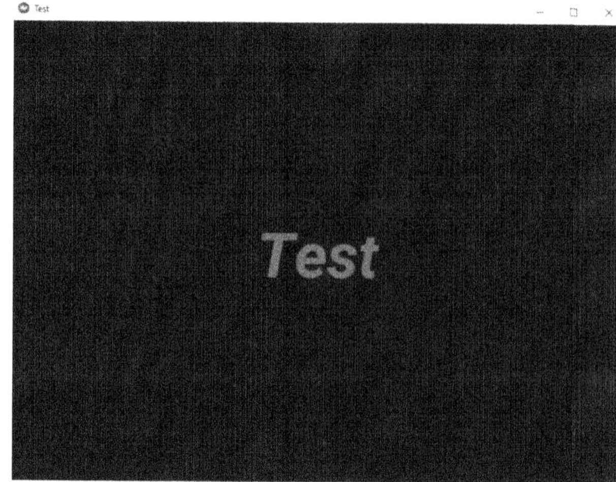


Here's the code:

```
# File name: test.kv

<Label>:
    text: 'Test'
    font_size: 80
    color: [126/255, 45/255, 210/255, 1]
    bold: True
    italic: True
```

# Chapter 8 - The Button Widget

In the previous chapter we left off with a basic Kivy app that displays a label. Now let's explore some other widgets. In particular, I'm going to briefly discuss the widgets we'll be making use of later in this book, so the button widget, the toggle button widget, as well as the check box, text input and slider widgets.

I'm going to start with the button widget in this chapter and I'll discuss the other widgets in the following chapters.

## A Button is Basically a Label...

In Kivy the **Button** class inherits from **Label**, so they have the same properties in common, plus the button has some extra functionality. In particular, they share the **text** property. Let's modify our **test.py** and **test.kv** files so that our program displays a button widget instead of a label. Let the changes be as few as possible.

Here's the **test.py** file:

```
# File name: test.py

from kivy.app import App
from kivy.uix.button import Button

class TestApp(App):
    def build(self):
        return Button()

if __name__ == '__main__':
    TestApp().run()
```

And here's the kv file. Let's just change **Label** to **Button**:

```
# File name: test.kv

<Button>:
    text: 'Test'
    font_size: 80
    color: [126/255, 45/255, 210/255, 1]
    bold: True
    italic: True
```

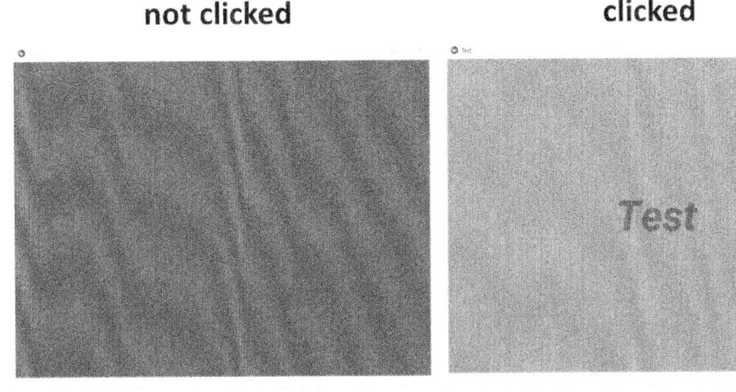


This works because, as mentioned before, the **Button** inherits all of the above properties from **Label**. The difference is, though, that this time we'll get a clickable button. Just run the app and check it out.

So this time the whole window is filled with our big button with the formatted text on it. Naturally nothing special happens when you click it because there isn't any code yet that would handle the button click event. Anyway, we now have a fully functional button.

## The background_color and background_normal Properties

By default the background of a button when not clicked is the shade of gray you can see above. If you want a different color, you should use the **background_color** property. Let's say we want a nice light shade of green with rgba values **(130, 180, 10, 1)**, which you can see here on the right.

Seems pretty easy. Let's add the **background_color** property:

```
# File name: test.kv

<Button>:
    text: 'Test'
    font_size: 80
    color: [126/255, 45/255, 210/255, 1]
    bold: True
    italic: True
    background_color: [130/255, 180/255, 10/255, 1]
```

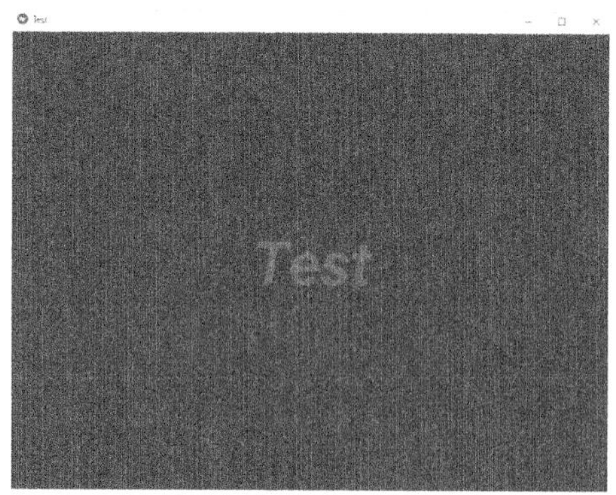


If you now run the program, you will get a much darker shade of green, which is not the color we wanted.

This is because the color we set is multiplied with the color of the button texture, which is gray, so the resulting new color will be always darker than expected.

If you don't want it to work this way, you should use the **background_normal** property and set it to an empty string:

```
# File name: test.kv

<Button>:
    text: 'Test'
    font_size: 80
    color: [126/255, 45/255, 210/255, 1]
    bold: True
    italic: True
    background_color: [130/255, 180/255, 10/255, 1]
    background_normal: ''
```

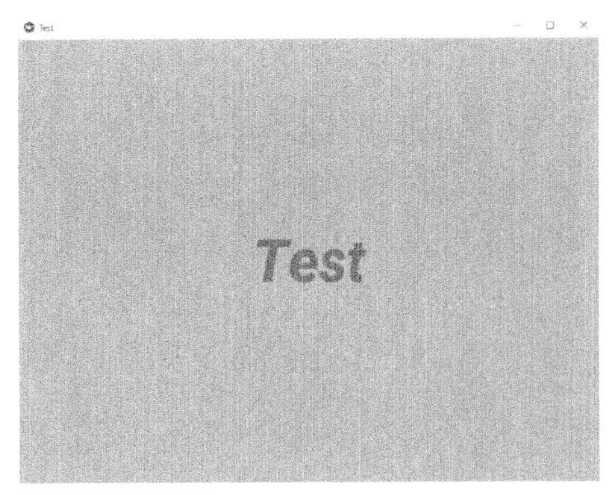


Now the color of the button should be the shade of green that we wanted.

That's it as far as the most basic button properties are concerned.

## Basic Button Events

Now, why do we even use buttons instead of labels? Well, as mentioned before, they have some extra functionality. They can be clicked, or pressed. I'm going to talk about events in Kivy a bit later, but as we are at it, let's just see how to handle pressing and releasing the button directly in kv. For more advanced scenarios, we'll be handling events in Python code later on.

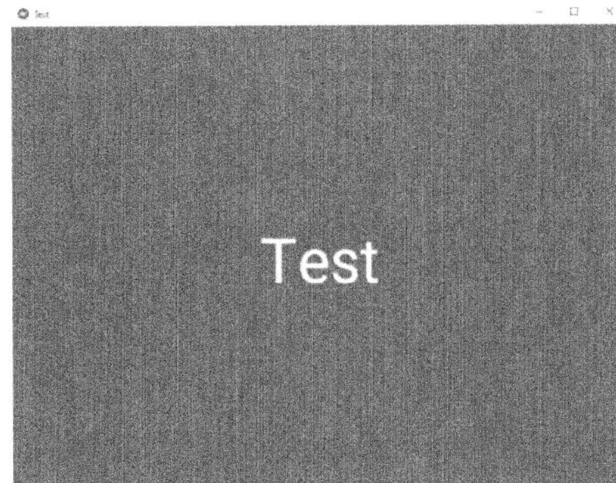


First of all, let's simplify our button slightly. Here's the full kv code:

```
# File name: test.kv

<Button>:
    text: 'Test'
    font_size: 80
```

If you run the program now, you will see a basic button.

Now, let's say we want the font size to be 200 instead of the original 80 when the button is pressed.

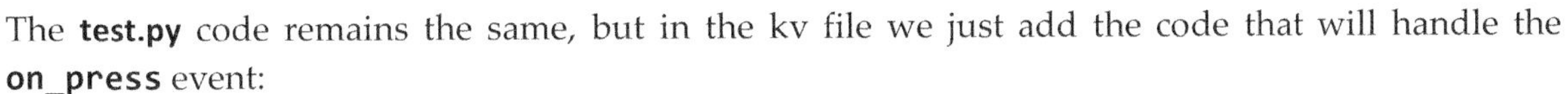

The **test.py** code remains the same, but in the kv file we just add the code that will handle the **`on_press`** event:

```
# File name: test.kv

<Button>:
    text: 'Test'
    font_size: 80
    on_press: self.font_size = 200
```

Here we're using the **`self`** variable. We'll be talking about it in more detail in one of the following chapters, but, to be brief, you should use this variable to refer to the object itself, so here it refers to the **`Button`** object itself. So, **`self.font_size`** refers to the **`Button`** object's **`font_size`** property.

Now run the program and click the button. Here's what it looks like before clicking, while clicked and then when released:

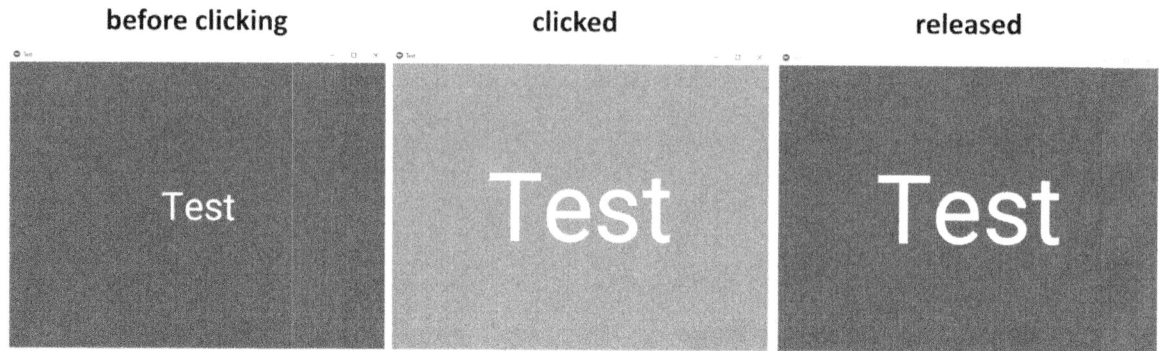


Now, when you release the button, the font size doesn't change back to 80. This is because we didn't tell the button what to do when it's released. You can do it by adding the **`on_release`** event:

```
# File name: test.kv

<Button>:
    text: 'Test'
    font_size: 80
    on_press: self.font_size = 200
    on_release: self.font_size = 80
```

Now the font size will change back when the button is released.

# Multiple Commands

And now suppose we want the button not only to resize its font when pressed, but also to change the text to **`'pressed'`**. When released, the font size should be set back to 80 and the text should change to **`'Test'`** again. You can do it in three basic ways.

The first way is just to add as many **`on_press`** and **`on_release`** events as needed:

```
# File name: test.kv

<Button>:
    text: 'Test'
    font_size: 80

    on_press: self.font_size = 200
    on_press: self.text = 'pressed'
    on_release: self.font_size = 80
    on_release: self.text = 'Test'
```

The second, more concise way is to separate the commands by semicolons:

```
# File name: test.kv

<Button>:
    text: 'Test'
    font_size: 80

    on_press: self.font_size = 200; self.text = 'pressed'
    on_release: self.font_size = 80; self.text = 'Test'
```

Finally, the third way, is to put all the commands one under another in an indented block of code:

```
# File name: test.kv

<Button>:
    text: 'Test'
    font_size: 80

    on_press:
        self.font_size = 200
        self.text = 'pressed'

    on_release:
        self.font_size = 80
        self.text = 'Test'
```

Whichever way you choose, the result will be the same:

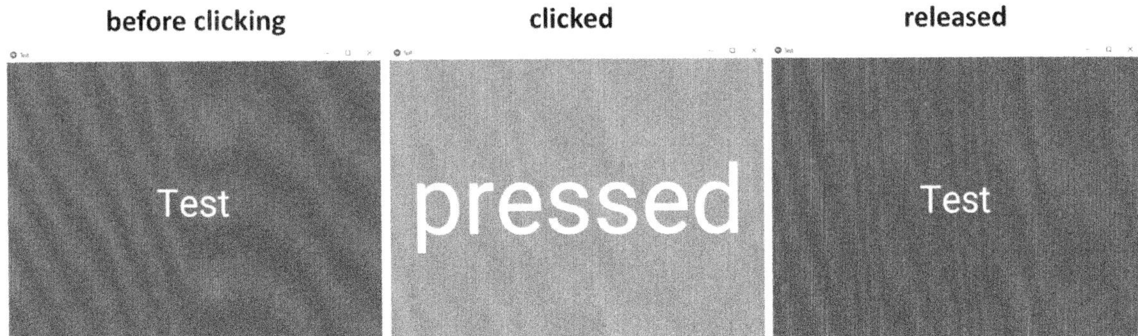


This is all you need to know about the **Button** class for now. We'll be using buttons a lot, so we're definitely going to learn more about them in near future.

And now it's time for some exercises.

# It's Your Turn Now...

### EXERCISE 1

Remove the **on_release** event. Now modify the **on_press** event so that each time the button is pressed the **font_size** increases by 10 pixels.

### SOLUTION

Here's the code:

```
# File name: test.kv

<Button>:
    text: 'Test'
    font_size: 80
    on_press: self.font_size += 10
```

If you now run this program, the font size will change each time you press the button.

### EXERCISE 2

Modify the code that is fired when the button is pressed so that the **font_size** is increased only if it's less than 200 pixels.

HINT: You can use a conditional here, just remember that everything must be on one line.

### SOLUTION

Here's the modified code:

```
# File name: test.kv

<Button>:
    text: 'Test'
    font_size: 80
    on_press: if self.font_size < 200: self.font_size += 10
```

Now, indeed, the font size is limited.

**EXERCISE 3**

Add an event that will fire each time the button is released. It should remove the last letter of the text provided there are at least two letters left. If there is only one letter, the text should change to **'The End'**.

HINT: You can use slicing and the ternary **if** statement.

**SOLUTION**

Here's the code:

```
# File name: test.kv

<Button>:
    text: 'Test'
    font_size: 80

    on_press: if self.font_size < 200: self.font_size += 10
    on_release: self.text = self.text[:-1] if len(self.text) > 1 else 'The End'
```

When you now run the program, each time the button is released, the text will be one letter shorter, until there is just the letter **'T'**. Then the text **'The End'** will appear. If you keep pressing and releasing the button, the text will continue getting shorter by one letter each time.

# Chapter 9 - The Check Box Widget

In the previous chapter we saw how to use buttons in Kivy. The button is a really common Kivy widget. In this chapter I'd like to touch upon another widget, the check box.

The check box is a two-state button that can be either checked or unchecked. Later we'll see that it can be used as a radio button as well, if it's in a group, but for now let's just have a look at a single check box.

The main property of a check box is **active**, which is **True** if it's checked and **False** otherwise. The basic check box event is **on_active**, which is fired if the state of the check box changes.

Let's replace our button from the previous chapter with a check box.

Here's the Python file:

```
# File name: test.py

from kivy.app import App
from kivy.uix.checkbox import CheckBox

class TestApp(App):
    def build(self):
        return CheckBox()

if __name__ == '__main__':
    TestApp().run()
```

And here's the kv file:

```
# File name: test.kv

<CheckBox>:
    # The check box should be checked.
    active: True
```

If you run the program, you will see a checked box in the app window. You can now uncheck it and check it again to make sure it works.

## The on_active Event

Let's make the check box do something when its state changes. For now something as simple as printing out a message in the terminal will do. Here's the kv file:

```
# File name: test.kv

<CheckBox>:
    active: True
    on_active: print('State changed')
```

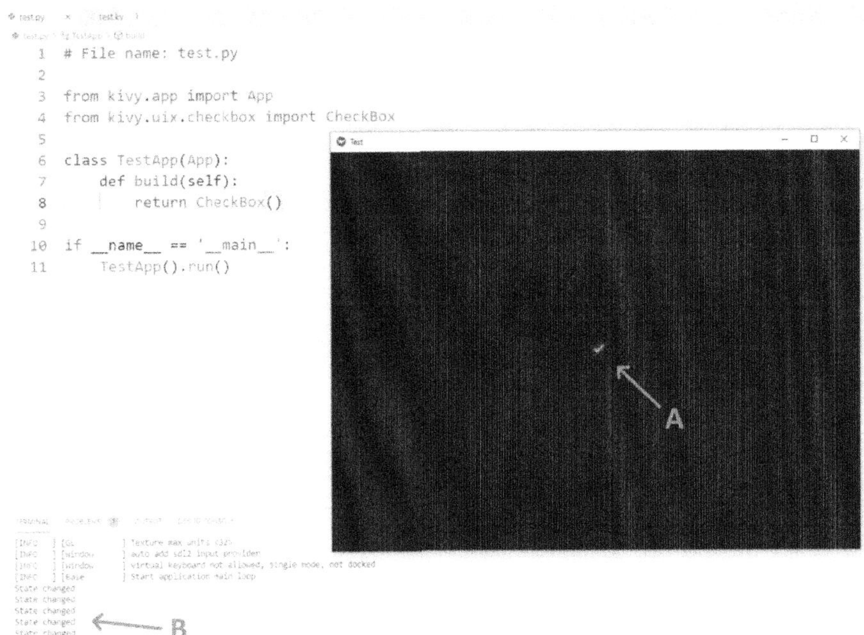


Now run the program and try checking and unchecking the check box several times (A). You will see the **'State changed'** message in the terminal each time you do (B).

## It's Your Turn Now...

### EXERCISE

Modify the **on_active** event so that the message in the terminal is **'state: active'** if the state changes from inactive to active and **'state: inactive'** otherwise.

HINT : Use the ternary **if** statement.

### SOLUTION

Here's the code:

```
# File name: test.kv

<CheckBox>:
    active: True
    on_active: print('state: active') if self.active else print('state: inactive')
```

Now, after several clicks the output in the terminal should look like so:

```
TERMINAL    PROBLEMS

[INFO   ] [Window
[INFO   ] [Base
state: inactive
state: active
state: inactive
state: active
state: inactive
state: active
state: inactive
state: active
```

# Chapter 10 - The Toggle Button Widget

The next widget I'd like to discuss is the toggle button, which shares features with both the regular button and the check box. It looks like a button at first glance, but when you press it, it remains pressed, just like the check box remains checked when you check it. So, it's a two-state button as well. The two states are **`normal`** and **`down`**.

You can set the state of the button to **`normal`** or **`down`** using the **`state`** property. You can use the **`on_state`** event if you want something to happen when the state changes. Besides, you can use the **`text`** property just like you did with the regular button.

Also, just like check boxes, toggle buttons may be grouped so that only one toggle button may be in the **`down`** state (i.e. pressed) at a time in a group. But for now we have just one widget in our program.

Creating and using a toggle button is easy. Let's remove the code we used for the check box and add a toggle button.

Here is the Python file:

```
# File name: test.py

from kivy.app import App
from kivy.uix.togglebutton import ToggleButton

class TestApp(App):
    def build(self):
        return ToggleButton()

if __name__ == '__main__':
    TestApp().run()
```

And here's the kv file:

```
# File name: test.kv

<ToggleButton>:
    text: 'not pressed'
    font_size: 80

    # The state is normalby default, so this line of code is redundant.
    state: 'normal'

    # Change the text on the toggle button if its state changes.
    on_state: self.text = 'not pressed' if self.state == 'normal' else 'pressed'
```

If you now run the program, you will see that if you press the button, both its color and its text will change.

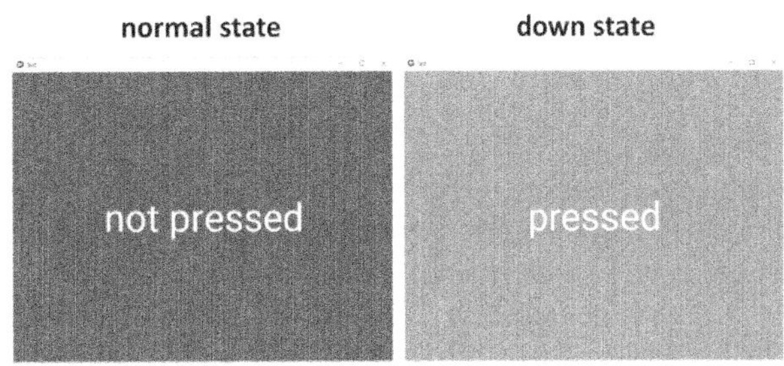


## It's Your Turn Now...

**EXERCISE**

The **ToggleButton** class inherits from **Button**, which in turn inherits from **Label**. This means **ToggleButton** has all the properties that **Label** has. One of them is **bold**, which changes the text style to bold if set to **True**. Modify the kv file so that:

1) the toggle button starts in the **down** state when the application is launched and

2) the style of the text changes to **bold** when the state changes to **normal** and back when the state changes to **down**.

Also change the text to **'Test'**.

HINT : You can use the ternary **if** statement.

**SOLUTION**

Here's the code:

```
# File name: test.kv

<ToggleButton>:
    text: 'Test'
    font_size: 80
    state: 'down'
    on_state: self.bold = True if self.state == 'normal' else False
```

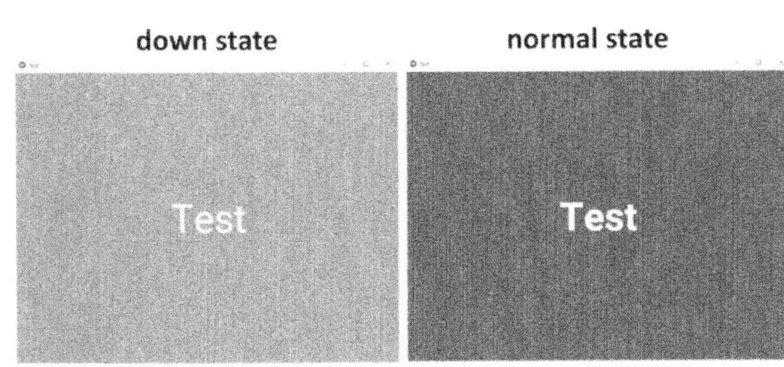


If you now run the program, the text style will differ in each state.

# Chapter 11 - The Text Input Widget

In the previous chapter we saw how to use toggle buttons in Kivy. Before that we discussed other widgets like labels, buttons and check boxes.

The next widget I'd like to briefly discuss is the **TextInput**. There's much more I could write about this widget than about all the other widgets so far. However, I'm not going to do that, at least not just yet. The **TextInput** widget is going to be used later in our project, so I will discuss all the properties and events that we need in due time. For now let me just concentrate on the very basics.

So, a text input is a widget in which the user can enter text. Then our program can use this text in one way or another, depending on what we need.

The **TextInput** widget may allow multiline text or just a single line of text. If you need the latter, just set the **multiline** property to **False**. The **text** property is used for the text in the **TextInput** widget, and there may also be a hint text, which is visible when the widget contains no text. This is usually used as a prompt as to what sort of data is expected in the widget. To set the hint text you use the **hint_text** property.

There are tons of other properties, which I'm not going to discuss now. There are also tons of events, which you can use when text is entered, when it's validated, when the widget gets focus, and so on.

## Multiline Text

OK, let's have a look at a simple example with a multiline text input first.

Here's the Python code:

```
# File name: test.py

from kivy.app import App
from kivy.uix.textinput import TextInput

class TestApp(App):
    def build(self):
        return TextInput()

if __name__ == '__main__':
    TestApp().run()
```

And here's the kv file:

```
# File name: test.kv

<TextInput>:
    text: 'hello darkness, \nmy old \nfriend...'

    # The multiline property is by default set to True, so this line is redundant.
    multiline: True

    # There should be a prompt when there's no text in the widget.
    hint_text: 'Type some lyrics.'
```

If you now run the program, the TextInput widget will occupy the whole available space, so the whole window. This is because it's the only widget now. As you can see, it works exactly the same as with the other widgets in this respect.

In the kv file we set the value of the **text** property to a multiline string. As you can see, you can use the newline escape sequence inside your string.

## Hint Text

Now click anywhere inside the widget and you can edit the text. In order to move to a new line you just need to hit Enter. And now delete all the text and you will see the hint text that you set in the kv file.

## Single Line Text

And now suppose we want to only allow single line text. All you have to do is set the **multiline** property to **False**:

```
# File name: test.kv

<TextInput>:
    # Remove the newline characters because
    # this is going to be single line text.
    text: 'hello darkness, my old friend...'
    multiline: False
    hint_text: 'Type some lyrics.'
```

I also changed the **text** property because now we can only have a single line of text.

Run the program again and if you now try to edit the text, you will notice that the Enter key will no longer let you go to a new line. Actually, what it now does is make the text input widget lose focus and validate the text entered in it, but in our case there isn't any validation code, so there's nothing to validate.

## Colors and Alignment

There are a couple of properties you can use to change the colors of the background and text. The colors are set as before, using lists with the rgba values from 0 to 1.

To change the color of the background of the text input, use the **background_color** property. If you want to change the color of the text, you should use the **foreground_color** property. You can also change the color of the hint text, using the **hint_text_color** property.

You can align the text horizontally using the **halign** property. You can align the text to the left, to the center or to the right.

Let's add the color and alignment properties to our kv code. I'll also set **font_size** to something bigger. The background should be blue and the text should be white. The hint text color should be another shade of blue. I also want the text to be centered horizontally.

```
# File name: test.kv

<TextInput>:
    text: 'hello darkness, my old friend...'

    multiline: False
    hint_text: 'Type some lyrics.'

    background_color: [0, 0, 1, 1]
    foreground_color: [1, 1, 1, 1]
    hint_text_color: [0, .5, .5, 1]
    font_size: 50
    halign: 'center'
```

If you run the app now, you will see the colors.

If you now click inside the text input and delete the text (you can also select it just like in any text editor and delete), you will see the hint text.

## Other Properties

Sometimes you may wish to disable text edition. Then you should use the **readonly** property:

```
# File name: test.kv

<TextInput>:
    ...
    readonly: True
```

The three dots in the code above just mean that some portion of the code is omitted for brevity. So, in this example it just means you should keep the code as it was and just add the **readonly** property at the end. This is a convention I'm going to use throughout this book.

If you now run the program, you will still be able to select the text, but you won't be able to edit or delete it.

You can also hide the text. This is what you do when you enter a password. Then each character is displayed as an asterisk, which is the default mask character. Let's remove the **readonly** property and add the **password** property which is used for that purpose:

```
# File name: test.kv

<TextInput>:
    ...
    halign: 'center'
    password: True
```

If you now run the program, both the text that is already there and the text you enter yourself will be displayed as a sequence of asterisks.

If you don't like asterisks, you can set the **password_mask** property to a different character:

```
# File name: test.kv

<TextInput>:
    ...
    password: True
    password_mask: '$'
```

Now you will see dollar signs instead.

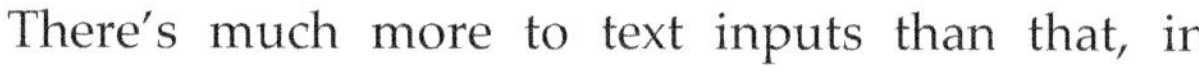

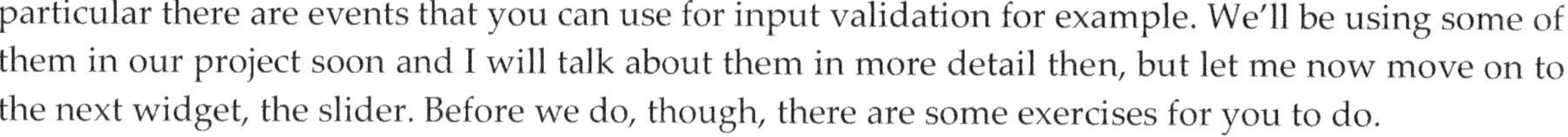

There's much more to text inputs than that, in particular there are events that you can use for input validation for example. We'll be using some of them in our project soon and I will talk about them in more detail then, but let me now move on to the next widget, the slider. Before we do, though, there are some exercises for you to do.

# It's Your Turn Now...

**EXERCISE 1**

Remove the **hint_text**, the **password** and **password_mask** properties. Also remove all the color and alignment properties. You can leave the **font_size** property as is. Then set the text to:

```
one

two

three
```

As you can see this is a multiline text. Remember that you don't have to use the **multiline** property at all in your code because it's set to **True** by default.

Now, there are two events that fire when you click the left mouse button and when you release the button. They are called **on_touch_down** and **on_touch_up** respectively. They also work for touches, hence the names.

Use these two events so that the text turns to all uppercase when you click and hold down the mouse and then back to lowercase when you release it.

HINT: You can use the standard Python **upper** and **lower** functions.

**SOLUTION**

So, here's the code:

```
# File name: test.kv

<TextInput>:
    text: 'one\ntwo\nthree'
    font_size: 50

    on_touch_down: self.text = self.text.upper()
    on_touch_up: self.text = self.text.lower()
```

If you now run the code and click the left mouse button inside the widget, you will see the text change from lowercase to uppercase.

**left mouse button released**

one
two
three

**left mouse button pressed**

ONE
TWO
THREE

**EXERCISE 2**

Remove the two events you just added. There's another event, **`on_double_tap`**, which is fired when you double-tap or double-click inside a text input. Use it to increase the font size by 10 pixels each time you double-click in the widget.

**SOLUTION**

Here's the code :

```
# File name: test.kv

<TextInput>:
    text: 'one\ntwo\nthree'
    font_size: 50
    on_double_tap: self.font_size += 10
```

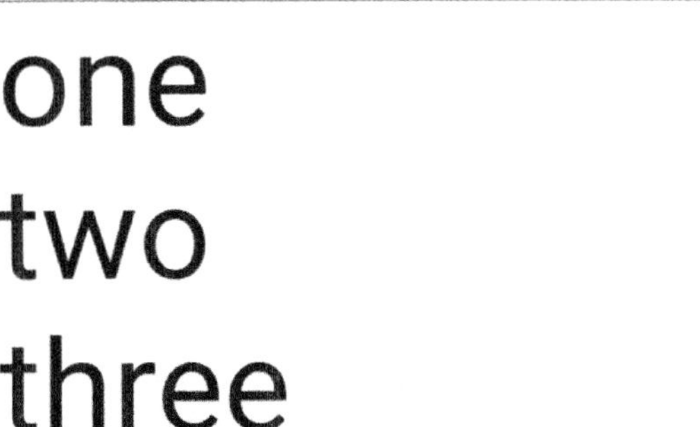


After a couple double clicks the text should be much bigger than before.

# Chapter 12 - The Slider Widget

In the previous chapter we were talking about the **TextInput** widget. In this chapter let's talk about the **Slider**.

The slider looks like a scrollbar. You can use it to set a value between a minimum and a maximum value. The main properties of a slider are **min**, **max** and **value**, which you can use to set the just mentioned values. The **min** and **max** properties are self-explanatory. The **value** property is the default value the slider is set to when it's created.

Sliders may be oriented horizontally (by default) or vertically, depending on what you set the **orientation** property to.

## Horizontal Orientation

So, this is enough for us to know to create a simple slider. Let it be a horizontal slider with values between **-100** and **200** and with the default value of **0**.

Here's the Python file:

```
# File name: test.py

from kivy.app import App
from kivy.uix.slider import Slider

class TestApp(App):
    def build(self):
        return Slider()

if __name__ == '__main__':
    TestApp().run()
```

And here's the kv file:

```
# File name: test.kv

<Slider>:
    min: -100
    max: 200
    value: 0

    # The default orientation is horizontal,
    # so you don't need this line of code,
    # but, of course, it will do no harm if
    # it's there.
    orientation: 'horizontal'
```

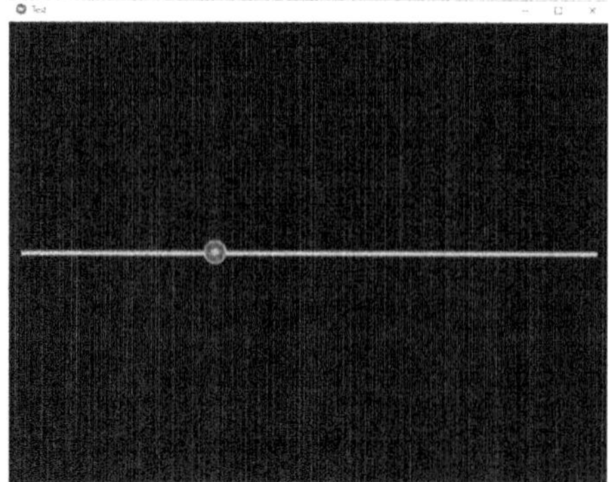

Now run the program. You will see the slider occupy the whole window. It's set to the default value of **0**, but you can slide it to the left and to the right. Give it a try.

## Vertical Orientation

And now change the orientation to vertical and run the program again. Here's the kv file:

```
# File name: test.kv

<Slider>:
    min: -100
    max: 200
    value: 0
    orientation: 'vertical'
```

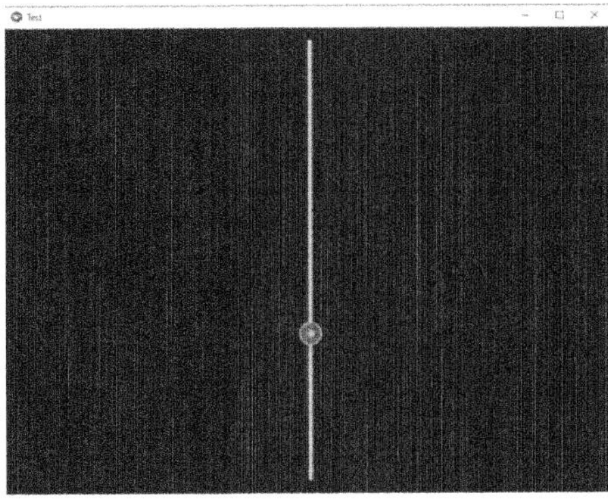

If you now run the program, you will see the slider oriented vertically. Now the minimum value is at the bottom and the maximum value is at the top. The default value is **0** again.

If you move the slider from left to right or from bottom to top, you can see that the movement is pretty smooth. This is because the default step of the slider is **1**. You can change it using the **step** property. Let's set the step to **50**:

```
# File name: test.kv

<Slider>:
    ...
    step: 50
```

If you run the program again, the slider will only move in 50-unit steps.

Fine, this was the last widget I wanted to discuss for now. There are lots of other widgets which are available out of the box in Kivy, but I'd like to talk about layouts now. As you probably noticed, there has always been just one single widget in our application. At first there was a label, then we got rid of the label and created a button, then we replaced the button with a check box, and so on. But usually even the most trivial apps have more than one widget. In our project there are definitely going to be more.

So, in order to place more widgets in our app, you have to lay them out somehow. Kivy uses a couple of predefined layouts that you can use. They are pretty flexible and may be nested as much as you need. This enables you to create practically any layout you might think of.

But before we discuss layouts, I want to talk about two things. First, in the next chapter, I'll show you how to define all the widgets in Python code. As you know, you can use Kivy without the assistance of the Kivy language, from which I discourage you, but I think you should know how to define the widgets just in Python. Second, in the last chapter in this part we'll see how to create our custom widgets. Creating custom widgets is also a way of putting multiple widgets on the screen, although, technically, we just create a single widget that consists of other widgets. And then, in the following part we'll start our discussion of Kivy layouts. In our application we'll be making use of several different layouts, so the sooner we start using them the better.

# It's Your Turn Now...

### EXERCISE 1

Delete the **step** and **orientation** properties. This will cause the default values to be used, so the step of 1 unit and horizontal orientation.

There is an interesting property in the **Slider** class, **value_track**. You can use it if you want the slider to draw a line between the values defined by the **min** and **value** properties. Using also the **value_track_color** and **value_track_width** properties you can change the color and width of this line respectively.

So, make the slider draw a red line with the width of **10**. The color should be a list with the rgba values. You can add some transparency, so a color like **[1, 0, 0, .8]** will do just fine.

### SOLUTION

Here's the code:

```
# File name: test.kv

<Slider>:
    min: -100
    max: 200
    value: 0

    value_track: True
    value_track_color: [1, 0, 0, .8]
    value_track_width: 10
```

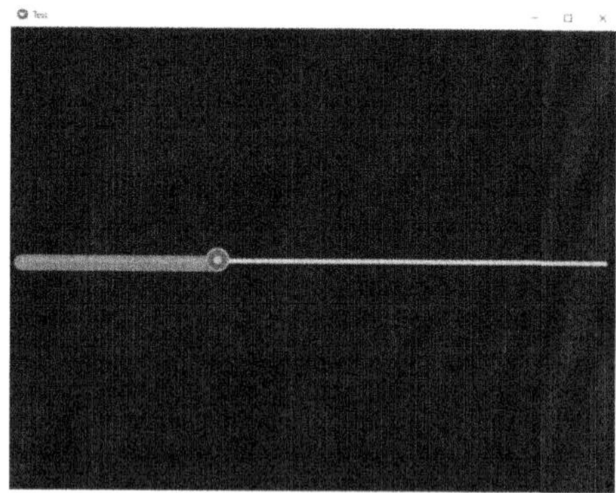

Now if you run the program, you will see the red, slightly transparent line. Drag the slider and watch the line move.

### EXERCISE 2

There are three slider events: **on_touch_down** (triggered when you touch or click the slider), **on_touch_move** (triggered when you drag it) and **on_touch_up** (triggered when you release the touch or click). Add these events to the kv code so that:

- the width of the track line changes to **20** when the slider is clicked,

- the color of the track line changes to green when the slider is dragged over positive values and to red when over negative values,

- the width of the track line changes back to **10** when the slider is released.

HINT : You can use the ternary **if** statement to change the color. For the green color you can use the rgba values [0, 1, 0, .8] .

**SOLUTION**

Here's the code:

```
# File name: test.kv

<Slider>:
    min: -100
    max: 200
    value: 0

    value_track: True
    value_track_color: [1, 0, 0, .8]
    value_track_width: 10

    on_touch_down: self.value_track_width = 20
    on_touch_move: self.value_track_color = [1, 0, 0, .8] if self.value < 0 else [0, 1, 0, .8]
    on_touch_up: self.value_track_width = 10
```

If you run the code now, you can watch the width and color of the track line change.

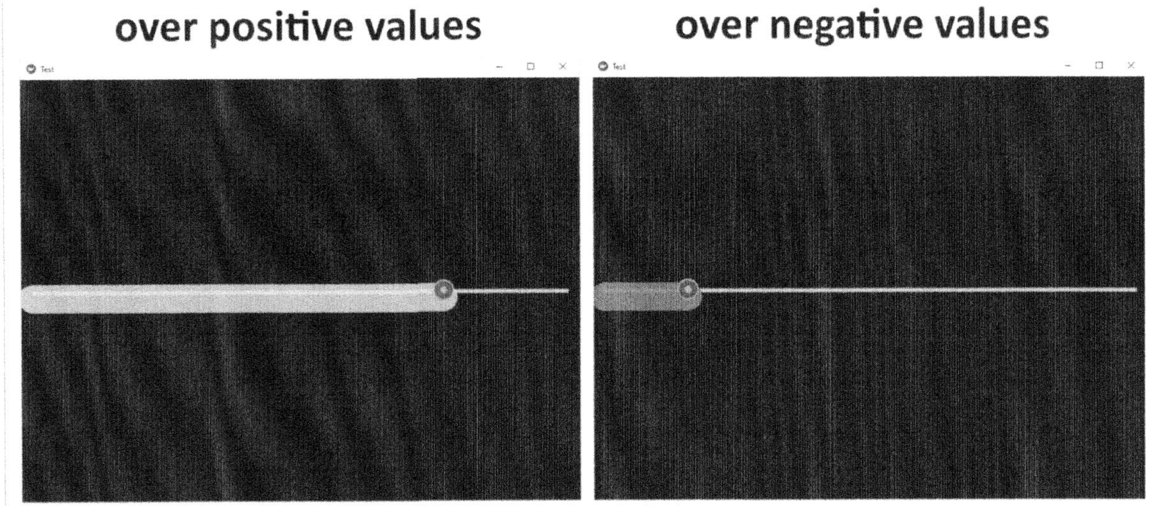

# Chapter 13 - Defining Widgets in Python Code

In this part of the book we've been creating widgets in the Kivy language, but we can also create widgets using just Python. In this chapter we'll try to reconstruct all the widgets we've created so far: the `Label`, the `Button`, the `CheckBox`, the `ToggleButton`, the `TextInput` and the `Slider`.

First of all let's remove all the code from the **test.kv** file. This file should be empty because we're going to use exclusively Python in this chapter.

I will be comparing the kv code with the corresponding Python code for clarity, but this is just for comparison, don't put the kv code in the kv file.

**The general rule is that the Kivy properties are passed as keyword arguments in Python.**

## The Label

To create a label you have to remember to import the `Label` class from the `kivy.uix.label` module. This is also true about all the other widgets, so keep that in mind when we move on to the other widgets.

First let's define a simple label in the **test.py** file. The code should look like so:

```
# File name: test.py

from kivy.app import App
from kivy.uix.label import Label

l = Label(text='Hello World!')

class TestApp(App):
    def build(self):
        return l

if __name__ == '__main__':
    TestApp().run()
```

If you run this code, you will see the same basic label as the one we created in Kivy language before.

So, as you can see, we first imported the **Label** class:

```
from kivy.uix.label import Label
```

Then we created an object of the **Label** class and set its **text** property to **'Hello World!'**:

```
l = Label(text='Hello World!')
```

And finally we defined the application class with the **build** method returning the label:

```
class TestApp(App):
    def build(self):
        return l
```

And now compare the Python code used to create the label above with its corresponding Kivy code that we could use instead:

Python

```
l = Label(text='Hello World!')
```

Kivy language

```
<Label>:
    text: 'Hello World!'
```

In a similar way you can define more complex labels in Python. Let's have a look at the following example from one of the previous chapters. It's in Kivy language:

```
<Label>:
    text: 'normal [b]bold[/b] [i]italic[/i] \n[u]underlined[/u] [s]strikethrough[/s] \n[s
ub]subscript[/sub] [sup]superscript[/sup] [size=100]big[/size] [color=#ff0f]yellow[/color
]'
    font_size: 50
    color: [126/255, 45/255, 210/255, 1]
    markup: True
```

Here's how we could create the same label in Python:

```
l = Label(text='normal [b]bold[/b] [i]italic[/i] \n[u]underlined[/u] [s]strikethrough[/s]
 \n[sub]subscript[/sub] [sup]superscript[/sup] [size=100]big[/size] [color=#ff0f]yellow[/
color]',
          font_size=50,
          color=[126/255, 45/255, 210/255, 1],
          markup=True)
```

As you can see, it's pretty straightforward. And now let's have a look at the other widgets.

# The Button

Before we continue with the next widget, remove or comment out the code that we used to create the label. We're now ready to create a button. Creating a button is easy too.

This is how we created a button in the Kivy language:

```
<Button>:
    text: 'Test'
    font_size: 80
```

In Python we would do it like so:

```
# File name: test.py

...
from kivy.uix.button import Button

b = Button(text='Test', font_size=50)

class TestApp(App):
    def build(self):
        return b
...
```

As you remember, we also had some events. We're going to discuss events in Kivy in more detail later on in the book, but for now let's just look at them briefly. The two events we had were **on_press** and **on_release**. Look at this kv code:

```
<Button>:
    text: 'Test'
    font_size: 80
    on_press: self.font_size = 200
    on_press: self.text = 'pressed'
    on_release: self.font_size = 80
    on_release: self.text = 'Test'
```

In Python we would have to bind the events to callback functions. Here's the full code that creates the same button as the kv code above:

```
# File name: test.py

...
from kivy.uix.button import Button

b = Button(text='Test', font_size=80)

# We must define the callback functions.
def press_callback(instance):
    instance.font_size = 200
    instance.text = 'pressed'

def release_callback(instance):
    instance.font_size = 80
    instance.text = 'Test'
```

```
# We must bind the events to the callback functions.
b.bind(on_press=press_callback)
b.bind(on_release=release_callback)

class TestApp(App):
    def build(self):
        return b
...
```

The **`instance`** argument in the callback functions references the **`Button`** object itself, just like **`self`** in the kv file.

Now if you run the program, you will see the same button as before. Make sure to press it to see the events in action.

# The Check Box

Now, remove or comment out the code we used to create a button. I'm sure you remember the check box you created as an exercise before. Here's the kv file:

```
<CheckBox>:
    active: True
    on_active: print('state: active') if self.active else print('state: inactive')
```

We can easily reconstruct it in Python:

```
# File name: test.py

...
from kivy.uix.checkbox import CheckBox

cb = CheckBox(active=True)

# Let's define the callback function.
def active_callback(instance, value):
    if value:
        print('state: active')
    else:
        print('state: inactive')

# Let's bind the active property to the callback function.
cb.bind(active=active_callback)

class TestApp(App):
    def build(self):
        return cb
...
```

Here we're binding the **active_callback** function directly to the **active** property. The **value** parameter is for the boolean value of the **active** property, so it may be **True** or **False**.

When we discuss events in more detail, you will see that names like **active** for the property and **on_active** for the event are closely related, but don't worry about that now.

If you run this code you will see the same output as before.

# The Toggle Button

Again, remove or comment out the **CheckBox** code. Now let's have a look at the toggle button we created in kv:

```
<ToggleButton>:
    text: 'not pressed'
    font_size: 80
    state: 'normal'
    on_state: self.text = 'not pressed' if self.state == 'normal' else 'pressed'
```

Here's how you could do the same in Python:

```
# File name: test.py

...
from kivy.uix.togglebutton import ToggleButton

tb = ToggleButton(text='not pressed', font_size=80, state='normal')

# Let's define the callback function.
def state_callback(instance, value):
    if value == 'normal':
        instance.text = 'not pressed'
    else:
        instance.text = 'pressed'

# Let's bind the callback function to the state property.
tb.bind(state=state_callback)

class TestApp(App):
    def build(self):
        return tb
...
```

# The Text Input

What about text inputs? Well, first remove or comment out the **ToggleButton** code. Here's the kv code that we're going to reconstruct in Python:

```
<TextInput>:
    text: 'one\ntwo\nthree'
    font_size: 50
    on_touch_down: self.text = self.text.upper()
    on_touch_up: self.text = self.text.lower()
```

So, again we have some properties and some events. Here's the corresponding Python code:

```
# File name: test.py

...
from kivy.uix.textinput import TextInput

ti = TextInput(text='one\ntwo\nthree', font_size=50)

# Let's define the callback functions.
def down_callback(instance, value):
    instance.text = instance.text.upper()

def up_callback(instance, value):
    instance.text = instance.text.lower()

# Let's bind the callback functions to the events.
ti.bind(on_touch_down=down_callback)
ti.bind(on_touch_up=up_callback)

class TestApp(App):
    def build(self):
        return ti
...
```

Naturally, if you run this program, you will get the same result as before.

# The Slider

Finally, let's remove or comment out all the **TextInput** code and revisit our slider. Here's the kv code:

```
<Slider>:
    min: -100
    max: 200
    value: 0

    value_track: True
    value_track_color: [1, 0, 0, .8]
    value_track_width: 10

    on_touch_down: self.value_track_width = 20
    on_touch_move: self.value_track_color = [1, 0, 0, .8] if self.value < 0 else [0, 1, 0, .8]
    on_touch_up: self.value_track_width = 10
```

And now let's rewrite the slider in Python:

```
# File name: test.py

...
from kivy.uix.slider import Slider

s = Slider(min=-100,
           max=200,
           value=0,
           value_track=True,
           value_track_color=[1, 0, 0, .8],
           value_track_width=10)

# Let's define the callback functions.
def down_callback(instance, val):
    instance.value_track_width = 20

def move_callback(instance, val):
    if instance.value < 0:
        instance.value_track_color = [1, 0, 0, .8]
    else:
        instance.value_track_color = [0, 1, 0, .8]

def up_callback(instance, val):
    instance.value_track_width = 10

# Let's bind the events to the callback functions.
s.bind(on_touch_down=down_callback)
s.bind(on_touch_move=move_callback)
s.bind(on_touch_up=up_callback)

class TestApp(App):
    def build(self):
        return s
...
```

So, now you know how to create widgets in the Kivy language and in Python. Turns out you can mix the two. In the next chapter I'll show you how you can use the Kivy language directly inside a Python file.

# It's Your Turn Now...

### EXERCISE

In the first chapter of this part of the book, where I introduced Kivy widgets, I briefly mentioned the **`Switch`** widget.

Here's the Python code that we used to create it:

```
# File name: test.py

from kivy.app import App
from kivy.uix.switch import Switch

class TestApp(App):
    def build(self):
        return Switch()

if __name__ == '__main__':
    TestApp().run()
```

And here's the very simplistic kv file :

```
# File name: test.kv

<Switch>:
```

As you can see, there were no properties or events. But if you read through the **Switch** documentation, you can see there are some properties and events you could use. Suppose we add some stuff to the kv file, so that it looks like this:

```
# File name: test.kv

<Switch>:
    active: True
    on_touch_down: print('*****')
    on_active: print('activated') if self.active else print('deactivated')
```

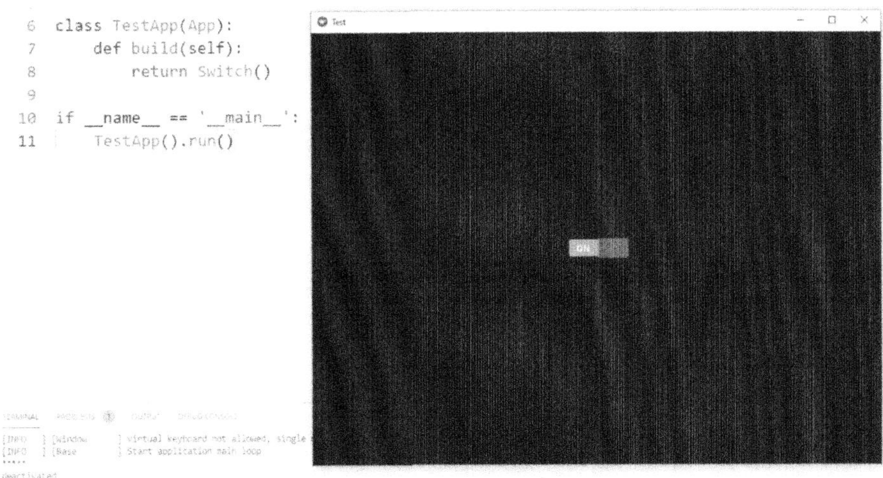


If you run the program, you will see a switch. Each time you click on it, a message will be printed in the terminal.

Now, remove the code from the kv file and reproduce the same switch in Python.

HINT: Just like with the **CheckBox**, you should bind the callback function directly to the **active** property.

## SOLUTION

So, after removing everything from the kv file, we only have the Python file.

```
# File name: test.py

from kivy.app import App
from kivy.uix.switch import Switch

sw = Switch(active=True)

# Let's define the callback functions.
def down_callback(instance, value):
    print('*****')

def active_callback(instance, value):
    if value:
        print('activated')
    else:
        print('deactivated')

# Let's bind the events to the callback functions.
sw.bind(on_touch_down=down_callback)
sw.bind(active=active_callback)

class TestApp(App):
    def build(self):
        return sw

if __name__ == '__main__':
    TestApp().run()
```

If you run the program, you will see the same output as before.

# Chapter 14 - Loading Kivy Language Strings in Python Code

In the previous chapter we learned how to create widgets in Python code. Earlier we were creating them in the Kivy language. The code written in the Kivy language was placed in a separate file with the extension kv.

In this chapter you'll see that you can also use the Kivy language directly inside the Python file. To do so, you need the **Builder** class from the **kivy.lang** module. We already used the **load_file** method from this class to load the kv file inside the Python file. This time we're going to need another method, **load_string**, which is used to load the kv code as a string in the Python file.

So, let's get to work right away. I'm not going to rewrite each and every widget like I did in the previous chapter, because it's pretty straightforward. Besides I must leave something for you to do as an exercise ☺

So, let's focus on just one widget, let it be the **Button**. First of all let's restore the state from before the previous chapter where we had a separate Python file and a separate kv file.

Your Python file should look like this:

```
# File name: test.py

from kivy.app import App
from kivy.uix.button import Button

class TestApp(App):
    def build(self):
        return Button()

if __name__ == '__main__':
    TestApp().run()
```

Your kv file, on the other hand, should look like this:

```
# File name: test.kv

<Button>:
    text: 'Test'
    font_size: 80

    on_press: self.font_size = 200
    on_press: self.text = 'pressed'
    on_release: self.font_size = 80
    on_release: self.text = 'Test'
```

And now we'll rewrite the Python file so that the kv code is embedded directly there.

You can now remove all the code from the kv file, but before that copy it so that you can later paste it in the Python file.

Speaking of which… Here's the Python file where we use the **load_string** method to load the kv code. It's exactly the same code as that in the separate kv file before we removed it.

By the way, here's a remark. As the code in future chapters is going to get longer and longer, I will sometimes put it in two columns separated by a line. The code in the second column is just the continuation of the code in the first column. This way we'll be saving space. The vertical line will also mark the zeroth level of indentation. Sometimes dotted lines will be added to mark indentation if it's not that clear. Here's the first time I'm using this convention:

```
# File name: test.py

from kivy.app import App
from kivy.uix.button import Button

# We need the Builder class.
from kivy.lang import Builder

# Here we load the kv code as a string.
Builder.load_string("""
<Button>:
    text: 'Test'
    font_size: 80
    on_press: self.font_size = 200
    on_press: self.text = 'pressed'
    on_release: self.font_size = 80
    on_release: self.text = 'Test'
""")

class TestApp(App):
    def build(self):
        return Button()

if __name__ == '__main__':
    TestApp().run()
```

The highlighted part is where we load the kv code. If you run the program now, it will work exactly the same as before.

# It's Your Turn Now...

## EXERCISE

You can now remove all the code from the Python file. The kv file is already empty.

Here's the Python code that we are going to use in this exercise:

```
# File name: test.py

from kivy.app import App
from kivy.uix.textinput import TextInput

class TestApp(App):
    def build(self):
        return TextInput()

if __name__ == '__main__':
    TestApp().run()
```

And here's the kv file :

```
# File name: test.kv

<TextInput>:
    text: '1\n2\n3'
    hint_text: 'Add some numbers...'
    background_color: [.5, .5, .5, 1]
    foreground_color: [.8, .8, .8, 1]
    hint_text_color: [.2, .2, .2, 1]
    font_size: 60
    halign: 'center'
```

Type it in. And now rewrite the Python file using the kv code in it as a string. Then remove all the code from the kv file.

**SOLUTION**

Here's the Python code that you probably came up with:

```
# File name: test.py

from kivy.app import App
from kivy.uix.textinput import TextInput
from kivy.lang import Builder

Builder.load_string("""
<TextInput>:
    text: '1\n2\n3'
    hint_text: 'Add some numbers...'
    background_color: [.5, .5, .5, 1]
    foreground_color: [.8, .8, .8, 1]
    hint_text_color: [.2, .2, .2, 1]
    font_size: 60
    halign: 'center'
""")

class TestApp(App):
    def build(self):
        return TextInput()

if __name__ == '__main__':
    TestApp().run()
```

Now, if you run this code, there will be a little nasty surprise. Look at what the terminal says:

```
...
      3:    text: '1
      4:2
 >>   5:3'
      6:    hint_text: 'Add some numbers...'
      7:    background_color: [.5, .5, .5, 1]
 ...
 Only one root object is allowed by .kv
```

The problem is that the kv string treats newline characters as escape characters, which they are, and the **text** property is split into three lines:

```
      3:    text: '1
      4:2
 >>   5:3'
```

If you watch the indentation, you see that the numbers 2 and 3 are indented as much as the root object, **<TextInput>**, so they are treated as root objects as well. This is not allowed because there may be only one root object.

This is easy to fix, though. Just add one more backslash before each newline character:

```
# File name: test.py

from kivy.app import App
from kivy.app import App
from kivy.uix.textinput import TextInput
from kivy.lang import Builder
```

```
Builder.load_string("""
<TextInput>:
    text: '1\\n2\\n3'
    hint_text: 'Add some numbers...'
    background_color: [.5, .5, .5, 1]
    foreground_color: [.8, .8, .8, 1]
    hint_text_color: [.2, .2, .2, 1]
    font_size: 60
    halign: 'center'
""")

class TestApp(App):
    def build(self):
        return TextInput()

if __name__ == '__main__':
    TestApp().run()
```

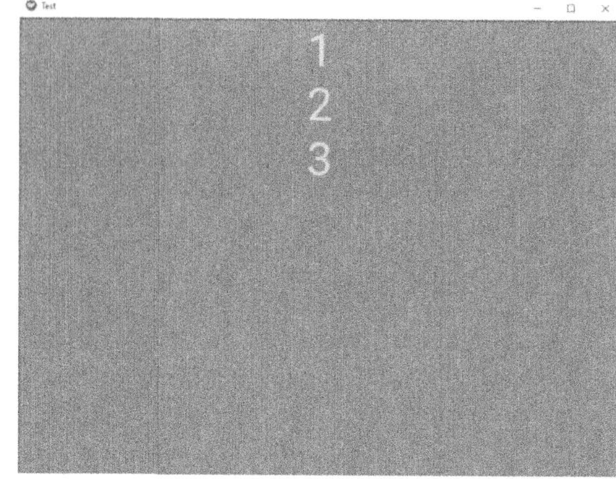


If you now run the program, it will work as expected.

# Chapter 15 – Custom Widgets

In the previous chapters we were using various Kivy widgets like labels, buttons, sliders, etc. But each time there was only one widget at a time. This is not what even the most trivial apps look like. Even a pretty basic app will have at least a couple widgets. In this chapter we're going to see how to address this issue.

## Defining Custom Widgets in Code

Actually there are two ways we can do it. We can either create our custom widgets or use layouts. In our project we'll stick to the latter, but still let's have a look at custom widgets too for a minute.

We can create our custom widgets by inheriting from the **Widget** class. Then we can put a couple of the standard widgets you already know into it. So, technically speaking, we're still going to have just one widget, but it will look as if there were more.

Suppose we need a text input and two buttons, so three widgets altogether. So, let's create a custom widget that contains these three elementary widgets.

Here's the Python code:

```
# File name: test.py

from kivy.app import App

# We'll need the Widget class
# to inherit from.
from kivy.uix.widget import Widget

# Here is the inheritance.
class MyCustomWidget(Widget):
    # We're going to implement it
    # in the kv file.
    pass

class TestApp(App):
    def build(self):
        # Now we want our custom
        # widget to be returned.
        return MyCustomWidget()

if __name__ == '__main__':
    TestApp().run()
```

As you can see, the **MyCustomWidget** class will be implemented in the kv file. Here it is:

```
# File name: test.kv

# We need to implement the
# MyCustomWidget class here.
<MyCustomWidget>:
    # There's going to be a text
    # input and two buttons.
    TextInput:
        hint_text: 'Type something'
    Button:
        text: 'Press Me'
    Button:
        text: 'Press Me Too'
```

In the code above **MyCustomWidget** is contained in angled brackets because this is the so-called **class rule notation**. This is how we use classes in the Kivy language. The text input and the two buttons are not contained in angled brackets because these are instances. This is how we make the distinction between class and instance in the Kivy language.

Now look what happens when you run this program: Where are the text input and the first button? Well, they are there, just stacked on top of each other under the second button. Our custom widget fills the whole window and its particular components are all in the bottom left corner of the window. We're now coming to the point where we have to do something with the position and size of our widgets.

# Widget Position and Size

All widgets have the **pos** and **size** properties which you can use to position and scale them appropriately. Each of the two properties is defined as a pair of fixed coordinates in pixels. In Kivy the coordinate **(0, 0)** is in the bottom left corner, which is just like in math, but unlike in a lot of other frameworks.

Anyway, let's set the positions of the three components of our custom widget so that we can see them all:

```
# File name: test.kv

<MyCustomWidget>:
    TextInput:
        hint_text: 'Type something'
        # Position the text input 20 pixels from the left
        # and 150 pixels from the bottom. This is where the
        # lower left corner of the widget will be.
        pos: 20, 150
    Button:
        text: 'Press Me'
        # Position the button 20 pixels from the left
        # and 20 pixels from the bottom.
        pos: 20, 20
    Button:
        text: 'Press Me Too'
        # Position the button 200 pixels from the left
        # and 20 pixels from the bottom.
        pos: 200, 20
```

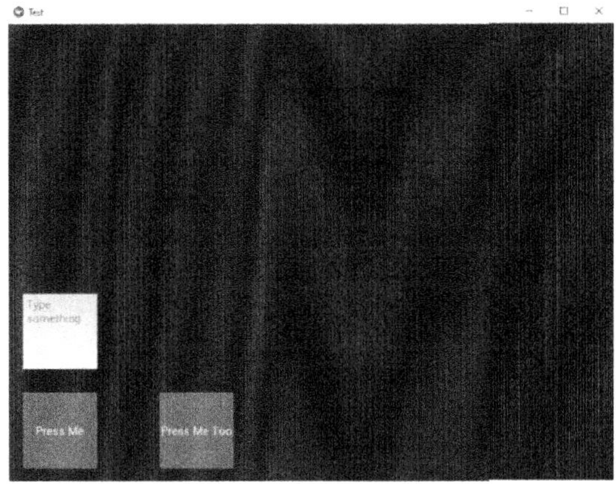


Let's run the program. Now at least you can see all three elementary widgets.

I don't particularly like their dimensions, though, so let me scale them using the **size** property.

```
# File name: test.kv

<MyCustomWidget>:
    TextInput:
        hint_text: 'Type something'
        pos: 20, 150
        # Make the text input 300 x 40 pixels.
        size: 300, 40
    Button:
        text: 'Press Me'
        pos: 20, 20
        # Make the button 120 x 40 pixels.
        size: 120, 40
    Button:
        text: 'Press Me Too'
        pos: 200, 20
        # Make the button 120 x 40 pixels.
        size: 120, 40
```

If you run the program again, the widgets will be scaled in a better way, I think.

# Other Properties in Custom Widgets

If you like, you can also change other properties, like the text color:

```
# File name: test.kv

<MyCustomWidget>:
    TextInput:
        hint_text: 'Type something'
        pos: 20, 150
        size: 300, 40
    Button:
        text: 'Press Me'
        pos: 20, 20
        size: 120, 40
        color: .7, .6, .4, 1
    Button:
        text: 'Press Me Too'
        pos: 200, 20
        size: 120, 40
        color: .7, .6, .4, 1
```

Now the text on the buttons is a different color.

You probably noticed that the code in the kv file is quite repetitive. We have two buttons with very similar properties. In the exercises below you will add two very similar sliders. Naturally, we should avoid repetitive code, so let's do something about it. In the next chapter I'll show you how to avoid repetitive code using class rules. We'll be talking about defining classes in Python code and in the Kivy language in more detail as well.

## It's Your Turn Now...

**EXERCISE 1**

Add a slider to our custom widget. It should be between the buttons and the text input, so it should start 20 pixels from the left and, say, 60 pixels from the bottom. The **`min`**, **`max`** and **`value`** properties should be set to **`0`**, **`100`** and **`25`** respectively. It should be the same width as the text input, so 300 pixels.

HINT: If you don't want to set both the width and height of a widget, but rather just one of them, you should use the **`width`** or **`height`** property with a single value assigned to it instead of **`size`**.

**SOLUTION**

Here's the modified kv code:

```
# File name: test.kv

<MyCustomWidget>:
    TextInput:
        ...
    Button:
        ...
    Button:
        ...
    Slider:
        min: 0
        max: 100
        value: 25
        pos: 20, 60
        width: 300
```

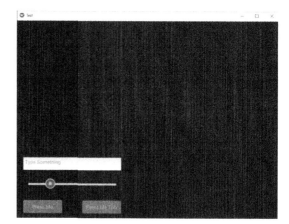

Run the app and you'll see the slider you just added.

**EXERCISE 2**

Add one more slider, this time with vertical orientation. It should be on the right-hand side, so it should start 320 pixels from the left and 20 pixels from the bottom. The **min**, **max** and **value** properties should be set to **0**, **100** and **25** respectively, so just like with the first slider. Its height should be 180 pixels.

**SOLUTION**

Here's the code:

```
# File name: test.kv

<MyCustomWidget>:
    ...
    Slider:
        ...
    Slider:
        orientation: 'vertical'
        min: 0
        max: 100
        value: 25
        pos: 320, 20
        height: 180
```

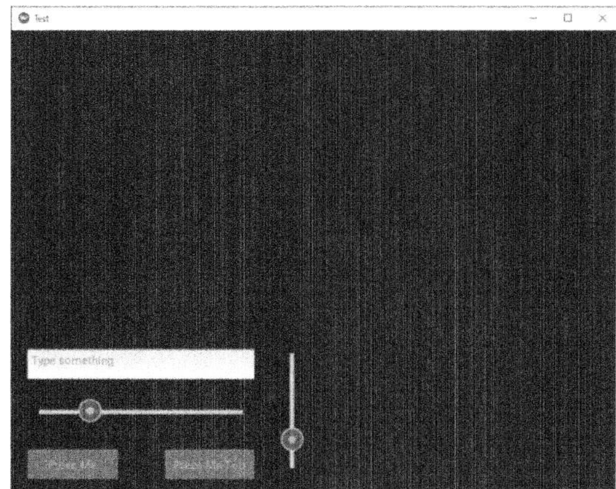

If you now run the program, you will see the two sliders.

# Chapter 16 – Classes and Class Rules

In the previous chapter we created a custom widget. We named it **MyCustomWidget**. It consists of a text input, two buttons and two sliders. Let's have a look at the code again. Here's the Python file:

```
# File name: test.py

from kivy.app import App
from kivy.uix.widget import Widget

class MyCustomWidget(Widget):
    pass

class TestApp(App):
    def build(self):
        return MyCustomWidget()

if __name__ == '__main__':
    TestApp().run()
```

And here's the kv file:

```
# File name: test.kv

<MyCustomWidget>:
    TextInput:
        hint_text: 'Type something'
        pos: 20, 150
        size: 300, 40
    Button:
        text: 'Press Me'
        pos: 20, 20
        size: 120, 40
        color: .7, .6, .4, 1
    Button:
        text: 'Press Me Too'
        pos: 200, 20
        size: 120, 40
        color: .7, .6, .4, 1

    # Slider added in exercise 1
    Slider:
        min: 0
        max: 100
        value: 25
        pos: 20, 60
        width: 300

    # Slider added in exercise 2
    Slider:
        orientation: 'vertical'
        min: 0
        max: 100
        value: 25
        pos: 320, 20
        height: 180
```

## Defining Classes in the Kivy Language

As you can see, the code in the kv file is quite repetitive. In particular, the two buttons share some properties and so do the sliders. So, if you decide to change the color of the button text, for example, you have to do it twice. What if there were 10 buttons or 20 sliders?

The kv code is easy to refactor. Let's just create a custom button and a custom slider and then use them in our custom widget. One more time I'd like to emphasize that you use angled brackets to define a class, but you don't use any brackets if you want to instantiate a widget of that class.

So, if you want to define a class in the Kivy language, you just put the name of the class in angled brackets. If you want the class to inherit from another class, you separate the subclass and the base class with the **@** character.

This will be more visible in the code:

```
# File name: test.kv

# First let's define our custom button. It should inherit from the Button
# class. To make a class inherit from another class in kv, you use the
# following syntax:
###
### <subclass@base_class>
###
# where subclass inherits from base_class.

<MyCustomButton@Button>:
    # Here we're going to put all the code that is repeated in each button.
    # Then you can remove this part of the code from the instances of the
    # custom button.
    size: 120, 40
    color: .7, .6, .4, 1

<MyCustomSlider@Slider>:
    # Here we're going to put all the code that is repeated in each slider.
    # Then you can remove this part of the code from the instances of the
    # custom slider.
    min: 0
    max: 100
    value: 25

<MyCustomWidget>:
    TextInput:
        hint_text: 'Type something'
        pos: 20, 150
        size: 300, 40

    # Now we'll use the custom button that we just created. Let's instantiate
    # the two buttons - there are no angled brackets for instances.
    MyCustomButton:
        text: 'Press Me'
        pos: 20, 20
    MyCustomButton:
        text: 'Press Me Too'
        pos: 200, 20

    # Now we'll use the custom slider that we just created.
    MyCustomSlider:
        pos: 20, 60
        width: 300
    MyCustomSlider:
        orientation: 'vertical'
        pos: 320, 20
        height: 180
```

If you now run the program, it will work just like before. So, in the example above we use class rules before the root widget. These are just class definitions in the Kivy language.

## Defining Classes in Python

Alternatively, you could define the **MyCustomButton** class in Python code and inherit it from **Button** there. Then you don't need the inheritance in kv anymore. Let's just do it so that you can see how. So, first let's modify the Python file:

```
# File name: test.py

from kivy.app import App
from kivy.uix.widget import Widget

# We're going to need the Button and
# the Slider.
from kivy.uix.button import Button
from kivy.uix.slider import Slider

# Here's the inheritance: we're defining
# the MyCustomButton and MyCustomSlider
# classes that inherit from Button and
# Slider respectively. We're leaving the
# implementation for the kv file.

class MyCustomButton(Button):
    pass

class MyCustomSlider(Slider):
    pass

class MyCustomWidget(Widget):
    pass

class TestApp(App):
    def build(self):
        return MyCustomWidget()

if __name__ == '__main__':
    TestApp().run()
```

And now let's modify the kv file:

```
# File name: test.kv

# The inheritance is now in the Python
# file, so let's remove it from here.
<MyCustomButton>:
    size: 120, 40
    color: .7, .6, .4, 1

<MyCustomSlider>:
    min: 0
    max: 100
    value: 25

<MyCustomWidget>:
    TextInput:
        hint_text: 'Type something'
        pos: 20, 150
        size: 300, 40
    MyCustomButton:
        text: 'Press Me'
        pos: 20, 20
    MyCustomButton:
        text: 'Press Me Too'
        pos: 200, 20
    MyCustomSlider:
        pos: 20, 60
        width: 300
    MyCustomSlider:
        orientation: 'vertical'
        pos: 320, 20
        height: 180
```

If you run the program now, it will again work exactly as it did before.

# The Problem with Fixed Positions

If you try resizing the window, you will notice that the widgets are not adjusted accordingly. In most scenarios you want them to be more flexible. The **pos** property that we've been using so far uses fixed positions in pixels, but you can also assign it a relative value. To this end you can use two internal Kivy variables, **root** and **self**, which we are going to discuss in the next chapter, along with the **app** variable.

# It's Your Turn Now...

### EXERCISE 1

The values of the properties set in the class rules will hold in all instances of a given widget. So, for example, if we define our custom slider like so:

```
<MyCustomSlider>:
    min: 0
    max: 100
    value: 25
```

and then instantiate it like so:

```
MyCustomSlider:
    pos: 20, 60
    width: 300
```

the values of **min**, **max** and **value** in the instance will be exactly the same as in the class rule. But if you want to tweak one or more of the values for a particular instance, you can just set them in the instance and the value from the class rule will be overwritten.

That said, add another **MyCustomSlider** to our custom widget. It should be oriented vertically and placed to the right of the previous one. You can set **pos** to **(400, 20)** and height to **180**. This slider should however have the **min** and **max** properties set to **0** and **200** respectively.

### SOLUTION

We only have to overwrite the **max** property, because the **min** property is the same as in the class rule.

Here's the code:

```
# File name: test.kv
...
<MyCustomWidget>:
    TextInput:
        ...
    MyCustomButton:
        ...
    MyCustomButton:
        ...
    MyCustomSlider:
        ...
    MyCustomSlider:
        ...
    MyCustomSlider:
        orientation: 'vertical'
        pos: 400, 20
        height: 180
        max: 200
```

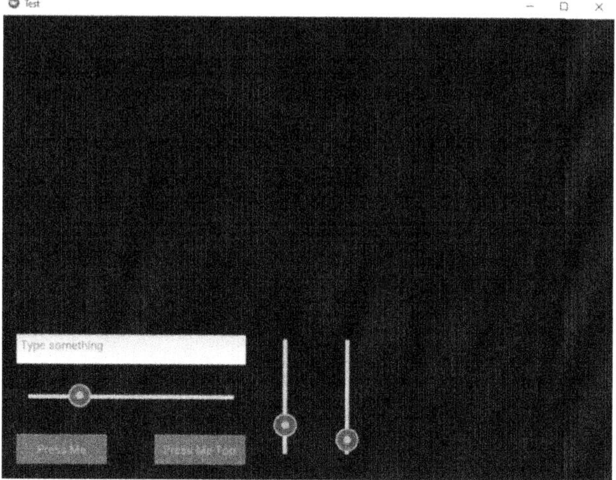

If you run your app now, you will see the third slider on the right.

### EXERCISE 2

You might have noticed that we now have three sliders, one horizontal and two vertical ones. The two vertical sliders also share some properties, like **orientation** and **height**. So, define another class, **MyCustomVerticalSlider**, which inherits (in the kv file) from **MyCustomSlider** and then use it in **MyCustomWidget**.

### SOLUTION

Here's the code:

```
# File name: test.kv
...
<MyCustomSlider>:
    ...

# Here's the new class that inherits
# from MyCustomSlider.
<MyCustomVerticalSlider@MyCustomSlider>:
    orientation: 'vertical'
    height: 180
```

```
<MyCustomWidget>:
    ...
    MyCustomSlider:
        ...

    # the two custom vertical sliders
    MyCustomVerticalSlider:
        pos: 320, 20
    MyCustomVerticalSlider:
        pos: 400, 20
        max: 200
```

If you run the program now, you will see the same as before.

# Chapter 17 – The root, self and app Variables

In the previous chapter we created a custom widget. Let's have a look at it again. Here's the Python code:

```
# File name: test.py

from kivy.app import App
from kivy.uix.widget import Widget
from kivy.uix.button import Button
from kivy.uix.slider import Slider

class MyCustomButton(Button):
    pass

class MyCustomSlider(Slider):
    pass

class MyCustomWidget(Widget):
    pass

class TestApp(App):
    def build(self):
        return MyCustomWidget()

if __name__ == '__main__':
    TestApp().run()
```

And here's the kv file:

```
# File name: test.kv

<MyCustomButton>:
    size: 120, 40
    color: .7, .6, .4, 1

<MyCustomSlider>:
    min: 0
    max: 100
    value: 25

<MyCustomVerticalSlider@MyCustomSlider>:

    orientation: 'vertical'
    height: 180

<MyCustomWidget>:
    TextInput:
        hint_text: 'Type something'
        pos: 20, 150
        size: 300, 40
    MyCustomButton:
        text: 'Press Me'
        pos: 20, 20
    MyCustomButton:
        text: 'Press Me Too'
        pos: 200, 20
    MyCustomSlider:
        pos: 20, 60
        width: 300
    MyCustomVerticalSlider:
        pos: 320, 20
    MyCustomVerticalSlider:
        pos: 400, 20
        max: 200
```

Run the program and try resizing the window. You will notice that the widgets are not adjusted accordingly. This is because the **pos** property that we've been using so far uses fixed positions in pixels. In the previous chapter I mentioned that you can also assign it a relative value, using the internal Kivy variables, **root** and **self**. In this chapter we'll see how to do that. And also, we'll discuss another Kivy variable, **app**.

# Positioning with the root and self Variables

What are the two variables, **root** and **self**, then? You may be familiar with the **self** variable that is used in Python as a reference to the object in which it's used. It works exactly the same in kv. The other variable, **root**, is a reference to the widget class at the top of the hierarchy.

For simplicity's sake, let's temporarily comment out the three sliders. Don't delete them completely, because we're going to need them in the exercises at the end of this chapter.

If you use the **self** variable inside one of the **MyCustomButton** instances, it'll be a reference to that very instance. If you use **root** inside a **MyCustomButton** instance, it will be a reference to **MyCustomWidget**, which is at the top of the hierarchy. We use dot notation to access the particular properties of the widgets referenced by **self** and **root**.

Having said that, we can now rewrite the kv code so that the positions of the internal widgets (the text input and the two custom buttons) are more flexible. Here's the kv file:

```
# File name: test.kv
...
<MyCustomWidget>:
    TextInput:
        hint_text: 'Type something'
        # The x coordinate of the text input should be equal to the x coordinate of the
        # whole custom widget (which fills the whole window). Let's add a 20-pixel
        # offset to it so that it doesn't touch the window.
        # ****************************************************
        # The y coordinate should be relative to the top side of the custom widget
        # (which is referenced by root). If you leave root.top, you won't see the text
        # input widget because its lower side will be on the top border of the window
        # and the rest of it will be outside the custom widget and outside the window.
        # This is why we have to subtract the text input's height. Additionally let's
        # subtract 20 to give some more room.
        pos: root.x + 20, root.top - self.height - 20
        size: 300, 40
    MyCustomButton:
        text: 'Press Me'
        # The button should be relative to the root's x and y coordinates.
        # The y coordinate is the one at the bottom of a widget. We'll add a 20-pixel
        # offset again.
        pos: root.x + 20, root.y + 20
    MyCustomButton:
        text: 'Press Me Too'
        # The other button will be relative to the right border of the custom widget.
        # Again, we have to subtract its width in order to see it. We'll add an offset
        # again. The y coordinate of the button will be relative to the bottom border
        # of the root widget, just like before.
        pos: root.right - self.width - 20, root.y + 20
    # MyCustomSlider:
    ...
```

Let's run the program. Try resizing the window and you'll see that this time the internal widgets are moving along.

This is because their positions are no longer fixed, but rather relative to different parts of the root widget.

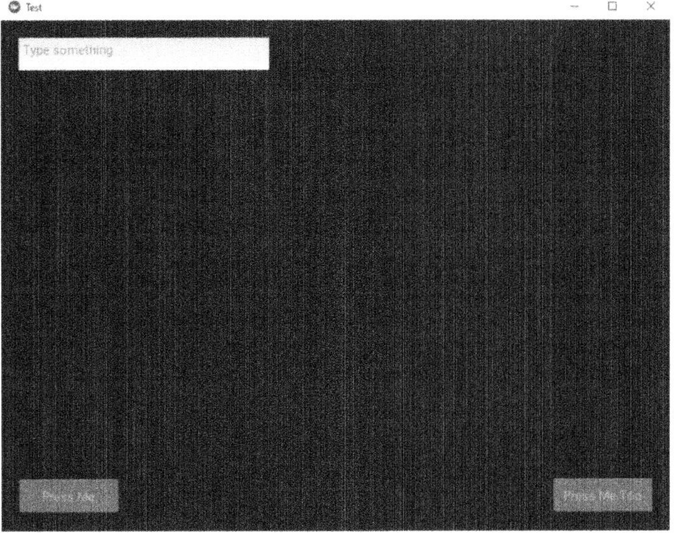

And here's a visualization of all the values that you can see in the code. This should help you understand what is what even more:

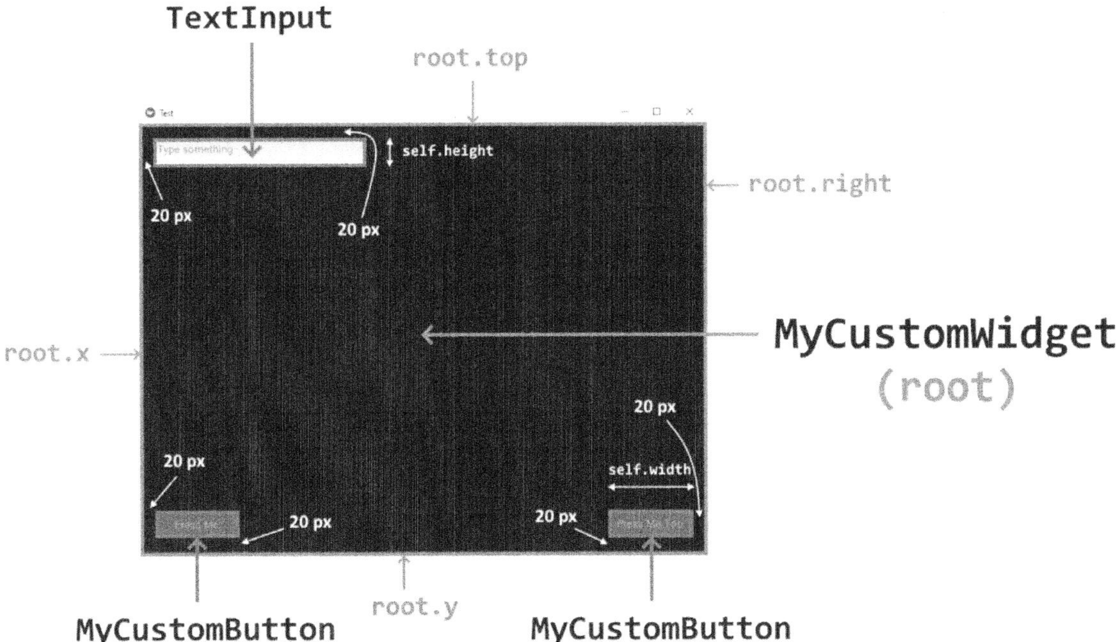


If this way of positioning widgets doesn't seem very clear and intuitive to you, the good news is that most of the time we'll be using a more straightforward way of doing it, but first we need to talk about layouts. We'll be talking about all the properties that you can use to position widgets in more detail when we need them. For now it's enough to know how the **x**, **y**, **top** and **right** properties are used.

# Using the root, self and app Variables

The **self** and **root** variables are not only used for positioning. Besides, there's the **app** variable. We're going to use all of them a lot throughout the project, but let's just have a quick look at what, among other things, we can do with them.

## self

Let's start with **self**. You can use it both in the class rules, so in the class definitions, and in instances. We already have it in the instance of text input (**self.height**) and the second button (**self.width**). Let's add some more:

```
# File name: test.kv

<MyCustomButton>:
    # Here, in the class rule, the text property is set to the string
    # representation of the button's size.
    text: str(self.size)
    size: 120, 40
    color: .7, .6, .4, 1

...

<MyCustomWidget>:
    TextInput:
        ...
    MyCustomButton:
        # We don't need the text property here, because the text defined
        # in the class rule will be used, so the size of the button.
        #text: 'Press Me'
        pos: root.x + 20, root.y + 20

    MyCustomButton:
        # Here we want to overwrite the default text defined in the class
        # rule. On this button instance we want to see its position.
        text: str(self.pos)
        pos: root.right - self.width - 20, root.y + 20

    # MyCustomSlider:
    ...
```

If you now run the program, you will see the size on the first button and the position on the second one. Try resizing the window and watch the position on the second button change.

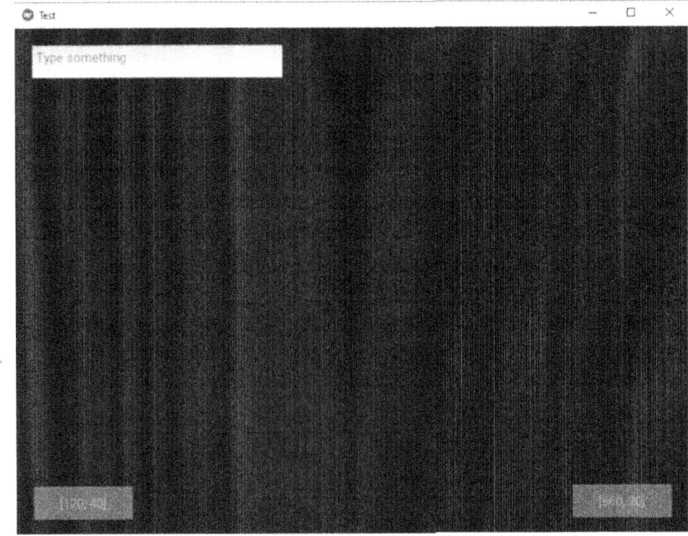


## root

You also already saw some examples of the **root** variable: **root.x**, **root.y**, **root.top**, **root.right**.

This variable always refers to the root widget, which in our example is **MyCustomWidget**. Let's use the **root** variable to set the text input's **text** property to the size of the whole root widget:

```
# File name: test.kv
...
<MyCustomWidget>:
    TextInput:
        hint_text: 'Type something'
        pos: root.x + 20, root.top - self.height - 20
        size: 300, 40

        # This time we want the text input to display the size of MyCustomWidget.
        text: str(root.size)

    MyCustomButton:
        ...
```

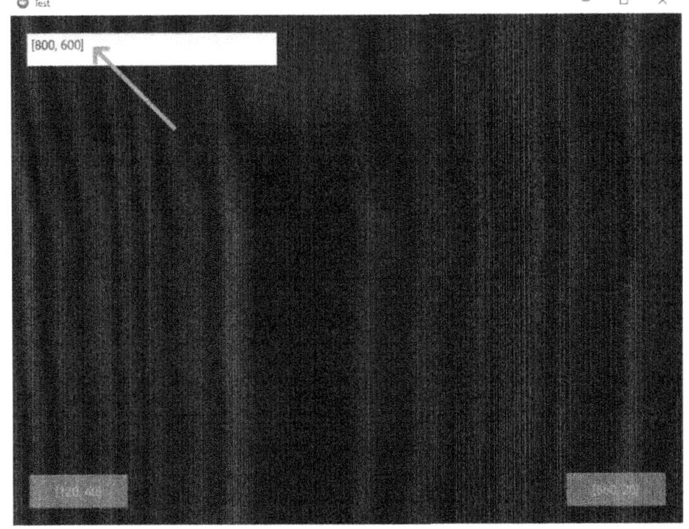


If you now run the program, you will see the root widget's size in the text input.

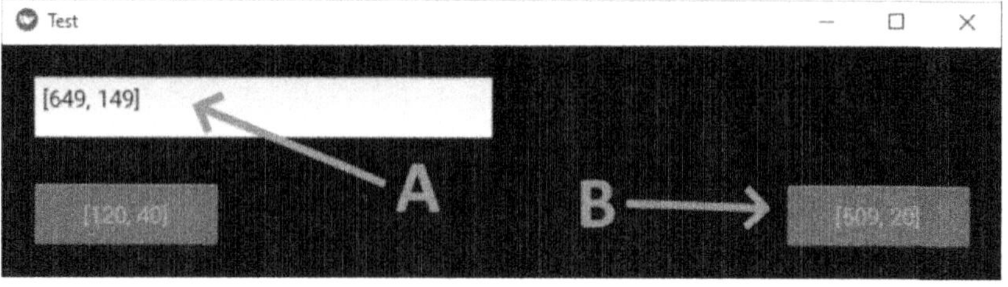


If you resize the window, the root widget will be resized too because it fills the whole window. The text in the text input will be updated (A). Also the text on the second button will be updated just like before (B):

## app

Now, what about the **app** variable? We're going to use it a couple times in our project. The **app** variable refers to the instance of the application. So, you can use it in kv code to access data defined in the **App** class or rather the class derived from **App**. Let's have a simple example. In the Python file, inside the **TestApp** class, let's define an attribute and a method:

```
# File name: test.py
...
class TestApp(App):
    # Let's define an attribute...
    message = 'WELCOME'

    # ...and a method.
    def changeText(self, button):
        button.text = '***'

    def build(self):
        return MyCustomWidget()

if __name__ == '__main__':
    TestApp().run()
```

Now we have access in the kv file to the attribute and method defined in **TestApp**:

```
# File name: test.kv
...
<MyCustomWidget>:
    TextInput:
        ...
    MyCustomButton:
        ...

    MyCustomButton:
        # We no longer want the button to display its position. Instead it should
        # display the string defined in the TestApp class in the Python file. Here
        # the app class can be accessed by means of the app variable.
        text: app.message
        pos: root.right - self.width - 20, root.y + 20
```

```
        # Also, let's add an event. When the button is pressed, it should call the
        # changeText method defined in TestApp in the Python file and pass itself
        # (hence the self variable) as the argument to the method.
        on_press: app.changeText(self)

    # MyCustomSlider:
    ...
```

Run the app and watch the second button.

**before pressing the second button** **after pressing the second button**

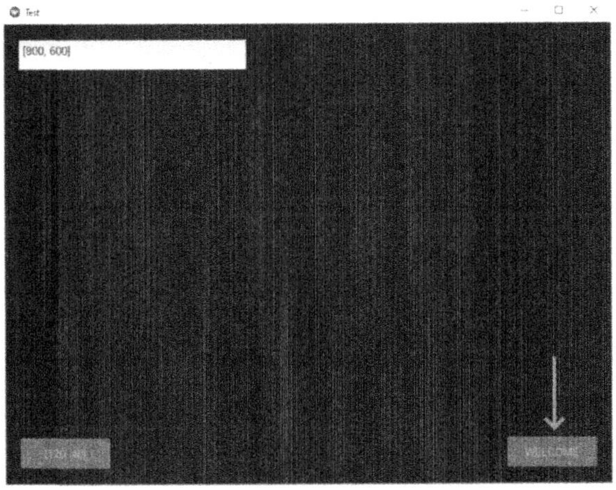

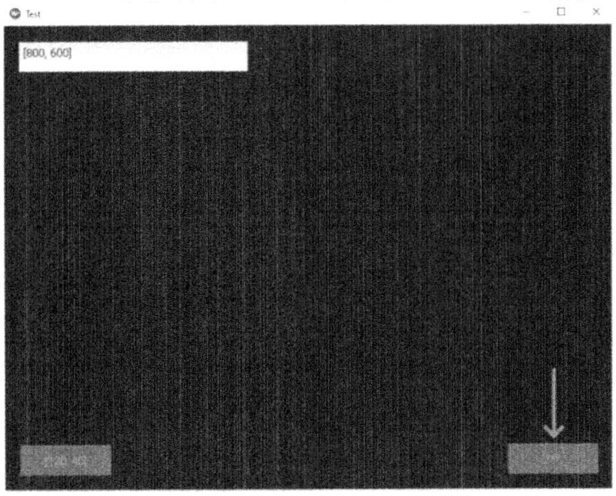

This will do for now, but don't worry, you're going to see lots of other interesting examples where the **root**, **self** and **app** variables are used.

# It's Your Turn Now...

### EXERCISE 1

We'll need the sliders now. Uncomment all the sliders in the kv code. They now have fixed positions. Change the positions so that they are relative. Use the following values:

- the horizontal slider: 20 pixels to the right of the left border of the root widget and 60 pixels above the lower border of the root widget.

- the first vertical slider: 400 pixels to the left of the right border of the root widget and 240 pixels below the upper border of the root widget.

- the second vertical slider: 300 pixels to the left of the right border of the root widget and 240 pixels below the upper border of the root widget.

**SOLUTION**

Here's the code:

```
# File name: test.kv
...
<MyCustomWidget>:
    ...
    MyCustomSlider:
        pos: root.x + 20, root.y + 60
        width: 300

    MyCustomVerticalSlider:
        pos: root.right - 400, root.top - 240

    MyCustomVerticalSlider:
        pos: root.right - 300, root.top - 240
        max: 200
```

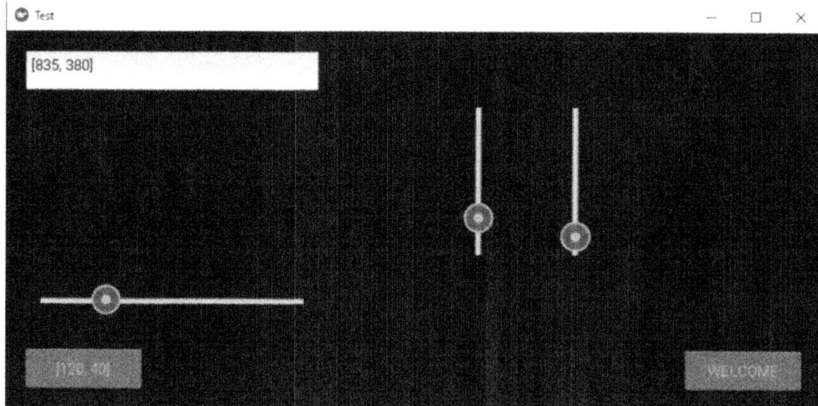


If you now run the program and resize the window, you will see that the positions of the sliders are no longer fixed.

**EXERCISE 2**

Add another attribute and two methods to the **TestApp** class:

- Name the attribute **slider_value** and set it to **85**.

- Name the first method **addTrack**. It should have two parameters: **slider** and **track_width**. In the method the value of the **value_track** property on the slider that you pass as the first argument should be set to **True**, which means we'll be able to see the default white track on the slider. Next the value of the **value_track_width** property on the slider should be set to **track_width**, which is the second argument.

- Name the second method **removeTrack**. It should take only one parameter, **slider**. The method first should check whether the **value_track** property on the slider is **True** and if so, remove the track by setting the property to **False**.

Then, in the kv file, add the **on_value** event to the **MyCustomVerticalSlider** class rule so that it is fired on each instance of the class. This event is fired whenever the value property of a slider changes. Now, if the value of the value property is greater than 50, the **addTrack** method from **TestApp** should be called (with a width of 5), otherwise the **removeTrack** method should be called.

Finally, inside the **MyCustomSlider** instance overwrite the **value** property of the slider with the value assigned to the **slider_value** attribute in **TestApp**.

**SOLUTION**

Here's the Python code:

```
# File name: test.py
...
class TestApp(App):
    message = 'WELCOME'

    # Let's create another attribute.
    slider_value = 85

    def changeText(self, button):
        button.text = '***'

    # Let's define two other methods:
    def addTrack(self, slider, track_width):
        slider.value_track = True
        slider.value_track_width = track_width

    def removeTrack(self, slider):
        if slider.value_track:
            slider.value_track = False

    def build(self):
        ...
```

And here's the kv file:

```
# File name: test.kv
...
<MyCustomVerticalSlider@MyCustomSlider>:
    orientation: 'vertical'
    height: 180

    # Let's add the on_value event.
    on_value: app.addTrack(self, 5) if self.value > 50 else app.removeTrack(self)

<MyCustomWidget>:
    ...
    MyCustomSlider:
```

```
        pos: root.x + 20, root.y + 60
        width: 300

        # Let's overwrite the value property with the value
        # defined in the TestApp class.
        value: app.slider_value

    MyCustomVerticalSlider:
        ...
```

If you now run the app, the value of the **value** property of the horizontal slider will be **85** (A) and if you move any of the vertical sliders, the **on_value** event will fire and depending on the actual value the track will be added or removed (B).

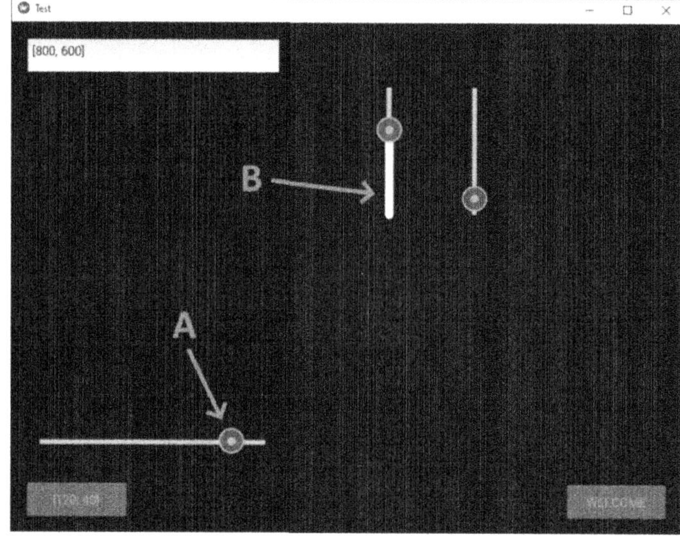

# Part III

# Kivy Layouts

In this part of the book we'll learn how to use layouts in Kivy. There are many types of layouts and we'll see what each of them best lends itself to. We'll be also talking about sizing and positioning widgets in layouts and about embedding layouts in other layouts.

# Chapter 18 - Introduction to Kivy Layouts

Before we jump into the Kivy layout basics, let's recap on what we know. In the previous chapter we left off with a custom widget consisting of a text input, two buttons and three sliders.

As mentioned before, this is still just one widget. But you are not limited to just one widget. If you need more, you can put them in a special container called **layout**.

A Kivy layout inherits from the `Widget` class and takes care of organizing the widgets embedded in it. There are a couple of different layouts available and they all organize the widgets in different ways. We're going to discuss all the particular layouts in the following chapters. For now let's just list and characterize them briefly so that you know what there is at your disposal. I'm also going to talk about the basics of positioning and scaling widgets inside layouts in this part. Actually, let's start with the latter.

## Introduction to Positioning and Scaling Widgets in Layouts

Up to now we've been using the `pos` and `size` properties to position and scale widgets respectively. You can also use them in layouts, but there are more options available. Usually instead of the two aforementioned properties, we use two other properties, `pos_hint` and `size_hint`. These use proportional coordinates, so expressed as percentages of the total size of the window. It's going to become clearer when we see some examples in the following chapters. Actually, there are even more options than just `pos`, `size`, `pos_hint` and `size_hint`. The one thing to remember here is that properties like `pos`, `size`, `width` or `height` are used with fixed numbers of pixels, whereas properties like `pos_hint` and `size_hint`, as well as some others, are used with proportional coordinates.

## Kivy Layout Types

So, what layouts do we have? Quite a few.

### `FloatLayout`

The first one to mention is `FloatLayout`. This layout works pretty much the same as we saw when we were creating custom widgets. It organizes the widgets inside the app window using the proportional coordinates, `pos_hint` and `size_hint`, so the values are percentages of the window's dimensions.

**RelativeLayout**

This layout differs from the previous one in that positions are relative to the layout and not the window.

**BoxLayout**

This is a layout we're going to use a lot throughout the whole project. It organizes the widgets in a single row or column.

**StackLayout**

This layout is similar to **BoxLayout** in that it also organizes the widgets in a row or column. The difference is that if it runs out of space, the next widgets are placed in the next row or column depending on its orientation.

**GridLayout**

This layout organizes the widgets in a grid, with a given number of rows or columns.

**AnchorLayout**

If you want your widgets to stick to the top, bottom or one of the sides, this is the layout to choose. It just anchors the widgets at specific positions.

**ScatterLayout**

This layout is the way to go if your application uses multitouch gestures for translating, scaling and rotating. Apart from that it's very much like **RelativeLayout**.

**PageLayout**

This layout is slightly different. You can use it to create a multipage effect where the particular pages may be flipped. You will usually put another layout in each page and put the widgets only inside of it.

If you read the last sentence about **PageLayout** carefully, you might have noticed that you can nest layouts, so put one layout inside another. It's a very flexible feature, which we'll be using a lot.

These are the Kivy layout basics, more or less. And remember, the descriptions of the layouts above are not exhaustive, to say the least. This is just for you so that you know what layouts there are. But we're only going to discuss most of the layouts in more detail in the following chapters, so don't worry if you don't understand layouts now. Actually we haven't even used any of them, which we are going to fix in the next chapter. So, let's head to the first layout, **FloatLayout**. In the next chapter we'll be also talking about scaling and positioning widgets in layouts.

# Chapter 19 – Widget Size and Position in Layouts

In the previous chapter we listed all the Kivy layouts and mentioned briefly the rules of positioning widgets inside layouts. Now we're going to talk in more detail about widget size and position in layouts.

Let's start with the first layout, the **`FloatLayout`**. It works in a similar way as when we created our custom widgets. The difference is in how widgets inside the FloatLayout, and actually inside other layouts as well, are scaled and positioned. This is the subject of this chapter.

As mentioned in the previous chapter, the FloatLayout organizes the widgets inside the app window using the proportional coordinates, **`pos_hint`** and **`size_hint`**, so the values are percentages of the window's dimensions.

What we are going to do now is write code that uses a FloatLayout. To demonstrate how the properties used for sizing and positioning work, let's put one, and then more buttons in it.

## The `size_hint` and `pos_hint` Properties

This time we're going to use the **`size_hint`** property instead of **`size`** to set the widget size.

Suppose the button should occupy 30% of the window in horizontal direction and 10% in vertical direction. These percentages should be expressed as **`.3`** and **`.1`** respectively.

We're also going to use the **`pos_hint`** property instead of **`pos`**. The **`pos_hint`** property must be assigned a dictionary with the **`x`**, **`right`**, **`y`** and **`top`** values specified.

Naturally, only up to two of them should be specified at any given time: **`x`** or **`right`** for the horizontal position and **`y`** or **`top`** for the vertical position.

## The `x`, `right`, `y` and `top` Properties

What are the four properties?

**`x`** - the left border of the widget

**`right`** - the right border of the widget

**`y`** - the bottom border of the widget

**`top`** - the top border of the widget

The values for each of the properties above are in the range from 0 to 1.

For example, if **x** is set to **0**, it means the left border, if it's set to **1**, it means the right border and if it's set to **.3**, it's 30% into the window from the left border. The other properties work the same.

To make it clearer, let's use different combinations of the **size_hint** and **pos_hint** properties. If you run the program after each change, you will quickly see how they work.

The content of the FloatLayout will be defined in the kv file, so in the Python file we're only going to return a **FloatLayout** instance without bothering what there is in it.

This is why the Python file will be the same for each of the examples below. What is going to change is the kv file. So, just remove all the code from **test.py** and **test.kv**. We're not going to need it anymore.

Then type in the following Python code:

```
# File name: test.py

from kivy.app import App

# We
need the FloatLayout, so let's import it.
from kivy.uix.floatlayout import FloatLayout

class TestApp(App):
    def build(self):
        # Let's return a FloatLayout.
        # We'll define it in the kv file.
        return FloatLayout()

if __name__ == '__main__':
    TestApp().run()
```

# Widget Size

Let's start with some basic examples. In the first couple examples we're not going to bother with position, we're only going to set the widget size. This means the default position will be assigned, which is the bottom left corner.

## Setting Widget Size with the size_hint Property

Here's the first kv snippet:

```
# File name: test.kv

# Here's our FloatLayout class
<FloatLayout>:
    Button:
        text: 'Press Me'

        # The button should occupy 50% of
        # the window in both horizontal
        # and vertical direction.
        size_hint: .5, .5
```

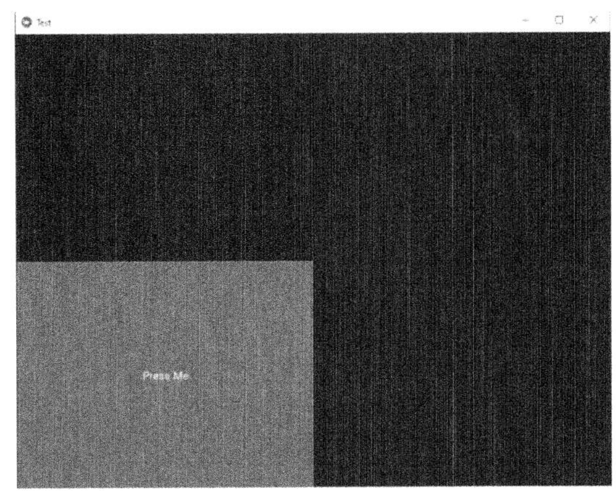


Run the program now and you will see that the

button indeed occupies 50% of the screen in each direction.

Notice that even if you resize the window, the button will still occupy 50% of it in each direction.

And now we want the button to occupy the whole width of the window and 30% of its height:

```
# File name: test.kv

<FloatLayout>:
    Button:
        text: 'Press Me'
        size_hint: 1, .3
```

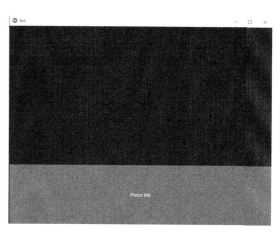

Again, try resizing the window and you will see that regardless of its size, the button will always occupy the whole width and 30% of the height.

Finally let's make the button fill the whole window. Actually it will fill the whole FloatLayout, which itself fills the whole window.

Here's the code:

```
# File name: test.kv

<FloatLayout>:
    Button:
        text: 'Press Me'
        size_hint: 1, 1
```

## Setting Widget Size with the `size_hint_x` and `size_hint_y` Properties

The **`size_hint`** property is set to a tuple of two values, one for scaling in horizontal and the other in vertical direction. But sometimes you may want to scale a widget in just one direction. Then you can use the **`size_hint_x`** or **`size_hint_y`** property, depending on which direction you need.

Let's scale the button only in horizontal direction first:

```
# File name: test.kv

<FloatLayout>:
    Button:
        text: 'Press Me'

        # The button should always occupy
        # 80% of the window's width.
        size_hint_x: .8
```

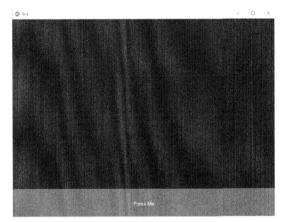

And now let's scale it only in vertical direction:

```
# File name: test.kv

<FloatLayout>:
    Button:
        text: 'Press Me'

        # The button should always occupy
        # 15% of the window's height.
        size_hint_y: .15
```

# Widget Position

Now that you know how to scale the widget, let's experiment with its position. As you know, the default position is at the coordinates **(0, 0)**, which is at the bottom left corner. Now let's try out all the four properties that we listed before: **x**, **right**, **y** and **top**. We're even going to learn two more properties in a minute.

## Horizontal Positioning

Let's start with horizontal positioning. Vertical positioning works pretty much the same, as you will see a bit later.

### The x Property

Anyway, let's modify our kv file so that there are three buttons. We want each button to have the same size, so we can define a custom button.

Here's the code with the **x** properties of the three buttons set to **0**, **.5** and **1** respectively. Remember that **x** is the left border of the widget, so the left border of the button in our case. If you don't set either the **y** or the **top** property, vertical position will default to **y = 0**.

```
# File name: test.kv

<CustomButton@Button>:
    # We want each button to occupy
    # 20% in horizontal direction
    # and 10% in vertical direction.
    size_hint: .2, .1

<FloatLayout>:
    CustomButton:
        text: 'Button 1'

        # left border of the button
        # on the left border of the
        # container
        pos_hint: {'x': 0}

    CustomButton:
        text: 'Button 2'

        # left border of the button
        # in the middle of the width
        # of the container
        pos_hint: {'x': .5}

    CustomButton:
        text: 'Button 3'

        # left border of the button
        # on the right border of the
        # container
        pos_hint: {'x': 1}
```

If you now run the program, this is what you get (here, with some annotations):

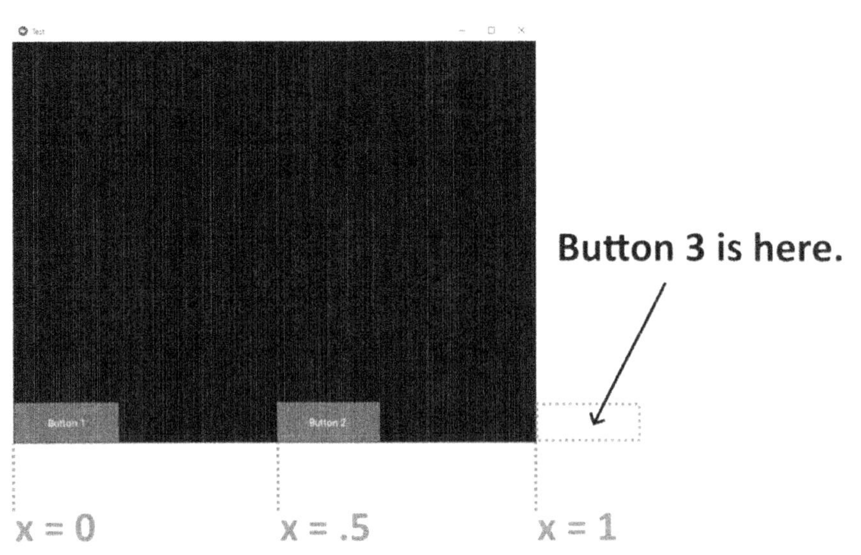


**x value outside the range from 0 to 1**

If you set **x** to a value outside the range from 0 to 1, the button or part of it will be outside the window.

By setting it to a negative value, the button will be moved to the left. If you set it to a number greater than 1, it will be moved to the right.

Finally, by setting it to a number close to 1, the right part of the button will be outside the window, etc. Have a look:

```
# File name: test.kv

<CustomButton@Button>:
    size_hint: .2, .1
```

```
<FloatLayout>:
    CustomButton:
        text: 'Button 1'

        # the whole button outside
        # the window on the left
        pos_hint: {'x': -2}

    CustomButton:
        text: 'Button 2'

        # left part of the button
        # outside the window on the left
        pos_hint: {'x': -.1}

    CustomButton:
        text: 'Button 3'

        # right part of the button
        # outside the window on the right
        pos_hint: {'x': .9}
```

## The center_x and right Properties

Now, suppose we want the buttons to be positioned uniformly: Button 1 on the left, Button 2 in the middle and Button 3 on the right. This would be difficult to achieve with just the **x** property, because you would have to take into consideration the width of the button to calculate the position of its center and right border.

This is where two other properties come in handy: the aforementioned **right** property for the right border of the widget and the **center_x** property for the center of the widget in horizontal direction. Let's see how we can use them:

```
# File name: test.kv

<CustomButton@Button>:
    size_hint: .2, .1

<FloatLayout>:
    CustomButton:
        text: 'Button 1'

        # This button should be
        # on the left.
        pos_hint: {'x': 0}

    CustomButton:
        text: 'Button 2'

        # This button should be
        # in the middle, so let's
        # use the center_x property.
        pos_hint: {'center_x': .5}

    CustomButton:
        text: 'Button 3'

        # This button should be
        # on the right, so let's
        # use the right property.
        pos_hint: {'right': 1}
```

Here (on the right) is the app when you run it (with some annotations again).

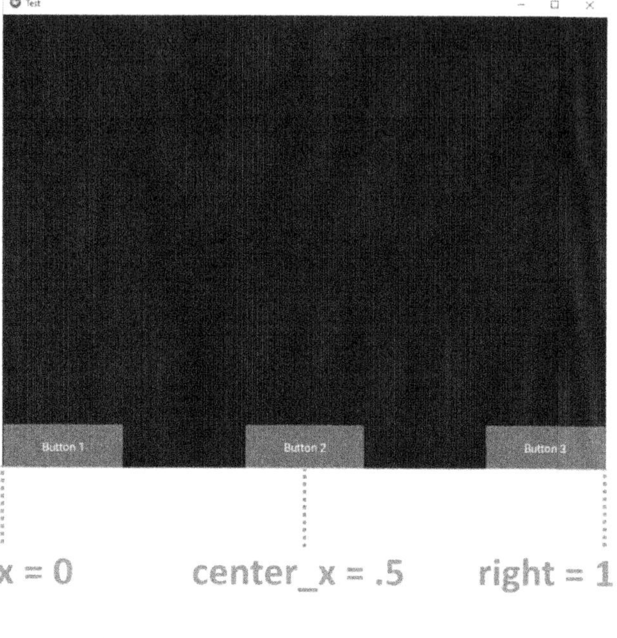


And just one more example with the **center_x** and **right** properties in action:

```
# File name: test.kv

<CustomButton@Button>:
    size_hint: .2, .1

<FloatLayout>:
    CustomButton:
        text: 'Button 1'

        # The right border of this
        # button should be near the
        # left border of the window.
        # Part of the button will be
        # invisible.
        pos_hint: {'right': .1}

    CustomButton:
        text: 'Button 2'

        # The right border of this
        # button should be at the
        # center of the window.
        pos_hint: {'right': .5}

    CustomButton:
        text: 'Button 3'

        # The center of this button
        # should be 75% away from the
        # left border of the window.
        pos_hint: {'center_x': .75}
```

And here (on the right) is how it looks.

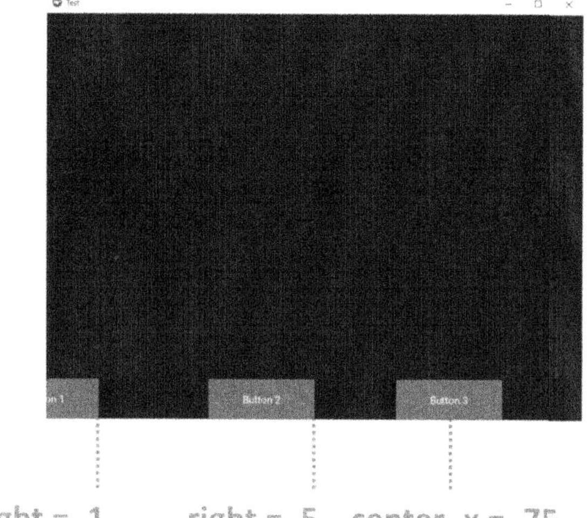


## Vertical Positioning

Now that you understand how the three properties **x**, **center_x** and **right** work, it will be easier to understand how their counterparts in the vertical direction work.

These are **y**, **center_y** and **top**. In the following examples we can omit the **x**, **center_x** and **right** properties in the **pos_hint** dictionary. Then the button will be placed at **x = 0**, which is the default value. Have a look:

```
# File name: test.kv

<CustomButton@Button>:
    size_hint: .2, .1

<FloatLayout>:
    CustomButton:
        text: 'Button 1'

        # The lower border of this
        # button should be on the
        # lower border of the window.
        pos_hint: {'y': 0}

    CustomButton:
        text: 'Button 2'

        # The center of this button
        # should be at the center of
        # the window in vertical
        # direction.
        pos_hint: {'center_y': .5}

    CustomButton:
        text: 'Button 3'

        # The top border of this
        # button should on the
        # top border of the window.
        pos_hint: {'top': 1}
```

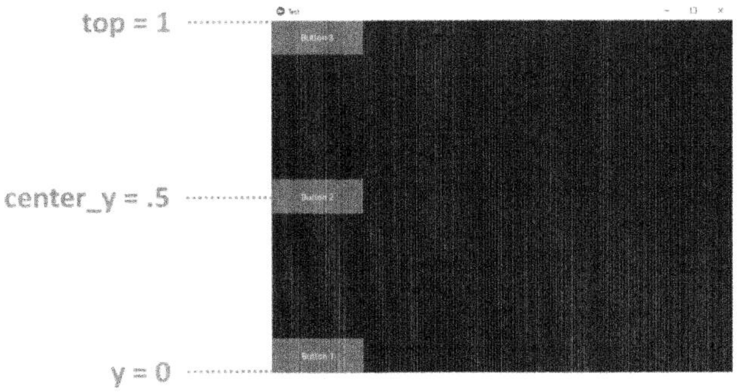

top = 1

center_y = .5

y = 0

## Positioning in Both Directions

Naturally, you can position widgets in both directions at the same time. Then you just have to set two properties in the **pos_hint** dictionary. Here's an example:

```
# File name: test.kv

<CustomButton@Button>:
    size_hint: .2, .1

<FloatLayout>:
    CustomButton:
        text: 'Button 1'

        # The button should be 10% from the left horizontally and its top should be in
        # the middle vertically.
        pos_hint: {'x': .1, 'top': .5}

    CustomButton:
        text: 'Button 2'

        # The button should be in the center of the window.
        pos_hint: {'center_x': .5, 'center_y': .5}

    CustomButton:
        text: 'Button 3'

        # The button should be on the right and 20% above the bottom.
        pos_hint: {'right': 1, 'y': .2}
```

And this is what we get:

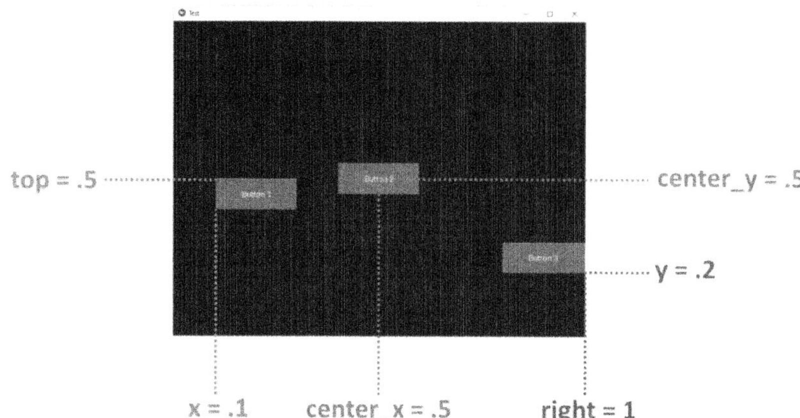


The position properties of each button are in distinct colors in the image to help you visualize what goes where.

Well, these are the basics of scaling and positioning widgets in layouts.

But there's more to it. You can also use the **size** and **pos** properties in layouts. In the next chapter we'll have a look at some more advanced examples of scaling and positioning widgets in layouts.

# It's Your Turn Now...

**EXERCISE 1**

Remove the **CustomButton** class rule and all three **CustomButton** instances from the kv file. Add the following widgets to the FloatLayout:

- A toggle button in the middle with the **text** property initially set to **'SMALL'**, which takes up 20% of the container horizontally and 30% vertically. When in pressed state, the text should change to **'BIG'** and the size of the toggle button should increase so that it occupies 40% of the containing FloatLayout both horizontally and vertically. When in normal state, **text** and **size** should take their original values.

- Four buttons near the four corners. They should be all 10% away from each of the borders of the container. The text properties of the buttons should be set to **'MOVE UP'** for the button near the lower left corner, **'MOVE RIGHT'** for the button near the upper left corner, **'MOVE DOWN'** for the button near the upper right corner and **'MOVE LEFT'** for the button near the lower right corner. Each button should take up 20% of the available space horizontally and 10% vertically. When pressed, three things should happen:

a) the button should move in the appropriate direction to the middle of the height or width of the border it's moving along (the button's center should be at that position),

b) the **text** property should change to **'MOVED'**,

c) the button should be disabled

HINT: To disable a widget, you can set the **disabled** property inherited from the **Widget** class to **True**.

**SOLUTION**

Here's the kv file:

```
# File name: test.kv

<FloatLayout>:
    ToggleButton:
        text: 'SMALL'
        pos_hint: {'center_x': .5, 'center_y': .5}
        size_hint: .2, .3
        on_state: self.text = 'SMALL' if self.state == 'normal' else 'BIG'
        on_state: self.size_hint = (.2, .3) if self.state == 'normal' else (.4, .4)

    Button:
        text: 'MOVE UP'
        size_hint: .2, .1
        pos_hint: {'x': .1, 'y': .1}
        on_press: self.pos_hint = {'x': .1, 'center_y': .5}
        on_press: self.text = 'MOVED'
        on_press: self.disabled = True

    Button:
        text: 'MOVE RIGHT'
        size_hint: .2, .1
        pos_hint: {'x': .1, 'top': .9}
        on_press: self.pos_hint = {'center_x': .5, 'top': .9}
        on_press: self.text = 'MOVED'
        on_press: self.disabled = True

    Button:
        text: 'MOVE DOWN'
        size_hint: .2, .1
        pos_hint: {'right': .9, 'top': .9}
        on_press: self.pos_hint = {'right': .9, 'center_y': .5}
        on_press: self.text = 'MOVED'
        on_press: self.disabled = True

    Button:
        text: 'MOVE LEFT'
        size_hint: .2, .1
        pos_hint: {'right': .9, 'y': .1}
        on_press: self.pos_hint = {'center_x': .5, 'y': .1}
        on_press: self.text = 'MOVED'
        on_press: self.disabled = True
```

If you run this program now, you will see the following:

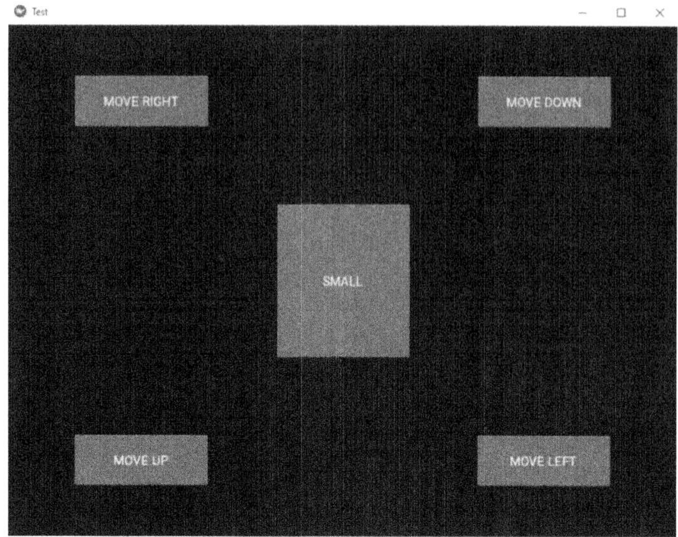


After pressing the toggle button in the middle and each of the four buttons, the app window should look like this:

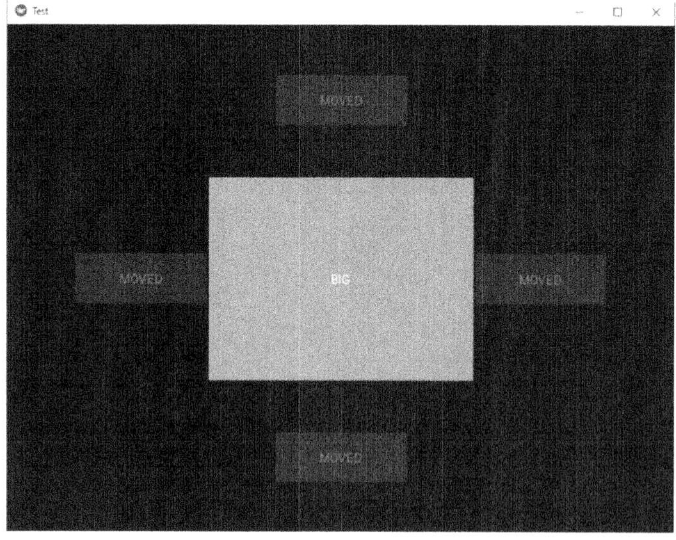


## EXERCISE 2

The code in the kv file that you just created is pretty repetitive, in particular there are four buttons that share the following:

- they all have their **size_hint** set to the same value,

- when pressed, they all change the text to **'MOVED'** and get disabled.

Factor these shared properties and events out into a class rule (you can name it simply **CustomButton**) and then use the custom widget inside the root widget instead of **Button**.

## SOLUTION

Here's the refactored code:

```
# File name: test.kv

<CustomButton@Button>:
    size_hint: .2, .1
    on_press: self.text = 'MOVED'
```

```
    on_press: self.disabled = True

<FloatLayout>:
    ToggleButton:
        text: 'SMALL'
        pos_hint: {'center_x': .5, 'center_y': .5}
        size_hint: .2, .3
        on_state: self.text = 'SMALL' if self.state == 'normal' else 'BIG'
        on_state: self.size_hint = (.2, .3) if self.state == 'normal' else (.4, .4)

    CustomButton:
        text: 'MOVE UP'
        pos_hint: {'x': .1, 'y': .1}
        on_press: self.pos_hint = {'x': .1, 'center_y': .5}

    CustomButton:
        text: 'MOVE RIGHT'
        pos_hint: {'x': .1, 'top': .9}
        on_press: self.pos_hint = {'center_x': .5, 'top': .9}

    CustomButton:
        text: 'MOVE DOWN'
        pos_hint: {'right': .9, 'top': .9}
        on_press: self.pos_hint = {'right': .9, 'center_y': .5}

    CustomButton:
        text: 'MOVE LEFT'
        pos_hint: {'right': .9, 'y': .1}
        on_press: self.pos_hint = {'center_x': .5, 'y': .1}
```

Naturally, if you now run the app, it'll works exactly the same as before.

# Chapter 20 – Advanced Scaling and Positioning

In the previous chapters we saw how widgets on their own and widgets in layouts are positioned and scaled. Before we move on, let's recapitulate briefly on what we already covered about scaling and positioning. So, if you want to scale a widget which is not inside a layout, you use the properties **size**, **width** and **height**. If you want to position such a widget, you use the **pos** property. All these properties use fixed numbers of pixels.

Now, if you want to scale a widget inside a layout, you should use one of the following properties: **size_hint**, **size_hint_x** or **size_hint_y**. They are used with proportions rather than fixed numbers of pixels, so the value you assign to them should be between 0 and 1.

If you want to position a widget inside a layout, you use the **pos_hint** property, to which you assign a dictionary with one or more of the following properties: **x**, **center_x**, **right** (for horizontal positioning), **y**, **center_y**, **top** (for vertical positioning). The values are proportions again, so they should be in the range from 0 to 1. One more thing we discussed in the previous chapter is that the proportions may also be outside the range from 0 to 1 if you want the widget or part of it to be outside the visible app window. Fine, you already know how to scale and position widgets, both on their own and inside layouts. But there are still some more options to explore. Let's have a look at them now.

## Using the x, center_x, right, y, center_y and top Properties in Layouts

You can use these properties with fixed numbers of pixels in layouts, but then you shouldn't use the same properties in **pos_hint**. Let's have a look at an example. You can leave the Python file as it was in the previous chapter. Here it is again:

```
# File name: test.py

from kivy.app import App
from kivy.uix.floatlayout import FloatLayout

class TestApp(App):
    def build(self):
        return FloatLayout()

if __name__ == '__main__':
    TestApp().run()
```

And here's the kv code we're going to use:

```
# File name: test.kv

<CustomButton@Button>:
    size_hint: .2, .1

<FloatLayout>:
    CustomButton:
        text: 'Button 1'
        x: 0
        y: 0

    CustomButton:
        text: 'Button 2'
        x: 200
        y: 200
```

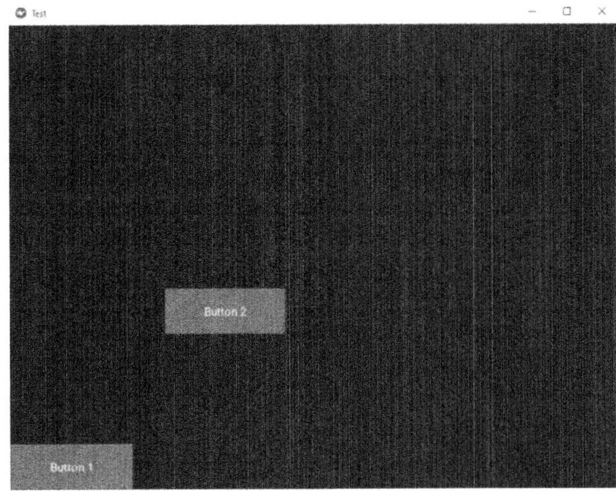


If you run this program now, you will get a window with two buttons. Now the left borders of the two buttons (**x**) and their bottom borders (**y**) will be always the same, even if you resize the window.

## Using the x, center_x, right, y, center_y and top Properties Outside Layouts

Some time ago we were using the **x**, **y**, **right** and **top** properties on the root object (it was in the chapter about the **root**, **self** and **app** variables). Let's simplify the code that we used in that chapter. Here's the Python file:

```
# File name: test.py

from kivy.app import App
from kivy.uix.button import Button
from kivy.uix.widget import Widget

class MyCustomButton(Button):
    pass

class MyCustomWidget(Widget):
    pass

class TestApp(App):
    def build(self):
        return MyCustomWidget()

if __name__ == '__main__':
    TestApp().run()
```

And here's the kv file:

```
# File name: test.kv

<MyCustomButton>:
    size: 120, 40
    color: .7, .6, .4, 1
```

```
<MyCustomWidget>:
    TextInput:
        hint_text: 'Type something'
        pos: root.x + 20, root.top - self.height - 20
        size: 300, 40
    MyCustomButton:
        text: 'Press Me'
        pos: root.x + 20, root.y + 20
    MyCustomButton:
        text: 'Press Me Too'
        pos: root.right - self.width - 20, root.y + 20
```

Here the properties are on the root object, which is the **MyCustomWidget** object. If you run this program, you will see a widget containing three elementary widgets, a text input and two custom buttons.

Try resizing the window and watch carefully how the elements behave.

And now let's rewrite the kv code as follows:

```
# File name: test.kv

<MyCustomButton>:
    size: 120, 40
    color: .7, .6, .4, 1

<MyCustomWidget>:
    TextInput:
        hint_text: 'Type something'
        x: 20
        y: 400
        size: 300, 40
    MyCustomButton:
        text: 'Press Me'
        center_x: 60
        center_y: 20
    MyCustomButton:
        text: 'Press Me Too'
        right: 300
        top: 20
```

If you now run the app, the elementary widgets will be positioned differently. Here's the app window with annotations:

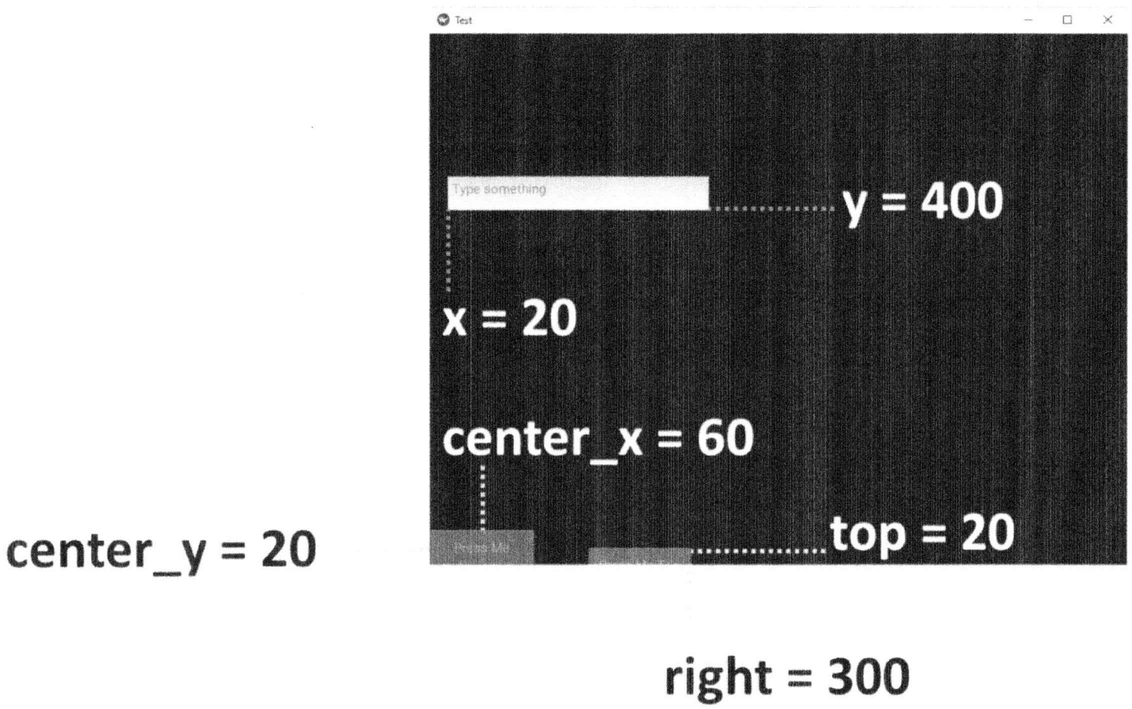

Type something
y = 400
x = 20
center_x = 60
center_y = 20
top = 20
right = 300

## Using the pos Property Inside Layouts

The **pos** property is usually used for widgets outside layouts. However, you can use it for widgets inside a layout if you need fixed numbers of pixels. Then, however, you must remember to not use **pos_hint** or otherwise it will override **pos**.

Here's a simple example.

Python code:

```
# File name: test.py

from kivy.app import App
from kivy.uix.floatlayout import FloatLayout

class TestApp(App):
    def build(self):
        return FloatLayout()

if __name__ == '__main__':
    TestApp().run()
```

kv code:

```
# File name: test.kv

<CustomButton@Button>:
    size_hint: .2, .1

<FloatLayout>:
    CustomButton:
        text: 'Button 1'
        pos: 20, 50

    CustomButton:
        text: 'Button 2'
        pos: 500, 500
```

And here's the program window with the two buttons.

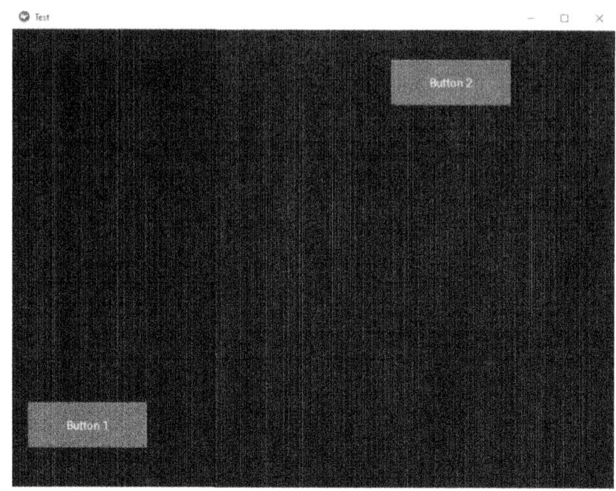


If you resize the window, the positions of the buttons won't change.

## Using the size, width and height Properties Inside Layouts for Scaling

You can also use the **size**, **width** and **height** properties for scaling in layouts. You must remember, however, to set **size_hint**, **size_hint_x** or **size_hint_y** (for size, width and height respectively) to **None**. In case of **size_hint** you should actually set it to **(None, None)**. Otherwise it won't take effect.

Here's an example. The Python file is just like before and here's the kv file:

```
# File name: test.kv

<FloatLayout>:
    Button:
        text: 'Button 1'
        pos: 20, 50
        size: 200, 20

    Button:
        text: 'Button 2'
        pos: 500, 500
        size_hint: None, None
        size: 200, 20
```

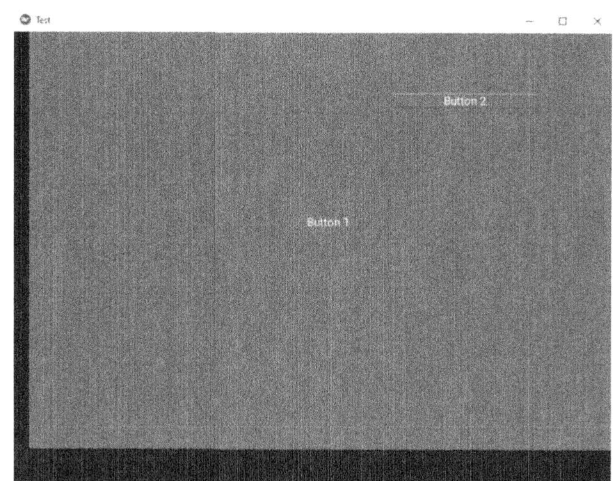


If you now run the application, you will see the two buttons.

As you can see, although we set **size** to the same value for both buttons, 200 pixels wide and 20 pixels high, it only works for Button 2. This is because we didn't set the first button's **size_hint** property to **(None, None)**.

Let's fix it:

```
# File name: test.kv

<FloatLayout>:
    Button:
        text: 'Button 1'
        pos: 20, 50
        size_hint: None, None
        size: 200, 20

    Button:
        ...
```

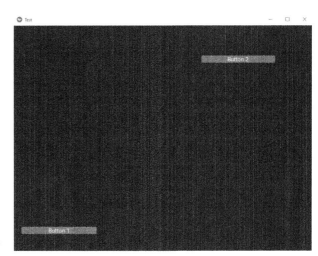

Now it will work as expected for both buttons.

And now watch what will happen if we change just one line of code:

```
# File name: test.kv

<FloatLayout>:
    Button:
        text: 'Button 1'
        pos: 20, 50

        # Here's the difference.
        size_hint_x: None
        size: 200, 20

    Button:
        ...
```

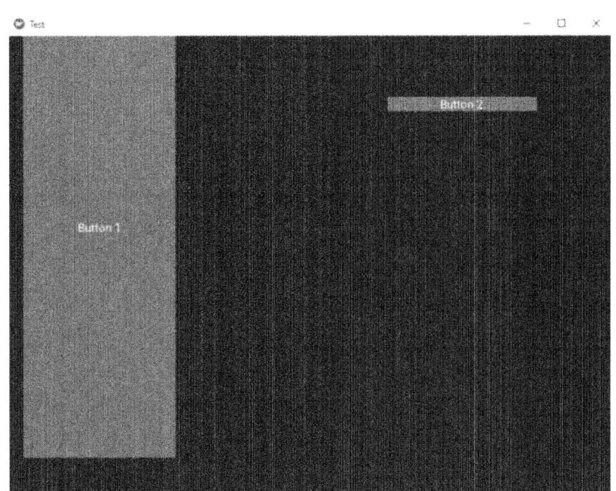


Now, for the first button, we only set the **size_hint_x** property to **None**, not **size_hint**. This will cause the **size** property to take effect only partially, in horizontal direction.

So now you know all you need about positioning and scaling widgets, both inside and outside layouts. I'm using the plural form, layouts, here, although the only layout we've been using so far is the **FloatLayout**. In the following chapters we'll have a look at the other layouts that we'll be making use of in our application.

# It's Your Turn Now...

### EXERCISE 1

Delete all the code in the kv file. Create a **CustomButton** class that derives from **Button**. In the class define the following properties:

- **`text`**

It should be set to a string that will display the position of the button in the following format:

```
x = 100
y = 100
right = 300
top = 300
center_x = 200.0
center_y = 200.0
```

Naturally, the actual numbers will differ for each button.

- **`size_hint`**

You should set it to **`(None, None)`**, so that we can use the **`size`** property with absolute values in pixels.

- **`size`**

The buttons should be 200 x 200 pixels.

Then create three instances of **`CustomButton`** inside a FloatLayout and set their absolute positions like so:

```
button 1: x = 100, y = 100

button 2: center_x = 400, center_y = 300

button 3: right = 700, top = 500
```

## SOLUTION

Here's the code:

```
# File name: test.kv

<CustomButton@Button>:
    text: 'x = ' + str(self.x) + '\ny = ' + str(self.y) + '\nright = ' + str(self.right)
+ '\ntop = ' + str(self.top) + '\ncenter_x = ' + str(self.center_x) + '\ncenter_y = ' + s
tr(self.center_y)
    size_hint: None, None
    size: 200, 200

<FloatLayout>:
    CustomButton:
        x: 100
```

```
        y: 100

    CustomButton:
        center_x: 400
        center_y: 300

    CustomButton:
        right: 700
        top: 500
```

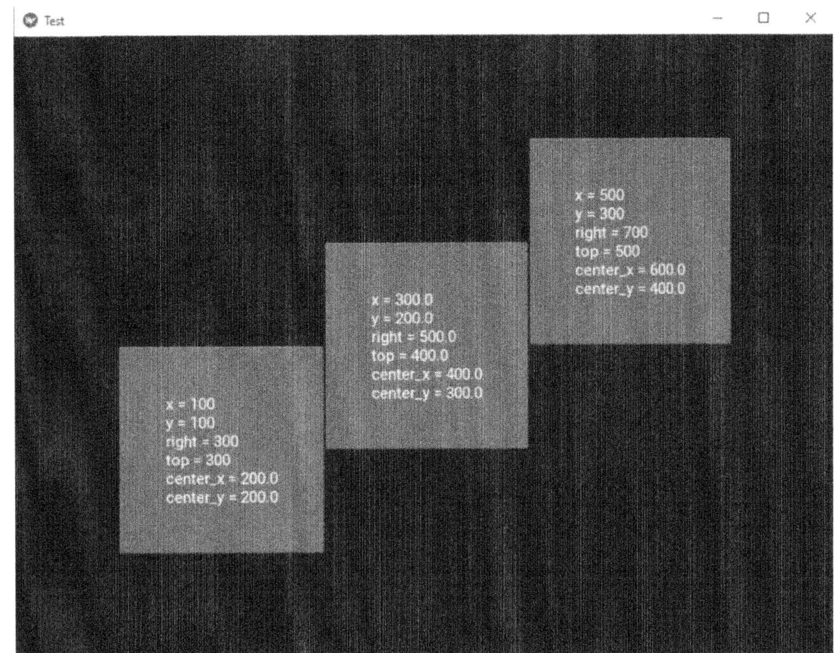


Remember to keep the whole text on one line.

Run the app and you will see the three buttons with position information on them.

**EXERCISE 2**

Delete the **`size_hint`** and **`size`** properties from the **`CustomButton`** class. Modify the **`text`** property so that it displays the width and height of the button in the following format:

```
width = 100

height = 200
```

Remove all the absolute positions from the three **`CustomButton`** instances and add to each of them the **`pos_hint`** property with the following values:

```
button 1: x = .1, y = .1

button 2: x = .4, y = .1

button 3: x = .7, y = .1
```

Then use the appropriate sizing properties (choose from **`size`**, **`size_hint`**, **`size_hint_x`**, **`size_hint_y`**, **`width`**, **`height`**) to set the size of each button like so:

button 1: 20% of the container's width and 20% of its height

button 2: 200 px wide, 50% of the container's height

button 3: 200 x 200 px

Try resizing the window and watch how the dimensions change.

## SOLUTION

Here's the code:

```
# File name: test.kv

<CustomButton@Button>:
    text: 'width = ' + str(self.width) + '\nheight = ' + str(self.height)

<FloatLayout>:
    CustomButton:
        pos_hint: {'x': .1, 'y': .1}
        size_hint: .2, .2

    CustomButton:
        pos_hint: {'x': .4, 'y': .1}
        size_hint_x: None
        size_hint_y: .5
        width: 200

    CustomButton:
        pos_hint: {'x': .7, 'y': .1}
        size_hint: None, None
        size: 200, 200
```

Run the app and watch the buttons.

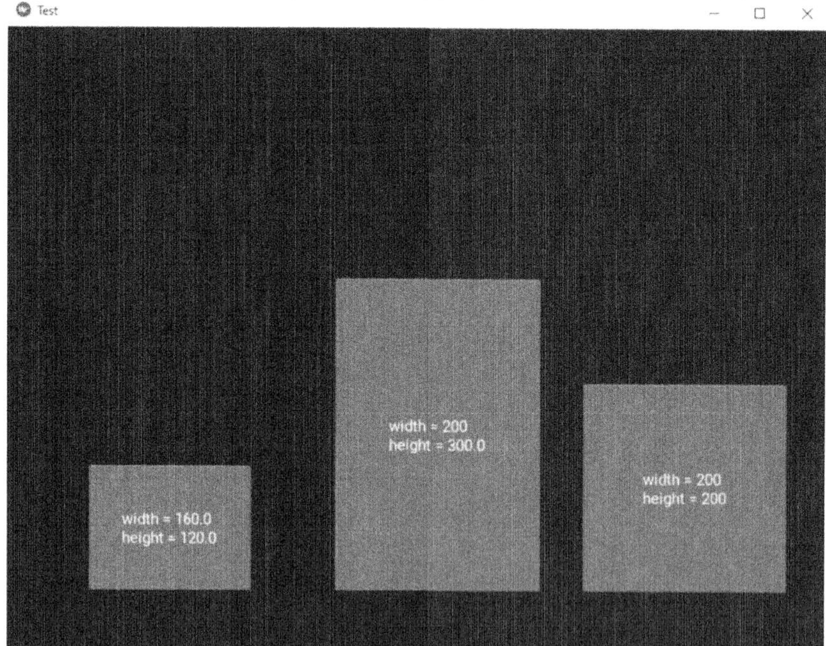

And here after resizing the window:

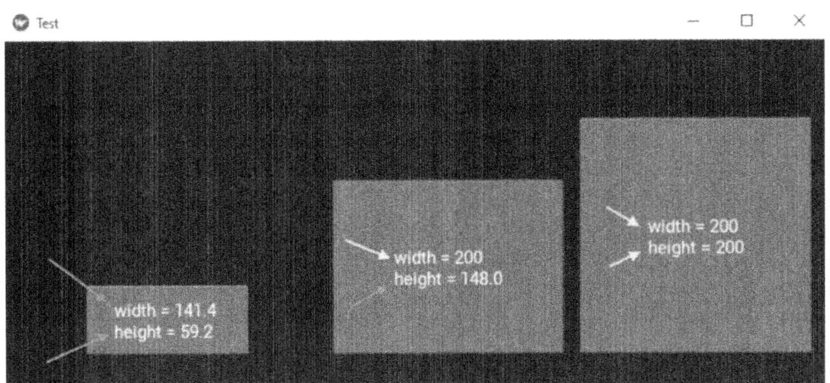


The red arrows indicate that the value has changed during resizing and the green arrows indicate that the value is constant.

# Chapter 21 - The RelativeLayout

You now know how to position and scale widgets inside layouts, but we've been using only the **FloatLayout** so far. Let's have a look now at how the other layouts work. Before we dive into the other layouts, though, there's one thing you should keep in mind. The positioning and sizing properties do not behave in the same way in all the layouts. Sometimes their behavior is not what you expect. This is why it's easier to combine the existing layouts and embed them one into another so that we can reach our goal instead of using the properties described before. Don't get me wrong, you can both use properties and combine layouts into larger hierarchies, but the latter is usually more intuitive than the former, especially in less trivial projects. Anyway, in our project we're going to use both techniques.

Now, in this and the following chapters I'm going to discuss each of the layouts one by one, keeping it as simple as I can, and then, in one of the last chapters in this part I'll show you a more complex example with embedded layouts. So, with **FloatLayout** covered for now, let's move on to **RelativeLayout**, which is the subject of this chapter.

## RelativeLayout

**RelativeLayout** works pretty much like **FloatLayout** and the difference will be clear only later when we embed it in another layout. Here's a simple example with a RelativeLayout and just one button in it. The button should be positioned at the fixed coordinates **(0, 0)** and occupy about a third of the available space in both horizontal and vertical direction.

Here's the Python code:

```
# File name: test.py

from kivy.app import App

# We must import the RelativeLayout class.
from kivy.uix.relativelayout import RelativeLayout

class TestApp(App):
    def build(self):
        # We're going to use the RelativeLayout now.
        return RelativeLayout()

if __name__ == '__main__':
    TestApp().run()
```

And here's the kv file:

```
# File name: test.kv

<RelativeLayout>:
    Button:
        text: 'Button'
        size_hint: .3, .3
        pos: 0, 0
```

If you run this code you'll see something that you would also see using the **FloatLayout**.

So, what's the difference? This is all about coordinates.

Let's compare the two layouts, the **FloatLayout** and the **RelativeLayout** on the following example.

First let's use the **FloatLayout** – this sounds familiar.

Here's the Python code:

```
# File name: test.py

from kivy.app import App
from kivy.uix.floatlayout import FloatLayout

class TestApp(App):
    def build(self):
        return FloatLayout()

if __name__ == '__main__':
    TestApp().run()
```

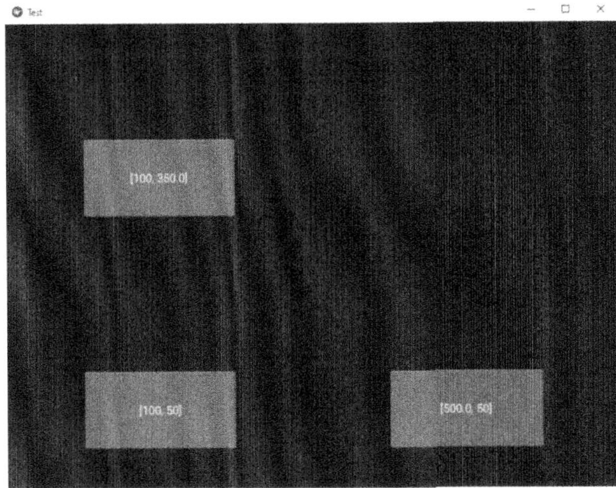


In the kv file we're going to create three buttons and set their **text** properties so that they display the coordinates of the buttons, so the positions of their bottom left corners.

```
# File name: test.kv

<FloatLayout>:
    pos: 100, 50
    Button:
        text: str(self.pos)
        size_hint: None, None
        size: 200, 100
        pos_hint: {'x': 0, 'y': 0}

    Button:
        text: str(self.pos)
        size_hint: None, None
        size: 200, 100
        pos_hint: {'x': .5, 'y': 0}

    Button:
        text: str(self.pos)
        size_hint: None, None
        size: 200, 100
        pos_hint: {'x': 0, 'y': .5}
```

Let's run the app and have a look at the three buttons.

As you can see, the coordinates are given in the coordinate system of the app window. The first thing to notice here is that I positioned the whole FloatLayout at **(100, 50)**. The first button (the lower left one) has the **pos_hint** values set to **0** (**x = 0** and **y = 0**), which means it should be positioned in the bottom left corner of the FloatLayout. And so it is, but as the FloatLayout itself is moved slightly away from the bottom left corner of the app window, the button is also 100 pixels to the right and 50 pixels in the upward direction from it. But still, although the first button is at the coordinates **(0, 0)** in the coordinate system of the FloatLayout, you can see the coordinates in the coordinate system of the window. The other buttons behave accordingly.

This is how a FloatLayout works – it uses the coordinate system of the window.

And now let's use the **RelativeLayout** instead of the **FloatLayout** to see the difference. Here's the Python file:

```
# File name: test.py

from kivy.app import App
from kivy.uix.relativelayout import RelativeLayout

class TestApp(App):
    def build(self):
        return RelativeLayout()

if __name__ == '__main__':
    TestApp().run()
```

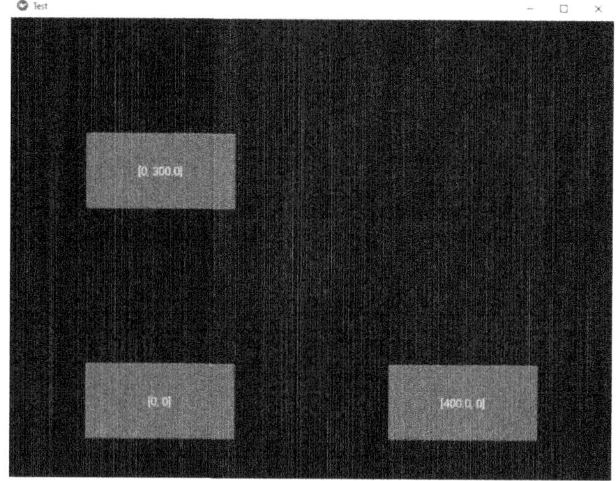


And here's the kv file. It's almost exactly the same as before. The difference is that now we have a RelativeLayout as the root widget, not a FloatLayout:

```
# File name: test.kv

<RelativeLayout>:
    pos: 100, 50
    ...
```

Let's run the app. Now it looks almost the same, but the coordinates are different. This time the coordinates of the buttons are relative to the RelativeLayout, not the app window. The RelativeLayout is at the coordinates **(100, 50)** in the coordinate system of the window and this is the position which marks the center of the coordinate system of the RelativeLayout.

To make it easier for you to understand how the coordinates are used with a FloatLayout and with a RelativeLayout, here's a simple visualization with annotations. Let's just compare these two screenshots:

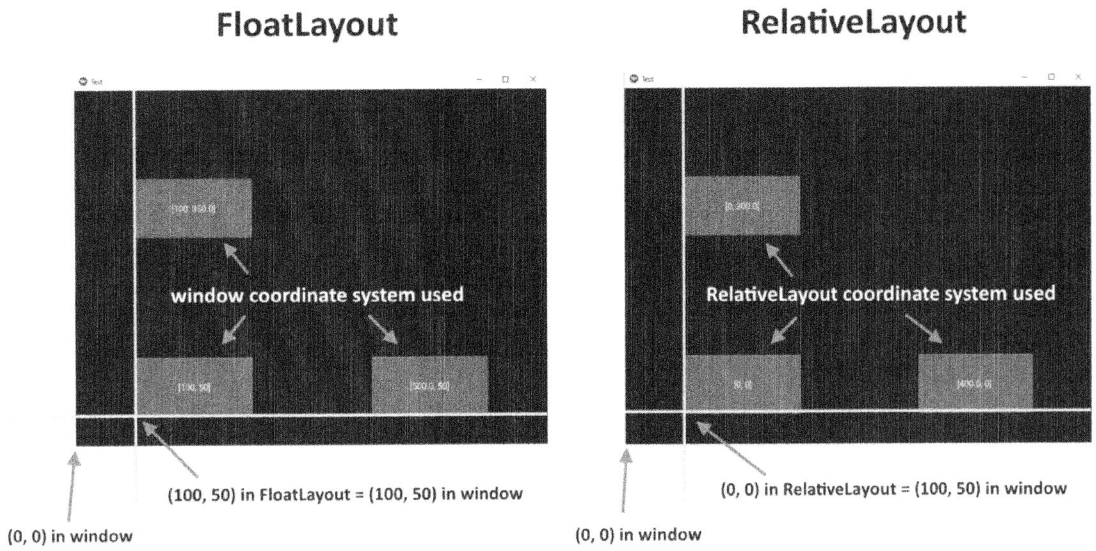

**FloatLayout**

window coordinate system used

(100, 50) in FloatLayout = (100, 50) in window

(0, 0) in window

**RelativeLayout**

RelativeLayout coordinate system used

(0, 0) in RelativeLayout = (100, 50) in window

(0, 0) in window

If you're working in a RelativeLayout, but need to know the position of a widget in the coordinate system of the window, you can use the **`to_window`** method inherited from the **`Widget`** class.

Let's modify the kv file so that each button displays its position in both coordinate systems: above in the coordinate system of the RelativeLayout and below in the coordinate system of the window. Here it is:

```
# File name: test.kv

<RelativeLayout>:
    pos: 100, 50
    Button:
        # Just a reminder: we use the * sign to unpack self.pos
        # to the corresponding x and y values. This is because
        # the to_window method must be given two arguments.
        text: str(self.pos) + '\n' + str(self.to_window(*self.pos))
        ...

    Button:
        text: str(self.pos) + '\n' + str(self.to_window(*self.pos))
        ...

    Button:
        text: str(self.pos) + '\n' + str(self.to_window(*self.pos))
        ...
```

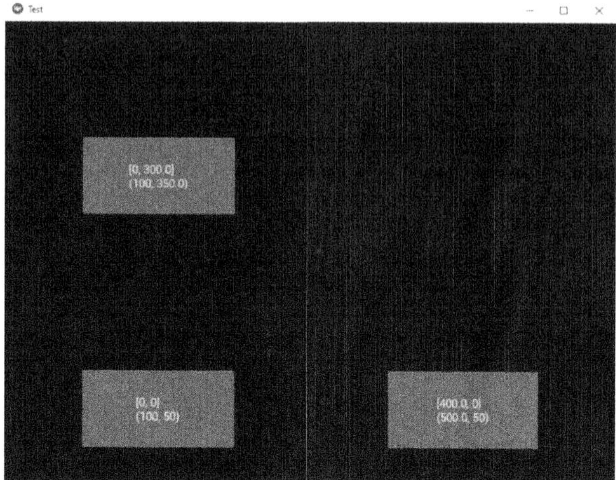


If we now run the app, we'll see the positions of the buttons in both coordinate systems.

So, when do we use the **RelativeLayout**? Well, we use it when it's more appropriate, more comfortable or just easier to use positions relative to the layout rather than to the window. In our application we'll use a RelativeLayout for the part of the GUI with the track on which the slugs will be running. It'll be easier for us to position the elements on the track in relation to the track itself, not the whole application window.

And now let's move on to the next layout, the GridLayout. But before we do, here's an exercise for you.

## It's Your Turn Now...

EXERCISE

Remove the last button. Add **on_press** events to the two remaining buttons:

- When the first button is pressed, the size of the RelativeLayout should change to occupy 50% of the window both horizontally and vertically.

- When the second button is pressed, the size of the RelativeLayout should change to occupy 100% of the window both horizontally and vertically.

HINT: Inside a button **self.size_hint** refers to the **size_hint** property of the button. Here you need to access the **size_hint** property of the RelativeLayout. The RelativeLayout is the parent of the button. This is why, instead of using the **root** variable, you can access it like so: **self.parent**.

SOLUTION

The Python file doesn't change.

Here's the kv file:

```
# File name: test.kv

<RelativeLayout>:
    pos: 100, 50
```

```
    Button:
        ...
        on_press: self.parent.size_hint = .5, .5

    Button:
        ...
        on_press: self.parent.size_hint = 1, 1
```

When you run the program, this is what you will see the two buttons.

So now the positions of the buttons are:

button 1:

- relative to RelativeLayout: **(0, 0)**

- relative to the window: **(100, 50)**

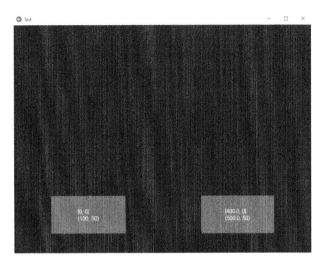

button 2:

- relative to RelativeLayout: **(400.0, 0)**

- relative to the window: **(500.0, 50)**

If you press the first button, the RelativeLayout will shrink to half its current size and the buttons it contains will move along.

In this case button 1 didn't move, but button 2 did. Its new position is:

button 2:

- relative to RelativeLayout: **(200.0, 0)**

- relative to the window: **(300.0, 50)**

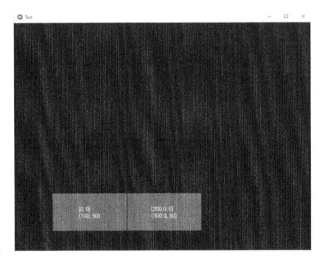

Finally, if you press the second button, you will restore the original state.

# Chapter 22 - The GridLayout

The two layouts we've been using so far are pretty similar, except for the coordinate system each of them uses. Today we'll be talking about a different type of layout, the **GridLayout**, which enables us to position widgets in a grid.

To demonstrate how a GridLayout works we'll need a couple widgets in it. Let's create ten simple buttons this time. Here's the Python code:

```
# File name: test.py

from kivy.app import App

# We must import the GridLayout class.
from kivy.uix.gridlayout import GridLayout

class TestApp(App):
    def build(self):
        # We're going to use the GridLayout now.
        return GridLayout()

if __name__ == '__main__':
    TestApp().run()
```

## GridLayout Rows

Now, with a GridLayout we must set the number of either rows or columns. The two properties that we use for that are **rows** and **cols** respectively. Then the available space will be filled in gradually so that the predefined number of rows or columns is maintained. Suppose we want the ten buttons to be in a grid consisting of two rows. Here's the kv code:

```
# File name: test.kv

<GridLayout>:
    # We need two rows.
    rows: 2

    # And now come the buttons.
    Button:
        text: 'Button 1'
    Button:
        text: 'Button 2'
    Button:
        text: 'Button 3'
    Button:
        text: 'Button 4'
    Button:
        text: 'Button 5'
    Button:
        text: 'Button 6'
    Button:
        text: 'Button 7'
    Button:
        text: 'Button 8'
    Button:
        text: 'Button 9'
    Button:
        text: 'Button 10'
```

If you now run the app, you will see the ten buttons.

So, as you can see, we indeed have two rows. The **GridLayout** is smart enough to know how many items to put in the first row before starting the second row.

I numbered the buttons on purpose. You can now easily see what order the buttons were added in: first row 1 from left to right, then row 2 from left to right, for as long as there are any widgets left.

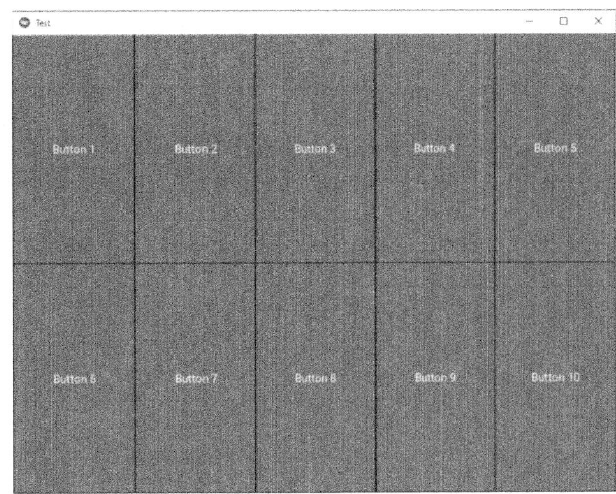


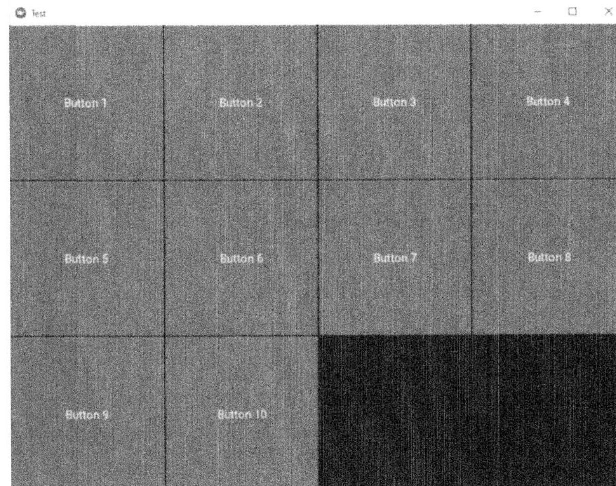


Let's change the number of rows to 3:

```
# File name: test.kv

<GridLayout>:
    # We need three rows.
    rows: 3

    # And now come the buttons.
    ...
```

This time we'll get three rows of buttons. So, again, the program calculates how many widgets must fit in a row so that the total number of three rows is not exceeded.

# GridLayout Columns

And now I'm going to achieve the same effect using the **cols** property. Let's rewrite the kv code so that we set the number of columns to 4. Here's the kv code:

```
# File name: test.kv

<GridLayout>:
    # We need four columns.
    cols: 4

    # And now come the buttons.
    ...
```

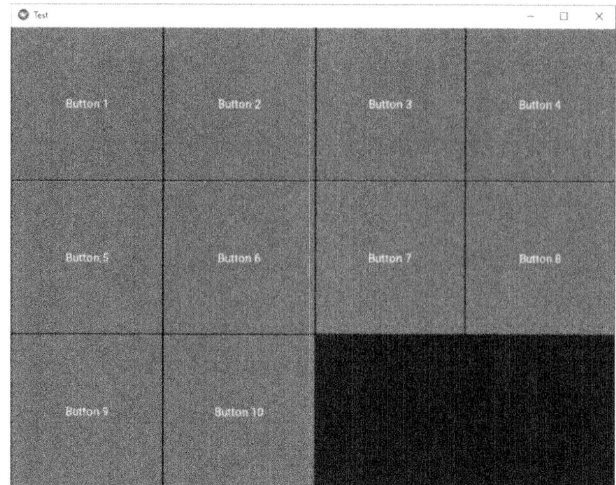


Let's run the program and see what we get.

See any difference? Well, in this particular case there isn't any. This is just how it works. The widgets are added from left to right, row after row.

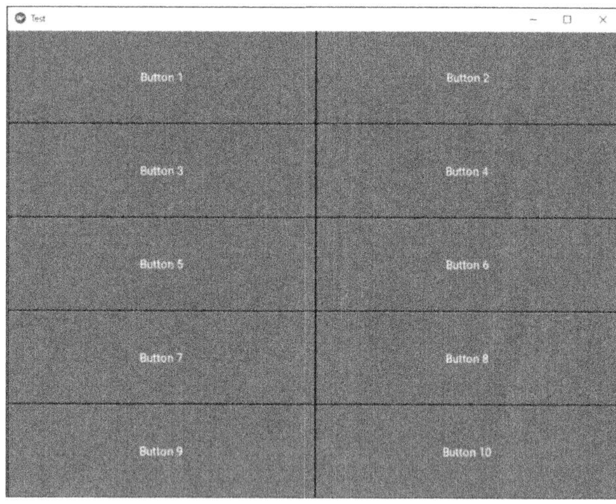


So, what if you set the number of columns to two? Let's find out:

```
# File name: test.kv

<GridLayout>:
    # We need two columns.
    cols: 2

    # And now come the buttons.
    ...
```

This time the buttons are arranged in two columns.

But still, you can see that the order of adding them is again row by row, from left to right.

## Column Width and Row Height

If you don't specify the sizes of the children (these are the widgets placed in the layout), all available space will be filled. But if you want, you can scale the children and then their size will be taken into consideration when the column width and row height are determined.

Let's define a custom button with a fixed size:

```
# File name: test.kv

# Let's define a custom button.
<SmallButton@Button>:
    size_hint: None, None
    size: 100, 50

<GridLayout>:
    # We need four rows.
    rows: 4

    # And now we'll be using
    # our custom buttons.
    SmallButton:
        text: 'Button 1'
    SmallButton:
        text: 'Button 2'
    SmallButton:
        text: 'Button 3'
    SmallButton:
        text: 'Button 4'
    SmallButton:
        text: 'Button 5'
    SmallButton:
        text: 'Button 6'
    SmallButton:
        text: 'Button 7'
    SmallButton:
        text: 'Button 8'
    SmallButton:
        text: 'Button 9'
    SmallButton:
        text: 'Button 10'
```

Let's run the program again and see if there is any difference.

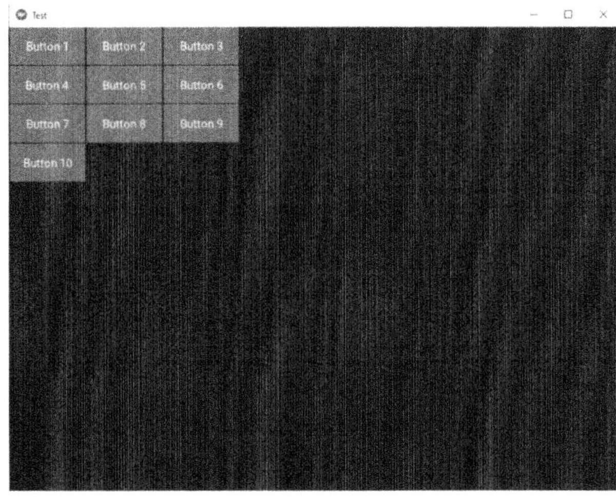


As you can see, the column widths and row heights are now adjusted to the sizes of the buttons. If the widgets are of different sizes, each row and each column has the respective height and width of the biggest widget in that row or column. To see that in action, let's overwrite the size of one of the buttons:

```
# File name: test.kv

<SmallButton@Button>:
    ...

<GridLayout>:
    rows: 4

    ...
    SmallButton:
        text: 'Button 5'
        size_hint: None, None
        size: 200, 100
    SmallButton:
        ...
```

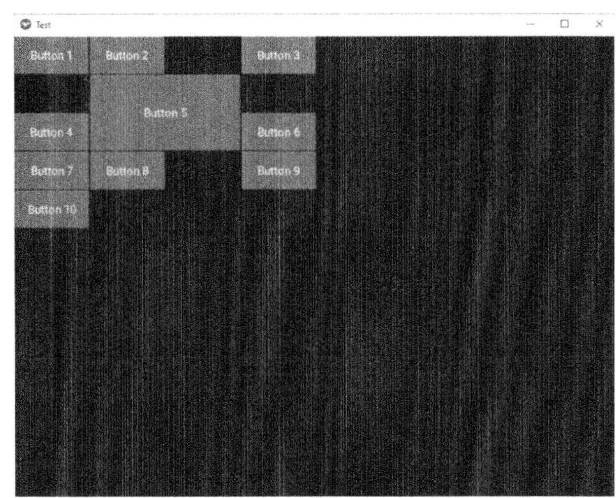


If you now run the program, you will see that the second row is as high as button 5, which is the biggest widget in that row and the second column is as wide as button 5, which is the biggest widget in that column.

OK, there is much more to the **GridLayout**, but we'll be talking about some other Grid-related stuff when we need it later in our project. For now, after you do the exercises below, let's move on to the next layout.

# It's Your Turn Now...

### EXERCISE 1

Remove the **size_hint** and **size** properties from button 5, so that all buttons are the same size again. There are two interesting properties that let you determine the width of the columns and the height of the rows regardless of the sizes of the children. These are: **col_default_width** and **row_default_height**. So, in our program the buttons are 100 x 50 pixels, so the width of each column is automatically set to 100 and the height of each row is automatically set to 50. But if you don't like this behavior, you can yourself decide how wide the columns should be or how high the rows. Using these two properties set the width of the columns to 200 px and the height of the rows to 100 px.

### SOLUTION

Here's the kv file:

```
# File name: test.kv

<SmallButton@Button>:
    size_hint: None, None
    size: 100, 50

<GridLayout>:
    rows: 4
    col_default_width: 200
    row_default_height: 100

    ...
    SmallButton:
        text: 'Button 5'
    SmallButton:
        ...
```

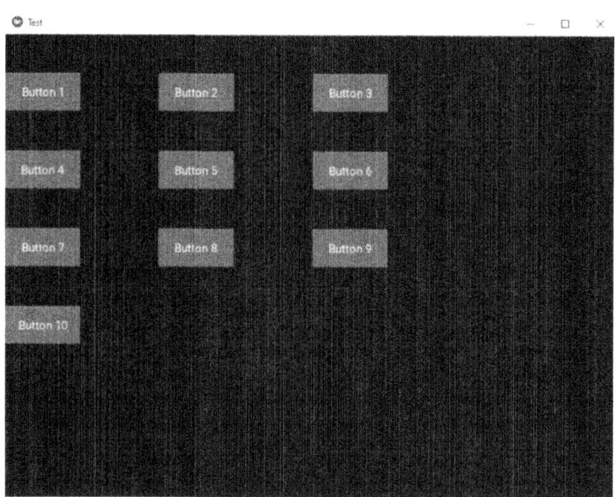


If you now run the program, you will see that the columns are now wider and the rows higher than before.

## EXERCISE 2

There are two other interesting properties that let you set the minimum width of a column or a minimum height of a row regardless of the actual size of the children. Unlike the two properties introduced in the previous exercise (by the way, remove them from the kv file now), these two properties let you decide how wide each individual column and how high each individual row should be.

The properties are **cols_minimum** and **rows_minimum**. Each of them is a dictionary of minimum widths or heights for each column or row. In the dictionary the keys are the numbers of the columns or rows (with 0 for the first column or row, 1 for the second, and so on) and the values are the minimum widths or heights.

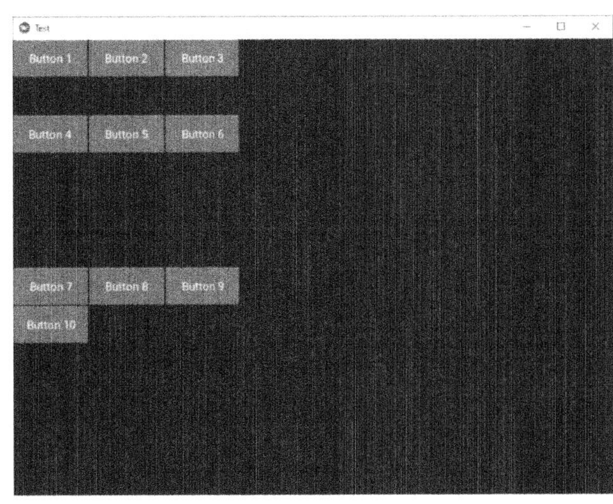


So, for example if you want the second row to be 100 px high and the third row to be 200 px, you can set it like so:

```
rows_minimum: {1: 100, 2: 200}
```

If you now run the program with this property set like above, the two middle rows will have the heights of 100 and 200 pixels respectively.

Now, using the two properties, set the widths of the columns and heights of the rows like so:

```
column 1: 200 px          row 1: 100 px          row 3: 200 px

column 2: 300 px          row 2: 70 px           row 4: 100 px

column 3: 150 px
```

## SOLUTION

Here's the code and the running app.

```
# File name: test.kv
...
<GridLayout>:
    rows: 4
    cols_minimum: {0: 200, 1: 300, 2: 150}
    rows_minimum: {0: 100, 1: 70, 2: 200, 3: 100}

    SmallButton:
        ...
```

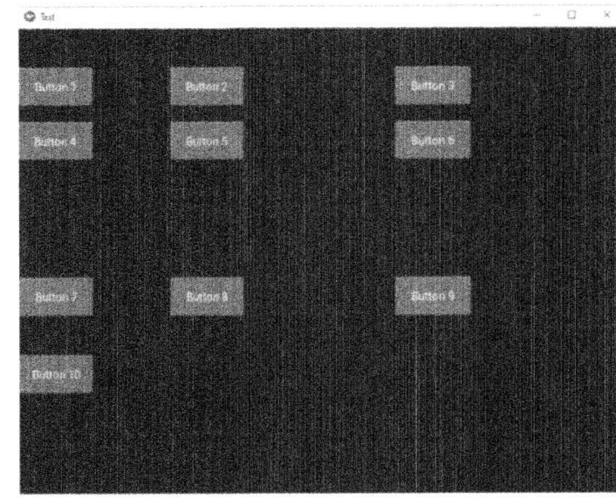

# Chapter 23 - The BoxLayout

The **BoxLayout** is a very common layout and we'll be using it a lot in our project. You can imagine it as a GridLayout with just one row or one column. If you want all the elements to be positioned in one row, you should set the **orientation** property to **'horizontal'**, or just leave it out altogether as this is the default value. If you want the elements to be in a column, you should set **orientation** to **'vertical'**. Let's see how it works.

Here's the Python file:

```
# File name: test.py

from kivy.app import App

# We must import the BoxLayout class.
from kivy.uix.boxlayout import BoxLayout

class TestApp(App):
    def build(self):
        # We're going to use the BoxLayout now.
        return BoxLayout()

if __name__ == '__main__':
    TestApp().run()
```

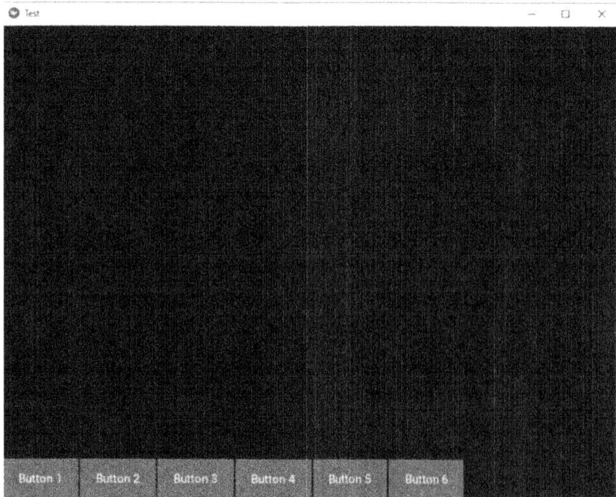


Now, we want the buttons that we created in the previous chapter to be all in one row. Let's reduce their number to 6, this will do. Here's the kv code:

```
# File name: test.kv

<SmallButton@Button>:
    size_hint: None, None
    size: 100, 50

<BoxLayout>:
    # The buttons should be in a row.
    # This is the default value, so
    # you can leave it out.
    orientation: 'horizontal'

    SmallButton:
        text: 'Button 1'
    SmallButton:
        text: 'Button 2'
    SmallButton:
        text: 'Button 3'
    SmallButton:
        text: 'Button 4'
    SmallButton:
        text: 'Button 5'
    SmallButton:
        text: 'Button 6'
```

If you run the app, you will see all six buttons in one row.

And now let's put the buttons in a column:

```
# File name: test.kv
...
<BoxLayout>:
    # The buttons should be in a column.
    orientation: 'vertical'

    SmallButton:
        ...
```

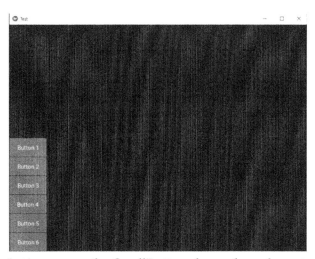

If you run the app again, the buttons will be in a column.

Naturally, if you don't specify the sizes of the children, all available space will be used. Let's remove the SmallButton class rule and create instances of regular buttons in the BoxLayout:

```
# File name: test.kv

<BoxLayout>:
    orientation: 'vertical'

    Button:
        text: 'Button 1'
    Button:
        text: 'Button 2'
    Button:
        text: 'Button 3'
    Button:
        text: 'Button 4'
    Button:
        text: 'Button 5'
    Button:
        text: 'Button 6'
```

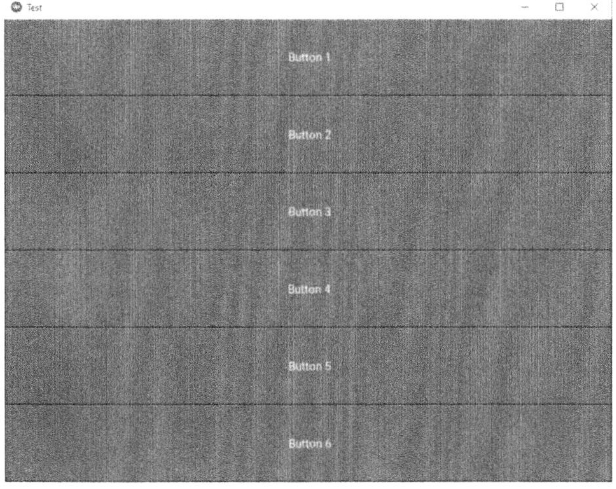


If you now run the program, the buttons will fill the whole layout. Or, you can set **`orientation`** to **`'horizontal'`**:

```
# File name: test.kv

<BoxLayout>:
    orientation: 'horizontal'
    ...
```

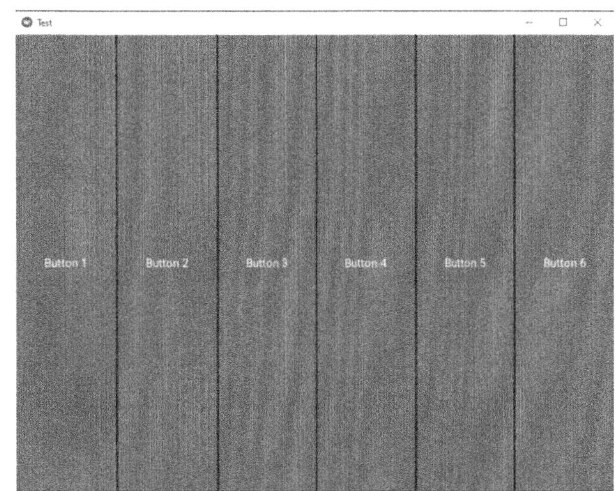

For now that's it as far as the **BoxLayout** is concerned. In the next chapter we'll be talking about a similar layout, the **StackLayout**. But before we do, don't forget to do the exercise below.

# It's Your Turn Now...

### EXERCISE

The **pos_hint** property works only partially in a BoxLayout, depending on its orientation. So, in a horizontal BoxLayout only the **y**, **center_y** and **top** properties work. In a vertical one, only **x**, **center_x** and **right** work.

First, remove the last three buttons, so that only three are left. Then define a **CustomButton** class that is a subclass of **Button**. In the class rule set the size of the custom button to 200 x 100. With that done, use the **CustomButton** class instead of the regular **Button** to create the three instances in the BoxLayout. Using the **pos_hint** property align the buttons like so:

- button 1 should be at the bottom
- button 2 should be in the center
- button 3 should be at the top.

### SOLUTION

Here's the code and the app window that you will see when you run the app, with the buttons aligned as expected. The buttons are all in one row.

```
# File name: test.kv

<CustomButton@Button>:
    size_hint: None, None
    size: 200, 100

<BoxLayout>:
    orientation: 'horizontal'

    CustomButton:
        text: 'Button 1'
        pos_hint: {'y': 0}

    CustomButton:
        text: 'Button 2'
        pos_hint: {'center_y': .5}

    CustomButton:
        text: 'Button 3'
        pos_hint: {'top': 1}
```

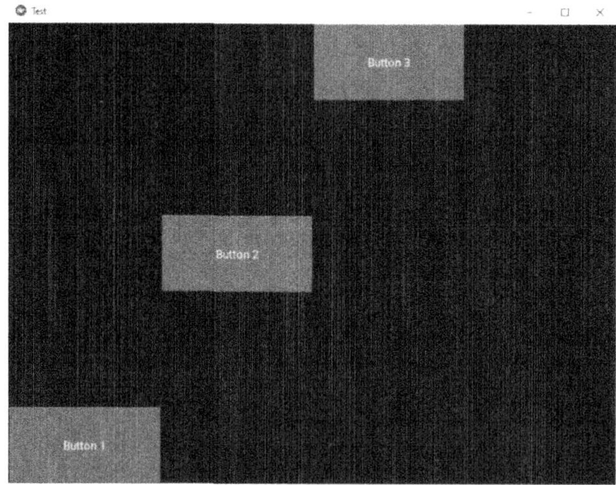

# Chapter 24 - The StackLayout

The next layout we're going to talk about is the **StackLayout**. Here's the Python file:

```
# File name: test.py

from kivy.app import App

# We must import the StackLayout class.
from kivy.uix.stacklayout import StackLayout

class TestApp(App):
    def build(self):
        # We're going to use the StackLayout now.
        return StackLayout()

if __name__ == '__main__':
    TestApp().run()
```

Just like the **BoxLayout**, the **StackLayout** also has the **orientation** property, but it works in a different way.

This layout arranges the widgets in a specific order and automatically moves on to the next row or column when it runs out of space in the current row or column.

The **orientation** property takes one of the following values:

**rl-tb** : right to left, top to bottom

**lr-tb** : left to right, top to bottom

**rl-bt** : right to left, bottom to top

**lr-bt** : left to right, bottom to top

**tb-rl** : top to bottom, right to left

**tb-lr** : top to bottom, left to right

**bt-rl** : bottom to top, right to left

**bt-lr** : bottom to top, left to right

Let's try out some of the orientations. First, we want the widgets to be arranged from right to left, top to bottom. Here's the kv code:

```
# File name: test.kv

<CustomButton@Button>:
    size_hint: None, None
    size: 300, 200
    font_size: 40

<StackLayout>:
    # The buttons should be arranged
    # from right to left, top to bottom.
    orientation: 'rl-tb'
    CustomButton:
        text: 'Button 1'
    CustomButton:
        text: 'Button 2'
    CustomButton:
        text: 'Button 3'
    CustomButton:
        text: 'Button 4'
    CustomButton:
        text: 'Button 5'
```

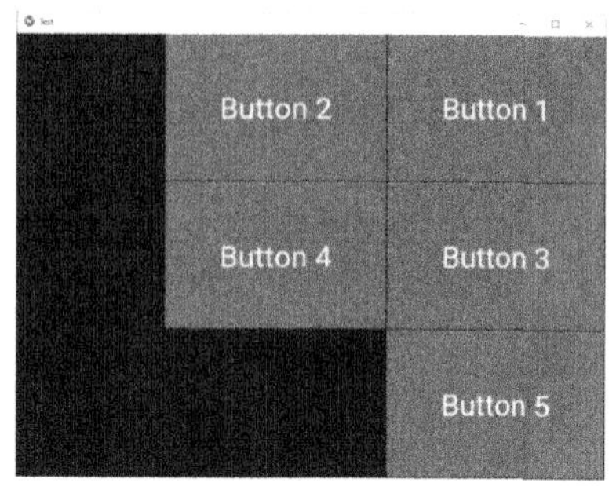


Run the app and watch what order the buttons appear in: first right to left and then top to bottom.

Now let's test some other combinations. There are only changes in the kv file. Each time when you run the app make sure to resize the window and watch how the widgets are repositioned.

So, how about the order from left to right, top to bottom? Here's the code:

```
# File name: test.kv
...
<StackLayout>:
    # The buttons should be arranged from
    # left to right, top to bottom.
    orientation: 'lr-tb'
    ...
```

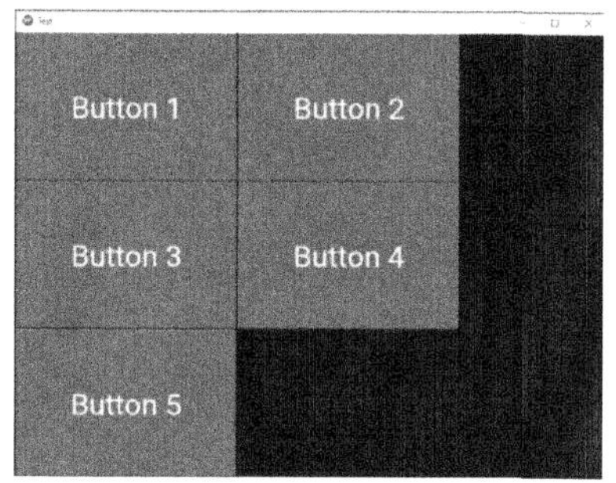


Run the app and watch the result now.

And see what happens if we set the orientation to **'tb-lr'**:

```
# File name: test.kv
...
<StackLayout>:
    # The buttons should be arranged from
    # top to bottom, left to right.
    orientation: 'tb-lr'
    ...
```

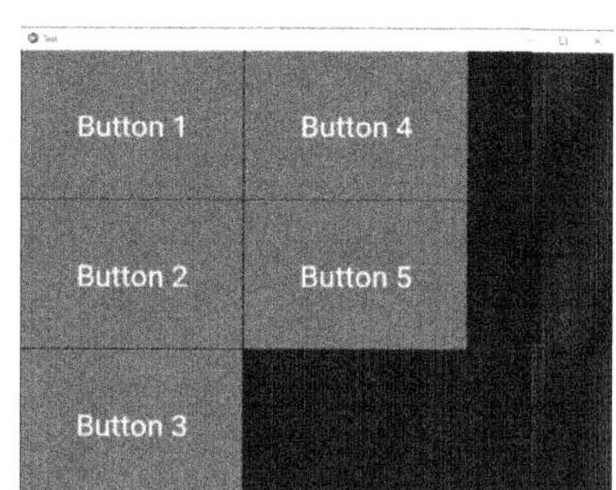


As you can see, here the order is first from top to bottom and then from left to right.

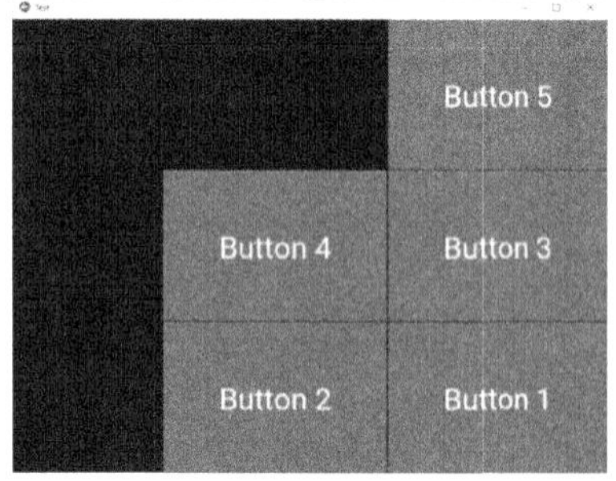


And now right to left, bottom to top:

```
# File name: test.kv
...
<StackLayout>:
    # The buttons should be arranged from
    # right to left, bottom to top.
    orientation: 'rl-bt'
    ...
```

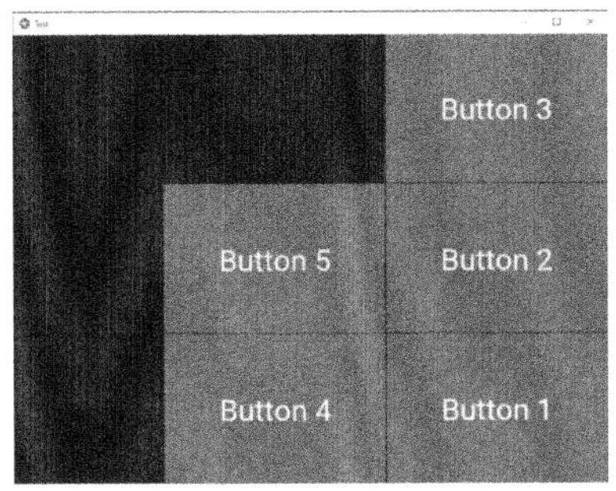


Finally, one more example, bottom to top, right to left:

```
# File name: test.kv
...
<StackLayout>:
    # The buttons should be arranged from
    # bottom to top, right to left.
    orientation: 'bt-rl'
    ...
```

And if you need more practice, feel free to try out all the other orientations. I'm going to wrap the **StackLayout** up for now and move on to a very interesting layout, the **AnchorLayout**.

# It's Your Turn Now...

## EXERCISE

Add five more CustomButtons to the layout. In the class rule change the size of the button to 300 x 100. Set the **orientation** property to bottom to top, left to right. Add some padding between the layout box and its children, like 20 pixels. You can do it by setting the **padding** property on the layout. Also add some spacing between the children, like 10 pixels. To do it, use the **spacing** property on the parent. When you run the app, make sure to resize the window and watch how the widgets are repositioned.

## SOLUTION

Here's the code:

```
# File name: test.kv
...
<StackLayout>:
    # The buttons should be arranged
    # from bottom to top, left to right.
    orientation: 'bt-lr'

    # Add padding and spacing.
    padding: 20
    spacing: 10

    CustomButton:
        text: 'Button 1'
    ...
    CustomButton:
        text: 'Button 6'
    CustomButton:
        text: 'Button 7'
    CustomButton:
        text: 'Button 8'
    CustomButton:
        text: 'Button 9'
    CustomButton:
        text: 'Button 10'
```

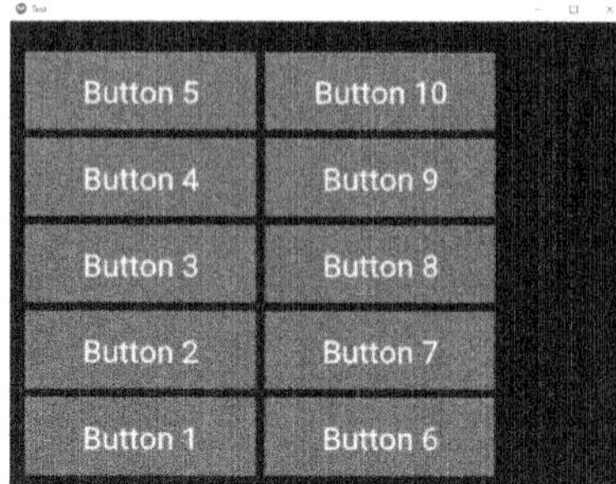


When you run the program, you will see the ten buttons arranged in two columns.

Feel free to resize the window and watch how the buttons are rearranged.

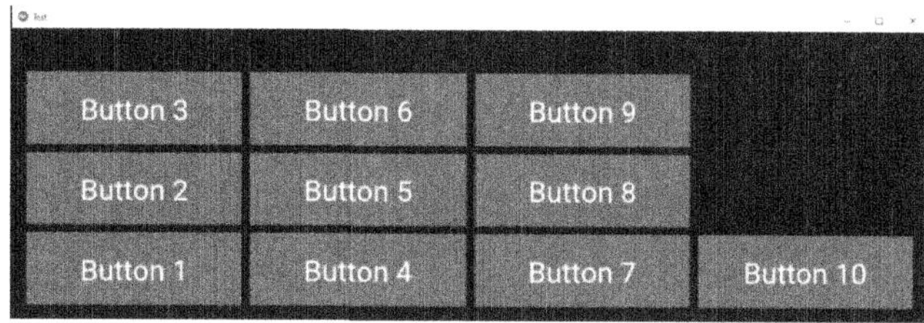

# Chapter 25 - The AnchorLayout

In this chapter we'll be talking about yet another type of layout, the **AnchorLayout**. We use this layout to anchor widgets in particular positions, like at the top or bottom, or on one of the sides. It lends itself well to creating menus. The two main properties used with this layout are **anchor_x** and **anchor_y**. Let's first rewrite the Python file to make use of the **AnchorLayout**:

```
# File name: test.py

from kivy.app import App

# We must import the AnchorLayout class.
from kivy.uix.anchorlayout import AnchorLayout

class TestApp(App):
    def build(self):
        # We're going to use the AnchorLayout now.
        return AnchorLayout()

if __name__ == '__main__':
    TestApp().run()
```

Suppose we want to position a widget in the upper right corner. Here's the kv file:

```
# File name: test.kv

<CustomButton@Button>:
    size_hint: None, None
    size: 200, 100
    font_size: 30

<AnchorLayout>:
    # Let's position the button
    # in the upper right corner.
    anchor_x: 'right'
    anchor_y: 'top'

    CustomButton:
        text: 'right\ntop'
```

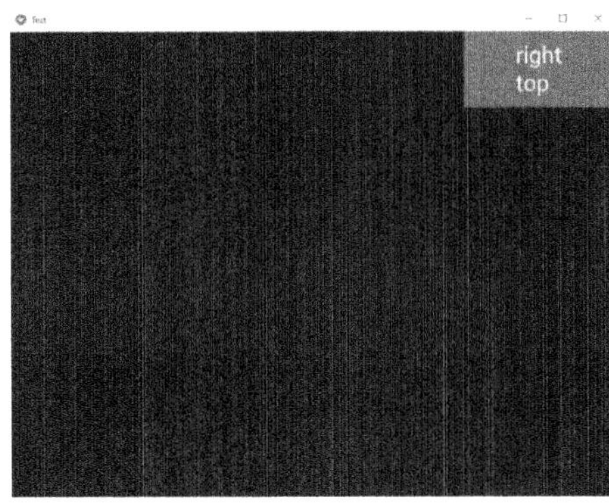


When you run the app, you will see the button in the upper right corner.

Well, I added just one button here because otherwise the buttons would be on top of one another and only the last one would be visible unless we changed the sizes of some of them. This layout is more practical if you want to position a custom widget, or even more if you want to position another embedded layout. For example you can imagine making a menu consisting of 5 labels positioned in a row inside a BoxLayout and then positioning the whole menu inside an AnchorLayout. We're going to see some embedding examples in one of the next chapters. And now some more examples with the **AnchorLayout**. Only the kv file is going to change.

Here's the first example. We want to position the button in the center (horizontally) and at the top:

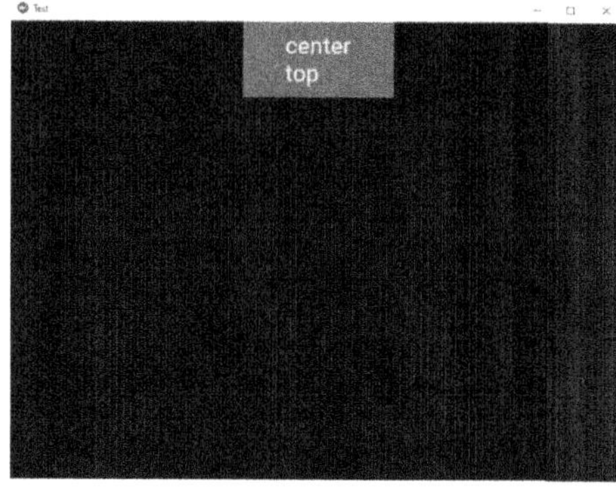


```
# File name: test.kv
...
<AnchorLayout>:
    anchor_x: 'center'
    anchor_y: 'top'

    CustomButton:
        text: 'center\ntop'
```

And now let's place the button in the lower left corner:

```
# File name: test.kv
...
<AnchorLayout>:
    anchor_x: 'left'
    anchor_y: 'bottom'

    CustomButton:
        text: 'left\nbottom'
```

And just one more example. Let's say the button should be in the very middle.

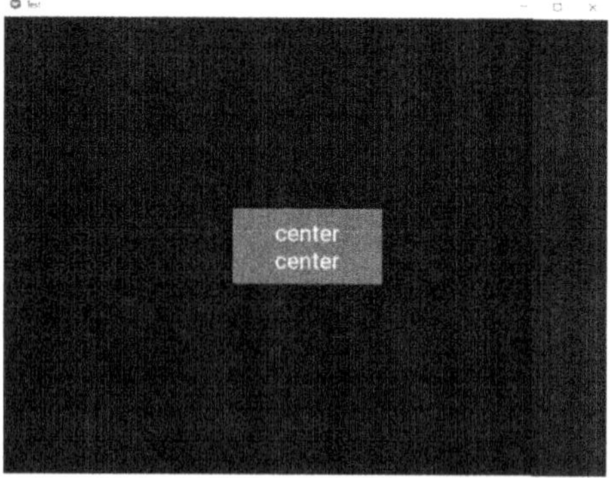


```
# File name: test.kv
...
<AnchorLayout>:
    anchor_x: 'center'
    anchor_y: 'center'

    CustomButton:
        # This time let's use the anchor_x and
        # anchor_y properties on the root widget.
        text: root.anchor_x + '\n' + root.anchor_y
```

This is it for now. We'll be talking about the **AnchorLayout** a bit more when we learn how to embed layouts in other layouts. In particular, we'll be creating a menu using the **AnchorLayout**. And now, in the next chapter, we'll be talking about the **PageLayout**, which is slightly different from the layouts covered so far.

# It's Your Turn Now...

### EXERCISE

Remove all the code from the kv file. Add a class rule for a **CustomSlider** that inherits from **Slider**. The slider should be sized 100 x 500 pixels, the minimum and maximum values should be set to 0 and 100 respectively and the current value should be 50. The slider should have vertical orientation.

Then create one instance of **CustomSlider** in an **AnchorLayout** with both **anchor_x** and **anchor_y** set to **'center'**. Add an event to the slider instance so that the slider gets anchored to the left when you move it down (when the value is less than or equal to 50) and to the right if the value is over 50.

HINT: In the chapter on sliders we used the **on_touch_move** event to handle slider movement. You can also use a ternary **if** statement. And one more thing: remember that the value changes on the slider, and the anchoring changes on the parent.

### SOLUTION

Here's the code and the app window that you will see when you run the app. When you first run the app, the slider is anchored to the center.

Then, when you move the slider down or up, the anchoring changes to the left or right respectively.

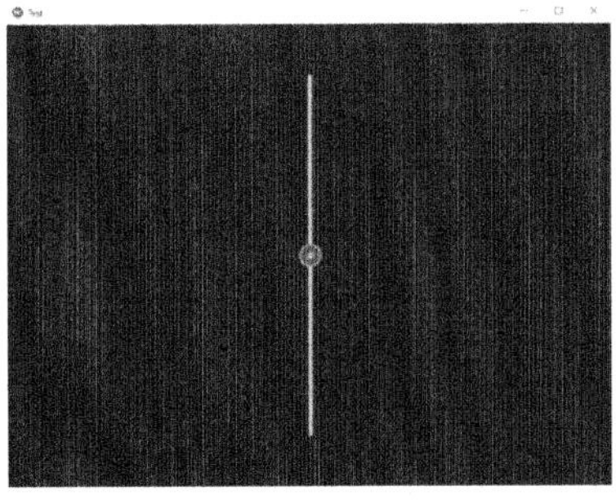

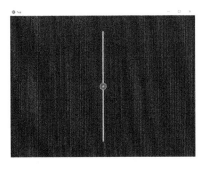

```
# File name: test.kv

<CustomSlider@Slider>:
    size_hint: None, None
    size: 100, 500
    min: 0
    max: 100
    value: 50
    orientation: 'vertical'

<AnchorLayout>:
    anchor_x: 'center'
    anchor_y: 'center'

    CustomSlider:
        on_touch_move: root.anchor_x = 'left' if self.value <= 50 else 'right'
```

**value <= 50**

**value > 50**

# Chapter 26 - The PageLayout

The **PageLayout** is a bit different than all the other layouts that we have covered so far. It's used to create multi-page apps. You can flip from one page to another by swiping in from the border areas on either side of the window. Let's create a simple app with three buttons, each on a separate page.

Here's the Python file:

```
# File name: test.py

from kivy.app import App

# We must import the PageLayout class.
from kivy.uix.pagelayout import PageLayout

class TestApp(App):
    def build(self):
        # We're going to use the PageLayout now.
        return PageLayout()

if __name__ == '__main__':
    TestApp().run()
```

And here's the kv file:

```
# File name: test.kv

# Let's make the font
# more visible for
# all buttons.
<Button>:
    font_size: 50

<PageLayout>:
    Button:
        text: 'Page 1'
    Button:
        text: 'Page 2'
    Button:
        text: 'Page 3'
```

As you can see, I added a class rule for the **Button** class. In the rule I set the **font_size** property to **50**, so this will hold for all buttons unless I overwrite this value on some of them.

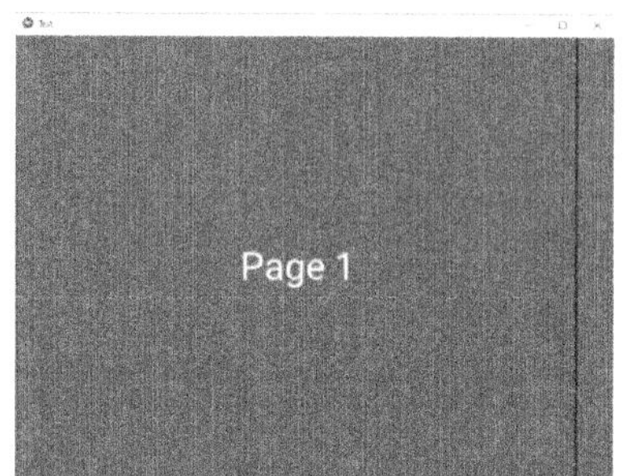


If you run this program, you will see just the first button and a small portion of the second one on the right.

This is the first page out of three. There's a distinct border area on the right. This means there's another page on the right, so just swipe in to the left to see page 2 replace page 1 in the window.

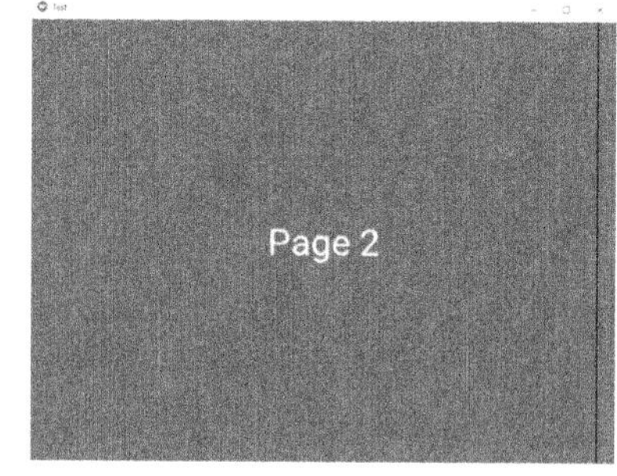


Now there's a distinct border area on the right and a slightly less visible, but still distinct border area on the left. This means there's at least one page on the left and at least one on the right.

Now you can swipe in both directions. Let's swipe to the left again to see page 3.

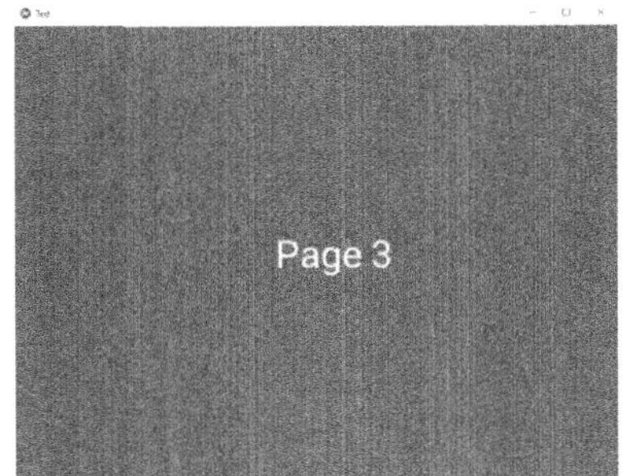


Now, this is the last page, so you can't swipe to the left anymore, but you can swipe to the right to go back to page 2.

In this example we're using just one widget on each page, but this layout works best with embedded layouts, so optimally there should be a distinct layout with its own widgets on each page. We're going to talk about embedding layouts in the next chapter.

So, now you more or less know how to use the layouts independently. In the next chapter, as I just mentioned, I'll show you how to embed layouts in other layouts. We'll be embedding layouts a lot in the project.

# It's Your Turn Now...

**EXERCISE 1**

The border on either side of a page defaults to 50 dp. You can change the width of the border by setting the **border** property on the layout. Using this property, set the border width to 200 dp. There's also another interesting property, **page**, which you can use to determine which page should be displayed when you launch the app. It defaults to **0**, which is the index of the first page. Set the **page** property so that the second page is displayed.

**SOLUTION**

Here's the code. If you now run the app, you will see that the border is now much wider and the second page is displayed, not the first one like before. This means you can now swipe in to the left or to the right.

```
# File name: test.kv
...
<PageLayout>:
    border: 200
    page: 1

    Button:
        ...
```

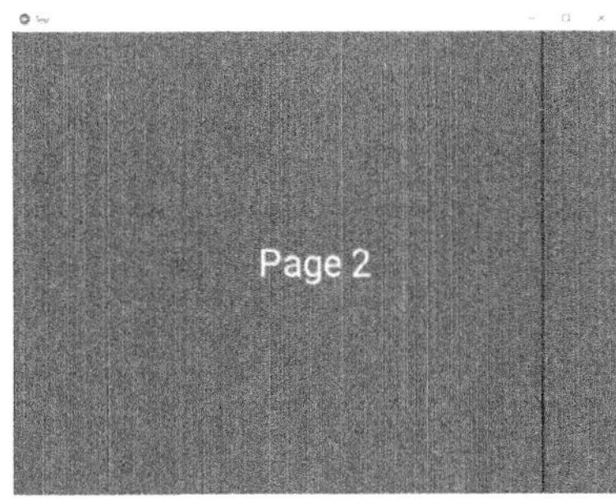


**EXERCISE 2**

When you flip to another page, you have to swipe to the left or right. If you let go too early, the old page will come back. The new page will take the place of the old one only if you swipe far enough. But what does it mean far enough? Well, by default it's 50% of the widget size. But you can change it. Suppose we want our app to be more sensitive and the new page should replace the old one if you swipe only 10% of the widget size. Do it by setting the value of the **swipe_threshold** property. The values you set this property to are expressed as percentages of the widget size, so **.1** for 10%, **.3** for 30%, etc.

**SOLUTION**

Here's the code:

```
# File name: test.kv
...
<PageLayout>:
    border: 200
    page: 1
    swipe_threshold: .1

    Button:
        ...
```

As you can see, all you had to do was add just one line of code. Now run the app and try flipping to another page. You will notice that now you don't have to swipe so far anymore.

# Chapter 27 – Embedding Layouts

In the preceding chapters we discussed some of the Kivy layouts that we're going to make use of throughout our project. Before we finally jump into the project, let's play with them for a while. In this chapter I'll show you some examples of embedding layouts so that you can practice a bit. This is important because we'll be using lots of embedded layouts in the project.

You can easily embed one layout in another. This system is very flexible and lets you create practically any GUI you might think of. You embed layouts just like any other widgets. You can even have multiple levels of nesting.

And now let's get down to work. Here are the examples of embedded layouts:

## FloatLayouts and RelativeLayouts inside GridLayout

As mentioned before, the **FloatLayout** and the **RelativeLayout** are pretty similar. The difference is that with the **FloatLayout** the coordinates are not relative to the position of the layout, whereas with **RelativeLayout** they are. Here's a simple demonstration. We'll use a GridLayout and embed four other layouts in it, two FloatLayouts and two RelativeLayouts. Here's the Python code:

```
# File name: test.py

from kivy.app import App

# We need a GridLayout to embed the other layouts in.
from kivy.uix.gridlayout import GridLayout

class TestApp(App):
    def build(self):
        return GridLayout()

if __name__ == '__main__':
    TestApp().run()
```

And now the kv code. Let's set the size in the class rule for the **Button** class for all **Button** instances. Let's add two FloatLayouts and two RelativeLayouts to the GridLayout with two buttons in each of them.

To make things clear the buttons in the FloatLayouts will have a text starting with **'F'** and the buttons in the RelativeLayouts with **'R'**.

```
# File name: test.kv

<Button>:
    size_hint: None, None
    size: 100, 50

<GridLayout>:
    rows: 2

    # FloatLayout 1
    FloatLayout:
        Button:
            text: 'F1a'
            pos: 0, 0
        Button:
            text: 'F1b'
            pos: 200, 200

    # RelativeLayout 1
    RelativeLayout:
        Button:
            text: 'R1a'
            pos: 0, 0
        Button:
            text: 'R1b'
            pos: 100, 50

    # RelativeLayout 2
    RelativeLayout:
        Button:
            text: 'R2a'
            pos: 100, 50
        Button:
            text: 'R2b'
            pos: 100, 100

    # FloatLayout 2
    FloatLayout:
        Button:
            text: 'F2a'
            pos: 200, 100
        Button:
            text: 'F2b'
            pos: 200, 150
```

If you run this program, it'll be quite difficult to see what it's all about. This is because although there are four cells in the GridLayout (2 rows and 2 columns), we don't actually see the borders between them. Let me add some border lines and annotations to the picture so that it's clearer for you.

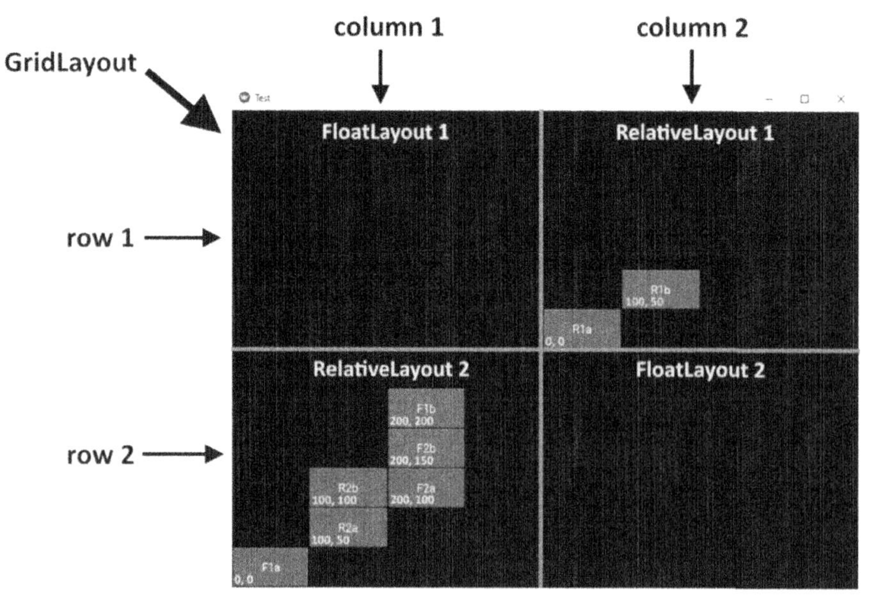


**Coordinates relative to the whole window are in blue.**
**Coordinates relative to the layout are in yellow.**

Have a look at the two buttons, F1a and R1a.

They both have the coordinates **`(0, 0)`**.

The former is relative to the whole window, though, whereas the latter is relative to the layout it's in, so RelativeLayout 1.

# Top Menu in AnchorLayout

In our next example we'll make a top menu using a BoxLayout for the menu items. The whole menu will be embedded in an AnchorLayout. Here's the Python code:

```
# File name: test.py

from kivy.app import App

# We need a AnchorLayout to embed the menu into.
from kivy.uix.anchorlayout import AnchorLayout

class TestApp(App):
    def build(self):
        return AnchorLayout()

if __name__ == '__main__':
    TestApp().run()
```

The menu should be in the upper left corner of the window. The menu itself is a BoxLayout with horizontal orientation.

For simplicity's sake it will just contain labels imitating the menu items in the top menu of the Visual Studio Code editor. We need a fixed size for the BoxLayout or otherwise it will fill the whole AnchorLayout.

As we are inside the AnchorLayout, we must set **size_hint** to **(None, None)** first and then use **size** to set the size in pixels.

```
# File name: test.kv

<AnchorLayout>:
    anchor_x: 'left'
    anchor_y: 'top'

    BoxLayout:
        size_hint: None, None
        size: 600, 50

        # And here come the
        # labels for our menu.
        Label:
            text: 'File'
        Label:
            text: 'Edit'
        Label:
            text: 'Selection'
        Label:
            text: 'View'
        Label:
            text: 'Go'
        Label:
            text: 'Run'
        Label:
            text: 'Terminal'
        Label:
            text: 'Help'
```

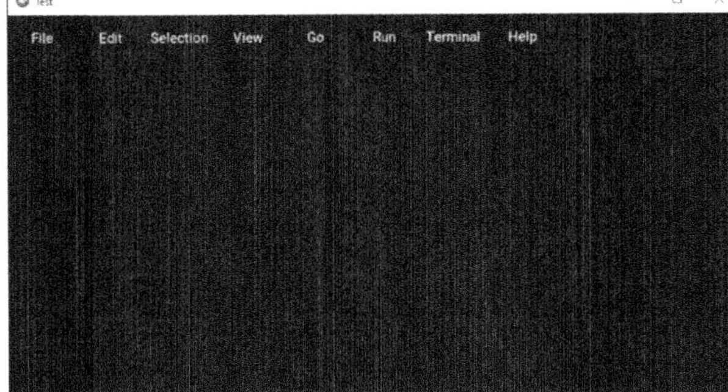


If you now run the program, you will see the app window with a top menu.

# Toolbar with StackLayout and AnchorLayout

In our next example we'll make a toolbar and place it on one side of the window. It will contain simple square buttons placed in a StackLayout.

The toolbar itself will be placed inside an AnchorLayout, just like before. This means that we don't actually have to change the Python file this time. And here's the kv file:

```
# File name: test.kv

# All the elements in the toolbar will
# be square buttons.
<Button>:
    size_hint: None, None
    size: 50, 50

<AnchorLayout>:
    # The toolbar should be on the right
    # side of the program window, at
    # the top.
    anchor_x: 'right'
    anchor_y: 'top'

    # The toolbar is a StackLayout with
    # top to bottom and then right to
    # left orientation.
    StackLayout:
        orientation: 'tb-rl'

        # We need a fixed size for the
        # StackLayout.
        size_hint: None, None
        size: 100, 300

        # And here are the buttons.
        Button:
            text: '1'
        Button:
            text: '2'
        Button:
            text: '3'
        Button:
            text: '4'
        Button:
            text: '5'
        Button:
            text: '6'
        Button:
            text: '7'
        Button:
            text: '8'
        Button:
            text: '9'
```

# Imitating Different Cell Sizes in GridLayout

And one more example. In this one we'll embed GridLayouts in a GridLayout to imitate different cell sizes, which you may be familiar with if you ever used the Windows 8 operating system or Windows Phone systems with tiles.

Let's modify the Python file first:

```
# File name: test.py

from kivy.app import App
from kivy.uix.gridlayout import GridLayout

# a custom GridLayout to act as the outer container
class OuterGridLayout(GridLayout):
    pass

class TestApp(App):
    def build(self):
        return OuterGridLayout()

if __name__ == '__main__':
    TestApp().run()
```

And now the kv file. We'll need big buttons and small buttons to represent the tiles. The big buttons will be placed directly in the outer GridLayout. The small buttons will be placed in inner GridLayouts embedded in the outer one.

```
# File name: test.kv

<BigButton@Button>:
    size_hint: None, None
    size: 200, 200

<SmallButton@Button>:
    size_hint: None, None
    size: 100, 100

<OuterGridLayout>:
    rows: 3
    size_hint: None, None
    size: 600, 600
    BigButton:
        text: '1'
    BigButton:
        text: '2'
    BigButton:
        text: '3'
    GridLayout:
        rows: 2
        SmallButton:
            text: '4a'
        SmallButton:
            text: '4b'
        SmallButton:
            text: '4c'
        SmallButton:
            text: '4d'
    BigButton:
        text: '5'
    BigButton:
        text: '6'
    BigButton:
        text: '7'
    BigButton:
        text: '8'
    GridLayout:
        rows: 2
        SmallButton:
            text: '9a'
        SmallButton:
            text: '9b'
        SmallButton:
            text: '9c'
        SmallButton:
            text: '9d'
```

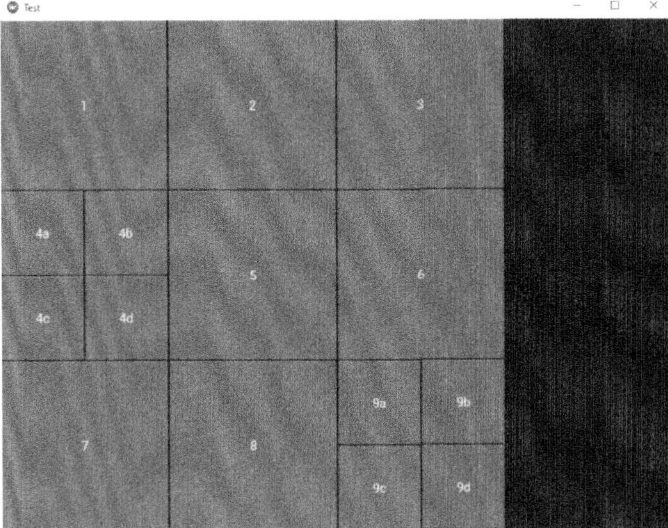


If you now run the program, you will see the well-known tiled interface.

This was the last example for now, but, as you might guess, the possibilities are countless, it all depends on what layout you need. You can nest layouts on multiple levels, which is very flexible.

In the next chapter we'll learn how to define layouts in Python code, without the Kivy language. As you know you can write Kivy apps just in Python, so this is something you might want to be able to do.

# It's Your Turn Now...

### EXERCISE

Create a pretty complex (and pretty useless, to be sincere) GUI in which four layouts are embedded in the four corners of the window. As the outer layout use a FloatLayout. The four layouts that should be embedded in the Floatlayout are:

1. In the upper left corner:

A vertical 200 x 300 px BoxLayout with three default sliders.

2. In the lower left corner:

A 300 x 300 px AnchorLayout with a button centered in the layout. The button should be 200 x 200 px and the text on it should read **':)'**.

3. In the lower right corner:

A 300 x 200 px PageLayout with three pages. On each page there should be a default button. The **text** properties of the three buttons should be set set to **'A'**, **'B'** and **'C'** respectively.

4. In the upper right corner:

A 300 x 300 px GridLayout with three columns. There should be six labels in the layout, numbered from 1 to 6 (so the **text** property should be set to the numbers from 1 to 6).

### SOLUTION

Here's the Python code:

```
# File name: test.py

from kivy.app import App

# We need a FloatLayout to embed the other layouts in.
from kivy.uix.floatlayout import FloatLayout

class TestApp(App):
    def build(self):
        return FloatLayout()

if __name__ == '__main__':
    TestApp().run()
```

And here's the kv file:

```
# File name: test.kv

<FloatLayout>:
    BoxLayout:
        orientation: 'vertical'
        size_hint: None, None
        size: 200, 300
        pos_hint: {'x': 0, 'top': 1}
        Slider:
        Slider:
        Slider:
    AnchorLayout:
        anchor_x: 'center'
        anchor_y: 'center'
        size_hint: None, None
        size: 300, 300
        pos_hint: {'x': 0, 'y': 0}
        Button:
            text: ':)'
            size_hint: None, None
            size: 200, 200
    PageLayout:
        size_hint: None, None
        size: 300, 200
        pos_hint: {'right': 1, 'y': 0}
        Button:
            text: 'A'
        Button:
            text: 'B'
        Button:
            text: 'C'
    GridLayout:
        cols: 3
        size_hint: None, None
        size: 300, 300
        pos_hint: {'right': 1, 'top': 1}
        Label:
            text: '1'
        Label:
            text: '2'
        Label:
            text: '3'
        Label:
            text: '4'
        Label:
            text: '5'
        Label:
            text: '6'
```

If you run the program, you should see this pretty weird GUI.

You can try resizing the window, pressing the buttons, moving the sliders and flipping pages in the PageLayout, it all works, although it doesn't do anything useful.

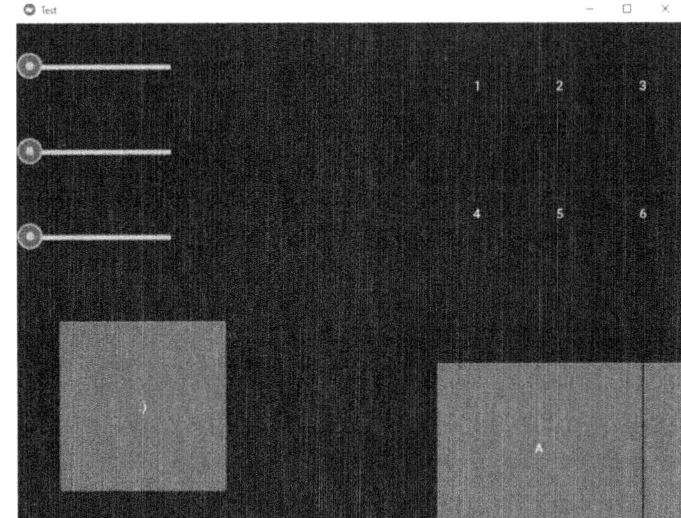

# Chapter 28 – Defining Layouts in Python Code

Now that you know how to create layouts and how to add widgets to layouts in the Kivy language, it's time to learn how to do the same just in Python, without the Kivy language. As you know, although the Kivy language is a flexible and powerful tool that enables you to separate presentation from logic, you are not forced to use it and if you like, you can use exclusively Python.

So, let's have a look at some examples with both Python and kv code and let's see how to rewrite them without the Kivy language. Let's start with the **FloatLayout**.

## The FloatLayout

Let's start with a very basic FloatLayout with just one widget.

Here is the Python file:

```
# File name: test.py

from kivy.app import App
from kivy.uix.floatlayout import FloatLayout

class TestApp(App):
    def build(self):
        return FloatLayout()

if __name__ == '__main__':
    TestApp().run()
```

And here's the kv file:

```
# File name: test.kv

<FloatLayout>:
    Button:
        text: 'Press Me'
        size_hint_y: .15
```

If you run the app, you will see a very simple interface with a single button.

Let's now get rid of the kv file (you can just remove all the code from it) and let's create the same GUI in Python.

Here's the Python file with explanations in comments.

One thing to note is the **add_widget** method defined in the **kivy.uix.layout.Layout** class **FloatLayout** inherits from. As its name suggests, we use it to add a widget to the layout.

```
# File name: test.py

from kivy.app import App

# We're going to need the FloatLayout and Button classes, so let's import them.
from kivy.uix.floatlayout import FloatLayout
from kivy.uix.button import Button

# This simple FloatLayout doesn't have any properties set on it, so we can
# create it by simply instancing the FloatLayout class without any arguments.
layout = FloatLayout()

# There's a button in the FloatLayout, so we must first create it. We already
# learned how to do it - you just have to pass all the properties that you
# want to set as keyword arguments to the class constructor.
button = Button(text='Press Me', size_hint_y=.15)

# Let's add the button to the layout using the add_widget method.
layout.add_widget(button)

class TestApp(App):
    def build(self):
        # The method must return the layout we created.
        return layout

if __name__ == '__main__':
    TestApp().run()
```

If you now run the program, the result will be exactly the same as before. In this example there's just one widget in the layout. In our next example we'll add more.

# The RelativeLayout

Here's an example with a RelativeLayout with two widgets, a button and a slider. At first the version with both Python and kv code. Here's the Python code:

```
# File name: test.py

from kivy.app import App
from kivy.uix.relativelayout import RelativeLayout

class TestApp(App):
    def build(self):
        return RelativeLayout()

if __name__ == '__main__':
    TestApp().run()
```

And here's the kv code:

```
# File name: test.kv

<RelativeLayout>:
    pos: 100, 50

    Button:
        text: 'Press Me'
        size_hint: None, None
        size: 200, 100
        pos_hint: {'x': 0, 'y': 0}

    Slider:
        min: 20
        max: 60
        value: 50
        size_hint: None, None
        height: 300
        orientation: 'vertical'
        pos_hint: {'x': 0, 'y': .3}
```

If you run the application, you will see the two widgets inside the RelativeLayout.

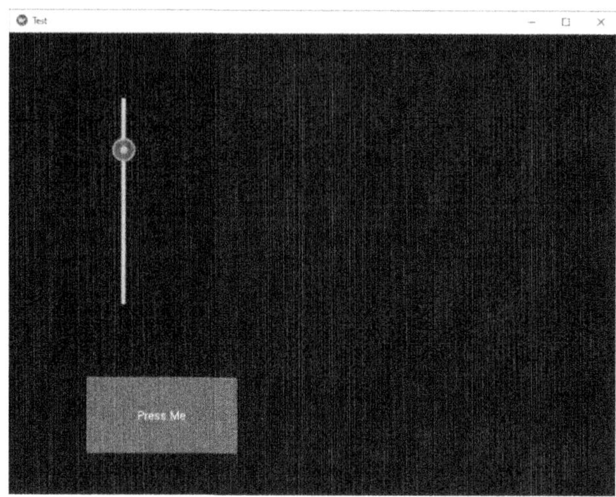


Let's now re-create it in pure Python. First, remove all the code from the kv file. And here's the Python file with explanations:

```
# File name: test.py

from kivy.app import App

# all the necessary imports
from kivy.uix.relativelayout import RelativeLayout
from kivy.uix.button import Button
from kivy.uix.slider import Slider

#  the RelativeLayout with pos set to (100, 50)
layout = RelativeLayout(pos=(100, 50))

# Let's create the widgets and add them to the layout.
button = Button(text='Press Me',
                size_hint=(None, None),
                size=(200, 100),
                pos_hint={'x': 0, 'y': 0})

slider = Slider(min=20,
                max=60,
                value=50,
                size_hint=(None, None),
                height=300,
                orientation='vertical',
                pos_hint={'x': 0, 'y': .3})
layout.add_widget(button)
layout.add_widget(slider)

class TestApp(App):
    def build(self):
        return layout

if __name__ == '__main__':
    TestApp().run()
```

Run the app and make sure it works like before.

# The GridLayout

Here's an example with a GridLayout. In the first version we have separate Python and kv files.

Here's the Python file:

```
# File name: test.py

from kivy.app import App
from kivy.uix.gridlayout import GridLayout

class TestApp(App):
    def build(self):
        return GridLayout()

if __name__ == '__main__':
    TestApp().run()
```

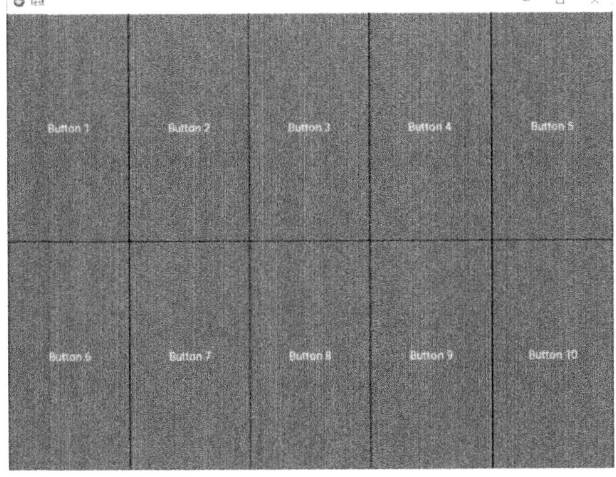

And here's the kv file:

```
# File name: test.kv

<GridLayout>:
    rows: 2

    Button:
        text: 'Button 1'
    Button:
        text: 'Button 2'
    Button:
        text: 'Button 3'
    Button:
        text: 'Button 4'
    Button:
        text: 'Button 5'
    Button:
        text: 'Button 6'
    Button:
        text: 'Button 7'
    Button:
        text: 'Button 8'
    Button:
        text: 'Button 9'
    Button:
        text: 'Button 10'
```

If you run the app, you will see the ten buttons in two rows.

Now, clear the kv file and modify the Python file like so:

```
# File name: test.py

from kivy.app import App

# the imports we need
from kivy.uix.gridlayout import GridLayout
from kivy.uix.button import Button

# Let's create the layout.
layout = GridLayout(rows=2)
```

```
# In this case it's easy to add the buttons in a loop.
for button_number in range(1, 11):
    layout.add_widget(Button(text=f'Button {button_number}'))

class TestApp(App):
    def build(self):
        return layout

if __name__ == '__main__':
    TestApp().run()
```

If you now run the app, it will work just like before.

## The BoxLayout

Next let's have a look at the BoxLayout. Let's start with two separate files again.

Here's the one with Python code:

```
# File name: test.py

from kivy.app import App
from kivy.uix.boxlayout import BoxLayout

class TestApp(App):
    def build(self):
        return BoxLayout()

if __name__ == '__main__':
    TestApp().run()
```

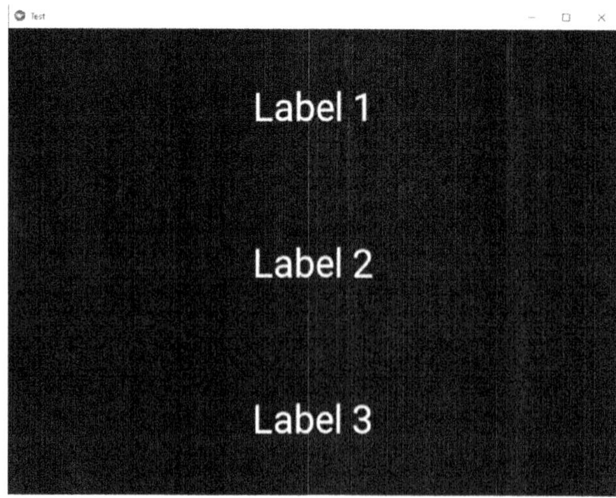


And now the kv file:

```
# File name: test.kv

<BoxLayout>:
    orientation: 'vertical'

    Label:
        text: 'Label 1'
        font_size: 50

    Label:
        text: 'Label 2'
        font_size: 50

    Label:
        text: 'Label 3'
        font_size: 50
```

When you run the app, you should see three big labels.

And now remove all the code from the kv file and rewrite the Python file like so:

```
# File name: test.py

from kivy.app import App

# the imports we need
from kivy.uix.boxlayout import BoxLayout
from kivy.uix.label import Label

# Let's create the layout.
layout = BoxLayout(orientation='vertical')

# We can use a loop to create and add the labels.
for label_number in range(1, 4):
    layout.add_widget(Label(text=f'Label {label_number}', font_size=50))

class TestApp(App):
    def build(self):
        return layout

if __name__ == '__main__':
    TestApp().run()
```

Naturally, the app works and looks just like before.

# The StackLayout

Now an example with a StackLayout. As usual, let's start with separate Python and kv files.

Here's the former:

```
# File name: test.py

from kivy.app import App
from kivy.uix.stacklayout import StackLayout

class TestApp(App):
    def build(self):
        return StackLayout()

if __name__ == '__main__':
    TestApp().run()
```

And here's the latter:

```
# File name: test.kv

<CustomButton@Button>:
    size_hint: None, None
    size: 300, 200
    font_size: 50

<StackLayout>:
    orientation: 'rl-tb'

    CustomButton:
        text: 'Button 1'
    CustomButton:
        text: 'Button 2'
    CustomButton:
        text: 'Button 3'
    CustomButton:
        text: 'Button 4'
    CustomButton:
        text: 'Button 5'
```

Here you can see the five buttons.

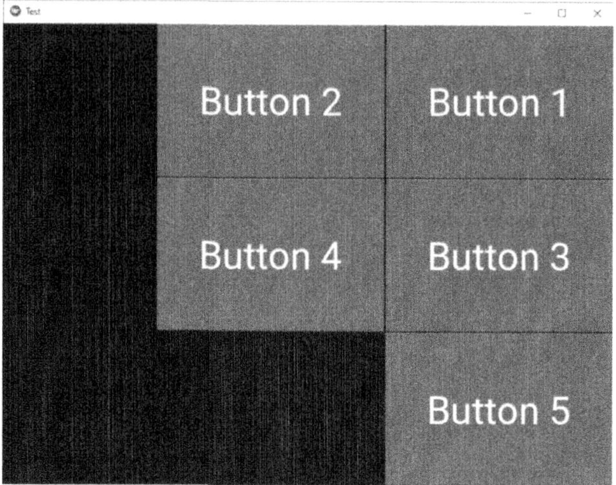


Now remove the kv code and rewrite the Python file like this:

```
# File name: test.py

from kivy.app import App

# our imports
from kivy.uix.stacklayout import StackLayout
from kivy.uix.button import Button

# Let's define the CustomButton class that inherits from Button.
class CustomButton(Button):
    def __init__(self, **kwargs):
        super().__init__(**kwargs)
        self.size_hint = (None, None)
        self.size = (300, 200)
        self.font_size = 50

# Let's create the layout.
layout = StackLayout(orientation='rl-tb')

# We can use a loop to create and add the custom buttons.
for button_number in range(1, 6):
    layout.add_widget(CustomButton(text=f'Button {button_number}'))

class TestApp(App):
    def build(self):
        return layout

if __name__ == '__main__':
    TestApp().run()
```

# The AnchorLayout

The next layout I'd like to talk about is the AnchorLayout. Here's an example we already saw in the chapter on the **AnchorLayout**. First, the two separate files.

Let's start with Python:

```
# File name: test.py

from kivy.app import App
from kivy.uix.anchorlayout import AnchorLayout

class TestApp(App):
    def build(self):
        return AnchorLayout()

if __name__ == '__main__':
    TestApp().run()
```

And here's the kv code:

```
# File name: test.kv

<CustomButton@Button>:
    size_hint: None, None
    size: 200, 100
    font_size: 30

<AnchorLayout>:
    anchor_x: 'right'
    anchor_y: 'top'

    CustomButton:
        text: 'right\ntop'
```

When you run the app, you can see a button in the top right corner.

And now let's remove the kv code and rewrite the Python file like this:

```
# File name: test.py

from kivy.app import App

# our imports
from kivy.uix.anchorlayout import AnchorLayout
from kivy.uix.button import Button

class CustomButton(Button):
    def __init__(self, **kwargs):
        super().__init__(**kwargs)
        self.size_hint = (None, None)
        self.size = (200, 100)
        self.font_size = 30

# Let's create the layout.
layout = AnchorLayout(anchor_x='right', anchor_y='top')

# Let's add the widget to the layout.
layout.add_widget(CustomButton(text='right\ntop'))
```

```
class TestApp(App):
    def build(self):
        return layout

if __name__ == '__main__':
    TestApp().run()
```

# The PageLayout

Finally, let's rewrite one of the examples we used in the chapter on the **PageLayout**. As usual, let's start with separate Python and kv files.

Here's the former:

```
# File name: test.py

from kivy.app import App
from kivy.uix.pagelayout import PageLayout

class TestApp(App):
    def build(self):
        return PageLayout()

if __name__ == '__main__':
    TestApp().run()
```

And here's the latter:

```
# File name: test.kv

<PageLayout>:
    border: 200
    page: 1

    Button:
        text: 'Page 1'
    Button:
        text: 'Page 2'
    Button:
        text: 'Page 3'
```

When you run the app, you will first see page 2. Now remove the kv code and rewrite the Python file like this:

```
# File name: test.py

from kivy.app import App

# our imports
from kivy.uix.pagelayout import PageLayout
from kivy.uix.button import Button

# Let's create the layout.
layout = PageLayout(border=200, page=1)

# Let's add the widgets to the layout.
for page in range(1, 4):
    layout.add_widget(Button(text=f'Page {page}'))

class TestApp(App):
    def build(self):
        return layout

if __name__ == '__main__':
    TestApp().run()
```

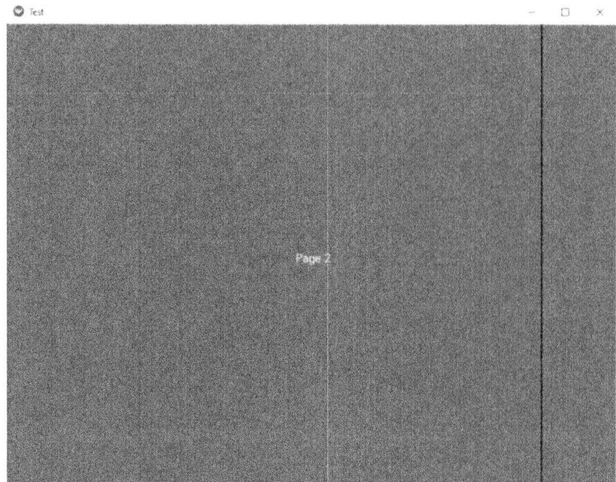

# Embedded Layouts

Now that you know how to define each layout in Python code, let's have a look at a slightly more complex example with embedded layouts.

In the chapter on embedding layouts we had the example where we created a top menu using a BoxLayout embedded in an AnchorLayout.

Here's the Python code again:

```
# File name: test.py

from kivy.app import App
from kivy.uix.anchorlayout import AnchorLayout

class TestApp(App):
    def build(self):
        return AnchorLayout()

if __name__ == '__main__':
    TestApp().run()
```

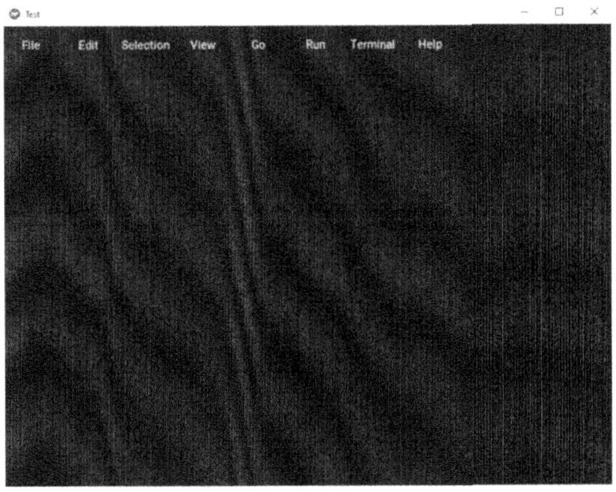

And here's the kv code:

```
# File name: test.kv

<AnchorLayout>:
    anchor_x: 'left'
    anchor_y: 'top'

    BoxLayout:
        size_hint: None, None
        size: 600, 50
        Label:
            text: 'File'
        Label:
            text: 'Edit'
        Label:
            text: 'Selection'
        Label:
            text: 'View'
        Label:
            text: 'Go'
        Label:
            text: 'Run'
        Label:
            text: 'Terminal'
        Label:
            text: 'Help'
```

Run the app to see the menu. Let's remove the kv code and re-create the app in pure Python:

```
# File name: test.py

from kivy.app import App

# our imports
from kivy.uix.anchorlayout import AnchorLayout
from kivy.uix.boxlayout import BoxLayout
from kivy.uix.label import Label

# Let's create the outer layout.
main_layout = AnchorLayout(anchor_x='left', anchor_y='top')

# Let's create the inner layout.
inner_layout = BoxLayout(size_hint=(None, None), size=(600, 50))

# Let's add the labels to the BoxLayout.
labels = ['File', 'Edit', 'Selection', 'View', 'Go', 'Run', 'Terminal', 'Help']
for label in labels:
    inner_layout.add_widget(Label(text=label))
```

```
# Let's add the inner layout to the outer layout.
main_layout.add_widget(inner_layout)

class TestApp(App):
    def build(self):
        # The method should return the outer layout.
        return main_layout

if __name__ == '__main__':
    TestApp().run()
```

As expected, the app now works just like before.

Now, with the basics of widgets and layouts covered, we could move on to the next topic, for example graphics or events in Kivy. I'm not going to do that, though. At least not just yet. Instead we're going to jump right into the project and we'll stop to discuss the stuff we need when we need it. In the next part we'll make a short break from programming and we'll have a look at the assets that will be used in the app and the general structure of the project. And then we'll start building the app from scratch.

# It's Your Turn Now...

## EXERCISE

In the chapter on embedding layouts we created a program imitating the Windows 8 – style tiled GUI. In this example we embedded GridLayouts in another GridLayout.

Here are the two separate files again. First the Python file:

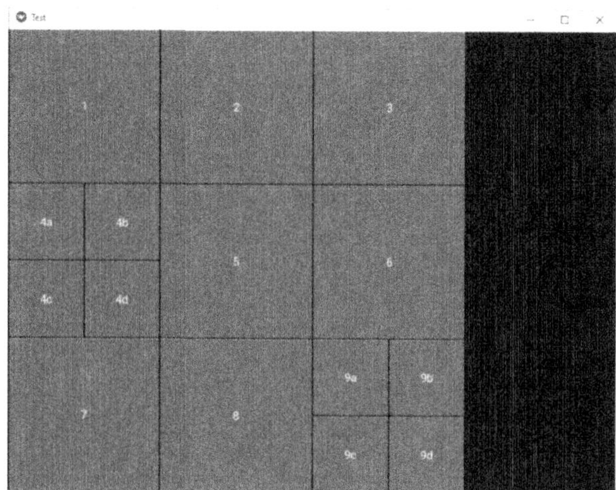


```
# File name: test.py

from kivy.app import App
from kivy.uix.gridlayout import GridLayout

class OuterGridLayout(GridLayout):
    pass

class TestApp(App):
    def build(self):
        return OuterGridLayout()

if __name__ == '__main__':
    TestApp().run()
```

And the kv file:

```
# File name: test.kv

<BigButton@Button>:
    size_hint: None, None
    size: 200, 200

<SmallButton@Button>:
    size_hint: None, None
    size: 100, 100
<OuterGridLayout>:
    rows: 3
    size_hint: None, None
    size: 600, 600

    BigButton:
        text: '1'
    BigButton:
        text: '2'
    BigButton:
        text: '3'
    GridLayout:
        rows: 2
        SmallButton:
            text: '4a'
        SmallButton:
            text: '4b'
        SmallButton:
            text: '4c'
        SmallButton:
            text: '4d'
    BigButton:
        text: '5'
    BigButton:
        text: '6'
    BigButton:
        text: '7'
    BigButton:
        text: '8'
    GridLayout:
        rows: 2
        SmallButton:
            text: '9a'
        SmallButton:
            text: '9b'
        SmallButton:
            text: '9c'
        SmallButton:
            text: '9d'
```

When we ran the app, we saw the tiled GUI. Now, re-create this app in pure Python, without the kv file (don't forget to remove the kv code first).

**SOLUTION**

So, the kv file is now empty. There are multiple ways to write the Python code, you can add the widgets one by one or in loops for example. Here's my version of the rewritten Python file, but yours might be equally good, or maybe even better, who knows?

```
# File name: test.py

from kivy.app import App

# our imports
from kivy.uix.gridlayout import GridLayout
from kivy.uix.button import Button

# Let's define the BigButton and SmallButton classes that inherit from Button.
class BigButton(Button):
    def __init__(self, **kwargs):
        super().__init__(**kwargs)
        self.size_hint = (None, None)
        self.size = (200, 200)
```

```
class SmallButton(Button):
    def __init__(self, **kwargs):
        super().__init__(**kwargs)
        self.size_hint = (None, None)
        self.size = (100, 100)


# Let's define the OuterGridLayout class that inherits from GridLayout.
class OuterGridLayout(GridLayout):
    def __init__(self, **kwargs):
        super().__init__(**kwargs)
        self.rows = 3
        self.size_hint = (None, None)
        self.size = (600, 600)

# Let's create the outer layout.
main_layout = OuterGridLayout()

# Let's create the two inner GridLayouts.
inner_layout1 = GridLayout(rows=2)
inner_layout2 = GridLayout(rows=2)

# Let's add the small buttons to the inner layouts.
labels1 = ['4a', '4b', '4c', '4d']
for label in labels1:
    inner_layout1.add_widget(Button(text=label))

labels2 = ['9a', '9b', '9c', '9d']
for label in labels2:
    inner_layout2.add_widget(Button(text=label))

# Let's add the big buttons and the inner layouts to the outer layout.
main_layout.add_widget(BigButton(text='1'))
main_layout.add_widget(BigButton(text='2'))
main_layout.add_widget(BigButton(text='3'))
main_layout.add_widget(inner_layout1)
main_layout.add_widget(BigButton(text='5'))
main_layout.add_widget(BigButton(text='6'))
main_layout.add_widget(BigButton(text='7'))
main_layout.add_widget(BigButton(text='8'))
main_layout.add_widget(inner_layout2)

class TestApp(App):
    def build(self):
        return main_layout

if __name__ == '__main__':
    TestApp().run()
```

Make sure to run the app to see if it works as before. It should.

# Part IV

# The Slugrace Project Structure and Assets

In this part of the book we'll build the file hierarchy for our project and add the game assets to the project. We'll also write some basic code to get started.

# Chapter 29 – Game Assets

As I mentioned in the previous chapter we're going to make a short break from programming now and have a look at the game assets that will be used in the app. There will be some graphics and sounds in the app. Let's start with the graphics.

## Visual Game Assets - the Images

We're going to need some images. Let's have a look at them now. These are PNG images because we need them to have transparent backgrounds. Here you can see all the images along with their names.

### The Race Track

The first image we need is the race track, on which the slugs will be running. This is a 1000x200 px image. We will place it in the background. On top of it will be the slugs and some text.

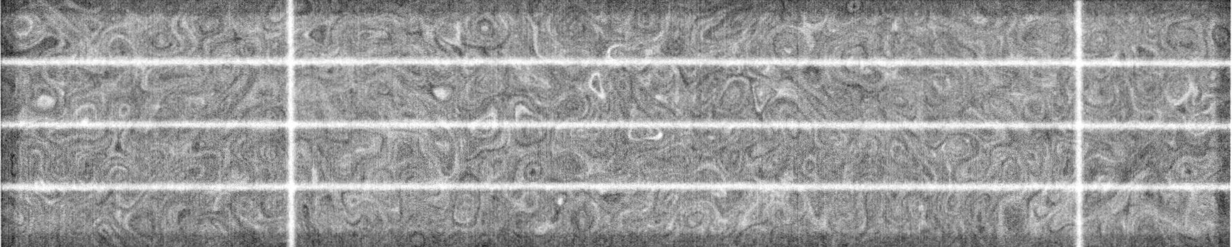

**racetrack.png**

### The Slugs

We definitely need the slugs. Actually, we need each slug in two versions: a silhouette which will be visible when a slug wins a race and a top view of the slug, which we'll see on the race track.

#### Silhouettes

Now, with the silhouettes it's simple. Each slug has a name and a corresponding image. The names are: Speedster, Trusty, Iffy and Slowpoke. Here are the images:

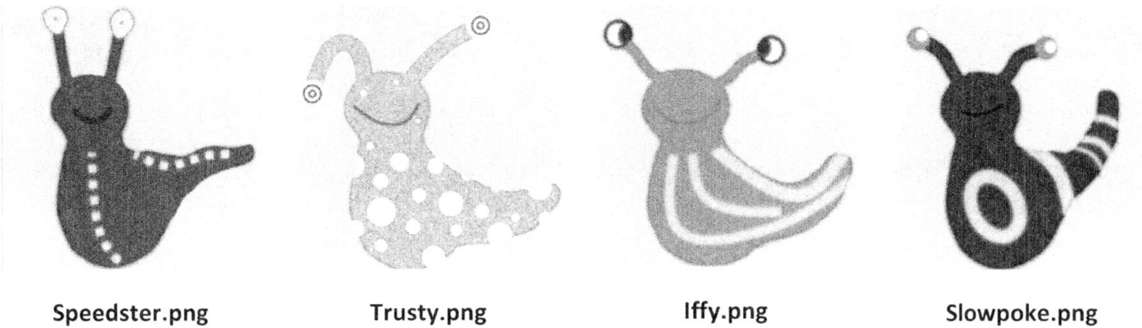

**Speedster.png** **Trusty.png** **Iffy.png** **Slowpoke.png**

We'll also need an image with all four slugs, which we'll use as a background decoration on one of the screens later in the game.

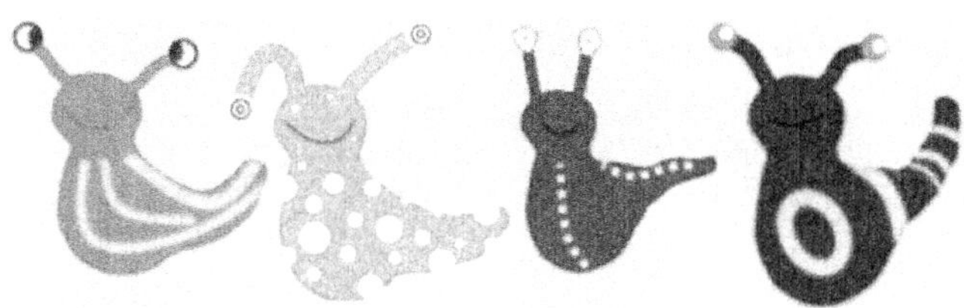

all slugs.png

### Top Views of the Slugs

As far as the top views are concerned, we'll need two images for each slug, one for the body and one for the eye (along with the tentacle it's on). This is because the tentacles (to which we're going to refer as eyes from now on for the sake of simplicity) are going to be moving parts. They will be attached to the bodies and animated later in the project. Here are the images:

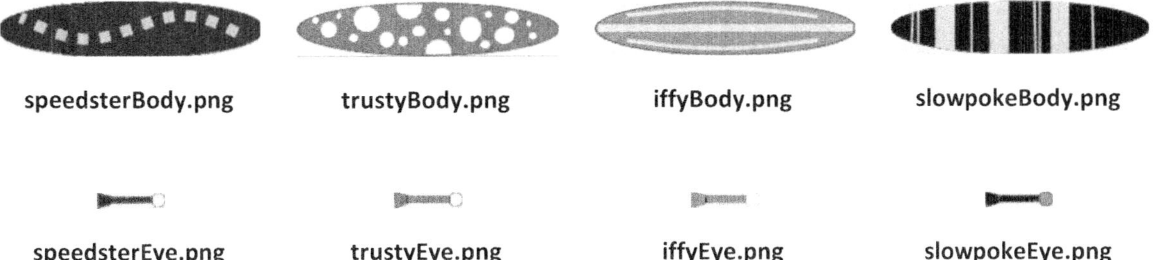

**speedsterBody.png** **trustyBody.png** **iffyBody.png** **slowpokeBody.png**

**speedsterEye.png** **trustyEye.png** **iffyEye.png** **slowpokeEye.png**

## The Accidents

As you know, the slugs will be racing along the track. But what you probably don't know yet is that they're going to suffer from some accidents from time to time, or, to be more precise, not necessarily suffer, because some accidents will be pretty convenient for them and will help them win the race. Anyways, we're going to discuss all the accidents later on, not so soon to tell the truth, but now let's just have a look at the visual game assets that we're going to use for the accidents.

First of all, we'll need a separate image for each slug for the Broken Leg accident:

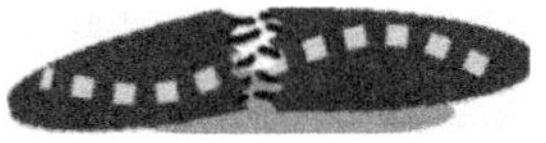
broken leg speedster.png

broken leg trusty.png

broken leg iffy.png

broken leg slowpoke.png

For the other accidents we'll just use generic images that will be used with all four slugs. They will be used as overlays on top of other images or, like the Overheat accident image, replace the slugs' images. Here are the visual game assets we'll be using with the accidents:

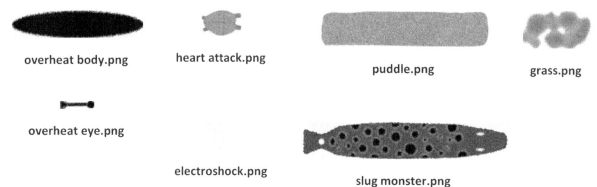

overheat body.png

heart attack.png

puddle.png

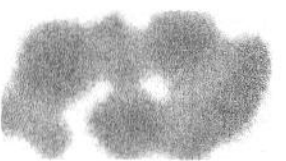
grass.png

overheat eye.png

electroshock.png

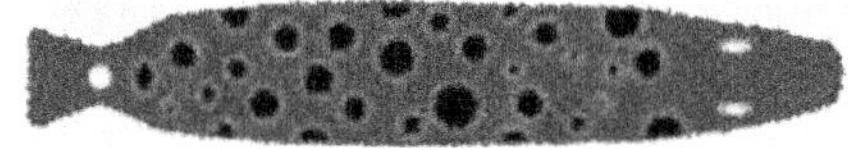
slug monster.png

## Splash Screen

splash screen.png

There will be a splash screen that will appear for a short while when you launch the game, before the actual game begins.

For the splash screen we'll use an image with the game title and the images of all four slugs on it.

## Button Images

The last two visual game assets we'll need are the images that we will put on the toggle button which will mute and unmute sound during the game.

sound_on.png

sound_off.png

# Audio Game Assets - the Sounds

We're going to add some sounds to the game. A game with sounds seems more complete.

## Game Background Music and Sound Effects

When we launch the game, there will be background music. It's in the Background Music.mp3 file.

Then, there will be some sound effects in the game:

| | |
|---|---|
| **Go.mp3** | This is a popping or rather shooting sound that will be heard whenever a race starts. |
| **Slugs Running.mp3** | This sound will be heard while the slugs are running in a race. |
| **Game Over.mp3** | This tune will be played when the game is over. |

## Slugs' Sound Effects

Then there will be some sound effects used by the slugs when they win. Each slug will produce a slightly different sound so that you can tell all the slugs apart by their sound after you get used to them:

| | |
|---|---|
| **Speedster Win.mp3** | This sound will be produced by Speedster if he wins. |
| **Trusty Win.mp3** | This sound will be produced by Trusty if he wins. |
| **Iffy Win.mp3** | This sound will be produced by Iffy if he wins. |
| **Slowpoke Win.mp3** | This sound will be produced by Slowpoke if he wins. |

## Accident Sound Effects

Finally, when an accident happens, there will be a sound effect to accompany the visual effect of the accident. Below is the list of the sound effects with short descriptions. Don't worry if you don't understand what it's all about. I will discuss the accidents later in the project. So, here are the sounds:

| | |
|---|---|
| **Asleep.mp3** | This sound will be produced by a slug that falls asleep. |
| **Blind.mp3** | This sound will be produced by a slug that goes blind. |
| **Broken Leg.mp3** | This sound will be produced by a slug that breaks his leg. |
| **Devoured.mp3** | This sound will be produced by a slug that is eaten by the slug monster. |
| **Drown.mp3** | This sound will be produced by a slug that drowns in the puddle. |
| **Electroshock.mp3** | This sound will be produced by a slug that is struck by lightning. |
| **Grass.mp3** | This sound will be produced by a slug that stops to eat some grass. |
| **Heart Attack.mp3** | This sound will be produced by a slug that has a heart attack. |
| **Overheat.mp3** | This sound will be produced by a slug that gets burned. |
| **Rubberizer.mp3** | This sound will be produced by a slug that stretches like rubber. |
| **Shooting Eyes.mp3** | This sound will be produced by a slug that shoots his eyes. |
| **Turning Back.mp3** | This sound will be produced by a slug that turns back. |

You can download all the game assets, both images and sounds, from Github:

**https://github.com/prospero-apps/python/tree/master/GUI%20Programming%20with%20Python%20and%20Kivy%20BOOK/assets**

You should save them in your project folder. We'll be doing just that in the next chapter.

# Chapter 30 - The Project Folder

In the previous chapter you saw the assets that we'll need for the project. They include both visual assets, like the images of the slugs and the race track and the button icons, and sounds, like the audio effects that you will hear when a slug finishes a race, when an accident happens or when the game is over.

In this chapter we're going to have a closer look at our working environment for our project, so, in other words, the folder in which our project lives. All the code files, both Python and kv, as well as all the assets will be in that folder.

## The Project Folder

For the purpose of this course I've been creating a new project folder for each chapter so that you can see how far we are into the project at the end of each chapter. This folder contains all the code files, both Python and kv. At this moment there are two files, **test.py** and **test.kv**. You're probably working on one folder throughout the whole course, so you can just keep doing so.

Just to remind you, I'm naming my project folder after the chapter it belongs to, so the folder for this chapter, which is chapter 30, is named **slugrace30**. If you named your folder just **slugrace**, as I suggested at the beginning of the book, then you will just modify it in each of the following chapters – also a thing you've been doing so far.

Now, we'll be adding more files to the folder and also the assets that we discussed in the previous chapter. You can keep the two test files. They're not going to be part of our project, but we're going to use them from time to time in order to test new stuff we learn.

And now download the assets from my Github repository if you haven't done so yet (you will find the link in the previous chapter) and put them in the project folder. At this moment the project folder should contain the following: the **assets** folder, the **test.py** file and the **test.kv** file.

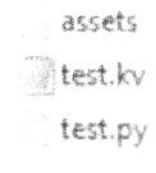


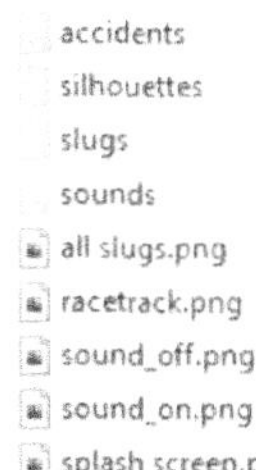


Your project folder path will probably look different than mine. You will have to take this into account each time we need access to one of our folders when working on the project. Now open the assets folder and you will see a hierarchy of folders and files. Make sure your folder hierarchy is the same if you want to follow along smoothly. As you can see, apart from the two test files there are no files with code yet in the project folder. We're going to fix this in the next chapter, where we'll be creating all the basic project files that we need.

# Chapter 31 - The File Hierarchy

In the previous chapter we had a closer look at our project folder and put the **assets** folder in it. But we didn't create any code files yet (apart from the two test files we've been working on since the beginning of this course). Let's add the code files now and build the file hierarchy. Don't worry if you don't understand what these files are going to be used for. You don't need to understand how they are going to be related to one another either. I mean for the time being.

We're going to need a couple of files. Most of them will be empty for now and we'll be filling them in with code as we proceed. But creating the file hierarchy with all the files now will give you an idea of how complex our project is going to be.

You can add the files manually or inside Visual Studio Code. I'm going to choose the latter option, so if you want to follow along, launch your VSC editor and open the project folder from the File menu. I showed you how to add files in VSC when we were adding the two test files.

## Adding Files

Now, let's add a Python file and name it **main.py**. This is going to be the main file in our project where the execution of our app will begin. Before you do it, make sure the main folder is selected, not the assets subfolder. If this were the case, the new file would be created inside the assets folder.

Our app's name will be **`SlugraceApp`**, so let's name the corresponding kv file **slugrace.kv**.

We'll also need files to take care of all the different parts of our project. They will all come in pairs: a Python file and a kv file. So now repeat the steps above to create the following files:

**settings.py**, **settings.kv**

**race.py**, **race.kv**

**bets.py**, **bets.kv**

**results.py**, **results.kv**

**widgets.py**, **widgets.kv**

**instructions.py**, **instructions.kv**

**gameover.py**, **gameover.kv**

**splash.py**, **splash.kv**

**slug.py**, **slug.kv**

We'll also need two Python files without kv counterparts:

**player.py**

**accident.py**

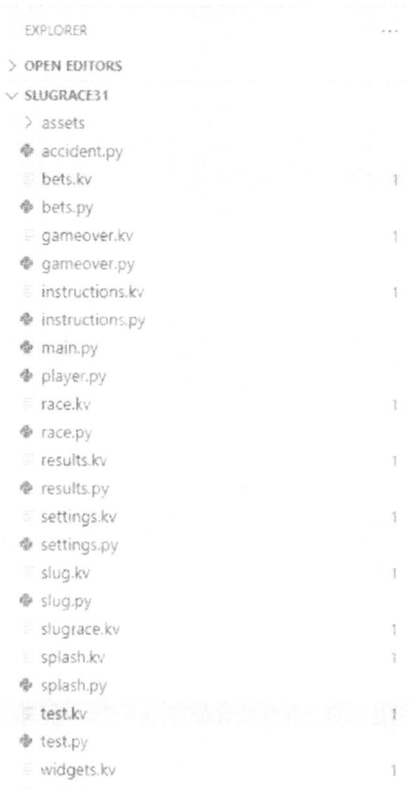


So, outside the assets folder there are 24 files altogether, including the two test files. These are all the files we'll need for our project. You can now see all the files in Visual Studio Code.

You can also see the number 1 to the right of the kv files, including the **test.kv** file, indicating some problems. If you open the terminal and select the PROBLEMS tab at the top, you will see what the problem is all about.

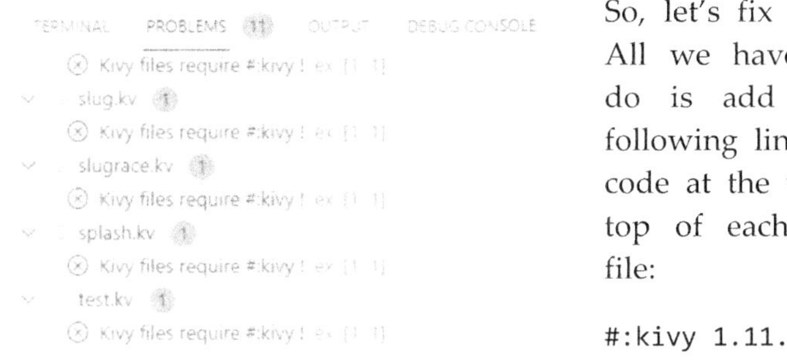

So, let's fix this. All we have to do is add the following line of code at the very top of each kv file:

```
#:kivy 1.11.1
```

This is the Kivy header and it must be followed by the version of Kivy you're using, so if you have a newer version of Kivy, use it instead. This line must be added even before the line with the file name. Here's what it should look like in the **test.kv** file:

```
#:kivy 1.11.1
# File name: test.kv
```

As soon as you type it in, the problem will be gone. Here's the **test.kv** file now. The number of problems in this file is no longer displayed, which means it's zero.

Now, as all your newly created files are still open, add the same code to each of the kv files, naturally changing the name of the file in each of them.

As for the Python files, just type the file name as a simple comment at the top, like we did in the **test.py** file. For example the first line in the **main.py** file should be:

```
# File name: main.py
```

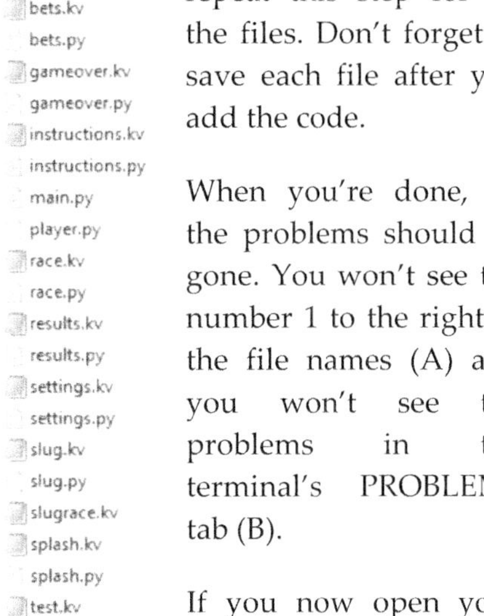


And so on. You can now repeat this step for all the files. Don't forget to save each file after you add the code.

When you're done, all the problems should be gone. You won't see the number 1 to the right of the file names (A) and you won't see the problems in the terminal's PROBLEMS tab (B).

If you now open your project folder, you will see all the files sitting there.

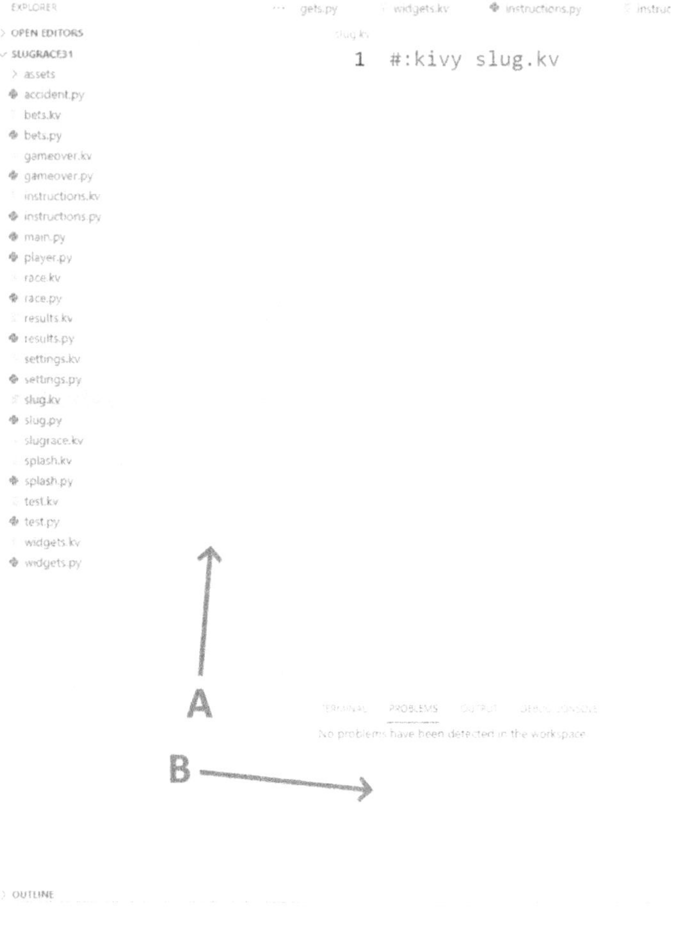


So, now we have all the files we need, but they are empty, except for the file names at the top of all files and additionally the Kivy headers at the very top in the kv files. In the next chapter we'll add some basic code to get started with the project.

# Chapter 32 – Some Basic Code to Get Started

In the previous chapter we created some files, both Python files and kv files. But they were left almost empty (except for the Kivy headers and file names). Now it's time to start filling them in with some code.

## The main.py File

Let's start with the **main.py** file. This is the file from which our application will eventually run and it will include all the classes that we will need access to from other files. So, if you need access from more than one file to a class, you'll find it here.

For example you will need access to the **Game** class from the Settings screen, but also from Bets, Results, and so on. So, the **Game** class will be defined in the **main.py** file. But we'll take care of the classes a bit later. Now let's just add some skeleton code:

```
# File name: main.py

import kivy
kivy.require('1.11.1')

from kivy.app import App

class SlugraceApp(App):
    def build(self):
        pass

if __name__ == '__main__':
    SlugraceApp().run()
```

Now, this code should look familiar to you because it's almost exactly the same as in the **test.py** file. The only difference is the first two lines of code where we import the **kivy** module and then call the **require** method on it. This piece if code is not necessary. The program would work the same without it, but we'll be adding it from now on to our Python files. The **require** method is used to check the minimum version required to run a Kivy application. If someone then tries to run it on an older version of Kivy, it won't work. I'm using the **1.11.1** version of Kivy, but if you are using a different version, just pass it as the argument to the **require** method.

If you run this code, no window will be created. The program doesn't have anything to create. We didn't specify any widget or layout to be created. But the app will run without errors and this is what will do for now. It doesn't seem very useful, but this code will be changed drastically very soon.

## The settings.py and settings.kv Files

Now, let's move on to the **settings.py** file. Although this file will eventually be just part of the whole application, let's write some code so that we can run it as a separate app for now.

Here's the code:

```
# File name: settings.py

import kivy
kivy.require('1.11.1')

from kivy.app import App
from kivy.uix.boxlayout import BoxLayout

class SettingsApp(App):
    def build(self):
        return BoxLayout()

if __name__ == '__main__':
    SettingsApp().run()
```

As you can see, it will return a BoxLayout.

Now let's write some code in the **settings.kv** file and put some elements in the layout. Before we do, though, just a quick reminder. By convention if the app's name and the kv file's name are the same (the latter being written all in lowercase and without the –**App** part at the end), the two files will be associated automatically.

Here the name of the app is **SettingsApp** and the name of the kv file is **settings.kv**, so the Python file will know it should load the **settings.kv** file without explicitly telling it to. And now the kv file:

```
#:kivy 1.11.1
# File name: settings.kv

<BoxLayout>:
    orientation: 'vertical'

    ### SETTINGS LABEL ###
    Label:
        text: 'Settings'
        font_size: 28

    ### THE PLAYERS ###
    Label:
        text: 'The Players'

    ### ENDING CONDITIONS ###
    Label:
        text: 'Ending Conditions'

    ### READY BUTTON ###
    Button:
        text: 'Ready'
```

Remember that this is just the skeleton code for the file. The Settings screen, however, is actually going to contain four big areas: the Settings Label area, the Players area, the Ending Conditions area and the Ready Button area. For now we're using just simple widgets in a vertical BoxLayout to imitate the areas, without any positioning or sizing for now. This should give you just the general idea of what the Settings screen should contain. We'll be filling in the details as we proceed with our project. Anyway, go back to the **settings.py** file and run the program. You should now see what is to become the Settings screen. Here you can see the four areas and this will do for now.

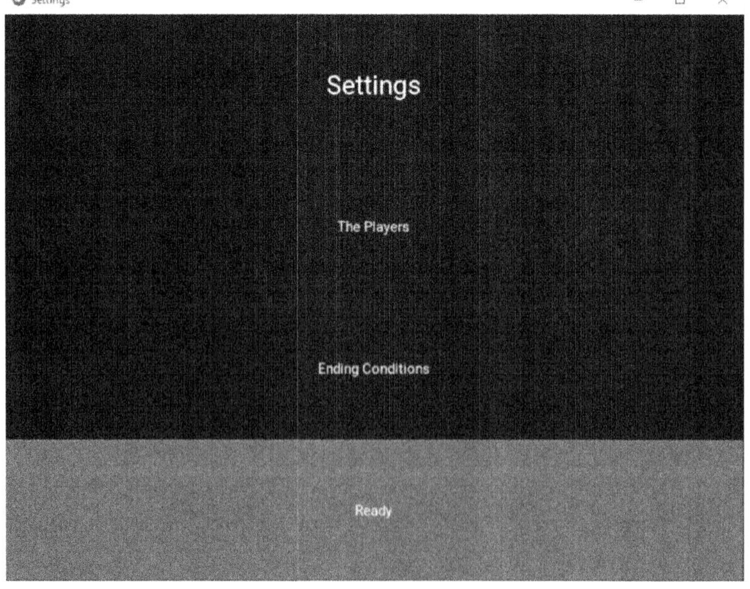

Before we move on, just one remark. To keep the code clear I will use comments with triple # symbols before and after the name of a GUI area, just like in the code above.

# The race.py and race.kv Files

Now let's move on to the next file, **race.py**. Again, let's treat it as a separate app at this time.

The Python file doesn't differ much:

```
# File name: race.py

import kivy
kivy.require('1.11.1')

from kivy.app import App
from kivy.uix.boxlayout import BoxLayout

class RaceApp(App):
    def build(self):
        return BoxLayout()

if __name__ == '__main__':
    RaceApp().run()
```

Here's the **race.kv** file:

```
#:kivy 1.11.1
# File name: race.kv

<BoxLayout>:
    orientation: 'vertical'

    ### INFO, STATS AND BUTTONS ###
    Label:
        text: 'Info, Stats and Buttons'

    ### THE TRACK ###
    Label:
        text: 'The Track'

    ### THE BETS ###
    Label:
        text: 'The Bets'
```

I'm keeping it very simple for now. If you run this app (from the **race.py** file) you will see the outline of the Race screen. Here you can see the layouts and widgets in action, although it's still very basic. But don't worry, things are going to become much more complex sooner than you might expect.

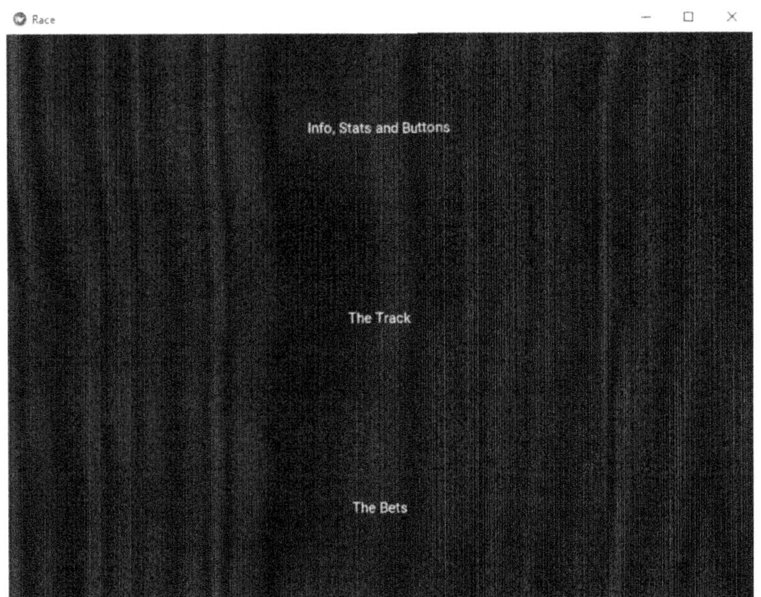


In the next part of the book we'll use our knowledge of layouts and widgets to build the basic GUIs of all the main screens our app will consist of: the Settings screen, the Race screen, the Bets screen, the Results screen and the Game Over screen.

# Part V

# The Slugrace Project GUIs

In this part of the book we'll use our knowledge of Kivy widgets and layouts to actually build the screens of our project. In particular, we're going to create the Settings, Race, Bets, Results and Game Over screens. For the time being the screens will just contain all the elements we need, but they won't look like in the final version of the game just yet.

# Chapter 33 - Introduction to the Settings Screen GUI

In the previous part of the book we created all the files we need for our project and we started adding some code to them. In this part we'll be adding all the code that we need to make pretty complete layouts with all the widgets that we need, although without any functionality for the time being. In this chapter, as well as in a couple following chapters, we'll focus on two files: **settings.py** and **settings.kv**.

Our goal here is to build the GUI for the Settings screen, which will be the screen that you will see after the app is launched (right after the splash screen disappears). Here you can choose the number of players, set the players' names and initial money amounts, as well as decide on an ending condition.

This is what the Settings screen is going to look like in the final version of the app:

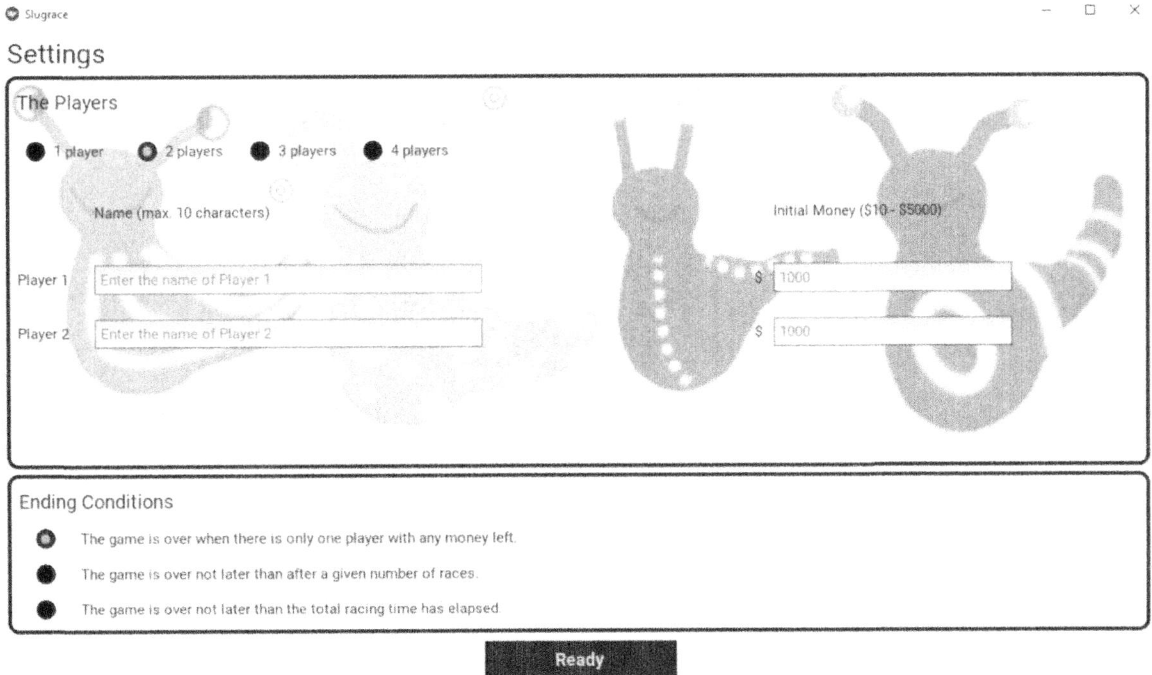


We won't achieve this stage in this part of the book, though, but at least we'll get started.

## Settings Screen Areas

As you know, the Settings screen is divided into several areas. We're going to discuss and build each area one by one, but first let's recap on what we have. Here are the **settings.py** and **settings.kv** files as they were where we left off.

First, the Python file:

```
# File name: settings.py

import kivy
kivy.require('1.11.1')

from kivy.app import App
from kivy.uix.boxlayout import BoxLayout

class SettingsApp(App):
    def build(self):
        return BoxLayout()

if __name__ == '__main__':
    SettingsApp().run()
```

And now the kv file:

```
#:kivy 1.11.1
# File name: settings.kv

<BoxLayout>:
    orientation: 'vertical'

    ### SETTINGS LABEL ###
    Label:
        text: 'Settings'
        font_size: 28

    ### THE PLAYERS ###
    Label:
        text: 'The Players'

    ### ENDING CONDITIONS ###
    Label:
        text: 'Ending Conditions'

    ### READY BUTTON ###
    Button:
        text: 'Ready'
```

And here's what this code creates for us. As you can see, there are four areas: The Settings Label area, the Players area, the Ending Conditions area and the Ready Button area.

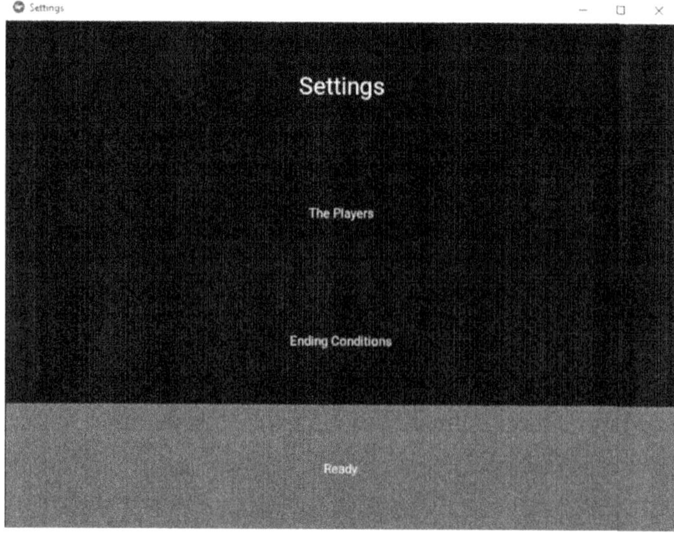


## The root Widget

If you look closer at the kv file, you will see that there is one top level widget, in our case it's a BoxLayout. The indentation suggests that everything that is below it is its child. And this is how we make GUIs in Kivy – there's always a root widget, which is the parent of other widgets, which themselves may be parents of yet other widgets, and so on.

But we don't want a regular BoxLayout to be the root widget. Let's create our own specific root widget that behaves like a BoxLayout but is unique for this screen. This can be easily done by means of inheritance.

So, let's create a **SettingsScreen** class in the Python file and use it as our root widget:

```
# File name: settings.py

import kivy
kivy.require('1.11.1')
from kivy.app import App
from kivy.uix.boxlayout import BoxLayout

# the layout for the whole Settings screen
class SettingsScreen(BoxLayout):
    pass

class SettingsApp(App):
    def build(self):
        # We must return the SettingsScreen now.
        return SettingsScreen()
...
```

And now the kv file. We're going to use the SettingsScreen as the root of the Settings screen instead of the regular BoxLayout.

```
#:kivy 1.11.1
# File name: settings.kv

<SettingsScreen>:
    orientation: 'vertical'
    ...
```

So, there's hardly any difference. Now we're using **SettingsScreen**, which is a subclass of **BoxLayout**, as our root widget. In a similar way we'll be creating the root widgets in the other kv files, but not now.

Now, in the following chapters, we're going to add the widgets that we need to all the four areas of the Settings screen. There's nothing to change in the first part, though. The Settings label is just what it is, a label. So, let's move on to the second area, the Players area, which is the subject of the next chapter.

# Chapter 34 - The Settings Screen – the Players Area

In the previous chapter we started working on the Settings screen, which is going to be the first screen you see after you launch the game (after the splash screen, naturally).

We already created the root widget, which inherits from **BoxLayout**. We named it **SettingsScreen**. We also know that the screen consists of four areas. The first area is just a label, so there's nothing special we can do about it at this point. Then we have the Players area, which we are going to focus on in this chapter. In the following chapters we'll handle the Ending Conditions and Ready Button areas.

## The Players Area

So, what do we actually want in the Players area? Well, this area will consist of three subareas:

1) Title – just a label telling us that we are inside the Players area,

2) Radio Buttons – they will let us choose the number of players,

3) Player Name and Initial Money Setup – here we will be able to give names to the players and set their initial money.

These three subareas will be placed one below another, so a vertically oriented BoxLayout seems a good choice as the container. We'll embed it inside the root **SettingsScreen** widget. Using labels as placeholders, we could represent the structure of the Players area like so:

```
#:kivy 1.11.1
# File name: settings.kv

<SettingsScreen>:
    ...
    ### THE PLAYERS ###
    BoxLayout:
        orientation: 'vertical'

        # Title
        Label:
            text: 'The Players'

        # Radio Buttons
        Label:
            text: 'Radio Buttons'

        # Player Name and Initial Money Setup
        Label:
            text: 'Player Name and Initial Money Setup'

    ### ENDING CONDITIONS ###
    Label:
        text: 'Ending Conditions'

    ### READY BUTTON ###
    Button:
        text: 'Ready'
```

If you run the **settings.py** file now, you will see the general structure so far.

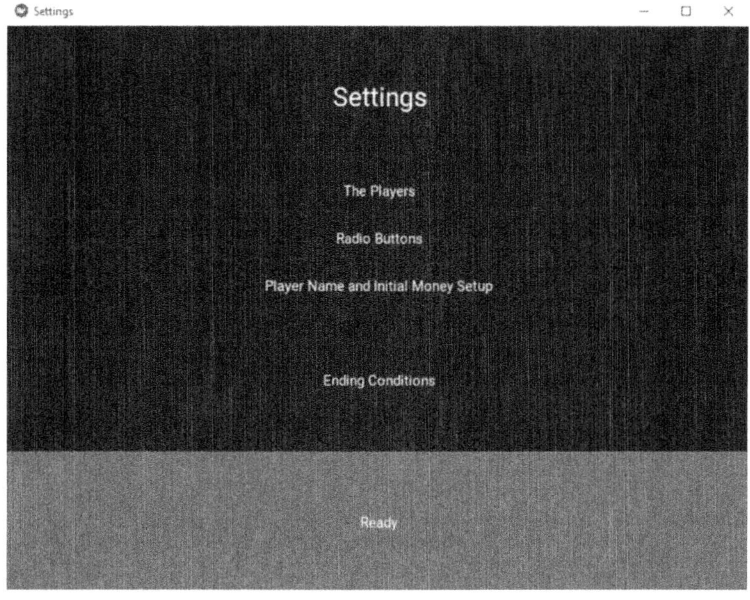


Again, the title is just a label, but let's have a look at the radio buttons now.

## The Radio Buttons

In Kivy radio buttons are implemented as check boxes. The difference is that with regular check boxes you can check any number of them simultaneously or uncheck all of them. Radio buttons work in a different way. At any given time only one radio button in a group may be checked. Besides, there's a graphical difference: check boxes are squares and radio buttons are circles.

You already saw how to create a check box when we were discussing some of the basic widgets like labels, buttons and some others. If you want to turn a check box into a radio button, all you have to do is assign a name to the **group** property. All check boxes with the same name of the group will be turned into radio buttons.

Now, there will be four radio buttons because we need four possible options: 1 player, 2 players, 3 players and 4 players. We'll put them in a horizontal BoxLayout. But we also need a label for each radio button, so instead of using just the check boxes, we'll put each check box along with its accompanying label in a horizontal BoxLayout. To turn the check boxes into radio buttons, we'll set their **group** property to **'players'**.

So, things are slowly becoming more and more complex. We'll have to embed more and more layouts inside other layouts, but don't worry, in the kv code it won't be as complicated as it sounds. Anyway, let's jump into the kv code. Here's the file:

```
#:kivy 1.11.1
# File name: settings.kv

<SettingsScreen>:
    ...
    ### THE PLAYERS ###
    BoxLayout:
        ...
        # Radio Buttons
        # the BoxLayout for all four radio buttons
        BoxLayout:
```

```
                # the BoxLayout for the radio button + label for 1 player
                BoxLayout:
                    CheckBox:
                        group: 'players'
                    Label:
                        text: '1 player'

                # the BoxLayout for the radio button + label for 2 players
                BoxLayout:
                    CheckBox:
                        group: 'players'
                    Label:
                        text: '2 players'

                # the BoxLayout for the radio button + label for 3 players
                BoxLayout:
                    CheckBox:
                        group: 'players'
                    Label:
                        text: '3 players'

                # the BoxLayout for the radio button + label for 4 players
                BoxLayout:
                    CheckBox:
                        group: 'players'
                    Label:
                        text: '4 players'

            # Player Name and Initial Money Setup
            Label:
                text: 'Player Name and Initial Money Setup'

        ### ENDING CONDITIONS ###
        ...
```

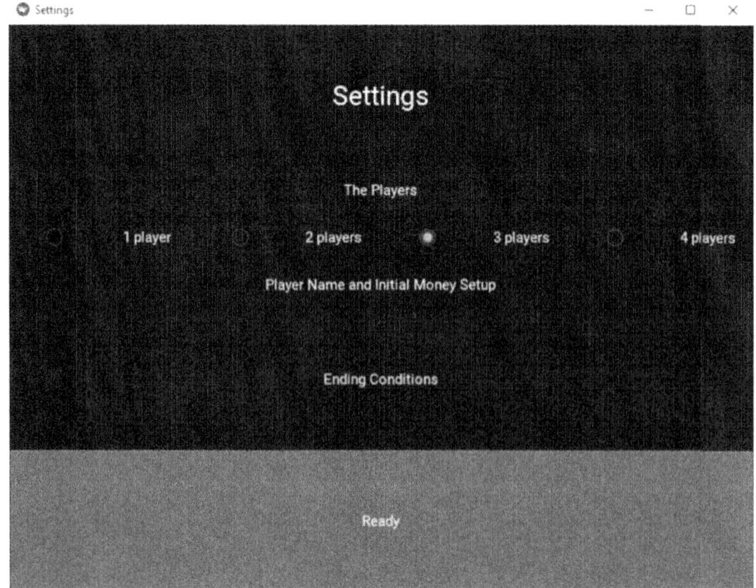


If you think this code is repetitive, you're right. We might use class rules to create custom widgets and simplify things. And this is what we eventually are going to do, but at first I'd like to write all the kv code for the Settings screens without class rules. Then, when we're done with that, we'll refactor it so that it uses class rules and custom widgets. I'm doing this because I want you to see the difference in the length of the files before and after refactoring. Then, when working on the other screens, we'll use class rules at an earlier stage.

If you run this program now, you will see the four radio buttons and none of them will be checked. But let's check one of them. Now if you check another one, the previous one will be unchecked, so that only one is checked at any given time. Try it out. It should be quite intuitive because radio buttons are used a lot in desktop and web applications. We're not done with the radio buttons yet, but let's leave them now as is and move on to the next subarea.

## Player Name and Initial Money Setup

The last subarea of the Players area is the Player Name and Initial Money Setup. This subarea is pretty complex, but I'm leaving it for you to do as an exercise. Although it may seem daunting at first, you know everything you need to do it, just follow the instructions below. And make sure to do it, because we'll need the code to proceed.

Before you jump into the exercise, here's some general information about the exercises in this course, so make sure to read it first. Actually, it's just a reminder.

*************************************************************************************

Exercises Info

At the end of each (or almost each) chapter, there's an exercise (or more than one) for you to do. Keep in mind that doing all the exercises is an integral part of this course. What I cover in the chapter is not the complete project. Only doing all the exercises will make the project complete.

So, make sure to do all the exercises and check out the key to the exercises after you're done with your own working solution. The point here is that sometimes there are several ways of doing something that all lead to the same final result, but as the solutions to the exercises are an integral part of the project, they're included in the final code that you can find in the code files for each chapter. This code is also the starting point for the following chapter. So, if your solution is different than what you see in the code files, it doesn't necessarily mean it's wrong, but you might want to use the version from the code files so that it's easier for you to follow along as we proceed. It'll be just easier if we start each chapter with the same code.

As the code you're going to write in the exercises may be lengthy, it also may be more error-prone, so don't get discouraged if something goes wrong and the program doesn't launch. If this is the case, just try to read the error message in the Kivy log at the bottom of Visual Studio Code or in a corresponding place in your editor of choice. But if you still can't figure out what's wrong, don't waste too much time on it, just check the key right away. The most important thing at this stage is that you understand what you did wrong and know how to fix it after you check the key.

*************************************************************************************

And now we can move on to the exercise.

# It's Your Turn Now...

**EXERCISE**

Here are the instructions for you to follow. After you finish the exercise and run the app, it won't look great because the widgets will be all squeezed together. This is fine, it doesn't mean you did something wrong, so don't worry about that. We're going to fix it in one of the following chapters.

And here are the instructions for the Player Name and Initial Money Setup subarea:

1. The whole Player Name and Initial Money Setup subarea will be in a vertical BoxLayout. All the layouts below will be its children.

2. At the top there's a horizontal BoxLayout for the headers. The header row at the top is there so that you know what the other widgets are all about. It should contain three labels:

- an empty label (so with the **`text`** property set to an empty string),

- a label with the text **`'Name'`**,

- a label with the text **`'Initial Money'`**.

3. There's a horizontal BoxLayout for each of the four players. Each of them contains:

- a label with a generic player name (like **`'Player 1'`**, **`'Player 2'`**, etc.),

- a text input for the new player name with no multiline text allowed (use the **`multiline`** property).

- a horizontal BoxLayout for the money part that contains:

--- an empty label (so with the **`text`** property set to an empty string),

--- a label with the dollar symbol,

--- a text input for the player's initial money amount, again with no multiline text allowed.

## SOLUTION

The structure above resembles the structure in code, so let's write the code now:

```
#:kivy 1.11.1
# File name: settings.kv

<SettingsScreen>:
    ...
    ### THE PLAYERS ###
    BoxLayout:
        ...
        # Player Name and Initial Money Setup
        # Everything will be in a vertical
        # BoxLayout.
        BoxLayout:
            orientation: 'vertical'

            # the headers row
            BoxLayout:
                # empty label just to add
                # some space
                Label:
                    text: ""

                # name header
                Label:
                    text: "Name"

                # money header
                Label:
                    text: "Initial Money"

            # the players rows
            # player 1
            BoxLayout:

                # generic player name
                Label:
                    text: 'Player 1'

                # new player name
                TextInput:
                    # multiline text not allowed
                    multiline: False

                # money
                BoxLayout:
                    # empty label to add
                    # some space
                    Label:
                        text: ""

                    # dollar sign
                    Label:
                        text: "$"

                    # initial money
                    TextInput:
                        multiline: False

            # The code for the other players
            # is without comments to make it
            # more concise.

            # player 2
            BoxLayout:
                Label:
                    text: 'Player 2'
                TextInput:
                    multiline: False
                BoxLayout:
                    Label:
                        text: ""
                    Label:
                        text: "$"
                    TextInput:
                        multiline: False

            # player 3
            BoxLayout:
                Label:
                    text: 'Player 3'
                TextInput:
                    multiline: False
                BoxLayout:
                    Label:
                        text: ""
                    Label:
                        text: "$"
                    TextInput:
                        multiline: False

            # player 4
            BoxLayout:
                Label:
                    text: 'Player 4'
                TextInput:
                    multiline: False
                BoxLayout:
                    Label:
                        text: ""
                    Label:
                        text: "$"
                    TextInput:
                        multiline: False

    ### ENDING CONDITIONS ###
    Label:
        text: 'Ending Conditions'

    ### READY BUTTON ###
    Button:
        text: 'Ready'
```

As mentioned above, this code is very repetitive. We're going to see about it later in the book, so let it be so for now. And now, if you run your app, you will get a basic GUI.

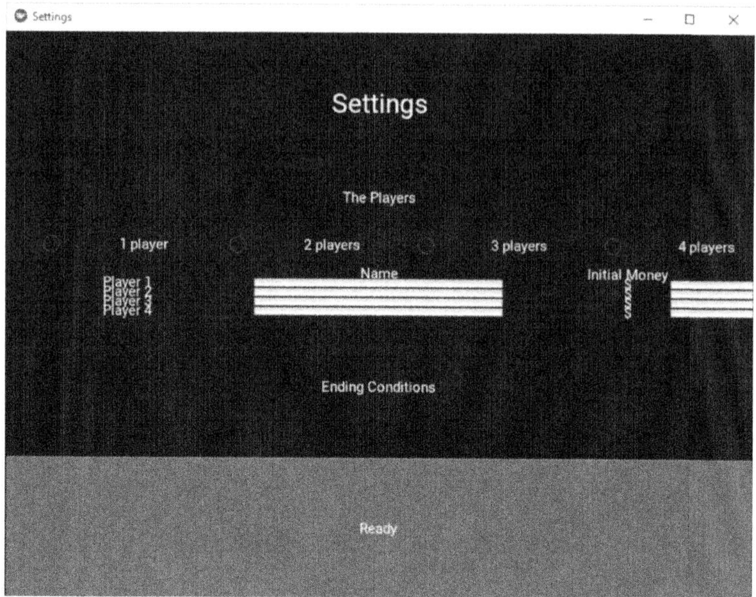


Well, as mentioned before, this doesn't look very good, because we didn't take care of positioning and sizing yet, but all the elements that we need are there. We'll position and scale all the widgets when we are done creating them, so now let's move on to the next area.

# Chapter 35 - The Settings Screen – the Ending Conditions Area

In the previous chapter we were working on the Players area of the Settings screen. There's still one pretty large area to handle, the Ending Conditions area, which is the subject of this chapter. And there's also one smaller area, the Ready Button area, which we are done with for the moment. So, open your project folder in your text editor and let's get down to work. The code we're going to be working on right now is in the **settings.kv** file.

## The Ending Conditions Area

You know that Slugrace is a racing game. But when does it end? Well, this will be left for the user of the app to decide. He or she will be given three options to choose from:

1) The game is over when there is only one player with any money left.

2) The game is over not later than after a given number of races.

3) The game is over not later than the total racing time that you set before the game starts has elapsed.

So, in the Settings screen you should be able to choose one of these options. The first option will be the default one.

If you should be allowed to choose only one option out of many, radio buttons seem to be a reasonable solution. So, let's use them. Additionally, for the second and third option there should be a text input where you can enter the number of races or the maximum game time respectively.

Actually I think I might have done my job for this chapter. There's nothing about the code that we need to write that you couldn't do yourself. So, just follow the instructions like in the previous chapter and take care of the Ending Conditions area yourself. Your code should replace the label in the Ending Conditions area.

After you do the exercise, with all the widgets we need in place, we'll have to size and position them inside their layouts so that it all looks better. We're going to do it in the next chapter.

# It's Your Turn Now...

**EXERCISE**

Here are the instructions:

1. The whole Ending Conditions area should be a vertical BoxLayout.

2. The first element in the BoxLayout should be a label with the text **`'Ending Conditions'`**.

3. Under the label should come the radio buttons with the accompanying labels and text inputs. They should be all placed inside a GridLayout with three rows. The GridLayout should contain six elements altogether. Three of them are check boxes, which we want to function as radio buttons, so that only one can be selected at any given time. In order to achieve that, you must set the **`group`** property of each of them to the same value. I suggest you use the string **`'conditions'`** as the group name.

Here are all the six widgets that are directly embedded in the GridLayout:

1) the first check box,

2) a label with the text `'The game is over when there is only one player with any money left.'`,

3) the second check box,

4) a horizontal BoxLayout with two widgets:

a) a label with the text `'The game is over not later than after a given number of races.'`,

b) a text input with no multiline text allowed,

5) the third check box,

6) a horizontal BoxLayout with two widgets:

a) a label with the text `'The game is over not later than the total racing time has elapsed.'`,

b) a text input with no multiline text allowed.

## SOLUTION

And here's the code:

```
#:kivy 1.11.1
# File name: settings.kv

<SettingsScreen>:
    ...
    ### ENDING CONDITIONS ###
    # Everything will be in a vertical BoxLayout.
    BoxLayout:
        orientation: 'vertical'

        # title label
        Label:
            text: "Ending Conditions"

        # radio buttons
        # The radio buttons will be placed in a GridLayout.
        GridLayout:
            rows: 3

            # option 1: money
            CheckBox:
                # All check boxes in this area will be assigned to a group,
                # which will turn them into radio buttons.
                group: 'conditions'
            # Each radio button will be accompanied by a label.
            Label:
                text: "The game is over when there is only one player with any money left."

            # option 2: races
            CheckBox:
                group: 'conditions'
            # The label and the text input will be placed in a horizontal BoxLayout.
            BoxLayout:
                Label:
                    text: "The game is over not later than after a given number of races."
                TextInput:
                    multiline: False

            # option 3: time
            CheckBox:
                group: 'conditions'
            BoxLayout:
                Label:
                    text: "The game is over not later than the total racing time has elapsed."
                TextInput:
                    multiline: False

    ### READY BUTTON ###
    ...
```

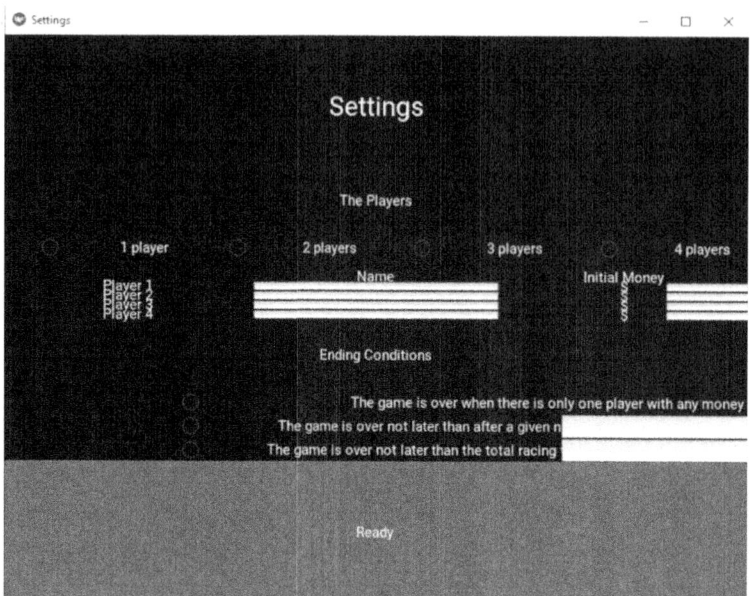


If you now run the program, you will see the Ending Conditions area.

Ugly? Well, definitely not extremely pretty, but it's slowly taking shape. The radio buttons are hardly visible, but they will be more visible when we take care of styles and colors. Besides, the text inputs hide parts of the labels, which also must be taken care of.

# Chapter 36 - The Settings Screen – Sizing and Positioning the Widgets

In the previous chapter we finished adding the widgets to the Settings screen. As you saw, even with all the widgets in place, the screen still looks ugly. It isn't even close to the final version, which you saw before.

We'll be worrying about colors and images only later, but now let's take care of sizing and positioning the widgets.

## Sizing and Positioning the Widgets

If you don't specify the size of a widget in an area or the size of the area itself, each area (so each layout or other widget) will occupy the same amount of space.

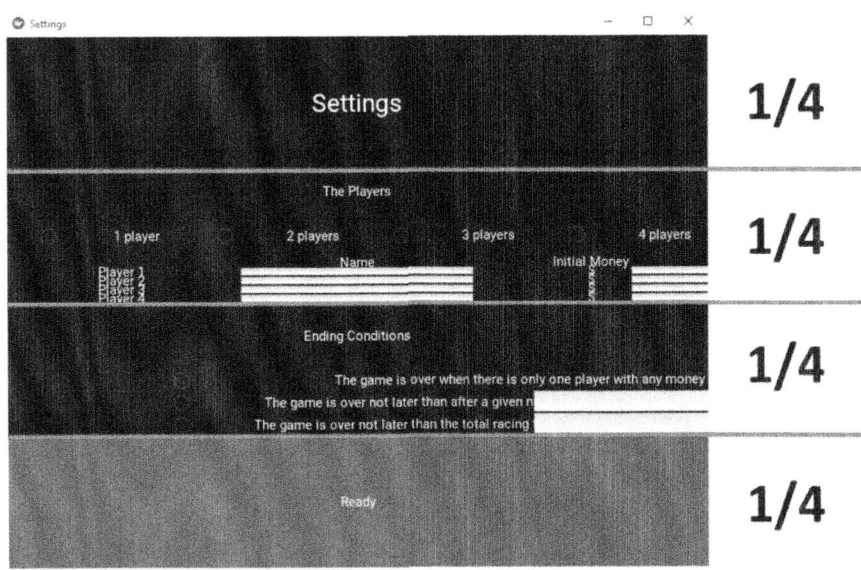


But we don't need so much space for the Settings Label or the Ready Button area. On the other hand, we need more space for the two areas in the middle. To sort this out, let's size the widgets that we want to be of a specific size. You may want to recap on the sizing techniques that I covered in one of the previous chapters.

Now, there are four areas that make up the Settings screen. Let's split the work evenly (or almost evenly). I'll take care of two areas and so will you, as an exercise. I think I'll take the first one and the last one, leaving the two in the middle for you.

Here's the kv file with all the size and position settings in the Settings Label and Ready Button areas. As for the Settings Label area, we want the label to occupy the whole width of its container, so the first element in the **size_hint** tuple must be set to **1**. But we want the height to be a fixed number of pixels, so the second element in **size_hint** must be set to **None**, because we're inside a layout. The height of 30 px will be just fine.

```
#:kivy 1.11.1
# File name: settings.kv

<SettingsScreen>:
    ...
    ### SETTINGS LABEL ###
    Label:
        text: 'Settings'
        font_size: 28

        # container width by 30 px
        size_hint: (1, None)
        height: 30
```

```
    ### THE PLAYERS ###
    ...
    ### READY BUTTON ###
    Button:
        text: 'Ready'

        # 200 by 40 px
        size_hint: (None, None)
        size: 200, 40

        # centered horizontally
        pos_hint: {'center_x': 0.5}
```

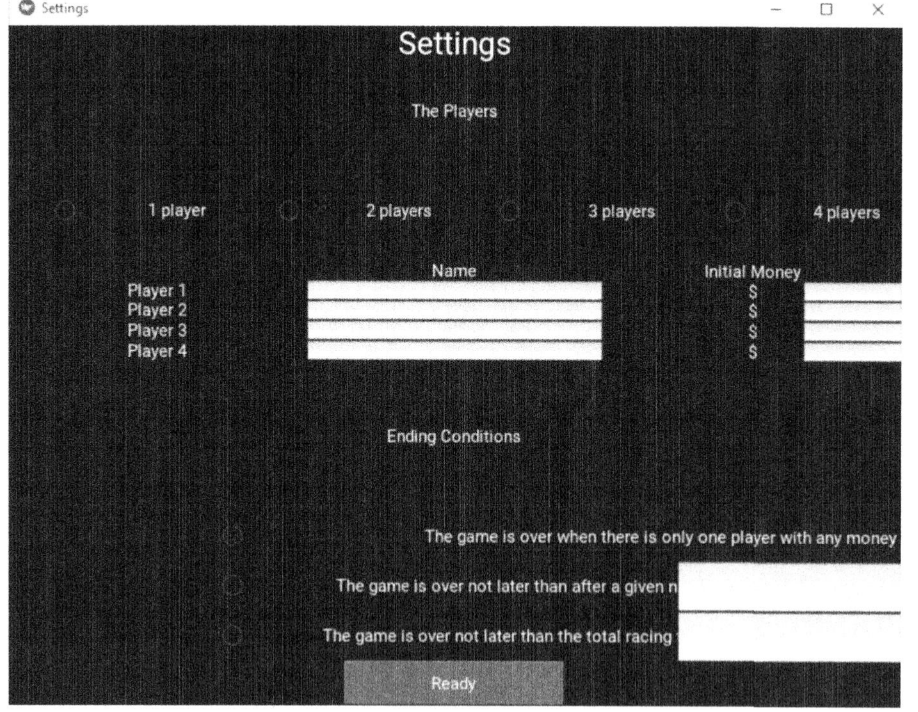


If you run the program now, you will see that the Settings label and the Ready button take up much less space than before.

The text on the label is centered, but we're going to align it to the left in the next chapter. For now this will do. And now it's your turn to size and position the widgets in the two larger areas.

# It's Your Turn Now...

### EXERCISE

This time you're going to see the kv code as it is right now and your task is to add sizing and positioning code according to the instructions in comments. The instructions are numbered so that you don't miss anything.

I've removed all the other comments (except the names of the areas and subareas) for now because I don't want the code to be cluttered with stuff you don't need to do in the exercise. Your code should go in the blanks. The blanks are represented by single horizontal lines, but you may need to write one or more lines of code in each.

If a number is repeated multiple times, the same code should be written each time. In such cases I'm not going to repeat the comment in each place, but rather just the number.

In the Radio Buttons subarea the same code should be repeated for each check box, which I'm going to skip here. Also, in the Player Name and Initial Money Setup subarea the same code should be repeated for all four players, which I'm also going to skip here. You should have no problem typing the same values for players 2-4, just don't forget to do it.

```
#:kivy 1.11.1
# File name: settings.kv

<SettingsScreen>:
    ...
    ### THE PLAYERS ###
    ...
        # Title
        Label:
            text: 'The Players'

            # <1> Let's make the font slightly bigger, like 20 pixels.
            ______________________________

            # <2> This label should occupy the whole width, its height should be 30 px.
            ______________________________

        # Radio Buttons
        BoxLayout:

            # <3> The whole Radio Buttons subarea should occupy 40% of the width
            # and should be 50 px high.
            ______________________________

            # 1 player
            BoxLayout:
                CheckBox:
                    group: 'players'

                    # <4> The check box should occupy half the width of the containing
```

```
                # BoxLayout and its whole height.
                ______________________________
            Label:
                text: '1 player'

        # Use the same values for the other check boxes.
        ...
    # Player Name and Initial Money Setup
    BoxLayout:
        ...
        # the headers row
        BoxLayout:
            Label:
                text: ""

                # <5> The width of the label should be 80 px.
                ______________________________

            # name header
            Label:
                text: "Name"

                # <6> The width of the label should be 700 px.
                ______________________________

            # money header
            ...
        # the players rows
        # player 1
        BoxLayout:
            Label:
                text: 'Player 1'

                # <7> This label should be 80x30 px.
                ______________________________

            TextInput:
                multiline: False

                # <8> This text input should be 400x30 px.
                ______________________________

            BoxLayout:
                Label:
                    text: ""

                    # <9> This label should be 280 px wide.
                    ______________________________

                Label:
                    text: "$"

                    # <10> This label should be 20x30 px.
                    ______________________________

                TextInput:
                    multiline: False
```

```
                # <11> This text input should be 250x30 px.
                ______________________________

        # Use the same values for players 2-4
        ...
### ENDING CONDITIONS ###
BoxLayout:
    orientation: 'vertical'

    # <12> This area should occupy the whole width
    # and 40% of the available height.
    ______________________________

    # title label
    Label:
        text: "Ending Conditions"

        # <1>
        ______________________________

        # <2>
        ______________________________

    # radio buttons
    GridLayout:
        rows: 3

        # option 1: money
        CheckBox:
            group: 'conditions'

            # <13> The width should be 5% of the available width.
            ______________________________

        Label:
            ...
        # option 2: races
        CheckBox:
            group: 'conditions'

            # <13>
            ______________________________


        BoxLayout:
            Label:
                ...
            TextInput:
                multiline: False

                # <11>
                ______________________________

        # option 3: time
        CheckBox:
            group: 'conditions'
```

```
            # <13>
            ______________________________

        BoxLayout:
            Label:
                ...
            TextInput:
                multiline: False

                # <11>
                ______________________________

    ### READY BUTTON ###
    ...
```

## SOLUTION

Here are the snippets of code you should have typed in (although you may have used slightly different ones that work the same):

```
<1>    font_size: 20
<2>    size_hint: (1, None)
       height: 30
<3>    size_hint: (.4, None)
       height: 50
<4>    size_hint: (.5, 1)
<5>    size_hint_x: None
       width: 80
<6>    size_hint_x: None
       width: 700
<7>    size_hint: None, None
       size: 80, 30
<8>    size_hint: None, None
       size: 400, 30
<9>    size_hint_x: None
       width: 280
<10>   size_hint: None, None
       size: 20, 30
<11>   size_hint: None, None
       size: 250, 30
<12>   size_hint: (1, .4)
<13>   size_hint_x: .05
```

Now run the program and watch what you did to it. Some of the widgets, like the Initial Money label and text inputs, have been cut off. But don't worry, the app window will eventually be bigger, so everything will fit in. For now, just resize the window manually by dragging its rigt border to see the missing parts.

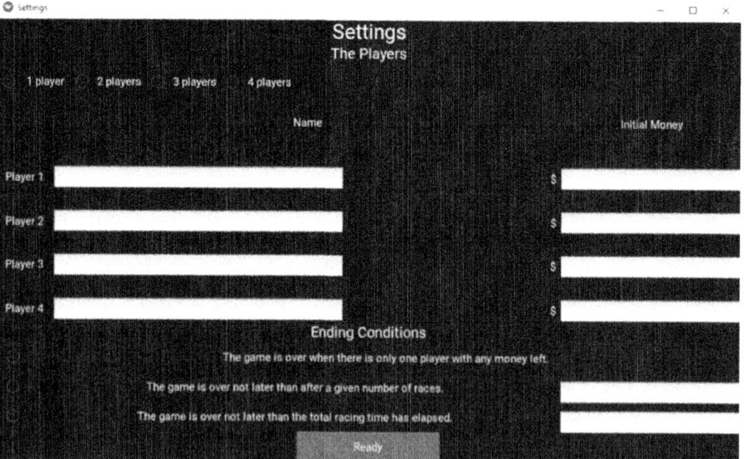


Now it looks better. But still, I don't quite like it yet. For example, the labels would look better if they were left-aligned. But let's put it off until the next chapter.

# Chapter 37 - The Settings Screen – Aligning Label Text

In the previous chapter we sized and positioned all the layouts and other widgets inside the Settings screen. One thing that definitely needs improving is text alignment on the labels.

## Aligning Label Text

You can align both horizontally and vertically in Kivy. You should use the **halign** and **valign** properties respectively. Let's align all the labels in the kv file horizontally to the left and vertically to the center. But before we do, there is one more thing you must be aware of. If you just set the **halign** or **valign** property, you won't see the effect. This is because the label text does not occupy the whole label. To work around it, you should set the **text_size** property to the size of the label. As this property is defined inside the label, you can refer to the label using the **self** variable.

So, if you want to align the label horizontally to the left and vertically to the center, the code should look like this:

```
text_size: self.size
halign: 'left'
valign: 'center'
```

And now let's align the label text in the Settings Label area. At first let's align it horizontally to the right and vertically to the center:

```
#:kivy 1.11.1
# File name: settings.kv

<SettingsScreen>:
    ...
    ### SETTINGS LABEL ###
    Label:
        ...
        height: 30
        text_size: self.size
        halign: 'right'
        valign: 'center'

    ### THE PLAYERS ###
    ...
```

Now the label text is aligned to the right, even if you resize the app window.

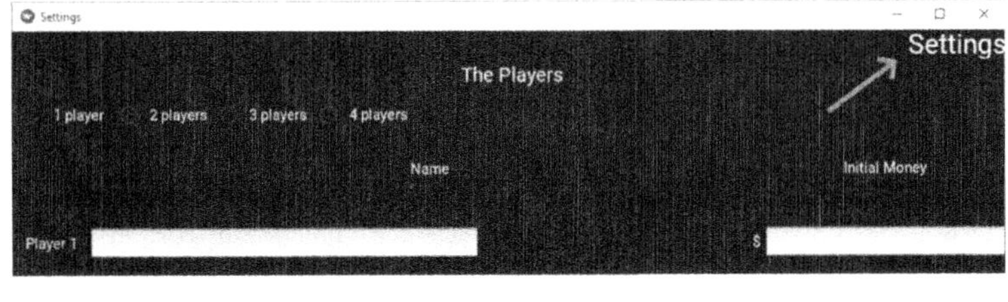


In our final version of the app the Settings label will be aligned to the left, though, so let's fix it:

```
#:kivy 1.11.1
# File name: settings.kv

<SettingsScreen>:
    ...
    ### SETTINGS LABEL ###
    Label:
        ...
        height: 30
        text_size: self.size
        halign: 'left'
        valign: 'center'

    ### THE PLAYERS ###
    ...
```

If you now run the app, you will see that the big label at the top has been aligned to the left.

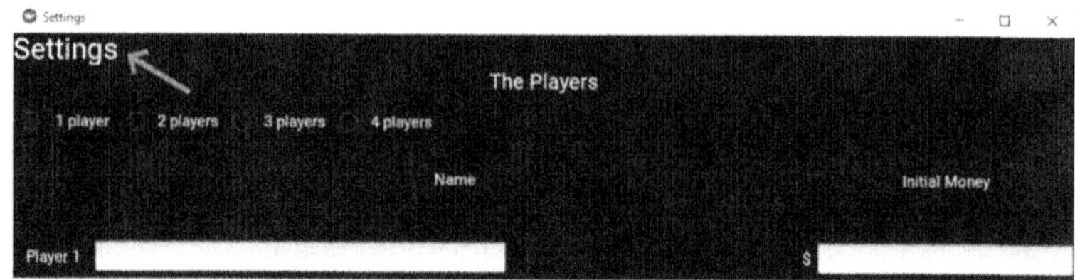


And now we'll align all the other labels in the Settings screen horizontally to the left and vertically to the center. Well, actually you will – this is your exercise for this chapter.

After you're done with it, you will see the labels aligned, but the widgets will be very close to the borders of the window and to one another. It wouldn't be a bad idea to add some padding and spacing, which we will take care of in the next chapter.

## It's Your Turn Now...

### EXERCISE

Align all the labels in the Settings screen horizontally to the left and vertically to the center.

### SOLUTION

I don't think it's necessary to show you the whole **settings.kv** file here because the code is very repetitive. All you have to do is add to each and every label that there is in the file the following lines of code:

```
text_size: self.size
halign: 'left'
valign: 'center'
```

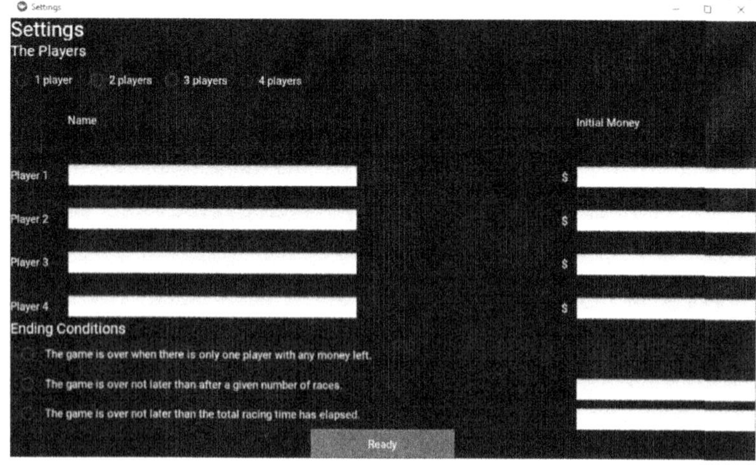


There should be 24 occurrences altogether. Run the program and resize the window so that you can see the missing parts of the widgets. It should now be beautifully aligned. Now the labels are aligned, but the widgets are packed very tightly, with very little space around them. This doesn't look good. So, our last thing to do for now is to add some padding and spacing. This is what we are going to do in the next chapter.

# Chapter 38 - The Settings Screen – Padding and Spacing

In the previous chapter we aligned the text on the labels horizontally to the left and vertically to the right. But there's still a lot to improve. For now the last thing we're going to do is add some padding and spacing so that the widgets don't stick to the borders of the app window and so that there is more space between them.

## Padding and Spacing

What's the difference between padding and spacing? Actually we already talked about it in the test file (**test.kv**) at the beginning of the book, but it was pretty long ago, so let's recap.

So, **padding** determines the distance between the layout box and the children. You can use it with 1, 2 or 4 arguments. If there is 1 argument, the padding is the same on each side. If there are 2 arguments, the first one is for horizontal padding and the second for vertical padding. If there are four arguments, they determine the padding in the following order: left, top, right, bottom.

On the other hand, **spacing** determines the distances between children. It takes just one argument. The default value is 0.

So, let's add padding and spacing to our code. Again, I'll handle the padding and spacing for the whole root widget and leave the rest as an exercise for you.

To add padding and spacing we use the **padding** and **spacing** properties respectively. Let's try a couple different combinations first. Suppose we want to add 50 pixels between the root widget and its children on all sides:

```
#:kivy 1.11.1
# File name: settings.kv

<SettingsScreen>:
    orientation: 'vertical'
    padding: 50

    ### SETTINGS LABEL ###
    ...
```

If you now run the code, you will clearly see the padding.

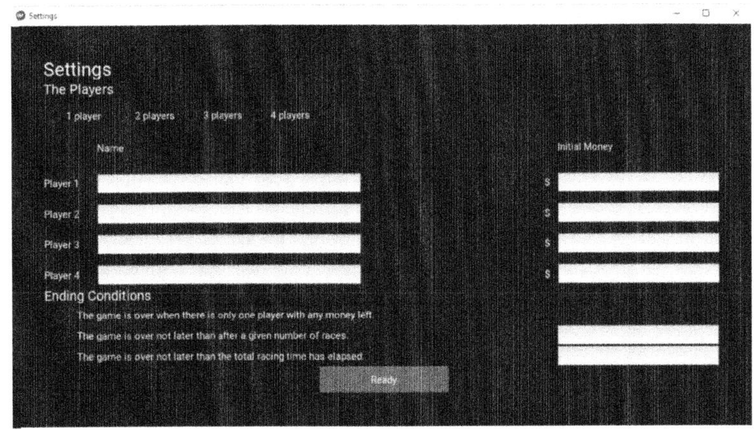

Here I resized the window so that we could see all the widgets. I'm also going to resize the window in the following examples further in this chapter. And now let's set the horizontal padding to 100 px and the vertical one to 50 px:

```
#:kivy 1.11.1
# File name: settings.kv

<SettingsScreen>:
    orientation: 'vertical'
    padding: 100, 50

    ### SETTINGS LABEL ###
    ...
```

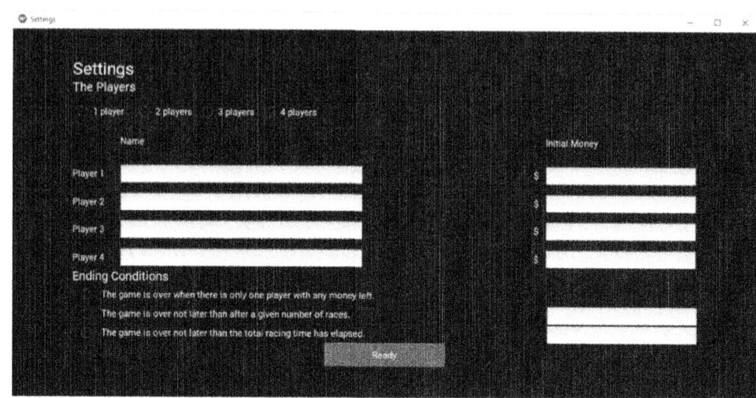

Now there's twice as much padding on the sides as at the bottom and top.

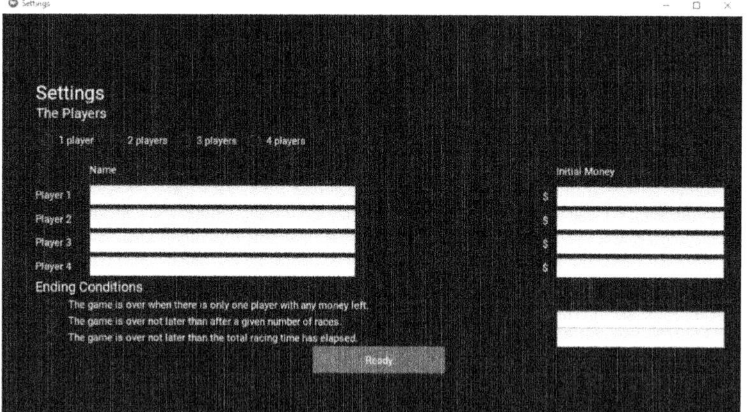

Finally, let's set a different amount of padding for each side, in the order: left, top, right, bottom:

```
#:kivy 1.11.1
# File name: settings.kv

<SettingsScreen>:
    orientation: 'vertical'
    padding: 50, 100, 25, 75

    ### SETTINGS LABEL ###
    ...
```

Let's additionally add 50 px of spacing between the children of the root widget:

```
#:kivy 1.11.1
# File name: settings.kv

<SettingsScreen>:
    orientation: 'vertical'
    padding: 50, 100, 25, 75
    spacing: 50

    ### SETTINGS LABEL ###
    ...
```

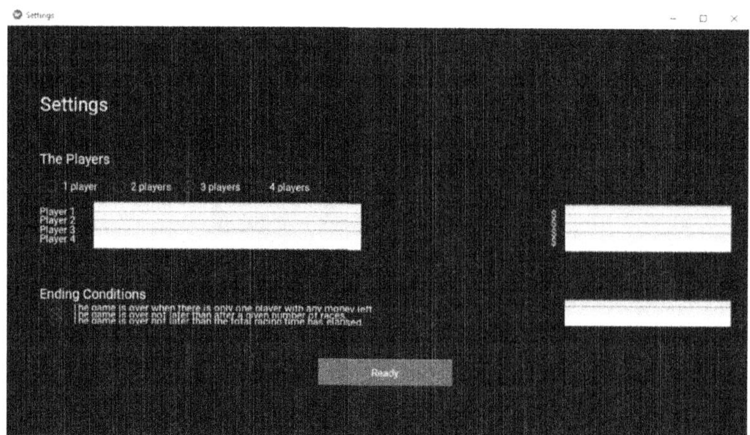

Here the spacing is set only between the direct children of the root widget, which means that the children of the children of the root widget aren't spaced yet, this is why they still look so squeezed. Resizing the window will move them apart, but eventually you'll add some padding and spacing to them in the exercise.

Good, but in our final version we don't need so much padding and spacing, so let's set the values to 10 px both:

```
#:kivy 1.11.1
# File name: settings.kv

<SettingsScreen>:
    orientation: 'vertical'
    padding: 10
    spacing: 10

    ### SETTINGS LABEL ###
    ...
```

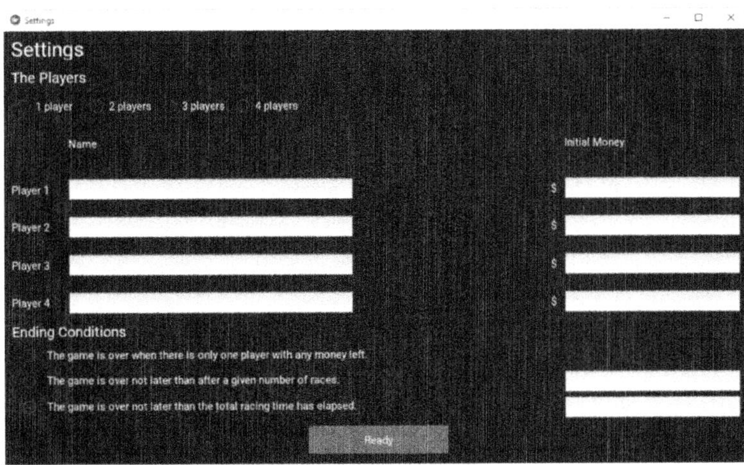


At this moment the app looks pretty decent, especially if you resize the window.

Now it's your turn to add some padding and spacing to the grandchildren of the root widget. After you finish the exercise, the app should look better. In the next chapter we'll do something about the kv code in the **settings.kv** file. It's extremely long and repetitive now, so we'll use some class rules to refactor it. You will be surprised (or maybe not) to see how much the code can be reduced.

# It's Your Turn Now...

## EXERCISE

Follow the instructions to add some padding and spacing to the code:

1. The Players area is implemented as a BoxLayout. Add 10 px of both padding and spacing to it.

2. The Ending Conditions area is also a BoxLayout. Add the same amount of padding and spacing as above.

3. Inside the Ending Conditions area you can see the GridLayout which contains the radio buttons. Add 10 px of spacing between the children of the GridLayout.

## SOLUTION

Here's the code:

```
#:kivy 1.11.1
# File name: settings.kv

<SettingsScreen>:
    ...
    ### THE PLAYERS ###
    BoxLayout:
        orientation: 'vertical'
        padding: 10
        spacing: 10

        # Title
        ...
```

```
    ### ENDING CONDITIONS ###
    BoxLayout:
        orientation: 'vertical'
        size_hint: (1, .4)
        padding: 10
        spacing: 10

        # title label
        ...
        # radio buttons
        GridLayout:
            rows: 3
            spacing: 10

            # option 1: money
            ...
```

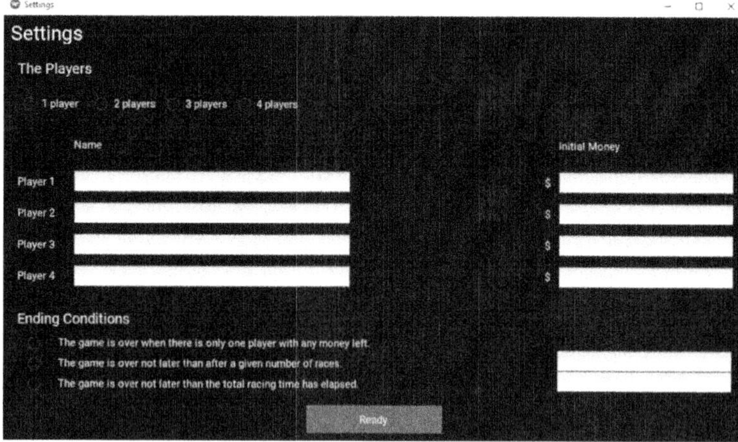


If you now run the app, it will look a bit better. Resize the app window to see it better.

Well, maybe the change isn't spectacular, but if you look closely at the two images above, so before and after you added the padding and spacing, you will be able to see a difference.

# Chapter 39 - The Settings Screen – Class Rules

In the preceding chapters we created our Settings screen GUI. We now have all the layouts we need and all the other widgets like buttons, labels or check boxes in place.

The code, especially in the kv file, is pretty long, right? Well, over 330 lines of code, including comments and blank lines. If you look closer at the code you can see right away that it's very repetitive. This is definitely a drawback. We're going to reduce the amount of code by extracting repetitive code into class rules. We're not going to change anything about what you see when you run the app, but rather just refactor the code.

## Class Rules

So, let's get to work. You already know what class rules are. We used the class rule notation when we were talking about custom widgets for the first time. So, the idea is that you can define a class that inherits from a widget class above the root widget and then use it inside the root widget just like any other widget. There are plenty of opportunities for us to use class rules in the Settings screen.

### Custom Labels

If you run the app, you can see there's a lot of text. This means there are a lot of labels. As far as font size is concerned, there are three sizes of text:

- most of the text is pretty small,

- the two titles (**`'The Players'`** and **`'Ending Conditions'`**) are larger,

- the screen title (**`'Settings'`**) is even larger.

Now let's have a look at how these labels are represented in code. Here are some examples of the small font size labels:

- the label that reads **`'1 player'`** in the Radio Buttons subarea:

```
Label:
    text: '1 player'
    text_size: self.size
    halign: 'left'
    valign: 'center'
```

- the name header:

```
Label:
    text: "Name"
    size_hint_x: None
    width: 700
    text_size: self.size
    halign: 'left'
    valign: 'center'
```

- one of the labels in the Ending Conditions area:

```
Label:
    text: "The game is over not later than after a given number of races."
    text_size: self.size
    halign: 'left'
    valign: 'center'
```

As you can see, all these labels share some properties:

```
text_size: self.size
halign: 'left'
valign: 'center'
```

They also have the **text** property, but it's set to a different value for each label. Also, the name header label contains some more properties like **size_hint_x** and **width**.

Now, we can extract the three shared properties listed above into a custom label, which is a subclass of **Label**.

As this is going to be the most used label in our code, let's name it **RegularLabel**. Now, above the root widget, type the following class rule that will create our custom **RegularLabel** class:

```
#:kivy 1.11.1
# File name: settings.kv

# RegularLabel inherits from Label.
<RegularLabel@Label>:
    text_size: self.size
    halign: 'left'
    valign: 'center'

<SettingsScreen>:
    ...
```

Now, with **RegularLabel** defined, we can use this class instead of **Label** in our code, so the above snippets will look like so:

- the label that reads **'1 player'** in the Radio Buttons subarea:

```
RegularLabel:
    text: '1 player'
```

- the name header:

```
RegularLabel:
    text: "Name"
    size_hint_x: None
    width: 700
```

- the label in the Ending Conditions area:

```
RegularLabel:
    text: "The game is over not later than after a given number of races."
```

So, all the repetitive code is gone and only the code that makes each label unique remains. And now have a look at the larger font size labels used for the titles:

- the Players area title label:

```
Label:
    text: 'The Players'
    font_size: 20
    size_hint: (1, None)
    height: 30
    text_size: self.size
    halign: 'left'
    valign: 'center'
```

- the Ending Conditions area title label:

```
Label:
    text: "Ending Conditions"
    font_size: 20
    size_hint: (1, None)
    height: 30
    text_size: self.size
    halign: 'left'
    valign: 'center'
```

The first thing you notice is that they also contain the code shared in the **RegularLabel** class, so we can create a new class that inherits from **RegularLabel**. Besides, there are three properties with the same values: **font_size**, **size_hint** and **height**, so we can move them to the new class.

So, let's add a new class rule under the **RegularLabel** definition. The name **TitleLabel** sounds fine to me, so I'll use it:

```
#:kivy 1.11.1
# File name: settings.kv

# RegularLabel inherits from Label.
<RegularLabel@Label>:
    ...
```

```
# TitleLabel inherits from RegularLabel.
<TitleLabel@RegularLabel>:
    font_size: 20
    size_hint: (1, None)
    height: 30

<SettingsScreen>:
    ...
```

Now we can rewrite the title labels like so:

- the Players area title label:

```
TitleLabel:
    text: 'The Players'
```

- the Ending Conditions area title label:

```
TitleLabel:
    text: "Ending Conditions"
```

Much more concise, isn't it? Now, as far as the largest label with the screen title **'Settings'** is concerned, we could create a class for it too, but let's take a different approach this time.

This label actually only differs from the title label in font size. If you set a property on a widget instance to a different value than defined in the class rule, it will overwrite it. So, here is the label as it is now in the code:

```
### SETTINGS LABEL ###
Label:
    text: 'Settings'
    font_size: 28
    size_hint: (1, None)
    height: 30
    text_size: self.size
    halign: 'left'
    valign: 'center'
```

Let's use our **TitleLabel** instead:

```
TitleLabel:
    text: 'Settings'
    font_size: 28
```

So, although the default font size defined in the **TitleLabel** class is **20**, in this particular **TitleLabel** instance it is set to **28**, which makes the text larger. This is how you can easily overwrite values for particular widgets.

Now, with our **RegularLabel** and **TitleLable** classes defined, let's rewrite the kv file using their instances in place of the **Label** instances:

```
#:kivy 1.11.1
# File name: settings.kv
...
<SettingsScreen>:
    ...
    ### SETTINGS LABEL ###
    TitleLabel:
        text: 'Settings'
        font_size: 28
    ### THE PLAYERS ###
    BoxLayout:
        ...
        # Title
        TitleLabel:
            text: 'The Players'
        # Radio Buttons
        BoxLayout:
            ...
            # 1 player
            BoxLayout:
                CheckBox:
                    ...
                RegularLabel:
                    text: '1 player'
            # the same for the other options,
            # just change the text accordingly
            ...
        # Player Name and Initial Money Setup
        BoxLayout:
            ...
            # the headers row
            BoxLayout:
                RegularLabel:
                    text: ""
                    size_hint_x: None
                    width: 80
                # name header
                RegularLabel:
                    text: "Name"
                    size_hint_x: None
                    width: 700
                # money header
                RegularLabel:
                    text: "Initial Money"
            # the players rows
            # player 1
            BoxLayout:
                RegularLabel:
                    text: 'Player 1'
                    size_hint: None, None
                    size: 80, 30
                TextInput:
                    ...
                BoxLayout:
                    RegularLabel:
                        text: ""
                        size_hint_x: None
                        width: 280
                    RegularLabel:
                        text: "$"
                        size_hint: None, None
                        size: 20, 30
                    TextInput:
                        ...
            # the same for the other players,
            # just change the text accordingly
            ...
    ### ENDING CONDITIONS ###
    BoxLayout:
        ...
        # title label
        TitleLabel:
            text: "Ending Conditions"
        # radio buttons
        GridLayout:
            ...
            # option 1: money
            CheckBox:
                ...
            RegularLabel:
                text: ...
            # option 2: races
            CheckBox:
                ...
            BoxLayout:
                RegularLabel:
                    text: ...
                TextInput:
                    ...
            # option 3: time
            CheckBox:
                ...
            BoxLayout:
                RegularLabel:
                    text: ...
                TextInput:
                    ...

    ### READY BUTTON ###
    ...
```

The number of lines of code in the kv file has been significantly reduced. If you now run the app, it will work as before.

## More Specific Custom Labels

If you scan the code carefully from top to bottom, you will see that there are some RegularLabels that still share some properties. These are:

1) the four RegularLabels with the generic names of the players, like this one:

```
RegularLabel:
    text: 'Player 1'
    size_hint: None, None
    size: 80, 30
```

Here only the text should be different, so we can create a custom label with all the other properties. A characteristic feature of these labels is that they have a specific size, so let's name the class **`Regular80x30Label`**.

Add the following class rule below the other class rules:

```
<Regular80x30Label@RegularLabel>:
    size_hint: None, None
    size: 80, 30
```

Now we can replace each occurrence of the four labels by a Regular80x30Label like this:

```
Regular80x30Label:
    text: 'Player 1'
```

2) the four RegularLabels with the dollar sign:

```
RegularLabel:
    text: "$"
    size_hint: None, None
    size: 20, 30
```

They all have the same size and besides they even have the same text. So, why not create a **`DollarLabel`** class? We could derive it from **`RegularLabel`** or **`Regular80x30Label`**. Maybe the former would make more sense as the characteristic feature of the latter is its size, which is even contained in its name, so let's opt for the **`RegularLabel`** class and subclass it.

Let's add the following class rule:

```
<DollarLabel@RegularLabel>:
    text: "$"
    size_hint: None, None
    size: 20, 30
```

As all four DollarLabels share all the properties and there are no differences between them, it's enough to use them like this:

```
DollarLabel:
```

So, at this stage we have the following class rules:

```
#:kivy 1.11.1
# File name: settings.kv

<RegularLabel@Label>:
    text_size: self.size
    halign: 'left'
    valign: 'center'

<TitleLabel@RegularLabel>:
    font_size: 20
    size_hint: (1, None)
    height: 30

<Regular80x30Label@RegularLabel>:
    size_hint: None, None
    size: 80, 30

<DollarLabel@RegularLabel>:
    text: "$"
    size_hint: None, None
    size: 20, 30

<SettingsScreen>:
    ...
```

And now, with the recent changes in place, the player BoxLayouts inside the Player Name and Initial Money Setup subarea should look like this:

```
#:kivy 1.11.1
# File name: settings.kv
...
<SettingsScreen>:
    ...
    ### THE PLAYERS ###
    ...
        # Player Name and Initial Money Setup
        BoxLayout:
            ...
            # the players rows
            # player 1
            BoxLayout:
                Regular80x30Label:
                    text: 'Player 1'
                TextInput:
                    ...
                BoxLayout:
                    RegularLabel:
                        text: ""
                        size_hint_x: None
                        width: 280
                    DollarLabel:
                    TextInput:
                        ...
            # player 2
            ...
```

Looks like we reduced the code by a couple lines this time. This is not as spectacular as before because:

1) there were fewer instances of the new classes in the code,

2) the new class rules also need some space.

But if you compare the length of the file now with that at the beginning, the code was reduced from about 330 to about 250 lines. Not bad. But we can reduce it even more because the labels are not the only widgets that share properties. There are also text inputs and check boxes (used as radio buttons in our code), but I'll leave them as an exercise for you to do.

I'm going to wrap it up now, but we'll come back to the Settings screen and simplify it even more when we cover Kivy properties and ids.

So, if after doing the exercises below you still can see some repetitiveness, don't worry about that, we'll fix that soon. In the next chapter we'll be building the screen where we're going to spend most of the time during the game, the Race screen.

# It's Your Turn Now...

## EXERCISE 1 - CUSTOM TEXT INPUTS

In the Settings screen there are several text inputs. There are two types of them actually:

a) the text inputs where we can enter the players' names:

```
TextInput:
    multiline: False
    size_hint: None, None
    size: 400, 30
```

b) the text inputs where we can enter numbers like the players' initial money or the number of races or the time of the game in the Ending Conditions area:

```
TextInput:
    multiline: False
    size_hint: None, None
    size: 250, 30
```

Create two class rules and define two classes, **`NameInput`** and **`NumInput`**, both inheriting directly from **`TextInput`**. Then use the custom widgets in the code.

## SOLUTION

Here are the two class rules:

```
# NameInput inherits from TextInput.
<NameInput@TextInput>:
    multiline: False
    size_hint: None, None
    size: 400, 30
```

```
# NumInput inherits from TextInput.
<NumInput@TextInput>:
    multiline: False
    size_hint: None, None
    size: 250, 30
```

Now the text inputs will be respectively simplified to:

```
NameInput:
```

and

```
NumInput:
```

If we replace all the occurrences of text inputs in the code, the kv file will look like so:

```
#:kivy 1.11.1
# File name: settings.kv

### LABELS ###
...
<DollarLabel@RegularLabel>:
    ...
### TEXT INPUTS ###
# NameInput inherits from TextInput.
<NameInput@TextInput>:
    multiline: False
    size_hint: None, None
    size: 400, 30

# NumInput inherits from TextInput.
<NumInput@TextInput>:
    multiline: False
    size_hint: None, None
    size: 250, 30

<SettingsScreen>:
    ...
    ### THE PLAYERS ###
    BoxLayout:
        ...
        # Player Name and Initial Money Setup
        BoxLayout:
            ...
            # the players rows
            # player 1
            BoxLayout:
                Regular80x30Label:
                    text: 'Player 1'

                NameInput:
                BoxLayout:
                    RegularLabel:
                        text: ""
                        size_hint_x: None
                        width: 280
                    DollarLabel:
                    NumInput:
            # the other players like above
            ...
    ### ENDING CONDITIONS ###
    BoxLayout:
        ...
        # radio buttons
        GridLayout:
            ...
            # option 2: races
            CheckBox:
                group: 'conditions'
                size_hint_x: .05

            BoxLayout:
                RegularLabel:
                    text: ...
                NumInput:
            # option 3 like above
            ...
```

Now the code was reduced from about 250 lines to less than 240.

## EXERCISE 2 - CUSTOM CHECK BOXES

Other pieces of repetitive code are the two radio button groups. There are radio buttons where you can choose the number of players in the Players area and radio buttons which you can use to choose an ending condition. As you know, radio buttons are just check boxes that all have the **group** property set to the same value.

Let's have a look at the radio buttons as they are right now. Here's the Players radio button:

```
CheckBox:
    group: 'players'
    size_hint: (.5, 1)
```

And here's the Ending Conditions radio button:

```
CheckBox:
    group: 'conditions'
    size_hint_x: .05
```

There are four Players radio buttons and three Ending Conditions radio buttons. Create custom radio buttons that inherit from **CheckBox**. Name them **PlayerRadioButton** and **ConditionRadioButton** respectively and then use them in the code.

## SOLUTION

Here are the two class rules:

```
<PlayerRadioButton@CheckBox>:
    group: 'players'
    size_hint: (.5, 1)

<ConditionRadioButton@CheckBox>:
    group: 'conditions'
    size_hint_x: .05
```

Now we can use the new radio buttons in code like this:

```
PlayerRadioButton:
```

and:

```
ConditionRadioButton:
```

Here's the full kv code:

```
#:kivy 1.11.1
# File name: settings.kv

### LABELS ###
...
### TEXT INPUTS ###
...
### CHECK BOXES ###
# PlayerRadioButton inherits from CheckBox.
<PlayerRadioButton@CheckBox>:
    group: 'players'
    size_hint: (.5, 1)

# ConditionRadioButton inherits from CheckBox.
<ConditionRadioButton@CheckBox>:
    group: 'conditions'
    size_hint_x: .05

<SettingsScreen>:
    ...
    ### THE PLAYERS ###
    BoxLayout:
        ...
            # Radio Buttons
            BoxLayout:
                ...
                # 1 player
                BoxLayout:
                    PlayerRadioButton:
                    RegularLabel:
                        text: '1 player'
                # like above for the other options
                ...
    ### ENDING CONDITIONS ###
    BoxLayout:
        ...
        # radio buttons
        GridLayout:
            ...
            # option 1: money
            ConditionRadioButton:
            RegularLabel:
                text: ...

            # like above for options 2 and 3
            ...
```

This time, again, the code didn't get much shorter, because although the code was simplified, we added the class rules at the beginning, so that the overall number of lines is more or less the same. But still, it was worth doing because we got rid of the code repetitiveness and thus, if we want to change anything in a check box, text input or label in the future, we can do it in just one place, in the class rule.

If you run the program now, after making all those changes, you should see the same window as before.

# Chapter 40 - The Race Screen GUI

In the last chapter of the previous part of the book we created a basic Race Screen GUI. This is the screen where we're going to spend most of the time during the game. So, what do we have now?

Here's the Python code in the **race.py** file:

```
# File name: race.py

import kivy
kivy.require('1.11.1')
from kivy.app import App
from kivy.uix.boxlayout import BoxLayout

class RaceApp(App):
    def build(self):
        return BoxLayout()

if __name__ == '__main__':
    RaceApp().run()
```

And here's the kv file:

```
#:kivy 1.11.1
# File name: race.kv

<BoxLayout>:
    orientation: 'vertical'

    ### INFO, STATS AND BUTTONS ###
    Label:
        text: 'Info, Stats and Buttons'

    ### THE TRACK ###
    Label:
        text: 'The Track'

    ### THE BETS ###
    Label:
        text: 'The Bets'
```

As you can see, it's very basic. Actually you can only see the three main areas:

1) Info, Stats and Buttons

2) The Track

3) The Bets

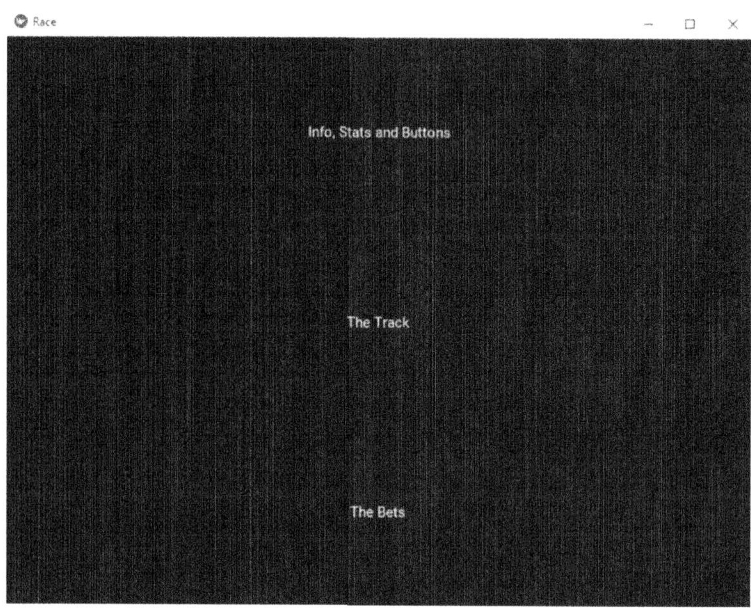


If you run this program, you will see the labels that we used as placeholders for the three areas.

OK, so this is what we have. And what are we aiming at?

Compare what we have with the final version of the Race screen, which you can see below.

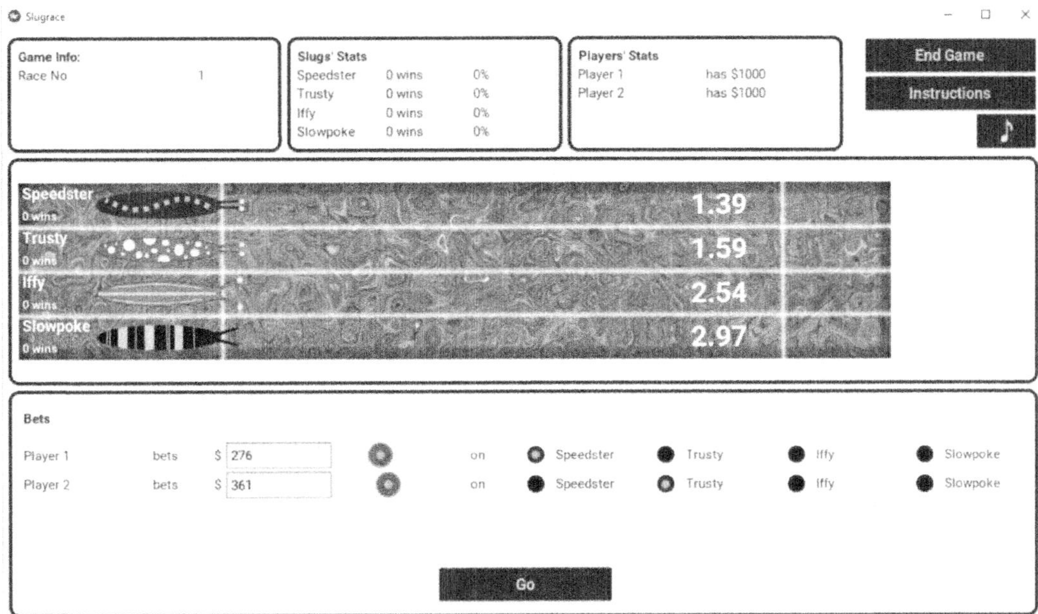


What we have and what we're aiming at are not very much alike. This means there's a lot of work to do. Actually it means much more work than we can do in one chapter, so here we're only going to start. But before we start, just one remark. In the final version image you can see the Bets area near the bottom. In the final version this part will be a separate screen which will be inserted here and will be replaced by the Results screen when a race is finished. So after the fastest slug crosses the finish line, the Race screen will look like this:

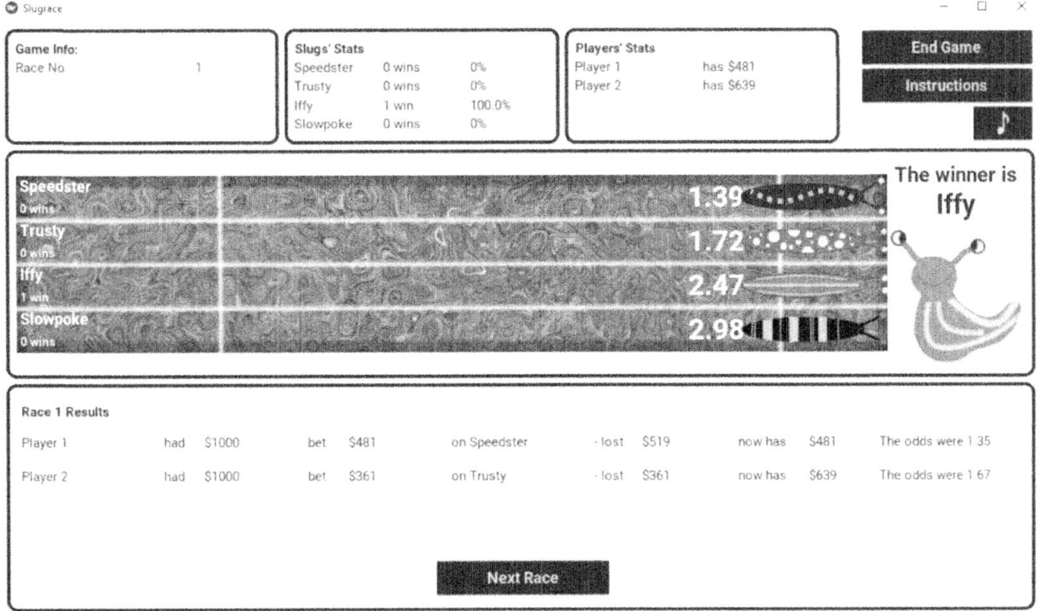

As you can see, now the lower part is different. For now, however, we're going to put a placeholder here and implement the Bets and Results screens as separate apps in the following chapters, just as we're doing now with all the screens. This is because we can run each of them separately and see how it looks. When we learn how to make all the Python and kv files communicate with one another, we'll change this behavior so that there will be just one main app and the screens will be swapped as needed.

And one more thing. We want all the screens to look consistent, so we're going to use the same styles for labels, buttons and other widgets. That's why we're going to use the custom widgets we defined in the Settings screen. At this point we'll just copy them and put above the root widget just like we did before, but this naturally means repetitive code again. It would be much better to define all the custom widgets in one place and then use them across the whole application, and this is what we actually are going to do, but not now. Before that we must learn how files communicate in Kivy. So, don't worry about the repetitive code for now, it will change.

# The root Widget

With that said, let's choose a root widget. As you remember, we used a BoxLayout in the Settings screen. We're going to use a BoxLayout in the Race screen too, at least for now.

So, let's modify the Python file:

```
# File name: race.py
...
from kivy.uix.boxlayout import BoxLayout

# root widget
class RaceScreen(BoxLayout):
    pass

class RaceApp(App):
    def build(self):
        return RaceScreen()
...
```

And now kv file:

```
#:kivy 1.11.1
# File name: race.kv

<RaceScreen>:
    orientation: 'vertical'
    ...
```

# The Areas Overview

At this point we used **RaceScreen** as the root widget, which is a subclass of **BoxLayout**. And now let's have a look at all the areas one by one. How are we going to implement them?

## The Info, Stats and Buttons Area Overview

Well, first comes the Info, Stats and Buttons area. This is what it should eventually look like:

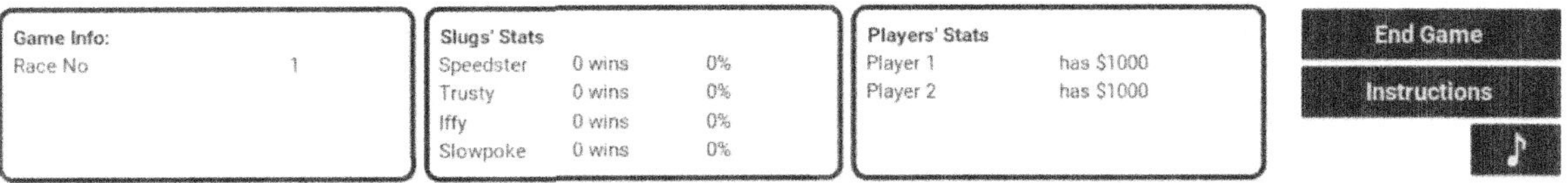


We'll implement it as a GridLayout with four columns. There will be one subarea in each column:

- in column 1: the Game Info subarea implemented as a BoxLayout,

- in column 2: the Slugs' Stats subarea implemented as a BoxLayout,

- in column 3: the Players' Stats subarea implemented as a BoxLayout,

- in column 4: the Buttons subarea implemented as a BoxLayout.

## The Track Area Overview

Then there's the Track area, so the part of the window where we'll be able to watch the slugs compete with one another. This is what it should look like before a race starts:

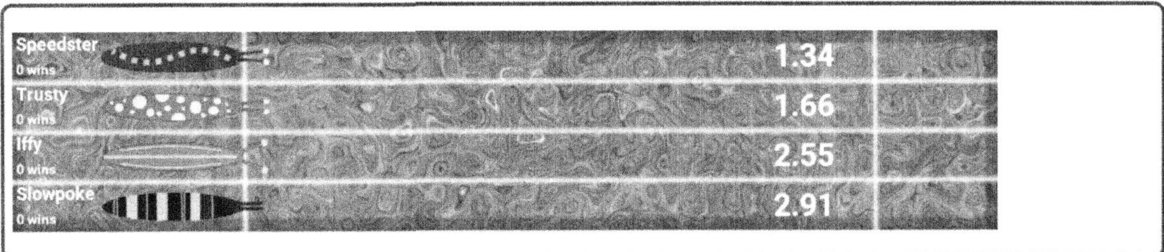


and after a race finishes:

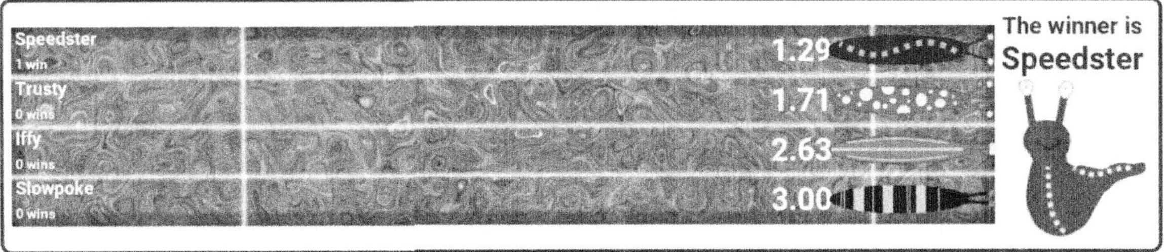


This area will be implemented as a horizontal BoxLayout with two subareas:

- the Track Image subarea implemented as a RelativeLayout,

- the Winner subarea implemented as a BoxLayout.

For now we're just going to use some placeholders without images. We will add the graphics when we learn how to do it, which is going to be soon.

## The Bets Area Overview

Finally we have the Bets area, or, to be more precise, the Bets/Results area, because here the two screens, Bets and Results, will be swapped after each race. So, this is how it should look before a race:

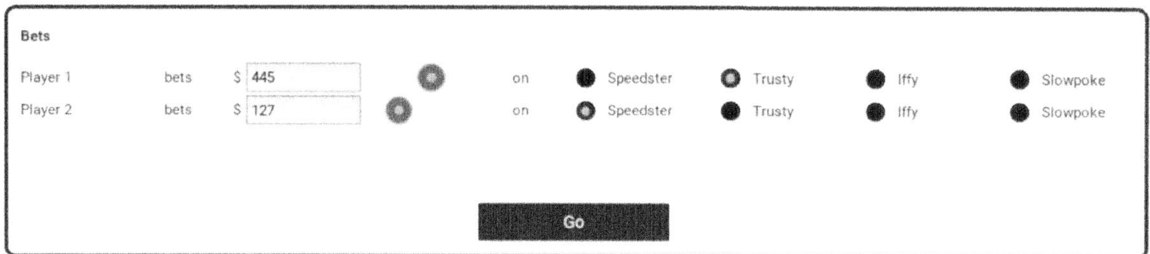


and after a race:

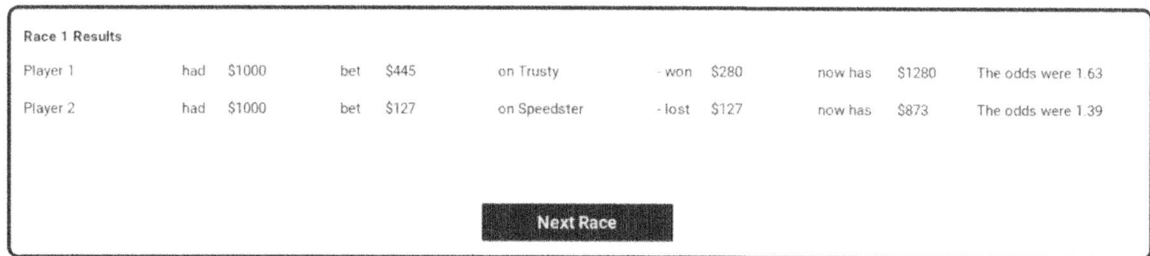


Here you can see how it should look if there are two players, but the number of players may be up to four. As you remember, this is one of the things that you can set in the Settings screen. We're not going to implement this area at all for now, because we'll implement the Bets and Results screens separately and then only inject them here. For the time being we'll be using just a placeholder for the whole area.

# The Areas One by One

So, now that we know what we want to achieve, let's give it a try. But wait a minute, you can do it yourself. In the first exercise you're going to create the Info, Stats and Buttons area and then, in the second exercise, you're going to implement the Track area, or rather a very basic version of it. The only area that you are going to implement relatively completely here is the Info, Stats and Buttons area. It's time to do it! Good luck.

After you finish the exercises, we'll be done with the Race screen for now. Before we move on to the next screen, which is the Bets screen, we'll see how to set the size of the app window so that we don't have to resize it anymore whenever we run the app. Resizing the window every time is pretty annoying, isn't it? So, this is going to be the topic of the next chapter.

# It's Your Turn Now...

## EXERCISE 1 - THE INFO, STATS AND BUTTONS AREA IMPLEMENTATION

This exercise is going to be pretty long, which doesn't mean difficult. Just follow the instructions and you should be good. Here are the instructions:

1. We're definitely going to need the **RegularLabel** class we created in the Settings screen. Just copy it in the **settings.kv** file and paste it here above the root widget.

2. As you can see, some of the labels are in bold type. Create a new class rule. The class should inherit from **RegularLabel**. Name it **BoldLabel** and set its **bold** property to **True**.

3. The Info, Stats and Buttons area should be implemented as a GridLayout with four BoxLayouts. So, under the root widget add a GridLayout with four columns. Set its **size_hint** property to **(1, .5)** and **spacing** to **4**. Inside the GridLayout create four vertical BoxLayouts with 10 px of padding, one for each of the four subareas. To keep your code clear add comments with the names of these subareas above each BoxLayout. The following names seem fine:

- Game Info

- Slugs' Stats

- Players' Stats

- Buttons (for this subarea additionally set **spacing** to **3** and **size_hint** to **(.7, 1)**)

4. Inside the Game Info subarea we need a BoldLabel (the one we just created in the class rules section) with the text **'Game Info:'**. Below the BoldLabel we need four horizontal (it's the default value of the **orientation** property, so you can just leave it out) BoxLayouts with two RagularLabels in each. In each BoxLayout the first RegularLabel (but not the second one) should have the **size_hint** property set to **(2.5, 1)**. The **text** properties of the labels should be set to the following strings:

- in the first BoxLayout: **'Race No'** and **'1'**

- in the second BoxLayout: **'Number of races set:'** and **'10'**

- in the third BoxLayout: **'Races Finished:'** and **'0'**

- in the fourth BoxLayout: **'Races to go:'** and **'10'**

The strings are just dummy data. They're here just for demonstrational purposes.

5. Inside the Slugs' Stats subarea we also need a BoldLabel, this time with the text **"Slugs' Stats"**. Below the BoldLabel we need four horizontal BoxLayouts with a 10 px spacing and with three RagularLabels in each. The **text** properties of the labels should be set to the following strings:

- in the first BoxLayout: **'Speedster'**, **'7 wins'** and **'70%'**

- in the second BoxLayout: **'Trusty'**,**'1 win'** and **'10%'**

- in the third BoxLayout: **'Iffy'**,**'0 wins'** and **'0%'**

- in the fourth BoxLayout: **'Slowpoke'**, **'2 wins'** and **'20%'**

The strings are just dummy data again.

6. Inside the Players' Stats subarea we again need a BoldLabel, this time with the text **"Players' Stats"**. Below the BoldLabel we need four horizontal BoxLayouts with two RagularLabels in each. The **text** properties of the labels should be set to the following strings:

- in the first BoxLayout: **'Player 1'** and **'has $1000'**

- in the second BoxLayout: **'Player 2'** and **'has $800'**

- in the third BoxLayout: **'Player 3'** and **'has $1300'**

- in the fourth BoxLayout: **'Player 4'** and **'has $1200'**

As before, the strings are just dummy data.

7. In the Buttons subarea we need three buttons. They will share some properties, so let's create a custom button first. Go to the class rules section above the root widget and add a class that inherits from **Button**. Name it **RightButton** because a characteristic feature of the instances of this class will be that they will stick to the right border of the container. Set the following properties:

- **font_size** to **18**,

- **size_hint** to **(None, None)**

- **size** to **(200, 40)**

- **pos_hint** to **{'right': 1}**

Then, back in the Buttons subarea add three instances of **RightButton** and set their **text** properties to **'End Game'**, **'Instructions'** and **'Sound'**, in this exact order.

## SOLUTION

Here's the full kv file:

```
#:kivy 1.11.1
# File name: race.kv
<RegularLabel@Label>:
    text_size: self.size
    halign: 'left'
    valign: 'center'
<BoldLabel@RegularLabel>:
    bold: True
<RightButton@Button>:
    font_size: 18
    size_hint: (None, None)
    size: 200, 40
    pos_hint: {'right': 1}
<RaceScreen>:
    orientation: 'vertical'
    ### INFO, STATS AND BUTTONS ###
    GridLayout:
        cols: 4
        size_hint: 1, .5
        spacing: 4
        # Game Info
        BoxLayout:
            orientation: 'vertical'
            padding: 10
            BoldLabel:
                text: 'Game Info:'
            BoxLayout:
                RegularLabel:
                    size_hint: (2.5, 1)
                    text: 'Race No'
                RegularLabel:
                    text: '1'
            BoxLayout:
                RegularLabel:
                    size_hint: (2.5, 1)
                    text: 'Number of races set:'
                RegularLabel:
                    text: '10'
            BoxLayout:
                RegularLabel:
                    size_hint: (2.5, 1)
                    text: 'Races finished:'
                RegularLabel:
                    text: '0'
            BoxLayout:
                RegularLabel:
                    size_hint: (2.5, 1)
                    text: 'Races to go:'
                RegularLabel:
                    text: '10'
        # Slugs' Stats
        BoxLayout:
            orientation: 'vertical'
            padding: 10
            BoldLabel:
                text: "Slugs' Stats"
            BoxLayout:
                spacing: 10
                RegularLabel:
                    text: "Speedster"
                RegularLabel:
                    text: '7 wins'
                RegularLabel:
                    text: '70%'
            BoxLayout:
                spacing: 10
                RegularLabel:
                    text: "Trusty"
                RegularLabel:
                    text: '1 win'
                RegularLabel:
                    text: '10%'
            BoxLayout:
                spacing: 10
                RegularLabel:
                    text: "Iffy"
                RegularLabel:
                    text: '0 wins'
                RegularLabel:
                    text: '0%'
            BoxLayout:
                spacing: 10
                RegularLabel:
                    text: "Slowpoke"
                RegularLabel:
                    text: '2 wins'
                RegularLabel:
                    text: '20%'
        # Players' Stats
        BoxLayout:
            orientation: 'vertical'
            padding: 10
            BoldLabel:
                text: "Players' Stats"
            BoxLayout:
                RegularLabel:
                    text: 'Player 1'
                RegularLabel:
                    text: 'has $1000'
            BoxLayout:
                RegularLabel:
                    text: 'Player 2'
                RegularLabel:
                    text: 'has $800'
            BoxLayout:
                RegularLabel:
                    text: 'Player 3'
                RegularLabel:
                    text: 'has $1300'
            BoxLayout:
                RegularLabel:
                    text: 'Player 4'
                RegularLabel:
                    text: 'has $1200'
        # Buttons
        BoxLayout:
            orientation: 'vertical'
            spacing: 3
            padding: 10
            size_hint: .7, 1
            RightButton:
                text: 'End Game'
            RightButton:
                text: 'Instructions'
            RightButton:
                text: 'Sound'
    ### THE TRACK ###
    ...
```

Well, this code is pretty lengthy, but also pretty straightforward. There's nothing new in it. If you now run the app (from the **race.py** file), the widgets will partially overlap, which doesn't look good, but remember that in the final version the app window will be bigger. At this moment you can just manually resize the window horizontally and vertically and then you will see the whole Info, Stats and Buttons subarea near the top of the window.

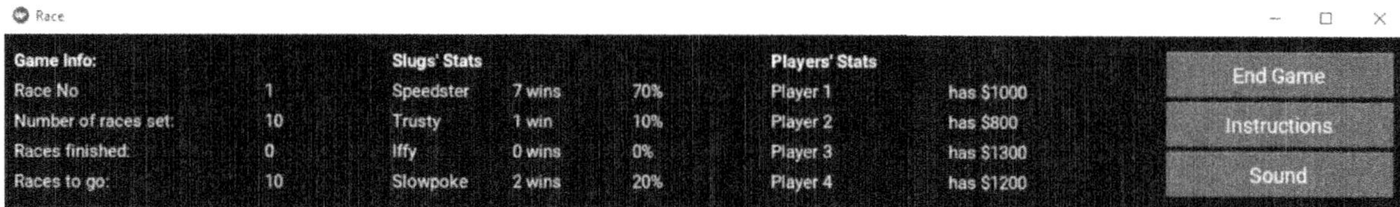


Looks a bit more like the final version, right? Anyway, don't pay attention to the numeric values in the code and screenshot, like the number of wins, race number, etc. I just put some arbitrary values here which doesn't make sense at all, but at least you can see what it's going to look like. These values will be then handled programmatically.

## EXERCISE 2 - THE TRACK AREA IMPLEMENTATION

The Track area will take shape only when we add the graphics to it, but for now let's add some dummy data so that there is at least something. Like before, just follow the instructions below. This time it's not going to be that long. Here are the instructions:

1. Implement the Track area as a horizontal BoxLayout with a 10 px padding.

2. The Track area will consist of two subareas: one for the track image and one for the image of the winner along with some info about the winning slug. For now implement the Track Image subarea just as a simple label with the **`text`** property set to **`'TRACK IMAGE'`**. This is just temporary code.

3. The other subarea, the one where the winning slug image and info will appear, should be implemented as a vertical BoxLayout. Set its **`size_hint`** property to **`(.18, 1)`**. Then add three labels to the BoxLayout:

- a label with the text **`'The winner is'`**, font size set to 24, the **`size_hint`** property set to **`(1, .2)`** and **`bold`** set to **`True`**,

- a label with the text **`'Trusty'`**, font size set to 32, the **`size_hint`** property set to **`(1, .2)`** and **`bold`** set to **`True`**,

- a label with the text **`'WINNER'`** – this is just a placeholder for the image that we're going to handle later.

**SOLUTION**

Here's the code:

```
#:kivy 1.11.1
# File name: race.kv
...
<RaceScreen>:
    ...
    ### THE TRACK ###
    BoxLayout:
        padding: 10

        # Track Image
        Label:
            text: 'TRACK IMAGE'

        # Winner
        BoxLayout:
            orientation: 'vertical'
            size_hint: (.18, 1)

            Label:
                text: "The winner is"
                font_size: 24
                size_hint: 1, .2
                bold: True

            Label:
                text: "Trusty"
                font_size: 32
                size_hint: 1, .2
                bold: True

            Label:
                text: 'WINNER'

    ### THE BETS ###
    ...
```

Run the code again and resize the window. You should now see all the elements of the Track area.

Although still very incomplete, this will have to do for now. I'm not going to touch the Bets area here because we'll build the Bets screen from scratch in one of the following chapters.

# Chapter 41 - The App Window Size Configuration

In the preceding chapters we were working on two screens, the Settings screen and the Race screen. When we were running the app, the widgets were squeezed all together, they overlapped with one another or were not visible at all. It didn't look good, so we resized the window each time we ran the app to see everything.

This is, however, not the best strategy to tell the user of our app to resize the window each time they run the app if they want to see everything. It would be much better if we could open the app window already resized. Fortunately, it's pretty easy to do.

## Configuration Object

You can change the size of the app window through the configuration object. It's instanced from the **Config** class defined in the **kivy.config** module. The configuration object can be used for lots of other settings as well, but it's beyond the scope of this chapter, so let's concentrate on the window size. Let's open the **settings.py** file. We need to import the **Config** class.

Then we have to set the width and height of the window. To this end we use the **set** method on the **Config** object. It takes three parameters:

- the configuration token that our option belongs to, which in our case is **graphics**,

- the option, which in our case will be **width** or **height**,

- the value – this is the value that we want to set our option to.

For the **Config** object to work correctly, it's important to use the **set** method before importing any other Kivy modules. This is why we'll put it at the very top of the Python file.

Now, what size should our window be? You can try it out. Let's start with the resolution 1000 x 300 pixels, for example.

Here's the modified Python file:

```
# File name: settings.py

# We need the configuration object.
from kivy.config import Config
# Let's configure the window size.
Config.set('graphics', 'width', '1000')
Config.set('graphics', 'height', '300')

import kivy
kivy.require('1.11.1')
from kivy.app import App
from kivy.uix.boxlayout import BoxLayout

class SettingsScreen(BoxLayout):
    pass

class SettingsApp(App):
    def build(self):
        return SettingsScreen()

if __name__ == '__main__':
    SettingsApp().run()
```

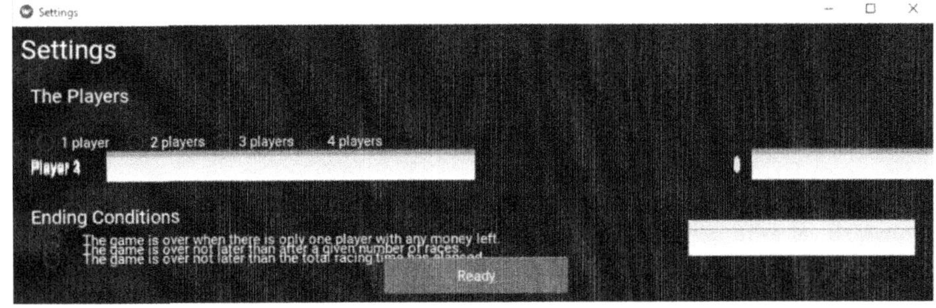


If you now run the app, the window will be wider but lower than before.

Well, it's different, but definitely not what we want. For our app I'd like to maintain the 16 : 9 ratio. So, it could be the 720p resolution, known as HD or high definition. This is a display resolution measuring 1280 x 720 pixels. But I thing this would be slightly too big for our app, so I decided to choose 1200 x 675 pixels. This is slightly less, but the ratio is 1200 : 675, so still 16 : 9. I'll go with this resolution, if you want the window slightly bigger, feel free to set it to a larger size, but remember to keep the 16 : 9 ratio. So, let's modify our app one more time:

```
# File name: settings.py

from kivy.config import Config
Config.set('graphics', 'width', '1200')
Config.set('graphics', 'height', '675')

import kivy
...
```

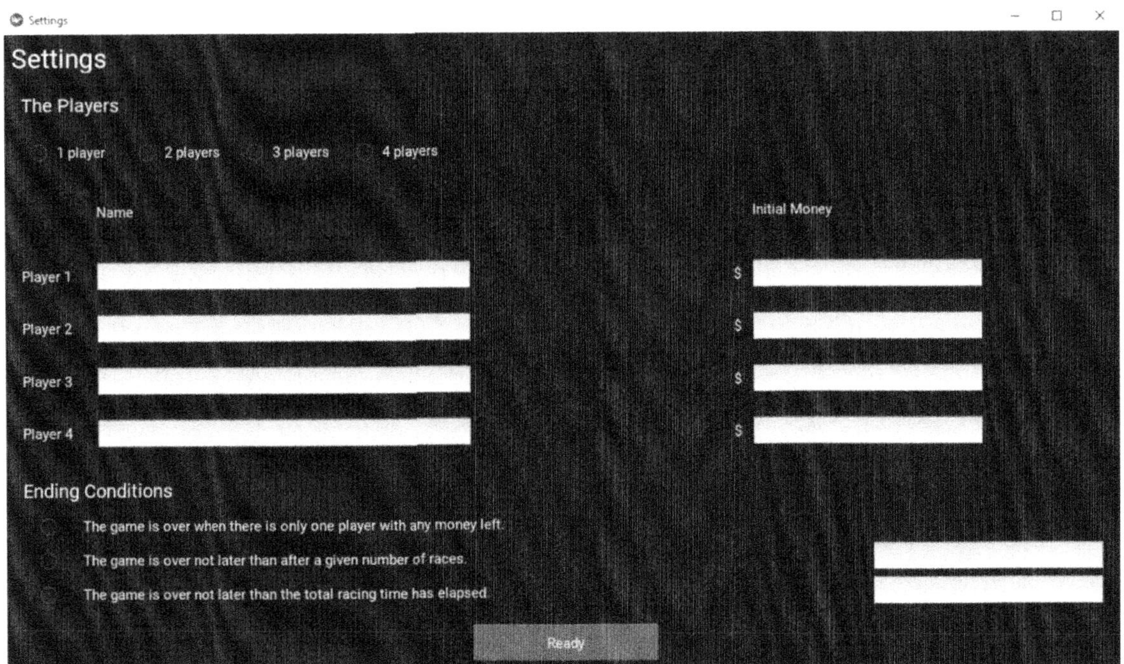


Now when you run the app, it looks much better.

# Fullscreen Mode

You might also want to run your app in fullscreen mode. Why not? Let's check it out.

There is a **`fullscreen`** option that you can set to **`1`**. The ratio of the window will be maintained.

Here's how you can use it:

```
# File name: settings.py

from kivy.config import Config
Config.set('graphics', 'width', '1200')
Config.set('graphics', 'height', '675')

# fullscreen mode
Config.set('graphics', 'fullscreen', '1')

import kivy
...
```

If you now run the app, it will open in fullscreen mode. To exit just hit the Escape key.

It doesn't look bad, but fullscreen mode is not so comfortable during the development stage, so I'll remove it from my code and keep the size of 1200 x 675. You could consider enabling fullscreen mode when your app is ready for deployment, though.

# Resizing the Window

And now let's run our app again and let's maximize the window:

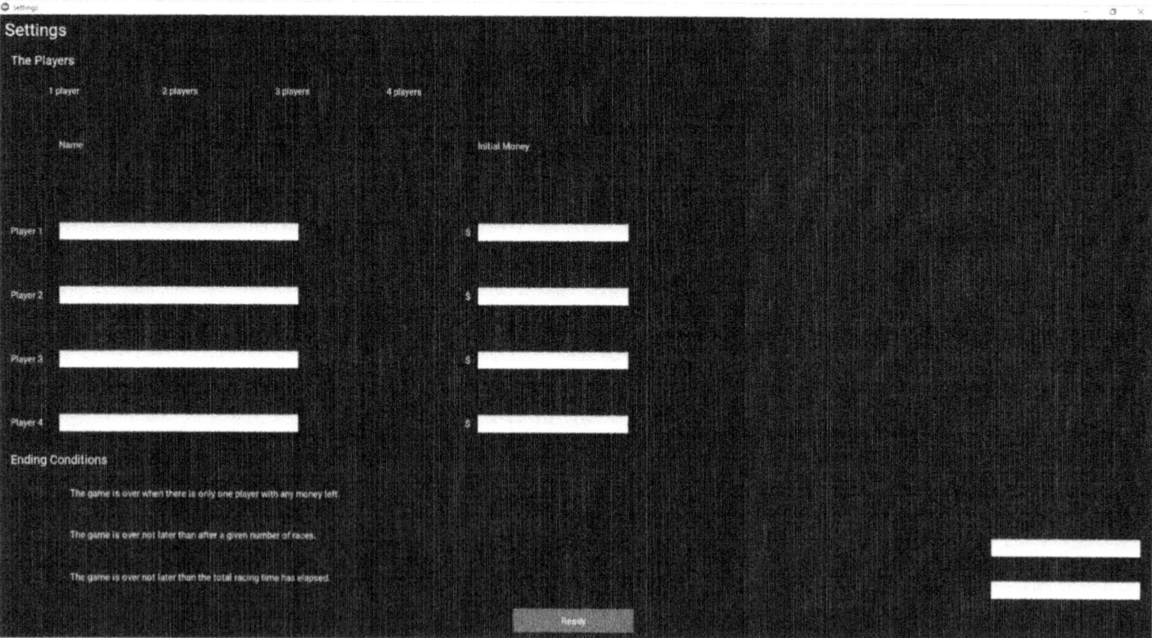


This time the widgets are too far apart. It doesn't look good. As we are going to use fixed-size graphics in our app, which we have to see completely at all times, we can make the window unresizable. I think it's a desired feature for this app, so I'll show you how to do it, but if you want to be able to resize the window, you don't have to use this setting.

So, if you want to make your app window unresizable, just set the **resizable** option to **0**. Here's the code after removing the **fullscreen** option and adding the **resizable** option:

```
# File name: settings.py

from kivy.config import Config
Config.set('graphics', 'width', '1200')
Config.set('graphics', 'height', '675')

# fixed size
Config.set('graphics', 'resizable', '0')

import kivy
...
```

Now if you run the app, you still can minimize the window, but you can't maximize it. You can't resize it by dragging the borders either, have a try.

This leaves us with a fixed-size window. As in this particular case there is no need to resize the window, which actually would only spoil the GUI, I'll leave the setting in the file, but in case you don't like this restriction, you can set the value of the option to **1** (which is the default value) so that the program will run just like if the setting was removed completely.

As at this moment each of our screens is used as a separate app, the configuration settings will only take effect in the Settings screen where the configuration code was placed. So, in the exercise below you will copy the settings to the Race screen so that it has the same size and behaves the same as far as resizing is concerned. In the final app this code will be removed from the screens and will be put only in the **main.py** file, from which the app will start. In the next chapter we'll move on to the next screen, the Bets screen.

# It's Your Turn Now...

### EXERCISE

This exercise is going to be extremely short and easy. Definitely the easiest one so far. Just copy the configuration code to the Race screen. It should be 1200 x 675 pixels in size and unresizable.

## SOLUTION

Here's the **race.py** file:

```
# File name: race.py

from kivy.config import Config
Config.set('graphics', 'width', '1200')
Config.set('graphics', 'height', '675')
Config.set('graphics', 'resizable', '0')

import kivy
...
```

And here's the window when you execute the code:

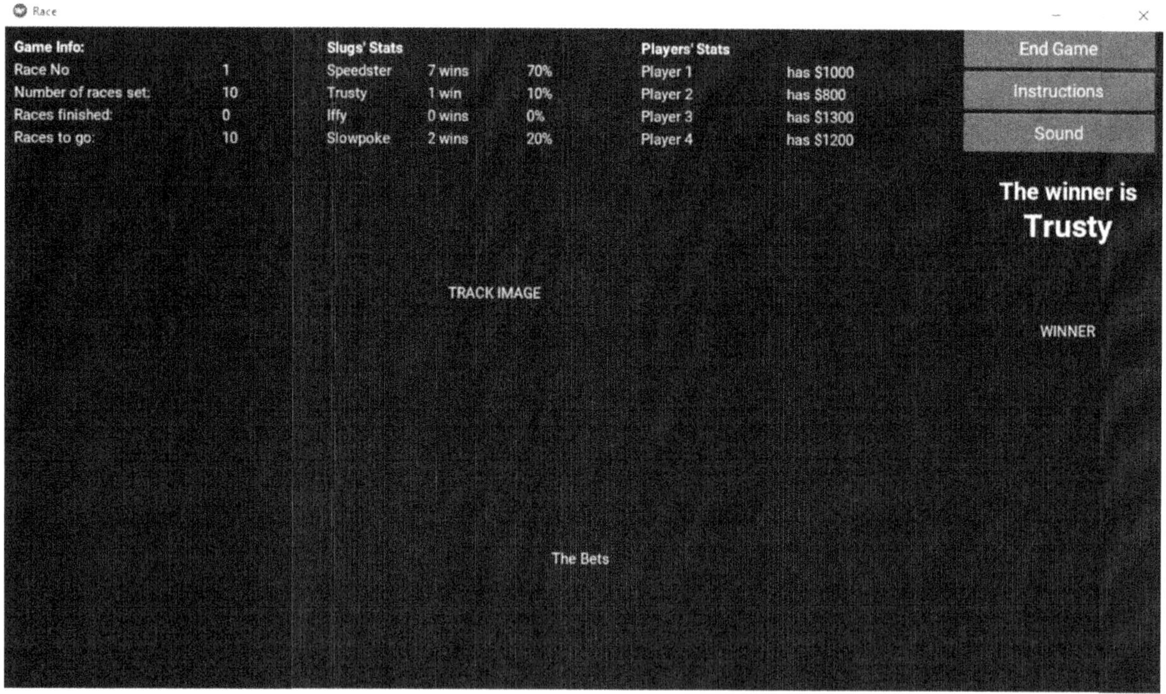

# Chapter 42 - The Bets Screen GUI

A while ago we created the Race screen. I also mentioned that the Bets and Results screens will be injected into the Race screen in the final version of the program, but for now let's create them as independent apps so that we can easily test them. So, in this chapter let's focus on the Bets screen and in the next one we'll create the Results screen.

When we were starting with some initial code in the last chapter of the previous part, we left the **bets.py** and **bets.kv** files empty. So now we have to start from scratch.

First let's have a look at the final version of the Bets screen:

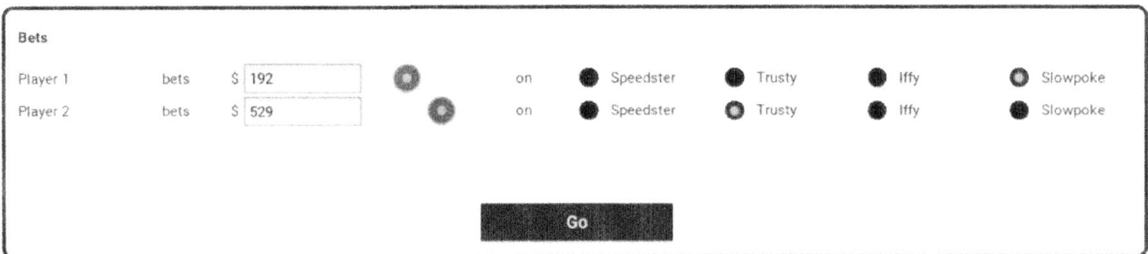


So, here we have three areas:

1) The Title Label area – with just a label that reads **'Bets'**

2) The Player Bets area – this one is pretty complex

3) The Go Button area – it contains just a simple button

So, the layout I think would take care of such a hierarchy well is a vertical BoxLayout.

## The root Widget

Let's define the **BetsScreen** class in the Python file then. It should inherit from **BoxLayout**. Here's the Python file, taking into account the window size configuration we were talking about in the previous chapter:

```
# File name: bets.py

from kivy.config import Config
Config.set('graphics', 'width', '1200')
Config.set('graphics', 'height', '675')
Config.set('graphics', 'resizable', '0')

import kivy
kivy.require('1.11.1')
from kivy.app import App
from kivy.uix.boxlayout import BoxLayout

class BetsScreen(BoxLayout):
    pass

class BetsApp(App):
    def build(self):
        return BetsScreen()

if __name__ == '__main__':
    BetsApp().run()
```

As you can see, the code is pretty much the same as in the previous Python files, for example when we were creating the Race screen.

Now that we have the **BetsScreen** class defined, let's use it as the root widget in the kv file. In its basic form the kv file looks like this:

```
#:kivy 1.11.1
# File name: bets.kv

<BetsScreen>:
    orientation: 'vertical'

    ### TITLE LABEL ###

    ### PLAYER BETS ###

    ### GO BUTTON ###
```

And now we can have a look at each area one by one. Or maybe rather let's handle the first and last areas right away, because they are very simple and straightforward, and then let's discuss the Player Bets area in more detail.

# The Title Label and Go Button Areas

First let's add some padding and spacing to the root widget, like 10 px. Now we can move on to the Title Label area.

For the Title Label we'll use the **BoldLabel** that we defined before. It inherits from **RegularLabel**, which itself inherits from **Label**. We need to add the appropriate class rules above the root widget. As mentioned before, all class rules that are shared by more than one screen will eventually be moved to a separate file, but for now let's just add them to the **bets.kv** file.

Our title label should read **'Bets'**. I'll also size it in horizontal direction appropriately.

As for the Go button, the text on it should read **'Go'**. Besides, it should have the same property values as the Ready button in the Settings screen, for consistency.

I'll also add a simple placeholder for the Player Bets area so that we can see it on the screen.

So, the kv file at this point looks like this:

```
#:kivy 1.11.1
# File name: bets.kv

### CLASS RULES ###

<RegularLabel@Label>:
    text_size: self.size
    halign: 'left'
    valign: 'center'

<BoldLabel@RegularLabel>:
    bold: True

<BetsScreen>:
    orientation: 'vertical'
    padding: 10
    spacing: 10

    ### TITLE LABEL ###
    BoldLabel:
        text: "Bets"
        size_hint: (1, None)
        height: 30

    ### PLAYER BETS ###
    # just a placeholder for now
    Label:
        text: 'PLAYER BETS'

    ### GO BUTTON ###
    # Let's make the button look the
    # same as in the Settings screen.
    Button:
        text: 'Go'
        size_hint: (None, None)
        size: 200, 40
        pos_hint: {'center_x': 0.5}
```

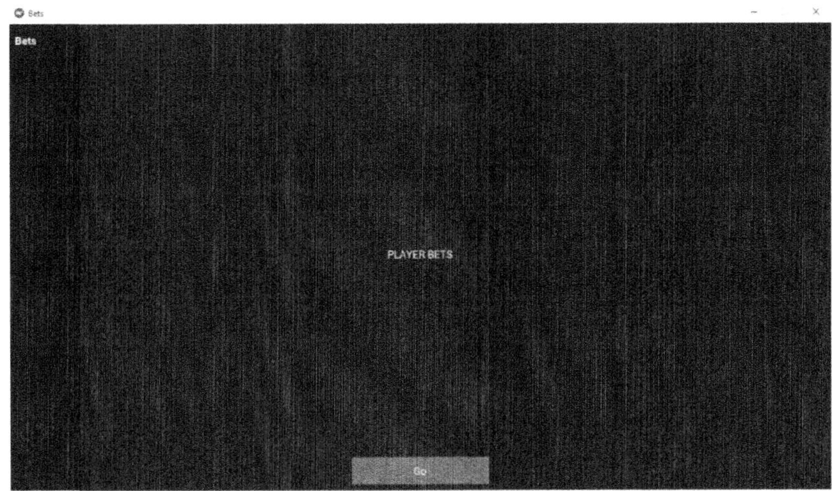


If you now run the app (from the **bets.py** file), you'll see the general structure of the Bets screen.

## The Player Bets Area

And now let's handle the middle part of the screen, the Player Bets area. In the image above you can see two players only, because that's what we set in the Settings screen, but there may be up to four players. Now, there's one row for each player. It contains some labels, a text input, a slider and four radio buttons with labels. For this area we're going to use a vertical BoxLayout for the four rows (as you can see, some of them may be invisible, which we'll take care of a bit later) and for each row we'll use a horizontal BoxLayout. The code is pretty long, but there's nothing new. This is why I think it would make a perfect exercise for you.

The Bets screen will be visible before a race starts. After it finishes, the Results screen will take its place. We'll be talking about the Results screen in the next chapter.

# It's Your Turn Now...

### EXERCISE

The Player Bets area now looks like so:

```
#:kivy 1.11.1
# File name: bets.kv
...
<BetsScreen>:
    ...
    ### PLAYER BETS ###
    # just a placeholder for now
    Label:
        text: 'PLAYER BETS'

    ### GO BUTTON ###
    ...
```

So there's nothing useful in it. After you finish this exercise, it'll look totally different. The code is going to be pretty long, but this is because it's very repetitive and let it be so for now. I promise we'll make it much more concise in due time.

And now follow the instructions:

1. We already have two class rules in our file (**`RegularLabel`** and **`BoldLabel`**). We're definitely going to need more. So, add the following class rules above the root widget:

a) As for the radio buttons add the **PlayerSlugButton** class that inherits from **CheckBox**. There will be a separate group set for each player because we want to be able to select one slug for each player. If we put all the radio buttons in one group, it would be only possible to select one slug for all the players altogether. There's only one property to set in the class rule. As you can see in the image, the radio buttons occupy the right half of each row, so set **size_hint** to **(.5, 1)**.

b) One more thing is the **BetInput** class. It will be used for the players' bet amounts and will inherit from **NumInput**, which inherits from **TextInput**. We defined **NumInput** in the **settings.kv** file, so just copy the class rule here and add the **BetInput** class. The **BetInput** will differ by width and the y-position.

Set **width** to **120** and **pos_hint** to **{'center_y': .5}**.

As you can see in the image above, there is a label with the dollar sign on it. We can use the **DollarLabel** class defined in the **settings.kv** file and overwrite some properties. So, make sure to copy the appropriate class rule to the **bets.kv** file.

2. With the class rules in place, create the layout for the Player Bets area. It should be a vertical BoxLayout. Inside the BoxLayout create four subareas, one for each player. Each subarea should be a horizontal BoxLayout with 10 px of spacing. For clarity add comments like **'player 1'**, **'player 2'**, etc. above each of the four BoxLayouts.

3. The first row (the one for Player 1) is our first subarea. Let's focus on it now, the other three subareas will be almost exactly the same. So, what does it consist of? We have some labels, a text input, a slider and some radio buttons with labels. Here's the hierarchy in a descriptive way, your task is to write the corresponding code. So, inside the Player 1 subarea we have:

- a RegularLabel with the text **'Player 1'**
- a RegularLabel with the text **'bets'** and the **size_hint** property set to **(.4, 1)**
- a horizontal BoxLayout with **spacing** set to **5** that contains:
    - -- a DollarLabel with right-aligned text (this label inherits from **RegularLabel** that has normally left-aligned text!) and the **size_hint** property set to **(1, 1)** because we don't want the fixed 20 x 30 size defined in the class
    - -- a BetInput (the class was defined in the class rules) with the text **'1000'** (just an arbitrary number)
- a slider with **min**, **max** and **value** set to **1**, **1000** and **1000** respectively that increments and decrements by 1, so set the **step** property to **1**.
- a RegularLabel with the text **'on'** and with the **size_hint** property set to **(.3, 1)**
- a horizontal BoxLayout that contains:
    - -- a PlayerSlugButton (defined in the class rules) with the **group** property set to **'player1'**
    - -- a RegularLabel with the text **'Speedster'**
- a horizontal BoxLayout that contains:
    - -- a PlayerSlugButton with the **group** property set to **'player1'**
    - -- a RegularLabel with the text **'Trusty'**

- a horizontal BoxLayout that contains:
  - -- a PlayerSlugButton with the **group** property set to **'player1'**
  - -- a RegularLabel with the text **'Iffy'**
- a horizontal BoxLayout that contains:
  - -- a PlayerSlugButton with the **group** property set to **'player1'**
  - -- a RegularLabel with the text **'Slowpoke'**

After you finish the Player 1 subarea, copy and paste the code three times and tweak it slightly to create the three remaining subareas. Here's what you have to change in each subarea:

- the number of the player in the first label (so **'Player 2'**, **'Player 3'**, **'Player 4'**)
- the group name in the radio buttons ( so **'player2'**, **'player3'**, **'player4'**)

## SOLUTION

Here's the full kv code:

```
#:kivy 1.11.1
# File name: bets.kv

### LABELS ###
<RegularLabel@Label>:
    text_size: self.size
    halign: 'left'
    valign: 'center'
<BoldLabel@RegularLabel>:
    bold: True
<DollarLabel@RegularLabel>:
    text: "$"
    size_hint: None, None
    size: 20, 30
### TEXT INPUTS ###
<NumInput@TextInput>:
    multiline: False
    size_hint: None, None
    height: 30
    width: 250
<BetInput@NumInput>:
    width: 120
    pos_hint: {'center_y': .5}
### OTHER WIDGETS ###
<PlayerSlugButton@CheckBox>:
    size_hint: (.5, 1)
<BetsScreen>:
    ...
    ### PLAYER BETS ###
    # just a placeholder for now
    BoxLayout:
        orientation: 'vertical'
        # player 1
        BoxLayout:
            spacing: 10
            RegularLabel:
                text: 'Player 1'
            RegularLabel:
                text: 'bets'
                size_hint: (.4, 1)
            BoxLayout:
                spacing: 5
                DollarLabel:
                    halign: 'right'
                    size_hint: 1, 1
                BetInput:
                    text: '1000'
            Slider:
                min: 1
                max: 1000
                value: 1000
                step: 1
            RegularLabel:
                text: 'on'
                size_hint: (.3, 1)
            BoxLayout:
                PlayerSlugButton:
                    group: 'player1'
                RegularLabel:
                    text: 'Speedster'
            BoxLayout:
                PlayerSlugButton:
                    group: 'player1'
                RegularLabel:
                    text: 'Trusty'
            BoxLayout:
                PlayerSlugButton:
                    group: 'player1'
                RegularLabel:
                    text: 'Iffy'
            BoxLayout:
                PlayerSlugButton:
                    group: 'player1'
                RegularLabel:
                    text: 'Slowpoke'
        # The code for the other players
        # is almost identical.
        ...
```

If you now run the app from the **bets.py** file, it will look pretty decent.

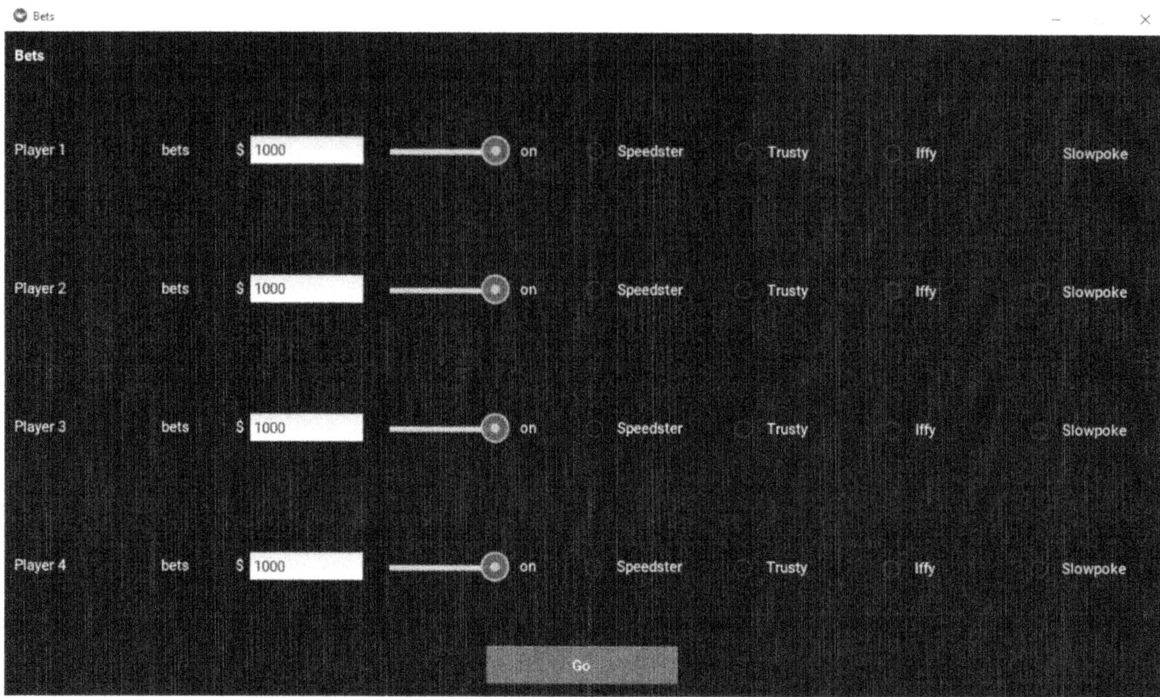


This is more or less what we were aiming at, at least as far as the visual representation is concerned. Naturally, here we can see all four players, because their visibility will be taken care of later in the book. In the next chapter we'll create the Results screen, which will be shown in place of the Bets screen after a race finishes. As I said before, in the final version both the Bets screen and the Results screen will be shown inside the Race screen which we already created.

# Chapter 43 – The Results Screen GUI

In the previous chapter we created the Bets screen, which will be injected into the lower part of the Race screen before each race starts. After a race finishes it will be replaced by the Results screen, which we still don't have. Here's what it should look like in the final version:

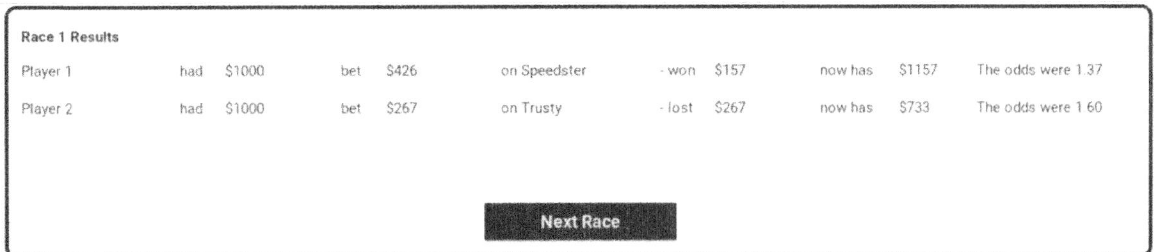
Race 1 Results
Player 1 had $1000 bet $426 on Speedster - won $157 now has $1157 The odds were 1.37
Player 2 had $1000 bet $267 on Trusty - lost $267 now has $733 The odds were 1.60
Next Race

Here again we see that in the Settings screen the 2-player mode has been selected, but there may be up to four players. So, we're going to create four players in the Results screen and then some of them may be programmatically made invisible like here.

There are lots of similarities between this screen and the Bets screen we discussed before. There are also three main areas:

1) The Title Label area – with a label that reads **'Race ... Results'** (with the actual race number in place of the three dots)

2) The Player Results area – slightly less complex than the Player Bets area in the Bets screen

3) The Next Race Button area – with simple button

## The root Widget

As usual, let's start with the Python file, in which we can define our root widget class. Just like before, we'll use a BoxLayout. Here's the Python code:

```
# File name: results.py

from kivy.config import Config
Config.set('graphics', 'width', '1200')
Config.set('graphics', 'height', '675')
Config.set('graphics', 'resizable', '0')

import kivy
kivy.require('1.11.1')
from kivy.app import App
from kivy.uix.boxlayout import BoxLayout

class ResultsScreen(BoxLayout):
    pass

class ResultsApp(App):
    def build(self):
        return ResultsScreen()

if __name__ == '__main__':
    ResultsApp().run()
```

# The kv File

As the kv file is going to be very much like the **bets.kv** file, I'm sure you can handle it on your own. This is going to be an exercise for you. Although it's pretty long, it's also very simple and straightforward. We're going to use the same widgets as before, so we also have to add the appropriate class rules before the root widget.

And in the next chapter we'll add one more screen, the Game Over screen. It's going to be very easy. After that we'll be left with just two more screens, the Instructions screen and the Splash screen. However, we're not going to take care of them now, because for the former I'd like to use the screenshots of the other screens, which will only be possible after they reach their final shape, and as far as the Splash screen is concerned, I don't want it to be displayed during development because we would have to wait until it disappears each time we run the app, and this is something we'll be doing a lot.

# It's Your Turn Now...

**EXERCISE**

Your task is to write the whole kv file for the Results screen. To get you started, here's the general structure of the file:

```
#:kivy 1.11.1
# File name: results.kv

<ResultsScreen>:
    orientation: 'vertical'
    padding: 10

    ### TITLE LABEL ###

    ### PLAYER RESULTS ###

    ### NEXT RACE BUTTON ###
```

All you have to do is write the rest. Just like with the Bets screen, the code is going to be pretty long, but this is also because it's repetitive.

And now follow the instructions:

1. We need two class rules in our file: for **RegularLabel** and **BoldLabel**. Just grab them from any kv file you wrote before and paste them here above the root widget.

2. In the Title Label area just add a BoldLabel and set the **text** property to **'Race 1 Results'**. Set the **height** property to **30**.

HINT: Remember you are inside a layout and there's something you must take care of before you can use the **height** property effectively!

3. It's time for the Player Results area, that's the long one. It should be a vertical BoxLayout. Inside the BoxLayout create four subareas, one for each player, exactly like you did in the Bets layout. Each subarea should be a horizontal BoxLayout. For clarity add comments like **'player 1'**,

`'player 2'`, etc. above each of the four BoxLayouts.

4. The first row (the one for Player 1) is our first subarea. Let's focus on it now, the other three subareas will hardly differ. What do we have here? All we have are labels. But we will group some of them inside BoxLayouts. Here's the hierarchy in a descriptive way, just like in the Bets screen, your task is to write the corresponding code. So, inside the Player 1 subarea we have:

- a RegularLabel with the text `'Player 1'`

- a horizontal BoxLayout that contains:

  -- a RegularLabel with the text `'had'` and the `size_hint` property set to `(.4, 1)`

  -- a RegularLabel with the text `'$1000'`

- a horizontal BoxLayout that contains:

  -- a RegularLabel with the text `'bet'` and the `size_hint` property set to `(.4, 1)`

  -- a RegularLabel with the text `'$300'`

- a RegularLabel with the text `'on Speedster'`

- a horizontal BoxLayout that contains:

  -- a RegularLabel with the text `'- won'` and the `size_hint` property set to `(.5, 1)`

  -- a RegularLabel with the text `'$400'`

- a horizontal BoxLayout that contains:

  -- a RegularLabel with the text `'now has'`

  -- a RegularLabel with the text `'$1400'`

- a RegularLabel with the text `'The odds were 2.54'`

After you finish the Player 1 subarea, copy and paste the code three times and tweak it slightly to create the three remaining subareas. Change the number of the player in the first label (so `'Player 2'`, `'Player 3'`, `'Player 4'`) in each subarea.

You can also change some of the dummy numeric data. Here's the data you can use for players 2-4:

player 2:

- had $1000, bet $300 on Speedster, lost (and not won, so change the text!) $400, now has $600, the odds were 1.59

player 3:

- had $1000, bet $300 on Trusty, won $400, now has $1400, the odds were 2.24

player 4:

- had $1000, bet $300 on Slowpoke, lost $400, now has $600, the odds were 1.85

5. In the Race Button area add a button with the text **`'Next Race'`**. Its size should be 200 x 40 px and it should be horizontally centered.

HINT: Use the **`pos_hint`** property to center the button horizontally. Also remember that you are inside a layout when you size it.

## SOLUTION

Here's the kv file:

```
#:kivy 1.11.1
# File name: results.kv

### CLASS RULES ###
<RegularLabel@Label>:
    text_size: self.size
    halign: 'left'
    valign: 'center'

<BoldLabel@RegularLabel>:
    bold: True

<ResultsScreen>:
    orientation: 'vertical'
    padding: 10

    ### TITLE LABEL ###
    BoldLabel:
        text: 'Race 1 Results'
        size_hint: (1, None)
        height: 30

    ### PLAYER RESULTS ###
    BoxLayout:
        orientation: 'vertical'

        # player 1
        BoxLayout:
            RegularLabel:
                text: 'Player 1'
            BoxLayout:
                RegularLabel:
                    text: 'had'
                    size_hint: (.4, 1)
                RegularLabel:
                    text: '$1000'
            BoxLayout:
                RegularLabel:
                    text: 'bet'
                    size_hint: (.4, 1)
                RegularLabel:
                    text: '$300'
            RegularLabel:
                text: 'on Speedster'
            BoxLayout:
                RegularLabel:
                    text: '- won'
                    size_hint: (.5, 1)
                RegularLabel:
                    text: '$400'
            BoxLayout:
                RegularLabel:
                    text: 'now has'
                RegularLabel:
                    text: '$1400'
            RegularLabel:
                text: 'The odds were 2.54'


        # Use the data given above for
        # the other players.
        # player 2
        ...
```

Don't worry about the numeric data I used in this code. All the money amounts, like bets, wins and losses, as well as other data like the odds, for example, are just dummy values and will be later calculated programmatically. Here what we only care for is the visual representation of the data.

If you run the app now (from the **results.py** file), you will see the Results screen.

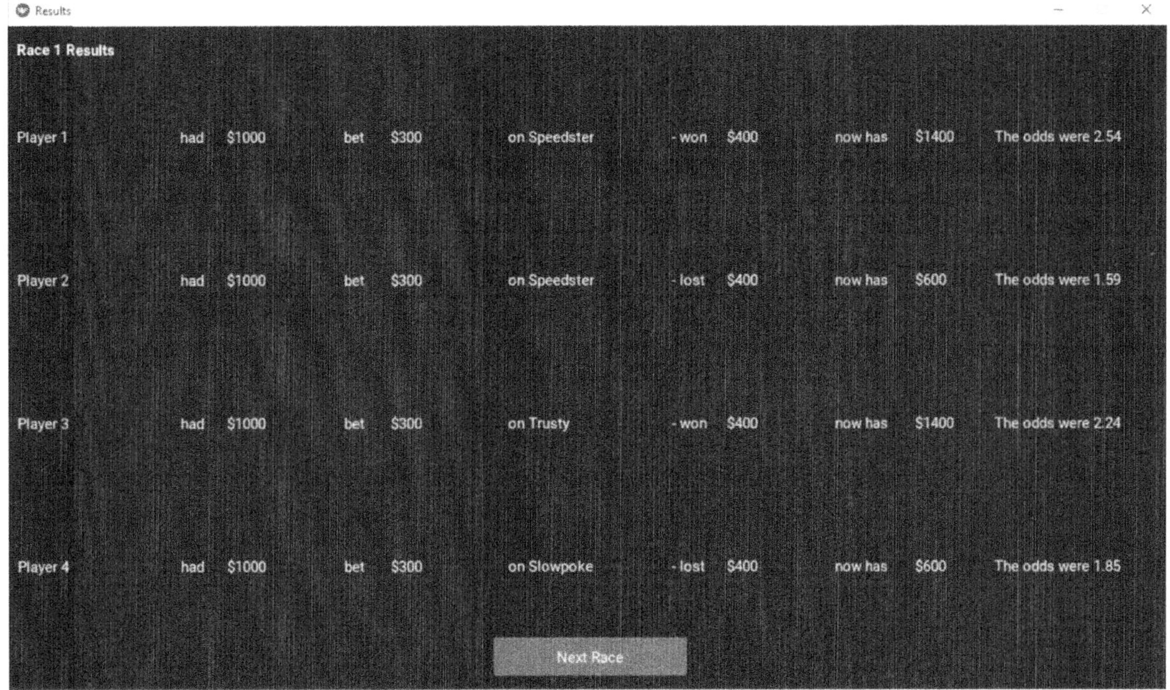


It contains all the elements we need.

# Chapter 44 – The Game Over Screen GUI

In the preceding chapters we created all the basic screens, or, to be precise, separate apps at this point. In particular, we have the Settings screen, the Race screen, the Bets screen and the Results screen. There's one more screen to make, at least for now, the Game Over screen. This is the screen that you will see when the game is over and it will display a message with information about the winner. There will be also two buttons, which you can use to either restart or quit the game. The screen in the final version should look something like this:

Game Over

There's only one player with any money left.

The winner is Player 2, having started at $1000, winning at $396

This GUI is pretty simple, we're going to use a subclass of **`BoxLayout`** as the root widget.

## The root Widget

So, here's the Python code:

```
# File name: gameover.py

from kivy.config import Config
Config.set('graphics', 'width', '1200')
Config.set('graphics', 'height', '675')
Config.set('graphics', 'resizable', '0')
```

```
import kivy
kivy.require('1.11.1')
from kivy.app import App
from kivy.uix.boxlayout import BoxLayout

class GameoverScreen(BoxLayout):
    pass

class GameoverApp(App):
    def build(self):
        return GameoverScreen()

if __name__ == '__main__':
    GameoverApp().run()
```

Well, there's nothing new or unexpected here.

## The kv File

Also, the kv file is pretty simple. As you probably suspect, I'll leave it as an exercise for you. We'll need some labels and some buttons. We're going to use the **BoldLabel** class, which we defined before, but we will overwrite the **font_size** property to make the text larger. You will also overwrite the **halign** property, which is inherited from **RegularLabel**, to center the widget. All we need to do in order to use the **BoldLabel** is add it to the class rules above the root widget. So, I'm sure you'll do it very quickly, this file is much less complex than the ones in the Bets and Results screens.

So, after you finish the Game Over screen in this chapter, with all the basic screens in place, let's make them look more like the images from the final versions that we've been using to illustrate what we are aiming at. As you can see, they are graphically more pleasing to the eye. In the next part of the book we're going to learn how to add colors and graphics to our Kivy app.

## It's Your Turn Now...

### EXERCISE

And here's the exercise that I promised. Follow the instructions to build the kv file from scratch.

1. Let's start with the root widget. In the Python file we defined it as a subclass of **BoxLayout** and we named the class **GameoverScreen**. Set its orientation to vertical.

2. Now add the class rules that we will need here. Just copy **RegularLabel** and **BoldLabel** from one of the other screens and paste them here above the root widget.

3. Under the root widget we'll need three BoldLabels and a BoxLayout with two buttons. Let's start with the BoldLabels. They should all have horizontally centered text. Set the **font_size** property of the top label to **100**, of the middle label to **40** and of the bottom label to **30**. The **text** property of the three labels should be respectively set to:

- **'Game Over'**

- **"There's only one player with any money left."**

- **"The winner is Player 2, having started at $1000, winning at $999"**

HINT: Use the **halign** property to align the text.

4. Under the three BoldLabels add a horizontal BoxLayout. Set its **spacing** property to **50** and center the whole layout both horizontally and vertically. Set its size to 450 x 200 px.

HINT: When setting the size of the BoxLayout remember that it's embedded in another layout.

5. Inside the BoxLayout you just created add two buttons. The text on the first one should be **'Play Again'** and on the second one **'Quit'**. Within the containing BoxLayout the two buttons should be centered vertically. The first button should stick to the left side of the BoxLayout and the second button to the right side. Both buttons should be 200 x 40 px.

**SOLUTION**

Here's the code:

```
#:kivy 1.11.1
# File name: gameover.kv

### CLASS RULES ###
<RegularLabel@Label>:
    text_size: self.size
    halign: 'left'
    valign: 'center'

<BoldLabel@RegularLabel>:
    bold: True

<GameoverScreen>:
    orientation: 'vertical'
    BoldLabel:
        font_size: 100
        text: 'Game Over'
        halign: 'center'
    BoldLabel:
        font_size: 40
        text: "There's only one player with any money left."
        halign: 'center'
```

```
BoldLabel:
    font_size: 30
    text: "The winner is Player 2, having started at $1000, winning at $999"
    halign: 'center'
BoxLayout:
    spacing: 50
    pos_hint: {'center_x': .5, 'center_y': .5}
    size_hint: None, None
    size: 450, 200
    Button:
        text: 'Play Again'
        pos_hint: {'x': 0, 'center_y': .5}
        size_hint: (None, None)
        size: 200, 40
    Button:
        text: 'Quit'
        pos_hint: {'right': 1, 'center_y': .5}
        size_hint: (None, None)
        size: 200, 40
```

It all looks very familiar, I'm sure. Now run the app (from the **gameover.py** file).

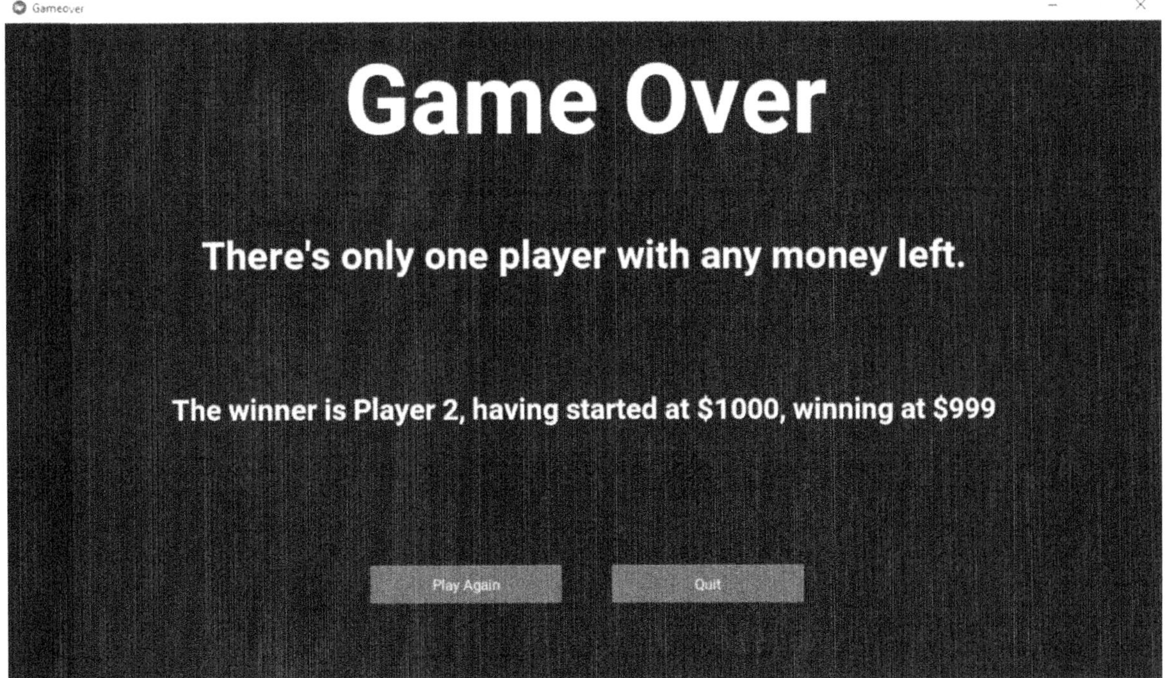
Gameover
Game Over
There's only one player with any money left.
The winner is Player 2, having started at $1000, winning at $999
Play Again
Quit

Naturally, the text is fixed and doesn't reflect the actual result of the game, but we're talking about just the GUI here.

# Part VI

# Graphics in Kivy

In this part of the book we'll add some life to our project, and in particular, some colors and graphics. We'll learn how to use canvas instructions to draw on widgets and manipulate the context. We'll also add the graphical assets to the screens.

# Chapter 45 - Introduction to the Canvas Object

In the previous part of the book we created all the basic screens our app needs. But they are not very eye-catching. And they don't look like in the final versions of the screens - by a long shot. Time to add some colors and graphics. But if we really want to talk about graphics in Kivy, we have to start with discussing the **Canvas** object that every Kivy widget has. This is the topic of this rather theoretical than practical chapter.

The canvas is not what you might think it is if you know this term from other environments, like HTML5, where it is the object we draw on. In Kivy a **canvas** is a set of drawing instructions that define the graphical representation of a widget. Have a look at this screenshot from the final version of the Race screen:

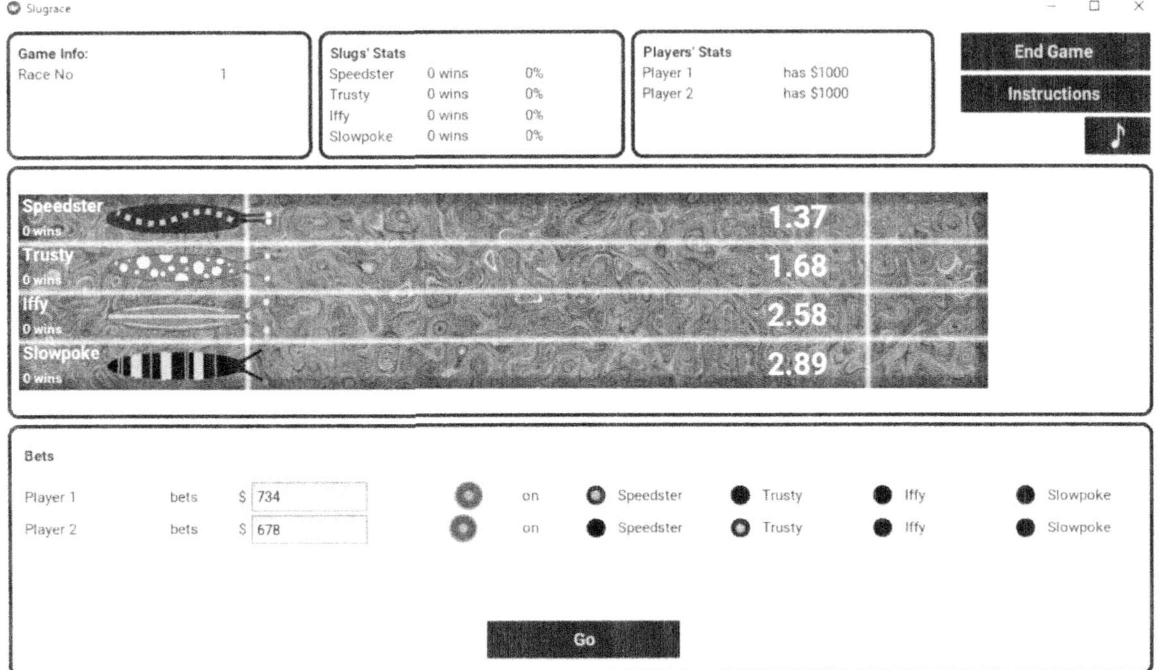


As you can see, the buttons have a dark background, let's say it's dark red, and the text is yellow. Also the check boxes look different than when we first created them. Actually, the whole layouts look different: They have a yellowish background and there are rectangles with rounded corners drawn on them. This is what we can achieve using canvas instructions.

## The Coordinate Space

In Kivy we draw in the coordinate space. This is the space which includes the app window that you can see but also extends beyond it, which means you can draw both inside and outside the visible window. All widgets share the same coordinate space. So, to make things clear, let's recap on this:

- each widget has its own canvas

- all widgets share the same coordinate space

Why this is important will become clear when we talk about drawing instructions.

## Drawing Instructions

Speaking of which... There are two types of drawing instructions in Kivy:

**vertex instructions** – instructions used to draw basic geometric shapes like lines, rectangles, ellipses and such like,

**context instructions** – instructions used to manipulate the whole coordinate space, so to add colors, rotate, translate and scale it.

We'll discuss both these groups of instructions in more detail in the following chapters. What is important is to remember that context instructions manipulate the whole coordinate space, not just the widget on which they are used. We will see this in action soon, but imagine you add a rotation instruction to a button to rotate it, say, 90 degrees in the counterclockwise direction. But this instruction will also affect all the subsequent graphics instructions, regardless if they will belong to the same or to any other widget. This is because the whole coordinate space is rotated. Naturally, there is a way to deal with that – all you have to do is save and then restore the context, but don't worry about that too much at this moment.

## What Is Actually a Widget?

Now that we know something about the coordinate space, we can slightly redefine the widget. Intuitively we know that a button is a widget, and so is a slider or any of the layouts, to mention just a few. But a widget is not restricted to the visible part of the button, slider, layout or any other visual element. In other words, the canvas instructions of a widget are not restricted to any specific area of the widget, but to the whole coordinate space. This means, for example, that we can draw on a button widget, but not necessarily on the rectangular representation of the button that we recognize as the button. Instead, we could draw outside it as well. This will become clearer as we proceed. OK, this theoretical introduction is getting pretty abstract, so let's jump into some code and see how it all really works. In the next chapter we'll see how to draw basic shapes in Kivy.

# Chapter 46 - Canvas Vertex Instructions - Drawing a Rectangle

In the previous chapter we were talking in general about the **Canvas** object, the coordinate space and canvas drawing instructions, so vertex instructions and context instructions. In this chapter we'll concentrate on the vertex instructions that we use to draw basic shapes on a widget.

We can draw on any widget. In this and the following chapters we're going to draw some shapes on a couple of different widgets. For educational purposes we'll be using the two test files that we created earlier, so **test.py** and **test.kv**. As you know, they're not going to be included in our project, they're just for you to practice.

## Drawing Shapes

In this chapter we'll create a 4 x 4 grid where we will draw 16 different shapes using vertex instructions. We will start to populate the grid with some filled shapes. In particular, we'll be drawing a filled rectangle in this chapter and some other filled shapes in the next one. After that we'll learn how to draw lines, borders of shapes and some more complex stuff.

In order to draw a shape, we have to choose a widget we want to draw it on. So we will place 16 widgets in the cells of the grid and draw on each of them. In most cases these are going to be layouts, labels and buttons, because drawing on them usually makes more sense than drawing on a slider or a check box, but, still, I'll show you that this is possible too.

The root widget is going to be a 4 by 4 GridLayout. We will implement it as a GridLayout with 4 columns. The shapes that we are going to draw will be all white for now, which we will be able to change after we discuss colors.

I'm not going to type the whole kv code in one go, but rather piece by piece so that you can see exactly what's going on. Let's start with the Python file, which is pretty simple and straightforward. Remove the code from the **test.py** file and then type the following new code:

```
# File name: test.py

from kivy.config import Config
Config.set('graphics', 'width', '1200')
Config.set('graphics', 'height', '675')
Config.set('graphics', 'resizable', '0')

import kivy
kivy.require('1.11.1')
```

```
from kivy.app import App
from kivy.uix.gridlayout import GridLayout

class TestScreen(GridLayout):
    pass

class TestApp(App):
    def build(self):
        return TestScreen()

if __name__ == '__main__':
    TestApp().run()
```

# Drawing a Rectangle

And now we'll start creating our kv file and draw the first shape, a rectangle. To draw a rectangle we need the **`Rectangle`** class. We also need two properties, **`pos`** and **`size`**, to specify the rectangle's position and size respectively.

In this and the following examples we will usually specify the position and size of the shapes that we draw as relative to the widget we draw them on. This way when the GridLayout expands from 1 cell to 16 cells and the widgets move and shrink, the shapes will still remain on the widgets they're on. If we used absolute coordinates, the shapes would not follow along with the visual parts of the widgets they're on. I'm going to demonstrate it soon.

So, let's draw a rectangle on a BoxLayout. Again, remove any existing code from **test.kv** and then type the following initial code in it:

```
#:kivy 1.11.1
# File name: test.kv

### A 4x4 GRIDLAYOUT WHERE WE ARE GOING TO DRAW SHAPES ###
<TestScreen>:
    cols: 4
    spacing: 4
    padding: 10

    # Shape 1 - A Rectangle on a BoxLayout
    BoxLayout:
        canvas:
            Rectangle:
                pos: self.x, self.y
                size: self.width, self.height
```

As you can see, I added some padding and spacing to the root widget. If you now run the app (from the **test.py** file), you will see a rectangle that is positioned at the beginning of the BoxLayout and is the same size as the BoxLayout (naturally taking into account the padding and spacing).

If you resize the window, the rectangle will be resized too. Let's temporarily comment out the lines where **pos** and **size** are set and let's set these two properties to some absolute values:

```
#:kivy 1.11.1
# File name: test.kv
...
    # Shape 1 - A Rectangle on a BoxLayout
    BoxLayout:
        canvas:
            Rectangle:
                # pos: self.x, self.y
                # size: self.width, self.height
                pos: 200, 100
                size: 300, 100
```

If you now run the app, you will see a different rectangle.

This time when you resize the window, the rectangle won't change.

But this is not the behavior we want, so let's restore the two values relative to the BoxLayout on which we are drawing the rectangle, or maybe, just for practice, let's set the size of the rectangle to half the size of the BoxLayout:

```
#:kivy 1.11.1
# File name: test.kv
...
    # Shape 1 - A Rectangle on a BoxLayout
    BoxLayout:
        canvas:
            Rectangle:
                pos: self.x, self.y
                size: self.width/2, self.height/2
```

And again, if you resize the window now, the rectangle will resize accordingly.

Now, before we move on to the next shape, an ellipse, it's time for a simple exercise for you.

# It's Your Turn Now...

### EXERCISE

We just drew a rectangle on a BoxLayout. But if you want, you can draw more than one rectangle. All you have to do is add another instance of the **Rectangle** class.

So, leave the first rectangle as is and add another one. This one should be the same size, but its bottom left corner should be in the middle (both horizontally and vertically) of the BoxLayout.

### SOLUTION

Here's the kv code:

```
#:kivy 1.11.1
# File name: test.kv
...
    # Shape 1 - A Rectangle on a BoxLayout
    BoxLayout:
        canvas:
            Rectangle:
                pos: self.x, self.y
                size: self.width/2, self.height/2
            Rectangle:
                pos: self.center_x, self.center_y
                size: self.width/2, self.height/2
```

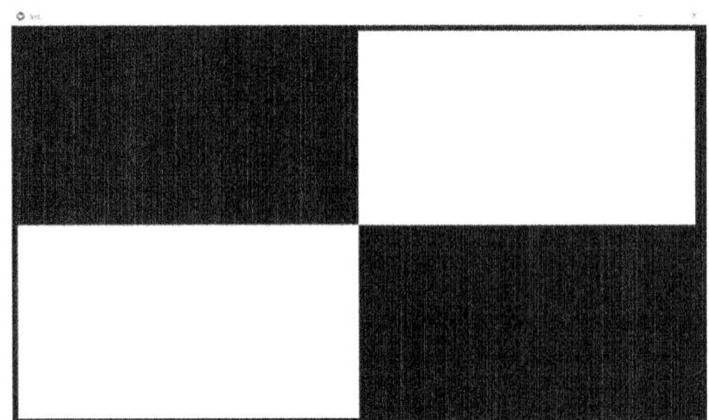

When you run the app, you can see two rectangles drawn on a single BoxLayout.

Feel free to resize the window. Both the BoxLayout and the two rectangles on it will follow along.

# Chapter 47 - Drawing Filled Shapes on Widgets

In the previous chapter we were drawing a filled rectangle on a widget. As an exercise you added a second rectangle. In this chapter we'll be drawing other filled shapes. Before we start, let's restore the kv file so that only one rectangle is drawn on the BoxLayout that is the same size as the widget. The Python code doesn't change. And here's the **test.kv** file. If you want to follow along, make sure to modify it in your editor:

```
#:kivy 1.11.1
# File name: test.kv

### A 4x4 GRIDLAYOUT WHERE WE ARE GOING TO DRAW SHAPES ###
<TestScreen>:
    cols: 4
    spacing: 4
    padding: 10

    # Shape 1 - A Rectangle on a BoxLayout
    BoxLayout:
        canvas:
            Rectangle:
                pos: self.x, self.y
                size: self.width, self.height
```

As you remember, we're drawing the shapes on widgets that are placed in a 4 x 4 grid. At this moment there is only one cell, but when we add another widget with a shape drawn on it, each of the two will take the same amount of space. So, let's draw a filled ellipse.

## Drawing an Ellipse

In order to draw an ellipse we need the **`Ellipse`** class. On the instance we can set a couple properties, but in this first example we'll just set **`pos`** and **`size`**, just like with the rectangle. This time we're going to draw the shape on a button. Here's the code:

```
#:kivy 1.11.1
# File name: test.kv

### A 4x4 GRIDLAYOUT WHERE WE ARE GOING TO DRAW SHAPES ###
...
    # Shape 1 - A Rectangle on a BoxLayout
    ...
```

```
    # Shape 2 - An Ellipse on a Button
    Button:
        canvas:
            Ellipse:
                pos: self.center_x - 50, self.center_y - 25
                size: 100, 60
```

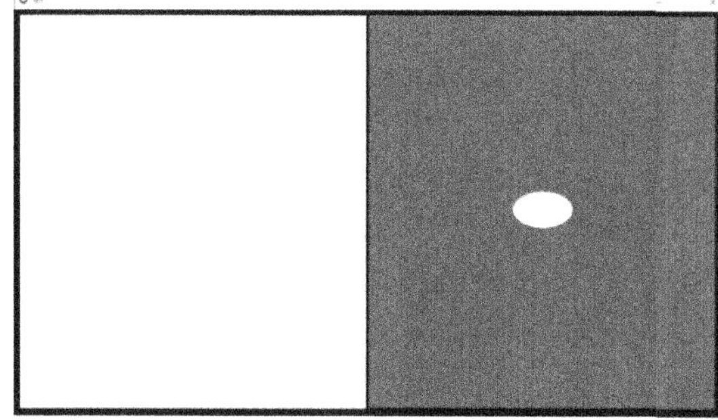

If you run this code now, you will see two widgets: the BoxLayout that we added before and the button we added just now. Each of them occupies half the available space.

## Drawing a Triangle

In Kivy ellipses are not real ellipses, they consist of many short segments which make them look like ellipses. If you reduce the number of segments, you can obtain interesting shapes. For example, if you reduce the number of segments to 3, you will get a triangle. To do so, you should just set the **segments** property to **3**. So, let's add a label with a triangle on it:

```
#:kivy 1.11.1
# File name: test.kv

### A 4x4 GRIDLAYOUT WHERE WE ARE GOING TO DRAW SHAPES ###
...
    # Shape 1 - A Rectangle on a BoxLayout
    ...
    # Shape 2 - An Ellipse on a Button
    ...
    # Shape 3 - A Triangle on a Label
    Label:
        canvas:
            Ellipse:
                segments: 3
                pos: self.x, self.y
                size: self.width - 10, self.height - 10
```

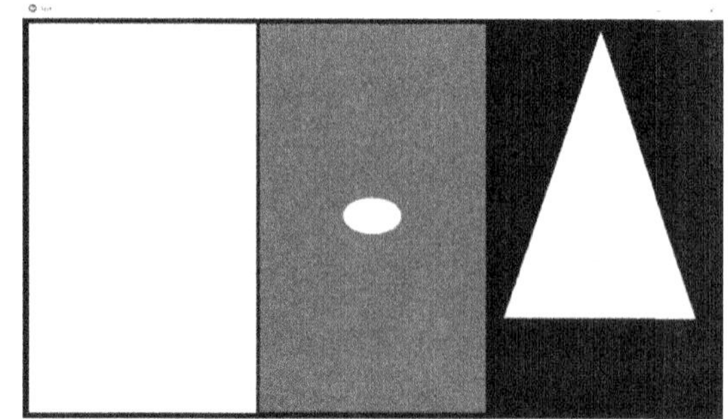

Run the app and watch the triangle in the third column.

## Drawing a Hexagon

In a similar way you can draw other polygons, like pentagons, hexagons, etc. Let's draw a hexagon on a button:

```
#:kivy 1.11.1
# File name: test.kv

### A 4x4 GRIDLAYOUT WHERE WE ARE GOING TO DRAW SHAPES ###
...
    # Shape 4 - A Hexagon on a Button
    Button:
        canvas:
            Ellipse:
                segments: 6
                pos: self.x, self.y
                size: self.width - 10, self.height - 10
```

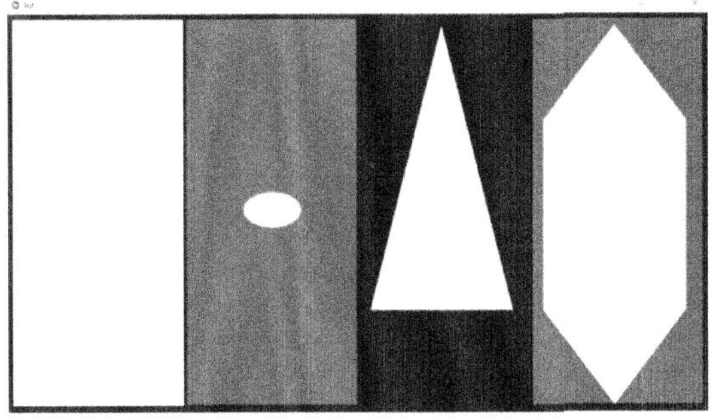

If you now run the app, you will see it sitting in the fourth column of the GridLayout.

## Drawing a Segment of a Circle

And now let's draw a segment of a circle. First of all, a circle is an ellipse with the width equal to the height. Second, in order to draw a segment of a circle or an ellipse in general, you need to use two properties that specify two angles: **angle_start** and **angle_end**. The former tells the program where the ellipse begins, the latter where it ends. First let's see it in action and then I'll comment on it briefly.

We're going to draw two circle segments on a label this time. As you know, you can draw as many shapes on a widget as you like. Here's the code:

```
#:kivy 1.11.1
# File name: test.kv

### A 4x4 GRIDLAYOUT WHERE WE ARE GOING TO DRAW SHAPES ###
...
    # Shape 5 - Two Circle Segments on a Label
    Label:
        canvas:
            Ellipse:
                angle_start: 90
                angle_end: 360
                pos: self.x, self.y
                size: 80, 80
            Ellipse:
                angle_start: 270
                angle_end: 540
                pos: self.x + 40, self.y + 40
                size: 80, 80
```

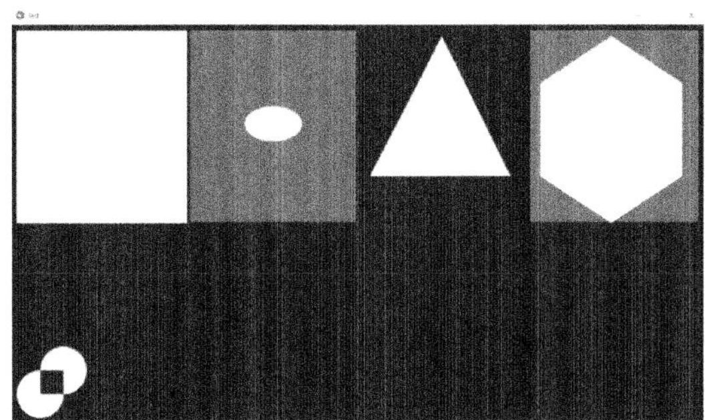

By the way, we're moving to the next row of our 4 by 4 grid. Looks nice, but why does it look the way it does? Let's have a look at these shapes in more detail, and in particular at how the angles work:

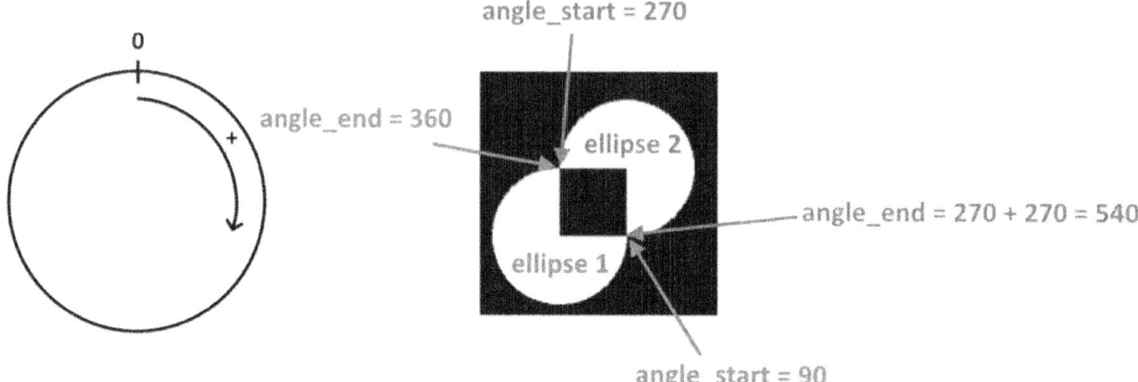


The angle 0° is on 12 o'clock, so to speak. The angle increases in clockwise direction. So, here are the two circles:

ellipse 1:

- **`angle_start`** = **`90`** (here the ellipse begins, not the empty part)

- **`angle_end`** = **`360`** (here the ellipse ends)

ellipse 2:

- **`angle_start`** = **`270`** (here the ellipse begins)

- **`angle_end`** = **`540`** (90 degrees left to the next 12 o'clock position and then 180 degrees to the end)

So, now we have five filled shapes. There's one more to draw, a rounded rectangle, but I think I'll leave it as an exercise for you. In the next chapter we're going to draw lines, irregular triangles, quadrilaterals, points, Bezier curves, meshes and arcs of a circle.

# It's Your Turn Now...

### EXERCISE

In this exercise your task is to draw two rounded rectangles on a BoxLayout, so rectangles with rounded corners. Use the **`RoundedRectangle`** class. You can specify its position and size just like that of a regular rectangle.

To make a corner rounded you have to specify its radius, using the **radius** property. There are a couple ways to do it. Read the instructions for more information. Here they are:

1. The first rounded rectangle should be positioned at the origin of the BoxLayout and be one third its width and height. It should have the radius of all four corners set to **20**. The value of the radius is passed as a list. If the radius of all four corners is the same, there's just one value in the list.

2. The second rounded rectagle should be positioned 100 px to the right of the left border of the BoxLayout and should sit on its bottom border. It should be the same size as the first rectangle. This time each corner should have a different radius, so the radius property should be set to a list of four values. The order of the radii is: top-left, top-right, bottom-right, bottom-left. Set the radii to **2**, **5**, **20** and **40** respectively.

### SOLUTION

Here's the code:

```
#:kivy 1.11.1
# File name: test.kv

### A 4x4 GRIDLAYOUT WHERE WE ARE GOING TO DRAW SHAPES ###
...
    # Shape 6 - Rounded Rectangles on a BoxLayout
    BoxLayout:
        canvas:
            RoundedRectangle:
                pos: self.x, self.y
                size: self.width / 3, self.height / 3
                radius: [10]
            RoundedRectangle:
                pos: self.x + 100, self.y
                size: self.width / 3, self.height / 3
                radius: [2, 5, 20, 40]
```

Run the app and look at the rounded rectangles you added.

As you can see, the first one has all corners rounded the same whereas in the second one all corners are different.

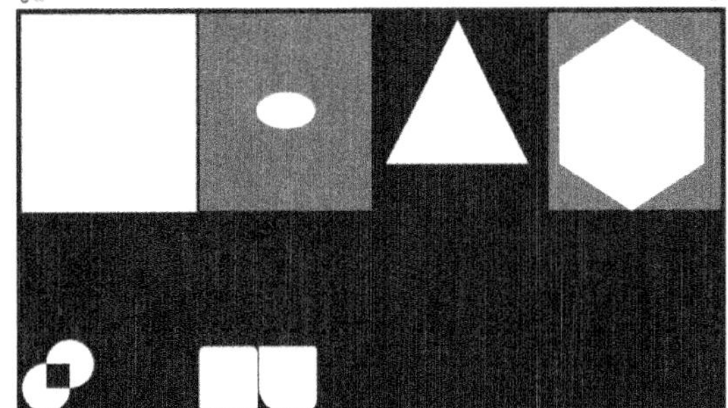

# Chapter 48 - Drawing Lines, Curves and Other Point-Defined Shapes

In the previous chapter we were drawing filled shapes on widgets. In this chapter we're going to add some more shapes, but this time they will be all defined by the points they consist of. In particular, we're going to draw lines, irregular triangles and quadrilaterals, points, Bezier curves, meshes and arcs of a circle.

To save space and make the shapes more visible, I'm going to only show you the particular widgets with the shapes on them, not the whole screenshots like I did in the previous chapter.

## Drawing Lines

Let's start with a line, or better three lines. A line is basically a sequence of points. Each point is a pair of X and Y coordinates. We can also specify the **width** property of the line, as well as a couple other properties like **cap** or **joint**. If you want to close the line, just set the **close** property to **True**.

So, we will draw the three lines on a button. We need the **Line** class to do that. As before, we'll be using point coordinates relative to the button.

The first line will be a default line, connecting the points that we specify in the **points** property.

The second line will be wider, and we will use round caps. Although the default value of the **cap** property is **'round'**, we will specify it explicitly anyway so that you can see how. Alternatively you could set the value to **'square'** or **'none'**. We will set the **joint** property to **'none'**.

The third line will be very much like the second one, but this time we'll set the **joint** property to **'bevel'** and we will close the line:

```
#:kivy 1.11.1
# File name: test.kv

### A 4x4 GRIDLAYOUT WHERE WE ARE GOING TO DRAW SHAPES ###
...
    # Shape 7 - Lines on a Button
    Button:
        canvas:
            Line:
                points: self.x + 20, self.y + 20, self.x + 120, self.y + 40, self.x + 150, self.y + 10

            Line:
                points: self.x + 20, self.y + 70, self.x + 120, self.y + 90, self.x + 150, self.y + 60
                width: 6
                cap: 'round'
                joint: 'none'
```

```
            Line:
                points: self.x + 20, self.y + 120, self.x + 120, self.y + 140, self.x + 150, self.y + 110
                width: 6
                joint: 'bevel'
                close: True
```

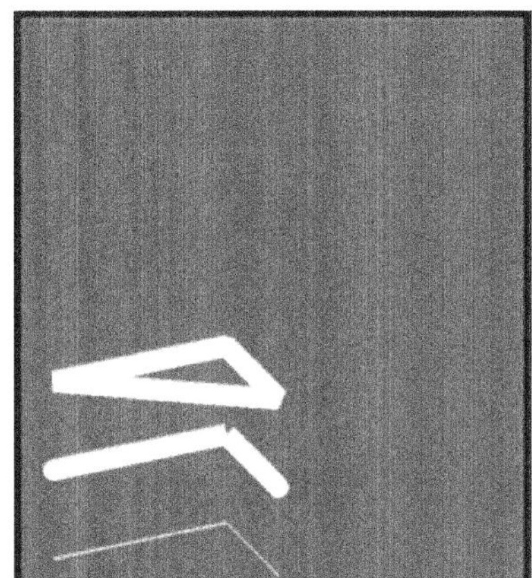

As you can see, the first line (at the bottom) is pretty thin. It consists of three points, the coordinates of which are relative to the coordinates of the button.

The second and third lines also consist of three points each, which are connected to form segments. These two lines are thicker. Watch the rounded caps in the second line and the joints in the second and third line.

# Drawing Irregular Triangles

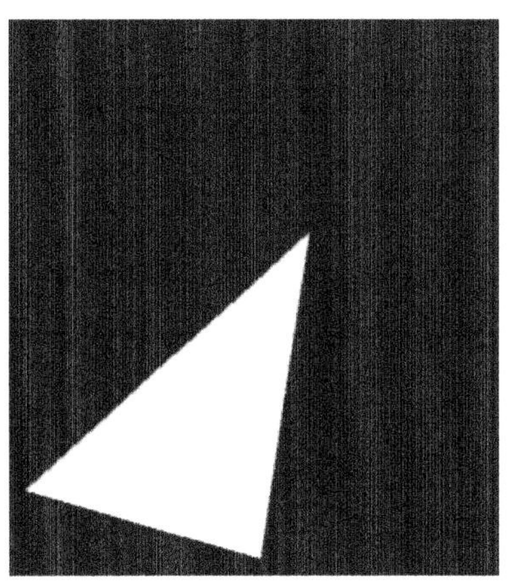

There are also other shapes that you can draw using points.

For example, you can draw triangles of any kind. You just pass the coordinates of the three corners of the triangle.

Have a look at this one:

```
#:kivy 1.11.1
# File name: test.kv

### A 4x4 GRIDLAYOUT WHERE WE ARE GOING TO DRAW SHAPES ###
...
    # Shape 8 - A Triangle on a BoxLayout
    BoxLayout:
        canvas:
            Triangle:
                points: self.x + 10, self.y + 50, self.x + 150, self.y + 10, self.x + 180, self.y + 200
```

# Drawing Quadrilaterals

In a similar way you can draw quadrilaterals, or quads for short. Just pass the X, Y – coordinates of the corners:

```
#:kivy 1.11.1
# File name: test.kv

### A 4x4 GRIDLAYOUT WHERE WE ARE GOING TO DRAW SHAPES ###
...
    # Shape 9 - A Quad on a Slider
```

```
    Slider:
        canvas:
            Quad:
                points: self.x + 20, self.y + 10, self.x + 25, self.y + 90, self.x + 140,
self.y + 170, self.x + 170, self.y + 50
```

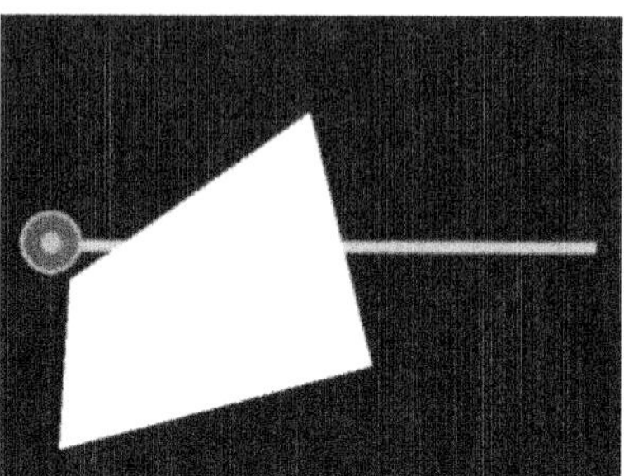

In the code above the coordinates are all on a single line.

This time I drew the shape on a slider so that you can see that it's also possible. By the way, try moving the slider from left to right or from right to left and you will see that the shape is indeed on top of the slider.

# Drawing Points

You can also draw single points using the **points** property. You can set the size of the points as well. In the code below we're going to create two sets of points: three points with the default point size and three bigger ones. All you have to do is pass the X, Y coordinates of the points:

```
#:kivy 1.11.1
# File name: test.kv

### A 4x4 GRIDLAYOUT WHERE WE ARE GOING TO DRAW SHAPES ###
...
    # Shape 10 - Points on a Button
    Button:
        canvas:
            Point:
                points: self.x + 50, self.y + 10, self.x + 100, self.y + 10, self.x + 150, self.y + 10
            Point:
                points: self.x + 50, self.y + 40, self.x + 100, self.y + 40, self.x + 150, self.y + 40
                pointsize: 5
```

# Drawing a Bezier Curve

Next, we're going to draw some Bezier curves. This shape uses the **points** property to define its attractors. The attractors are points, which attract the curve, but don't touch it (except for the first and last one). A more detailed explanation of Bezier curves is outside the scope of this article, you can find plenty of information about them online, so let's just jump into the code. We're going to create three curves. The first one will be a simple one, the second one will be a 'low-resolution' one, consisting of only 10 segments and the third one will be dashed. For the dashes we use the **dash_length** and **dash_offset** properties:

```
#:kivy 1.11.1
# File name: test.kv

### A 4x4 GRIDLAYOUT WHERE WE ARE GOING TO DRAW SHAPES ###
...
    # Shape 11 - Bezier Curves on a Button
    Button:
        canvas:
            Bezier:
                points: self.x + 20, self.y + 10, self.x + 25, self.y + 90, self.x + 140, self.y + 170, self.x + 1
70, self.y + 50
            Bezier:
                points: self.x + 20, self.y + 60, self.x + 60, self.y + 140, self.x + 20, self.y + 210, self.x + 1
00, self.y + 220
                segments: 10
            Bezier:
                points: self.x + 20, self.y + 90, self.x + 20, self.y + 150, self.x + 80, self.y + 230, self.x + 2
00, self.y + 90
                segments: 200
                dash_length: 10
                dash_offset: 15
```

Just remember to keep all the coordinates of each curve on a single line.

## Drawing a Mesh

The next shape is a mesh. It's a compound of triangles. Again, if you're interested, you can read more about meshes in the documentation. Here it's enough to say that a mesh consists of vertices, which are drawn in a specific order. The **vertices** property takes the X, Y, U, V coordinates, so you need four numbers for each vertex. The U and V are texture coordinates and we're going to set them to **0** in our example to keep things simple.

The **indices** property specifies the order in which the mesh is drawn. The **mode** property is used to tell the program how to draw the vertices. The **mode** property may be set to **'points'** if you want the vertices to be represented as separate points, **'line_strip'** if you want them to be connected with lines or **'triangle-fan'** if you want the mesh to be filled with color, like in our example. There are also some other modes available. Here's the code:

```
#:kivy 1.11.1
# File name: test.kv

### A 4x4 GRIDLAYOUT WHERE WE ARE GOING TO DRAW SHAPES ###
...
    # Shape 12 - A Mesh on a BoxLayout
    BoxLayout:
        canvas:
            Mesh:
                mode: 'triangle_fan'
                vertices: self.x + 80, self.y + 50, 0, 0, self.x + 20, self.y + 50, 0, 0, self.x + 40, self.y + 10
, 0, 0, self.x + 100, self.y + 10, 0, 0, self.x + 140, self.y + 120, 0, 0
                indices: 0, 1, 2, 3, 4
```

The last shape we're going to draw in this chapter is an arc of a circle. But this is going to be an exercise for you. In the next chapter we'll continue adding shapes to our GridLayout, this time just borders of shapes.

# It's Your Turn Now...

### EXERCISE

To draw a circle we use the **Line** class with the **circle** property, which specifies the X and Y coordinates of the center of the circle, followed by **radius**, **angle_start**, **angle_end** and **segments**. We already used the **angle_start** and **angle_end** properties when we were drawing a segment of an ellipse, so if you need a refresher, go back to the previous chapter and check it out.

Anyway, the circle you are going to draw will be on a label, 100 px to the right of the left border of the label and 70 px above its bottom border. The radius should be set to 60.

And now imagine the face of the clock. The arc should go from the 2 o'clock position to the 6 o'clock position. Just remember that the 12 o'clock position corresponds to 0 degrees and the angles are measured in clockwise direction. Set the angle_start and angle_end properties accordingly.

The arc should consist of 20 segments. Finally, make sure the arc is a bit wider than the default value. A width of 3 will be fine.

### SOLUTION

Here's the code:

```
#:kivy 1.11.1
# File name: test.kv

### A 4x4 GRIDLAYOUT WHERE WE ARE GOING TO DRAW SHAPES ##
#
...
    # Shape 13 - An Arc of a Circle on a Label
    Label:
        canvas:
            Line:
                # The 2 o'clock position corresponds to 60 degrees
                # and the 6 o'clock position to 180 degrees.
                circle: self.x + 100, self.y + 70, 60, 60, 180, 20
                width: 3
```

At this point our app window looks like this:

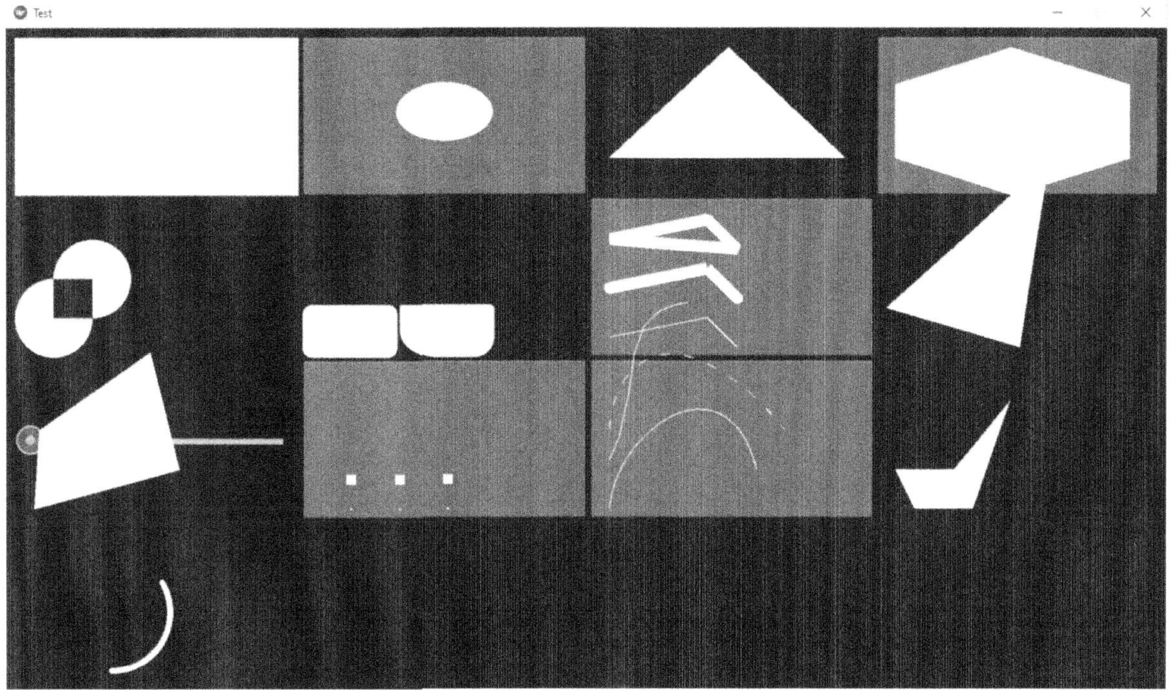

# Chapter 49 - Drawing Just the Borders of Shapes

In the two previous chapters we were drawing shapes on widgets placed in a GridLayout. These were filled shapes or shapes defined by points. In this chapter we'll be drawing just the borders of shapes.

If you don't want a shape to be filled in, so you need just the border of the shape, you should use the **Line** class with appropriate properties, just like we used the **Line** class with the **circle** property to draw the arc of a circle.

## Drawing the Border of a Rounded Rectangle

Let's start by drawing the border of a rounded rectangle. This is actually the shape that we will use to decorate the areas or panels in our project, like the Game Info panel in the Race screen or the Ending Conditions area in the Settings screen, to mention just a few.

To draw a rounded rectangle we use the **Line** class with the **rounded_rectangle** property. The **rounded_rectangle** property specifies the X and Y coordinates, the width and height of the rounded rectangle and the radius. Again, you can either set one radius for all corners or a separate radius for each corner. You can also specify how many segments should be used to draw the circle arc at each corner, but we will not use this property here.

So, let's draw a rounded rectangle on a button. It should be positioned 80 px to the right of the left border of the button and 20 px above its bottom border. Both the width and height should be 120 px, which will make it a rounded square. We will set the radii of all the corners to **20**.

Besides, we will also use the **width** property on the **Line** object to make the shape more visible. Here's the code:

```
#:kivy 1.11.1
# File name: test.kv

### A 4x4 GRIDLAYOUT WHERE WE ARE GOING TO DRAW SHAPES ###
...
    # Shape 14 - The Border of a Rounded Rectangle on a Button
    Button:
        canvas:
            Line:
                rounded_rectangle: self.x + 80, self.y + 20, 120, 120, 20
                width: 3
```

# Drawing the Border of a Decagon

The last but one shape we're going to draw is the border of a decagon. A decagon is a ten-sided polygon. We can do it using the **Line** class and the **circle** property that we already know. All we have to do to convert the circle into a decagon is set the number of segments to **10**. We're going to use the **circle** property with five arguments: the X and Y coordinates of the center of the circle, the radius, **angle_start**, **angle_end** and the number of segments. We're going to position the center of the circle in the center of the label. Here's the code:

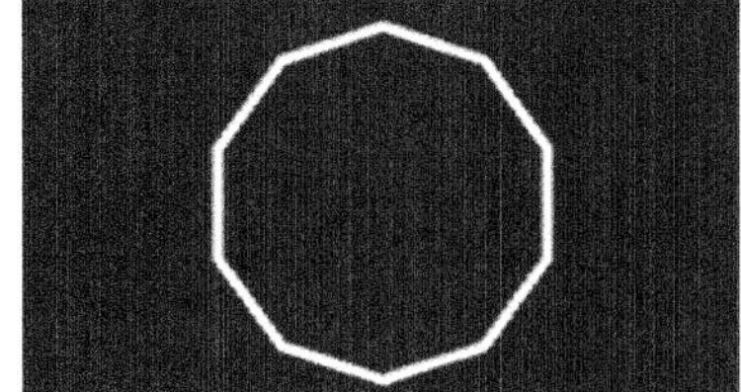

```
#:kivy 1.11.1
# File name: test.kv

### A 4x4 GRIDLAYOUT WHERE WE ARE GOING TO DRAW SHAPES ###
...
    # Shape 15 - A Decagon on a Label
    Label:
        canvas:
            Line:
                circle: self.center_x, self.center_y, 70, 0, 360, 10
                width: 2
```

There is one more shape to draw. As you might have guessed, it's an exercise for you. This one is going to be slightly more complex. And in the next chapter we'll see how to use vertex instructions in Python code.

# It's Your Turn Now...

### EXERCISE

Your task is to draw a smiley on a label, something like the one in the picture on the right. Follow the instructions:

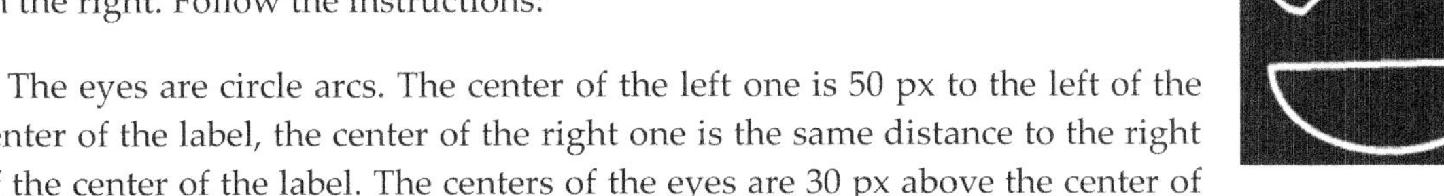

1. The eyes are circle arcs. The center of the left one is 50 px to the left of the center of the label, the center of the right one is the same distance to the right of the center of the label. The centers of the eyes are 30 px above the center of the label. Each eye has a radius of 20 px. You can set the **angle_start** and **angle_end** properties yourself, just look at the image. Here each circle is used with five arguments: the X and Y coordinates of the center of the circle, the radius, **angle_start** and **angle_end**. Remember to set the widths of the lines to **2** and close them.

2. The mouth is a semi-ellipse. To draw it you need a **Line** object again, but this time with the **ellipse** property with the following arguments: X and Y coordinates of the bottom left of the

ellipse, the width and height of the ellipse, **angle_start** and **angle_end**. By looking at the image and taking the positions and radii of the eyes into consideration, you can easily calculate the X coordinate of the bottom left of the ellipse and the width of the ellipse. The Y coordinate should be 70 px below the center of the label and the height should be 100 px. The **angle_start** and **angle_end** are also easy to figure out. Again, remember to set the width of the line to **2** and close it.

## SOLUTION

Here's the code:

```
#:kivy 1.11.1
# File name: test.kv

### A 4x4 GRIDLAYOUT WHERE WE ARE GOING TO DRAW SHAPES ###
...
    # Shape 16 - A Smiley on a Label
    Label:
        canvas:
            Line:
                circle: self.center_x - 50, self.center_y + 30, 20, 180, 450
                width: 2
                close: True
            Line:
                circle: self.center_x + 50, self.center_y + 30, 20, 270, 540
                width: 2
                close: True
            Line:
                ellipse: self.center_x - 70, self.center_y - 70, 140, 100, 90, 270
                width: 2
                close: True
```

And here's our grid with all 16 widgets with the shapes on them, the last one being the smiley you just drew.

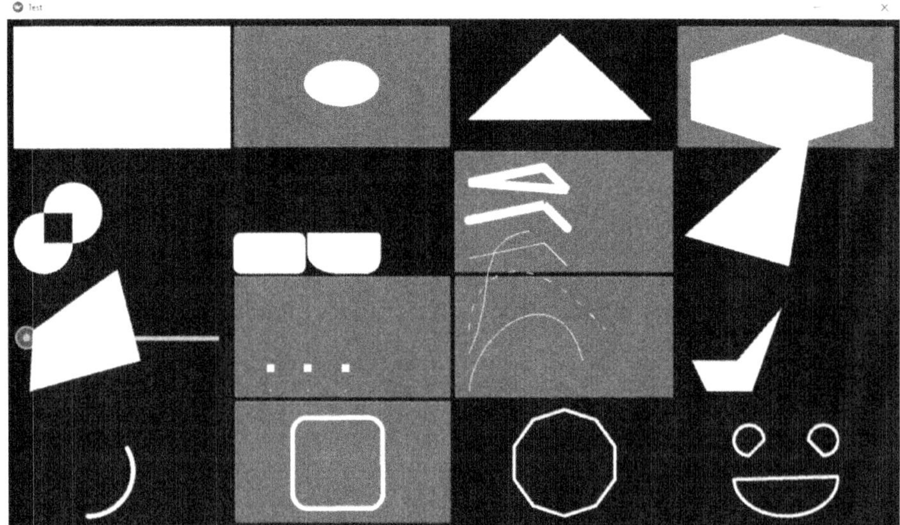

# Chapter 50 - Vertex Instructions in Python Code

In the preceding chapters we were drawing shapes on widgets. In this chapter we'll see how to do the same thing using just Python, so without the Kivy language.

As you know, you can make Kivy apps using just Python, although I think this way we're not making things easier. If you add vertex instructions in the kv file, they are automatically updated when any property they depend on changes. In Python, you have to take care of it yourself. This is why it's more convenient to add the instructions in kv code. However, I think you should be able to do it in Python too, so I decided to add this chapter.

To start with, let's create a simple app with just one widget using both Python and kv. Then we'll re-create it exclusively in Python. We'll be using the two test files again.

In this example we'll define a custom widget and draw an ellipse on it. Make sure your **test.py** file looks like this:

```
# File name: test.py

from kivy.config import Config
Config.set('graphics', 'width', '1200')
Config.set('graphics', 'height', '675')
Config.set('graphics', 'resizable', '1')

import kivy
kivy.require('1.11.1')
from kivy.app import App

# We need the Widget class.
from kivy.uix.widget import Widget

# Let's create a custom widget that
# inherits from the Widget class.
class CustomWidget(Widget):
    pass

class TestApp(App):
    def build(self):
        return CustomWidget()

if __name__ == '__main__':
    TestApp().run()
```

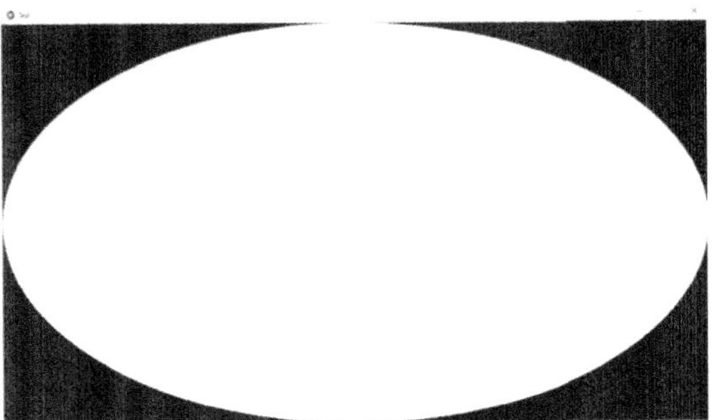

Remove all the code from the **test.kv** file and type in the following:

```
#:kivy 1.11.1
# File name: test.kv

<CustomWidget>:
    canvas:
        Ellipse:
            pos: self.pos
            size: self.size
```

There isn't anything new about it. When you run the app, you will see the widget with the ellipse on it. If you resize the window, the properties of the ellipse, which depend on the properties of the widget, will adjust themselves – the ellipse will always be the size of the widget.

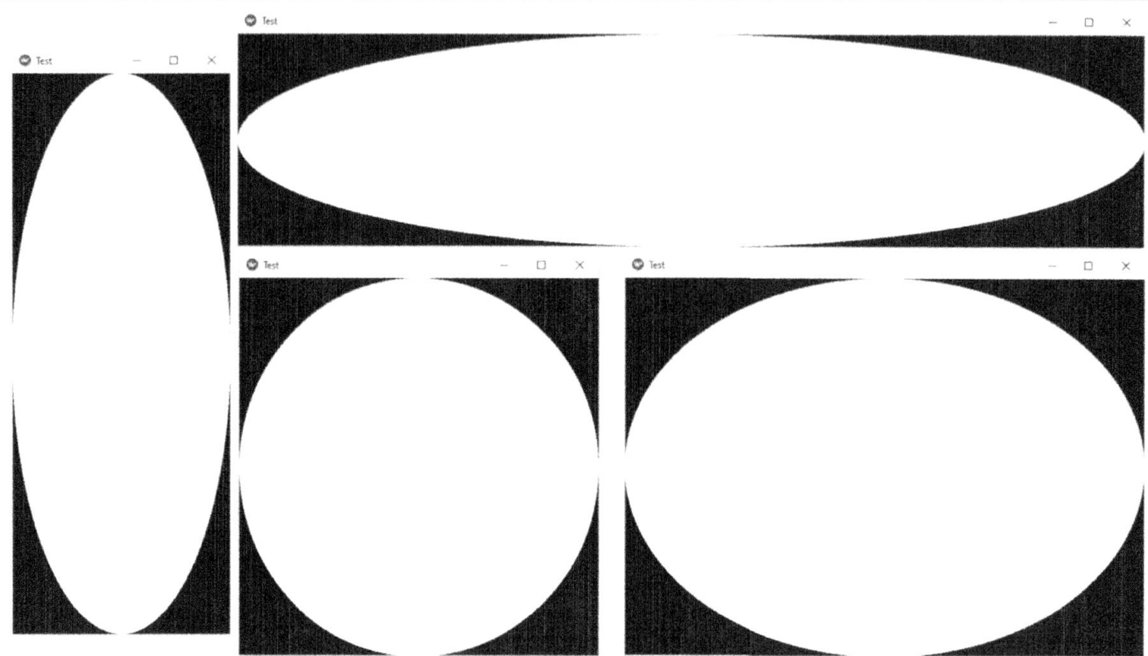

And now let's remove all the code from the kv file and try to re-create the same widget with the same ellipse on it in Python. Let's start with something like this:

```
# File name: test.py
...
from kivy.uix.widget import Widget

# We need the Ellipse class to draw the shape.
from kivy.graphics import Ellipse

class CustomWidget(Widget):
    def __init__(self, **kwargs):
        super().__init__(**kwargs)
        self.canvas.add(Ellipse(pos=self.pos, size=self.size))

class TestApp(App):
    def build(self):
        return CustomWidget()
...
```

If we now run the app, we see a different ellipse, which is not what we might have expected.

If we want the ellipse to adjust itself to the properties of the widget, we must take care of it ourselves. We haven't talked about Kivy property binding in Python code, so don't worry if you don't fully understand what the code below is all about. This will become clearer after we discuss this subject later in the course. To be brief, though, this code will make the ellipse react to the changing values of the widget's properties. What I want you to pay attention to is rather how we add the ellipse to the canvas instructions in Python. Here's the code with explanations in the comments:

```
# File name: test.py
...
class CustomWidget(Widget):
    def __init__(self, **kwargs):
        super().__init__(**kwargs)

        # Whenever the pos or size property of the widget changes, the update_canvas
        # method should be called.
        self.bind(pos=self.update_canvas)
        self.bind(size=self.update_canvas)

        # We also want to call the update_canvas right away when the widget is created.
        self.update_canvas()

    # Now we have to define the update_canvas method.
    def update_canvas(self, *args):

        # We must remove everything from canvas or otherwise what we added before
        # will remain.
        self.canvas.clear()

        # Now we can add the ellipse.
        self.canvas.add(Ellipse(pos=self.pos, size=self.size))

class TestApp(App):
    def build(self):
        return CustomWidget()

if __name__ == '__main__':
    TestApp().run()
```

Now, if you run the app, it should work like before, also when you resize the window.

# Using a Context Manager

In the code above we added the ellipse directly, like so:

```
self.canvas.add(Ellipse(pos=self.pos, size=self.size))
```

We usually use a context manager to do it, so we use the **with** statement. Here's how we usually write code like that:

```
with self.canvas:
    Ellipse(pos=self.pos, size=self.size)
```

So, using a context manager we could rewrite the Python file like this:

```
# File name: test.py
...
class CustomWidget(Widget):
    def __init__(self, **kwargs):
        ...

    def update_canvas(self, *args):
        self.canvas.clear()

        # Let's use a context manager.
        with self.canvas:
            Ellipse(pos=self.pos, size=self.size)

class TestApp(App):
    ...
```

Whether you use a context manager or add objects directly to the canvas, you must admit that doing it in the Kivy language is much more comfortable. That's why we're going to do it there in the book. In the next chapter we'll draw some shapes on some of the widgets in our project screens. In particular we'll draw rounded rectangles to visually separate all the different areas or panels within each of the screens. And now, just for practice, do the exercise below.

# It's Your Turn Now...

### EXERCISE

Modify the Python file so that instead of an ellipse a filled rounded rectangle is drawn. It should be half the width and one third the height of the widget. Position it 20 px to the right of the widget's left border and the same amount above the bottom border. The radius of each corner should be 10% of the widget's width, so that it will change when you resize the window. Remember to import the **RoundedRectangle** class from **kivy.graphics**. Use a context manager to add the rounded rectangle to the canvas.

HINT: Remember to use a list to set the radius.

## SOLUTION

Here's the code:

```
# File name: test.py
...
from kivy.uix.widget import Widget

# We need the RoundedRectangle class.
from kivy.graphics import RoundedRectangle

class CustomWidget(Widget):
    def __init__(self, **kwargs):
        ...

    def update_canvas(self, *args):
        self.canvas.clear()

        with self.canvas:
            RoundedRectangle(pos = (self.x + 20, self.y + 20),
                             size = (self.width / 2, self.height / 3),
                             radius = [self.width / 10])

class TestApp(App):
    ...
```

If you now run the app, you will see the rounded rectangle.

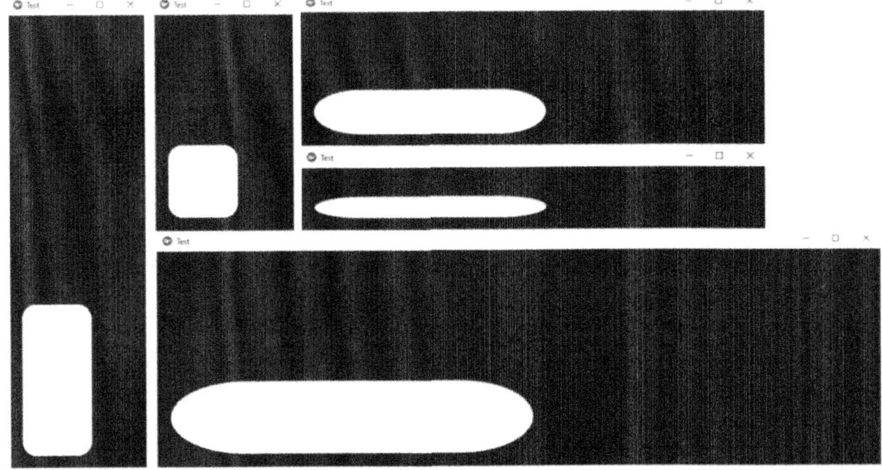

And now play with the window size.

When you resize the window, the radii of the corners should change accordingly.

# Chapter 51 - Adding Shapes to the Project Screens

In the preceding chapters we were talking about drawing all sorts of shapes on widgets. We know how to draw ellipses, rectangles, lines, polygons, and many, many more on all sorts of widgets, including layouts. In this chapter we'll make use of this knowledge to add some simple shapes to our Slugrace GUI.

## Rounded Rectangles in Settings Screen

Let's start with the Settings screen. Let's add two rounded rectangles (just the borders, without filling them in). Just a quick reminder from one of the previous chapters. Here's the kv code we used to draw a rounded rectangle:

```
# Shape 14 - The Border of a Rounded Rectangle on a Button
Button:
    canvas:
        Line:
            rounded_rectangle: self.x + 100, self.y + 10, 30, 90, 10
            width: 3
```

Now we can use this code in the **settings.kv** file. Actually, we're going to create two rounded rectangles, one around the Players area and one around the Ending Conditions area. In the image on the left you can see what the screen looks like now, before adding the rounded rectangles.

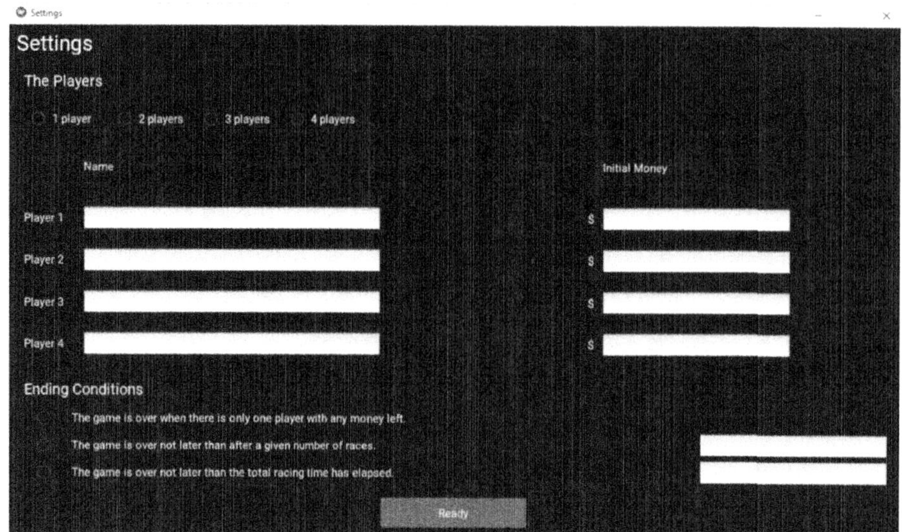


The areas are implemented as BoxLayouts, so we have to add canvas vertex instructions to the BoxLayouts. The radius of each corner should be set to **10** (it's the last argument that we pass to the **rounded_rectangle** property of the **Line** object). And here's the code to add the two rounded rectangles:

```
#:kivy 1.11.1
# File name: settings.kv
...
<SettingsScreen>:
    ...
    ### THE PLAYERS ###
    BoxLayout:
        canvas:
            Line:
                rounded_rectangle: self.x, self.y, self.width, self.height, 10
                width: 2

        orientation: 'vertical'
        ...

    ### ENDING CONDITIONS ###
    BoxLayout:
        canvas:
            Line:
                rounded_rectangle: self.x, self.y, self.width, self.height, 10
                width: 2

        orientation: 'vertical'
        ...
```

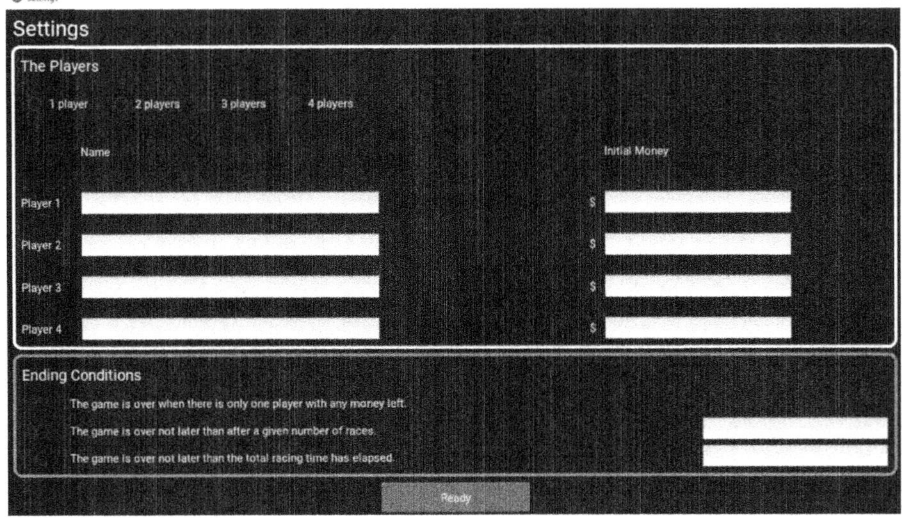


If you now run the code with these changes in place, you will see the two rounded rectangles.

Don't worry about the colors for now. What matters is that we have the two rounded rectangles.

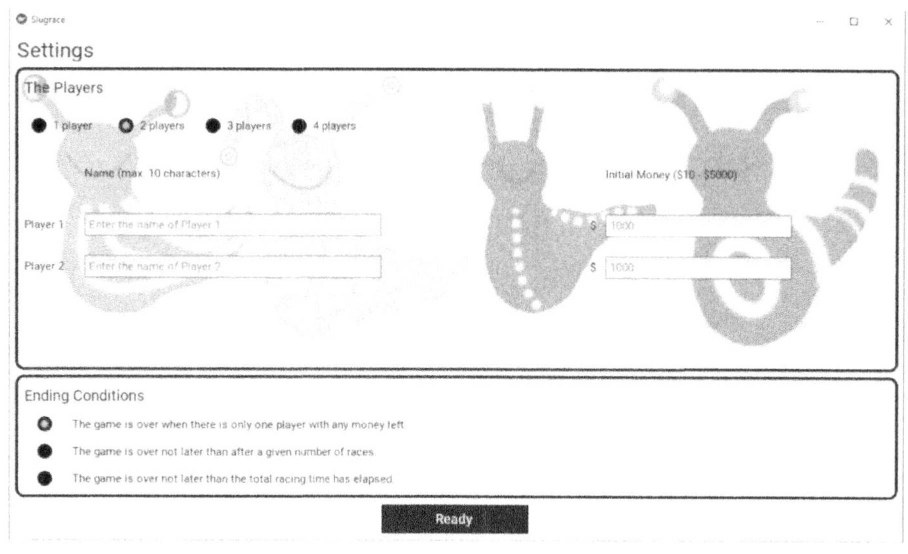


Now we are just a little bit closer to the final version of the screen, which you can see on the left.

And now let's add rounded rectangles to the Race screen, too. Actually, I'll leave it as an exercise for you.

And in the next chapter we'll start our discussion of canvas context instructions that we will use, among other things, to add colors.

# It's Your Turn Now...

## EXERCISE

You are now going to draw rounded rectangles in the Race screen that visually separate the main areas of the screen.

At this moment the screen looks pretty basic.

Follow carefully the instructions below.

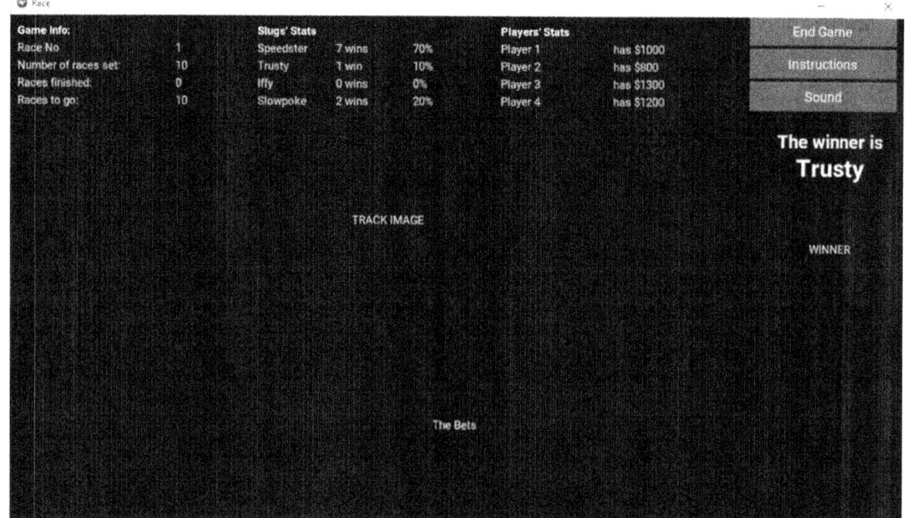

But first have a look at the final version of the screen so that you can clearly see the five rounded rectangles.

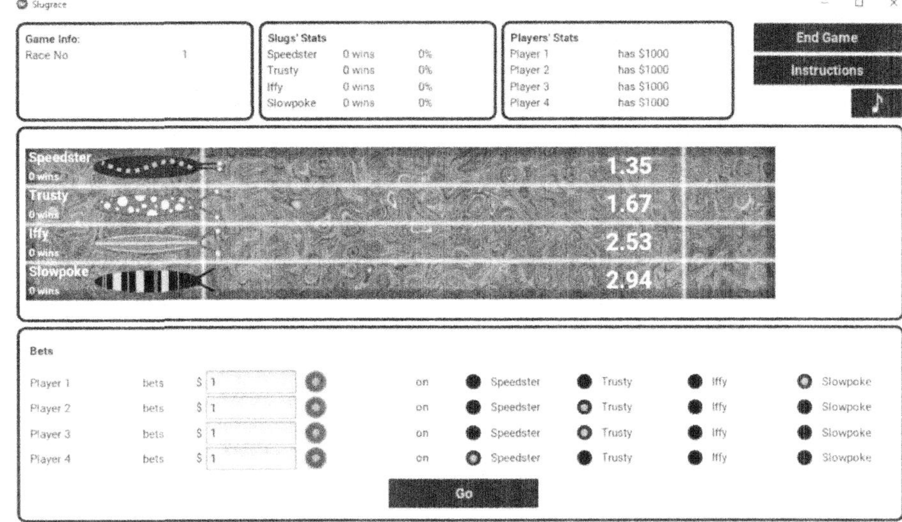


So, now that you know what we want to achieve, let's jump right in. Here are the instructions:

1. The three smaller rounded rectangles should surround the Game Info panel, the Slugs' Stats panel and the Players' Stats panel. Each of these areas is implemented as a BoxLayout, so find them one by one and add canvas vertex instructions to draw a rounded rectangle on each of them. Each of the rectangles should be positioned at the origin of the BoxLayout it's drawn on and be the same size (width and height). Each corner should have a radius of `10`. The width of the line should be set to `2`.

2. Then come the two bigger rounded rectangles. The first one should be drawn around the Track area, which is implemented as a BoxLayout. The other should be drawn around the label that we're temporarily using as the placeholder for the Bets screen. Just like before, each of the rectangles should be positioned at the origin of the widget it's drawn on and be the same size (width and height). Each corner should have a radius of `10`. The width of the line should be set to `2`.

3. If you did everything correctly up to this point and if you now run the app, you should see the rounded rectangles around the particular areas, but they are a little tight. So, add some spacing and padding. First add 10 px of padding and the same amount of spacing to the root widget. Then, in the GridLayout that contains the Info, Stats and Buttons area you can see that the **`spacing`** property is set to `4`. Increase the value to `10`. Also the three buttons are a little too close to the top border. This area has the **`padding`** property set to `10`, which adds the padding on all sides, pushing the buttons too far in the upward direction. Considering the size of the window, they will look better without any padding, so just remove the **`padding`** property completely from the BoxLayout in which the Buttons area is implemented. Now the Race screen should look better.

## SOLUTION

Here's the code:

```
#:kivy 1.11.1
# File name: race.kv
...
<RaceScreen>:
    orientation: 'vertical'
    spacing: 10
    padding: 10

    ### INFO, STATS AND BUTTONS ###
    GridLayout:
        cols: 4
        size_hint: 1, .5
        spacing: 10

        # Game Info
        BoxLayout:
            canvas:
                Line:
                    rounded_rectangle: self.x, self.y, self.width, self.height, 10
                    width: 2

            orientation: 'vertical'
            ...
        # Slugs' Stats
        BoxLayout:
            canvas:
                Line:
                    rounded_rectangle: self.x, self.y, self.width, self.height, 10
                    width: 2

            orientation: 'vertical'
            ...
        # Players' Stats
        BoxLayout:
            canvas:
                Line:
                    rounded_rectangle: self.x, self.y, self.width, self.height, 10
                    width: 2

            orientation: 'vertical'
            ...
        # Buttons
        BoxLayout:
            orientation: 'vertical'
            spacing: 3
            # padding: 10
            size_hint: .7, 1
            ...
    ### THE TRACK ###
```

```
    BoxLayout:
        canvas:
            Line:
                rounded_rectangle: self.x, self.y, self.width, self.height, 10
                width: 2

        padding: 10
        ...
    ### THE BETS ###
    Label:
        canvas:
            Line:
                rounded_rectangle: self.x, self.y, self.width, self.height, 10
                width: 2

        text: 'The Bets'
```

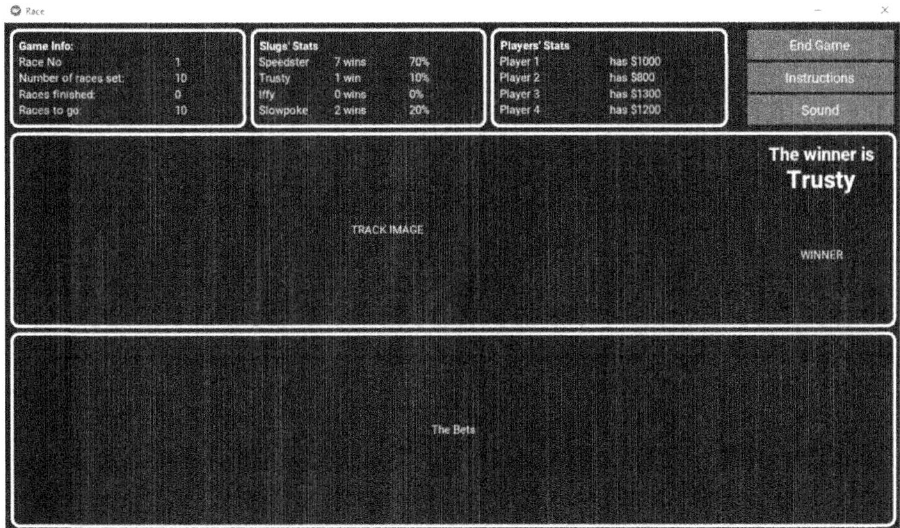


If you now run the app (from the **race.py** file), the Race screen should look pretty decent.

# Chapter 52 - Canvas Context Instructions – the Color Instruction

Over a couple preceding chapters we've been drawing shapes on widgets. But they were all white. As there are other colors out there to choose from, let's see how to make the shapes red, blue or any other color you may wish.

First of all, let's draw some shapes. We're going to use our test files again. Make sure your **test.py** file looks like so:

```
# File name: test.py

from kivy.config import Config
Config.set('graphics', 'width', '1200')
Config.set('graphics', 'height', '675')
Config.set('graphics', 'resizable', '1')

import kivy
kivy.require('1.11.1')
from kivy.app import App
from kivy.uix.floatlayout import FloatLayout

class TestLayout(FloatLayout):
    pass

class TestApp(App):
    def build(self):
        return TestLayout()

if __name__ == '__main__':
    TestApp().run()
```

This is a very simple setup with a subclass of **FloatLayout** as the root widget. Now, in the kv file let's add some canvas instructions to draw a rectangle:

```
#:kivy 1.11.1
# File name: test.kv

<TestLayout>:
    canvas:
        Rectangle:
            pos: self.x + 50, self.y + 50
            size: 500, 100
```

If you run the code, you will see a rectangle drawn on the root widget.

So, nothing you couldn't have expected. Let's now make the rectangle red. All you have to do is add the **Color** context instruction with the **rgba** property.

The value for the red color is **(1, 0, 0, 1)**. Have a look:

```
#:kivy 1.11.1
# File name: test.kv

<TestLayout>:
    canvas:
        Color:
            rgba: 1, 0, 0, 1
        Rectangle:
            pos: self.x + 50, self.y + 50
            size: 500, 100
```

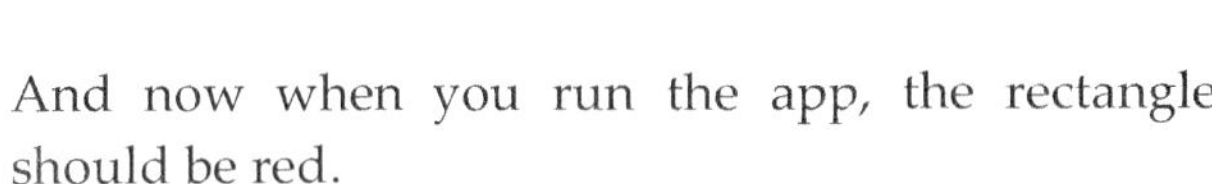

And now when you run the app, the rectangle should be red.

And so it is. But watch what happens if I put the **Color** context instruction after the **Rectangle** vertex instruction:

```
#:kivy 1.11.1
# File name: test.kv

<TestLayout>:
    canvas:
        Rectangle:
            pos: self.x + 50, self.y + 50
            size: 500, 100
        Color:
            rgba: 1, 0, 0, 1
```

Now the rectangle will remain white, just like it was at the beginning. Try it out.

Why is that? Well, that's because context instructions change the whole coordinate space context. If you change the color at a given point, the change will be only visible from that moment on and will continue to be visible until another change occurs. So, when we put the **Color** instruction before the **Rectangle** instruction, we changed the color property for the whole coordinate space and then we drew the Rectangle in this changed context. That's why the rectangle was red. In the other example, we first drew the rectangle and only then changed the coordinate space context, that's why the rectangle remained white. If this sounds complicated, maybe the next example will make things clearer.

First let's move the **Color** instruction above the **Rectangle** instruction so that the rectangle is red again. And then let's use some vertex instructions to draw more shapes:

```
#:kivy 1.11.1
# File name: test.kv

<TestLayout>:
    canvas:
        # Set color to red.
        Color:
            rgba: 1, 0, 0, 1
        Rectangle:
            pos: self.x + 50, self.y + 50
            size: 500, 100
        Rectangle:
            pos: 50, 350
            size: 100, 100
        Ellipse:
            pos: 200, 350
            size: 100, 100
        Line:
            points: 20, 400, 550, 400
            width: 10
        Line:
            circle: 400, 400, 50
            width: 10
        Triangle:
            points: 500, 350, 500, 450, 550, 450
```

If you run the app, you'll see all the shapes are red.

This is because they are all in one coordinate space, for which we set the color to red. And it will be red until we set it to a different one.

So let's do it – after the long rectangle near the bottom is drawn, we want to change the color to blue. This will set the color for the whole coordinate space context, so all shapes that follow will be blue:

```
#:kivy 1.11.1
# File name: test.kv

<TestLayout>:
    canvas:
        # Set color to red.
        Color:
            rgba: 1, 0, 0, 1
        # red
        Rectangle:
            pos: self.x + 50, self.y + 50
            size: 500, 100
        # Change color to blue.
        Color:
            rgba: 0, 0, 1, 1
        # blue
        Rectangle:
            pos: 50, 350
            size: 100, 100
        # still blue
        Ellipse:
            pos: 200, 350
            size: 100, 100
        # still blue
        Line:
            points: 20, 400, 550, 400
            width: 10
        # still blue
        Line:
            circle: 400, 400, 50
            width: 10
        # still blue
        Triangle:
            points: 500, 350, 500, 450, 550, 450
```

And now we have two colors, red and blue.

Now let's move the second **Color** instruction further down:

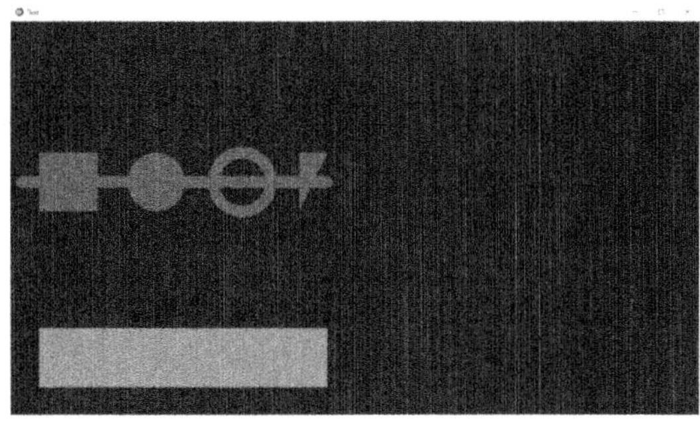

```
#:kivy 1.11.1
# File name: test.kv

<TestLayout>:
    canvas:
        # Set color to red.
        Color:
            rgba: 1, 0, 0, 1
        # red
        Rectangle:
            pos: self.x + 50, self.y + 50
            size: 500, 100
        # still red
        Rectangle:
            pos: 50, 350
            size: 100, 100
        # still red
        Ellipse:
            pos: 200, 350
            size: 100, 100
        # Change color to blue.
        Color:
            rgba: 0, 0, 1, 1
        # blue
        Line:
            points: 20, 400, 550, 400
            width: 10
        # still blue
        Line:
            circle: 400, 400, 50
            width: 10
        # still blue
        Triangle:
            points: 500, 350, 500, 450, 550, 450
```

Now we're changing the context only after the ellipse is drawn, so the new color will take effect starting from the first line.

By the way, you can see that the shapes are drawn in the same order as they are added to the canvas, so the line is drawn after the rectangle and the ellipse. Now, with the different colors it's possible to see.

And now let's move the **Color** instruction up again, and then let's add more **Color** instructions:

```
#:kivy 1.11.1
# File name: test.kv

<TestLayout>:
    canvas:
        # Set color to red.
        Color:
            rgba: 1, 0, 0, 1
        Rectangle:
            pos: self.x + 50, self.y + 50
            size: 500, 100
        # Change color to blue.
        Color:
            rgba: 0, 0, 1, 1
        Rectangle:
            pos: 50, 350
            size: 100, 100
        Ellipse:
            pos: 200, 350
            size: 100, 100
        # Change color to green.
        Color:
            rgba: 0, 1, 0, 1
        Line:
            points: 20, 400, 550, 400
            width: 10
        # Change color to pinkish.
        Color:
            rgba: 1, .5, .5, 1
        Line:
            circle: 400, 400, 50
            width: 10
        # Change color to a shade of purple.
        Color:
            rgba: .5, .5, 1, 1
        Triangle:
            points: 500, 350, 500, 450, 550, 450
```

Let's run the app and see all the colors.

So, what's going on here? Let's analyze it step by step:

- Before the first shape is drawn, the color is set to red. So, everything will be drawn in red until the color changes again.

- Before the second shape is drawn, the color is set to blue. So, everything will be drawn in blue until the context color changes again.

- The two shapes, the rectangle and the ellipse, are drawn in blue one by one.

- Then the context color changes to green. From now on everything will be green, until we change the context again.

- After the green line is drawn, the context color changes to a shade of pink. The circle is drawn in this new color.

- After the circle is drawn, the context color changes one more time, this time to a shade of purple. The last shape is drawn in this color.

Here the order of drawing is even more visible. Watch the green line. It was drawn after the rectangle and ellipse, but before the circle and triangle, so the latter two are sitting on top of it.

But the instructions may be executed in a different order. In the next chapter we'll be talking in detail about the order of execution. But before you move on to the next chapter, here's an exercise for you so that you can play around with the colors for a while.

# It's Your Turn Now...

### EXERCISE

You can leave the Python file as is. In this exercise you will change the color of the root widget and then add a button to the root widget and set its color. When the button is pressed, its canvas should be cleared, which means its graphical representation will be gone, although the now invisible button will be still there. To achieve all this follow the instructions below:

1. Remove the two labels in the **test.kv** file.

2. Let's say we want the root widget to be blue (`0, 0, 1, 1`). To see the color you must draw something on the root widget. As we want the whole root widget to be blue, you should draw a shape that fills it completely. A good candidate is a rectangle with the same position and size as the root widget. Remember to add the vertex and context instructions in the correct order.

3. Add a button to the root widget. It should be half the width of the root widget. Center it horizontally.

HINT: Use the `size_hint` and `pos_hint` properties accordingly.

4. The button should be red (`1, 0, 0, 1`). Again, you have to draw a rectangle on it with the same position and size.

5. Add an event so that when the button is pressed, two things should happen:

a) the first time the button is pressed, it should become invisible, which means its canvas should be cleared,

b) each time the button is pressed (even when invisible), the text `'Still here...'` should be printed to the terminal.

HINTS:

- Use the `on_press` event to make the button react to presses.

- Use the `clear` method on the button's canvas to clear it.

- Use the `print` function to print to the terminal.

## SOLUTION

Here's the code:

```
#:kivy 1.11.1
# File name: test.kv

<TestLayout>:
    # Add first the color, then the shape
    # to the root widget's canvas.
    canvas:
        Color:
            rgba: 0, 0, 1, 1
        Rectangle:
            pos: self.pos
            size: self.size

    orientation: 'vertical'

    Button:
        canvas:
            Color:
                rgba: 1, 0, 0, 1
            Rectangle:
                pos: self.pos
                size: self.size

        size_hint_x: .5
        pos_hint: {'center_x': .5}

        # You can do both things on one line,
        # using a semicolon to separate them.
        on_press: self.canvas.clear(); print('Still here...')
```

When you run the app, you will see the blue root widget with the red button.

When you press the button, two things happen:

First, it disappears, or rather becomes invisible (A), and, second, the text **'Still here...'** is printed in the terminal (B).

The message in the terminal suggests the button is still there.

Check it out: Just press a couple times in the middle of the window where you saw the button before. Even though you can't see the button, you can still press it. You can tell it by the output in the terminal.

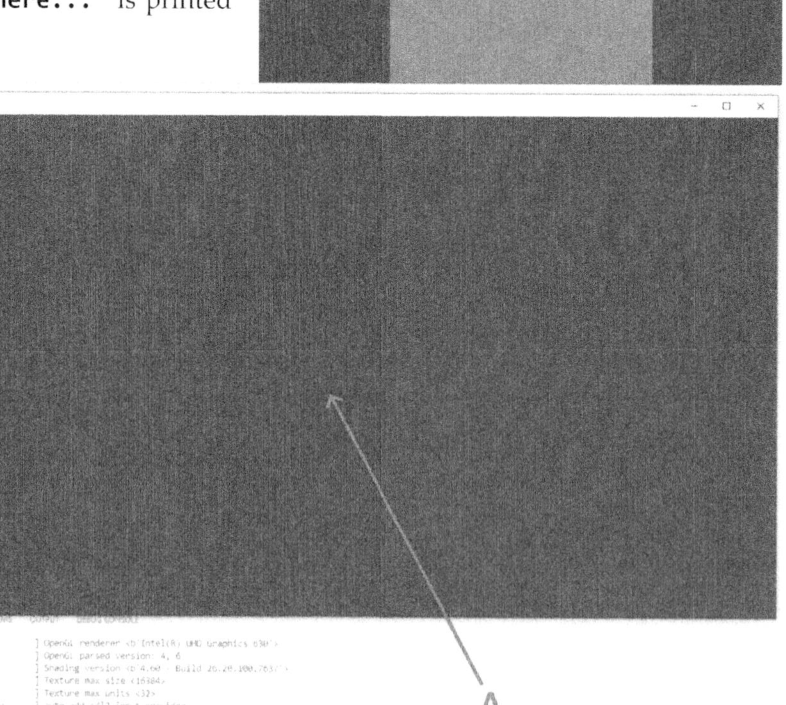

# Chapter 53 - Canvas Instructions – Order of Execution

In the previous chapter we were using the **Color** context instruction to add some colors to the shapes we were drawing on widgets. Let's have a look at a similar example.

Here's the Python file:

```
# File name: test.py

from kivy.config import Config
Config.set('graphics', 'width', '1200')
Config.set('graphics', 'height', '675')
Config.set('graphics', 'resizable', '1')

import kivy
kivy.require('1.11.1')
from kivy.app import App
from kivy.uix.floatlayout import FloatLayout

class TestLayout(FloatLayout):
    pass

class TestApp(App):
    def build(self):
        return TestLayout()

if __name__ == '__main__':
    TestApp().run()
```

Here we're drawing four squares on the root widget and adding a label with a rectangle drawn on it. When we run the app, we get something like this:

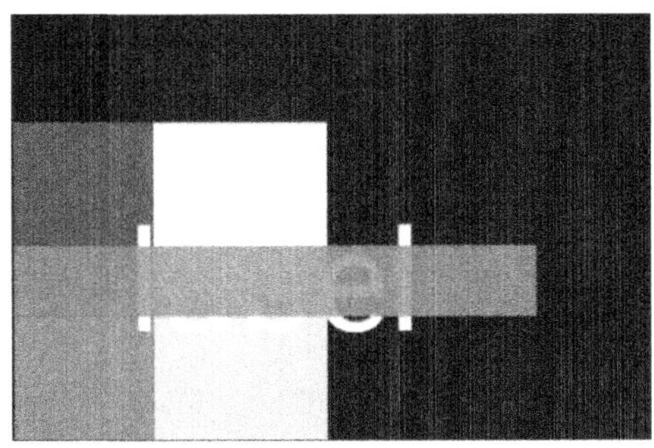

Here's the kv file:

```
#:kivy 1.11.1
# File name: test.kv

<TestLayout>:
    canvas:
        # red square
        Color:
            rgba: 1, 0, 0, 1
        Rectangle:
            pos: 0, 0
            size: 100, 100
        # green square
        Color:
            rgba: 0, 1, 0, 1
        Rectangle:
            pos: 80, 0
            size: 100, 100
        # blue square
        Color:
            rgba: 0, 0, 1, 1
        Rectangle:
            pos: 0, 80
            size: 100, 100
        # yellow square
        Color:
            rgba: 1, 1, 0, 1
        Rectangle:
            pos: 80, 80
            size: 100, 100

    # label with a gray rectangle
    Label:
        canvas:
            Color:
                rgba: .5, .5, .5, .9
            Rectangle:
                pos: self.pos
                size: self.size

        text: 'label'
        font_size: 80
        size_hint: None, None
        y: 70
        size: 300, 40
```

As you can see, some of the shapes sit on top of others, covering them partially. I also made the font size on the label pretty large so that you can see what happened to the text. It's partially covered by the gray, semitransparent rectangle.

Now let's analyze what order all these elements were drawn in. Looks like they were added in the following order:

1) the red square
2) the green square
3) the blue square
4) the yellow square
5) the label text
6) the gray rectangle on the label

We can easily tell the order because elements drawn later come on top of elements drawn earlier. All four squares are the same size, so we can clearly see which covers which, partially of course.

# The Three Sets of Canvas Instructions

But this order of execution may be changed. Each widget that has a visual representation on the screen has a canvas instance, even if we don't define it explicitly. To be more precise, each widget has three sets of canvas instructions: **`canvas.before`**, **`canvas`** and **`canvas.after`**. You can use them to change the order of execution. You don't have to explicitly define all of them, but they will be still there – Kivy takes care of it.

So, let's modify our kv file so that the order of execution is changed:

```
#:kivy 1.11.1
# File name: test.kv

<TestLayout>:
    canvas.before:
        # red square
        Color:
            rgba: 1, 0, 0, 1
        Rectangle:
            pos: 0, 0
            size: 100, 100
        # green square
        Color:
            rgba: 0, 1, 0, 1
        Rectangle:
            pos: 80, 0
            size: 100, 100
    canvas:
        # blue square
        Color:
            rgba: 0, 0, 1, 1
        Rectangle:
            pos: 0, 80
            size: 100, 100
    canvas.after:
        # yellow square
        Color:
            rgba: 1, 1, 0, 1
        Rectangle:
            pos: 80, 80
            size: 100, 100

    # label with a gray rectangle
    Label:
        canvas.before:
            Color:
                rgba: .5, .5, .5, .9
            Rectangle:
                pos: self.pos
                size: self.size
        text: 'label'
        font_size: 80
        size_hint: None, None
        y: 70
        size: 300, 40
```

If you now run the app, you will see that the order of execution has really changed.

So, here we have the root widget with a label. Now the order of execution is as follows:

1. First the **canvas.before** instructions of the root widget are executed, so first the red square is drawn, followed by the green square. Within one set of instructions the elements are drawn in order of appearance.

2. After that, the **canvas** instructions of the root widget are executed, so the blue square is drawn as next. It sits on top of everything that was drawn before.

3. And now is the interesting part. The **canvas.after** instructions of the root widget will be drawn only after all children of the root widget are handled. In our case there's only one child, the label, so now the execution will move to the label. The **canvas.before** instructions of the label will be executed first, so this time the gray rectangle is drawn before the text is displayed, that's why now the text is on top of it.

4. Then the **canvas** and **canvas.after** instructions of the label are executed, although they're not explicitly defined here.

5. After that the execution goes back to the root widget and the root widget's **canvas.after** instructions are executed, so the yellow square is drawn as last, on top of anything else. Now, in the exercise below, you will have another opportunity to practice the three sets of canvas instructions and in the next chapter we'll be talking about other context instructions, like the ones used for translating, rotating and scaling.

## It's Your Turn Now...

### EXERCISE

Modify the kv code using different combinations of the canvas instructions so that the final result looks like in the picture on the right.

As you can see, there's another rectangle on the label. It's half the height of the label. Its color is a lighter shade of gray and it's fully opaque. You can set the **rgba** property to **(.8, .8, .8, 1)**.

## SOLUTION

Here's the code:

```
#:kivy 1.11.1
# File name: test.kv

<TestLayout>:
    canvas.before:
        ...
    canvas.after:
        # blue square
        ...
        # yellow square
        ...
    # label with a gray rectangle
    Label:
        canvas.before:
            ...
        canvas.after:
            Color:
                rgba: .8, .8, .8, 1
            Rectangle:
                pos: self.pos
                size: self.width, self.height / 2

        text: 'label'
        font_size: 80
        size_hint: None, None
        y: 70
        size: 300, 40
```

Now the order of execution is as follows:

1. First the **canvas.before** instructions of the root widget are executed, just like before, so the red and green squares are drawn first.

2. After that, the **canvas** instructions of the root widget are executed, although we didn't specify them explicitly. This is why we don't see any visual effect of them working.

3. Next come the three sets of the label's canvas instructions. The **canvas.before** instructions of the label will be executed first, so the dark gray rectangle being part of the label is drawn on top of the red and green squares.

4. Then the **canvas** instructions of the label are executed. We didn't specify them explicitly, but they are there anyway. This is why the text is displayed as next, on top of the dark gray rectangle.

5. After that the **canvas.after** instructions of the label are executed, so the light gray rectangle is drawn on top of the label text.

6. Finally, after handling the only child of the root widget, the root widget's **canvas.after** instructions are executed and the blue and yellow squares are drawn on top of everything else, in this exact order: first blue, then yellow.

# Chapter 54 - The Translate, Rotate and Scale Instructions

In the previous chapter we were talking about the order of execution. The only context instruction we've been using so far was **Color**. Today we'll be talking about three context instructions that manipulate the whole coordinate space. As you know, the coordinate space is shared by all widgets, it extends even beyond the borders of the app window because you can add stuff not only inside the window, but also outside it if you have a reason to do that (for example if you want to add a widget that is initially invisible but then moves toward the visible part of the coordinate space in the app window).

Anyway, the three context instructions that we will be discussing today are **Translate**, **Rotate** and **Scale**. Their names are self-explanatory, but how they work may be counter-intuitive at the beginning. This is why the example in this chapter is rather lengthy, but I want you to go through the whole of it carefully so that you really understand what's going on.

We'll be still using the same Python code as in the previous chapter.

As for the kv code, we'll be adding the instructions step by step and watch the results. Let's start with something you already know – drawing a red triangle:

```
#:kivy 1.11.1
# File name: test.kv

<TestLayout>:
    canvas:
        # (1) - context instruction - red color
        Color:
            rgba: 1, 0, 0, 1

        # (2) - vertex instruction - draw triangle
        Triangle:
            points: 0, 0, 0, 400, 200, 0
```

Let's run the app and we should see the triangle in the bottom left corner of the window.

We're going to use context instructions to manipulate the whole coordinate space and things will be getting pretty complex soon. So, it'll be much easier to follow what's going on if I add, as annotations to the screenshots, the X and Y axes and the origin point, which is the point at the coordinates (0, 0), here represented as a black circle at the point where the axes cross. The axes will be slightly offset from the borders for better visibility.

So, now that we haven't used any of the three context instructions yet, the axes are pretty obvious. You can see them in the image on the right.

# Translation

The instruction that we are going to use first is **Translate**. It's used to move the coordinate space along one or more axes. The properties that you can use here are:

**x**, **y**, **z** – used to traslate along the X, Y or Z axis respectively,

**xy** – used to traslate along both the X and Y axes,

**xyz** – used to traslate along all three axes.

We're going to move the coordinate space to the right, so along the X axis, then we'll change the color and draw another triangle. Now watch the coordinates of the points that make up the triangle in our kv code – they are exactly the same as before:

```
#:kivy 1.11.1
# File name: test.kv

<TestLayout>:
    canvas:
        # (1) - context instruction - red color
        ...
        # (2) - vertex instruction - draw triangle
        ...
        # (3) context instruction - translating by 400 px to the right
        Translate:
            x: 400

        # (4) context instruction - green color
        Color:
            rgba: 0, 1, 0, 1

        # (5) vertex instruction - draw triangle
        Triangle:
            points: 0, 0, 0, 400, 200, 0
```

Let's run the app again. Now, although the coordinates of the points that make up the second triangle were exactly the same in the code as before, the green triangle was drawn at a different position. Why did this happen? Well, using the **Translate** instruction we actually moved the whole coordinate space 400 px to the right.

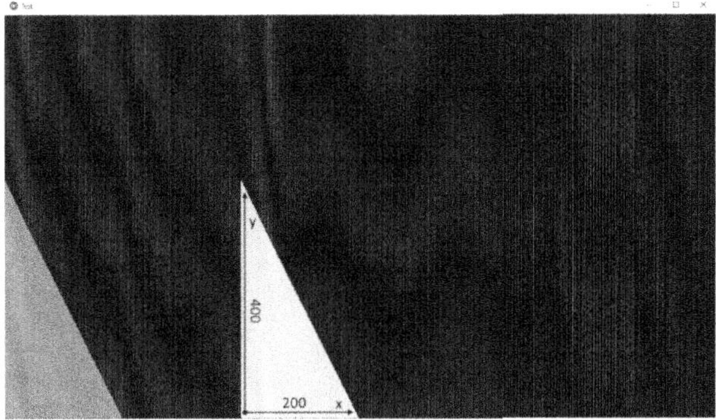


The annotations show us visually that now the position (0, 0) is no longer in the bottom left corner of the window. It's now 400 px further to the right. So now the whole coordinate system has moved and now the origin point (0, 0) is where the coordinates (400, 0) were before. The previous origin point is now at the coordinates (-400, 0) after the translation.

Let's now translate the coordinate space 500 px to the right and 250 px up. This time we'll use the **xy** property. Then let's change the color to blue and draw another triangle with exactly the same coordinates:

```
#:kivy 1.11.1
# File name: test.kv

<TestLayout>:
    canvas:
        ...
        # (6) context instruction - translating by
        # 500 px to the right and 250 px up
        Translate:
            xy: 500, 250

        # (7) context instruction - blue color
        Color:
            rgba: 0, 0, 1, 1

        # (8) vertex instruction - draw triangle
        Triangle:
            points: 0, 0, 0, 400, 200, 0
```

So, again, the whole coordinate system has been translated.

It's still not that complicated, right? But wait until we start discussing rotation, which is actually going to be our next topic.

# Rotation

So, how about rotation? There are three properties that we will be making use of when rotating the coordinate space:

**angle** – used to specify the angle of rotation (positive values are used for the counterclockwise direction),

**axis** – used to specify around which axes the rotation should occur – we use the format (x, y, z), so in our case we should set it to (0, 0, 1) because we are only going to rotate around the Z axis (the one going into the screen),

**origin** – used to specify the origin of rotation, which can be understood as the pivot point to which the rotation should be relative; by default the origin is the point at the coordinates (0, 0), but it can be changed.

For now let's rotate the coordinate space 90 degrees is counterclockwise direction along the Z axis with the origin of rotation at point (0, 0) and draw another triangle:

```
#:kivy 1.11.1
# File name: test.kv

<TestLayout>:
    canvas:
        ...
        # (9) context instruction - rotating 90 degrees
        # in counterclockwise direction on the Z axis
        Rotate:
            angle: 90
            axis: 0, 0, 1

        # (10) context instruction - yellow color
        Color:
            rgba: 1, 1, 0, 1

        # (11) vertex instruction - draw triangle
        Triangle:
            points: 0, 0, 0, 400, 200, 0
```

If you run the app, you will see another triangle, this time a yellow one, drawn in the rotated coordinate space.

As you can see, the whole coordinate space has been rotated. Now the X axis is vertical and the Y axis is horizontal. The coordinate space was rotated around the origin point, so now the origin is still at the same position.

Suppose we want to translate the coordinate space up in the next step. But what does it mean to move up in this context? Well, the coordinate space is rotated, so if you translate along the X axis, you will move up or down and if you translate along the Y axis , you will move left or right.

Let's translate along the X axis then so that our next triangle is drawn above the one we added as last:

```
#:kivy 1.11.1
# File name: test.kv

<TestLayout>:
    canvas:
        ...
        # (12) context instruction - translating
        # by 200 px on the X axis
        Translate:
            x: 200

        # (13) vertex instruction - draw triangle
        Triangle:
            points: 0, 0, 0, 400, 200, 0
```

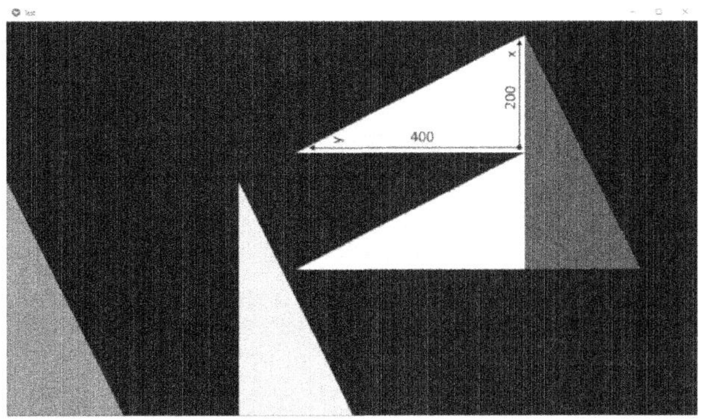


This time we didn't change the color, so it's still yellow.

And now let's rotate the coordinate space again, but this time we'll change the origin of rotation.

Instead of around the point (0, 0), we want to rotate the space 180 degrees around the vertex of the new yellow triangle which in the image is the farthest to the left, near the letter 'y' being part of the annotations. So we need the coordinates of this point.

Remember that our coordinate space is now rotated, so the X values change vertically. But the vertex is at the same height as the point (0, 0), so the X coordinate is still 0. The Y values change horizontally (increasing to the left), so the Y value is 400. This means we want to rotate the space arount the point (0, 400) and draw another yellow triangle:

```
#:kivy 1.11.1
# File name: test.kv

<TestLayout>:
    canvas:
        ...
        # (14) context instruction - rotating 180 degrees
        # on the Z axis around the point (0, 400)
        Rotate:
            angle: 180
            axis: 0, 0, 1
            origin: 0, 400

        # (15) vertex instruction - draw triangle
        Triangle:
            points: 0, 0, 0, 400, 200, 0
```

As you can see, the origin of rotation was at the point (0, 400) in the current coordinate space.

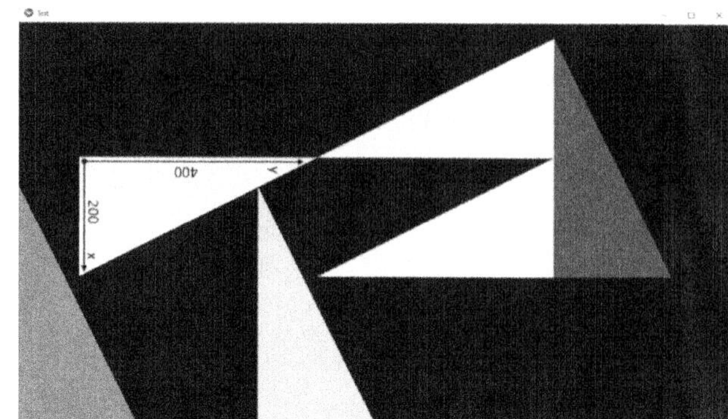

You already know how to translate and rotate the coordinate space. What about scaling? Let's talk about it next.

## Scale

There are several useful properties you can use with scaling:

**x**, **y**, **z** – the scale on the X, Y or Z axis respectively,

**xyz** – the scale on all three axes,

**origin** – the origin of the scale, by default the point (0, 0).

The values that we use for scaling are proportions to the current size of the coordinate space. So, if you want to make something half its current size, you should use the value **.5**, but then, to restore it to its original size, you have to use the value **2**, to make it twice as big again.

If you don't want to change the scale on an axis, you can set the value to **1** for that axis. And now let's scale the coordinate space down on the X axis (this is the vertical one now) and draw another rectangle:

```
#:kivy 1.11.1
# File name: test.kv

<TestLayout>:
    canvas:
        ...
        # (16) context instruction - scaling down on the X axis
        Scale:
            xyz: .5, 1, 1

        # (17) context instruction - light blue color
        Color:
            rgba: 0, 1, 1, 1

        # (18) vertex instruction - draw triangle
        Triangle:
            points: 0, 0, 0, 400, 200, 0
```

Now, the interesting thing you probably noticed is that the whole coordinate space has been scaled down on the X axis. I even squeezed the annotations in the vertical direction to make it more visible. The light blue triangle is still 200 px wide (I'm referring to the dimension along the x axis here), but in the new manipulated coordinate space the 200 px just occupies half the space it occupied before.

And now let's scale the coordinate space down on the Y axis, but as the origin of scale let's set the point which is in the middle of the triangles's height. Its coordinates are (0, 200). Then, let's draw another triangle:

```
#:kivy 1.11.1
# File name: test.kv

<TestLayout>:
    canvas:
        ...
        # (19) context instruction - scaling down on the Y axis
        # relative to the point (0, 200)
        Scale:
            xyz: 1, .5, 1
            origin: 0, 200

        # (20) context instruction - purple color
        Color:
            rgba: 1, 0, 1, 1

        # (21) vertex instruction - draw triangle
        Triangle:
            points: 0, 0, 0, 400, 200, 0
```

As you can see, the coordinate space shrank again.

And now let's flip the coordinate space vertically. It's very easy to do, you just have to set the scale to **-1** on the appropriate axis, in our case on the X axis, because this is the axis that will now change its direction from downward to upward. Here's the code:

```
#:kivy 1.11.1
# File name: test.kv

<TestLayout>:
    canvas:
        ...
        # (22) context instruction - flipping vertically
        Scale:
            xyz: -1, 1, 1

        # (23) context instruction - greenish color
        Color:
            rgba: .5, 1, .5, 1

        # (24) vertex instruction - draw triangle
        Triangle:
            points: 0, 0, 0, 400, 200, 0
```

Again, I even flipped the annotations to better visualize what's going on.

Now, after so many manipulations of the coordinate space, you could have gotten lost if not for the annotations. As you can see, now the point (0, 0) is in the lower left vertex of the triangle, the X values increase in the upward direction and the Y values increase as we move to the right.

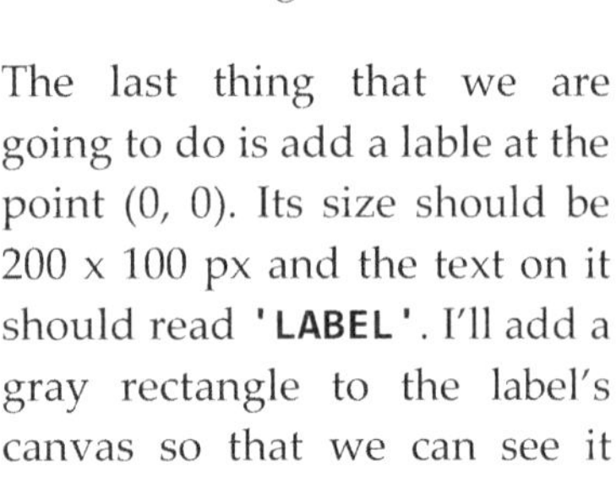

The last thing that we are going to do is add a lable at the point (0, 0). Its size should be 200 x 100 px and the text on it should read **'LABEL'**. I'll add a gray rectangle to the label's canvas so that we can see it better. Have a look:

```
#:kivy 1.11.1
# File name: test.kv

<TestLayout>:
    canvas:
        ...
        # (24) vertex instruction - draw triangle
        Triangle:
            points: 0, 0, 0, 400, 200, 0

    # label with a gray rectangle
    Label:
        canvas.before:
            Color:
                rgba: .5, .5, .5, .9
            Rectangle:
                pos: self.pos
                size: self.size

        text: 'LABEL'
        size_hint: None, None
        size: 200, 100
        font_size: 70
```

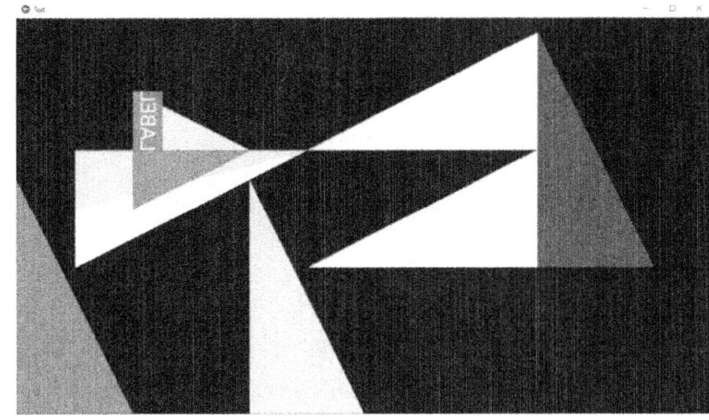


Watch how the label is oriented according to the manipulated coordinating space.

We're not yet completely done with our file, but the rest will be an exercise for you. Anyway, if you manipulate the coordinate space it's very difficult to then remember how the coordinate space is rotated or scaled and adjust all our widgets to be positioned and sized correctly. This is why there should be a way to remember the context before the manipulation and then restore it after the manipulation. Luckily, there is. We'll see how to do it in the next chapter.

## It's Your Turn Now...

EXERCISE

Your task is to add some context instructions to the root widget's canvas before the label is added. Your goal is to restore the coordinate space to its original position and size. Try to do it yourself.

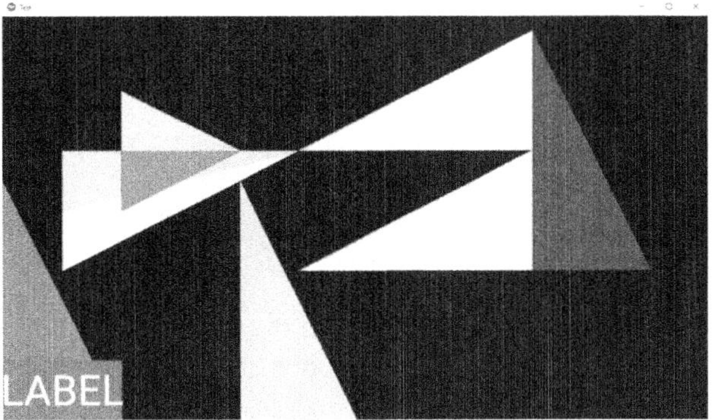


There are a couple ways of doing this, you can use the instructions in a different order, but as long as your final result is the same, you're good. To make things slightly more difficult, try to use exactly one **`Scale`**, one **`Rotate`** and one **`Translate`** instruction. If you prefer to follow my instructions, you will find them below. In the image on the right you can see what the result should look like.

And now the instructions:

1. We scaled the coordinate space by a factor of .5 on the X and Y axes, so now let's scale it up. If you don't remember what factor to use, go back to where I discussed the **`Scale`** instruction and check it out. At the same time as scaling the coordinate space, flip it horizontally, so on the Y axis.

HINT: You can scale and flip in one go, just multiply the scaling factor by -1 on the appropriate axis.

2. Next rotate the coordinate space 90 degrees clockwise on the Z axis.

3. Finally translate the coordinate space 200 px to the left and 450 px down.

## SOLUTION

Here's the kv file:

```
#:kivy 1.11.1
# File name: test.kv

<TestLayout>:
    canvas:
        ...

        # (26) context instruction - rotating
        # 90 degrees in clockwise direction
        Rotate:
            angle: -90
            axis: 0, 0, 1

        # (27) context instruction - translating
        # 200 px to the left and 450 px down
        Translate:
            xy: -200, -450

    # label with a gray rectangle
    Label:
        canvas.before:
            Color:
                rgba: .5, .5, .5, .9
            Rectangle:
                pos: self.pos
                size: self.size

        text: 'LABEL'
        size_hint: None, None
        size: 200, 100
        font_size: 70
```

If you now run the code, you should see the label in the bottom left corner, oriented as in the image above.

# Chapter 55 - The PushMatrix and PopMatrix Instructions

In the previous chapter we were talking about context instructions, in particular about the **Translate**, **Rotate** and **Scale** instructions. As you remember, whenever you use one of these instructions, they manipulate the whole coordinate space. As you also remember, we had to add even more instructions to restore the coordinate space to its original state. This was actually what you were supposed to do in the exercise.

Well, we did restore the original state of the coordinate space, but in order to do that we had to do some math to reverse the changes we had made earlier. But there's a faster way of doing it. Suppose you want to rotate the coordinate space, add some widgets or draw some shapes, and then continue your work using the original state. I will use a simplified version of the code from the previous file to demonstrate how it works.

The Python file is not going to change change. The kv file was pretty complex, so let's simplify it so that there is just one **Translate**, one **Rotate** and one **Scale** instruction:

```
#:kivy 1.11.1
# File name: test.kv

<TestLayout>:
    canvas:
        Color:
            rgba: 1, 0, 0, 1
        Triangle:
            points: 0, 0, 0, 400, 200, 0

        # TRANSLATE
        Translate:
            xy: 600, 200
        Color:
            rgba: 0, 1, 0, 1
        Triangle:
            points: 0, 0, 0, 400, 200, 0

        # ROTATE
        Rotate:
            angle: 45
            axis: 0, 0, 1
            origin: -100, 100
        Color:
            rgba: 1, 1, 0, 1
        Triangle:
            points: 0, 0, 0, 400, 200, 0

        # SCALE
        Scale:
            xyz: .3, .3, 0
        Color:
            rgba: 0, 1, 1, 1

        Triangle:
            points: 0, 0, 0, 400, 200, 0


    Label:
        canvas.before:
            Color:
                rgba: .5, .5, .5, .9

            Rectangle:
                pos: self.pos
                size: self.size

        text: 'LABEL'
        size_hint: None, None
        size: 200, 100
        font_size: 70
```

If we now run the program, exactly the same will happen as in the previous chapter. After each instruction the coordinate space is manipulated and the following shape is drawn relative to that new space. Also the label is added using the modified coordinate space.

But suppose we want the label to be in the bottom-left corner, so as if the original coordinate space was used. To do that, we have to save the current coordinate space context and after we're done with all the manipulations, restore it. The former can be done by means of the **PushMatrix** context instruction and the latter by means of **PopMatrix**. So, let's do just that:

```
#:kivy 1.11.1
# File name: test.kv

<TestLayout>:
    canvas:
        # Save context.
        PushMatrix

        # all the manipulations
        Color:
            rgba: 1, 0, 0, 1
        Triangle:
            points: 0, 0, 0, 400, 200, 0
        Translate:
            xy: 600, 200
        Color:
            rgba: 0, 1, 0, 1
        Triangle:
            points: 0, 0, 0, 400, 200, 0
        Rotate:
            angle: 45
            axis: 0, 0, 1
            origin: -100, 100
        Color:
            rgba: 1, 1, 0, 1
        Triangle:
            points: 0, 0, 0, 400, 200, 0
        Scale:
            xyz: .3, .3, 0
        Color:
            rgba: 0, 1, 1, 1
        Triangle:
            points: 0, 0, 0, 400, 200, 0

        # Restore context.
        PopMatrix

    Label:
        canvas.before:
            Color:
                rgba: .5, .5, .5, .9

            Rectangle:
                pos: self.pos
                size: self.size

        text: 'LABEL'
        size_hint: None, None
        size: 200, 100
        font_size: 70
```

In this example we save the context before we do any manipulations, so we can easily restore the original state. Now the label should be positioned, rotated and scaled as if no manipulations had taken place.

Naturally, we can save the context anywhere and even more than once. In the latter case the **PopMatrix** instruction will always restore the last saved context.

Now suppose we want to translate the coordinate space like we did before and save its state at this stage, then do all the other manipulations, and finally restore the state that we had after the translation but before the rotation and scaling. All you have to do is move the **PushMatrix** instruction to where you need to save the context:

```
#:kivy 1.11.1
# File name: test.kv

<TestLayout>:
    canvas:
        # translation
        Color:
            rgba: 1, 0, 0, 1
        Triangle:
            points: 0, 0, 0, 400, 200, 0
        Translate:
            xy: 600, 200

        # Save context.
        PushMatrix

        # the other manipulations
        Color:
            rgba: 0, 1, 0, 1
        Triangle:
            points: 0, 0, 0, 400, 200, 0
        Rotate:
            angle: 45
            axis: 0, 0, 1
            origin: -100, 100
        Color:
            rgba: 1, 1, 0, 1
        Triangle:
            points: 0, 0, 0, 400, 200, 0
        Scale:
            xyz: .3, .3, 0
        Color:
            rgba: 0, 1, 1, 1
        Triangle:
            points: 0, 0, 0, 400, 200, 0

        # Restore context.
        PopMatrix

    Label:
        canvas.before:
            Color:
                rgba: .5, .5, .5, .9

            Rectangle:
                pos: self.pos
                size: self.size

        text: 'LABEL'
        size_hint: None, None
        size: 200, 100
        font_size: 70
```

If you now run the program, the you will see the label added relative to the restored context.

The possibility to save the current context and then restore it comes really handy if you want to draw a shape or add a widget which is very much like another shape or widget, but only differs by its position, rotation or scale. Then doing the math to recalculate all the coordinates would be tedious.

Now, using the **PushMatrix** and **PopMatrix** instructions, you can use the same values with the position and size properties, just manipulate the whole coordinate space for a while. This is actually something that I want you to do as an exercise. And in the next chapter, I'll show you how to use context instructions in Python code, without the Kivy language.

## It's Your Turn Now...

### EXERCISE

Leave the Python file as is. Remove all the code from the kv file and type in the following:

```
#:kivy 1.11.1
# File name: test.kv

<TestLayout>:
    canvas:
        Color:
            rgba: 0, 1, 0, 1
        Line:
            points: 100, 100, 120, 200, 150, 120, 180, 150, 200, 100
            close: True
            width: 5

    Label:
        text: 'Done'
        font_size: 40
        pos: 100, 200
        size_hint: None, None
        size: 100, 50
```

This program uses absolute coordinates. If you run it, you will see a line and a label. Now suppose you want to draw another line that should look exactly the same, but be twice as big and positioned farther to the right. You could calculate the absolute coordinates of the points the line should consist of, but to calculate them involves some math, maybe not extremely difficult, but still time-consuming.

Imagine you'd like to draw five more copies, each one slightly modified. This would involve much more math on your part to calculate all the point coordinates. And what if the shape was even more complex? Luckily, in cases like this, you can use the same point coordinates for all shapes, just modify the coordinate space accordingly.

What we want to achieve here is just a modified copy of a shape. Besides, there's the label. We want the label to stay where it is and be the same size. This means we have to save the coordinate space context before we manipulate it and then restore the context after we're done manipulating it, but before we add the label.

Here are the instructions for you to follow:

1. At first we won't save the context to see how the label behaves. We have to scale and translate the coordinate space before we draw the second line. Let's start with the former. Scale the coordinate space to make it twice as big. Also remember that by default the scale origin is at point (0, 0). Change it to (100, 100) – this way we'll be scaling relative to the first point of the line.

2. Now translate the coordinate space 200 px to the right.

3. Draw another line. Use exactly the same point coordinates and line width (the width will be affected too) as before.

When you now run the program, you should see something like in the picture on the left.

4. We're almost there. The second line is fine, but the label is now drawn in the modified coordinate space. As you remember, we wanted it to be drawn in the original context. So, save the context before you manipulate it and then restore it before you add the label. Now the result should be like in the picture on the right.

## SOLUTION

Here's the code for the first version, so the one where we don't save the context:

```
#:kivy 1.11.1
# File name: test.kv

<TestLayout>:
    canvas:
        Color:
            rgba: 0, 1, 0, 1
        Line:
            points: 100, 100, 120, 200, 150, 120, 180, 150, 200, 100
            close: True
            width: 5

        Scale:
            xyz: 2, 2, 0
            origin: 100, 100

        Translate:
            x: 200

        Line:
            points: 100, 100, 120, 200, 150, 120, 180, 150, 200, 100
            close: True
            width: 5

    Label:
        ...
```

If you run the app now, the label will be translated and scaled. And here's the version where we save and then restore the context:

```
#:kivy 1.11.1
# File name: test.kv

<TestLayout>:
    canvas:
        PushMatrix

        Color:
            rgba: 0, 1, 0, 1
        Line:
            points: 100, 100, 120, 200, 150, 120, 180, 150, 200, 100
            close: True
            width: 5

        Scale:
            xyz: 2, 2, 0
            origin: 100, 100
```

```
        Translate:
            x: 200

        Line:
            points: 100, 100, 120, 200, 150, 120, 180, 150, 200, 100
            close: True
            width: 5

        PopMatrix

    Label:
        ...
```

Now the label will be drawn in the original context. By the way, you can put the **PushMatrix** instruction anywhere in the code, but before you start manipulating the context, so in our example it should be anywhere above the **Scale** instruction, for example:

```
#:kivy 1.11.1
# File name: test.kv

<TestLayout>:
    canvas:
        Color:
            rgba: 0, 1, 0, 1
        Line:
            points: 100, 100, 120, 200, 150, 120, 180, 150, 200, 100
            close: True
            width: 5

        PushMatrix

        Scale:
            xyz: 2, 2, 0
            origin: 100, 100

        Translate:
            x: 200

        Line:
            points: 100, 100, 120, 200, 150, 120, 180, 150, 200, 100
            close: True
            width: 5

        PopMatrix

    Label:
        ...
```

This will work the same.

# Chapter 56 - Context Instructions in Python Code

In the preceding chapters we were talking about context instructions. We discussed the following instructions: **Color**, **Translate**, **Rotate**, **Scale**, **PushMatrix** and **PopMatrix**. Today we'll see how to use them directly in Python, so without the Kivy language.

Let's start with a quick setup, just a FloatLayout with a rectangle drawn on it. Here's the Python code:

```
# File name: test.py

from kivy.config import Config
Config.set('graphics', 'width', '1200')
Config.set('graphics', 'height', '675')
Config.set('graphics', 'resizable', '1')

import kivy
kivy.require('1.11.1')
from kivy.app import App
from kivy.uix.floatlayout import FloatLayout

# We need the Rectangle class to draw the shape.
from kivy.graphics import Rectangle

class TestLayout(FloatLayout):
    def __init__(self, **kwargs):
        super().__init__(**kwargs)

        with self.canvas:
            Rectangle(pos=(100, 100), size=(400, 200))

class TestApp(App):
    def build(self):
        return TestLayout()

if __name__ == '__main__':
    TestApp().run()
```

We don't need any code in the kv file, because we're going to use only Python in this chapter, so make sure the kv file is empty or completely commented out.

If you now run the app, you will see a white rectangle.

Let's make the rectangle red. First, we have to import the **Color** class from **kivy.graphics**. Then we have to add a **Color** instruction:

```
# File name: test.py
...
from kivy.graphics import Rectangle, Color

class TestLayout(FloatLayout):
    ...
        with self.canvas:
            Color(1, 0, 0, 1)
            Rectangle(pos=(100, 100), size=(400, 200))

class TestApp(App):
    ...
```

Again, it's important to place the **Color** instruction before the rectangle is drawn. Run the app and you will see the red rectangle.

And now let's translate the coordinate space and draw another rectangle, with the same color and size. Don't forget to import the **Translate** class first. The X and Y translations are passed as arguments to the **Translate** instruction. So, let's translate the coordinate space 500 px to the right and 200 px up:

```
# File name: test.py
...
from kivy.graphics import Rectangle, Color, Translate

class TestLayout(FloatLayout):
    ...
        with self.canvas:
            Color(1, 0, 0, 1)
            Rectangle(pos=(100, 100), size=(400, 200))
            Translate(500, 200)
            Rectangle(pos=(100, 100), size=(400, 200))

class TestApp(App):
    ...
```

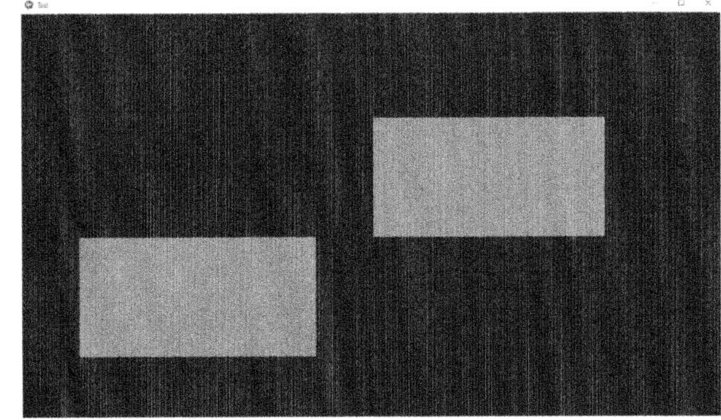

Now there are two red rectangles.

And now let's change the color to green, scale the coordinate space on the X and Y axes to make it half its current size and then draw another rectangle. Naturally, we have to import the **Scale** class first. Then we have to pass the scale factors for all three axes as arguments. Additionally, let's set the scale origin to the bottom right corner of the second rectangle, which is at (500, 100). You can do it by passing the **origin** keyword argument:

```
# File name: test.py
...
from kivy.graphics import Rectangle, Color, Translate, Scale

class TestLayout(FloatLayout):
    ...
        with self.canvas:
            Color(1, 0, 0, 1)
            Rectangle(pos=(100, 100), size=(400, 200))
            Translate(500, 200)
            Rectangle(pos=(100, 100), size=(400, 200))
            Color(0, 1, 0, 1)
            Scale(.5, .5, 0, origin=(500, 100))
            Rectangle(pos=(100, 100), size=(400, 200))

class TestApp(App):
    def build(self):
        return TestLayout()

if __name__ == '__main__':
    TestApp().run()
```

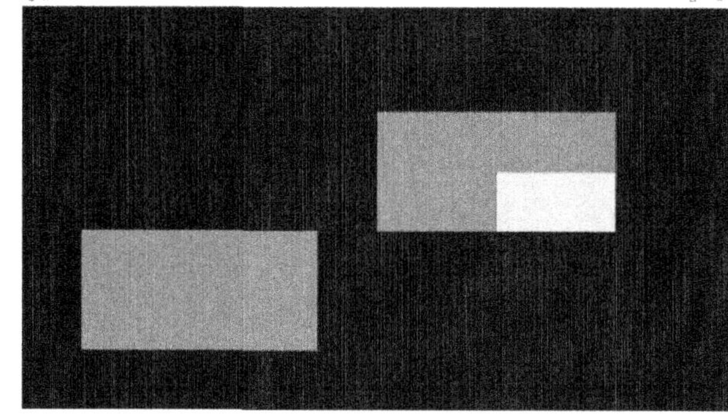

The app window now displays three rectangles.

Finally, let's rotate the coordinate space, change the color and draw another rectangle. You need to import the **Rotate** class first. Then all you have to do is pass the angle, axis and origin as arguments. We want to rotate the rectangle 45 degrees clockwise, on the Z axis, relative to its center, which is at (250, 150).

Here's the code:

```
# File name: test.py
...
from kivy.graphics import Rectangle, Color, Translate, Scale, Rotate

class TestLayout(FloatLayout):
    ...
        with self.canvas:
            Color(1, 0, 0, 1)
            Rectangle(pos=(100, 100), size=(400, 200))
            Translate(500, 200)
            Rectangle(pos=(100, 100), size=(400, 200))
            Color(0, 1, 0, 1)
            Scale(.5, .5, 0, origin=(500, 100))
```

```
            Rectangle(pos=(100, 100), size=(400, 200))
            Color(0, 0, 1, 1)
            Rotate(angle=-45, axis=(0, 0, 1), origin=(250, 150))
            Rectangle(pos=(100, 100), size=(400, 200))

class TestApp(App):
    ...
```

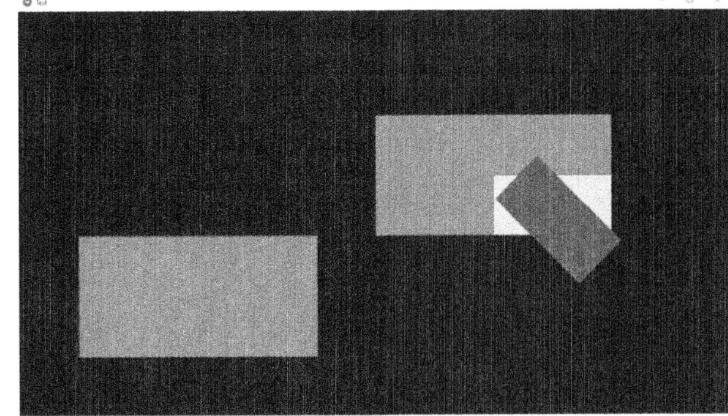

If you run the app now, you will see the new rotated rectangle too.

What about the **PushMatrix** and **PopMatrix** instructions in Python code? You will have an opportunity to practice it in this chapter's exercise.

And in the next chapter we'll go back to our Slugrace project and add some colors here and there.

# It's Your Turn Now...

### EXERCISE

In the previous chapter's exercise we saved the coordinate space context, drew a line, then manipulated the coordinate space by translating and scaling it, finally restored the original context and added a label. Go back to that exercise and have a look at the code again, both Python and kv.

And now, remove the kv code and re-create the same result using pure Python. If you don't remember how to draw shapes or add widgets programmatically, go back to the chapter where this was discussed for a refresher. The only thing that is going to be new here are the two matrix instructions, **PushMatrix** and **PopMatrix**. Remember to import the two classes along with all the other classes that you will need. Then, in the code, just use the instructions without any arguments, like so: **PushMatrix()** and **PopMatrix()**.

### SOLUTION

So, the first thing to do is remove all the code from the kv file. And here's the Python file, with explanations in the comments:

```
# File name: test.py

from kivy.config import Config
Config.set('graphics', 'width', '1200')
Config.set('graphics', 'height', '675')
Config.set('graphics', 'resizable', '1')
```

```
import kivy
kivy.require('1.11.1')
from kivy.app import App
from kivy.uix.floatlayout import FloatLayout

# We will need some classes.
from kivy.graphics import Line, Color, Translate, Scale, PushMatrix, PopMatrix
from kivy.uix.label import Label

class TestLayout(FloatLayout):
    def __init__(self, **kwargs):
        super().__init__(**kwargs)

        with self.canvas:
            # Save the context.
            PushMatrix()

            # Set color to green.
            Color(0, 1, 0, 1)

            # Draw the first line.
            Line(points=(100, 100, 120, 200, 150, 120, 180, 150, 200, 100),
                 width=5, close=True)

            # Scale the coordinate space.
            Scale(2, 2, 0, origin=(100, 100))

            # Translate the coordinate space.
            Translate(200, 0)

            # Draw the second line.
            Line(points=(100, 100, 120, 200, 150, 120, 180, 150, 200, 100),
                 width=5, close=True)

            # Restore the saved context.
            PopMatrix()

        # Add the label.
        self.add_widget(Label(text='Done', font_size=40, pos=(100, 200),
                              size_hint=(None, None), size=(100, 50)))

class TestApp(App):
    def build(self):
        return TestLayout()

if __name__ == '__main__':
    TestApp().run()
```

The app is written completely in Python. If you run it, you'll see the same result as before.

# Chapter 57 - Adding Colors to the Slugrace Project

In the preceding chapters we were talking about graphics in Kivy. In particular, we learned how to draw shapes on widgets, how to add colors and how to manipulate the coordinate space using context instructions. In this chapter we'll implement some of what we learned in the Slugrace project.

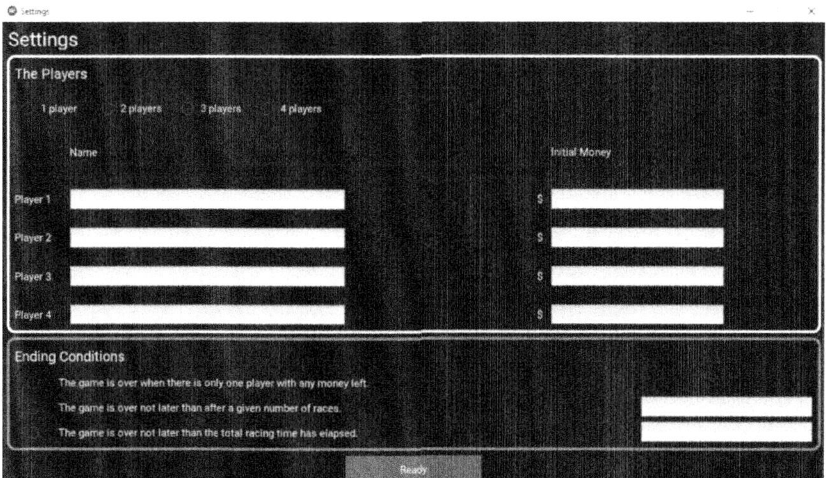


The first thing that we're going to take care of are the colors. Open the **settings.py** file and run the program.

You'll see a window with a black background and white rounded rectangles around the Players and Ending Conditions areas.

If you compare this with the final version, you will see that the color of the whole window in the latter is a shade of yellow. This color is applied to the root widget, so let's do it now.

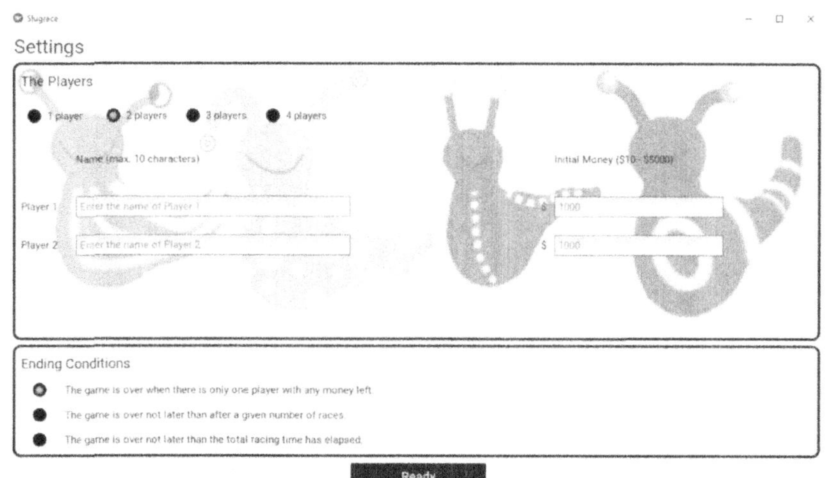


Open the **settings.kv** file and draw a yellow rectangle the size of the root widget.

Let's set the color of the rectangle to `(1, 1, .8, 1)`, which is the same shade of yellow as that in the final version.

Here's the code:

```
#:kivy 1.11.1
# File name: settings.kv
...
<SettingsScreen>:
    canvas:
        Color:
            rgba: 1, 1, .8, 1
        Rectangle:
            pos: self.pos
            size: self.size

    orientation: 'vertical'
    padding: 10
    spacing: 10

    ### SETTINGS LABEL ###
    ...
```

If you now run the app, the background color will be the shade of yellow we wanted.

But now, with the yellow background color, there is very little contrast between the background and the text. This is because, as you could see before, the text color on our labels was the default white. Let's change it to something darker. As all our labels are instances of the **RegularLabel** class or one of its subclasses, let's set the color in the **RegularLabel** class rule. Remember, though, that we're not changing the **Color** property of the coordinate space context, but just the **color** property of the label:

```
#:kivy 1.11.1
# File name: settings.kv

### LABELS ###
<RegularLabel@Label>:
    color: .2, .1, 0, 1
    text_size: self.size
    halign: 'left'
    valign: 'center'

<TitleLabel@RegularLabel>:
    ...
```

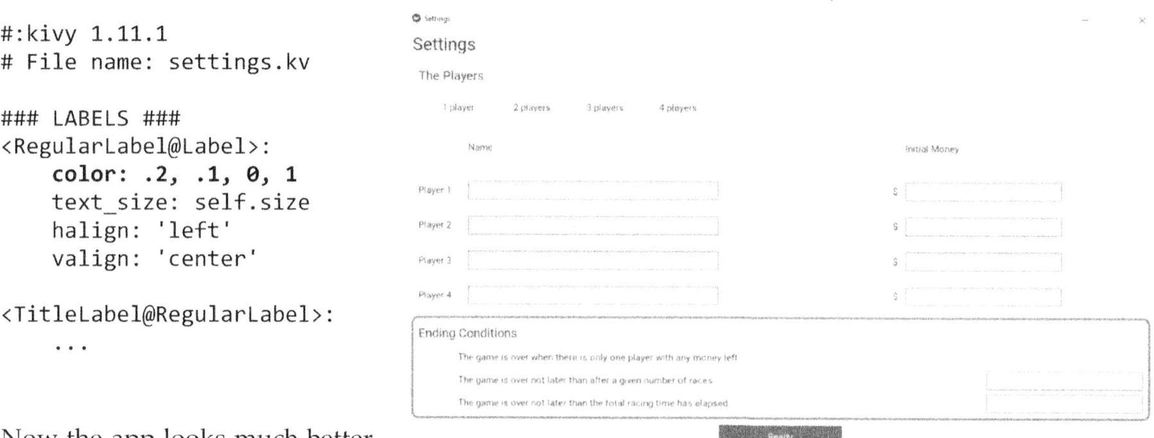


Now the app looks much better.

Better, but not yet perfect. There's still some work to do, but this is very simple, so I'll leave it for you as an exercise. First, you will add some more colors to the Settings screen and then to the other screens. Most of this code will be repetitive, for example you will have to change the text color in the **RegularLabel** class rule in each screen. Later, we will put the **RegularLabel** class, as well as all the other classes that are shared by multiple screens, in a separate file, but for now do it in each screen one by one – just for practice.

In the next chapter we will add even more colors to our widgets in order to style them a bit. As you can see, the radio buttons are hardly visible right now. And the button could look better, too.

# It's Your Turn Now...

### EXERCISE

Follow the instructions to add more colors:

1. The rounded rectangles around the main areas of the Settings screen are a shade of brown. There are two locations in the kv file where the rounded rectangles are drawn: one in the Players area and the other in the Ending Conditions area. Find these two locations, and add the `Color` instruction before the instruction that draws the shape. Set the `rgba` property to `(.2, .1, 0, 1)` – this is the shade of brown that we need.

2. We're done with the Settings screen for now. Let's open the other screens, so Race, Bets, Results and Game Over and do the same changes there. In the kv files of the screens that I just mentioned add the yellow rectangle to the root widget, then change the color of the text on the `RegularLabel` class and finally change the color of the rounded rectangles. Use the same colors as in the Settings screens.

Remark:

- In the Race screen the labels in the Track and Bets areas are not RegularLabels, but just instances of the `Label` class. Make sure to change the text color on all instances.

### SOLUTION

The **settings.kv** file should look like so:

```
#:kivy 1.11.1
# File name: settings.kv

### LABELS ###
<RegularLabel@Label>:
    color: .2, .1, 0, 1
    text_size: self.size
    halign: 'left'
    valign: 'center'
...
<SettingsScreen>:
    canvas:
        Color:
            rgba: 1, 1, .8, 1
        Rectangle:
            pos: self.pos
            size: self.size
```

```
        orientation: 'vertical'
        padding: 10
        spacing: 10

        ### SETTINGS LABEL ###
        ...
        ### THE PLAYERS ###
        BoxLayout:
            canvas:
                Color:
                    rgba: .2, .1, 0, 1
                Line:
                    rounded_rectangle: self.x, self.y, self.width, self.height, 10
                    width: 2

            ...
        ### ENDING CONDITIONS ###
        BoxLayout:
            canvas:
                Color:
                    rgba: .2, .1, 0, 1
                Line:
                    rounded_rectangle: self.x, self.y, self.width, self.height, 10
                    width: 2
            ...
```

If you now run the app, the Settings screen will look much better.

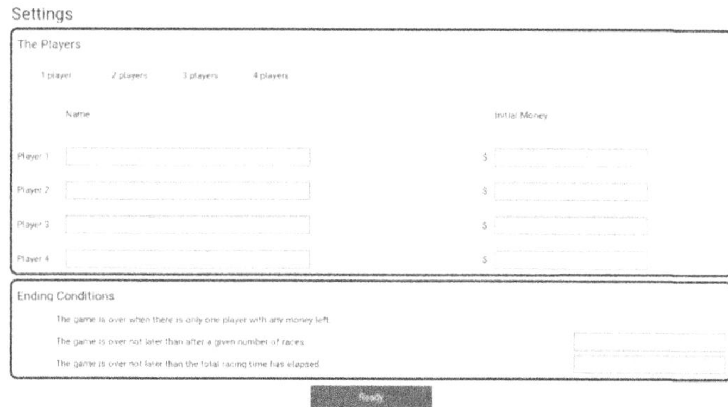


Let's move on to the Race screen. If you run the code now, you will see the black window.

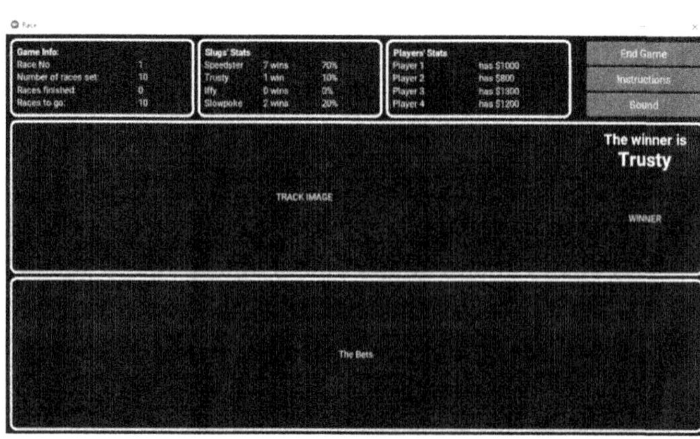

Here's the code with all the changes highlighted and commented:

```
#:kivy 1.11.1
# File name: race.kv

### CLASS RULES ###

<RegularLabel@Label>:
    # darker text color
    color: .2, .1, 0, 1
    text_size: self.size
    ...
<RaceScreen>:
    # The yellow rectangle on the root widget.
    canvas:
        Color:
            rgba: 1, 1, .8, 1
        Rectangle:
            pos: self.pos
            size: self.size

    orientation: 'vertical'
    ...
    ### INFO, STATS AND BUTTONS ###
    GridLayout:
        ...
        # Game Info
        BoxLayout:
            canvas:
                # a shade of brown for the rounded rectangle
                Color:
                    rgba: .2, .1, 0, 1
                Line:
                    ...
        # Slugs' Stats
        BoxLayout:
            canvas:
                # a shade of brown for the rounded rectangle
                Color:
                    rgba: .2, .1, 0, 1
                Line:
                    ...
        # Players' Stats
        BoxLayout:
            canvas:
                # a shade of brown for the rounded rectangle
                Color:
                    rgba: .2, .1, 0, 1
                Line:
                    ...
```

```
### THE TRACK ###
BoxLayout:
    canvas:
        # a shade of brown for the rounded rectangle
        Color:
            rgba: .2, .1, 0, 1
        Line:
            ...
    # Track Image
    Label:
        # darker text color
        color: .2, .1, 0, 1
        text: 'TRACK IMAGE'

    # Winner
    BoxLayout:
        ...
        Label:
            # darker text color
            color: .2, .1, 0, 1
            text: "The winner is"
            ...
        Label:
            # darker text color
            color: .2, .1, 0, 1
            text: "Trusty"
            ...
        Label:
            # darker text color
            color: .2, .1, 0, 1
            text: 'WINNER'

### THE BETS ###
Label:
    canvas:
        # a shade of brown for the rounded rectangle
        Color:
            rgba: .2, .1, 0, 1
        Line:
            rounded_rectangle: self.x, self.y, self.width, self.height, 10
            width: 2

    # darker text color
    color: .2, .1, 0, 1
    text: 'The Bets'
```

With these changes in place, the Race screen now looks better too.

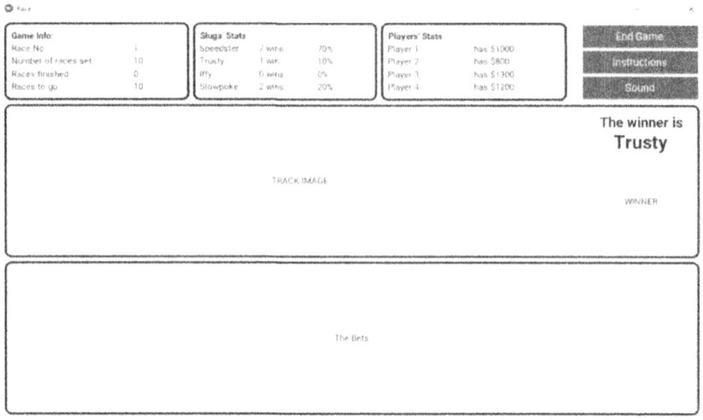

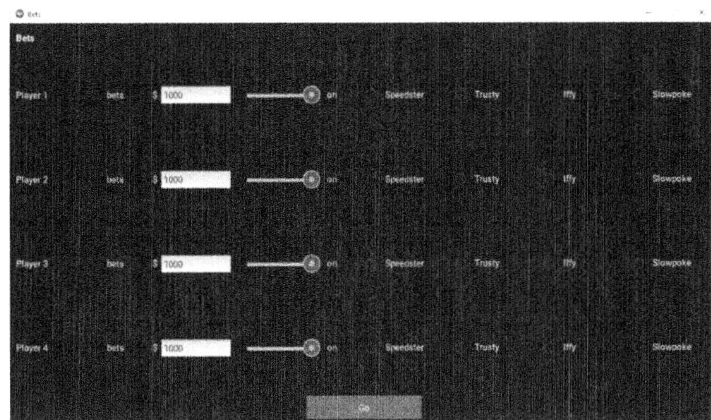

And now the Bets screen. Just like the other screens, it's black right now.

We don't have any rounded rectangles here, so we only have to take care of the background color and the text color on the **RegularLabel** class.

Here's the code with all necessary changes:

```
#:kivy 1.11.1
# File name: bets.kv

### LABELS ###
<RegularLabel@Label>:
    # darker text color
    color: .2, .1, 0, 1
    text_size: self.size
    ...
<BetsScreen>:
    # The yellow rectangle
    # on the root widget.
    canvas:
        Color:
            rgba: 1, 1, .8, 1
        Rectangle:
            pos: self.pos
            size: self.size

    orientation: 'vertical'
    ...
```

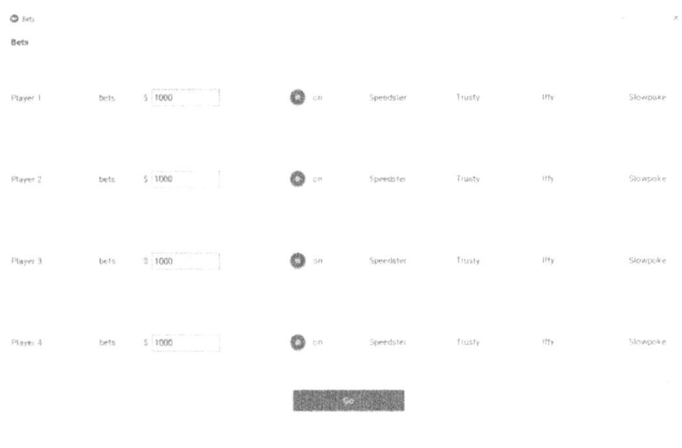

Now the Bets screen is as yellow as the other screens. And now the Results screen. It's no less black than the others used to be.

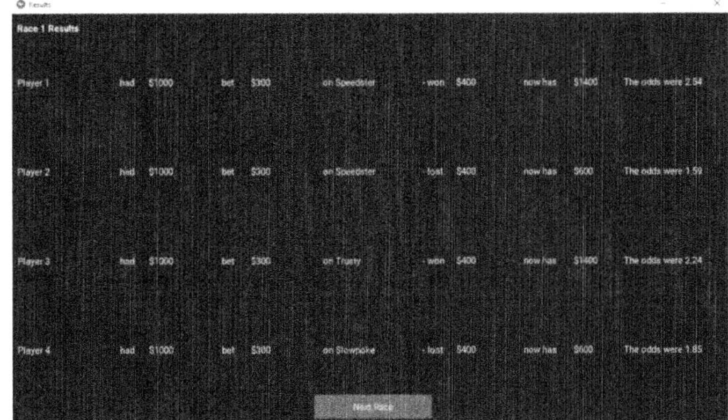

There aren't any rounded rectangles here either, so let's just change the background color to yellow and the color of the text on the **RegularLabel** class:

```
#:kivy 1.11.1
# File name: results.kv

### CLASS RULES ###
<RegularLabel@Label>:
    # darker text color
    color: .2, .1, 0, 1
```

```
        text_size: self.size
    ...
<ResultsScreen>:
    # The yellow rectangle
    # on the root widget.
    canvas:
        Color:
            rgba: 1, 1, .8, 1
        Rectangle:
            pos: self.pos
            size: self.size

    orientation: 'vertical'
    ...
```

And now the screen is yellow. Finally, the Game Over screen.

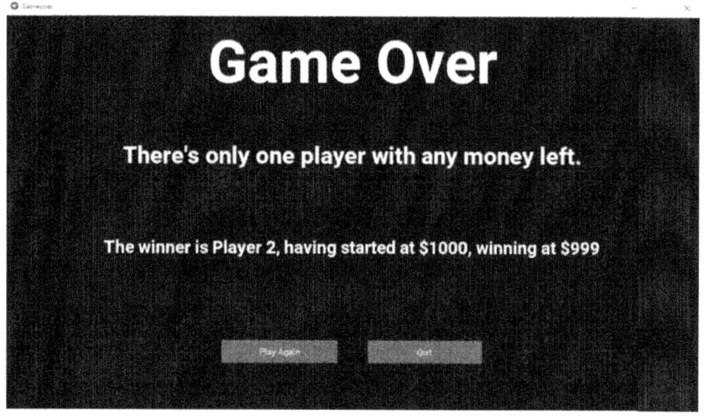
Game Over
There's only one player with any money left.
The winner is Player 2, having started at $1000, winning at $999

Again, all we have to do is change the color of the background and of the text on the **RegularLabel** class:

```
#:kivy 1.11.1
# File name: gameover.kv

### CLASS RULES ###
<RegularLabel@Label>:
    # darker text color
    color: .2, .1, 0, 1
    text_size: self.size
    halign: 'left'
    ...
<GameoverScreen>:
    # The yellow rectangle
    # on the root widget.
    canvas:
        Color:
            rgba: 1, 1, .8, 1
        Rectangle:
            pos: self.pos
            size: self.size

    orientation: 'vertical'
    ...
```

Game Over
There's only one player with any money left.
The winner is Player 2, having started at $1000, winning at $999

And now it's as yellow as the other screens.

# Chapter 58 - Styling the Widgets in the Slugrace Project

In the previous chapter we added some colors to our screens. However, except for the text color on the labels, we didn't touch the widgets. Let's add some styling to them too. By styles I mean colors and other properties that have a visual effect.

As I have already mentioned multiple times, in the final version of the app all class rules that are shared by more than one screen will be moved to one file and referenced from there. This way we will be able to define their styles only in one place. For the time being, though, we'll have to repeat the same code for each screen if we want the same styles.

## The Buttons

Let's start with the buttons. Generally, we want all buttons to look similar, for the sake of consistency. Have a look at the Ready button in the final version of the Settings screen and in the current version:

final version | current version

Ready | Ready

As you can see, the colors of both the text and the background are different. Let's make the button look like in the final version then. In the class rules, above the root widget, we'll add a custom button class. The background color of the button is going to be a shade of red, so let's name the class **RedButton**. Then let's use an instance of this new button instead of the regular button that we now have. Here's the code:

```
#:kivy 1.11.1
# File name: settings.kv

### LABELS ###
...
### BUTTONS ###
<RedButton@Button>:
    # The background color should be a shade of red.
    background_color: .8, 0, 0, 1

    # The text color should be a shade of yellow.
    color: 1, .8, .1, 1
```

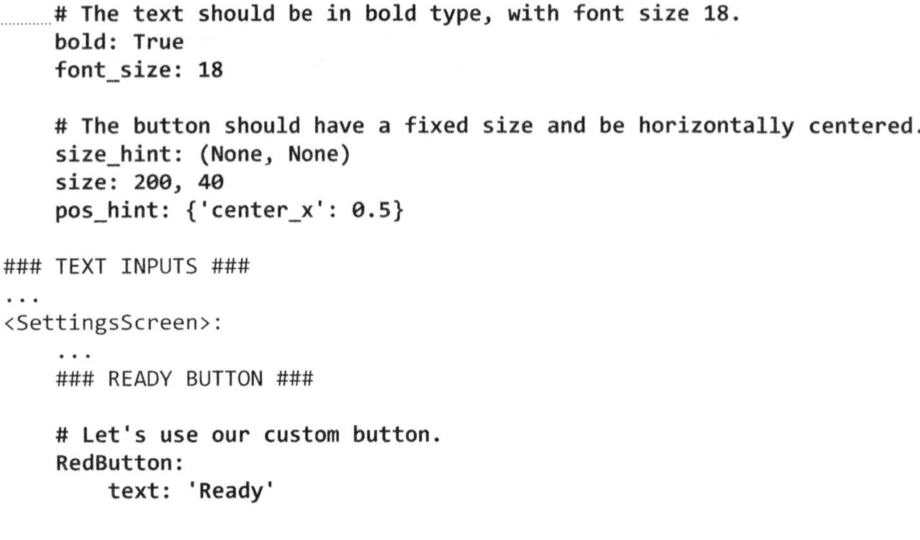

```
    # The text should be in bold type, with font size 18.
    bold: True
    font_size: 18

    # The button should have a fixed size and be horizontally centered.
    size_hint: (None, None)
    size: 200, 40
    pos_hint: {'center_x': 0.5}

### TEXT INPUTS ###
...
<SettingsScreen>:
    ...
    ### READY BUTTON ###

    # Let's use our custom button.
    RedButton:
        text: 'Ready'
```

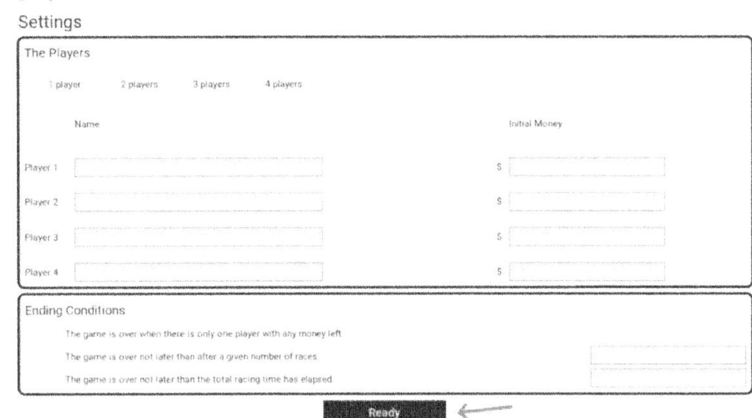


Now the button should look like in the final version.

Later, in the exercise I'll ask you to do the same with all the buttons in the other screens. And now let's have a look at the other widgets that we definitely have to handle, the check boxes, or rather the radio buttons, because it's how the check boxes are used in our project.

At this moment the radio buttons are hardly visible. In the final version the circles that you can check are filled, so let's do it now. Or, you know what? You can do it yourself as an exercise too. And after you're done with that, in the next chapter we'll add some graphics to the background using canvas instructions.

# It's Your Turn Now...

### EXERCISE 1 - STYLING THE BUTTONS

In this exercise you will style the buttons in the remaining screens.

Styling the other buttons is easy. All you have to do is copy the **RedButton** class rule to the other screens with buttons, so all the other screens to be precise. After that you have to replace all the instances of **Button** with **RedButton**.

If any properties should differ from the ones set in the class rule, remember that you can overwrite them on the instance.

One thing to notice is that in the Race screen we already created a custom button, the **RightButton**. If you compare the **RedButton** with the **RightButton**, you will see that, apart from the styling properties (**background_color**, **color** and **bold**), which the latter is currently lacking, they only differ in position. Have a look:

**RedButton**

```
<RedButton@Button>:
    background_color: .8, 0, 0, 1
    color: 1, .8, .1, 1
    bold: True
    font_size: 18
    size_hint: (None, None)
    size: 200, 40
    pos_hint: {'center_x': 0.5}
```

**RightButton**

```
<RightButton@Button>:
    font_size: 18
    size_hint: (None, None)
    size: 200, 40
    pos_hint: {'right': 1}
```

I don't think we need two custom buttons that only differ in one property (we would add the styling properties anyway), so let's get rid of the **RightButton** class and let's replace the three **RightButton** instances by three **RedButton** instances. Make sure to overwrite the **pos_hint** property in each of them, though.

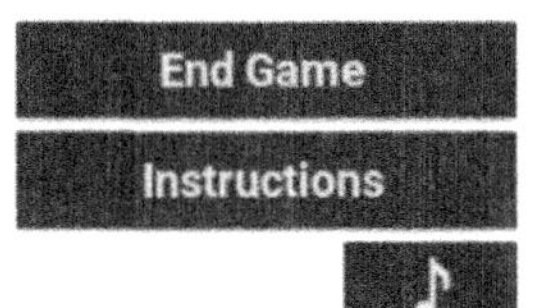


There's one more thing about the buttons in the Race screen, and in particular about the third one. If you look at the final version of the screen, you can see that it's much shorter.

This means that we have to overwrite not only the **pos_hint** property on that button instance, but also the **size** property. The size of the button should be 70 x 40 px.

As for the other screens, there's nothing special you have to think about.

## SOLUTION

Let's have a look at all the screens one by one. We already covered the Settings screen in the chapter text, so next comes the Race screen. That's the one with the most changes:

```
#:kivy 1.11.1
# File name: race.kv
...
<BoldLabel@RegularLabel>:
    bold: True

# The RedButton class rule.
# Make sure to remove the RightButton class.
<RedButton@Button>:
    background_color: .8, 0, 0, 1
```

```
    color: 1, .8, .1, 1
    bold: True
    font_size: 18
    size_hint: (None, None)
    size: 200, 40
    pos_hint: {'center_x': 0.5}

<RaceScreen>:
    ...
    ### INFO, STATS AND BUTTONS ###
    ...
        # Buttons
        BoxLayout:
            orientation: 'vertical'
            spacing: 3
            size_hint: .7, 1

            # We're replacing the three RightButtons with RedButtons.
            # We have to overwrite the pos_hint property.
            RedButton:
                text: 'End Game'
                pos_hint: {'right': 1}

            RedButton:
                text: 'Instructions'
                pos_hint: {'right': 1}

            # Here we have to overwrite the size property too.
            RedButton:
                text: 'Sound'
                pos_hint: {'right': 1}
                size: 70, 40

    ### THE TRACK ###
    ...
```

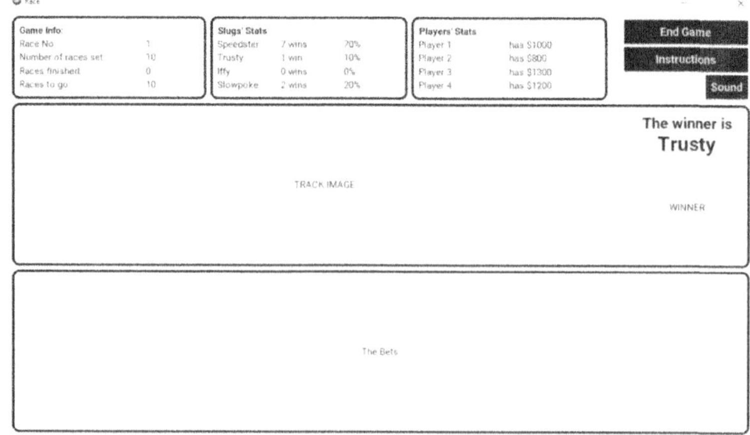


Now the Race screen should look a little more like in the final version.

Next, let's have a look at the Bets screen. Here's the code:

```
#:kivy 1.11.1
# File name: bets.kv
..
### OTHER WIDGETS ###
<PlayerSlugButton@CheckBox>:
    size_hint: (.5, 1)

# The RedButton class rule.
<RedButton@Button>:
```

```
    background_color: .8, 0, 0, 1
    color: 1, .8, .1, 1
    bold: True
    font_size: 18
    size_hint: (None, None)
    size: 200, 40
    pos_hint: {'center_x': 0.5}

<BetsScreen>:
    ...
    ### GO BUTTON ###

    # We're replacing Button with RedButton.
    RedButton:
        text: 'Go'
```

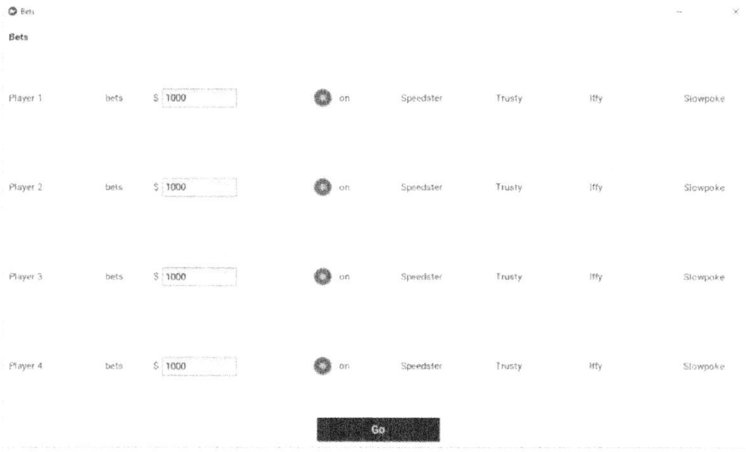

If you now run the code, you will see a nice red button also here.

And here's the code of the Results screen:

```
#:kivy 1.11.1
# File name: results.kv

### CLASS RULES ###
...
<BoldLabel@RegularLabel>:
    bold: True

# The RedButton class rule.
<RedButton@Button>:
    background_color: .8, 0, 0, 1
    color: 1, .8, .1, 1
    bold: True
    font_size: 18
    size_hint: (None, None)
    size: 200, 40
    pos_hint: {'center_x': 0.5}

<ResultsScreen>:
    ...
    ### NEXT RACE BUTTON ###

    # We're replacing Button with RedButton.
    RedButton:
        text: 'Next Race'
```

If you run the code, you will see the following a red button again, just like you wanted.

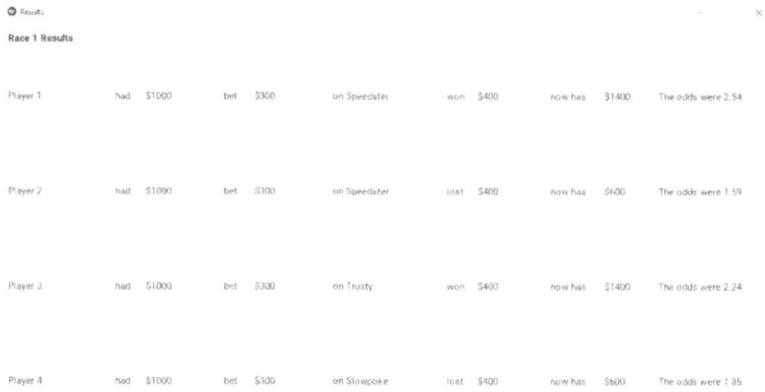


And finally the Game Over screen. Here's the kv code:

```
#:kivy 1.11.1
# File name: gameover.kv

### CLASS RULES ###
...
<BoldLabel@RegularLabel>:
    bold: True

# The RedButton class rule.
<RedButton@Button>:
    background_color: .8, 0, 0, 1
    color: 1, .8, .1, 1
    bold: True
    font_size: 18
    size_hint: (None, None)
    size: 200, 40
    pos_hint: {'center_x': 0.5}

<GameoverScreen>:
    ...
    BoxLayout:
        spacing: 50
        pos_hint: {'center_x': .5, 'center_y': .5}
        size_hint: None, None
        size: 450, 200

        # We're replacing Button with RedButton, but
        # we have to overwrite the pos_hint property.
        RedButton:
            text: 'Play Again'
            pos_hint: {'x': 0, 'center_y': .5}
        RedButton:
            text: 'Quit'
            pos_hint: {'right': 1, 'center_y': .5}
```

Here you can see two red buttons if you execute the code.

Game Over

There's only one player with any money left.

The winner is Player 2, having started at $1000, winning at $999

Play Again Quit

### EXERCISE 2 - STYLING THE RADIO BUTTONS

In this exercise you will style all the radio buttons throughout the project. There are radio buttons in two screens, the Settings screen and the Bets screen. Let's start with the former. You will find two classes defined in the class rules section in the **settings.kv** file, **`PlayerRadioButton`** and **`ConditionRadioButton`**.

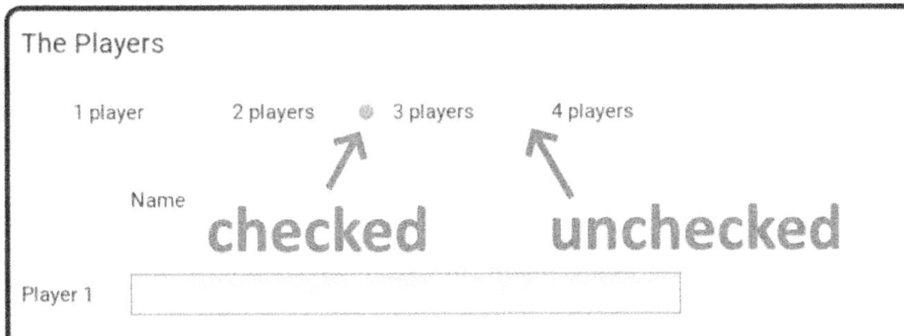


If you run the app, you will see that there's a little circle where you can click to check the radio button.

When unchecked, the circle is hardly visible. Let's replace it with a filled circle that you can see without difficulty.

You're going to start with the **`PlayerRadioButton`** class. To draw a filled circle you have to use the **`Color`** instruction and the **`Ellipse`** class. So, you need to add some canvas instructions. First, set the color to black (**`0, 0, 0, 1`**). The ellipse should be a circle. It should sit in the very center of the widget, but as you know, when you specify the position of an ellipse, you actually specify the position of its bottom-left corner, not the center. However, knowing that the radius of the circle is 20, it's easy to calculate the coordinates of its center. Remember to set the **`size`** property as well. It's also easy to calculate.

If you have done everything correctly so far, you should now see filled circles, which you can't check, though. Actually, you can check them, but you won't see the blue dot that appears when a radio button is checked. This is because the blue dot is drawn before the circle. But this can be easily fixed. You know that we can change the order in which things are drawn. Assuming you used the basic **`canvas`** instruction, just use one of the other canvas instructions instead. Now it should work as expected.

When you're done with the **PlayerRadioButton**, copy the canvas instructions to the **ConditionRadioButton** class and then to **PlayerSlugButton** in the **bets.kv** file.

## SOLUTION

Here's the **settings.kv** file:

```
#:kivy 1.11.1
# File name: settings.kv
...
### CHECK BOXES ###
<PlayerRadioButton@CheckBox>:
    # We want to draw something, so we need canvas instructions.
    # The black circle should be drawn first, so we should
    # use the canvas.before set of instructions.
    canvas.before:
        # At first let's set the color for the context.
        Color:
            rgba: 0,0,0,1

        # Then let's draw the ellipse. If the radius is 10, the bottom left
        # corner of the ellipse is 10 px to the left and 10 px in the
        # downward direction from the center of the radio button. The size
        # is twice the radius in both directions.
        Ellipse:
            pos:self.center_x - 10, self.center_y - 10
            size:[20,20]

    group: 'players'
    size_hint: (.5, 1)

<ConditionRadioButton@CheckBox>:
    # the same canvas instructions as with the PlayerRadioButton
    canvas.before:
        Color:
            rgba: 0,0,0,1
        Ellipse:
            pos:self.center_x - 10, self.center_y - 10
            size:[20,20]

    group: 'conditions'
    size_hint_x: .05

<SettingsScreen>:
    ...
```

1 player 2 players 3 players 4 players

If you now run the app, the radio buttons will be filled and you will see the blue dot when you check one of them.

And here's the **bets.kv** file:

```
#:kivy 1.11.1
# File name: bets.kv
..
### OTHER WIDGETS ###
<PlayerSlugButton@CheckBox>:
    canvas.before:
        Color:
            rgba: 0,0,0,1
        Ellipse:
            pos:self.center_x - 10, self.center_y - 10
            size:[20,20]

    size_hint: (.5, 1)

<RedButton@Button>:
    ...
```

If you run the app now, you'll see lots of beautifully styled radio buttons.

# Chapter 59 - Adding Background Graphics Using Canvas Instructions

In the preceding chapters we added some colors to our screens and widgets. But besides colors you can also add images. The **VertexInstruction** class, from which classes like **Rectangle** or **Ellipse** inherit, has the **source** property which you can use to add an image. Let's start with an example right away.

Open the **test.py** file and type in the following code:

```
# File name: test.py

from kivy.config import Config
Config.set('graphics', 'width', '1200')
Config.set('graphics', 'height', '675')
Config.set('graphics', 'resizable', '1')

import kivy
kivy.require('1.11.1')
from kivy.app import App
from kivy.uix.floatlayout import FloatLayout

class TestLayout(FloatLayout):
    pass

class TestApp(App):
    def build(self):
        return TestLayout()

if __name__ == '__main__':
    TestApp().run()
```

Then, in the **test.kv** file type in the following:

```
#:kivy 1.11.1
# File name: test.kv

<TestLayout>:
    canvas:
        Rectangle:
            pos: 100, 100
            size: 400, 100

        Rectangle:
            pos: 800, 100
            size: 350, 350

        Ellipse:
            pos: 200, 400
            size: 600, 250
```

If you run the app now, you will see a couple shapes.

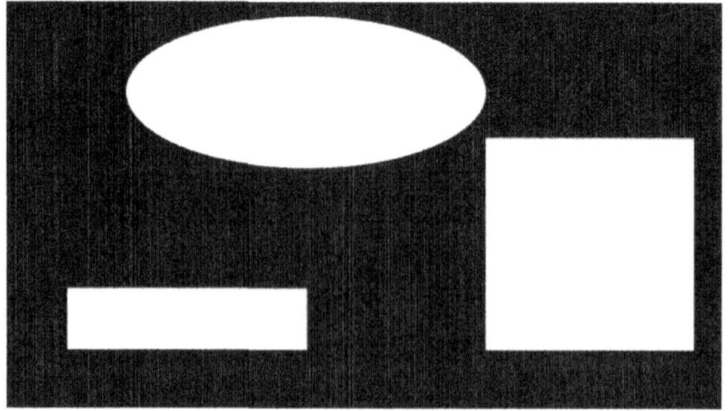

Let's set the **source** property of each of them to an image. We can use one of the images from our assets folder, for example the **racetrack.png** image.

Now the image will be drawn on each of the shapes.

Here's the kv code:

```
#:kivy 1.11.1
# File name: test.kv

<TestLayout>:
    canvas:
        Rectangle:
            pos: 100, 100
            size: 400, 100
            source: 'assets/racetrack.png'

        Rectangle:
            pos: 800, 100
            size: 350, 350
            source: 'assets/racetrack.png'

        Ellipse:
            pos: 200, 400
            size: 600, 250
            source: 'assets/racetrack.png'
```

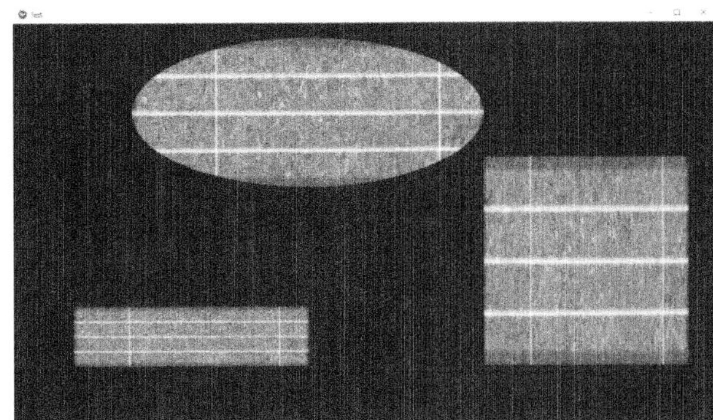

## Image and Color

If you additionally use the **Color** context instruction before the image is drawn, you will obtain an interesting effect. The color will not cover the image, but rather act like a light that illuminates the image. Let's change the color before each of the three shapes is drawn:

```
#:kivy 1.11.1
# File name: test.kv

<TestLayout>:
    canvas:
        # red
        Color:
            rgba: 1, 0, 0, 1
        Rectangle:
            pos: 100, 100
            size: 400, 100
            source: 'assets/racetrack.png'

        # green
        Color:
            rgba: 0, 1, 0, 1
        Rectangle:
            pos: 800, 100
            size: 350, 350
            source: 'assets/racetrack.png'

        # blue
        Color:
            rgba: 0, 0, 1, 1
        Ellipse:
            pos: 200, 400
            size: 600, 250
            source: 'assets/racetrack.png'
```

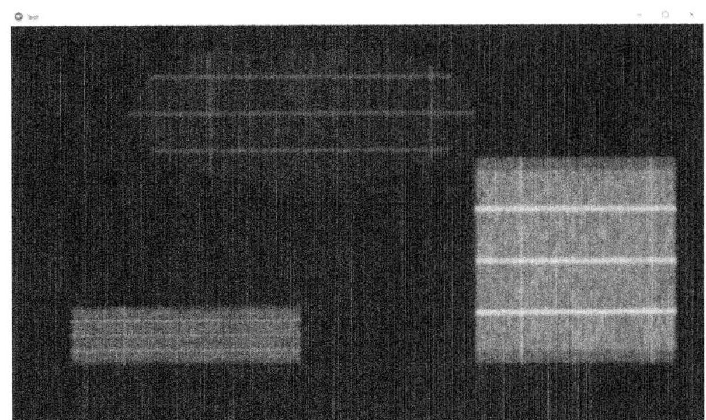

In the Slugrace app there's only going to be one background image. We have to add it to the Settings screen.

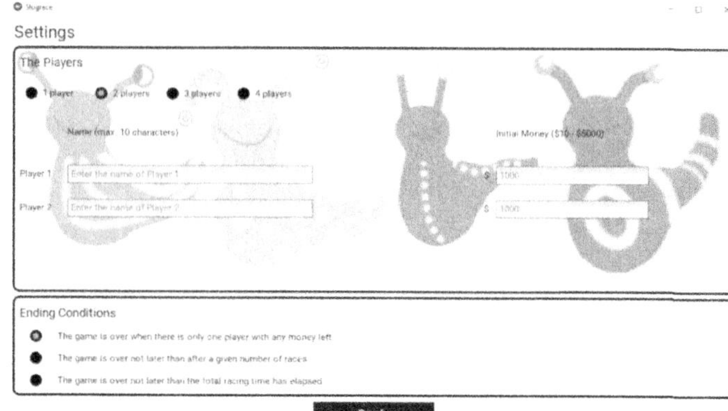


If you look at the final version of the screen, you can see the image with the silhouettes of all four slugs in the Players area.

But now that you already know how to do it, I'll leave it for you as an exercise.

And in the next chapter, we'll add the graphical assets to the Race screen. They include the track and the slugs.

# It's Your Turn Now...

### EXERCISE

Follow the instructions below to add the image with the silhouettes of the four slugs to the background of the Players area in the Settings screen:

1. First of all find the Players area in the **settings.kv** file. It should look like this:

```
#:kivy 1.11.1
# File name: settings.kv
...
<SettingsScreen>:
    ...
    ### THE PLAYERS ###
    BoxLayout:
        canvas:
            Color:
                rgba: .2, .1, 0, 1
            Line:
                rounded_rectangle: self.x, self.y, self.width, self.height, 10
                width: 2

        orientation: 'vertical'
        padding: 10
        spacing: 10

        # Title
        ...
```

There already are some canvas instructions, the one that sets the color and the one that draws the rounded rectangle.

2. In order to add an image, we need some shape to draw it on, like a rectangle. In this case it doesn't really matter whether we first draw the rectangle with the image and then the rounded rectangle or the other way around, because the two graphical elements don't overlap anywhere. However, it would matter if, for example, the rectangle with the image were bigger. Just to keep things orderly, add the rectangle with the image before the instructions that are already there. Just make sure the rectangle has the same position and size as the BoxLayout it's drawn on. The image file that you are going to add is called '**all slugs.png**' and it's in the assets folder.

3. If you were to run the program at this point, the image of the slugs would be very crisp with vivid colors. As you look at the final version of the screen, you can see that the colors are somewhat faded. We could have handled this in an image editor before we even added the image to the assets folder, but we can still do it here. As you remember, when you add both an image and a color, the color acts like light that illuminates the image. So, if we use the white color (1, 1, 1, 1), there is no difference. But if you only change the alpha value, the transparency and thus vividness of the image will change. To make this happen, add another **`Color`** instruction before the **`Rectangle`** instruction and set the color to **`(1, 1, 1, .4)`**.

The '**all slugs.png**' image has a transparent background so the only parts of it that can be influenced by the new color are the very silhouettes of the slugs.

## SOLUTION

Here's the code:

```
#:kivy 1.11.1
# File name: settings.kv
...
<SettingsScreen>:
    ...
    ### THE PLAYERS ###
    BoxLayout:
        canvas:
            # Let's change the alpha value to make the colors faded.
            Color:
                rgba: 1, 1, 1, .4

            # Let's add the rectangle with the image.
            Rectangle:
                pos: self.pos
                size: self.size
                source: 'assets/all slugs.png'

            Color:
                rgba: .2, .1, 0, 1
            Line:
                rounded_rectangle: self.x, self.y, self.width, self.height, 10
                width: 2
```

```
        orientation: 'vertical'
        padding: 10
        spacing: 10

        # Title
        ...
```

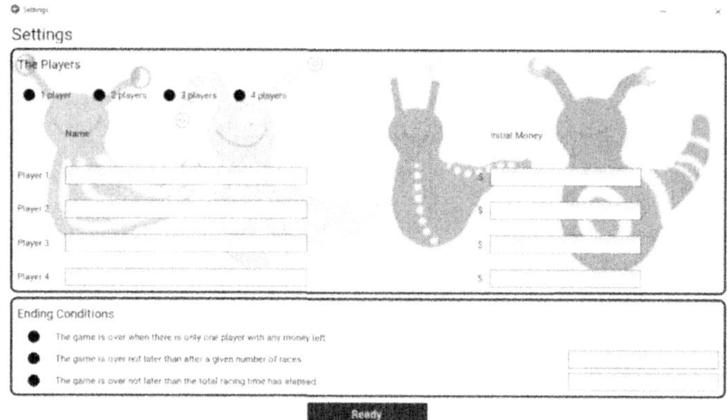


And now you can see the background image in the Settings screen.

# Chapter 60 - Adding the Graphical Assets to the Slugrace Project

In the previous chapter we added a background image to the Players area of the Settings screen. In this chapter we'll see how to add graphical assets to our project. We'll need graphical assets in the Race screen. Here's what they look like in the final version:

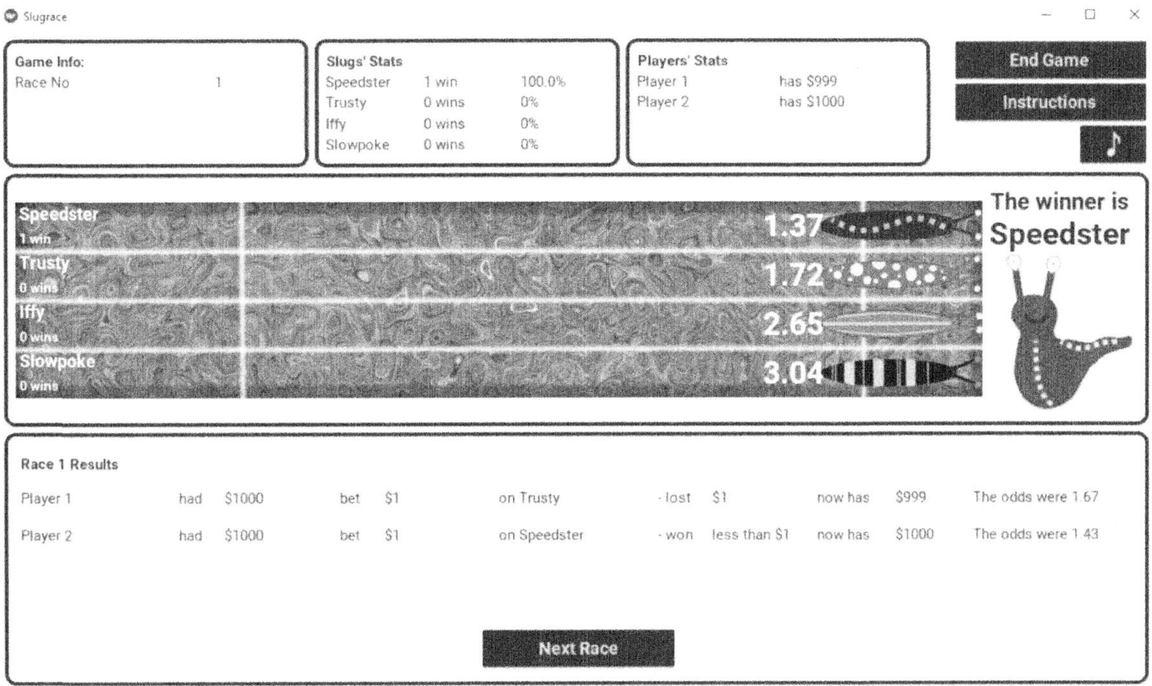


So, there is the track image, the four images of the slugs in top view and the silhouette image of the winning slug. Besides, there are some labels on top of the track, which we are going to add as well.

## The Track Image

Let's start with the **racetrack.png** image. You can find the file in the **assets** folder. If you hover your mouse over the file, you can see how big the image is. It's 1000 x 200 px. And this is the size we want it to be at all times during the game. Even if you resize the app window, the size of the racetrack image shouldn't change. So, we need a fixed size for the widget.

Now, what widget are we actually going to use? Well, there are several options, but the easiest one seems to be the `Image` widget, which is available in Kivy out of the box. All you have to do is set its

**source** property to the path to the image file.

So, let's implement the track image. At this moment we have some placeholder code in the Track area of the Race screen that displays a label with the text **'TRACK IMAGE'**. Here's the kv code:

```
#:kivy 1.11.1
# File name: race.kv
...
<RaceScreen>:
    ...
    ### THE TRACK ###
    BoxLayout:
        ...
        # Track Image
        Label:
            color: .2, .1, 0, 1

            text: 'TRACK IMAGE'

        # Winner
        ...
```

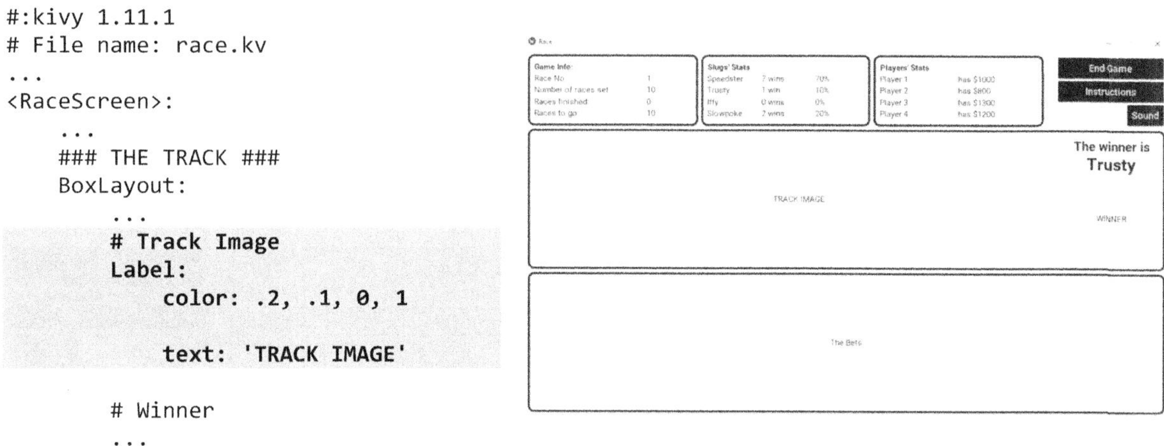


If you run the app now, you will see just the text. So, let's replace the label with an **Image** widget:

```
#:kivy 1.11.1
# File name: race.kv
...
<RaceScreen>:
    ...
    ### THE TRACK ###
    BoxLayout:
        ...
        # Track Image
        Image:
            #  the path to the image file
            source: 'assets/racetrack.png'

            # fixed size
            size_hint: None, None
            size: 1000, 200

            # centered vertically
            pos_hint: {'center_y': .5}

        # Winner
        ...
```

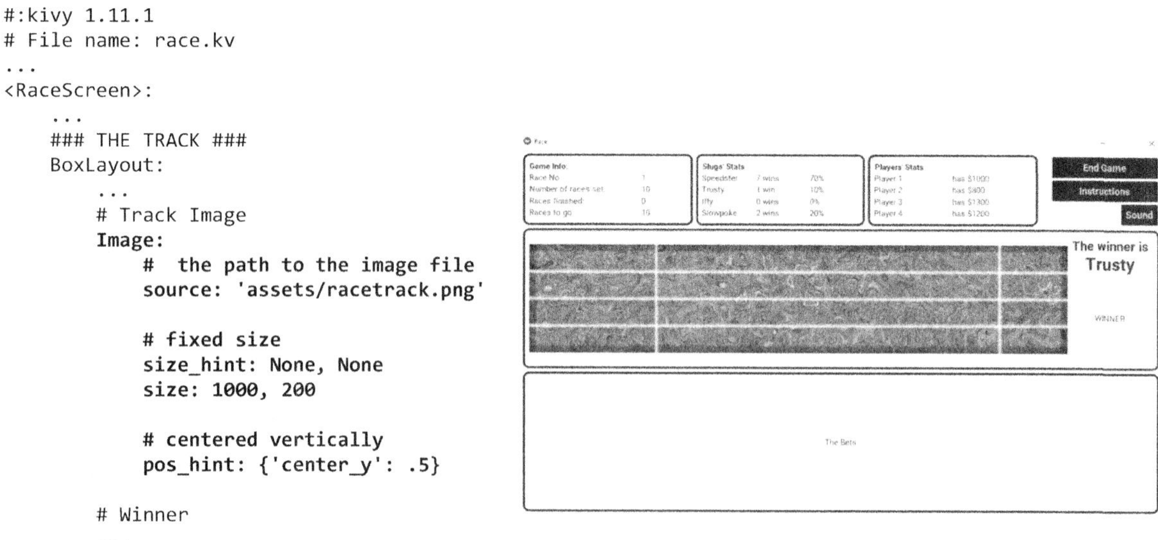


If you now run the app, you'll see the image in place. As you can see in the code, the Track area is implemented as a BoxLayout with two subareas: the Track Image subarea to the left and the Winner subarea to the right. The Winner subarea is the one you're going to take care of yourself as an exercise, but now let's concentrate on the Track Image subarea.

The track image itself is not the only thing we need in the Track Image subarea. There are also the top view images of the four slugs and some labels. So, it would be convenient to enclose all these elements in another container. It will be easier for us to use coordinates relative to the Track Image subarea when we add the other widgets, so a good candidate for the container is the **RelativeLayout**. So, let's add the layout and put the track image in it:

```
#:kivy 1.11.1
# File name: race.kv
...
<RaceScreen>:
    ...
    ### THE TRACK ###
    BoxLayout:
        ...
        # Track Image
        RelativeLayout:
            # Let's move the sizing and positioning
            # code to the container.
            size_hint: None, None
            size: 1000, 200
            pos_hint: {'center_y': .5}
            Image:
                source: 'assets/racetrack.png'

        # Winner
        ...
```

You may have noticed that I moved the sizing and positioning code to the layout now. There will be no difference if you run the app now, but it will make our life easier when we then add the other widgets. Speaking of which, let's add the white labels and the four slug images.

## The White Labels

Now, with the track image in place, let's position the labels on it. First of all, let's add some class rules. We're going to need three types of labels: the medium-sized ones for the names of the slugs, the small ones for the wins and the big ones for the odds. Let's name the classes **WhiteNameLabel**, **WhiteWinsLabel** and **WhiteOddsLabel** respectively.

Here are the class rules:

```
#:kivy 1.11.1
# File name: race.kv

### CLASS RULES ###

<RegularLabel@Label>:
    ...
<BoldLabel@RegularLabel>:
    ...

# the white labels
<WhiteOddsLabel@BoldLabel>:
    font_size: 32
    color: 1, 1, 1, 1

<WhiteNameLabel@BoldLabel>:
    font_size: 18
    color: 1, 1, 1, 1

<WhiteWinsLabel@BoldLabel>:
    font_size: 14
    color: 1, 1, 1, 1

<RedButton@Button>:
    ...
```

As you can see, these are just simple labels that inherit from the **BoldLabel** class, each of them with a different font size. Later in the book, when we discuss properties, we will create a custom widget that will hold the slug name and wins information, but for now let's just create four separate BoxLayouts, one for each slug and add some hardcoded text to them. The positions of the widgets in the RelativeLayout will be relative to the container.

To better understand where the vertical positions that I'm using come from, here's a little image of the RelativeLayout with the track image and the proportions that you can see in the code:

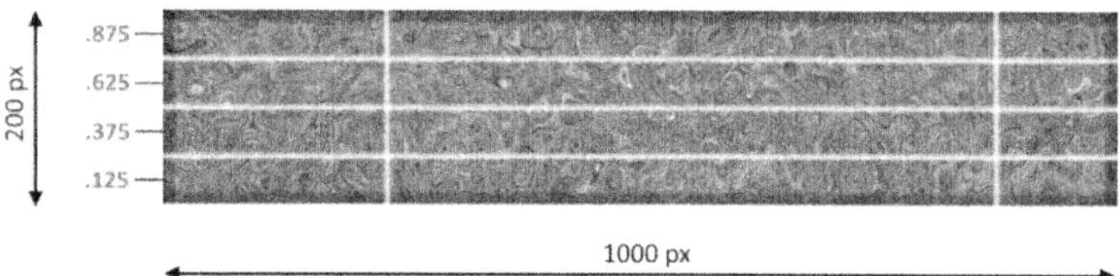


We just want each BoxLayout with the two slug info labels to be centered on the slug's own lane. By the way, the four lanes are separated by white lines, which are part of the image. The starting line and the finish line are also there.

Each BoxLayout will have a fixed size that will help us keep the text where we want it. To position the BoxLayout we'll use the **pos_hint** property values that will place it just slightly to the right of the left border of the parent layout (**RelativeLayout**) and centered vertically on its lane. These values are relative to the RelativeLayout.

Here's the code:

```
#:kivy 1.11.1
# File name: race.kv
...
<RaceScreen>:
    ...
    ### THE TRACK ###
    BoxLayout:
        ...
        # Track Image
        RelativeLayout:
            size_hint: None, None
            size: 1000, 200
            pos_hint: {'center_y': .5}
            Image:
                source: 'assets/racetrack.png'
            # white labels with slug info
            # Speedster
            BoxLayout:
                orientation: 'vertical'
                size_hint: None, None
                size: 100, 50
                pos_hint: {'x': .004, 'center_y': .875}
```

```
            WhiteNameLabel:
                text: 'Speedster'
            WhiteWinsLabel:
                text: '0 wins'
        # Trusty
        BoxLayout:
            orientation: 'vertical'
            size_hint: None, None
            size: 100, 50
            pos_hint: {'x': .004, 'center_y': .625}
            WhiteNameLabel:
                text: 'Trusty'
            WhiteWinsLabel:
                text: '0 wins'
        # Iffy
        BoxLayout:
            orientation: 'vertical'
            size_hint: None, None
            size: 100, 50
            pos_hint: {'x': .004, 'center_y': .375}
            WhiteNameLabel:
                text: 'Iffy'
            WhiteWinsLabel:
                text: '0 wins'
        # Slowpoke
        BoxLayout:
            orientation: 'vertical'
            size_hint: None, None
            size: 100, 50
            pos_hint: {'x': .004, 'center_y': .125}
            WhiteNameLabel:
                text: 'Slowpoke'
            WhiteWinsLabel:
                text: '0 wins'
    # Winner
    ...
```

If you now run the app, you will see the names and wins on the track image:

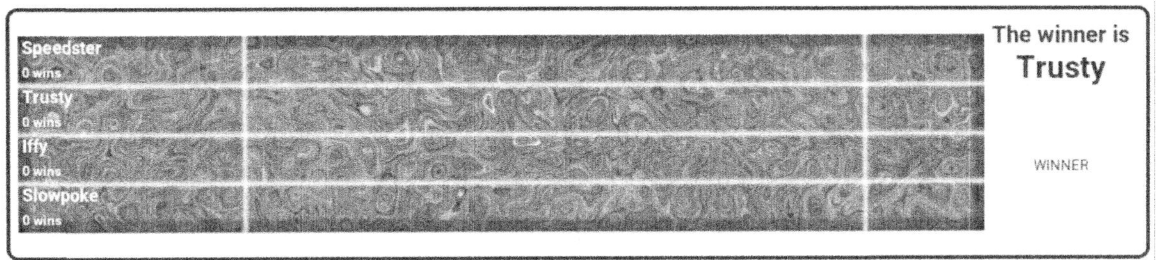


Even if you resize the window (probably you would have to change the **resizable** property to **1** in the configuration section in the **race.py** file first), the labels will remain on the track, relative to the RelativeLayout their containing BoxLayouts are in. If you want, feel free to check it out.

The last thing to do, as far as the white labels are concerned, are the big odds labels. They should be positioned near the finish line. Here's the code:

```
#:kivy 1.11.1
# File name: race.kv
...
<RaceScreen>:
    ...
    ### THE TRACK ###
    BoxLayout:
        ...
        # Track Image
        RelativeLayout:
            ...
            # white labels with slug info
            ...
            # the odds labels
            # Speedster
            WhiteOddsLabel:
                text: '1.42'
                pos_hint: {'x': .77, 'center_y': .875}
            # Trusty
            WhiteOddsLabel:
                text: '1.61'
                pos_hint: {'x': .77, 'center_y': .625}
            # Iffy
            WhiteOddsLabel:
                text: '2.53'
                pos_hint: {'x': .77, 'center_y': .375}
            # Slowpoke
            WhiteOddsLabel:
                text: '2.89'
                pos_hint: {'x': .77, 'center_y': .125}
        # Winner
        ...
```

Now we have all the labels in place:

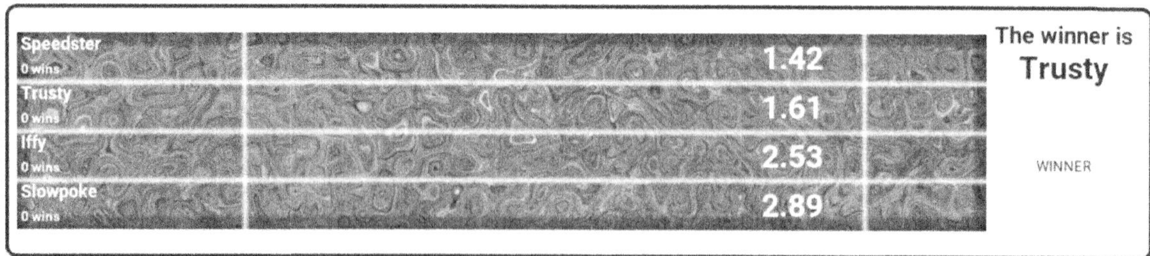


Next, we're going to add the top view images of the four slugs.

# The Top View Slug Images

You can find the images in the **slugs** subfolder of the **assets** folder. There are actually two images for each slug: body (235 x 49 px) and eye (54 x 12 px). Each slug image should then actually consist of three smaller images: the body and two eyes. To make the code less repetitive, we will later create a custom widget and then add four instances of it in the Track Image subarea, but for now, let's add just four RelativeLayouts each containing the respective body and two eyes.

In the final version of the Race screen, the slugs will move their eyes. For now, the eyes will be immobile, but still, we will rotate them so that they are positioned at an angle relative to the body. To do that, we'll use some canvas context instructions like **PushMatrix** and **PopMatrix** to save and restore the context respectively, as well as **Rotate**, to actually rotate the eyes. And one more thing, when I use the word 'eye' in the context of our project, I mean the whole tentancle with the eye at the end. Sorry for not being biologically correct.

Here's the code with explanations in comments. It's lengthy, but pretty straightforward, so just take your time to examine it carefully:

```
#:kivy 1.11.1
# File name: race.kv
...
<RaceScreen>:
    ...
    ### THE TRACK ###
    BoxLayout:
        ...
        # Track Image
        RelativeLayout:
            ...
            # white labels with slug info
            ...
            # the odds labels
            ...
            # slug images
            # Speedster
            # By putting the body image and two instances of the eye image in a RelativeLayout, we
            # will be able to position the eyes relative to the body easily. The exact values that
            # I'm using in the size and pos_hint properties were determined by trial and error and
            # just seem to be working fine for our purposes.
            RelativeLayout:
                pos_hint: {'x': .09, 'center_y': .875}
                size_hint: None, None
                size: 143, 30
                # the body image
                Image:
                    source: 'assets/slugs/speedsterBody.png'
                # the left eye image
                Image:
                    canvas.before:
                        # Let's save the context before rotation.
                        PushMatrix
                        # Let's rotate the eye 30 degrees counterclockwise on the Z axis around the
                        # point which is horizontally on the left border of the eye image and
```

```
                    # vertically halfway its height.
                    Rotate:
                        angle: 30
                        axis: 0, 0, 1
                        origin: self.x, self.center_y
                canvas.after:
                    # Let's restore the context.
                    PopMatrix
                source: 'assets/slugs/speedsterEye.png'
                # The position of the eye is relative to the RelativeLayout it's in along with
                # the body image and the other eye image.
                pos_hint: {'x': .95, 'y': .45}
                # Let's scale the eye image down so that it looks well-proportioned.
                size_hint: 0.25, 0.25
            # the right eye image
            Image:
                canvas.before:
                    PushMatrix
                    Rotate:
                        angle: -30
                        axis: 0, 0, 1
                        origin: self.x, self.center_y
                canvas.after:
                    PopMatrix
                source: 'assets/slugs/speedsterEye.png'
                pos_hint: {'x': .95, 'y': .3}
                size_hint: 0.25, 0.25
        # Trusty
        RelativeLayout:
            pos_hint: {'x': .09, 'center_y': .625}
            size_hint: None, None
            size: 143, 30
            # the body image
            Image:
                source: 'assets/slugs/trustyBody.png'
            # the left eye image
            Image:
                canvas.before:
                    PushMatrix
                    Rotate:
                        angle: 30
                        axis: 0, 0, 1
                        origin: self.x, self.center_y
                canvas.after:
                    PopMatrix
                source: 'assets/slugs/trustyEye.png'
                pos_hint: {'x': .95, 'y': .45}
                size_hint: 0.25, 0.25
            # the right eye image
            Image:
                canvas.before:
                    PushMatrix
                    Rotate:
                        angle: -30
                        axis: 0, 0, 1
                        origin: self.x, self.center_y
                canvas.after:
                    PopMatrix
                source: 'assets/slugs/trustyEye.png'
                pos_hint: {'x': .95, 'y': .3}
```

```
                size_hint: 0.25, 0.25
        # Iffy
        RelativeLayout:
            pos_hint: {'x': .09, 'center_y': .375}
            size_hint: None, None
            size: 143, 30
            # the body image
            Image:
                source: 'assets/slugs/iffyBody.png'
            # the left eye image
            Image:
                canvas.before:
                    PushMatrix
                    Rotate:
                        angle: 30
                        axis: 0, 0, 1
                        origin: self.x, self.center_y
                canvas.after:
                    PopMatrix
                source: 'assets/slugs/iffyEye.png'
                pos_hint: {'x': .95, 'y': .45}
                size_hint: 0.25, 0.25
            # the right eye image
            Image:
                canvas.before:
                    PushMatrix
                    Rotate:
                        angle: -30
                        axis: 0, 0, 1
                        origin: self.x, self.center_y
                canvas.after:
                    PopMatrix
                source: 'assets/slugs/iffyEye.png'
                pos_hint: {'x': .95, 'y': .3}
                size_hint: 0.25, 0.25
        # Slowpoke
        RelativeLayout:
            pos_hint: {'x': .09, 'center_y': .125}
            size_hint: None, None
            size: 143, 30
            # the body image
            Image:
                source: 'assets/slugs/slowpokeBody.png'
            # the left eye image
            Image:
                canvas.before:
                    PushMatrix
                    Rotate:
                        angle: 30
                        axis: 0, 0, 1
                        origin: self.x, self.center_y
                canvas.after:
                    PopMatrix
                source: 'assets/slugs/slowpokeEye.png'
                pos_hint: {'x': .95, 'y': .45}
                size_hint: 0.25, 0.25
            # the right eye image
            Image:
                canvas.before:
                    PushMatrix
                    Rotate:
```

```
                            angle: -30
                            axis: 0, 0, 1
                            origin: self.x, self.center_y
                    canvas.after:
                        PopMatrix
                    source: 'assets/slugs/slowpokeEye.png'
                    pos_hint: {'x': .95, 'y': .3}
                    size_hint: 0.25, 0.25
        # Winner
        ...
```

If you now run the app, you will see the images of the slugs on the track:

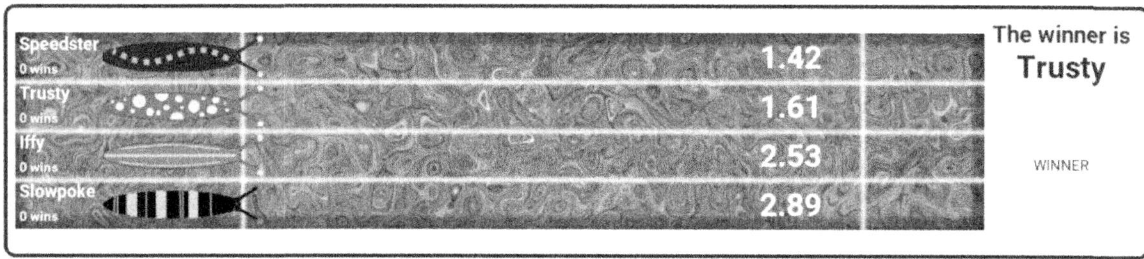


This looks much better. The only thing that we still have to take care of is the winner image, but this is extremely easy to do. You will do it in no time as an exercise and after that we'll be done with our graphical assets... Or, almost done. In the next chapter I'll show you how to organize graphical assets in an atlas and how to use the atlas.

# It's Your Turn Now...

### EXERCISE

At this moment we have the following code that creates the Winner subarea of the Track area:

```
#:kivy 1.11.1
# File name: race.kv
...
<RaceScreen>:
    ...
    ### THE TRACK ###
    ...
        # Winner
        BoxLayout:
            orientation: 'vertical'
            size_hint: (.18, 1)
            Label:
                color: .2, .1, 0, 1
                text: "The winner is"
                font_size: 24
                size_hint: 1, .2
                bold: True
            Label:
                color: .2, .1, 0, 1
                text: "Trusty"
                font_size: 32
                size_hint: 1, .2
                bold: True
            Label:
                color: .2, .1, 0, 1
                text: 'WINNER'

    ### THE BETS ###
    ...
```

In the image on the right you can see what it looks like when you run the app.

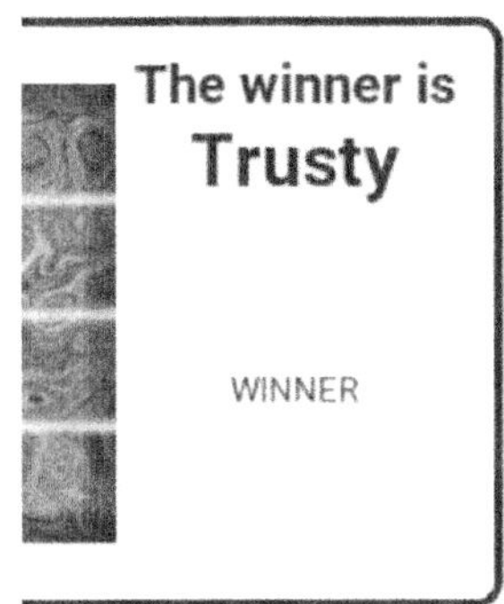


Now, your task is very easy, just replace the label with the text **'WINNER'** with an image of a slug. Which slug exactly appears here will later depend on which one has won a particular race, but for now let's just choose one of them as a placeholder, for example Trusty.

You will find the image file in the **silhouettes** subfolder of the **assets** folder. The name of the file is **Trusty.png**.

## SOLUTION

Here's the code:

```
#:kivy 1.11.1
# File name: race.kv
...
<RaceScreen>:
    ...
    ### THE TRACK ###
    ...
        # Winner
        BoxLayout:
            ...

            Label:
                ...
            Label:
                color: .2, .1, 0, 1
                text: "Trusty"
                ...
            Image:
                source: 'assets/silhouettes/Trusty.png'

    ### THE BETS ###
    ...
```

And you should now see the silhouette of Trusty on the right. This slug is going to be a permanent winner for some time now.

# Chapter 61 - Making and Using an Atlas

In the previous chapter we added the graphical assets to our project. In our app there are just a few images and they are all loaded only once, so we don't have to worry about things like loading time. In larger projects there may be more images, some of which may be requested from a remote server, so in such cases loading time is something that might matter. To efficiently manage the loading of images, we can group all the images that an app makes use of in one big image, the so-called **atlas**.

As mentioned before, in our case this isn't necessary, but I will create and use an atlas anyway so that you can see how to do it in case you develop an app with lots of images.

If you open the **assets** folder, you will find some images directly in this folder, and some more in a couple subfolders. I will create three atlases, one for each of the subfolders. I won't create an atlas for the images that are directly in the **assets** folder, so we'll be referencing images both directly and through the atlases.

We could equally well create one big atlas with all the images, but in our simple application it doesn't really matter so much.

## Creating an Atlas

To create an atlas, you should follow a few steps. Let's demonstrate this on the example of the top view slug images that are in the **slugs** subfolder of the **assets** folder. Here are the images that you can see in the folder:

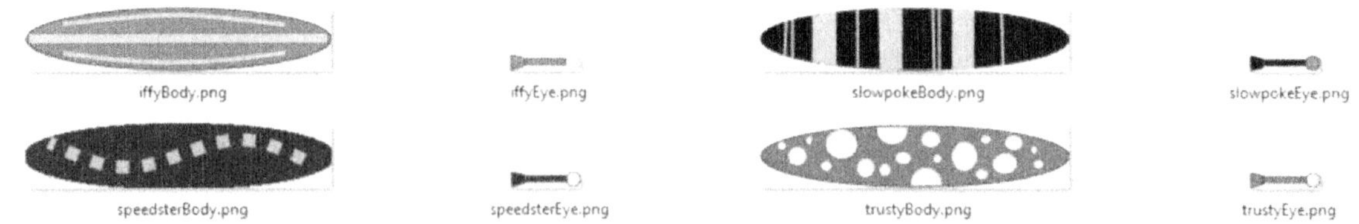


So, here are the steps:

1. First of all we have to know how big an atlas we need. It should be as small as possible. If you open the **slugs** subfolder you can hover over the images that you want to put into your atlas and check their dimensions.

In our case there are four 235 x 49 px images of slug bodies and four 54 x 12 px images of slug eyes. This means that if we stacked them vertically (the bodies one below another, and then all eyes in one row), we would need a minimum height of:

4 x 49 px + 12 px = 208 px

We would also need a minimum width of 235 px because this is more than 4 times the width of an eye image and will be enough for the body images.

So, we need an atlas that is minimum 235 x 208 px, let's make it 240 x 220 px. If we miscalculate the size, two things may happen:

- If the size in any dimension is less than the size of the largest image in that dimension, we'll get an error and no atlas will be created.

- If the size in each dimension is greater than the size of the largest image in that direction, but if it's still not enough for all the images to fit in, two or more atlas images will be created.

Before we actually create the atlas image, we'll see what happens if we miscalculate the size.

2. To create the atlas image we need to open the terminal and go to the directory where our images are:

Anaconda Prompt (Anaconda3)

```
(base) C:\Users\PC>d:

(base) D:\>cd D:\Coder\Python\Courses\Kivy Basics Course\book\code\slugrace61\assets\slugs

(base) D:\Coder\Python\Courses\Kivy Basics Course\book\code\slugrace61\assets\slugs>
```

Naturally, it will be a different directory on your computer.

3. There is a command that you can use in the terminal to create an atlas, but before you can use it, make sure to install the pillow library. You can use pip do do that:

```
pip install pillow
```

4. With pillow installed, you can use the command that will create the atlas. Here's the syntax:

```
python -m kivy.atlas basename size images
```

As you can see, we use this command with three parameters: **basename**, **size** and **images**. Let me explain briefly what mean:

- **basename**

The command will create two files, the atlas image file and a json file. We're going to discuss the two files a bit later. Anyway, the basename will be used as the prefix of the two files, as you will see in a minute.

- **size**

This is the size of the atlas image that we are going to create. If you pass just one number here, like for example 500, the atlas image will be a square (500 x 500 px in this case). You can also pass the width and hight, for example 500x200, then the atlas will be a rectangle.

- **images**

This is just the list of all the files that you want to go into the atlas. You can either list the files separating them by spaces or you can use the * wildcard to select for example all the files with the extension **.png**. We'll see this in action in a moment.

And now, before we actually create the atlas, we'll try out a couple options, just to practice. We're going to use the basename **'slugs'**.

First, let's try to create an atlas image which is not big enough for the largest image to fit in. The largest images are the body images, each 235 x 49 px, so a size 100 x 100 px is definitely not enough. We want all the png files to go into the atlas. Here's the command:

```
python -m kivy.atlas slugs 100 *.png
```

Here's what happens:

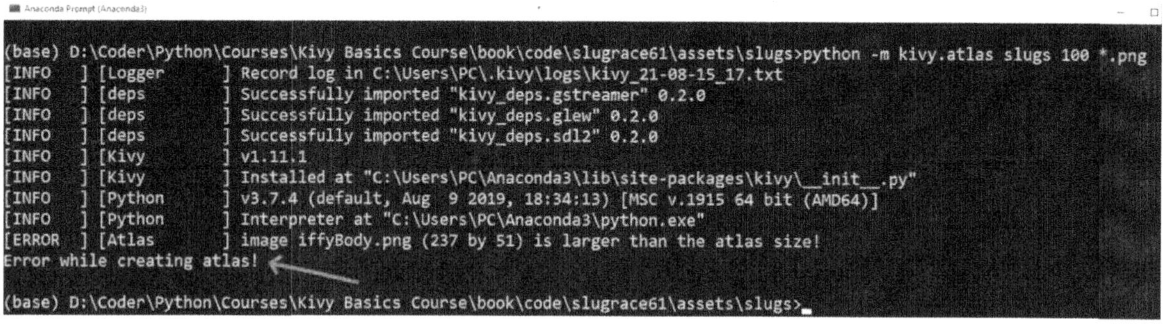

```
(base) D:\Coder\Python\Courses\Kivy Basics Course\book\code\slugrace61\assets\slugs>python -m kivy.atlas slugs 100 *.png
[INFO   ] [Logger      ] Record log in C:\Users\PC\.kivy\logs\kivy_21-08-15_17.txt
[INFO   ] [deps        ] Successfully imported "kivy_deps.gstreamer" 0.2.0
[INFO   ] [deps        ] Successfully imported "kivy_deps.glew" 0.2.0
[INFO   ] [deps        ] Successfully imported "kivy_deps.sdl2" 0.2.0
[INFO   ] [Kivy        ] v1.11.1
[INFO   ] [Kivy        ] Installed at "C:\Users\PC\Anaconda3\lib\site-packages\kivy\__init__.py"
[INFO   ] [Python      ] v3.7.4 (default, Aug  9 2019, 18:34:13) [MSC v.1915 64 bit (AMD64)]
[INFO   ] [Python      ] Interpreter at "C:\Users\PC\Anaconda3\python.exe"
[ERROR  ] [Atlas       ] image iffyBody.png (237 by 51) is larger than the atlas size!
Error while creating atlas!

(base) D:\Coder\Python\Courses\Kivy Basics Course\book\code\slugrace61\assets\slugs>
```

We get an error because the size that we specified was not enough.

OK, so now let's try to create a larger atlas, but still not large enough for all the images to fit in, like for example 300 x 200 px. Here's the command:

```
python -m kivy.atlas slugs 300x200 *.png
```

Now the atlas is created:

```
(base) D:\Coder\Python\Courses\Kivy Basics Course\book\code\slugrace61\assets\slugs>python -m kivy.atlas slugs 300x200 *.png
[INFO   ] [Logger      ] Record log in C:\Users\PC\.kivy\logs\kivy_21-08-15_18.txt
[INFO   ] [deps        ] Successfully imported "kivy_deps.gstreamer" 0.2.0
[INFO   ] [deps        ] Successfully imported "kivy_deps.glew" 0.2.0
[INFO   ] [deps        ] Successfully imported "kivy_deps.sdl2" 0.2.0
[INFO   ] [Kivy        ] v1.11.1
[INFO   ] [Kivy        ] Installed at "C:\Users\PC\Anaconda3\lib\site-packages\kivy\__init__.py"
[INFO   ] [Python      ] v3.7.4 (default, Aug  9 2019, 18:34:13) [MSC v.1915 64 bit (AMD64)]
[INFO   ] [Python      ] Interpreter at "C:\Users\PC\Anaconda3\python.exe"
[INFO   ] [Atlas       ] create an 300x200 rgba image
Atlas created at slugs.atlas
2 images have been created

(base) D:\Coder\Python\Courses\Kivy Basics Course\book\code\slugrace61\assets\slugs>
```

But as the size of the atlas image was not enough for all the images to fit in, we got two atlas images. If you now open the folder where the images are, you will see three new files:

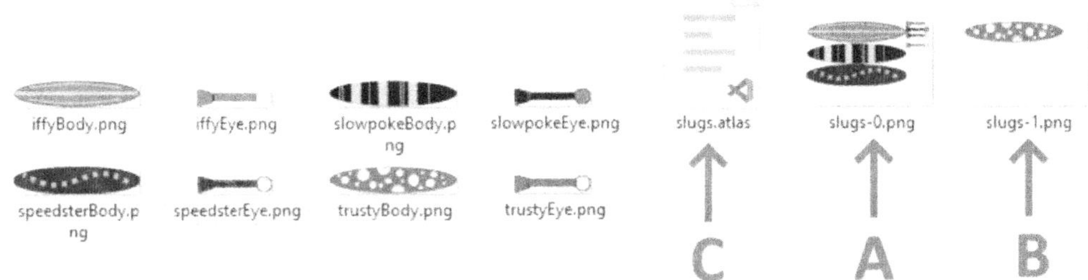


Two of them are atlas images (A and B), and one is a json file (C). As you look at the names of the files, they all have the basename as the prefix. So, the first atlas image is called **slugs-0.png**. There are as many images in it as it was possible to pack. But there was too little room, so another atlas image, **slugs-1.png**, had to be created. It contains the last image. You could leave it like this, it will work perfectly, but we're going to create just one atlas image that is large enough for all the images to fit.

But before that, let's play a little more with the atlases. Now, let's create an atlas that contains just a couple selected images.

First, delete the three files you just created. And then let's create an atlas with three images: **iffyBody.png**, **trustyBody.png** and **speedsterEye.png**, for example. A size of 250 x 150 will be more than enough:

```
python -m kivy.atlas slugs 250x150 iffyBody.png trustyBody.png speedsterEye.png
```

Here's what the terminal shows:

```
(base) D:\Coder\Python\Courses\Kivy Basics Course\book\code\slugrace61\assets\slugs>python -m kivy.
atlas slugs 250x150 iffyBody.png trustyBody.png speedsterEye.png
[INFO   ] [Logger      ] Record log in C:\Users\PC\.kivy\logs\kivy_21-08-15_19.txt
[INFO   ] [deps        ] Successfully imported "kivy_deps.gstreamer" 0.2.0
[INFO   ] [deps        ] Successfully imported "kivy_deps.glew" 0.2.0
[INFO   ] [deps        ] Successfully imported "kivy_deps.sdl2" 0.2.0
[INFO   ] [Kivy        ] v1.11.1
[INFO   ] [Kivy        ] Installed at "C:\Users\PC\Anaconda3\lib\site-packages\kivy\__init__.py"
[INFO   ] [Python      ] v3.7.4 (default, Aug  9 2019, 18:34:13) [MSC v.1915 64 bit (AMD64)]
[INFO   ] [Python      ] Interpreter at "C:\Users\PC\Anaconda3\python.exe"
[INFO   ] [Atlas       ] create an 250x150 rgba image
Atlas created at slugs.atlas
1 image has been created

(base) D:\Coder\Python\Courses\Kivy Basics Course\book\code\slugrace61\assets\slugs>
```

So, this time one image has been created. Here's the folder:

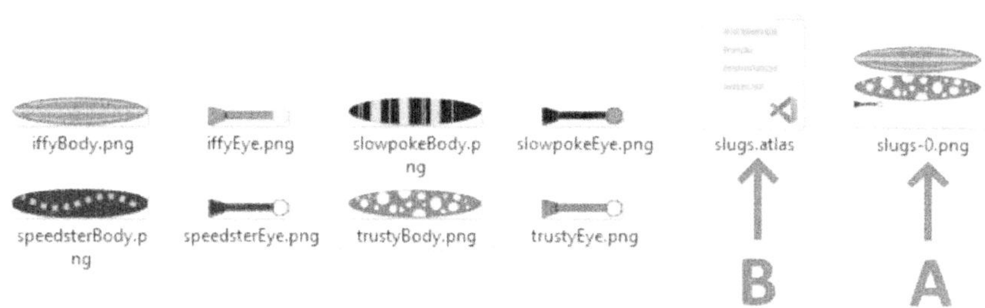


Now we have one atlas image, **slugs-0.png** (A), and the accompanying json file (B).

Fine, and now we can create the atlas that we are actually going to use. First, delete the two files that were just created in your folder. Now, we want our atlas to be just a single image with all the PNG images that are in the folder. Its size should be 240 x 220 px, which, as we calculated, should be enough. So, here's the command:

```
python -m kivy.atlas slugs 240x220 *.png
```

Here's what we can see in the console:

```
(base) D:\Coder\Python\Courses\Kivy Basics Course\book\code\slugrace61\assets\slugs>python -m kivy.atlas
slugs 240x220 *.png
[INFO   ] [Logger      ] Record log in C:\Users\PC\.kivy\logs\kivy_21-08-15_20.txt
[INFO   ] [deps        ] Successfully imported "kivy_deps.gstreamer" 0.2.0
[INFO   ] [deps        ] Successfully imported "kivy_deps.glew" 0.2.0
[INFO   ] [deps        ] Successfully imported "kivy_deps.sdl2" 0.2.0
[INFO   ] [Kivy        ] v1.11.1
[INFO   ] [Kivy        ] Installed at "C:\Users\PC\Anaconda3\lib\site-packages\kivy\__init__.py"
[INFO   ] [Python      ] v3.7.4 (default, Aug  9 2019, 18:34:13) [MSC v.1915 64 bit (AMD64)]
[INFO   ] [Python      ] Interpreter at "C:\Users\PC\Anaconda3\python.exe"
[INFO   ] [Atlas       ] create an 240x220 rgba image
Atlas created at slugs.atlas
1 image has been created

(base) D:\Coder\Python\Courses\Kivy Basics Course\book\code\slugrace61\assets\slugs>
```

And here's what we can see in the folder: The four body and the four eye images have been nicely packed in one single image.

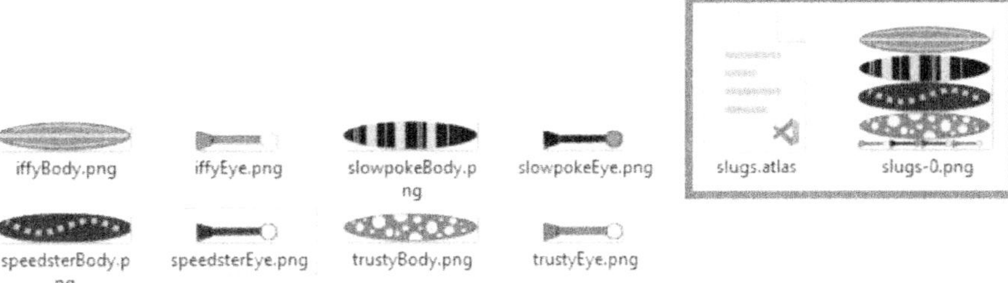


And, as usual, there's the json file as well. So, now we have the atlas that we will be using in our project. We could delete all the eight single images now, but who knows, maybe we need them one day, so let's just keep them. In the project, however, we're not going to use the single images, but just the atlas.

Later, in the exercises, you will be creating two more atlases, one for the silhouette images and one for the accident images, but for now, let's have a look at the two files that were created.

# The Atlas Image and the json File

You might have noticed that each time an atlas was created, an additional json file was created with the extension **.atlas**. So, there may be one or more atlas image files and just one json file. Why is the json file there? Well, this file specifies the coordinates of the single images inside the atlas image. To see the contents of the json file, just open it in any text editor, like Notepad or directly inside VSC. Here's what you should see:

```
{"slugs-0.png": {"iffyBody": [2, 169, 235, 49], "slowpokeBody": [2, 118, 235,
49], "speedsterBody": [2, 67, 235, 49], "trustyBody": [2, 16, 235, 49],
"iffyEye": [2, 2, 54, 12], "slowpokeEye": [58, 2, 54, 12], "speedsterEye": [114,
2, 54, 12], "trustyEye": [170, 2, 54, 12]}}
```

And here's the same slightly formatted for better readability:

```
{"slugs-0.png":
    {"iffyBody": [2, 169, 235, 49],
     "slowpokeBody": [2, 118, 235, 49],
     "speedsterBody": [2, 67, 235, 49],
     "trustyBody": [2, 16, 235, 49],
     "iffyEye": [2, 2, 54, 12],
     "slowpokeEye": [58, 2, 54, 12],
     "speedsterEye": [114, 2, 54, 12],
     "trustyEye": [170, 2, 54, 12]
     }
}
```

Here we have each atlas image specified (there's only one in our case, **slugs-0.png**) and inside the atlas image we have each single image that we put into the atlas. Here you can see the names of the single images, by which we will refer to them later in the code. And there are the coordinates of the images in the format `[x, y, width, height]`. This is enough for our program to know where to look for each image.

## How to Use the Atlas

And finally, now that we have the atlas, let's use it in our project. We're going to modify the code in the **race.kv** file where the images of the slugs were created. Here's the code for the first slug image as it looks now:

```
#:kivy 1.11.1
# File name: race.kv
...
<RaceScreen>:
    ...
    ### THE TRACK ###
    BoxLayout:
        ...
        # Track Image
        RelativeLayout:
            ...
            # slug images
            # Speedster
            RelativeLayout:
                ...
                # the body image
                Image:
                    source: 'assets/slugs/speedsterBody.png'

                # the left eye image
                Image:
                    ...
                    source: 'assets/slugs/speedsterEye.png'
                    ...
                # the right eye image
                Image:
                    ...
                    source: 'assets/slugs/speedsterEye.png'
                    ...
            # Trusty
            ...
```

Now, if you want to set the source of the speedsterBody image, here's the syntax:

```
source: 'atlas://assets/slugs/slugs/speedsterBody'
```

So, first we have the prefix **'atlas:'** followed by a double slash, then the path to the atlas (highlighted in yellow), the name of the atlas (highlighted in green – this is just the basename we used to create the atlas, without the number attached to it, so it will be the same even if there are more atlas images) and finally the name of the image without the extension (highlighted in blue – this is the name that you saw in the json file).

And now let's modify the source properties for all the images. Here's the code:

```
#:kivy 1.11.1
# File name: race.kv
...
<RaceScreen>:
    ...
    ### THE TRACK ###
    ...
            # slug images
            # Speedster
            RelativeLayout:
                ...
                # the body image
                Image:
                    source: 'atlas://assets/slugs/slugs/speedsterBody'

                # the left eye image
                ...
                    source: 'atlas://assets/slugs/slugs/speedsterEye'
                    ...
                # the right eye image
                Image:
                    ...
                    source: 'atlas://assets/slugs/slugs/speedsterEye'
                    ...
            # Trusty
            RelativeLayout:
                ...
                # the body image
                Image:
                    source: 'atlas://assets/slugs/slugs/trustyBody'

                # the left eye image
                Image:
                    ...
                    source: 'atlas://assets/slugs/slugs/trustyEye'
                    ...
                # the right eye image
                Image:
                    ...
                    source: 'atlas://assets/slugs/slugs/trustyEye'
                    ...
            # Iffy
            RelativeLayout:
                ...
                # the body image
                Image:
                    source: 'atlas://assets/slugs/slugs/iffyBody'

                # the left eye image
                Image:
                    ...
                    source: 'atlas://assets/slugs/slugs/iffyEye'
```

```
                    ...
                # the right eye image
                Image:
                    ...
                    source: 'atlas://assets/slugs/slugs/iffyEye'
                    ...
            # Slowpoke
            RelativeLayout:
                ...
                # the body image
                Image:
                    source: 'atlas://assets/slugs/slugs/slowpokeBody'

                # the left eye image
                Image:
                    ...
                    source: 'atlas://assets/slugs/slugs/slowpokeEye'
                    ...
                # the right eye image
                Image:
                    ...
                    source: 'atlas://assets/slugs/slugs/slowpokeEye'
                    ...
        # Winner
        ...
```

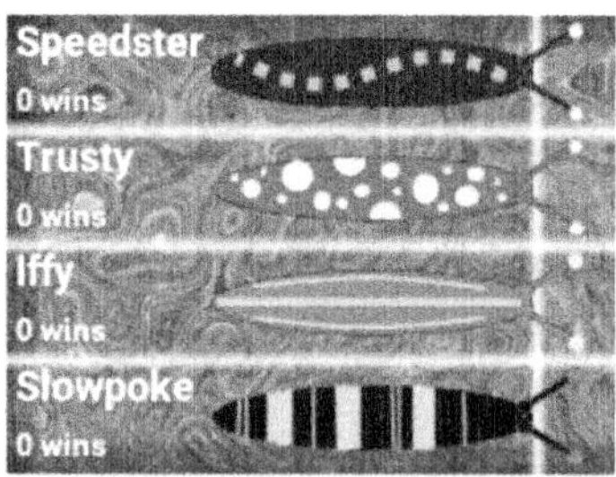


If you now run the app, you will see exactly the same images as before.

Well, that's it. We're done with the graphics. Or, almost done. In the exercises below you will create two more atlases and use them in the project. And then, in the next part, we will finally start working on the logic of the game.

## It's Your Turn Now...

In these exercises you will create two more atlases and use them in the project.

**EXERCISE 1**

You're going to start with the silhouette images of the slugs. They are in the **silhouettes** subfolder of the **assets** folder, the full path on your computer will be different than on mine, so keep that in mind when you specify the path in the terminal. Each of the 4 images is 400 x 400 px.

**SOLUTION**

If you have already closed your terminal, open it again and go to the **silhouettes** subdirectory. If your terminal is still open and you are still in the **slugs** directory, you can easily change directory like so:

```
(base) D:\Coder\Python\Courses\Kivy Basics Course\book\code\slugrace61\assets\slugs>cd ..\silhouettes

(base) D:\Coder\Python\Courses\Kivy Basics Course\book\code\slugrace61\assets\silhouettes>_
```

The two dots stand for the directory that is one level up in the hierarchy, so **assets**, and then we choose the **silhouettes** subdirectory.

You must create the atlas image that will contain all the PNG images in the **silhouettes** directory. Use the basename `'silhouettes'`. What size should it be? Looks like 800 x 800 px will do, then the four images will fit exactly in the atlas image. But it turns out that this is not enough because there is some space added between the images, so let's make it 820 x 820 px.

So, here's the command you should use in the terminal:

```
python -m kivy.atlas silhouettes 820 *.png
```

Here the atlas image should be a square, so you don't have to type both dimensions. If you run the command in the terminal, you will see the message telling you that 1 atlas image has been created:

```
(base) D:\Coder\Python\Courses\Kivy Basics Course\book\code\slugrace61\assets\silhouettes>python -m kivy.atlas
silhouettes 820 *.png
[INFO   ] [Logger      ] Record log in C:\Users\PC\.kivy\logs\kivy_21-08-15_22.txt
[INFO   ] [deps        ] Successfully imported "kivy_deps.gstreamer" 0.2.0
[INFO   ] [deps        ] Successfully imported "kivy_deps.glew" 0.2.0
[INFO   ] [deps        ] Successfully imported "kivy_deps.sdl2" 0.2.0
[INFO   ] [Kivy        ] v1.11.1
[INFO   ] [Kivy        ] Installed at "C:\Users\PC\Anaconda3\lib\site-packages\kivy\__init__.py"
[INFO   ] [Python      ] v3.7.4 (default, Aug  9 2019, 18:34:13) [MSC v.1915 64 bit (AMD64)]
[INFO   ] [Python      ] Interpreter at "C:\Users\PC\Anaconda3\python.exe"
[INFO   ] [Atlas       ] create an 820x820 rgba image
Atlas created at silhouettes.atlas
1 image has been created

(base) D:\Coder\Python\Courses\Kivy Basics Course\book\code\slugrace61\assets\silhouettes>
```

You can see the image file, along with its corresponding json file, in the **sihouettes** subfolder.

**EXERCISE 2**

And now you will create the atlas with the all the accident images. First, change directory to the **accidents** subdirectory of the **assets** folder. You can do it just like before:

```
(base) D:\Coder\Python\Courses\Kivy Basics Course\book\code\slugrace61\assets\silhouettes>cd ..\accidents

(base) D:\Coder\Python\Courses\Kivy Basics Course\book\code\slugrace61\assets\accidents>
```

This time use the basename **'accidents'**. There are quite a few images in this folder. What size will be good? An image 820 x 260 px should be fine.

**SOLUTION**

So, here's the command you should use in the terminal:

```
python -m kivy.atlas accidents 820x260 *.png
```

Again, one atlas image was created:

```
(base) D:\Coder\Python\Courses\Kivy Basics Course\book\code\slugrace61\assets\accidents>python -m kivy.atlas
accidents 820x260 *.png
[INFO   ] [Logger      ] Record log in C:\Users\PC\.kivy\logs\kivy_21-08-15_24.txt
[INFO   ] [deps        ] Successfully imported "kivy_deps.gstreamer" 0.2.0
[INFO   ] [deps        ] Successfully imported "kivy_deps.glew" 0.2.0
[INFO   ] [deps        ] Successfully imported "kivy_deps.sdl2" 0.2.0
[INFO   ] [Kivy        ] v1.11.1
[INFO   ] [Kivy        ] Installed at "C:\Users\PC\Anaconda3\lib\site-packages\kivy\__init__.py"
[INFO   ] [Python      ] v3.7.4 (default, Aug  9 2019, 18:34:13) [MSC v.1915 64 bit (AMD64)]
[INFO   ] [Python      ] Interpreter at "C:\Users\PC\Anaconda3\python.exe"
[INFO   ] [Atlas       ] create an 820x260 rgba image
Atlas created at accidents.atlas
1 image has been created

(base) D:\Coder\Python\Courses\Kivy Basics Course\book\code\slugrace61\assets\accidents>
```

You can see it in the folder along with the json file.

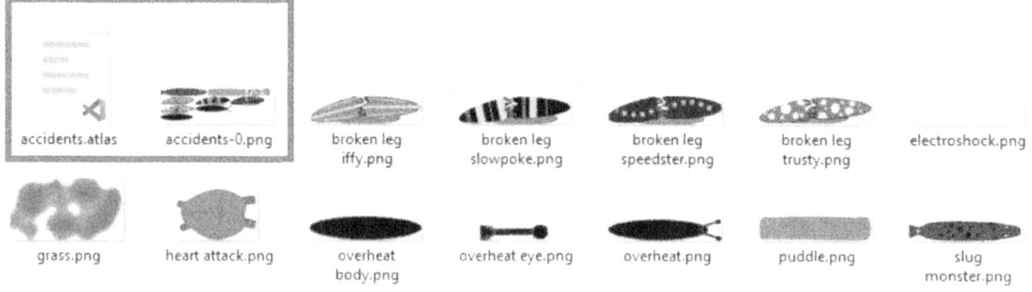


**EXERCISE 3**

We didn't create the accidents yet, so we'll leave the **accidents** atlas for later in the book, but we will use the **silhouettes** atlas to display the image of the winning slug. Modify the code in the Winner subarea of the Track area so that the source of the image is set to the atlas. Here's the code as it is right now:

```
#:kivy 1.11.1
# File name: race.kv
...
<RaceScreen>:
    ...
    ### THE TRACK ###
    ...
        # Winner
        BoxLayout:
            ...
            Image:
                source: 'assets/silhouettes/Trusty.png'
    ### THE BETS ###
    ...
```

**SOLUTION**

And here's the code after the modification:

```
#:kivy 1.11.1
# File name: race.kv
...
<RaceScreen>:
    ...
    ### THE TRACK ###
    ...
        # Winner
        BoxLayout:
            ...
            Image:
                source: 'atlas://assets/silhouettes/silhouettes/Trusty'

    ### THE BETS ###
    ...
```

Now you should still see the silhouette of Trusty.

# Part VII

# Kivy Properties and Referencing Objects

In this part of the book we'll learn how to use Kivy ids and Kivy properties to reference objects and how to observe property changes. Then we'll add some Kivy properties to the Slugrace project.

# Chapter 62 - Parents and Children

In the previous part we took care of what our app should look like. In this part we'll take care of how it should work. We know that all the widgets in our app are not going to be lonely islands, they have to communicate with each other somehow. This means we need references. You already know how to reference the widget itself, the root object and the running app. To do that we need the internal Kivy variables **self**, **root** and **app** respectively. Let's shortly revise how they work.

For this and a couple following chapters we'll use a simple setup. So, we're going to take a break from our project for a while and use our two test files again, **test.py** and **test.kv**.

Here's the code in the **test.py** file:

```
# File name: test.py

from kivy.config import Config
Config.set('graphics', 'width', '1200')
Config.set('graphics', 'height', '675')
Config.set('graphics', 'resizable', '1')

import kivy
kivy.require('1.11.1')
from kivy.app import App
from kivy.uix.floatlayout import FloatLayout

class TestLayout(FloatLayout):
    pass

class TestApp(App):
    def build(self):
        return TestLayout()

if __name__ == '__main__':
    TestApp().run()
```

And here's the kv file:

```
#:kivy 1.11.1
# File name: test.kv

<TestLayout>:
    Label:
        text: 'label 1'
        size_hint: .5, .5
        pos_hint: {'x': 0, 'top': 1}

    BoxLayout:
        size_hint: .5, .5
        pos_hint: {'x': .5, 'top': 1}

        Button:
            text: 'button 1'

        BoxLayout:
            orientation: 'vertical'

            Button:
                text: 'button 2'

            Slider:
                min: 100
                max: 200
                value: 150
                orientation: 'vertical'

            Button:
                text: 'button 3'

        Button:
            text: 'button 4'

    Button:
        text: 'button 5'
        size_hint: .5, .5
        pos_hint: {'x': 0, 'y': 0}

    Label:
        text: 'label 2'
        size_hint: .5, .5
        pos_hint: {'x': .5, 'y': 0}
```

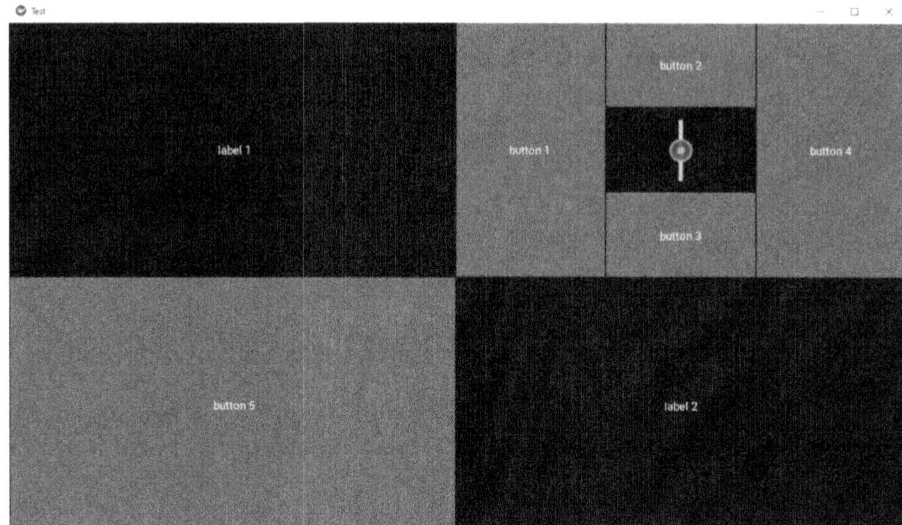


It's a pretty simple example. If you run it, you will see quite a bunch of widgets.

## The `self` Variable Revisited

Let's start with the **self** variable. It's used to reference the widget it's used on, so if you use it on the first label, for example, it references the label itself.

Let's use it to set the first label's **text** property to its position:

```
#:kivy 1.11.1
# File name: test.kv

<TestLayout>:
    Label:
        text: str(self.pos)
        size_hint: .5, .5
        pos_hint: {'x': 0, 'top': 1}

    BoxLayout:
        size_hint: .5, .5
```

Let's also use this variable on the last button to set its **text** property to the string representation of the widget's **size_hint** property:

```
#:kivy 1.11.1
# File name: test.kv

<TestLayout>:
    ...
    BoxLayout:
        ...
        Button:
            text: 'button 4'

    Button:
        text: str(self.size_hint)
        size_hint: .5, .5
        pos_hint: {'x': 0, 'y': 0}

    Label:
        text: 'label 2'
        ...
```

Now run the app and you will see the new texts on the first label (A) and the last button (B).

What's more, if you resize the window, you will see the text react to the changes. The **y** position of the first label will change, and so will the text on the label. Natually, the values of the **x** position and of the **size_hint** property on the button will not change, so there will be no change in the text on the button either. This is how properties in Kivy work – they react to changes! We are going to cover this topic extensively later in this part.

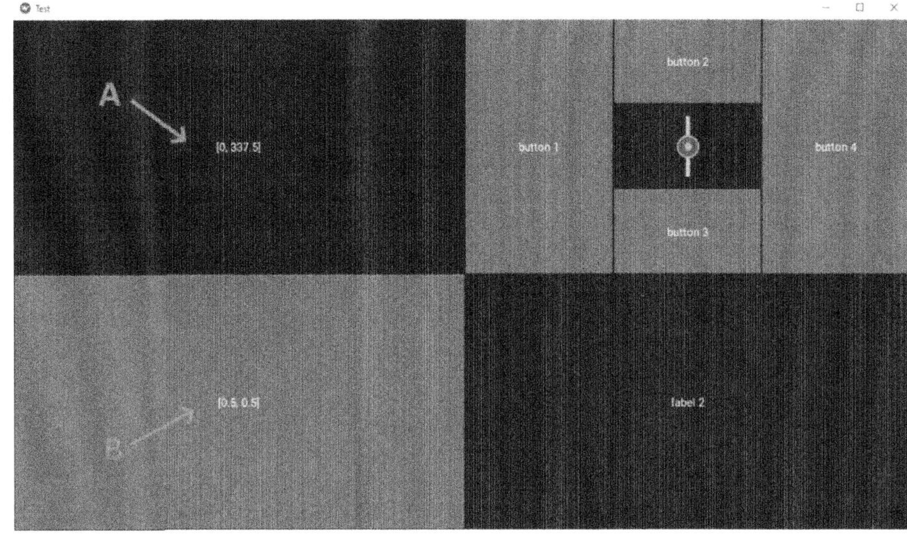


## The root Variable Revisited

Now let's have a look at the **root** variable. It always references the root widget, which in this case is the **TestLayout**. Let's change the text on the last label to the string representation of the root widget's class:

```
#:kivy 1.11.1
# File name: test.kv

<TestLayout>:
    ...
    Button:
        ...
    Label:
        text: str(root)
        size_hint: .5, .5
        pos_hint: {'x': .5, 'y': 0}
```

If you now run the app, you'll see it on the last label.

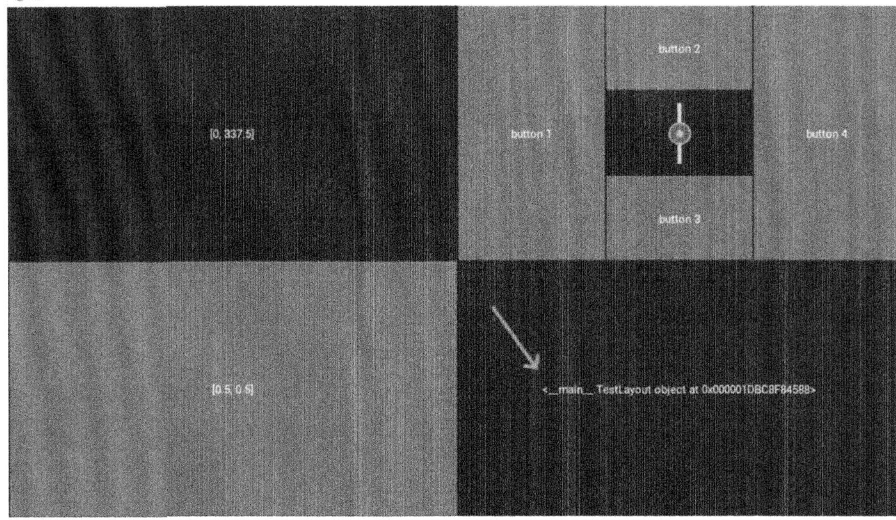

# The app Variable Revisited

And finally, the **app** variable. It references the running app.

Let's modify the Python file so that it contains an attribute:

```
# File name: test.py
...
class TestLayout(FloatLayout):
    pass

class TestApp(App):

    # Here's an attribute.
    number = 5

    def build(self):
        return TestLayout()

if __name__ == '__main__':
    TestApp().run()
```

And now let's set the **text** property of the first label to this attribute:

```
#:kivy 1.11.1
# File name: test.kv

<TestLayout>:
    Label:
        text: str(app.number)
        size_hint: .5, .5
        pos_hint: {'x': 0, 'top': 1}

    BoxLayout:
        ...
```

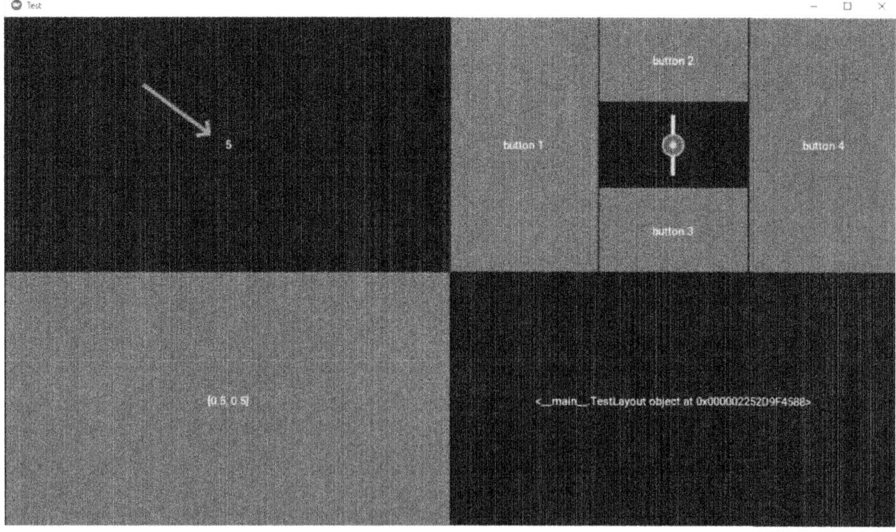


Now we have access to the attribute. If you run the app, you'll see its value displayed on the first label.

This is all good, but what if the first label needs access to the second button or if the second button needs access to the slider, for example? There aren't any special variables that we can use, but there are a couple other solutions to this problem. We're going to discuss them one by one. In this chapter we'll see how a widget can use the parent-child relationships to reference other widgets. Then, in the following chapters we'll be talking about ids and Kivy properties. The latter is what we are going to use in our project extensively.

# Parent-Child Relationships

Let's start with the parent-child relationships. Every widget in Kivy, except for the root, has a parent widget. It also may have child widgets.

Have a look at kv code again. In our example the root widget, **TestLayout**, has four children: 2 labels, a BoxLayout and a button. The BoxLayout itself has three children: two buttons and another BoxLayout, the latter also having three children: a slider and two buttons.

So, if the root widget has four children, it's their parent, like in a human family. Let's take the slider as an example. Its parent is the BoxLayout, which is a child of another BoxLayout, which in turn is a child of the root widget. Like there are parents, grandparents, great-grandparents, great-great-grandparents and so on in a family on one hand, and children, grandchildren, great-grandchildren, and so on on the other, similar hierarchies are found in Kivy, just the terminology is a bit different.

So, if you want to refer to a parent, you use the **parent** property. To refer to a grandparent, you just use the **parent** property on the parent, so **parent.parent**. A great-grandparent would be **parent.parent.parent**, etc. As far as children are concerned, you can access them using the **children** property. It's a list, so if you need access to a particular child, just use its index.

And now, just for practice, we'll try out some combinations the the **parent** and **children** properties in the kv file. Read the comments carefully and everything will be clear. We'll be setting the **text** properties of the widgets to different values. Each comment is going to consist of three parts, separated by three asterisks (***). In the first part you'll see what we want the **text** property to display. In the middle part you'll see an explanation. Finally, in the last part, you'll see what the expected result is. Here's the code:

```
#:kivy 1.11.1
# File name: test.kv

<TestLayout>:
    Label:
        # the type of the last child of the root
        # ***
        # The last child of the root is this very label because widgets are added in this
        # order. So, the first child is the last label, then the big button, then the
        # BoxLayout and finally this label.
        # ***
        # So, you should see the Label class displayed on the label.
        text: str(type(root.children[-1]))
        size_hint: .5, .5
        pos_hint: {'x': 0, 'top': 1}
    BoxLayout:
        size_hint: .5, .5
        pos_hint: {'x': .5, 'top': 1}
        Button:
            # the value of the orientation property on the slider
            # ***
            # The slider is this button's parent's (BoxLayout) second child's (BoxLayout)
```

```
            # second child.
            # ***
            # You should see the text 'vertical' on this button.
            text: str(self.parent.children[1].children[1].orientation)
        BoxLayout:
            orientation: 'vertical'
            Button:
                # the value of the value property on the slider
                # ***
                # The slider is the second child of this button's parent, which in turn is the
                # BoxLayout.
                # ***
                # You should see the number 150 on this button.
                text: str(self.parent.children[1].value)
            Slider:
                min: 100
                max: 200
                value: 150
                orientation: 'vertical'
            Button:
                # This button's great-grandparent should be the root, is it?
                # ***
                # Here we have a boolean expression that checks whether this button's parent's
                # (BoxLayout) parent's (BoxLayout) parent (TestLayout) is the root.
                # ***
                # The TestLayout is the root, so you will see the text 'True'.
                text: str(self.parent.parent.parent == root)
        Button:
            # number of the root's children
            # ***
            # The root is the TestLayout. It has four children.
            # ***
            # So you will see the number 4 on the button.
            text: str(len(root.children))
    Button:
        # the index of this button in the root's list of children
        # ***
        # This button is one of the root's children. Using the index method we can check its
        # index. As mentioned before, the children are in reversed order, so this is
        # the second child.
        # ***
        # You'll see the index of the second child, so 1.
        text: str(root.children.index(self))
        size_hint: .5, .5
        pos_hint: {'x': 0, 'y': 0}
    Label:
        # Is this label a child of the root?
        # ***
        # Here we're just checking if this label is an element of the root's children list.
        # ***
        # It definitely is, so you should see 'yes' displayed on the label.
        text: 'yes' if self in root.children else 'no'
        size_hint: .5, .5
        pos_hint: {'x': .5, 'y': 0}
```

If you run the app, you will see the all the **text** properties set.

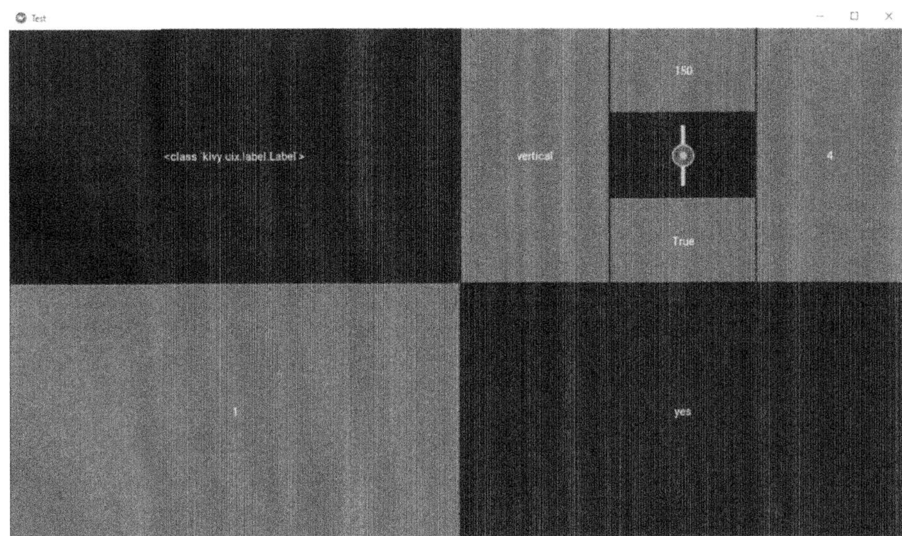


Everything looks just like expected. So, now we know how to reference parents and children in the kv file. But can we also reference them in Python code? Sure, we can.

# Parents and Children in Python Code

We will now set the **text** properties of the widgets programmatically. So, completely remove all the **text** properties from the kv file. Additionally we'll define a custom button in the Python file and use it instead of the big button. In the **CustomButton** class we'll define a method, **set_text**, that will set the **text** properties of all the widgets. We will be talking about events a bit later in the course, but when the custom button is pressed, it will call the **set_text** method.

The kv file now should look like so:

```
#:kivy 1.11.1
# File name: test.kv

<TestLayout>:
    Label:
        size_hint: .5, .5
        pos_hint: {'x': 0, 'top': 1}

    BoxLayout:
        size_hint: .5, .5
        pos_hint: {'x': .5, 'top': 1}

        Button:

        BoxLayout:
            orientation: 'vertical'

            Button:

            Slider:
                min: 100
                max: 200
                value: 150
                orientation: 'vertical'

            Button:

        Button:

    Button:
        size_hint: .5, .5
        pos_hint: {'x': 0, 'y': 0}

    Label:
        size_hint: .5, .5
        pos_hint: {'x': .5, 'y': 0}
```

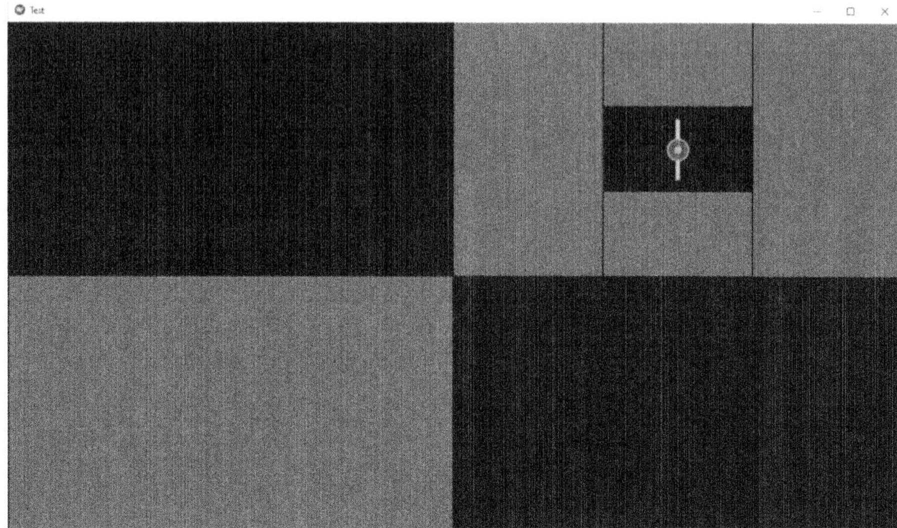

If you now run the app, you will see the widgets without any text on them.

And now let's try to re-create what we just had in Python code.

We'll start doing this together and then you'll finish it as an exercise.

First, let's remove the **number** attribute we created before in the **TestApp** class, we don't need it anymore. Then, let's define the **CustomButton** class with the **set_text** method. Here's the code with comments:

```
# File name: test.py
...
from kivy.uix.floatlayout import FloatLayout

# We'll need Button class to inherit from.
from kivy.uix.button import Button

class TestLayout(FloatLayout):
    pass

class CustomButton(Button):
    def set_text(self):
        ### set the text on the first label
        self.parent.children[-1].text = str(type(self.parent.children[-1]))

        ### set the text on the first button
        self.parent.children[2].children[-1].text = str(
            self.parent.children[2].children[1].orientation)

        ### set the text on the second button
        self.parent.children[2].children[1].children[-1].text = str(
            self.parent.children[2].children[1].children[1].value)

class TestApp(App):
    def build(self):
        return TestLayout()

if __name__ == '__main__':
    TestApp().run()
```

Now, in the kv file, replace the big button with an instance of the **CustomButton** class. Also, add the **on_press** event to the custom button so that the **set_text** method is called when the button is pressed:

```
#:kivy 1.11.1
# File name: test.kv

<TestLayout>:
    ...
    BoxLayout:
        ...
        Button:
    CustomButton:
        size_hint: .5, .5
        pos_hint: {'x': 0, 'y': 0}
        on_press: self.set_text()
    Label:
        ...
```

If you run and press the big button, it will set the **text** property on the first three widgets.

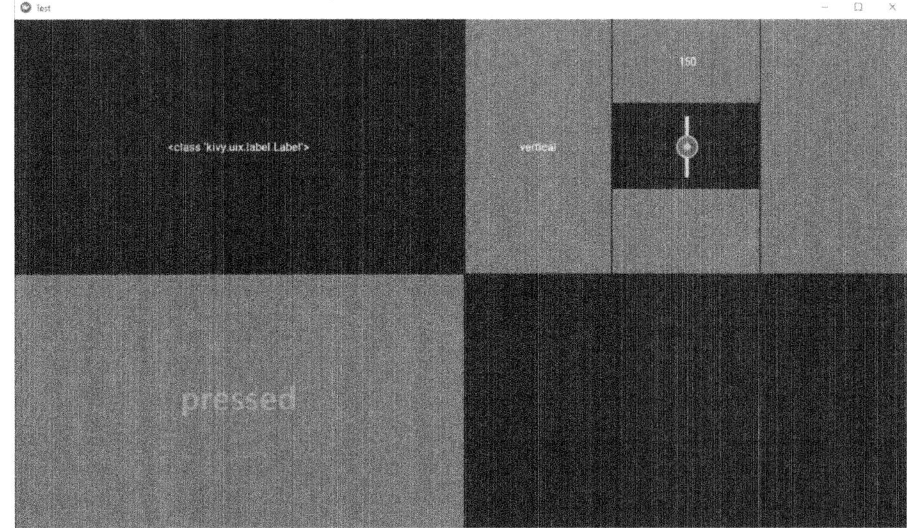


As you can see, the Python code is not very readable.

We could make the code more readable, which, as you might have guessed, you will be asked to do in the exercise, but still this is not how we'll be referencing widgets in our project. However, before we move on to see what other options we have, make sure to do the exercises below. Anyway, from time to time you will be referencing widgets using their parent-child relatioships. And in the next chapter we'll be talking about ids, which will make things much easier.

# It's Your Turn Now...

### EXERCISE 1

Using the **parent** and **children** properties, finish the implementation of the **set_text** method (starting from the third button) so that when the big button is pressed, the **text** property on all the widgets is set to the same value that we used when we set the **text** property in kv code.

## SOLUTION

Here's the method:

```
# File name: test.py
...
class CustomButton(Button):
    def set_text(self):
        ### set the text on the first label
        self.parent.children[-1].text = str(type(self.parent.children[-1]))

        ### set the text on the first button
        self.parent.children[2].children[-1].text = str(
            self.parent.children[2].children[1].orientation)

        ### set the text on the second button
        self.parent.children[2].children[1].children[-1].text = str(
            self.parent.children[2].children[1].children[1].value)

        ### set the text on the third button
        self.parent.children[2].children[1].children[0].text = str(
            self.parent.children[2].children[1].children[0].parent.parent.parent
            == self.parent)

        ### set the text on the fourth button
        self.parent.children[2].children[0].text = str(len(self.parent.children))

        ### set the text on this very button
        self.text = str(self.parent.children.index(self))

        ### set the text on the second label
        self.parent.children[0].text = ('yes'
            if self.parent.children[0] in self.parent.children else 'no')

class TestApp(App):
    ...
```

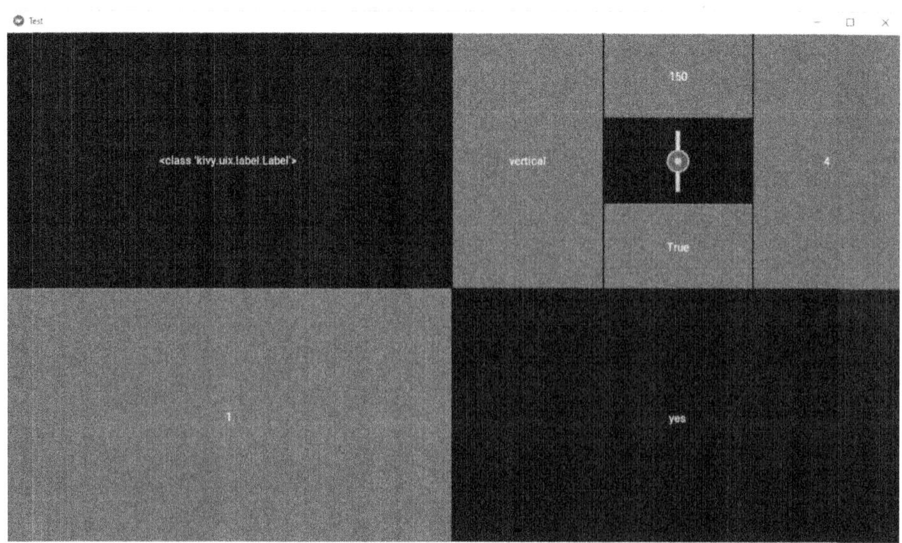


If you run the app and press the big button, you should see the same as before.

## EXERCISE 2

You can simplify the code and make it more readable by first assigning the widgets to variables and then using them in the code. Here's how you could do it for the first three widgets:

```
# File name: test.py
...
class CustomButton(Button):
    def set_text(self):
        # variables used for better readability
        root = self.parent
        label1 = root.children[-1]
        button1 = root.children[2].children[-1]
        button2 = root.children[2].children[1].children[-1]
        slider = root.children[2].children[1].children[1]

        ### set the text on the first label
        label1.text = str(type(label1))

        ### set the text on the first button
        button1.text = str(slider.orientation)

        ### set the text on the second button
        button2.text = str(slider.value)

        ### set the text on the third button
        ...
```

Use the same naming convention and simplify the other widgets like this.

## SOLUTION

Here's the code:

```
# File name: test.py
...
class CustomButton(Button):
    def set_text(self):
        # variables used for better readability
        ...
        slider = root.children[2].children[1].children[1]
        button3 = root.children[2].children[1].children[0]
        button4 = root.children[2].children[0]
        button5 = self
        label2 = root.children[0]

        ### set the text on the first label
        ...
        ### set the text on the third button
        button3.text = str(button3.parent.parent.parent == root)

        ### set the text on the fourth button
        button4.text = str(len(root.children))

        ### set the text on this very button
        button5.text = str(root.children.index(self))

        ### set the text on the second label
        label2.text = 'yes' if label2 in root.children else 'no'

class TestApp(App):
    ...
```

# Chapter 63 - Kivy ids

In the previous chapter we learned how to reference widgets using their parent-child relationships. Today we'll learn how to do it using ids. We'll be using the same code as in the previous chapter, just slightly modified. Make sure your Python file looks like this:

```
# File name: test.py

from kivy.config import Config
Config.set('graphics', 'width', '1200')
Config.set('graphics', 'height', '675')
Config.set('graphics', 'resizable', '1')

import kivy
kivy.require('1.11.1')
from kivy.app import App
from kivy.uix.floatlayout import FloatLayout
from kivy.uix.button import Button

class TestLayout(FloatLayout):
    pass

class CustomButton(Button):
    def set_text(self):
        pass

class TestApp(App):
    def build(self):
        return TestLayout()

if __name__ == '__main__':
    TestApp().run()
```

The kv file should be exactly like before. If you look at it, you'll see that we didn't set the **text** property on any of the widgets. We will do it using ids, both in kv and in Python.

If you run the app, you will see just the widgets, without any text on them.

## Kivy ids in the Kivy Language

Now let's add some ids. We only have to add them to the widgets that we want to reference. We can use any string for an id, but to make them stand out in our code, I will start their names with an underscore. This is by no means necessary, but this convention is pretty often used.

To set an id, we use the **id** property. So, here's the code with the ids added to some widgets. You can also see how these widgets are referenced by other widgets. Everything is explained in a detailed way in the comments.

```
#:kivy 1.11.1
# File name: test.kv

<TestLayout>:
    Label:
        # This label should display the text from the second label. _label2 is the id of
        # the second label. Scroll down to see it set on the second label.
        text: _label2.text
        size_hint: .5, .5
        pos_hint: {'x': 0, 'top': 1}
```

```
    BoxLayout:
        size_hint: .5, .5
        pos_hint: {'x': .5, 'top': 1}
        Button:
            # This button should display the string representation of the size_hint
            # property on the custom button. We are referencing the custom button
            # by its id.
            text: str(_customButton.size_hint)
        BoxLayout:
            orientation: 'vertical'
            Button:
                # The text on this button should display the string representation of the
                # pos_hint property on the second label, which is referenced by its id.
                text: str(_label2.pos_hint)
            Slider:
                # This slider may be referenced by its id.
                id: _slider
                min: 100
                max: 200
                value: 150
                orientation: 'vertical'
            Button:
                # The text on this button should display the value of the value property,
                # which we set on the slider. The slider itself is referenced by its id.
                text: str(_slider.value)
        Button:
            # The text on this button should display the slider's orientation. The
            # slider is referenced by its id.
            text: str(_slider.orientation)
    CustomButton:
        # We want to be able to reference the custom button, so it needs an id.
        id: _customButton
        # The text on the custom button should display the value of the max property that
        # we set on the slider. The slider is referenced by its id.
        text: str(_slider.max)
        size_hint: .5, .5
        pos_hint: {'x': 0, 'y': 0}
        on_press: self.set_text()
    Label:
        # This label needs an id because we want to be able to reference it. Let’s also
        # set its text to something.
        id: _label2
        text: 'ABC'
        size_hint: .5, .5
        pos_hint: {'x': .5, 'y': 0}
```

If you now run the program, you'll see the **text** properties set.

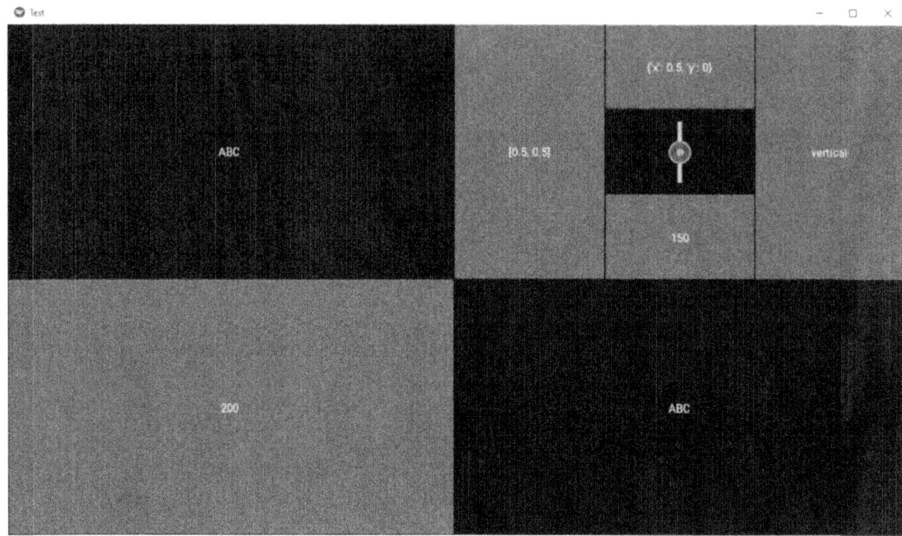


# Kivy ids in Python Code

If you want to reference the ids in Python code, you can use the **ids** property.

Let's demonstrate it on the example of the **set_text** method on the custom button. This method is called when the button is pressed. Suppose we want the method the set the **text** property on the second label to **'CHANGED'**. We have to reference the second label in Python code by its id.

Here's how to do it:

```
# File name: test.py
...
class CustomButton(Button):
    def set_text(self):
        self.parent.ids._label2.text = 'CHANGED'

class TestApp(App):
    ...
```

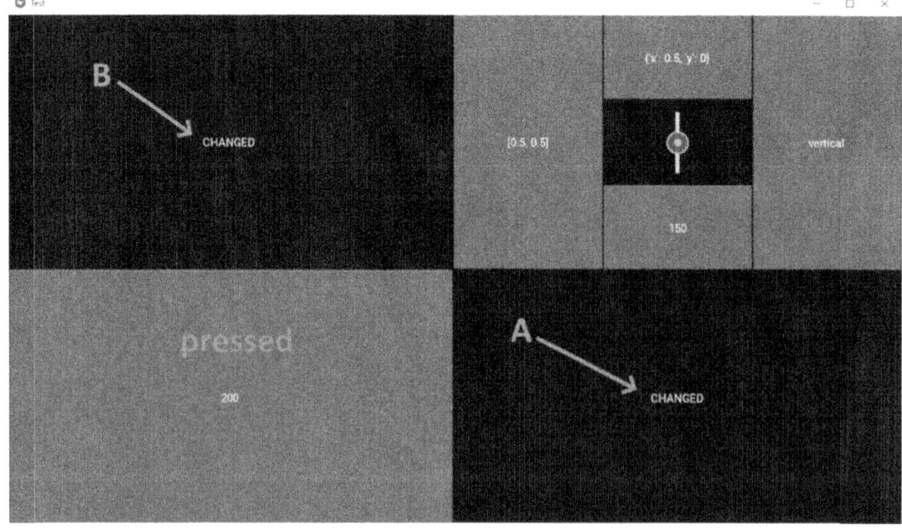


We have access to the ids inside the rule where they were added in the kv code. In our case, they are accessible inside **TestLayout**, which is the parent of the custom button. So, from the ids inside the **TestLayout** we selected **_label2** that references the second label and set its **text** property to a new value. And now watch what happens when we run the app and press the big custom button. The text changed not only on the second label (A), but also on the first one (B). Why is that? Well, if you look at the **text** property on the first label, you will see that it is set to the value of the **text** property on the second label:

```
#:kivy 1.11.1
# File name: test.kv

<TestLayout>:
    Label:
        text: _label2.text
        size_hint: .5, .5
        pos_hint: {'x': 0, 'top': 1}

    BoxLayout:
        ...
    Label:
        id: _label2
        text: 'ABC'
        size_hint: .5, .5
        pos_hint: {'x': .5, 'y': 0}
```

You may remember that properties react to changes, so if there is a change in the **text** property on the second label, and the **text** property on the first label is set to the same value as on the second label, the change will be visible also there.

And now let's check out all the ids that are available for us. Let's just print them out to the terminal when the big button is pressed. The **ids** property is a dictionary property (of type **DictProperty** to be precise), which is one of the property types available in Kivy.

We will discuss some of them in this part, but for now it's enough to know that we can treat it like a dictionary. So, let's print out both the keys and values, which you can do using the **items** method in the **for** loop:

```
# File name: test.py
...
class CustomButton(Button):
    def set_text(self):
        self.parent.ids._label2.text = 'CHANGED'

        for id in self.parent.ids.items():
            print(id)

class TestApp(App):
    ...
```

Now, when you run the app and press the big button, not only will the text on the two labels change, but we will also see all the ids printed out in the terminal.

Each key-value pair will be printed out as a 2-tuple with the key and value:

```
('_slider', <WeakProxy to <kivy.uix.slider.Slider object at 0x000001C16245A3C8>>)
('_customButton', <WeakProxy to <__main__.CustomButton object at 0x000001C166D19358>>)
('_label2', <WeakProxy to <kivy.uix.label.Label object at 0x000001C166D19588>>)
```

So, the keys are the strings that we used for the ids, and the values just tell us what the ids are. As you can see, they are not the widgets themselves, but rather weak references to them.

As the **ids** property is a dictionary property, you can use dictionary syntax alternatively, so instead of this:

```
self.parent.ids._label2.text = 'CHANGED'
```

you can use this:

```
self.parent.ids['_label2'].text = 'CHANGED'
```

Give it a try, but I'll stick to the former notation, though.

# The Scope of Kivy ids

As mentioned before, the scope of the ids is limited to the rule in which they were added. So, let's modify our kv file like so:

```
#:kivy 1.11.1
# File name: test.kv

<CustomLayout@BoxLayout>:
    size_hint: .5, .5
    pos_hint: {'x': .5, 'top': 1}

    Button:
        text: str(_customButton.size_hint)

    BoxLayout:
        orientation: 'vertical'

        Button:
            text: str(_label2.pos_hint)

        Slider:
            id: _slider
            min: 100
            max: 200
            value: 150
            orientation: 'vertical'

        Button:
            text: str(_slider.value)

        Button:
            text: str(_slider.orientation)

<TestLayout>:
    Label:
        text: _label2.text
        size_hint: .5, .5
        pos_hint: {'x': 0, 'top': 1}

    CustomLayout:

    CustomButton:
        id: _customButton
        text: str(_slider.max)
        size_hint: .5, .5
        pos_hint: {'x': 0, 'y': 0}
        on_press: self.set_text()

    Label:
        id: _label2
        text: 'label 2'
        size_hint: .5, .5
        pos_hint: {'x': .5, 'y': 0}
```

So, here we extracted one of the root's children into a custom widget. To be precise, we extracted the BoxLayout that contains two buttons and another BoxLayout into **CustomLayout** and then we used an instance of the latter in the code.

If you try to run this code, it won't work. The problem is that we are trying to reference widgets that are in a different rule. Inside the **CustomLayout** rule we have access to the **_slider** id, but not to **_customButton** or **_label2**.

Similarly, inside **TestLayout** we can access **_label2**, but not **_slider**.

Let's now use only the ids to which we have access to see if it works. Change the code again:

```
#:kivy 1.11.1
# File name: test.kv

<CustomLayout@BoxLayout>:
    size_hint: .5, .5
    pos_hint: {'x': .5, 'top': 1}


............Button:
        text: str(_slider.orientation)
```

```
........ BoxLayout:
        orientation: 'vertical'
        Button:
            text: str(_slider.orientation)
        Slider:
            ...
<TestLayout>:
    ...
    CustomButton:
        id: _customButton
        text: _label2.text
        size_hint: .5, .5
        ...
```

This should work.

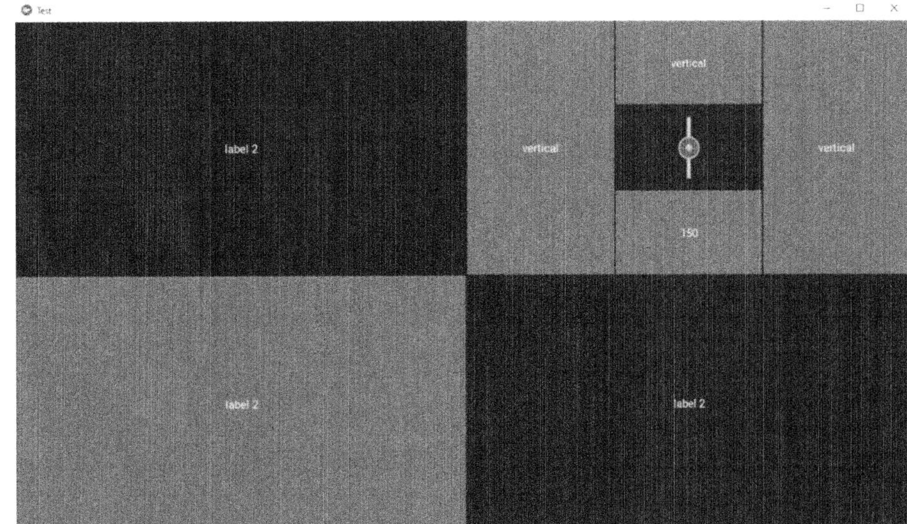


We will be using ids in our project extensively. But first of all, we'll be using them to reference widgets by means of custom properties. Kivy properties are very powerful and we'll be using them a lot. In the following chapters we'll be talking about Kivy properties and we'll see how to use them to reference widgets. But before that, there's an exercise for you to do.

# It's Your Turn Now...

## EXERCISE

In this exercise you will play around with ids a little. Your goal is to make the slider move up a little each time a button is clicked. Follow the instructions:

1. The **CustomLayout** class is defined in the kv file only. It inherits from **BoxLayout**. Define the class in the Python file and make it inherit there instead of in the kv file. Remember to import the class you want to inherit from.

2. Still in the Python file, create a method in the **CustomLayout** class that will be called each time one of the buttons is pressed. Name the method **move_slider**. It doesn't take any parameters (except **self**, of course). The method should check if the current value of the slider is less than or

equal to the max value minus 5. If so, the value should increase by 5 units. Use the slider's id to get a reference to it.

3. In the kv file find the first button inside the **CustomLayout** rule. When this button is pressed, the **move_slider** method you just created should be called.

**SOLUTION**

Here's the Python file:

```
# File name: test.py
...
from kivy.uix.floatlayout import FloatLayout

# We need the BoxLayout class to inferit from.
from kivy.uix.boxlayout import BoxLayout

from kivy.uix.button import Button

class TestLayout(FloatLayout):
    pass

# We now define the CustomLayout class here, in Python code.
class CustomLayout(BoxLayout):
    # Here's the move_slider method. It will increase the slider's value by 5 units as
    # long as it's less than max - 5. The ids are now accessible inside this class,
    # the ids property is now set on self.
    def move_slider(self):
        if self.ids._slider.value <= self.ids._slider.max - 5:
            self.ids._slider.value += 5

class CustomButton(Button):
    ...
```

And here's the kv file:

```
#:kivy 1.11.1
# File name: test.kv

<CustomLayout>:
    size_hint: .5, .5
    pos_hint: {'x': .5, 'top': 1}
    Button:
        text: str(_slider.orientation)
        # When the button is pressed, the method move_slider is called. This method
        # is defined in the CustomLayout class in the Python file, which is the root,
        # so we call the function on the root.
        on_press: root.move_slider()
    BoxLayout:
        ...
```

If you now run the app and press the first button a couple times, the slider will move up each time and the new value will be visible on the button below the slider.

If you press this button...

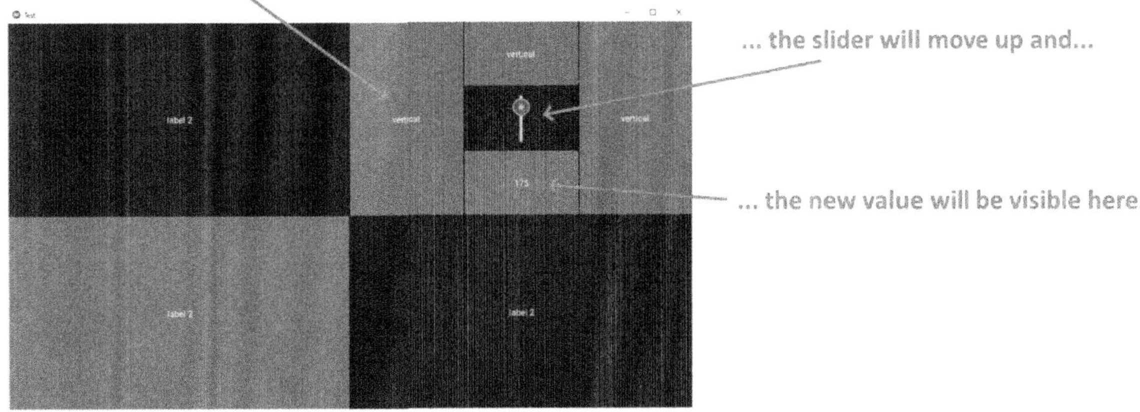
... the slider will move up and...
... the new value will be visible here.

# Chapter 64 - Introduction to Kivy Properties

In the previous chapter we were referencing widgets by ids. You can also reference widgets using Kivy properties, but before we learn how to do it, let's talk about Kivy properties in general.

## What Are Kivy Properties?

To start with, what are Kivy properties? Don't be misled by the name, they are not to be confused with the regular Python properties that you know. We've been using the word PROPERTY a lot since the first chapters of this book. You know that there's a **text** property in the **Label** class, there's a **size** property in the **Widget** class, there are the **min**, **max** and **value** properties in the **Slider** class and many, many more. These are all examples of inherited properties – you get them out of the box when you inherit from a class where they are defined.

Now, before we go any further, let's have a look at our test files from the previous chapter. I removed the code that prints the ids out to the terminal in the **set_text** method of the **CustomButton** class, we don't need it anymore. Here's the Python code:

```
# File name: test.py
...
class TestLayout(FloatLayout):
    pass

class CustomLayout(BoxLayout):
    def move_slider(self):
        if self.ids._slider.value <= self.ids._slider.max - 5:
            self.ids._slider.value += 5

class CustomButton(Button):
    def set_text(self):
        self.parent.ids._label2.text = 'CHANGED'

class TestApp(App):
    def build(self):
        return TestLayout()

if __name__ == '__main__':
    TestApp().run()
```

And here's the kv code:

```
#:kivy 1.11.1
# File name: test.kv

<CustomLayout>:
    size_hint: .5, .5
    pos_hint: {'x': .5, 'top': 1}

    Button:
        text: str(_slider.orientation)
        on_press: root.move_slider()

    BoxLayout:
        orientation: 'vertical'

        Button:
            text: str(_slider.orientation)

        Slider:
            id: _slider
            min: 100
            max: 200
            value: 150
            orientation: 'vertical'

        Button:
            text: str(_slider.value)

    Button:
        text: str(_slider.orientation)

<TestLayout>:
    Label:
        text: _label2.text
        size_hint: .5, .5
        pos_hint: {'x': 0, 'top': 1}

    CustomLayout:

    CustomButton:
        id: _customButton
        text: _label2.text
        size_hint: .5, .5
        pos_hint: {'x': 0, 'y': 0}
        on_press: self.set_text()

    Label:
        id: _label2
        text: 'label 2'
        size_hint: .5, .5
        pos_hint: {'x': .5, 'y': 0}
```

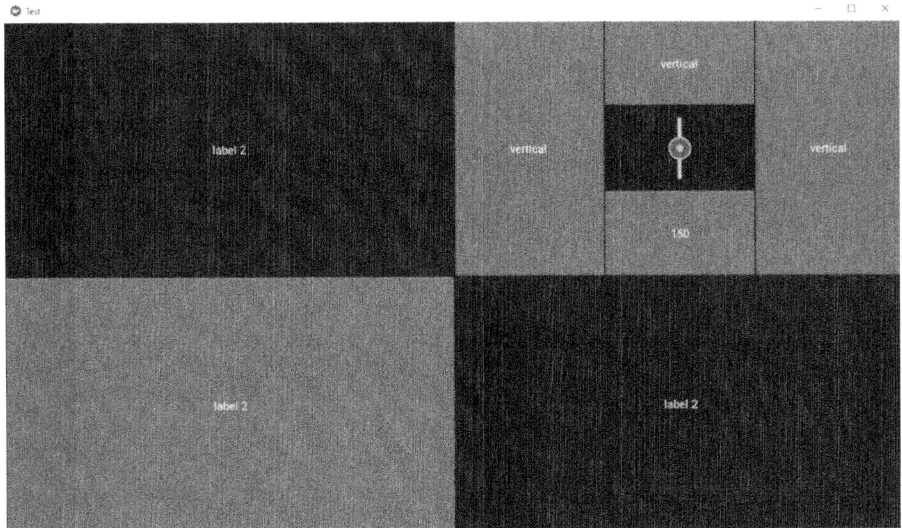


If you run this program, you will see the familiar app window from the previous chapter.

As you remember, when you press the first button (the one to the left of the slider), the value of the **value** property on the slider will increase by 5 units. You will see the change on the slider itself (it will move up), but also on the button below the slider, which displays the current value of the **value** property. Here are the parts of the code that are responsible for that:

- in the kv file:

```
#:kivy 1.11.1
# File name: test.kv

<CustomLayout>:
    ...
    Button:
        text: str(_slider.orientation)
        on_press: root.move_slider()

    BoxLayout:
        ...
        Slider:
            id: _slider
            min: 100
            max: 200
            value: 150
            orientation: 'vertical'

        Button:
            text: str(_slider.value)

    Button:
        ...
```

- in the Python file:

```
# File name: test.py
...
class CustomLayout(BoxLayout):
    def move_slider(self):
        ...
            self.ids._slider.value += 5

class CustomButton(Button):
    ...
```

So, the text on the button below the slider displays the slider's value. When the button is pressed, the **move_slider** method defined in the **CustomLayout** class is called. This method changes the **value** property on the slider. But we didn't write any code to tell the button below the slider to change its text. Still, it does it anyway. This is how properties work, they react to changes. Even if you had tens of other widgets with their **text** properties set to the slider's value, they would all react to any change of the **value** property.

There's another example in the same code. Have a closer look at the following lines of code:

- in the kv file:

```
#:kivy 1.11.1
# File name: test.kv
...
<TestLayout>:
    Label:
        text: _label2.text
        ...
    CustomButton:
        id: _customButton
        text: _label2.text
        ...
        on_press: self.set_text()

    Label:
        id: _label2
        text: 'label 2'
        ...
```

- in the Python file:

```
# File name: test.py
...
class CustomButton(Button):
    def set_text(self):
        self.parent.ids._label2.text = 'CHANGED'

class TestApp(App):
    ...
```

So, initially the **text** property on the second label is set to **'label 2'**. This label has the id **_label2**, which is used in the first label and in the custom button to set their own **text** properties to the same value. Now, when the custom button is pressed, the **set_text** method defined in the **CustomButton** class is called and it finds the widget with the id **_label2**, which is the second label, and sets its text to a new value. And again, even though we didn't explicitly tell it to do so, the program also changes the text on the first label and the custom button:

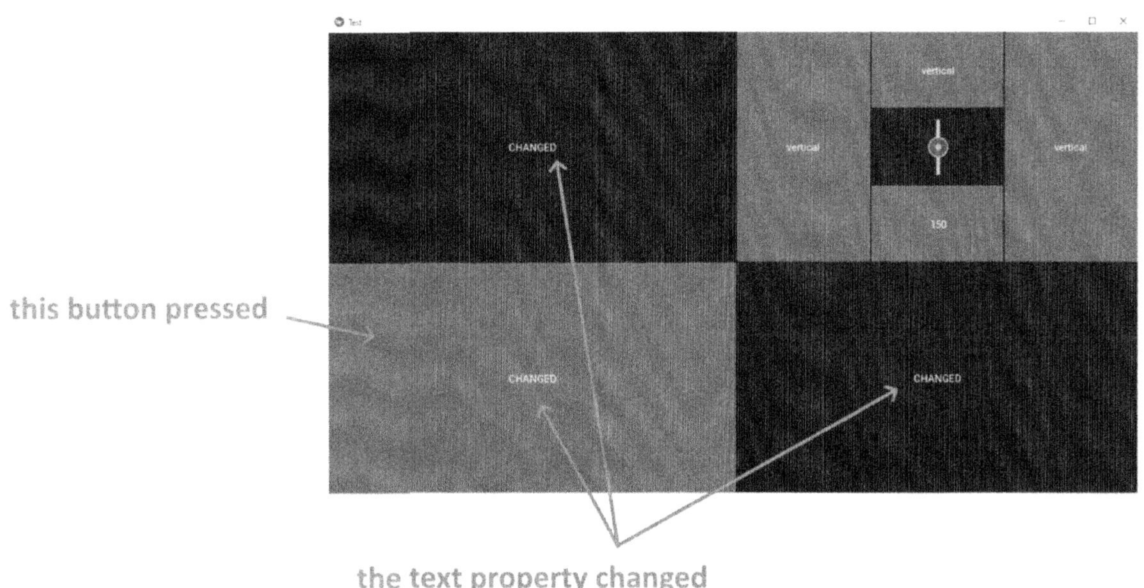


So, the property again reacted to the change. Now, before we really dive into the realm of properties, let's just briefly discuss their main features.

# Features of Kivy Property

The one feature that you already know is that Kivy properties automatically observe any changes and react accordingly. Kivy properties implement the Observer Design Pattern. You can specify what should happen when a property's value changes. There's a very convenient naming convention that we are going to discuss in more detail soon. You can bind your own function as a callback to changes of a property's value.

Besides, Kivy properties can be used with validation constraints. We use this feature to validate the values that we try to set our property to.

Finally, Kivy properties optimize memory management, because a single instance of a property is shared across all the instances of the class where they were defined.

# Types of Kivy Properties

There are actually a couple types of Kivy properties. If you look at the documentation of the `Label` class, for example, you will find the following description of the `text` property:

*text*
*Text of the label.*

*Creation of a simple hello world:*

*widget = Label(text='Hello world')*
*If you want to create the widget with an unicode string, use:*

*widget = Label(text=u'My unicode string')*
***text is a StringProperty and defaults to ''.***

The last sentence, the one in bold type, is what interests us most at this moment. It says that the **`text`** property is a **`StringProperty`**.

Now, let's have a look at some more properties in the documentation. For example, there's the **`size`** property in the **`Widget`** class:

*size*
*Size of the widget.*

***size is a ReferenceListProperty of (width, height) properties.***

This is a **`ReferenceListProperty`**. What about the **`max`** property in the **`Slider`** class? Here's what we can see in the documentation:

*max*
*Maximum value allowed for value.*

***max is a NumericProperty and defaults to 100.***

So, this time it's a **`NumericProperty`**.

These are just a couple examples, but there are more property types. In particular, there are the following types of Kivy properties:

- NumericProperty
- StringProperty
- ListProperty
- ObjectProperty
- BooleanProperty
- BoundedNumericProperty
- OptionProperty
- ReferenceListProperty
- AliasProperty
- DictProperty

We're going to use many of them in our project. Some of them have pretty self-explanatory names, like the **NumericProperty** or **BooleanProperty**. But there are also some that we can use in more advanced scenarios like the **OptionProperty** or **AliasProperty**, for example. First, though, we'll see how to use Kivy properties to reference widgets.

Before you move on, there's a simple exercise for you. This time it's pretty theoretical, but still take your time to do it.

# It's Your Turn Now...

### EXERCISE

This time you're not going to change anything in the code. Instead you're going to examine the kv file carefully and find all the properties on all the different widgets that are used in the program. So, identify each property and check out the appropriate widget's documentation to determine what type of property they are. Be aware that although you can use the **size** property on a label, for example, you won't find it in the **Label** class. This is because this property is inherited from the base class, which is **Widget**. You can always check out the base class in the documentation.

Create a table to give even more information. Here are the three properties that we already discussed in the chapter to get you started:

| name of property | defined in class... | type of property | default value |
|---|---|---|---|
| text | Label | StringProperty | '' |
| size | Widget | ReferenceListProperty | |
| max | Slider | NumericProperty | 100 |

### SOLUTION

Here's the kv file with all the properties highlighted. I only highlighted the first occurrences of them and I also omitted the ones mentioned in the chapter:

```
#:kivy 1.11.1
# File name: test.kv

<CustomLayout>:
    size_hint: .5, .5
    pos_hint: {'x': .5, 'top': 1}

    Button:
        ...
    BoxLayout:
        orientation: 'vertical'
        ...
        Slider:
            id: _slider
            min: 100
            max: 200
            value: 150
            orientation: 'vertical'

        Button:
            ...
```

And here's the table:

| name of property | defined in class... | type of property | default value |
|---|---|---|---|
| `text` | `Label` | `StringProperty` | `''` |
| `size` | `Widget` | `ReferenceListProperty` | |
| `max` | `Slider` | `NumericProperty` | `100` |
| `size_hint` | `Widget` | `ReferenceListProperty` | |
| `pos_hint` | `Widget` | `ObjectProperty` | |
| `orientation` | `BoxLayout` | `OptionProperty` | `'horizontal'` |
| `id` | `Widget` | `StringProperty` | `None` |
| `min` | `Slider` | `NumericProperty` | `0` |
| `value` | `Slider` | `NumericProperty` | `0` |
| `orientation` | `Slider` | `OptionProperty` | `'horizontal'` |

As you can see, both the **`BoxLayout`** class and the **`Slider`** class define an **`orientation`** property.

# Chapter 65 - Referencing Objects Using Kivy Properties

In the previous chapter we were talking about Kivy properties. In this chapter we'll see how to use Kivy properties to reference widgets and properties set on other widgets.

We're going to be working on our test files again. Let's simplify them slightly.

Here's the kv file:

```
#:kivy 1.11.1
# File name: test.kv

<TestLayout>:
    Label:
        id: _label1
        text: 'label 1'
        size_hint: .5, .5
        pos_hint: {'x': 0, 'top': 1}
    BoxLayout:
        size_hint: .5, .5
        pos_hint: {'x': .5, 'top': 1}
        Button:
            id: _button1
            text: 'button 1'
        BoxLayout:
            orientation: 'vertical'
            Button:
                id: _button2
                text: 'button 2'
            Slider:
                id: _slider
                min: 100
                max: 200
                value: 150
                orientation: 'vertical'
            Button:
                text: 'button 3'
        Button:
            text: 'button 4'
    Button:
        text: 'button 5'
        size_hint: .5, .5
        pos_hint: {'x': 0, 'y': 0}
    Label:
        id: _label2
        text: 'label 2'
        size_hint: .5, .5
        pos_hint: {'x': .5, 'y': 0}
```

And here's the Python file:

```
# File name: test.py

from kivy.config import Config
Config.set('graphics', 'width', '1200')
Config.set('graphics', 'height', '675')
Config.set('graphics', 'resizable', '1')

import kivy
kivy.require('1.11.1')
from kivy.app import App
from kivy.uix.floatlayout import FloatLayout

class TestLayout(FloatLayout):
    def on_touch_down(self, touch):
        self.ids._label1.text = str(int(touch.x))
        self.ids._label2.text = str(int(touch.y))
        self.ids._button1.font_size += 1
        self.ids._button2.text += '+'
        self.ids._slider.value += 1

class TestApp(App):
    def build(self):
        return TestLayout()

if __name__ == '__main__':
    TestApp().run()
```

Now, here, inside the **TestLayout** class, you can see the **on_touch_down** method. This method will be called whenever you click your left mouse button or touch the screen, if applicable. The **touch** parameter contains the coordinates of the point where you clicked or touched.

In this example widgets are referenced from within Python code by means of the **ids** property.

We're referencing five widgets by their ids and change some of their properties in code. If you run the program and click your left mouse button several times, you will see the effects.

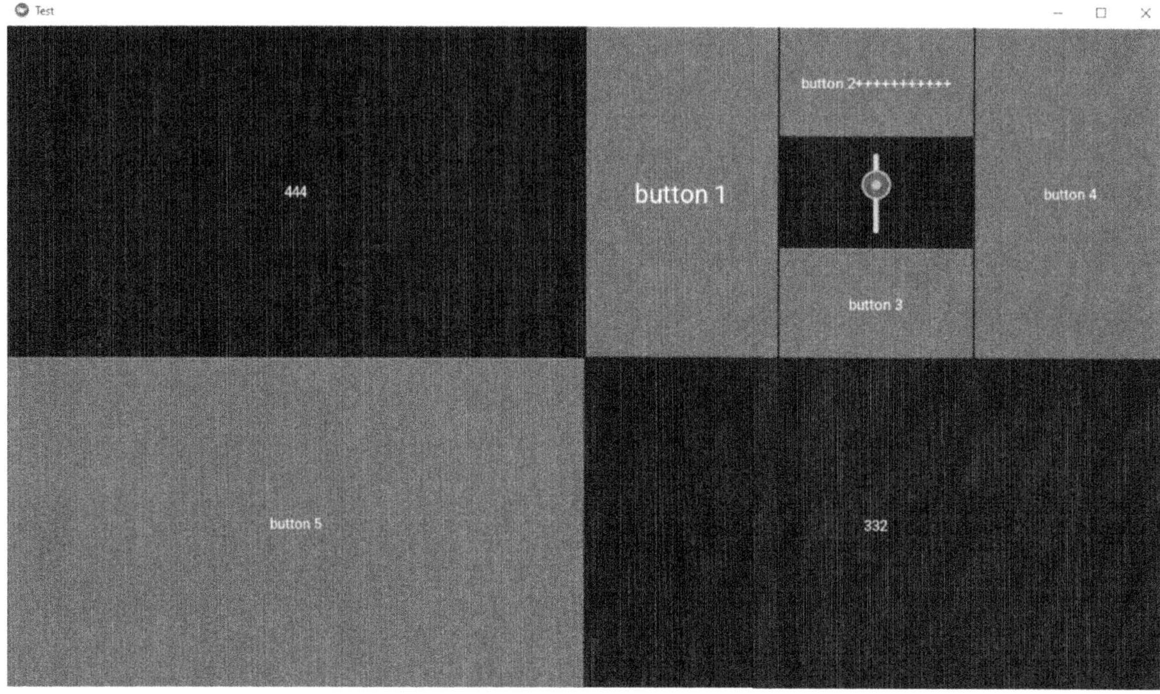


# The ObjectProperty

Instead of using the **ids** property, we could have used our own properties. Let's now rewrite the two files to use Kivy properties. Let's start with the kv file. Here's the code with comments:

```
#:kivy 1.11.1
# File name: test.kv

<TestLayout>:
    # Let's define five properties that will reference the five
    # widgets that we referenced by ids before. You can name them
    # whatever you like.

    # You use a widget's id to set the property. For example, to
    # associate the first property with the first label, you use
    # the first label's id:
    label1: _label1

    # And here are the other four properties.
    label2: _label2
    button1: _button1
    button2: _button2
    slider: _slider
```

```
    Label:
        id: _label1
        ...
    BoxLayout:
        ...
        Button:
            id: _button1
            ...
        BoxLayout:
            ...
            Button:
                id: _button2
                ...
            Slider:
                id: _slider
                ...
    Label:
        id: _label2
        ...
```

In the Python file we define the properties we need directly in the class. This will be discussed later. In our case, the properties are supposed to reference widgets, which are objects, generally speaking. If you want to reference a widget, you should use an **ObjectProperty**. The default value of an **ObjectProperty** is **None**, and this will do. Here's the Python file:

```
# File name: test.py
...
from kivy.uix.floatlayout import FloatLayout

# You have to import the property classes that you want to use.
from kivy.properties import ObjectProperty

class TestLayout(FloatLayout):
    # We define the properties here.
    label1 = ObjectProperty()
    label2 = ObjectProperty()
    button1 = ObjectProperty()
    button2 = ObjectProperty()
    slider = ObjectProperty()

    def on_touch_down(self, touch):
        # Now you can use the properties instead of the ids property. They must be used
        # on an instance, so you need to add self.
        self.label1.text = str(int(touch.x))
        self.label2.text = str(int(touch.y))
        self.button1.font_size += 1
        self.button2.text += '+'
        self.slider.value += 1

class TestApp(App):
    ...
```

If you now run the app, it will work just like before.

Now, in case of the **ObjectProperty** class, it's enough to define the property in the kv file and the property will be understood as an **ObjectProperty**. This means that even if you don't declare the properties explicitly in the Python file, they will be still available. To see how it works, temporarily comment out the declarations of the properties in the Python file:

```
# File name: test.py
...
class TestLayout(FloatLayout):
    # We define the properties here.
    # label1 = ObjectProperty()
    # label2 = ObjectProperty()
    # button1 = ObjectProperty()
    # button2 = ObjectProperty()
    # slider = ObjectProperty()

    def on_touch_down(self, touch):
        ...
```

You will be able to run the app anyway.

You may be confused by the way Kivy properties are declared and then used in Python code. I will discuss this subject in more detail in the next chapter. But before I do that, here's a simple exercise for you.

# It's Your Turn Now...

**EXERCISE**

Create three properties and use them to reference the three remaining buttons (button 3, button 4 and button 5). In the chapter we used the **`on_touch_down`** method, which is called whenever you click the left mouse button (or touch the touch screen). There are two similar methods:

**`on_touch_move`** – called when you move your mouse after clicking the left button or your finger on a touch screen,

**`on_touch_up`** – called when you release the mouse button or move your finger away from the screen.

Use these methods to do the following:

1. When you move the mouse after clicking the left mouse button, the text on button 3 should display the position of the mouse in the following format:

```
x = 256

y = 114
```

HINTS:

a) Use the **`touch.x`** and **`touch.y`** properties to retrieve the coordinates and convert them to integers. You can use an f-string to format the text. Don't forget to add the newline character.

b) The **`on_touch_move`** and **`on_touch_up`** methods also take the **`touch`** parameter which stores the position of the mouse or touch.

2. Also while the mouse is moving, button 4 should follow the mouse ; its center should be where the mouse currently is.

HINT: You can use the **`center`** property on the button. Its value must be set to a list or tuple with two values, the X-position and the Y-position. You can use **`touch.x`** and **`touch.y`** again.

3. Finally, when the mouse button is released, the width of button 5 should be halved.

HINT: Use the **`size_hint_x`** property on the button.

## SOLUTION

Here's the kv file:

```
#:kivy 1.11.1
# File name: test.kv

<TestLayout>:
    label1: _label1
    label2: _label2
    button1: _button1
    button2: _button2
    slider: _slider

    # Here are the three properties:
    button3: _button3
    button4: _button4
    button5: _button5

    Label:
        ...

    BoxLayout:
        ...
        BoxLayout:
            ...
            Button:
                # id to reference the button
                id: _button3
                text: 'button 3'

        Button:
            # id to reference the button
            id: _button4
            text: 'button 4'

    Button:
        # id to reference the button
        id: _button5
        text: 'button 5'
        ...
```

And here's the Python file:

```
# File name: test.py
...
class TestLayout(FloatLayout):
    label1 = ObjectProperty()
    ...
    slider = ObjectProperty()

    # Here are the three new properties.
    button3 = ObjectProperty()
    button4 = ObjectProperty()
    button5 = ObjectProperty()

    def on_touch_down(self, touch):
        ...
    # This method is called when you move the mouse with the left mouse button down.
    def on_touch_move(self, touch):
        # The text on button 3 should display the position of the mouse.
        self.button3.text = f'x = {int(touch.x)}\ny = {int(touch.y)}'
        # Button 4 should follow the mouse.
        self.button4.center = [touch.x, touch.y]

    # This method is called when you release the mouse button.
    def on_touch_up(self, touch):
        # The width of button 5 should be halved.
        self.button5.size_hint_x /= 2

class TestApp(App):
    ...
```

Here's what you can see when you run the app, click the left mouse button, move the mouse and then release the left mouse button:

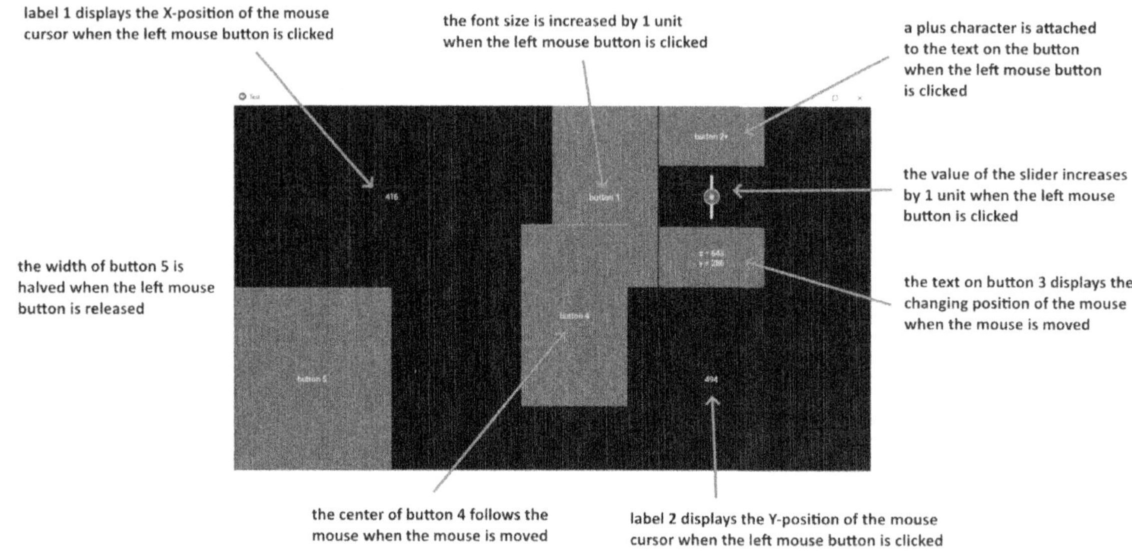
label 1 displays the X-position of the mouse cursor when the left mouse button is clicked
the font size is increased by 1 unit when the left mouse button is clicked
a plus character is attached to the text on the button when the left mouse button is clicked
the value of the slider increases by 1 unit when the left mouse button is clicked
the width of button 5 is halved when the left mouse button is released
the text on button 3 displays the changing position of the mouse when the mouse is moved
the center of button 4 follows the mouse when the mouse is moved
label 2 displays the Y-position of the mouse cursor when the left mouse button is clicked

# Chapter 66 - Defining and Using Kivy Properties

In the previous chapter we were creating and using some properties. In this chapter we'll have a look at how properties are actually defined and used. But before we do, let's recap on how class and instance attributes work in general.

## Class Attributes

Let's modify the Python file from the previous chapter a bit so that there aren't any Kivy properties anymore. Instead we'll define a class attribute.

Just a reminder: A class attribute is a Python variable that belongs to a class rather than a particular object. It's shared by all the instances of that class. We define class attributes outside the constructor.

So, in the code below we'll create a class attribute, **counter**, and see how it works:

```
# File name: test.py
...
from kivy.properties import ObjectProperty
from kivy.uix.button import Button

class CustomButton(Button):
    counter = 0

    def on_press(self):
        self.__class__.counter += 1

class TestLayout(FloatLayout):
    pass

class TestApp(App):
    def build(self):
        return TestLayout()

if __name__ == '__main__':
    TestApp().run()
```

As you can see, we have a **CustomButton** class here that we will use instead of **Button**. Inside the class definition, but outside the constructor (which we don't explicitly define here), we define the class attribute **counter**. We can access a class attribute in two ways:

1) like we just did, so using **self.__class__** - which is preferred, because it's independent of the class name:

```
self.__class__.counter
```

2) using the name of the class, so in our case it would be:

```
CustomButton.counter
```

I'll stick to the former, though.

We also define the **on_press** event that will be triggered whenever the **CustomButton** is pressed. It will increment the value of **counter** by 1.

Now let's modify the kv file so that it makes use of the **CustomButton** instances instead of the regular buttons. Also, let's remove any code that we don't need at this moment, like the ids of the widgets. Let's set the **text** properties on each **CustomButton** to the value of the class attribute **counter**:

```
#:kivy 1.11.1
# File name: test.kv

<TestLayout>:
    Label:
        ...
    BoxLayout:
        ...
        CustomButton:
            text: str(self.__class__.counter)
        BoxLayout:
            orientation: 'vertical'
            CustomButton:
                text: str(self.__class__.counter)
            Slider:
                ...
            CustomButton:
                text: str(self.__class__.counter)
        CustomButton:
            text: str(self.__class__.counter)
    CustomButton:
        text: str(self.__class__.counter)
        size_hint: .5, .5
        ...
```

Let's run the app.

As you can see, the **text** property on all five custom buttons is set to **0**, which is the current value of the **counter** class attribute.

Now, if we press a custom button, the value of the class attribute should increment by 1. Try it out.

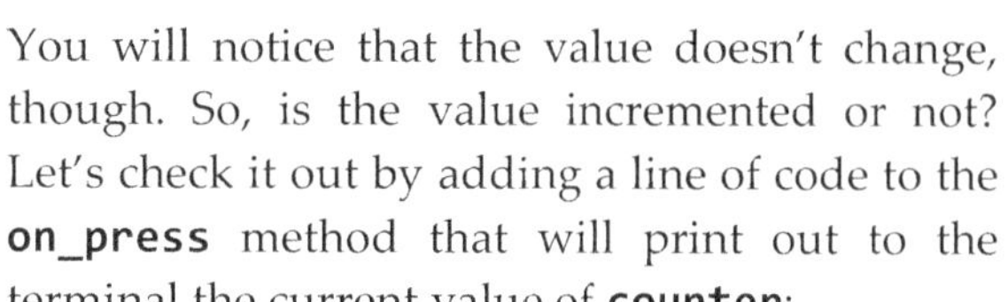

You will notice that the value doesn't change, though. So, is the value incremented or not? Let's check it out by adding a line of code to the **on_press** method that will print out to the terminal the current value of **counter**:

```
# File name: test.py
...
class CustomButton(Button):
    counter = 0

    def on_press(self):
        self.__class__.counter += 1
        print(self.__class__.counter)

class TestLayout(FloatLayout):
    ...
```

Run the program again, press any of the custom buttons and watch the output in the terminal.

Here I pressed a couple buttons in an arbitrary order and each time I did I could see the current value of **counter** printed out to the terminal (A). So, looks like it works. I didn't see any of the changes on any of the buttons, though (B).

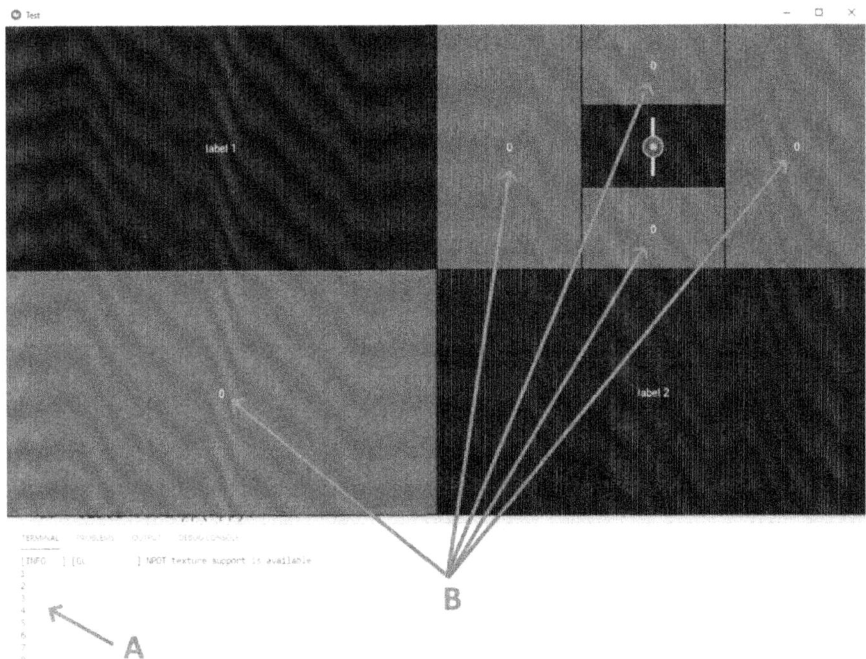


This is something I actually might have expected.

I know that when I use a Kivy property, any change of the property will automatically update the **text** property on the button, but I'm not using a Kivy property here, but rather a class attribute.

This means that if I want to see the change on the buttons, I must update their **text** properties manually.

Let's do that:

```
# File name: test.py
...
class CustomButton(Button):
    counter = 0

    def on_press(self):
        self.__class__.counter += 1

        # We must update the text property manually.
        self.text = str(self.__class__.counter)

class TestLayout(FloatLayout):
    ...
```

I also removed the **print** function from the **on_press** method.

Now, if you run the app, the value will be updated on the button that is being pressed. So, let's launch the app and press the big button 5 times.

As you can see, the value was updated on the big button, so the one that we pressed.

It's not updated on the other buttons, though. And what will happen if you now press another button, like the one to the left of the slider? It should be updated, because this is what the **on_press** method will take care of, but what value should I expect? Let's find out.

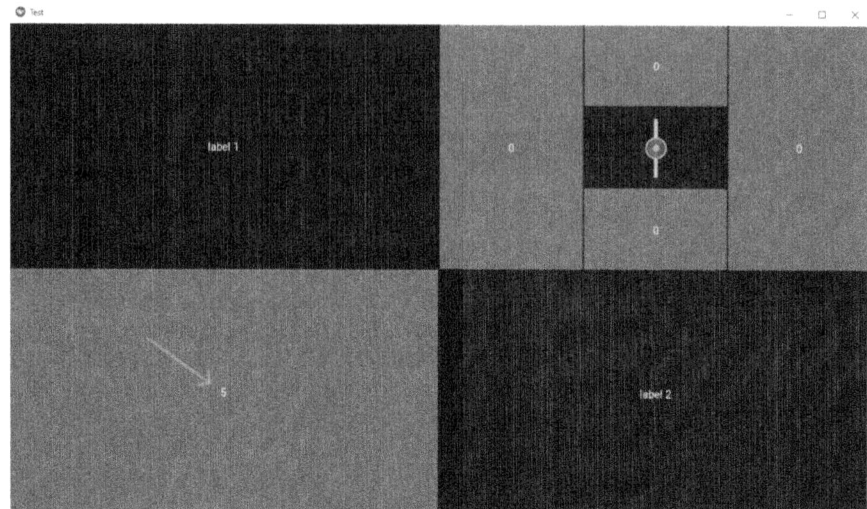

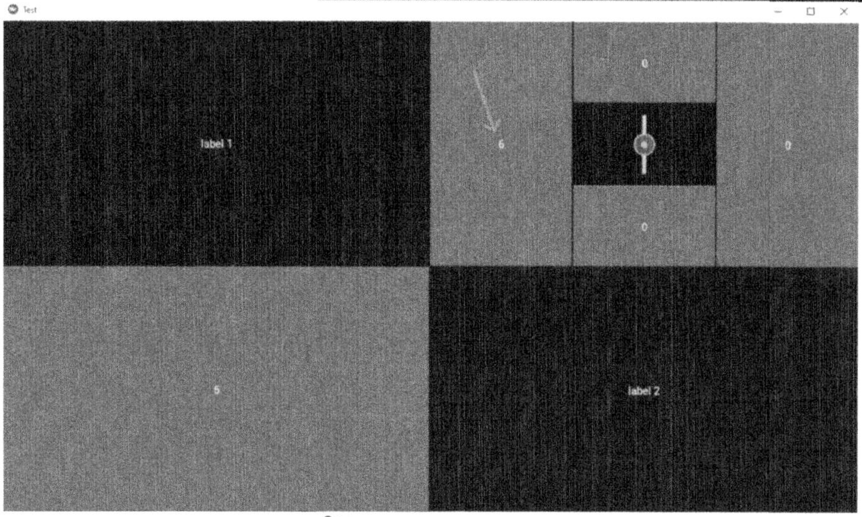

The value is **6**.

Why not **1**?

Well, this is because, as mentioned before, a class attribute is shared by all instances of the class.

So, each time you press ANY instance of the **CustomButton** class, the class attribute will be incremented on the class level and will be shared by all the instances of that class. If you now keep pressing the buttons, the value will be incremented each time, but it will only update on the instance that was pressed.

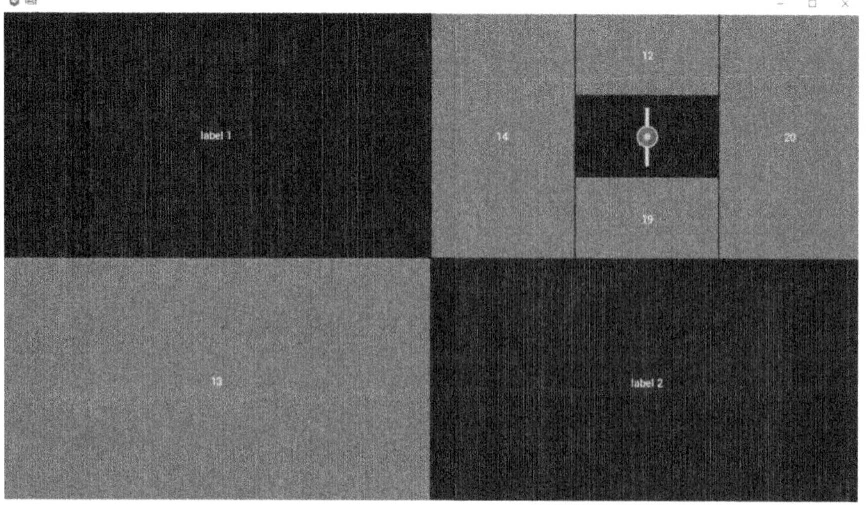


This might be what you want, but it might be not.

In the latter case, you

would probably prefer each button to be independent of the others and update its own counter.

This would let us know how many times each particular button was pressed, unlike in the example above where we only knew how many button presses there were altogether. This is what instance attributes are better suited for.

# Instance Attributes

So, let's use an instance attribute instead. But what is an instance attribute in the first place? Well, this is a Python variable that belongs to only one instance of the class, so each instance has its own, independent copy. Instance attributes are defined inside the constructor. Have a look:

```
# File name: test.py
...
class CustomButton(Button):
    def __init__(self, **kwargs):
        super().__init__(**kwargs)

        # This is an instance attribute.
        self.counter = 0

    def on_press(self):
        self.counter += 1

        # Add this line to print the value
        # of counter to the terminal.
        print(self.counter)

class TestLayout(FloatLayout):
    ...
```

Now **counter** is an instance attribute. I set its initial value to **0** in the constructor and I also added the line that will print out the current value of the **counter** attribute that belongs only to the button that was pressed. You also need to modify the kv file so that now the **text** properties on the buttons are set to the instance attribute:

```
#:kivy 1.11.1
# File name: test.kv

<TestLayout>:
    ...
    BoxLayout:
        ...
        CustomButton:
            text: str(self.counter)
        BoxLayout:
            ...
            CustomButton:
                text: str(self.counter)
            Slider:
                ...
            CustomButton:
                text: str(self.counter)

        CustomButton:
            text: str(self.counter)
    CustomButton:
        text: str(self.counter)
        ...
```

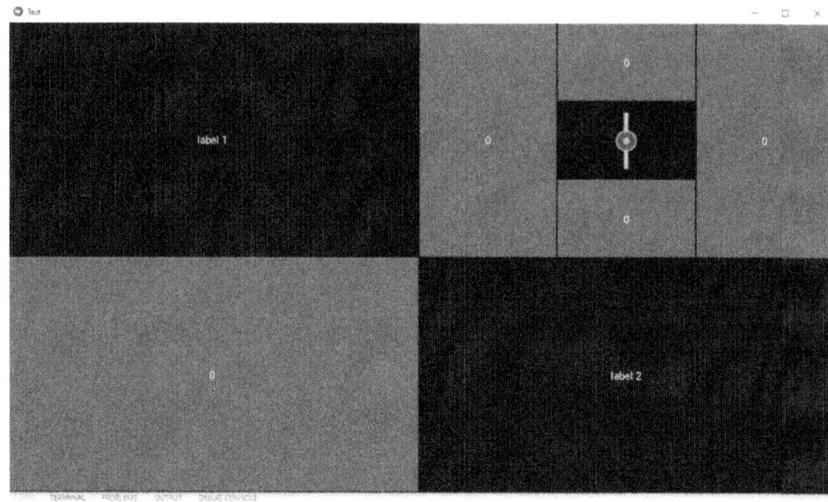


This code looks very much like before, but there's a big difference. When you now run the app and press a button, you'll see how the value of **counter** increases. But when you press another button, it will increase independently, so the values will be incremented from 0 again. You will see the changes only in the terminal now, because instance attributes don't automatically react to changes either. So, we have to update the **text** property manually again:

```
# File name: test.py
...
class CustomButton(Button):
    def __init__(self, **kwargs):
        ...
    def on_press(self):
        self.counter += 1
        # We must update the text property manually.
        self.text = str(self.counter)

class TestLayout(FloatLayout):
    ...
```

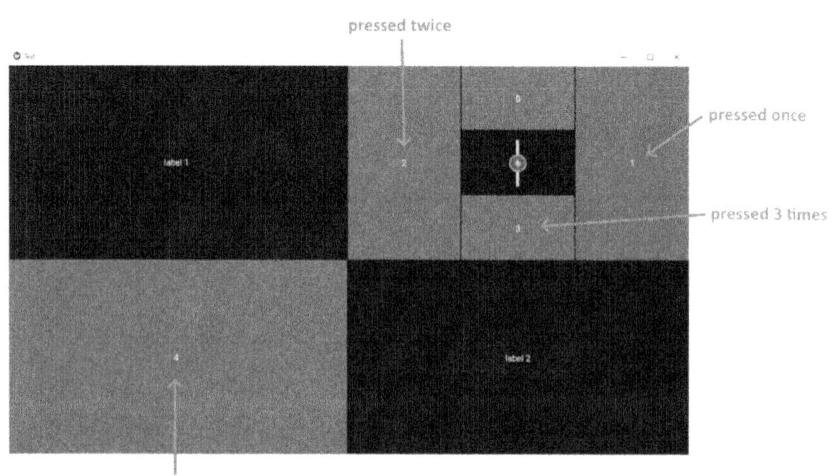


I also removed the **print** function that printed out the value of **counter** to the terminal. If you run the app now and press the buttons, the values of **counter** will update individually for each button.

This is almost what

we wanted. If only the values of the **counter** property could be updated automatically... Actually, you know they can – this is how Kivy properties work. Let's have a closer look at them now.

# Kivy Properties

So now, after we briefly recapped on class and instance attributes, have a look at the following piece of code that we used in the previous chapter:

```
# File name: test.py
...
class TestLayout(FloatLayout):
    label1 = ObjectProperty()
    label2 = ObjectProperty()
    button1 = ObjectProperty()
    button2 = ObjectProperty()
    slider = ObjectProperty()

    def on_touch_down(self, touch):
        self.label1.text = str(int(touch.x))
        self.label2.text = str(int(touch.y))
        self.button1.font_size += 1
        self.button2.text += '+'
        self.slider.value += 1
...
```

As you can see, we defined the Kivy properties like we define class attributes, so on the class level, but then we used them like instance attributes inside the **on_touch_down** method. So, do they behave like class attributes or like instance attributes? Well, Kivy properties are an interesting combination of both. We define them as class attributes, but they are not shared by all the instances of the class, so they behave like instance properties. This is because Kivy internally transforms them to instance attributes.

What makes them more useful than instance properties, though, is that whenever we define a Kivy property, Kivy internally also associates an event with this property, using a naming convention of adding the prefix **on_** to the name of the property. So, if the property's name is **state**, the corresponding method will be **on_state**, and so on. This event is fired whenever the value of a property changes, this is why we don't need to take care of the changes ourselves.

Let's rewrite the code that we've been using throughout this chapter so that it makes use of a property rather than a class or instance attribute. We're going to need a **NumericProperty** this time.

```
# File name: test.py
...
from kivy.uix.floatlayout import FloatLayout

# Don't forget to import NumericProperty.
from kivy.properties import NumericProperty

from kivy.uix.button import Button

class CustomButton(Button):
    # We need a number, so a NumericProperty
    # is the way to go. Let's initialize it
    # to 0 by passing 0 as the default value.
    counter = NumericProperty(0)

    def on_press(self):
        # Here we use the property just like
        # an instance attribute.
        self.counter += 1

class TestLayout(FloatLayout):
    ...
```

As you can see, I defined the property as a **NumericProperty** on the class level, just like a class attribute, but then used it inside a method like an instance attribute. I also removed the code that I needed before to manually change the value of the **text** property on the button whenever the **counter** property changed. I don't need it anymore. Now that **counter** is a Kivy property, the **text** property on the button will be updated automatically each time the value of the **counter** property changes.

We don't need to change anything in the kv file, because Kivy properties are used just like instance properties. If you now run the program, it will work like before. The text on the custom buttons will be updated automatically.

In the next chapter we'll have a closer look at observing and reacting to property changes. We will see how to use callbacks when there's a property change. The naming convention with the **on_** prefix is not the only way. But first, do the exercise below.

# It's Your Turn Now...

EXERCISE

In this exercise you will create the **CustomLabel** class, which you will then use in the kv file instead of **Label**. You will define a Kivy property in the class that will be used to add a star symbol to the label text each time you click on the label. Here are the instructions:

1. In the Python file define the **CustomLabel** class that inherits from **Label**. In the class define the **info** property of type **StringProperty**. The initial value of the **info** property should be a single star symbol. In order to be able to use a **StringProperty**, you must first import it.

2. Inside the **CustomLabel** class add the **on_touch_down** method that will be called whenever you click on the label. If this happens, another star symbol will be attached to the label text. The problem is it will also be called if you click outside the label. To make sure that the star is appended only if you click on that particular label, you can use the **collide_point** method that is defined in the **Widget** class, from which **Label** inherits, so you have access to it. The **collide_point** method should be called on the instance of the **CustomLabel** class. You should pass two parameters to it: the X-position and the Y-position of the mouse click, which are stored in the **touch** parameter passed to the **on_touch_down** method. Simply put, in order to check if the click was inside the bounding box of the label, you should type:

```
if self.collide_point(touch.x, touch.y):
        ...
```

In place of the three dots above you should type the actual code that will append the star symbol to the label text.

## SOLUTION

Here's the Python file:

```
#:kivy 1.11.1
# File name: test.kv

<TestLayout>:
    # Let's use the CustomLabel.
    CustomLabel:
        # The text on the label should be the info text defined and updated
        # in the Python file.
        text: self.info
        size_hint: .5, .5
        pos_hint: {'x': 0, 'top': 1}

    BoxLayout:
        ...
    CustomButton:
        text: str(self.counter)
        size_hint: .5, .5
        pos_hint: {'x': 0, 'y': 0}

    # Again, let's use the CustomLabel.
    CustomLabel:
        text: self.info
        size_hint: .5, .5
        pos_hint: {'x': .5, 'y': 0}
```

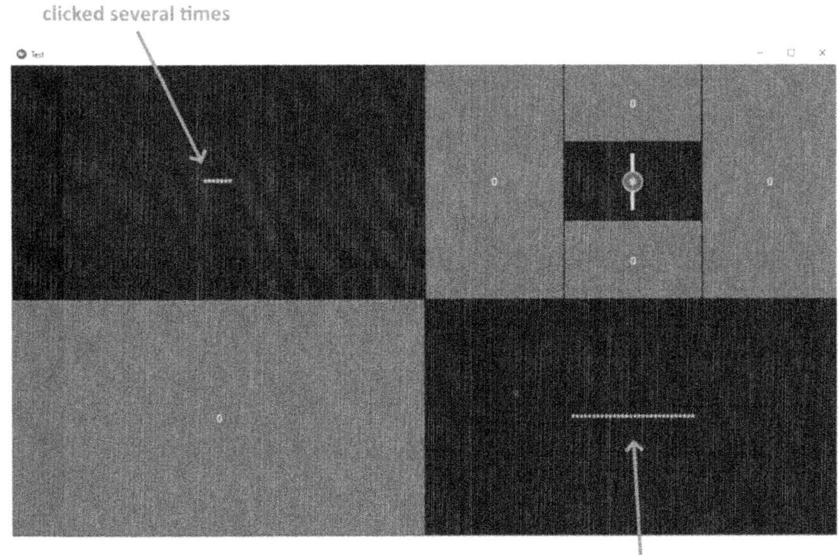


If you now run the app, each time you click on a label, a star will be added only on that particular label. Check it out.

# Chapter 67 - Observing Property Changes

In the previous chapter we were talking about defining and using Kivy properties. We created a couple of properties and then used them in our test files. In one of the previous chapters I mentioned that Kivy properties implement the Observer Design Pattern. This means that property changes are observed. You can bind to a property and deliver your own method that will be called when the value of the property changes.

In the previous chapter I mentioned that there is a naming convention that the callback method is named after the name of the property, using the prefix **on_**. Using this convention, the method is defined in the same class as the property it corresponds to.

But you can also observe a property change outside the class where the property is defined. Then you have to use the **bind** method.

In the chapter we're going to have a look at both options. Let's start with the former.

## The on_<property_name> Methods

Let's use our test files again. In the example from the previous chapter we have the **counter** property in the **CustomButton** class. So, if we want to define a method that will be called whenever the value of the property changes, the name of the method should be **on_counter**. The method will take the **instance** and **value** parameters. The former refers to the instance of the class, the latter to the value of the property. Actually, the names of the parameters don't have to be **instance** and **value**, they can be anything, but you will often see them. It's like the name of the **self** parameter that doesn't have to be named **self** either, but usually is.

So, let's add the **on_counter** method that will print the values hiding behind the two parameters, **instance** and **value**. Let's first change the text on the big button in the kv file:

```
#:kivy 1.11.1
# File name: test.kv

<TestLayout>:
    ...
    CustomButton:
        text: 'big button'
        size_hint: .5, .5
        pos_hint: {'x': 0, 'y': 0}

    CustomLabel:
        ...
```

And now let's add the **on_counter** method in **test.py** that will be called when the value of the counter property changes:

```
# File name: test.py
...
class CustomButton(Button):
    counter = NumericProperty(0)

    # The instance parameter refers to the instance of the class which triggered
    # the event, the value parameter refers to the value of the counter property
    # on that instance.
    def on_counter(self, instance, value):
        print(f'''instance: {instance}
               text on instance: {instance.text}
               value of counter: {value}''')

    def on_press(self):
        ...
```

Now watch the output in the terminal that you get when you run the app and press on a couple buttons:

```
instance: <__main__.CustomButton object at 0x000002F42B01E518>
               text on instance: big button
               value of counter: 1
instance: <__main__.CustomButton object at 0x000002F42B01E518>
               text on instance: big button
               value of counter: 2
instance: <__main__.CustomButton object at 0x000002F425BC4588>
               text on instance: 0
               value of counter: 1
instance: <__main__.CustomButton object at 0x000002F42B01E2E8>
               text on instance: 0
               value of counter: 1
instance: <__main__.CustomButton object at 0x000002F42B01E2E8>
               text on instance: 1
               value of counter: 2
instance: <__main__.CustomButton object at 0x000002F42B01E2E8>
               text on instance: 2
               value of counter: 3
instance: <__main__.CustomButton object at 0x000002F42B01E518>
               text on instance: big button
               value of counter: 3
```

So, I first pressed the big button twice, then another button once, then yet another button three times and finally the big button again. As you can see, **instance** refers to the **CustomButton** instance that triggers the event and **value** refers to the value of the **counter** property on that instance.

Now that we know what the parameters stand for, let's remove the **print** function from the method and add some code that will do something when the value of the **counter** property changes. Now the text on a button will be changed every time it's pressed, but after the third click it will also get bigger. After the eighth click the color of the text will change to red and after the tenth click the text will be in bold type. Here's the code:

```
# File name: test.py
...
class CustomButton(Button):
    counter = NumericProperty(0)

    def on_counter(self, instance, value):
        if value > 3:
            self.font_size += 5
        if value > 8:
            self.color = [1, 0, 0, 1]
        if value > 10:
            self.bold = True

    def on_press(self):
        ...
```

Let's run and test the app. The **on_counter** method is now called each time the value of the **counter** property changes.

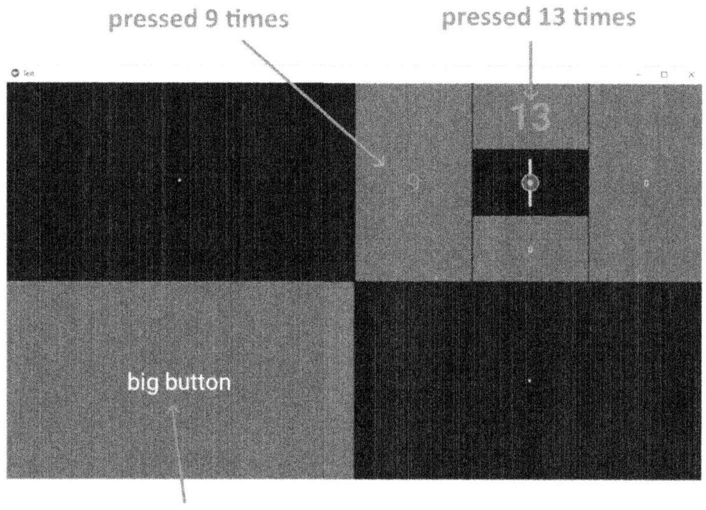


## The bind Method

The other way to observe property change is by means of the **bind** method. This method is used outside the class where the property was defined.

Let's demonstrate it on a simplified example. Our app should now have two custom buttons. Here's the kv code:

```
#:kivy 1.11.1
# File name: test.kv

<TestLayout>:
    button1: _button1
    button2: _button2

    CustomButton:
        id: _button1
        text: str(self.counter)
        size_hint_x: .5

    CustomButton:
        id: _button2
        text: str(self.counter)
        size_hint_x: .5
        pos_hint: {'x': .5}
```

So, we have two ObjectProperties here, **button1** and **button2**, which reference the two **Button** widgets by ids. The **test.py** file (here with explanations in the comments) should look like so:

```
# File name: test.py

from kivy.config import Config
Config.set('graphics', 'width', '1200')
Config.set('graphics', 'height', '675')
Config.set('graphics', 'resizable', '1')

import kivy
kivy.require('1.11.1')
from kivy.app import App
from kivy.uix.floatlayout import FloatLayout
from kivy.properties import NumericProperty
from kivy.uix.button import Button

class CustomButton(Button):
    counter = NumericProperty(0)

    def on_press(self):
        self.counter += 1

# This function will be called when the counter property on either button changes.
def make_bigger(instance, value):
    if value < 5:
        instance.font_size += 20

# This function will be called when the counter property on the second button changes.
def change_color(instance, value):
    if instance.color == [1, 0, 0, 1]:
        instance.color = [0, 1, 0, 1]
    else:
        instance.color = [1, 0, 0, 1]

class TestLayout(FloatLayout):
    def __init__(self, **kwargs):
        super().__init__(**kwargs)

        # Bind the make_bigger function to the counter property on the first button.
        self.button1.bind(counter=make_bigger)

        # You can bind more than one function to a property.
        self.button2.bind(counter=make_bigger)
        self.button2.bind(counter=change_color)

class TestApp(App):
    def build(self):
        return TestLayout()

if __name__ == '__main__':
    TestApp().run()
```

So, here we have the **CustomButton** class where the **counter** property is defined. The value of the **counter** property is incremented by 1 each time the button is pressed. In the kv code two instances of **CustomButton** are defined as children of the root widget. By means of the two ObjectProperties we can access them in the Python file.

We have also defined two functions outside either class, **make_bigger** and **change_color**, which are supposed to modify the font size and color of the button text respectively. But how should the functions know that they should be called? We have to bind them to the **counter** property. In the code above we bind one function to the **counter** property on the first button and two functions on the second button. This means that whenever the value of the **counter** property changes on the first button, the **make_bigger** function will be called on that button. In order for the function to know that it should work on that button only, the instance of the button is passed to the function as the **instance** parameter. The **value** parameter, on the other hand, refers to the value of the property.

Now, as far as the other button is concerned, we also want the **make_bigger** function to be called when the **counter** property changes, so we also bind the function to the second button's **counter** property. But we can bind more than one function to a property, which is exactly what we are doing here. Besides the **make_bigger** function, we also want the **change_color** function to be called.

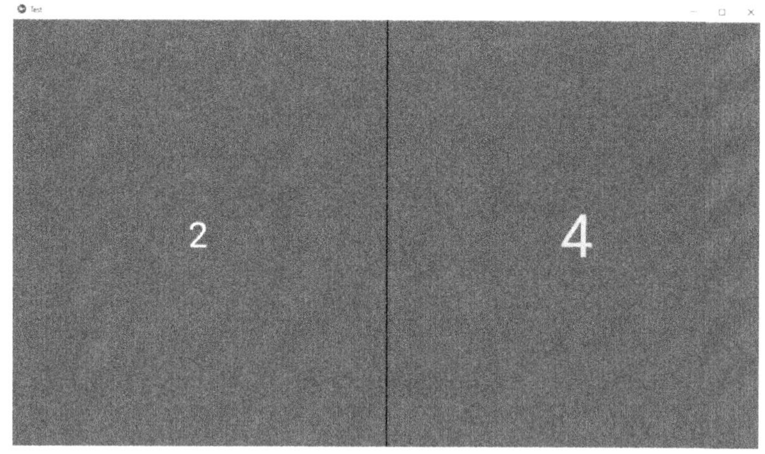


Now run the program to see whether the functions were bound correctly.

When you press the first button and the value of the **counter** property changes, only the **make_bigger** function will be called. When you press the other button and its **counter** property changes, both functions will be called. The image on the right shows what you can see after several clicks.

We will be using the **bind** method a lot throughout our project, so you will have an opportunity to see it in action more than once.

In the next chapter we'll add some properties to the Slugrace project, but first here's an exercise for you.

# It's Your Turn Now...

## EXERCISE

Your goal in this exercise is to add a random vowel to the button text each time a button is pressed. When the text on the button is longer than 8 characters, only the last three characters are shown.

Here's your initial kv code:

```
#:kivy 1.11.1
# File name: test.kv

<TestLayout>:
    CustomButton:
        text: str(self.vowels)
        font_size: 50
        size_hint_x: .5

    CustomButton:
        text: str(self.vowels)
        font_size: 50
        size_hint_x: .5
        pos_hint: {'x': .5}
```

And here's your initial Python code:

```
# File name: test.py
...
from kivy.app import App
from kivy.uix.floatlayout import FloatLayout
from kivy.properties import StringProperty
from kivy.uix.button import Button

class CustomButton(Button):
    vowels = StringProperty('a')

class TestLayout(FloatLayout):
    pass

class TestApp(App):
    ...
```

If you run this app now, you will see two buttons with the text `'a'`.

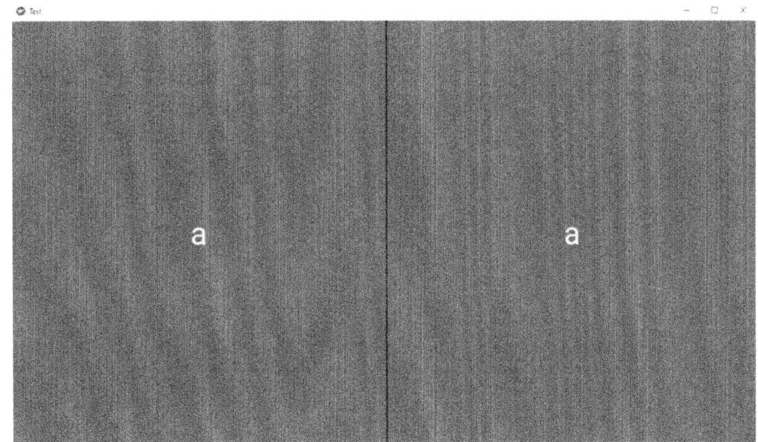


Here are the instructions for you to follow:

1. Each time you press a button, a random vowel should be added to the text on the button. To do that, you can use the **`choice`** function from the **`random`** module. Go ahead and import it.

2. Inside the **`CustomButton`** class add the **`on_press`** method. When the button is pressed, a single random vowel is appended at the end of the **`vowels`** property.

HINT: You can use the **`choice`** method to pick a random letter from a string, so if it be a vowel, **`choice('aeiou')`** will work.

3. Use the naming convention with the **`on_`** prefix to create a method that will set the value of the

**vowels** property to its final three characters if the length of the button text exceeds 8 characters.

HINT: You can use slicing to do that.

## SOLUTION

The kv code didn't change. And here's the Python code:

```
# File name: test.py
...
from kivy.uix.button import Button
# You'll need the choice function that will pick a random letter from the string.
from random import choice

class CustomButton(Button):
    vowels = StringProperty('a')

    def on_vowels(self, instance, value):
        if len(value) > 8:
            instance.vowels = value[-3:]

    def on_press(self):
        self.vowels += choice('aeiou')

class TestLayout(FloatLayout):

    ...
```

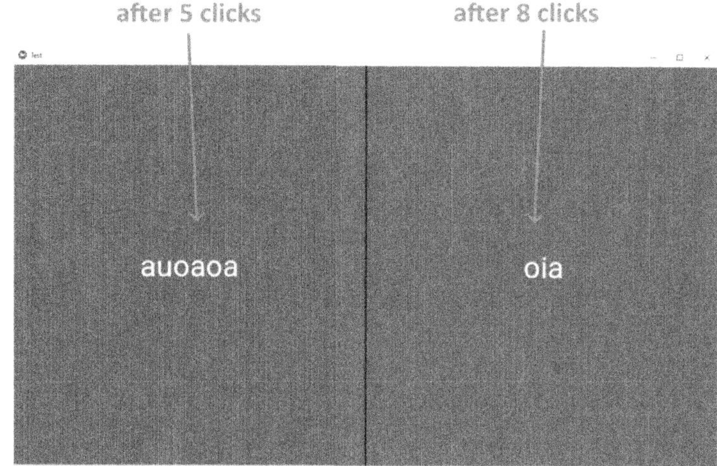


If you now run the app and click the buttons several times, a random vowel will be appended to the text on the button.

When the text is longer than 8 characters, the text is shortened to just the last three characters.

# Chapter 68 - Adding Some Properties to the Slugrace Project

In the preceding chapters we were talking about Kivy properties. Let's add some properties to our Slugrace project. This will make the code much less repetitive and error-prone.

Let's start with the Settings screen. There are a couple opportunities for us to make use of Kivy properties.

## The Player Radio Buttons

In the **settings.kv** file, inside the Players area, you will find the Radio Buttons section:

```
#:kivy 1.11.1
# File name: settings.kv
...
<SettingsScreen>:
    ...
    ### THE PLAYERS ###
    ...
        # Radio Buttons
        BoxLayout:
            ...
            # 1 player
            BoxLayout:
                PlayerRadioButton:
                RegularLabel:
                    text: '1 player'
            # 2 players
            BoxLayout:
                PlayerRadioButton:
                RegularLabel:
                    text: '2 players'
            # 3 players
            BoxLayout:
                PlayerRadioButton:
                RegularLabel:
                    text: '3 players'
            # 4 players
            BoxLayout:
                PlayerRadioButton:
                RegularLabel:
                    text: '4 players'
        # Player Name and Initial Money Setup
        ...
```

This code is responsible for the radio buttons in the Players area where you will choose the number of players. As you can see, the code for each player only differs in the label text. We could leave it as is because it isn't much code and we will have to set the text for each label anyway, but let's simplify it slightly using Kivy properties.

So, now each player is represented by a BoxLayout with a PlayerRadioButton and RegularLabel. Let's create a class that inherits from **`BoxLayout`** and contains the two widgets. We can name it **`PlayerCount`**. We can then create a StringProperty in the class and set the RegularLabel's text to it.

Next we can replace the code for each player in the code above by an instance of our class and just set the StringProperty there.

But enough talking, let's do it.

First let's define the class in the Python file. Open the **settings.py** file and add the following code:

```
# File name: settings.py
...
from kivy.uix.boxlayout import BoxLayout

# Import the StringProperty.
from kivy.properties import StringProperty

# Here's the new class with a StringProperty.
class PlayerCount(BoxLayout):
    count_text = StringProperty('')

class SettingsScreen(BoxLayout):
    ...
```

As you can see, there's the StringProperty that we can now use. Now, in the kv file let's add a rule for the **PlayerCount** class:

```
#:kivy 1.11.1
# File name: settings.kv
...
<ConditionRadioButton@CheckBox>:
    ...
### OTHER RULES ###
# Here's our PlayerCount class that inherits
# from BoxLayout.There we have the
# PlayerRadioButton and RegularLabel. We can
# now set the text on the RegularLabel to the
# count_text StringProperty we just defined
# in Python.
<PlayerCount>:
    PlayerRadioButton:
    RegularLabel:
        text: root.count_text

<SettingsScreen>:
    ...
```

And now we can replace each piece of code that represents one player by an instance of the **PlayerCount** class and set the **count_text** property accordingly:

```
#:kivy 1.11.1
# File name: settings.kv
...
<PlayerCount>:
    PlayerRadioButton:
    RegularLabel:
        text: root.count_text

<SettingsScreen>:
    ...
    ### THE PLAYERS ###
    ...
        # Radio Buttons
        BoxLayout:
            ...
            # 1 player
            PlayerCount:
                count_text: '1 player'

            # 2 players
            PlayerCount:
                count_text: '2 players'

            # 3 players
            PlayerCount:
                count_text: '3 players'

            # 4 players
            PlayerCount:
                count_text: '4 players'

        # Player Name and Initial Money Setup
        ...
```

Now our code is a bit shorter and more readable. We're using the instances of the **PlayerCount** class just like any other widgets.

# The Player Settings

Next, further down in the **settings.kv** file, there's even more repetitive code. Scroll down until you see the Player Name and Initial Money Setup section. There we have the players rows subsection with a lot of repetitive code. Here's just the piece of code for player 1 in full, the pieces of code for the other players are the same except for the text on the Regular80x30Labels:

```
#:kivy 1.11.1
# File name: settings.kv
...
<SettingsScreen>:
    ...
    ### THE PLAYERS ###
    BoxLayout:
        ...
        # Player Name and Initial Money
        BoxLayout:
            ...
            # the players rows
            # player 1
            BoxLayout:
                Regular80x30Label:
                    text: 'Player 1'
                NameInput:
                BoxLayout:
                    RegularLabel:
                        text: ""
                        size_hint_x: None
                        width: 280
                    DollarLabel:
                    NumInput:
            # player 2
            BoxLayout:
                Regular80x30Label:
                    text: 'Player 2'
                ...
            # player 3
            BoxLayout:
                Regular80x30Label:
                    text: 'Player 3'
                ...
            # player 4
            BoxLayout:
                Regular80x30Label:
                    text: 'Player 4'
                ...
    ### ENDING CONDITIONS ###
    ...
```

Here again each player is represented by their own piece of code. So, for each player we have a BoxLayout with a Regular80x30Label, a NameInput, and another BoxLayout with three further widgets. The code is pretty much the same for each player. What differs is the text on the Regular80x30Label.

So, you probably have a feeling that this could be simplified, right? Let's do it in a similar way as with the radio buttons.

First, let's define a class in the Python file that inherits from **BoxLayout** and define a StringProperty in it. We can name it **PlayerSettings**:

```
# File name: settings.py
...
from kivy.properties import StringProperty

class PlayerCount(BoxLayout):
    count_text = StringProperty('')

class PlayerSettings(BoxLayout):
    label_text = StringProperty('')

class SettingsScreen(BoxLayout):
    ...
```

And now let's add the following rule in the kv file:

```
#:kivy 1.11.1
# File name: settings.kv
...
### OTHER RULES ###
<PlayerCount>:
    ...
<PlayerSettings>:
    Regular80x30Label:
        text: root.label_text
    NameInput:
    BoxLayout:
        RegularLabel:
            text: ""
            size_hint_x: None
            width: 280
        DollarLabel:
        NumInput:

<SettingsScreen>:
    ...
```

With that in place, we are ready to replace each player's BoxLayout with an instance of the **PlayerSettings** class. All we have to do is set the **label_text** property accordingly:

```
#:kivy 1.11.1
# File name: settings.kv
...
<SettingsScreen>:
    ...
    ### THE PLAYERS ###
    ...
        # Player Name and Initial Money Setup
        BoxLayout:
            ...
            # the players rows
            # player 1
            PlayerSettings:
                label_text: 'Player 1'
            # player 2
            PlayerSettings:
                label_text: 'Player 2'
            # player 3
            PlayerSettings:
                label_text: 'Player 3'
            # player 4
            PlayerSettings:
                label_text: 'Player 4'

    ### ENDING CONDITIONS ###
    ...
```

Now the code became much shorter and more readable.

That's it for now as far as the Settings screen is concerned.

In the exercises below you will create similar classes with Kivy properties for the other screens.

This time there are going to be considerably more exercises than ever before, but take your time to do them all. We'll need the results of your work later in the book.

We're going to use properties a lot in our project. We're also going to use some other types of properties soon, but now I'd like to transform the loose collection of several simple apps, which we actually have right now, into one app that will be launched from one place, but will still be able to use all the files that are included in it. So, we must make the files communicate with one another. This is what we are going to talk about in the next part.

# It's Your Turn Now...

### EXERCISE 1

Let's add some properties to the Race screen now. Open the **race.kv** file and scroll down until you find the Slugs' Stats section:

```
#:kivy 1.11.1
# File name: race.kv
...
<RaceScreen>:
    ...
    ### INFO, STATS AND BUTTONS ###
    ...
        # Slugs' Stats
        BoxLayout:
            ...
            BoxLayout:
                spacing: 10
                RegularLabel:
                    text: "Speedster"
                RegularLabel:
                    text: '7 wins'
                RegularLabel:
                    text: '70%'
            BoxLayout:
                spacing: 10
                RegularLabel:
                    text: "Trusty"
                RegularLabel:
                    text: '1 win'
                RegularLabel:
                    text: '10%'
            BoxLayout:
                spacing: 10
                RegularLabel:
                    text: "Iffy"
                RegularLabel:
                    text: '0 wins'
                RegularLabel:
                    text: '0%'
            BoxLayout:
                spacing: 10
                RegularLabel:
                    text: "Slowpoke"
                RegularLabel:
                    text: '2 wins'
                RegularLabel:
                    text: '20%'
        # Players' Stats
        ...
```

Here the code is pretty simple and actually we could leave it as is, but we can also simplify it slightly with some properties. You can see four BoxLayouts, one for each slug. Each contains three RegularLabels. So, in the **race.py** file add the **SlugStats** class that inherits from **BoxLayout** and define three Kivy properties in it, a StringProperty and two NumericProperties. Name the StringProperty **name** and the NumericProperties **wins** and **win_percent** and set their default values to an empty string, **0** and **0** respectively. Don't forget to import the **NumericProperty** and **StringProperty** classes first.

Then, in the kv file add the **SlugStats** rule and set the **text** properties of the three RegularLabels to **name**, **wins** and **win_percent** respectively.

Now, as for the three properties, make sure that:

- the text on the first RegularLabel displays just the value of the **name** property,

- the text on the second RegularLabel displays the value of the **wins** property followed by the word **'win'** or **'wins'** depending on whether the value of **wins** is **1** or anything else,

HINT: Use concatenation to add the word **'win'** or **'wins'** and use the ternary **if** statement to decide which of the two should be chosen.

- the text on the third RegularLabel displays the value of the **win_percent** property followed by the **%** sign.

Finally replace the BoxLayouts in the Slugs' Stats subarea by instances of the **SlugStats** class. Use the same values as before.

## SOLUTION

Here's the Python file:

```
# File name: race.py
...
from kivy.uix.boxlayout import BoxLayout

# Import the classes that you will need.
from kivy.properties import NumericProperty, StringProperty

class SlugStats(BoxLayout):
    name = StringProperty('')
    wins = NumericProperty(0)
    win_percent = NumericProperty(0)

class RaceScreen(BoxLayout):
    ...
```

And here's the kv file:

```
#:kivy 1.11.1
# File name: race.kv

### CLASS RULES ###
...
<SlugStats>:
    spacing: 10
    RegularLabel:
        text: root.name
    RegularLabel:
        text: str(root.wins) + (' win' if root.wins == 1 else ' wins')
    RegularLabel:
        text: str(root.win_percent) + '%'

<RaceScreen>:
    ...
    ### INFO, STATS AND BUTTONS ###
    ...
        # Slugs' Stats
        BoxLayout:
            ...
            BoldLabel:
```

```
            text: "Slugs' Stats"

        SlugStats:
            name: 'Speedster'
            wins: 7
            win_percent: 70

        SlugStats:
            name: 'Trusty'
            wins: 1
            win_percent: 10

        SlugStats:
            name: 'Iffy'
            wins: 0
            win_percent: 0

        SlugStats:
            name: 'Slowpoke'
            wins: 2
            win_percent: 20

    # Players' Stats
    ...
```

Run the program to make sure it works as before.

### EXERCISE 2

Just below the Slug's Stats section is the Players' Stats section. Let's simplify this part too. In the Python file add the **PlayerStats** class that inherits from **BoxLayout** and add two properties to it: the StringProperty **name** and the NumericProperty **money**. Initialize them to an empty string and **0** respectively.

Then, in the kv file, add the corresponding rule. There are two RegularLabels. The first one's text should be set to the **name** property and the second one's text should read: **'has $'** followed by the value of the **money** property.

Finally, use instances of the **PlayerStats** class in the code instead of the BoxLayouts. Set the properties to the same values.

### SOLUTION

Here's the Python code:

```
# File name: race.py
...
class SlugStats(BoxLayout):
    ...
class PlayerStats(BoxLayout):
    name = StringProperty('')
    money = NumericProperty(0)

class RaceScreen(BoxLayout):
    ...
```

And here's the kv code:

```
#:kivy 1.11.1
# File name: race.kv

### CLASS RULES ###
...
<SlugStats>:
    ...
<PlayerStats>:
    RegularLabel:
        text: root.name
    RegularLabel:
        text: 'has $' + str(root.money)

<RaceScreen>:
    ...
    ### INFO, STATS AND BUTTONS ###
    ...
        # Players' Stats
        BoxLayout:
            ...
            BoldLabel:
                text: "Players' Stats"
            PlayerStats:
                name: 'Player 1'
                money: 1000
            PlayerStats:
                name: 'Player 2'
                money: 800
            PlayerStats:
                name: 'Player 3'
                money: 1300
            PlayerStats:
                name: 'Player 4'
                money: 1200
        # Buttons
        ...
```

## EXERCISE 3

We're still in the Race screen. If you scroll down, you will find the Track area with the labels with slug info. They look like they can be simplified as well. Here's the code:

```
#:kivy 1.11.1
# File name: race.kv
...
<RaceScreen>:
    ...
    ### THE TRACK ###
    BoxLayout:
        ...
        # Track Image
        RelativeLayout:
            ...
            # white labels with slug info
            # Speedster
            BoxLayout:
                orientation: 'vertical'
                size_hint: None, None
                size: 100, 50
                pos_hint: {'x': .004, 'center_y': .875}
                WhiteNameLabel:
                    text: 'Speedster'
                WhiteWinsLabel:
                    text: '0 wins'
            # Trusty
            BoxLayout:
                orientation: 'vertical'
                size_hint: None, None
                size: 100, 50
                pos_hint: {'x': .004, 'center_y': .625}
                WhiteNameLabel:
                    text: 'Trusty'
                WhiteWinsLabel:
                    text: '0 wins'
            # Iffy
            BoxLayout:
                orientation: 'vertical'
                size_hint: None, None
                size: 100, 50
                pos_hint: {'x': .004, 'center_y': .375}
                WhiteNameLabel:
                    text: 'Iffy'
                WhiteWinsLabel:
                    text: '0 wins'
            # Slowpoke
            BoxLayout:
                orientation: 'vertical'
                size_hint: None, None
                size: 100, 50
                pos_hint: {'x': .004, 'center_y': .125}
                WhiteNameLabel:
                    text: 'Slowpoke'
                WhiteWinsLabel:
                    text: '0 wins'
            # the odds labels
            ...
```

As you can see, they look pretty much the same. There are some differences, though:

- the **center_y** property inside the **pos_hint** property is different for each slug,

- the names of the slugs are different,

- the wins stats are different.

When defining our class, we have to take the differences into account. So, in the Python file, add the **SlugInfo** class that inherits from **BoxLayout** and add three properties to it:

- the NumericProperty **y_position**, initialized to **0**,

- the StringProperty **name**, initialized to an empty string,

- the NumericProperty **wins**, initialized to **0**.

Then, in the kv file add the corresponding rule. In the rule you should set the **orientation**, **size_hint** and **size** properties to the same values as they are in the BoxLayouts. You should also set the **pos_hint** property, which requires a dictionary. So, in the dictionary **x** should be set to **.004**, so just as it is in the BoxLayouts, but **center_y** should be set to the **y_position** property.

Then, in the two WhiteLabels, set the **text** properties to the **name** and **wins** properties respectively. In the latter case use the same concatenated string as in the **SlugStats** rule (so with the ternary **if** statement).

Finally, replace the four BoxLayouts in the code with instances of the **SlugInfo** class. For the **name** and **y_position** properties use the same values as before, but the **wins** properties for the particular slugs should be set to **7**, **1**, **0** and **2** respectively so that they match the numbers in the Slugs' Stats subarea.

## SOLUTION

So, here's the Python file:

```
# File name: race.py
...
class SlugStats(BoxLayout):
    ...
class PlayerStats(BoxLayout):
    ...
class SlugInfo(BoxLayout):
    y_position = NumericProperty(0)
    name = StringProperty('')
    wins = NumericProperty(0)

class RaceScreen(BoxLayout):
    ...
```

And here's the kv file:

```
#:kivy 1.11.1
# File name: race.kv

### CLASS RULES ###
...
<SlugStats>:
    ...
<PlayerStats>:
    ...
<SlugInfo>:
    orientation: 'vertical'
    size_hint: None, None
    size: 100, 50
    pos_hint: {'x': .004, 'center_y': root.y_position}
    WhiteNameLabel:
        text: root.name
    WhiteWinsLabel:
        text: str(root.wins) + (' win' if root.wins == 1 else ' wins')

<RaceScreen>:
    ...
    ### THE TRACK ###
    BoxLayout:
        ...
        # Track Image
        RelativeLayout:
            ...
            # white labels with slug info
            # Speedster
            SlugInfo:
                y_position: .875
                name: 'Speedster'
                wins: 7
            # Trusty
            SlugInfo:
                y_position: .625
                name: 'Trusty'
                wins: 1
            # Iffy
            SlugInfo:
                y_position: .375
                name: 'Iffy'
                wins: 0
            # Slowpoke
            SlugInfo:
                y_position: .125
                name: 'Slowpoke'
                wins: 2
            # the odds labels
            ...
```

Run the app. It should work as before.

## EXERCISE 4

We're not yet done with the Race screen. There are the four slug images. Here's just the piece of code for the first slug because the code is pretty lengthy, but you can see the whole code in your text editor.

```
#:kivy 1.11.1
# File name: race.kv
...
<RaceScreen>:
    ...
    ### THE TRACK ###
    BoxLayout:
        ...
        # Track Image
        RelativeLayout:
            ...
            # slug images
            # Speedster
            RelativeLayout:
                pos_hint: {'x': .09, 'center_y': .875}
                size_hint: None, None
                size: 143, 30
                # the body image
                Image:
                    source: 'atlas://assets/slugs/slugs/speedsterBody'
                # the left eye image
                Image:
                    canvas.before:
                        PushMatrix
                        Rotate:
                            angle: 30
                            axis: 0, 0, 1
                            origin: self.x, self.center_y
                    canvas.after:
                        PopMatrix
                    source: 'atlas://assets/slugs/slugs/speedsterEye'
                    pos_hint: {'x': .95, 'y': .45}
                    size_hint: 0.25, 0.25
                # the right eye image
                Image:
                    canvas.before:
                        PushMatrix
                        Rotate:
                            angle: -30
                            axis: 0, 0, 1
                            origin: self.x, self.center_y
                    canvas.after:
                        PopMatrix
                    source: 'atlas://assets/slugs/slugs/speedsterEye'
                    pos_hint: {'x': .95, 'y': .3}
                    size_hint: 0.25, 0.25
            # Trusty
            ...
        # Winner
        ...
```

These look pretty complex, right? That's mainly because they are. But don't worry, your task is easier than it looks.

Each slug is represented by a RelativeLayout that contains three images, the body image and two eye images. Now, what are the differences? If we know this, we'll know what properties we need. So, the four slug images differ in the following:

- the body and eye images have different sources,

- just like with the **SlugInfo** widgets, the **center_y** property inside the **pos_hint** property of the RelativeLayout for each slug is different.

And that's essentially it. All the other properties are shared in some way. So, we will need three properties, two for the sources of the body and eye images and one for the **center_y** value inside the **pos_hint** property. So, in the Python file add the **SlugImage** class that inherits from **RelativeLayout** (don't forget to import the **RelativeLayout** class first) and add the following properties:

- the StringProperty **body_image**, initialized to an empty string,

- the StringProperty **eye_image**, initialized to an empty string,

- the NumericProperty **y_position**, initialized to **0**.

Then, in the kv file add the **SlugImage** rule. Here are some instructions that should help you:

1. The root's **size_hint** and **size** properties should be set like before, so to **(None, None)** and **(143, 30)** respectively.

2. In the root's **pos_hint** property **x** should be set like before, so to **.09**, and **center_y** should be set to the **y_position** property.

3. To make the code more concise later in the code, set the source of the body image to the string **'atlas://assets/slugs/slugs/'** followed by the value of the **body_image** property. This will allow us to set the **body_image** property later in the code to something like **'speedsterBody'** instead of the full path.

4. Use the same strategy to set the **source** properties of the two eye images accordingly. The rest of the eye images should be implemented exactly like before.

Finally, replace the four RelativeLayouts in the code by instances of the **SlugImage** class. Set the properties to the same values. Remember to set the **body_image** and **eye_image** properties just to the names of the particular images, not the full paths.

## SOLUTION

So, here's the Python file:

```
# File name: race.py
...
from kivy.uix.boxlayout import BoxLayout

# We're going to need the RelativeLayout class.
from kivy.uix.relativelayout import RelativeLayout

from kivy.properties import NumericProperty, StringProperty

class SlugStats(BoxLayout):
    ...
class PlayerStats(BoxLayout):
    ...
class SlugInfo(BoxLayout):
    ...
class SlugImage(RelativeLayout):
    body_image = StringProperty('')
    eye_image = StringProperty('')
    y_position = NumericProperty(0)

class RaceScreen(BoxLayout):
    ...
```

And here's the kv file:

```
#:kivy 1.11.1
# File name: race.kv

### CLASS RULES ###
...
<SlugStats>:
    ...
<PlayerStats>:
    ...
<SlugInfo>:
    ...
<SlugImage>:
    pos_hint: {'x': .09, 'center_y': root.y_position}
    size_hint: None, None
    size: 143, 30
    # the body image
    Image:
        source: 'atlas://assets/slugs/slugs/' + root.body_image
    # the left eye image
    Image:
        canvas.before:
            PushMatrix
            Rotate:
```

```
                angle: 30
                axis: 0, 0, 1
                origin: self.x, self.center_y
        canvas.after:
            PopMatrix
        source: 'atlas://assets/slugs/slugs/' + root.eye_image
        pos_hint: {'x': .95, 'y': .45}
        size_hint: 0.25, 0.25
    # the right eye image
    Image:
        canvas.before:
            PushMatrix
            Rotate:
                angle: -30
                axis: 0, 0, 1
                origin: self.x, self.center_y
        canvas.after:
            PopMatrix
        source: 'atlas://assets/slugs/slugs/' + root.eye_image
        pos_hint: {'x': .95, 'y': .3}
        size_hint: 0.25, 0.25

<RaceScreen>:
    ...
    ### THE TRACK ###
    BoxLayout:
        ...
        # Track Image
        RelativeLayout:
            ...
            # slug images
            # Speedster
            SlugImage:
                body_image: 'speedsterBody'
                eye_image: 'speedsterEye'
                y_position: .875
            # Trusty
            SlugImage:
                body_image: 'trustyBody'
                eye_image: 'trustyEye'
                y_position: .625
            # Iffy
            SlugImage:
                body_image: 'iffyBody'
                eye_image: 'iffyEye'
                y_position: .375
            # Slowpoke
            SlugImage:
                body_image: 'slowpokeBody'
                eye_image: 'slowpokeEye'
                y_position: .125
        # Winner
        ...
```

## EXERCISE 5

We're done with the Race screen for now. Let's move on to the Bets screen. Here we have just one thing to do. There's a vertical BoxLayout with four horizontal BoxLayouts that represent the players' bets. Again, as this code is pretty lengthy, here's just the part of it that represents the first player. You can check out the parts for the other players directly in the code.

```
#:kivy 1.11.1
# File name: bets.kv
...
<BetsScreen>:
    ...
    ### PLAYER BETS ###
    BoxLayout:
        orientation: 'vertical'
        # player 1
        BoxLayout:
            spacing: 10
            RegularLabel:
                text: 'Player 1'
            RegularLabel:
                text: 'bets'
                size_hint: (.4, 1)
            BoxLayout:
                spacing: 5
                DollarLabel:
                    halign: 'right'
                    size_hint: 1, 1
                BetInput:
                    text: '1000'
            Slider:
                min: 1
                max: 1000
                value: 1000
                step: 1
            RegularLabel:
                text: 'on'
                size_hint: (.3, 1)
            BoxLayout:
                PlayerSlugButton:
                    group: 'player1'
                RegularLabel:
                    text: 'Speedster'
            BoxLayout:
                PlayerSlugButton:
                    group: 'player1'
                RegularLabel:
                    text: 'Trusty'
            BoxLayout:
                PlayerSlugButton:
                    group: 'player1'
                RegularLabel:
                    text: 'Iffy'
            BoxLayout:
                PlayerSlugButton:
                    group: 'player1'
                RegularLabel:
                    text: 'Slowpoke'

        # player 2
        ...
        # player 3
        ...
        # player 4
        ...
    ### GO BUTTON ###
    ...
```

Let's refactor this code using Kivy properties again. First, let's find out how these horizontal BoxLayouts differ. Here are the differences:

- The text on the first RegularLabel is different for each player – it's the player's name.

- The value of the BetInput's **text** property doesn't differ now, but as it represents a particular player's bet (amount of money that the player bets), it will be different for each player, depending on how much money each player wants to bet. So, let's assume this property's value will be different for each player.

- As far as the sliders are concerned, they all look the same at this moment, but the truth is that only two out of the four slider properties will be the same for each player, **min** and **step**. The **max** property will represent the maximum amount of money a player can bet, so it will change pretty often. The **value** property will represent the bet that the player wants to put on a slug, so the same value as the value displayed in the BetInput. The player will just have the option to set the bet either by typing it in or by moving the slider. So, these two properties, **max** and **value**, will be different for each player.

- In the BoxLayouts with a PlayerSlugButton and a RegularLabel, the **group** property will be different for each player, but the names of the slugs will be the same.

As you can see, there are quite a few differences. So, in the Python file create the **Bet** class that inherits from **BoxLayout** and define the following properties (remember to import the classes first):

- the StringProperty **player_name** initialized to an empty string,

- the NumericProperty **bet_amount** initialized to **0**,

- the NumericProperty **max_bet_amount** initialized to **0**,

- the StringProperty **player_group** initialized to an empty string.

Then, in the kv file add the corresponding rule for the **Bet** class. You should be able to do it by yourself after so much practice in the exercises above. Just one hint: Use the **bet_amount** property to set both the BetInput's **text** property and the slider's **value** property.

## SOLUTION

Here's the Python file:

```
# File name: bets.py
...
from kivy.uix.boxlayout import BoxLayout
from kivy.properties import NumericProperty, StringProperty

class Bet(BoxLayout):
    player_name = StringProperty('')
    bet_amount = NumericProperty(0)
    max_bet_amount = NumericProperty(0)
    player_group = StringProperty('')

class BetsScreen(BoxLayout):
    ...
```

And here's the kv file:

```
#:kivy 1.11.1
# File name: bets.kv
...
<RedButton@Button>:
    ...
### OTHER RULES ###
<Bet>:
    spacing: 10
    RegularLabel:
        text: root.player_name
    RegularLabel:
        text: 'bets'
        size_hint: (.4, 1)
    BoxLayout:
        spacing: 5
        RegularLabel:
            text: '$'
            halign: 'right'
        BetInput:
            text: str(root.bet_amount)
    Slider:
        min: 1
        max: root.max_bet_amount
        value: root.bet_amount
        step: 1
    RegularLabel:
        text: 'on'
        size_hint: (.3, 1)
    BoxLayout:
        PlayerSlugButton:
            group: root.player_group
        RegularLabel:
            text: 'Speedster'
    BoxLayout:
        PlayerSlugButton:
            group: root.player_group
        RegularLabel:
            text: 'Trusty'
    BoxLayout:
        PlayerSlugButton:
            group: root.player_group
        RegularLabel:
            text: 'Iffy'
    BoxLayout:
        PlayerSlugButton:
            group: root.player_group
        RegularLabel:
            text: 'Slowpoke'

<BetsScreen>:
    ...
    ### PLAYER BETS ###
    BoxLayout:
        orientation: 'vertical'

        # player 1
        Bet:
            player_name: 'Player 1'
            bet_amount: 1000
            max_bet_amount: 1000
            player_group: 'player1'
        # player 2
        Bet:
            player_name: 'Player 2'
            bet_amount: 1000
            max_bet_amount: 1000
            player_group: 'player2'
        # player 3
        Bet:
            player_name: 'Player 3'
            bet_amount: 1000
            max_bet_amount: 1000
            player_group: 'player3'
        # player 4
        Bet:
            player_name: 'Player 4'
            bet_amount: 1000
            max_bet_amount: 1000
            player_group: 'player4'

    ### GO BUTTON ###
    RedButton:
        text: 'Go'
```

Don't you think the code looks much cleaner now? Run it to make sure everything works like before.

**EXERCISE 6**

OK, just one more exercise, the Results screen. Open the **results.kv** file and go to the Player Results area. Just like in the Bets screen, here we also have a vertical BoxLayout with four horizontal BoxLayouts representing the results of the four players. Here's the code for the first player:

```
#:kivy 1.11.1
# File name: results.kv
...
<ResultsScreen>:
    ...
    ### PLAYER RESULTS ###
    BoxLayout:
        orientation: 'vertical'

        # player 1
        BoxLayout:
            RegularLabel:
                text: 'Player 1'
            BoxLayout:
                RegularLabel:
                    text: 'had'
                    size_hint: (.4, 1)
                RegularLabel:
                    text: '$1000'
            BoxLayout:
                RegularLabel:
                    text: 'bet'
                    size_hint: (.4, 1)
                RegularLabel:
                    text: '$300'
            RegularLabel:
                text: 'on Speedster'
            BoxLayout:
                RegularLabel:
                    text: '- won'
                    size_hint: (.5, 1)
                RegularLabel:
                    text: '$400'
            BoxLayout:
                RegularLabel:
                    text: 'now has'
                RegularLabel:
                    text: '$1400'
            RegularLabel:
                text: 'The odds were 2.54'

        # player 2
        ...
        # player 3
        ...
        # player 4
        ...
    ### NEXT RACE BUTTON ###
    ...
```

We'll refactor this code too. First, what are the differences? Here they are:

- The name of the player in the first RegularLabel will be different for each player.

- All the RegularLabels that display amounts of money will differ.

- The name of the slug on which the bet was put will be different.

- One of the RegularLabels informs us whether the player won or lost. So, there are two options possible here.

- The RegularLabel that displays the odds will also differ.

That said, create the **Result** class that inherits from **BoxLayout** in the **results.py** file and add the following properties:

- the StringProperty **player_name** initialized to an empty string, representing the player's name,

- the NumericProperty **money_before** initialized to **0**, representing the amount of money the player had before the race,

- the NumericProperty **bet_amount** initialized to **0**, representing the bet amount,

- the StringProperty **slug_name** initialized to an empty string, representing the slug on which the bet was put,

- the StringProperty **result_info** initialized to an empty string, informing us whether the player won or lost money,

- the NumericProperty **gain_or_loss** initialized to **0**, representing the amount of money gained or lost,

- the NumericProperty **current_money** initialized to **0**, representing the amount of money the player has after the race,

- the NumericProperty **odds** initialized to **0**, representing the odds before the race that just finished.

Then, add the corresponding rule in the kv file. I'm sure you can do it all by yourself. For now you can set all the properties to the same values that they had before. Don't worry they don't make much sense at this moment. As far as the last RegularLabel is concerned, its **text** property should be set by concatenating the string **'The odds were '** with the value of the **odds** property.

## SOLUTION

So, here's the Python file:

```
# File name: results.py
...
from kivy.uix.boxlayout import BoxLayout
from kivy.properties import NumericProperty, StringProperty

class Result(BoxLayout):
    player_name = StringProperty('')
    money_before = NumericProperty(0)
    bet_amount = NumericProperty(0)
    slug_name = StringProperty('')
    result_info = StringProperty('')
    gain_or_loss = NumericProperty(0)
    current_money = NumericProperty(0)
    odds = NumericProperty(0)

class ResultsScreen(BoxLayout):
    ...
```

And here's the kv file:

```
#:kivy 1.11.1
# File name: results.kv

### CLASS RULES ###
...
<RedButton@Button>:
    ...
<Result>:
    RegularLabel:
        text: root.player_name
    BoxLayout:
        RegularLabel:
            text: 'had'
            size_hint: (.4, 1)
        RegularLabel:
            text: '$' + str(root.money_before)
    BoxLayout:
        RegularLabel:
            text: 'bet'
            size_hint: (.4, 1)
        RegularLabel:
            text: '$' + str(root.bet_amount)
    RegularLabel:
        text: 'on ' + root.slug_name
    BoxLayout:
        RegularLabel:
            text: root.result_info
            size_hint: (.5, 1)
        RegularLabel:
            text: '$' + str(root.gain_or_loss)
    BoxLayout:
        RegularLabel:
            text: 'now has'
        RegularLabel:
            text: '$' + str(root.current_money)
    RegularLabel:
        text: 'The odds were ' + str(root.odds)

<ResultsScreen>:
    ...
    ### PLAYER RESULTS ###
    BoxLayout:
        orientation: 'vertical'
        # player 1
        Result:
            player_name: 'Player 1'
            money_before: 1000
            bet_amount: 300
            slug_name: 'Speedster'
            result_info: '- won'
            gain_or_loss: 400
            current_money: 1400
            odds: 2.54

        # player 2
        Result:
            player_name: 'Player 2'
            money_before: 1000
            bet_amount: 300
            slug_name: 'Speedster'
            result_info: '- lost'
            gain_or_loss: 400
            current_money: 600
            odds: 1.59

        # player 3
        Result:
            player_name: 'Player 3'
            money_before: 1000
            bet_amount: 300
            slug_name: 'Trusty'
            result_info: '- won'
            gain_or_loss: 400
            current_money: 1400
            odds: 2.24

        # player 4
        Result:
            player_name: 'Player 4'
            money_before: 1000
            bet_amount: 300
            slug_name: 'Speedster'
            result_info: '- lost'
            gain_or_loss: 400
            current_money: 600
            odds: 1.85

    ### NEXT RACE BUTTON ###
    ...
```

Run all the files that you modified today again to make sure everything works as before.

# Part VIII

# Screens, Files and Classes

In this part of the book we'll organize the structure of the app, we'll add a centralized style sheet file and we'll turn what we've been calling screens up to now into actual Kivy screens.

# Chapter 69 - Game Structure Organization

In the preceding parts of the book we were working not on a single app, but, technically speaking, on a set of apps. What we called screens were actually separate apps, each inheriting from the **App** class and launched by means of the **run** method.

Just as an example, here's the Seetings screen:

```
# File name: settings.py
...
from kivy.app import App
...
class SettingsApp(App):
    ...

if __name__ == '__main__':
    SettingsApp().run()
```

And we have four more apps like that: the Race screen, the Bets screen, the Results screen and the Game Over screen. What's more, we're also going to implement the Splash screen and the Instructions screen. also have But, naturally, we don't want so many apps, we need just one.

In this part of the book we'll put all the pieces together and create a single working app. To do that we must know how the files communicate with one another. Then, there will be one and only one place where the app will start, in the **main.py** file. And the other files will be turned into real screens, managed by a screen manager.

But before we start working on that, let's think about it. How should the app be structured? I already mentioned it several times, but let's recap:

1) When the game is launched, the Splash screen should show up for a while and right after that the Settings screen should be displayed. Here the user will be able to set the number of players, their names and how much money each player should start the game with. Also here the user will be able to set the ending condition.

2) After everything is set in the Settings screen and the Ready button is pressed, the Settings screen will be replaced by the Race screen. Inside the Race screen the Bets screen will be injected in the Bets area where the players can place their bets.

3) After all bets are placed and the Go button is pressed, the race starts and you can see the slugs running for victory. As soon as there is a winner, the Bets screen will be replaced by the Results screen.

4) When the user presses the Next Race button, the Results screen will again be replaced by the Bets screen, and so on.

5) When the game is over, which is the case when an ending condition is met or the End Game button in the Race screen is pressed, the whole Race screen is replaced by the Game Over screen.

6) If the user presses the Play Again button in the Game Over screen, the Game Over screen is replaced by the Settings screen again and the game starts over.

In the next chapter we'll put all the styling code with the definitions of our custom widgets in one file and then reference the file from other files.

# Chapter 70 - A Centralized Style Sheet File

In the previous chapter we were talking about the structure of our app. You know there will be just one place, in the **main.py** file, where the app will start. You also know there will be just one app instead of the collection of separate apps that we now have.

So, as just mentioned, we now have five separate apps, because each of the so-called screens, like the Settings screen, the Race screen, etc., is a separate app with code to run it.

In each of the apps, where needed, we define the same custom widgets like **`RegularLabel`** or **`RedButton`**, for example. This makes the code repetitive and error-prone. If you wanted to change some properties of the **`RedButton`**, you would have to find all the places where it's defined and make the changes multiple times. Not only would it be tedious, but it would also be easy to accidentally omit some of them.

That's why it's always good to keep your code **DRY**, which stands for **Don't Repeat Yourself**. It means what it says, we should avoid repeating the same code multiple times.

This is why in this chapter we'll move all the class rules to a separate file and then use them in the other files of our project.

Actually, we already have the file we need, it's called **widgets.kv**. We created it when we were adding all the files to our project, but it's empty now. So, let's have a look at all the other kv files again, and in particular at the class rules defined above the root widgets.

If a class rule is going to be used in just one file, we could leave it there, but I'm going to move all the widgets that inherit from the basic Kivy widgets, so all kinds of labels, buttons, radio buttons, text inputs, etc. to the **widgets.kv** file too, just to keep the other kv files clean. I'm going to leave the rules in the particular files only if they are specific for those files, used only in those files and do not inherit from the basic Kivy widgets.

Moving the class rules to the **widgets.kv** file will temporarily break our app, which we are going to fix soon.

So, after scanning all the kv files throughout the project, I selected the rules that were used in more than one file and moved them from the original files to the **widget.kv** file.

Now the file looks like so:

```
#:kivy 1.11.1
# File name: widgets.kv

### LABELS ###
<RegularLabel@Label>:
    color: .2, .1, 0, 1
    text_size: self.size
    halign: 'left'
    valign: 'center'

<TitleLabel@RegularLabel>:
    font_size: 20
    size_hint: (1, None)
    height: 30

<Regular80x30Label@RegularLabel>:
    size_hint: None, None
    size: 80, 30

<DollarLabel@RegularLabel>:
    text: "$"
    size_hint: None, None
    size: 20, 30

<BoldLabel@RegularLabel>:
    bold: True

<WhiteOddsLabel@BoldLabel>:
    font_size: 32
    color: 1, 1, 1, 1

<WhiteNameLabel@BoldLabel>:
    font_size: 18
    color: 1, 1, 1, 1

<WhiteWinsLabel@BoldLabel>:
    font_size: 14
    color: 1, 1, 1, 1

### BUTTONS ###
<RedButton@Button>:
    background_color: .8, 0, 0, 1
    color: 1, .8, .1, 1
    bold: True
    font_size: 18
    size_hint: (None, None)
    size: 200, 40
    pos_hint: {'center_x': 0.5}

### TEXTINPUTS ###
<NameInput@TextInput>:
    multiline: False
    size_hint: None, None
    size: 400, 30

<NumInput@TextInput>:
    multiline: False
    size_hint: None, None
    size: 250, 30

<BetInput@NumInput>:
    width: 120
    pos_hint: {'center_y': .5}

### CHECK BOXES ###
<PlayerRadioButton@CheckBox>:
    canvas.before:
        Color:
            rgba: 0,0,0,1
        Ellipse:
            pos:self.center_x - 10, self.center_y - 10
            size:[20,20]

    group: 'players'
    size_hint: (.5, 1)

<ConditionRadioButton@CheckBox>:
    canvas.before:
        Color:
            rgba: 0,0,0,1
        Ellipse:
            pos:self.center_x - 10, self.center_y - 10
            size:[20,20]

    group: 'conditions'
    size_hint_x: .05

<PlayerSlugButton@CheckBox>:
    canvas.before:
        Color:
            rgba: 0,0,0,1
        Ellipse:
            pos:self.center_x - 10, self.center_y - 10
            size:[20,20]

    size_hint: (.5, 1)
```

All these class rules are now only in this one file, I removed them from the other kv files. Make sure to also remove the rules from **settings.kv**, **race.kv**, **bets.kv**, **results.kv** and **gameover.kv**.

Make also sure not to remove the rules that are used only in one file. In particular, don't remove:

- the **`PlayerCount`** and **`PlayerSettings`** rules from **settings.kv**,

- the **SlugStats**, **PlayerStats**, **SlugInfo** and **SlugImage** rules from **race.kv**,

- the **Bet** rule from **bets.kv**,

- the **Result** rule from **results.kv**.

Naturally, at this point our app won't work because it can't use the custom widgets. They are not referenced in any way. So, let's fix it.

## Access to the Rules Defined in the widgets.kv File

You might be tempted to load the **widgets.kv** file in each screen like so:

```
# File name: settings.py
...
from kivy.properties import StringProperty

# We need the Builder class.
from kivy.lang import Builder

#Let's load the widgets.kv file.
Builder.load_file('widgets.kv')

class PlayerCount(BoxLayout):
    ...
```

I said you might be tempted to do so, which suggests it isn't the way to go. Yes, that's not the way to go, but we will do it just for the time being anyway because now these are all separate apps. Then, when they are all combined into one big app, we will change it. Actually, even then it would still work, but you would get a warning that the kv file is loaded multiple times, which might lead to unwanted behaviors.

We don't want to put ourselves at risk of unwanted behaviors, so let's not go this way eventually, just for now. The rule is that each kv file should be loaded only once in the app.

So, as I said, this is only a temporary solution. In the exercise below you will add the code to the other files and then, in the next chapter we'll talk a little more about communication between files.

## It's Your Turn Now...

### EXERCISE

I assume you have removed all the class rules that are now defined in the **widgets.kv** file from the other kv files. Now load the **widgets.kv** file in each of the screens.

You won't get the warning that a kv file is loaded multiple times because it's actually loaded only once in each app. Make sure the apps run as before.

## SOLUTION

### Settings screen

So, here's the Settings screen again, first the Python file:

```
# File name: settings.py
...
from kivy.properties import StringProperty
from kivy.lang import Builder
Builder.load_file('widgets.kv')

class PlayerCount(BoxLayout):
    ...
```

And now the kv file:

```
#:kivy 1.11.1
# File name: settings.kv

<PlayerCount>:
    ...
<PlayerSettings>:
    ...
<SettingsScreen>:
    ...
```

As you can see, I didn't move the **PlayerCount** and **PlayerSettings** rules to the **widgets.kv** file because they are specific just for this screen.

### Race screen

And now the Race screen. Here's the Python file:

```
# File name: race.py
...
from kivy.properties import NumericProperty, StringProperty
from kivy.lang import Builder
Builder.load_file('widgets.kv')

class SlugStats(BoxLayout):
    ...
```

So, again, I left the screen-specific widgets in the **race.kv** file and moved the others to the **widgets.kv** file.

And the kv file:

```
#:kivy 1.11.1
# File name: race.kv

<SlugStats>:
    ...
<PlayerStats>:
    ...
<SlugInfo>:
    ...
<SlugImage>:
    ...
<RaceScreen>:
    ...
```

### Bets screen

Now, the Bets screen. Here's the Python file:

```
# File name: bets.py
...
from kivy.properties import NumericProperty, StringProperty
from kivy.lang import Builder
Builder.load_file('widgets.kv')

class Bet(BoxLayout):
    ...
```

And the kv file:

```
#:kivy 1.11.1
# File name: bets.kv

<Bet>:
    ...
<BetsScreen>:
    ...
```

### Results screen

Next, the Results screen. Here's the Python file:

```
# File name: results.py
...
from kivy.properties import NumericProperty, StringProperty
from kivy.lang import Builder
Builder.load_file('widgets.kv')

class Result(BoxLayout):
    ...
```

And the kv file:

```
#:kivy 1.11.1
# File name: results.kv

<Result>:


    ...
<ResultsScreen>:
    ...
```

### Game Over screen

And finally the Game Over screen. Here's the Python file:

```
# File name: gameover.py
...
from kivy.uix.boxlayout import BoxLayout
from kivy.lang import Builder
Builder.load_file('widgets.kv')

class GameoverScreen(BoxLayout):
    ...
```

And the kv file:

```
#:kivy 1.11.1
# File name: gameover.kv

<GameoverScreen>:
    ...
```

As you can see, there are no class rules in the **gameover.kv** file now.

All the apps run as before and display the widgets defined in the **widgets.kv** file correctly.

# Chapter 71 - Let Screens Be Screens

Throughout the whole project up to now we've been using the term ***screen*** a lot. We have the Settings screen, the Race screen, the Bets screen, the Results screen and the Game Over screen. But are they really screens or do we just call them screens?

We've been using the term because it's intuitive. In the final version of the app the visible contents of the app window will change. But we've been using the term also because now we will turn the so-called screens into real screens and we don't have to change the terminology we're using.

In Kivy a screen is an object of the **Screen** class that inherits from **RelativeLayout**. So, if we want to use screens in our project, our classes need to inherit from the **Screen** class. Besides, we need a screen manager, so an object of the **ScreenManager** class to handle the screens inside the app window.

A screen manager must contain widgets that inherit from the **Screen** class, no other types are allowed. In this chapter we'll create the real screens and then, in the next chapter, we'll see how to use them with a screen manager.

Now, as you look at the root widgets of our screens, they all inherit from **BoxLayout**. This means that if we change the base class to **Screen**, things won't work for us anymore. Let's have a look at the Game Over screen first because it's pretty simple and then we'll move on to the other screens.

Here's our **gameover.py** file:

```
# File name: gameover.py
...
class GameoverScreen(BoxLayout):
    pass

class GameoverApp(App):
    ...
```

Let's now change it so that it inherits from **Screen**:

```
# File name: gameover.py
...
from kivy.lang import Builder

# We need the Screen class.
from kivy.uix.screenmanager import Screen

Builder.load_file('widgets.kv')

# Now the root widget should inherit from
# Screen instead of BoxLayout.
class GameoverScreen(Screen):
    pass

class GameoverApp(App):
    ...
```

If you now run the app, everything will fall apart.

This is because we now have a **Screen**, which actually is a **RelativeLayout**, and we had a **BoxLayout** before. The two layouts work differently, hence the disaster.

But it's easy to fix. All you have to do is put the whole code inside the root widget in a BoxLayout.

Here's the kv file after the modification:

```
#:kivy 1.11.1
# File name: gameover.kv

<GameoverScreen>:
    canvas:
        Color:
            rgba: 1, 1, .8, 1
        Rectangle:
            pos: self.pos
            size: self.size

    # Now the contents of the root widgets will be enclosed in a BoxLayout
    # and we will move the properties that we had on the GameoverScreen
    # before (when it was still a BoxLayout) to this new BoxLayout.
    # Here we only had one property - orientation. So,
    # after that we will have a BoxLayout inside the Screen.

    # Don't forget to indent the code inside the BoxLayout.
    BoxLayout:
        orientation: 'vertical'

        BoldLabel:
            font_size: 100
            text: 'Game Over'
            halign: 'center'
        BoldLabel:
            ...
```

Now if you run the app, you will see all the widgets in their places again.

Well, this may seem reduntatnt code to you. We actually now have to type in more code than before to get the same result. But this is necessary for a screen manager to work. A screen manager won't swap the screens if they do not inherit from the **Screen** class. In the next chapter we'll create a screen manager and you will see that it was worth it.

But before that we have to change the other root widgets to screens, which is an exercise for you. This is pretty straightforward, just repeat the steps from the Game Over screen.

# It's Your Turn Now...

## EXERCISE

Turn the other so-called screens to real Kivy screens. The first step is to import the **Screen** class. The second step is to make the root widget inherit from the **Screen** class. And the third step is to move the contents of the root widget in the kv file into another **BoxLayout**. The one thing to remember is that if there were any **BoxLayout** properties on the root screen, they must be moved to the new BoxLayout.

## SOLUTION

### Settings screen

So, here's the Settings screen. First the Python file:

```
# File name: settings.py
...
from kivy.lang import Builder
from kivy.uix.screenmanager import Screen
Builder.load_file('widgets.kv')
...
class SettingsScreen(Screen):
    ...
```

And here's the kv file. Remember to indent the code correctly inside the new BoxLayout:

```
#:kivy 1.11.1
# File name: settings.kv
...
<SettingsScreen>:
    canvas:
        Color:
            rgba: 1, 1, .8, 1
        Rectangle:
            pos: self.pos
            size: self.size

    # Here's the BoxLayout with the
    # previous root widget's properties
    # now moved to it.
    BoxLayout:
        orientation: 'vertical'
        padding: 10
        spacing: 10

        # Change the indentation of the
        # rest of the code below.
        ### SETTINGS LABEL ###
        TitleLabel:
            ...
```

Now run the app again to see if it works. It should.

### Race screen

And now let's move on to the next screen, the Race screen. Here's the Python file:

```
# File name: race.py
...
from kivy.lang import Builder
from kivy.uix.screenmanager import Screen
Builder.load_file('widgets.kv')
...
class RaceScreen(Screen):
    ...
```

And the kv file:

```
#:kivy 1.11.1
# File name: race.kv
...
<RaceScreen>:
    canvas:
        Color:
            rgba: 1, 1, .8, 1
        Rectangle:
            pos: self.pos
            size: self.size

    # Here's the BoxLayout with the
    # previous root widget's properties
    # now moved to it.
    BoxLayout:
        orientation: 'vertical'
        spacing: 10
        padding: 10

        # Change the indentation of the
        # rest of the code below.
        ### INFO, STATS AND BUTTONS ###
        GridLayout:
            ...
```

### Bets screen

Next let's modify the code in the Bets screen. Here's the Python file:

```
# File name: bets.py
...
from kivy.lang import Builder
from kivy.uix.screenmanager import Screen
Builder.load_file('widgets.kv')
...
class BetsScreen(Screen):
    ...
```

And the kv file:

```
#:kivy 1.11.1
# File name: bets.kv
...
<BetsScreen>:
    canvas:
        Color:
            rgba: 1, 1, .8, 1
        Rectangle:
            pos: self.pos
            size: self.size

    # Here's the BoxLayout with the
    # previous root widget's properties
    # now moved to it.
    BoxLayout:
        orientation: 'vertical'
        padding: 10
        spacing: 10

        # One more indentation level!
        ### TITLE LABEL ###
        BoldLabel:
            ...
```

**Results screen**

And finally the Results screen. Let's start with the Python file again:

```
# File name: results.py
...
from kivy.lang import Builder
from kivy.uix.screenmanager import Screen
Builder.load_file('widgets.kv')
...
class ResultsScreen(Screen):
    ...
```

And the kv file:

```
#:kivy 1.11.1
# File name: results.kv
...
<ResultsScreen>:
    canvas:
        Color:
            rgba: 1, 1, .8, 1
        Rectangle:
            pos: self.pos
            size: self.size

    # Here's the BoxLayout.
    BoxLayout:
        orientation: 'vertical'
        padding: 10

        # Indentation!
        ### TITLE LABEL ###
        BoldLabel:
            ...
```

Before you move on to the next chapter, make sure all the apps work as before.

# Chapter 72 – Screen Managers

In the previous chapter we turned our so-called screens into real screens. As you remember, the **Screen** class inherits from **RelativeLayout**, unlike the root widgets of the five screens before, which inherited from **BoxLayout**. Now that the root widgets are **Screen** objects, which is required of them by the **ScreenManager** object that we are going to create, we had to enclose all the widgets inside the root widgets into additional BoxLayouts so that our GUIs don't fall apart.

So, this is where we left off in the previous chapter. But the functionality of the program didn't change. This is what we are going to take care of in this chapter.

## The ScreenManager Class

So, to work with screens, we need a screen manager. This is an object of the **ScreenManager** class that handles the transitions from one screen to another.

Now, in our app we will need two screen managers. The first one will switch between the Settings screen, Race screen, Game Over screen and later also Instructions screen. These are the screens that will take up the whole space of the app window. But then we'll need another screen manager that will switch between the Bets screen and the Results screen inside the Race screen.

So, what do we need to do? Let's start with the first screen manager, the one that will handle the full-window screens. When you open the **main.py** file, you will see the following code:

```
# File name: main.py

import kivy
kivy.require('1.11.1')
from kivy.app import App

class SlugraceApp(App):
    def build(self):
        pass

if __name__ == '__main__':
    SlugraceApp().run()
```

So, here we have the **SlugraceApp** that inherits from **App**, which we run by calling the **run** method on it. But if you run this app, nothing interesting happens. The **build** method doesn't return anything. In the terminal you can see the following message:

```
[CRITICAL] [Application ] No window is created. Terminating application run.
```

This is actually the place where our app will start. When our screen system is up and running, we won't be running the five screens separately, as we've been doing so far, but rather from one location, which is right here.

So, for this to run, the **build** method must return something. It's going to return a **ScreenManager** object that we're just about to create. So, here's how we do it:

```
# File name: main.py

# We'll add the configuration code here, just like
# we did in all the other Python files before.
from kivy.config import Config
Config.set('graphics', 'width', '1200')
Config.set('graphics', 'height', '675')
Config.set('graphics', 'resizable', '0')

import kivy
kivy.require('1.11.1')
from kivy.app import App

# We need to import the ScreenManager class.
from kivy.uix.screenmanager import ScreenManager

# Now we must define a screen manager class that
# inherits from ScreenManager.
class SlugraceScreenManager(ScreenManager):
    # We'll implement it in the kv file.
    pass

class SlugraceApp(App):
    def build(self):
        # The method should return the screen manager.
        return SlugraceScreenManager()

if __name__ == '__main__':
    SlugraceApp().run()
```

When we run the app now, we will see just a black app window. This is because a ScreenManager is returned that hasn't been implemented yet. We're going to implement it in the kv file.

As you can see, the name of the app is **SlugraceApp**, so, following the naming convention discussed before, the kv file should be called **slugrace.kv**.

Actually we already created it, but for now it's empty. So, let's implement the screen manager in the file. The screen manager should contain the three full-window screens. Each screen must have a name so that we can then reference it.

```
#:kivy 1.11.1
# File name: slugrace.kv

# Here's our screen manager with
# the three full-window screens.
<SlugraceScreenManager>:
    SettingsScreen:
        name: 'settingsscreen'
    RaceScreen:
        name: 'racescreen'
    GameoverScreen:
        name: 'gameoverscreen'
```

In the code on the left you can see that our screen manager contains three screens. By default it will use the first one, so **SettingsScreen**. But there are still a couple of things we must do. First of all, we must load the kv files of the three screens in the Python file. Second, we must import the Python files in the kv files, which is something new that we haven't done before.

Let's start with the former, we already did it before:

```
# File name: main.py
...
from kivy.uix.screenmanager import ScreenManager

# We need the Builder class to load kv files.
from kivy.lang import Builder
```

```
# We must load the kv files of the three screens.
Builder.load_file('settings.kv')
Builder.load_file('race.kv')
Builder.load_file('gameover.kv')

class SlugraceScreenManager(ScreenManager):
    ...
```

But this is not enough for the app to work. If tou ran it now, you would get an error informing you that **SettingsScreen** is an unknown class. The other classes, **RaceScreen** and **GameoverScreen**, are unknown too. So, now we have to inform the corresponding kv files what they are, which we do by importing the Python files in the kv files.

# Importing in kv Files

To import Python modules and classes in the Kivy language we use a special syntax:

```
#:import alias name
```

It looks like a comment, but as you can see there's a colon folowing the **#** sign. Unlike in Python code, the alias comes first and only then the name of the module or class without the **.py** extension. So, for example if you wanted to import the numpy module, you would do it like so:

```
#:import np numpy
```

which is equivalent to:

```
import numpy as np
```

in Python.

If you want to import just a function from a module, which you would in Python do like so:

```
from module import function
```

you should use the following syntax in kv:

```
#:import function module.function
```

So, now that you know how to import stuff in kv, we can import the Python files. In kv we must use an alias, which is not required in Python, so often you just repeat the name of the module as the alias in the Kivy language. This is how we are going to import **settings.py** in **settings.kv**:

```
#:import settings settings
```

So, we're importing the **settings** module with the alias **settings**. Now the **settings.kv** file should look like this:

```
#:kivy 1.11.1
# File name: settings.kv
#:import settings settings

<PlayerCount>:
    ...
```

Similarly, let's import the appropriate modules in the other two kv files. Here's the **race.kv** file:

```
#:kivy 1.11.1
# File name: race.kv
#:import race race

<SlugStats>:
    ...
```

And here's the **gameover.kv** file:

```
#:kivy 1.11.1
# File name: gameover.kv
#:import gameover gameover

<GameoverScreen>:
    ...
```

With the modules imported, the screen manager should display the first screen on its list, so the Settings screen. Here's what we get when we run the app from the **main.py** file:

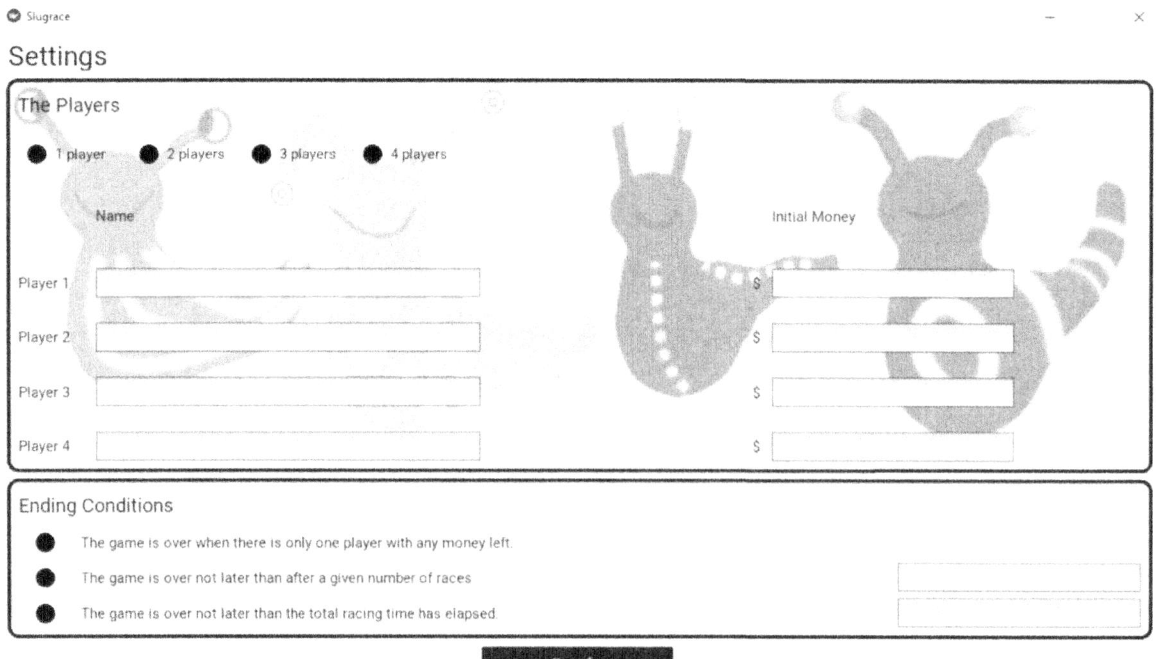


Although the app works, in the terminal you can see quite a few errors and warnings. Some of them are related to the fact that the **widgets.kv** file is loaded multiple times. We'll handle this in the next chapter. And now let's make the screen manager actually switch the screens.

## Switching Screens

As I said, the first screen in the screen manager is used by default if not otherwise specified. But how do we switch to another screen?

When we press the Ready button in the Settings screen, we want to switch to the Race screen. To do that we must somehow reference the screen manager and set its **current** property to the name of the screen.

You can access a screen's manager by using the **manager** property on the **Screen** object. Each screen has the **manager** property which is used to access the instance of the screen manager.

So, in the **settings.kv** file let's locate the Ready button and set the manager's **current** property to indicate the Race screen. We have to use the name of the screen that we defined before:

```
#:kivy 1.11.1
# File name: settings.kv
#:import settings settings
...
<SettingsScreen>:
    ...
        ### READY BUTTON ###
        RedButton:
            text: 'Ready'
            on_press: root.manager.current = 'racescreen'
```

Now if you run the app (from now on we'll be always running the app from the **main.py** file), the Settings screen will appear again. Let's press the Ready button and we should switch to the Race screen. Later on we'll see how to switch screens in Python code. And now let's make the screen manager switch to the Game Over screen when we press the End Game button in the Race screen. You will find the code in the **race.kv** file. Here's what we have to add:

```
#:kivy 1.11.1
# File name: race.kv
#:import race race
...
<RaceScreen>:
    ...
            # Buttons
            BoxLayout:
                ...
                RedButton:
                    text: 'End Game'
                    pos_hint: {'right': 1}
                    on_press: root.manager.current = 'gameoverscreen'

                RedButton:
                    text: 'Instructions'
                    ...
```

Now when you run the app and press the Ready button, you will switch to the Race screen. In the Race screen you can now press the End Game button and you will switch to the Game Over screen.

Finally, in the Game Over screen, we want to switch back to the Settings screen when the Play Again button is pressed, which will also close the cycle of switches between screens in our app, at least the full-window screens. Here's the code in the **gameover.kv** file:

```
#:kivy 1.11.1
# File name: gameover.kv
#:import gameover gameover

<GameoverScreen>:
    ...
            RedButton:
                text: 'Play Again'
                pos_hint: {'x': 0, 'center_y': .5}
                on_press: root.manager.current = 'settingsscreen'
            RedButton:
                text: 'Quit'
                ...
```

Try it out. You should now be able to switch from the Settings screen to the Race screen, from the Race screen to the Game Over screen and from the Game Over screen back to the Settings screen.

We're not done with the code yet, there's quite a lot of code to refactor, which we'll take care of in the next chapter, but now, in the exercise below, you will implement the other screen manager, so the one that switches between the Bets screen and the Results screen inside the Race screen.

# It's Your Turn Now...

**EXERCISE**

In this exercise you will implement the other screen manager, the one responsible for switching between the Bets screen and the Results screen. These two screens will be embedded in the Bets area of the Race screen. Follow the steps to implement the screen manager:

1. In the **race.py** file add the **RaceScreenManager** class that inherits from **ScreenManager**. Don't forget to import the **ScreenManager** class first. Leave the implementation of the class for the kv file.

2. Still in the **race.py** file load the two kv files, **bets.kv** and **results.kv**.

3. Implement the RaceScreenManager in the **race.kv** file. Add a class rule at the top of the file for the **RaceScreenManager**. It should contain two screens:

**BetsScreen** – with the **name** property set to **'betsscreen'**

**ResultsScreen** – with the **name** property set to **'resultsscreen'**.

4. In the two kv files, **bets.kv** and **results.kv** import the **bets** and **results** Python files respectively. Leave the aliases the same as the names of the files.

5. Now, when we enter the Race screen from the Settings screen, we want the Bets screen to sit in the Bets area by default. At this moment we only have a placeholder there. To do that, we'll place the **RaceScreenManager** widget defined in the class rules section in the Bets area and set its **current** property to **'betsscreen'**. First locate the Bets area in the **race.kv** file.

It now looks like this:

```
#:kivy 1.11.1
# File name: race.kv
#:import race race
...
<RaceScreen>:
    ...
        ### THE BETS ###
        Label:
            canvas:
                Color:
                    rgba: .2, .1, 0, 1
                Line:
                    rounded_rectangle: self.x, self.y, self.width, self.height, 10
                    width: 2

            color: .2, .1, 0, 1
            text: 'The Bets'
```

We'll put the screen manager inside a BoxLayout and add some padding. We could also put the screen manager directly and move the canvas instructions responsible for drawing the rounded rectangle to it, but then, when a screen is loaded, it would partially cover the rounded rectangle of its parent, which is the manager. It wouldn't look good, hence the additional BoxLayout.

So, replace the **Label** instance with a **BoxLayout**, move the label's canvas instructions to the BoxLayout and set the BoxLayout's padding to 5 pixels. This way there will be some extra space around the screen and the rounded rectangle will be fully visible. Then add the **RaceScreenManager** widget inside the BoxLayout. You could set its **current** property to **'betsscreen'**, but this is not necessary as the first screen will be used by default.

6. Now we need some code two switch between the two screens. In the **bets.kv** file add the **on_press** event to the Go button. When the button is pressed, the Bets screen should switch to the Results screen. Here the root is the Bets screen and its manager is the RaceScreenManager.

7. Then add similar code to the Next Race button in the **results.kv** file. This time when the button is pressed, the Results screen should switch back to the Bets screen. This will enable you to switch between the two screens in a cycle by pressing the two buttons.

## SOLUTION

So, here's the **race.py** file:

```
# File name: race.py
...
from kivy.lang import Builder

# Besides Screen we have to import ScreenManager.
from kivy.uix.screenmanager import Screen, ScreenManager

Builder.load_file('widgets.kv')

# Load the Bets and Results kv files.
Builder.load_file('bets.kv')
Builder.load_file('results.kv')

# Here's the screen manager class.
class RaceScreenManager(ScreenManager):
    pass

class SlugStats(BoxLayout):
    ...
```

And here's the **race.kv** file:

```
#:kivy 1.11.1
# File name: race.kv
#:import race race

# Here's the implementation of the screen manager.
<RaceScreenManager>:
    BetsScreen:
        name: 'betsscreen'
    ResultsScreen:
        name: 'resultsscreen'

<SlugStats>:
    ...
<RaceScreen>:
    ...
        ### THE BETS ###
        # Let's enclose the RaceScreenManager inside a BoxLayout. Let's move the canvas
        # instructions from the Label to the BoxLayout and add 5 pixels of padding so
        # that the rounded rectangle is not partially covered by the screen loaded by
        # the screen manager.
        BoxLayout:
            canvas:
                Color:
                    rgba: .2, .1, 0, 1
                Line:
                    rounded_rectangle: self.x, self.y, self.width, self.height, 10
```

```
                width: 2
            padding: 5
            # Here's the screen manager. We could set its current property to
            # 'betsscreen', but this would be redundant as the manager uses the first
            # screen by default.
            RaceScreenManager:
                # current: 'betsscreen'
```

Here's the **bets.kv** file:

```
#:kivy 1.11.1
# File name: bets.kv
#:import bets bets

<Bet>:
    ...
<BetsScreen>:
    ...
        ### GO BUTTON ###
        RedButton:
            text: 'Go'

            # When the button is pressed, this screen should
            # switch to the Results screen.
            on_press: root.manager.current = 'resultsscreen'
```

And the **results.kv** file:

```
#:kivy 1.11.1
# File name: results.kv
#:import results results

<Result>:
    ...
<ResultsScreen>:
    ...
        ### NEXT RACE BUTTON ###
        RedButton:
            text: 'Next Race'

            # When the button is pressed, this screen
            # should switch to the Bets screen.
            on_press: root.manager.current = 'betsscreen'
```

Now when you run the app (from the **main.py**) file and then press the Ready button in the Settings screen, you will switch to the Race screen with the Bets screen embedded in the Bets area.

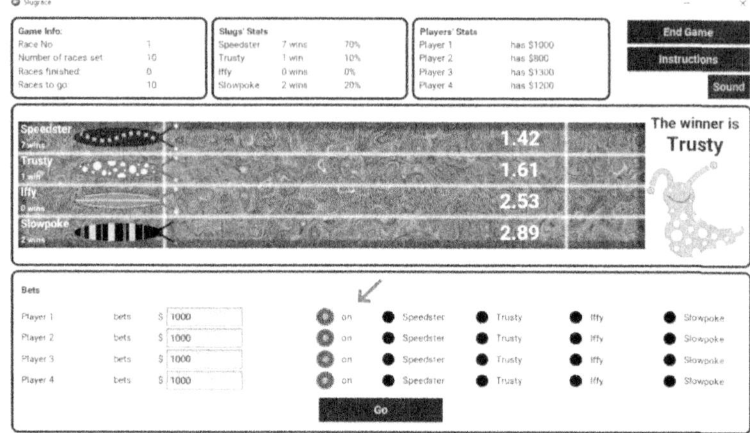


If you now press the Go button, the Bets screen will be replaced by the Results screen.

If you now press the Next Race button, you will go back to the Bets screen, and so on.

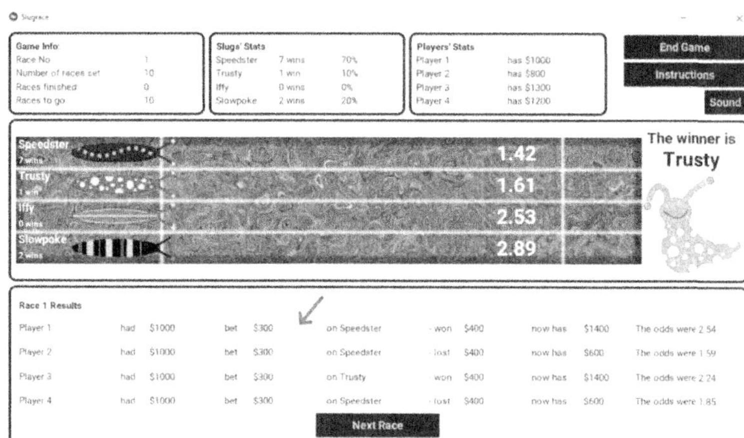

# Chapter 73 - Managing Screens - Some Code Cleanup

In the previous chapter we added two screen managers that switch between screens. Now the general flow of our application is as it should be, but still there are some warnings and errors visible in the terminal. This is because we have to clean the code up a bit.

First of all, now the application is always launched in one place, in the **main.py** file. But we still have the code in the particular screens that we used before to run them as individual apps.

Here's an example from the Settings screen:

```
# File name: settings.py

from kivy.config import Config
Config.set('graphics', 'width', '1200')
Config.set('graphics', 'height', '675')
Config.set('graphics', 'resizable', '0')

import kivy
kivy.require('1.11.1')
from kivy.app import App
from kivy.uix.boxlayout import BoxLayout
from kivy.properties import StringProperty
from kivy.lang import Builder
from kivy.uix.screenmanager import Screen
Builder.load_file('widgets.kv')

class PlayerCount(BoxLayout):
    count_text = StringProperty('')

class PlayerSettings(BoxLayout):
    label_text = StringProperty('')

class SettingsScreen(Screen):
    pass

class SettingsApp(App):
    def build(self):
        return SettingsScreen()

if __name__ == '__main__':
    SettingsApp().run()
```

The code that we don't need anymore is highlighted gray. Let's remove it. Now the **settings.py** file should look like this:

```
# File name: settings.py

from kivy.config import Config
Config.set('graphics', 'width', '1200')
Config.set('graphics', 'height', '675')
Config.set('graphics', 'resizable', '0')

from kivy.uix.boxlayout import BoxLayout
from kivy.properties import StringProperty
from kivy.lang import Builder
from kivy.uix.screenmanager import Screen
Builder.load_file('widgets.kv')

class PlayerCount(BoxLayout):
    count_text = StringProperty('')

class PlayerSettings(BoxLayout):
    label_text = StringProperty('')

class SettingsScreen(Screen):
    pass
```

Now we should remove the corresponding parts in the **race.py**, **bets.py**, **results.py** and **gameover.py** files, so first the import of the **kivy** module (along with the line of code that specifies which version of Kivy is required) and the **App** class, then the class that inherits from **App** and the code that runs the program. It's very easy, just do it yourself.

One more thing. The **GameoverScreen** class now inherits from **Screen**, not from **BoxLayout** anymore and we don't have any other widgets that inherit from the latter, so remove the import of the **BoxLayout** class in the **gameover.py** file too.

# kv Files loaded Multiple Times

As you look at the warnings in the terminal you can see a warning that is repeated multiple times regarding the **widgets.kv** file. As you remember, we used the **load_file** method in the **Builder** class to load the file in each of the screens, so multiple times. Here's how we did it:

```
Builder.load_file('widgets.kv')
```

And here's what the warning says (naturally the path on your machine will be different):

```
[WARNING] [Lang        ]

The file D:\Coder\Python\Courses\Kivy Basics Course\book\code\slugrace73\widgets.kv is loaded multiples times, you might have unwanted behaviors.
```

As I mentioned in one of the previous chapters, a kv file should be loaded only once. So, first we'll load the file in the **main.py** file, which is going to be the only place where this file will be loaded.

Here's the code:

```
# File name: main.py
...
Builder.load_file('gameover.kv')

# We will load the widgets.kv file only
# once, right here.
Builder.load_file('widgets.kv')

class SlugraceScreenManager(ScreenManager):
    ...
```

Now we'll remove the code from the other Python files that loads the **widgets.kv** file, so from **settings.py**, **race.py**, **bets.py**, **results.py** and **gameover.py**. Just make sure you don't forget any of these locations.

Also, in all of the above mentioned five Python files except **race.py**, you can remove the code that imports the **Builder** class because it was only used with the **widgets.kv** file in mind. But don't remove the import from the **race.py** file because it's used there to load the Bets and Results screens.

Now the **widgets.kv** file is loaded only once, in the **main.py** file, and all screens have access to the widgets defined in it. If you run the app now, it'll work like before except you won't get these warning messages.

# Configuration Code

Now that we put the configuration code in the **main.py** file, we don't need it in the other locations. So, again, go through the screens one by one and remove the code that imports the **Config** class, which looks like so:

```
from kivy.config import Config
```

And then remove the following lines of code in each screen:

```
Config.set('graphics', 'width', '1200')
Config.set('graphics', 'height', '675')
Config.set('graphics', 'resizable', '0')
```

Just make sure you don't remove it from the **main.py** file as well by accident. Now our Python files are simplified and the app is configured in one place only.

# Error Loading Texture

If you now run the app, it will work like before, but in the terminal you will see the following error, repeated multiple times:

```
[ERROR  ] [Image       ] Error loading texture atlas://assets/slugs/slugs/
```

You can see the error although the images are displayed correctly. So, what's the problem?

Well, the problem is that the program tries to load the image in the class rule. We have the following code in the **race.kv** file:

```
#:kivy 1.11.1
# File name: race.kv
#:import race race
...
<SlugImage>:
    ...
    # the body image
    Image:
        source: 'atlas://assets/slugs/slugs/' + root.body_image

    # the left eye image
    Image:
        ...
        source: 'atlas://assets/slugs/slugs/' + root.eye_image
        ...
```

```
    # the right eye image
    Image:
        ...
        source: 'atlas://assets/slugs/slugs/' + root.eye_image
        ...
<RaceScreen>:
    ...
```

So the program tries to resolve the source string by concatenating the first part of the path with **root.body_image** or **root.eye_image**.

But these two properties were set to empty strings in the Python file:

```
# File name: race.py
...
class SlugImage(RelativeLayout):
    body_image = StringProperty('')
    eye_image = StringProperty('')
    y_position = NumericProperty(0)

class RaceScreen(Screen):
    ...
```

This means that the **source** property is set to just the first part of the path, which is **'atlas://assets/slugs/slugs/'**. Then the source is set correctly for each slug in each **SlugImage** widget further in the kv code, where the **body_image** and **eye_image** properties are set, but we still have the error in the terminal. So, as it works, we could just ignore the errors, but it's not good to have errors, so let's fix it.

We can do it in two ways. First, we could just set some default values for the two properties in the Python file, like for example the names of the images of one of the slugs. Let's try it out. Here's the modified Python code:

```
# File name: race.py
...
class SlugImage(RelativeLayout):
    body_image = StringProperty('speedsterBody')
    eye_image = StringProperty('speedsterEye')
    y_position = NumericProperty(0)

class RaceScreen(Screen):
    ...
```

Now the two properties are no longer empty strings and the error will go away because the source for the body will now be set to:

```
'atlas://assets/slugs/slugs/speedsterBody'
```

and the source for the eye will be set to:

```
'atlas://assets/slugs/slugs/speedsterEye'
```

and now the two images will be loaded. Then, in the **SlugImage** widgets they will be overwritten by the names of the appropriate slugs.

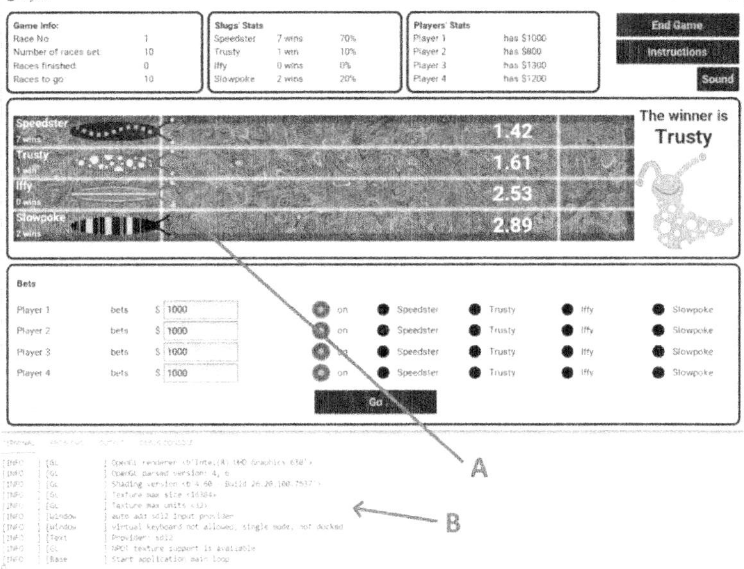


Let's run the app now and see if the error is really gone in the terminal.

So now we can see the same images as before (A) and the errors are gone (B). Although this solution works, it seems slightly inelegant to me. Why do we have to choose one of the slugs to use its images in the Python file? That's why I'll do it in a slightly different way. First, let's set the default values of the **body_image** and **eye_image** properties back to empty strings:

```
# File name: race.py
...
class SlugImage(RelativeLayout):
    body_image = StringProperty('')
    eye_image = StringProperty('')
    y_position = NumericProperty(0)

class RaceScreen(Screen):
    ...
```

And now, in the kv file we'll set the source to the concatenated string only if the **body_image** and **eye_image** properties are not empty strings. If they are, the source will be set to **None**. Here's the code:

```
#:kivy 1.11.1
# File name: race.kv
#:import race race
...
<SlugImage>:
    ...
    # the body image
    Image:
        # The source will be set to the concatenated string only if the body_image is
        # not an empty string. Otherwise it will be set to None. In Python an empty
        # string is understood as the boolean value False, hence the simplified syntax
        # inside the condition in the ternary if statement.
        source: 'atlas://assets/slugs/slugs/' + root.body_image if root.body_image else None
```

```
    # the left eye image
    Image:
        canvas.before:
            PushMatrix
            Rotate:
                angle: 30
                axis: 0, 0, 1
                origin: self.x, self.center_y
        canvas.after:
            PopMatrix

        # The source will be set to the concatenated string only if the body_image is
        # not an empty string. Otherwise it will be set to None.
        source: 'atlas://assets/slugs/slugs/' + root.eye_image if root.eye_image else None

        pos_hint: {'x': .95, 'y': .45}
        size_hint: 0.25, 0.25

    # the right eye image
    Image:
        canvas.before:
            PushMatrix
            Rotate:
                angle: -30
                axis: 0, 0, 1
                origin: self.x, self.center_y
        canvas.after:
            PopMatrix

        # The source will be set to the concatenated string only if the body_image is
        # not an empty string. Otherwise it will be set to None.
        source: 'atlas://assets/slugs/slugs/' + root.eye_image if root.eye_image else None

        pos_hint: {'x': .95, 'y': .3}
        size_hint: 0.25, 0.25

<RaceScreen>:
    ...
```

If you run the program now and navigate to the Race screen (by pressing the Ready button), it will work and look like before and the errors will be gone too.

In this chapter there are no exercises for you to do, we just cleaned the code up a little. In the next chapter we'll be talking about transitions. This is what you see when a screen manager switches from one screen to another.

# Chapter 74 - Transitions

In this part we've been working on screens and screen managers. Let's run our app again and see exactly what happens when we press the Ready button in the Settings screen. Yes, we know what happens, the screen manager switches to the Race screen.

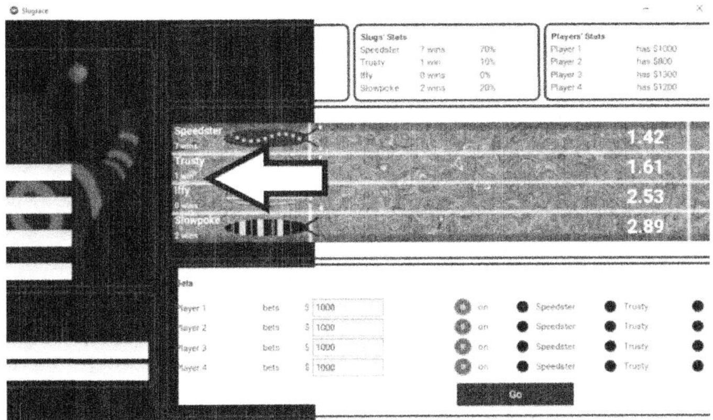


But I want you to observe how this happens. So, watch carefully.

As you can see, the screens slide from right to left. This animation is called a **transition**. You get it out of the box when you use a screen manager. But what if you wanted the screens to slide in the opposite direction? Or what if you don't want the transition at all? Finally, what if you would like a different animation? I'm going to address all of these in this chapter, demonstrating it on the two screens illustrated above, but then, eventually, I'll restore the settings to how they are now, because I like the basic sliding animation from right to left. But as an exercise, you will then implement sliding transitions in both directions between the Bets and Results screens.

Besides, I'm going to address another problem here. As you can see in the image above, when you switch screens, the background color of the first screen changes to black. It doesn't look good. We'll change it so that the background is yellow all the time during the transition.

## Transition Direction

Let's start with changing the direction of the transition. What if we want the screens to slide from left to right? You just have to specify the direction in code. Here's the **settings.kv** file:

```
#:kivy 1.11.1
# File name: settings.kv
#:import settings settings
...
<SettingsScreen>:
    ...
        ### READY BUTTON ###
        RedButton:
            text: 'Ready'
            # Now we not only want to switch to another screen,
            # but also change the sliding direction.
```

```
            on_press:
                root.manager.current = 'racescreen'
                root.manager.transition.direction = 'right'
```

Now when you run the app and press the Ready button, the screens will slide from left to right.

This time it's the Race screen that looks bad. We want the background to be yellow at all times, so let's fix it as next.

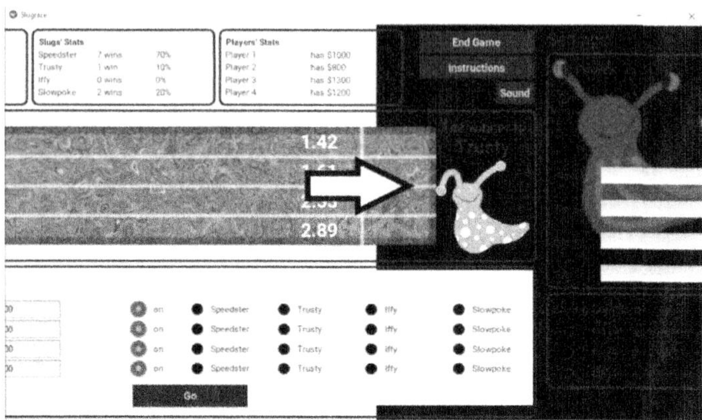


## Fixing the Background Color

The problem with the background color is that during the transition we see the background of the app window, not any of the screens. The default color is black. If we don't want to see the black color during the transition, we have to set the window's color to the same color as the background color of the screens. We'll do it in the **main.py** file.

First we need to import the **Window** class that takes care of all sorts of app window configurations and then use the **clearcolor** property to change the background color.

Now, one important thing: You have to import the **Window** class only after setting the configuration. Otherwise the configuration won't be set as expected. A good place to do that is directly before the app is run:

```
# File name: main.py
...
if __name__ == '__main__':
    # We need the Window class to change the background color.
    from kivy.core.window import Window

    # Now we can change the color to the same shade of yellow as the screens.
    Window.clearcolor = (1, 1, .8, 1)

    SlugraceApp().run()
```

If you now run the app and press the Ready button, you won't see the ugly black background anymore.

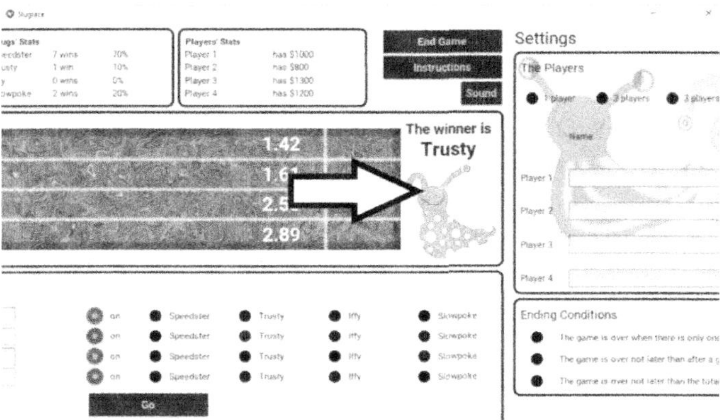


As you can see, here the screens are still sliding from left to right. You can also experiment with the two vertical directions, up and down. All you have to do is just set the transition direction to **'up'** or **'down'** respectively. Finally, let's change back to **'left'**, which we can do by either setting the transition direction explicitly to **'left'** or just removing the line of code completely as **'left'** is the default value. Let's do the latter.

Fine, and now what if we don't want any transition at all? That's what we are going to look at next.

# No Transition at All

As mentioned before, there are several transitions available out of the box. The one we've been using so far is called **SlideTransition** and it's the default one. If we don't want any transition at all, we just have to use the **NoTransition** transition.

I'll be demonstrating all the different types of transitions on the example of the **SlugraceScreenManager**, which is defined in the **slugrace.kv** file. First we have to import the **NoTransition** class and then set the transition property accordingly. You already know the syntax for importing stuff in kv files. Here's the code:

```
#:kivy 1.11.1
# File name: slugrace.kv
#:import NoTransition kivy.uix.screenmanager.NoTransition

<SlugraceScreenManager>:
    # We don't want any transition.
    transition: NoTransition()

    SettingsScreen:
        name: 'settingsscreen'
    RaceScreen:
        name: 'racescreen'
    GameoverScreen:
        name: 'gameoverscreen'
```

Now when we run the app, the screens will switch instantly, without any animation. Try it out.

# Other Transitions

Besides the **SlideTransition** and the **NoTransition**, there are several other transitions. Let's play with them for a while.

## CardTransition

Let's start with the **CardTransition**. This transition can work in two modes: **'push'** and **'pop'**, the former being set by default. In push mode, the new screen slides on the old one. Here's the code:

```
#:kivy 1.11.1
# File name: slugrace.kv
#:import CardTransition kivy.uix.screenmanager.CardTransition

<SlugraceScreenManager>:
    transition: CardTransition()

    SettingsScreen:
        ...
```

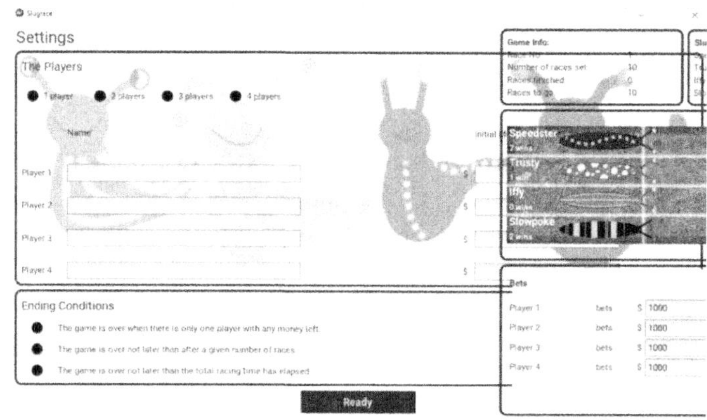


So, unlike in the **SlideTransition**, the old screen doesn't move. In pop mode, on the other hand, the old screen slides off the new one. Here's the code:

```
#:kivy 1.11.1
# File name: slugrace.kv
#:import CardTransition kivy.uix.screenmanager.CardTransition

<SlugraceScreenManager>:
    transition: CardTransition(mode='pop')

    SettingsScreen:
        ...
```

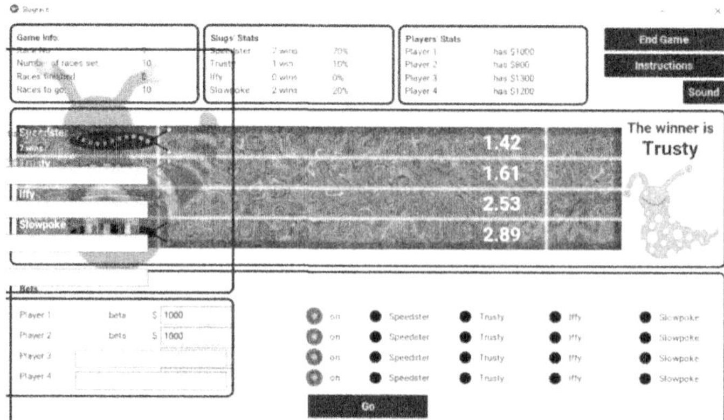


Now it looks a bit different.

## SwapTransition

Next we have the **SwapTransition**. Here the old screen shrinks and the new one appears in its place. Let's modify our code again:

```
#:kivy 1.11.1
# File name: slugrace.kv
#:import SwapTransition kivy.uix.screenmanager.SwapTransition

<SlugraceScreenManager>:
    transition: SwapTransition()

    SettingsScreen:
        ...
```

Let's run the app. In the image on the right you can see how the transition looks in its first phase, before the new screen appears.

## FadeTransition

In the **FadeTransition** the new and old screens fade in and out respectively. Here's the code:

```
#:kivy 1.11.1
# File name: slugrace.kv
#:import FadeTransition kivy.uix.screenmanager.FadeTransition

<SlugraceScreenManager>:
    transition: FadeTransition()

    SettingsScreen:
        ...
```

You can see the effect in the image on the right.

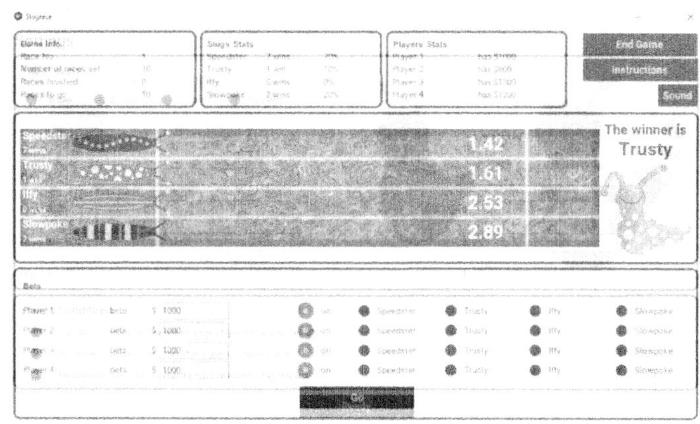


## WipeTransition

With the **WipeTransition** set, the screens are wiped from right to left. Here's the code:

```
#:kivy 1.11.1
# File name: slugrace.kv
#:import WipeTransition kivy.uix.screenmanager.WipeTransition

<SlugraceScreenManager>:
    transition: WipeTransition()

    SettingsScreen:
        ...
```

And here, in the image on the right, you can see the transition in action.

## FallOutTransition

In the **FallOutTransition** the old screen shrinks and fades out, revealing the new one behind it. Here's the code:

```
#:kivy 1.11.1
# File name: slugrace.kv
#:import FallOutTransition kivy.uix.screenmanager.FallOutTransition

<SlugraceScreenManager>:
    transition: FallOutTransition()

    SettingsScreen:
        ...
```

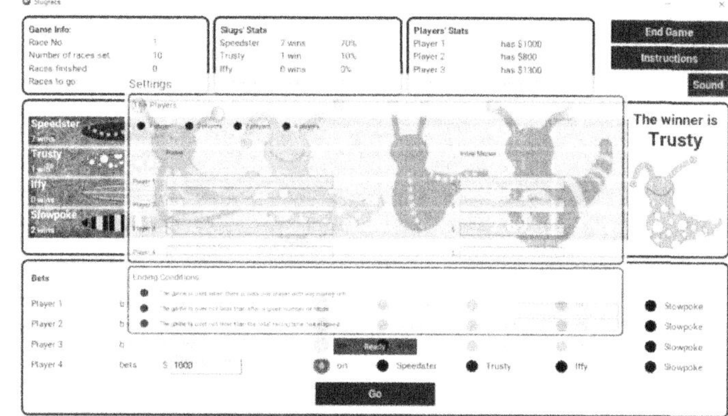


By default the transition takes 0.15 seconds (= 150 ms) to complete. You can change it by setting the duration property. If you want it to take 1 second, here's what you need to add:

```
#:kivy 1.11.1
# File name: slugrace.kv
#:import FallOutTransition kivy.uix.screenmanager.FallOutTransition

<SlugraceScreenManager>:
    transition: FallOutTransition(duration=1)

    SettingsScreen:
        ...
```

## RiseInTransition

Finally, the **RiseInTransition**. In this transition the new screen starts off transparent in the middle of the window and then grows to cover the old one.

Here you can also set the duration, which, for this transition, defaults to 0.2 seconds (= 200 ms).

Here's the code:

```
#:kivy 1.11.1
# File name: slugrace.kv
#:import RiseInTransition kivy.uix.screenmanager.RiseInTransition

<SlugraceScreenManager>:
    transition: RiseInTransition(duration=1)

    SettingsScreen:
        ...
```

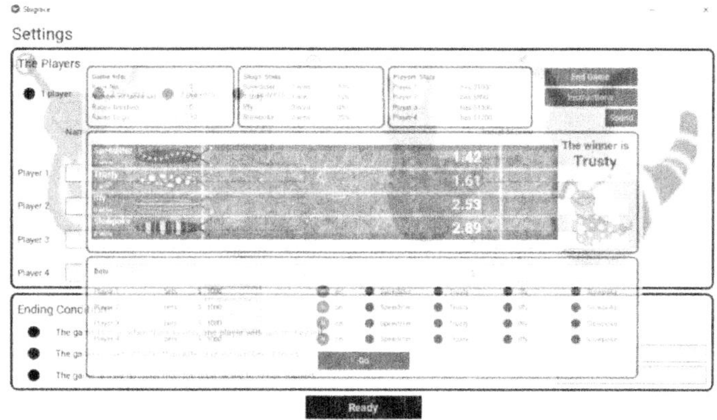


Fine, we're done trying out all the different transitions. Now let's go back to our basic **SlideTransition** for the **SlugraceScreenManager**. As this is the default one, you can just remove the transition code completely:

```
#:kivy 1.11.1
# File name: slugrace.kv

<SlugraceScreenManager>:
    SettingsScreen:
        ...
```

As mentioned before, in the exercise you will change the transitions for the other screen manager. And in the next part of the book we'll handle game logic.

# It's Your Turn Now...

### EXERCISE

In this exercise you will change the transitions between the Bets and Results screens. We're still going to use the default **SlideTransition**, but when the screen switches from Bets to Results, it should switch from right to left, and when it switches from Results to Bets, it should switch from left to right, as if the Bets screen was coming back to where it was before.

This exercise involves typing very little code. First, identify the file or files and the locations inside the files where something must be changed and then add the code that we need.

### SOLUTION

So, there are only two locations where you have to add some code. The first one is in the **results.kv** file:

```
#:kivy 1.11.1
# File name: results.kv
#:import results results
...
<ResultsScreen>:
    ...
        ### NEXT RACE BUTTON ###
        RedButton:
            text: 'Next Race'
            on_press:
                root.manager.current = 'betsscreen'
                root.manager.transition.direction = 'right'
```

The second location is in the **bets.kv** file:

```
#:kivy 1.11.1
# File name: bets.kv
#:import bets bets
...
<BetsScreen>:
    ...
        ### GO BUTTON ###
        RedButton:
            text: 'Go'
            on_press:
                root.manager.current = 'resultsscreen'
                root.manager.transition.direction = 'left'
```

Although the direction from right to left is the default one, if you only set the direction in the Results screen, it wouldn't change back in the Bets screen, so we have to explicitly set it there.

Now run the app and in the Race screen try switching between the Bets and Results screens several times. You will see they slide in different directions.

# Part IX

# Game Logic

In this part of the book we'll handle the game logic. We'll cover topics like events, user input validation and scheduling, to mention just a few. This is the real meat of the book.

# Chapter 75 - The Main Classes for the Game Logic

In the previous part of the book we were working on the screens of our app. We're now pretty much done with the graphical layer of our game, but what about the logic? In this and a couple following chapters we'll implement the infrastracture for the game logic and program the logic.

To start with, we'll add two classes to our project: **Slug** and **Player**. The **Slug** class will contain all the code, both Python and kv, that is related to the slugs. The **Player** class will contain all the player code. There will be four instances of the **Slug** class in the game, one for each of the slugs. There will also be four instances of the **Player** class because there may be up to four players in the game. By players I mean you and your friends, so the people who will actually play the game and put the bets on the slugs. There will be no graphical representation of the player.

## The Slug Class

Anyway, let's start with the **Slug** class. When you play the game now, you can see the four slugs on the track.

As there will be four slugs and they will all have the same functionalities, it's convenient to extract the code that handles them into a separate class.

But first, let's have a look at how the slugs are handled now. They are now embedded in the Race screen, as images. Have a look at the following Python code:

```
# File name: race.py
...
class SlugImage(RelativeLayout):
    body_image = StringProperty('speedsterBody')
    eye_image = StringProperty('speedsterEye')
    y_position = NumericProperty(0)

class RaceScreen(Screen):
    ...
```

So, we have the **SlugImage** class defined with three properties. Here's how the slug images are implemented in the kv file. First we have the class rule at the top and then we instantiate it four times inside **RaceScreen**:

```
#:kivy 1.11.1
# File name: race.kv
#:import race race
...
<SlugImage>:
    pos_hint: {'x': .09, 'center_y': root.y_position}
    size_hint: None, None
    size: 143, 30

    # the body image
    Image:
        source: 'atlas://assets/slugs/slugs/' + root.body_image if root.body_image else None

    # the left eye image
    Image:
        canvas.before:
            PushMatrix
            Rotate:
                angle: 30
                axis: 0, 0, 1
                origin: self.x, self.center_y
        canvas.after:
            PopMatrix

        source: 'atlas://assets/slugs/slugs/' + root.eye_image if root.eye_image else None
        pos_hint: {'x': .95, 'y': .45}
        size_hint: 0.25, 0.25

    # the right eye image
    Image:
        canvas.before:
            PushMatrix
            Rotate:
                angle: -30
                axis: 0, 0, 1
                origin: self.x, self.center_y
        canvas.after:
            PopMatrix

        source: 'atlas://assets/slugs/slugs/' + root.eye_image if root.eye_image else None
        pos_hint: {'x': .95, 'y': .3}
        size_hint: 0.25, 0.25

<RaceScreen>:
    ...
        ### THE TRACK ###
        ...
                # slug images
                # Speedster
                SlugImage:
                    body_image: 'speedsterBody'
                    eye_image: 'speedsterEye'
                    y_position: .875

                # Trusty
                SlugImage:
                    body_image: 'trustyBody'
```

```
                eye_image: 'trustyEye'
                y_position: .625

            # Iffy
            SlugImage:
                body_image: 'iffyBody'
                eye_image: 'iffyEye'
                y_position: .375

            # Slowpoke
            SlugImage:
                body_image: 'slowpokeBody'
                eye_image: 'slowpokeEye'
                y_position: .125

        # Winner
        ...
```

This works pretty well and now we have two options, either will be fine. The first option is that we could have a separate **SlugImage** class for the image of the slug and a separate **Slug** class for the logic of the slug object and then programmatically bind them together. The second option that we could have just one **Slug** class and put all the logic and representation in it. In this project we'll choose the second option, so we'll create a **Slug** class and move all the slug-related code into it.

In the **race.kv** file there are five class rules above the root widget: **RaceScreenManager**, **SlugStats**, **PlayerStats**, **SlugInfo** and **SlugImage**. Although most of them need access to slug-related data, actually only the **SlugImage** class is a real representation of a slug itself. The others are just widgets with some information about the slugs. So, we will move the **SlugImage** code into a separate file and leave the other class rules in the Race screen. Later we'll feed the slug data to them as well.

So, some time ago, when we created all the basic files for our project, we also created the **slug.py** and **slug.kv** files. They're empty now. Now, let's add all the necessary imports to it and let's move the **SlugImage** class from the **race.py** file to the **slug.py** class. Here's what the code in the **slug.py** file should look like:

```
# File name: slug.py

# We'll need this stuff, so let's import it.
from kivy.uix.relativelayout import RelativeLayout
from kivy.properties import StringProperty, NumericProperty

# This exact code was in the race.py file before. Now it's here.
# Don't forget to remove it in the race.py file.
class SlugImage(RelativeLayout):
    body_image = StringProperty('')
    eye_image = StringProperty('')
    y_position = NumericProperty(0)
```

As mentioned in the comments, don't forget to remove the class from the **race.py** file. You don't have to import the **RelativeLayout** class in the **race.py** file anymore, so remove it from there to keep the code clean.

Now the class takes care of the image only, but later it will also be used for the logic. So, a more appropriate name for the class will be just **Slug**. Modify the code like so:

```
# File name: slug.py
...
class Slug(RelativeLayout):
    body_image = StringProperty('')
    ...
```

Next, move the whole **SlugImage** rule from **race.kv** to **slug.kv**. Remember to change the name **SlugImage** to **Slug**. Also import the **slug.py** file in the kv file with the alias **slug**. So, the file should now look like so:

```
#:kivy 1.11.1
# File name: slug.kv
#:import slug slug

<Slug>:
    pos_hint: {'x': .09, 'center_y': root.y_position}
    size_hint: None, None
    size: 143, 30

    # the body image
    ...
```

Now, for this to work, we must slightly modify our code. In the **race.kv** file we must replace all the instanced of the **SlugImage** class with instances of the **Slug** class:

```
#:kivy 1.11.1
# File name: race.kv
#:import race race
...
<RaceScreen>:
    ...
        ### THE TRACK ###
        ...
                # slug images
                # Speedster
                Slug:
                    body_image: 'speedsterBody'
                    ...
                # Trusty
                Slug:
                    body_image: 'trustyBody'
                    ...
                # Iffy
                Slug:
                    body_image: 'iffyBody'
                    ...
                # Slowpoke
                Slug:
                    body_image: 'slowpokeBody'
                    ...
            # Winner
            ...
```

We also have to load the new kv file to the **main.py** file, so let's just add the line of code that we need:

```
# File name: main.py
...
Builder.load_file('settings.kv')
Builder.load_file('race.kv')
Builder.load_file('gameover.kv')
Builder.load_file('widgets.kv')

# We need this for the slugs.
Builder.load_file('slug.kv')

class SlugraceScreenManager(ScreenManager):
    ...
```

Now if you run the app, you will see the slugs like before.

# The Player Class

We also created the **player.py** file. There we're going to create the **Player** class that will be used to hold information about the players, so their names, initial money, how much money they currently have, how much they bet, and so on. We'll be adding stuff to this class as our program grows. For now, let's create a basic version of the class. Actually, I'll leave it as an exercise for you.

And in the next chapter we'll create the **Game** class.

# It's Your Turn Now...

### EXERCISE

In this exercise you're going to implement the **Player** class. We're not going to use this class just yet, but we will soon.

We only have the **player.py** file. There's not going to be a corresponding kv file because the **Player** objects will have no visual representation.

However, we want to use Kivy properties inside the class. For this to be possible at all, the **Player** class must inherit from the **EventDispatcher** class, which is defined in the **kivy.event** module. So, don't forget to add this class in the imports section. We could also inherit from the **Widget** class or any other class that inherits from it, but the **EventDispatcher** class will do.

So, define the **Player** class and make it a subclass of **EventDispatcher**. Inside the **Player** class we'll need a couple properties. In particular, define the following Kivy properties (and also don't forget to import all the the necessary property classes before):

**name** – a StringProperty defaulting to an empty string,

**initial_money** – a NumericProperty defaulting to **0** (this is for the amount of money the player starts with),

**money** – a NumericProperty defaulting to **0** (this is for amount of money the player has at a particular time),

**money_before_race** – a NumericProperty defaulting to **0** (this is for the amount of money the player has before the race starts),

**money_won** – a NumericProperty defaulting to **0** (this is for the amount of money won by the player in the race, negative if the player loses),

**bet** – a NumericProperty defaulting to **1** (this is for the amount of money the player puts on their chosen slug).

## SOLUTION

Here's the **player.py** file:

```
# File name: player.py

# We need some property classes.
from kivy.properties import StringProperty, NumericProperty

# We need this to use Kivy properties at all.
from kivy.event import EventDispatcher

# The class must inherit from EventDispatcher.
class Player(EventDispatcher):
    name = StringProperty('')
    initial_money = NumericProperty(0)
    money = NumericProperty(0)
    money_before_race = NumericProperty(0)
    money_won = NumericProperty(0)
    bet = NumericProperty(1)
```

# Chapter 76 - The Game Class

In the previous part of the book we created all the screens that our app will be using. In the previous chapter we added two classes, **Slug** and **Player**. We will need the classes to create four slug objects and four player objects.

In our game there will always be four slugs. As you know, they even have names: Speedster, Trusty, Iffy and Slowpoke. Regardless of any settings, there will always be all four.

As far as players are concerned, there may be one, two, three or four players, depending on what we choose in the Settings screen. However, to keep things simple, in our implementation there will always be four instances of the **Player** class. If there are fewer players than four, not all of them will be used. Naturally, there are other ways of implementing it, but I decided to it like that.

Now, the problem is that we need access to the slugs and players in multiple screens. There are widgets that need slug and player info in more than one place, so it would be reasonable to find a place where this info can be stored and can be accessed from any screen. For example, player info must be available in the Settings screen, where the names and initial money of each player are set, in the Race screen in the Players' Stats area, as well as in the Bets screen, Results screen or in the Game Over screen.

So, where are we going to put all that shared data? There are two major options. We can put the data in the **SlugraceApp** class. Then we will be able to access it from anywhere in the app. The second option is to put all the shared data in the root widget of our application, so in the class that is returned by the **build** method of the **SlugraceApp** class. We'll be using both approaches to some extent, but the player data and slug info will be stored in the root widget class, which is **SlugraceScreenManager**.

Let's have a look at the **SlugraceScreenManager** class again then.

In the Python file we only have the declaration:

```
# File name: main.py
...
class SlugraceScreenManager(ScreenManager):
    pass

class SlugraceApp(App):
    def build(self):
        return SlugraceScreenManager()

if __name__ == '__main__':
    ...
```

The definition of the class is now completely in the kv file:

```
#:kivy 1.11.1
# File name: slugrace.kv

<SlugraceScreenManager>:
    SettingsScreen:
        name: 'settingsscreen'
    RaceScreen:
        name: 'racescreen'
    GameoverScreen:
        name: 'gameoverscreen'
```

Now, as mentioned before, there will be four players and four slugs in the game. Let's start with the former. In order to create an instance of the **Player** class, we need to import the class to the **main.py** file first. Then, inside the **SlugraceScreenManager** class, we will create the objects:

```
# File name: main.py
...
from kivy.lang import Builder

# We need the Player class to instantiate the four players.
from player import Player

Builder.load_file('settings.kv')
...
class SlugraceScreenManager(ScreenManager):
    # Now let's instantiate the four players.
    player1 = Player()
    player2 = Player()
    player3 = Player()
    player4 = Player()

class SlugraceApp(App):
    ...
```

We instantiated the four players and are ready to use them now. How about the slugs? Well, we actually defined the four slugs in the Race screen already. Have a look:

```
#:kivy 1.11.1
# File name: race.kv
#:import race race
...
<RaceScreen>:
    ...
        ### THE TRACK ###
        ...
                # the slugs
                # Speedster
                Slug:
                    body_image: 'speedsterBody'
                    ...
                # Trusty
                Slug:
                    body_image: 'trustyBody'
                    ...
                # Iffy
                Slug:
                    body_image: 'iffyBody'
                    ...
                # Slowpoke
                Slug:
                    body_image: 'slowpokeBody'
                    ...
            # Winner
            ...
```

So, as you can see, the four slugs are there. We just need to tell the **SlugraceScreenManager** class how to access them. This shouldn't be difficult. The slugs are defined in the Race screen, so we can use properties in the **RaceScreen** class to access the slugs. As we look at the implementation of the **SlugraceScreenManager** class in kv, we can easily access the Race screen by an id. So, indirectly we can access the four slugs in the **SlugraceScreenManager** class too.

Let's start by adding the properties in the **RaceScreen** class:

```
#:kivy 1.11.1
# File name: race.kv
#:import race race
...
<RaceScreen>:
    canvas:
        ...
            size: self.size

    # We'll access the four slugs by ids.
    # To this end let's define four
    # object properties.
    speedster: _speedster
    trusty: _trusty
    iffy: _iffy
    slowpoke: _slowpoke

    BoxLayout:
        ...
        ### THE TRACK ###
        ...
                # the slugs
                # Speedster
                Slug:
                    id: _speedster
                    body_image: 'speedsterBody'
                    ...
                # Trusty
                Slug:
                    id: _trusty
                    body_image: 'trustyBody'
                    ...
                # Iffy
                Slug:
                    id: _iffy
                    body_image: 'iffyBody'
                    ...
                # Slowpoke
                Slug:
                    id: _slowpoke
                    body_image: 'slowpokeBody'
                    ...
            # Winner
            ...
```

Now we need to modify the **SlugraceScreenManager** class so that it has access to the slugs:

```
#:kivy 1.11.1
# File name: slugrace.kv

<SlugraceScreenManager>:
    # Here are the properties on the root widget class that we
    # will use to access the slugs from outside the Race screen.
    speedster: _racescreen.speedster
    trusty: _racescreen.trusty
    iffy: _racescreen.iffy
    slowpoke: _racescreen.slowpoke

    SettingsScreen:
        name: 'settingsscreen'
    RaceScreen:
        # Let's add the id to be able to access the Race screen.
        id: _racescreen
        name: 'racescreen'
    GameoverScreen:
        name: 'gameoverscreen'
```

Now, one more thing before we continue. This is not necessary, but as the **SlugraceScreenManager** class is going to contain all the game data, like the players, the slugs, but also all sorts of other stuff that we are going to add to it in the following chapters, let's rename it **Game**. This name is just shorter and more comfortable to use.

Here's the Python file:

```
# File name: main.py
...
class Game(ScreenManager):
    player1 = Player()
    ...
class SlugraceApp(App):
    def build(self):
        return Game()

if __name__ == '__main__':
    ...
```

And here's the kv file:

```
#:kivy 1.11.1
# File name: slugrace.kv

<Game>:
    speedster: _racescreen.speedster
    ...
```

Now, the last thing to do is to make sure all screens have access to the **Game** class because they will need player info, slug info and other data defined in it. You're going to do it as an exercise and in the next chapter we'll be talking about events in Kivy in more detail.

# It's Your Turn Now...

### EXERCISE

In this exercise you will enable all the screens to access the **Game** class, which is the main screen manager. In case of the Settings, Race and Game Over screens, it's very easy because you can use the **manager** property to access the **Game** class (which is the three classes' screen manager after all). As far as the Bets and Results screens are concerned, it's a bit more complicated, but if you look at how their screen manager is embedded in the Race screen and use the **parent** and **manager** properties, you will quickly figure it out.

For consistency, add a **game** property to each of the screens and set it to the **Game** class. To get you started, here's how you should do it in the Settings screen. Just add the following line of code below the canvas instructions in the **SettingsScreen** rule:

```
#:kivy 1.11.1
# File name: settings.kv
#:import settings settings
...
<SettingsScreen>:
    canvas:
        ...
            size: self.size

    game: root.manager

    BoxLayout:
        ...
```

Here **root** refers to the root widget, which is **SettingsScreen**, and **manager** is its screen manager, so the **Game** class.

**SOLUTION**

So, here's the Race screen, which is very similar:

```
#:kivy 1.11.1
# File name: race.kv
#:import race race
...
<RaceScreen>:
    canvas:
        ...
            size: self.size

    game: root.manager

    speedster: _speedster
    ...
```

And here's the Game Over screen, which is also very similar:

```
#:kivy 1.11.1
# File name: gameover.kv
#:import gameover gameover

<GameoverScreen>:
    canvas:
        ...
            size: self.size

    game: root.manager

    BoxLayout:
        ...
```

And now let's have a look at how the Bets and Results screens are embedded in the Race screen. Or rather their screen manager:

```
#:kivy 1.11.1
# File name: race.kv
#:import race race
...
<RaceScreen>:
    ...
    BoxLayout:
        ...
        ### THE BETS ###
        BoxLayout:
            ...
            RaceScreenManager:
```

What we want to do is get access to the **RaceScreen** class and next to its manager.

As you can see in the simplified hierarchy above, **RaceScreen** is **RaceScreenManager's** parent's parent's parent.

Keeping that in mind, we can access the **Game** class from the Bets screen like so:

```
#:kivy 1.11.1
# File name: bets.kv
#:import bets bets
...
<BetsScreen>:
    canvas:
        ...
            size: self.size

    game: root.manager.parent.parent.parent.manager

    BoxLayout:
        ...
```

Here's a visualization that will make things clearer for you:

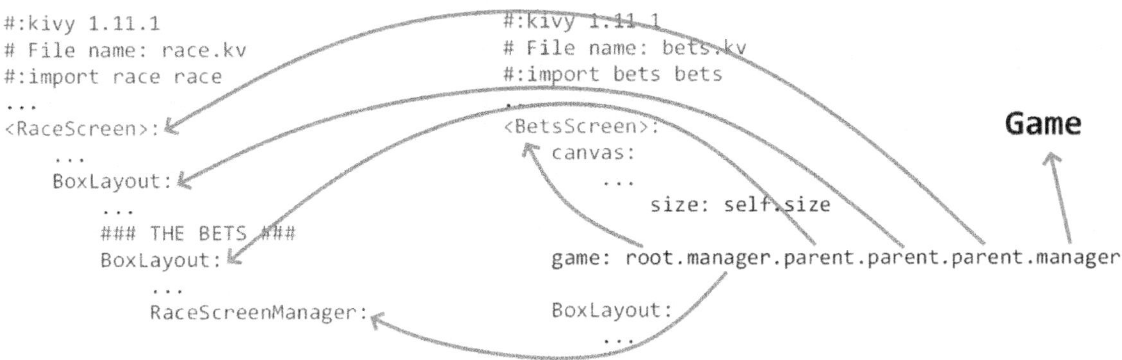


Similarly, in the Results screen we'll have:

```
#:kivy 1.11.1
# File name: results.kv
#:import results results
...
<ResultsScreen>:
    canvas:
        ...
            size: self.size

    game: root.manager.parent.parent.parent.manager

    BoxLayout:
        ...
```

Now we can access the **Game** class from any screen using the **game** property.

# Chapter 77 - Events in Kivy

In the previous chapter we created the **Game** class, or rather renamed the **SlugraceScreenManager** class that we defined long ago. This is the class most of our game logic will go into. Part of the logic is that if we do something, like press a button or check a radio button, something should happen. This is what events are for.

We've been using events a lot since the beginning of this book. In this chapter we'll try to systematize what we know about the basic usage of events in Kivy. Let's take a break from the Slugrace project and use the test files (**test.py** and **test.kv**) for a while to practice events.

## Overriding Inherited Event Methods

Open the **test.py** file and type in the following code:

```
# File name: test.py

from kivy.config import Config
Config.set('graphics', 'width', '1200')
Config.set('graphics', 'height', '675')
Config.set('graphics', 'resizable', '1')

import kivy
kivy.require('1.11.1')
from kivy.app import App
from kivy.uix.boxlayout import BoxLayout
from kivy.properties import NumericProperty
from kivy.uix.button import Button

class CustomButton(Button):
    counter = NumericProperty(1)

class TestLayout(BoxLayout):
    pass

class TestApp(App):
    def build(self):
        return TestLayout()

if __name__ == '__main__':
    TestApp().run()
```

And here's the kv file:

```
#:kivy 1.11.1
# File name: test.kv

<CustomButton>:
    font_size: 200
    size_hint_x: .5
    text: str(self.counter)

<TestLayout>:
    CustomButton:
    CustomButton:
```

If you run the app, you will see the two buttons next to each other.

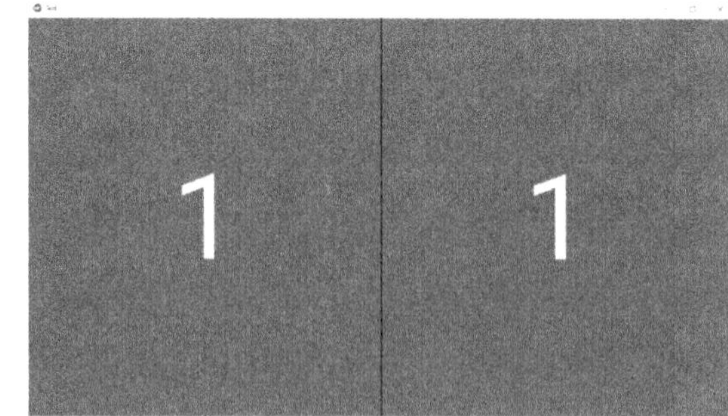

If you read the documentation, you will see that the **Button** class (**kivy.uix.button.Button**) inherits from the **ButtonBehavior** class (**kivy.uix.behaviors.button.ButtonBehavior**). In the latter you will find two methods which you already know, **on_press** and **on_release**. So, whenever you're using a button, you get these two methods out of the box, through inheritance. These are inherited methods – they already exist, you don't have to define them. But you can redefine them, so override their functionality. You can do it in two ways, either for the whole class (then they will be redefined for all instances of the class) or just for a single instance.

If you want the **on_press** event to do something on one instance only, you can easily do it in kv code. Let's define a simple functionality that increases the counter value for the second button when it's pressed. All you have to do is define the **on_press** event on just that button:

```
#:kivy 1.11.1
# File name: test.kv
...
<TestLayout>:
    CustomButton:
    CustomButton:
        on_press: self.counter += 1
```

Now if you run the program and click on the second button, the counter value will change. But it won't change if you press the first button.

You can also define an event on each instance individually so that it works in a different way. Have a look at this:

```
#:kivy 1.11.1
# File name: test.kv
...
<TestLayout>:
    CustomButton:
        on_press: self.counter -= 1
    CustomButton:
        on_press: self.counter += 1
```

Now the counter will be increased on the second button, but decreased on the first one.

If you want the event to work the same for all instances, a better solution that defining it on each instance and thus making the code repetitive, is to define it in the class rule or in Python code. Suppose we want the counter value to be increased on any instance of the button when pressed.

Here's how we can do it in kv:

```
#:kivy 1.11.1
# File name: test.kv

<CustomButton>:
    ...
    text: str(self.counter)
    on_press: self.counter += 1

<TestLayout>:
    CustomButton:
    CustomButton:
```

Now if you run the app and press both buttons several times, you will see something like in the image on the right.

Alternatively, you could remove the code from the kv file and put it in the Python file:

```
# File name: test.py
...
class CustomButton(Button):
    counter = NumericProperty(1)

    def on_press(self):
        self.counter += 1

class TestLayout(BoxLayout):
    ...
```

You can also put the code in both Python code and kv code. For example, if we want the counter value to be increased for each button, but additionally we want the font size to be increased only on the second button, we can put the shared behavior in the Python file (or in the class rule in kv) and the individual behavior on the particular instance in kv. Here's how we do it. First, the Python code. It's like in the snippet above. The method will work for each button. And here's the kv file:

```
#:kivy 1.11.1
# File name: test.kv

<CustomButton>:
    ...
    text: str(self.counter)

<TestLayout>:
    CustomButton:
    CustomButton:
        # This will work only on this button.
        on_press: self.font_size += 100
```

If you now run the program and press the two buttons let's say six times each, you can see that the font sizes differ.

Here we've been working on the **Button**'s **on_press** event only, but naturally you can override any other event method on any other widget like that.

# Triggering Methods

In the previous example we just changed the button's **counter** and **font_size** properties by passing some simple Python code directly in kv. But sometimes we need something more complex to happen each time an event is triggered. If this is the case, we can define a method in the Python file and call it from the kv file.

Here we're defining a method in the **CustomButton** class:

```
# File name: test.py
...
class CustomButton(Button):
    counter = NumericProperty(1)

    def handle_counter(self):
        self.counter += 1

        if self.counter > 5:
            self.counter = 1

class TestLayout(BoxLayout):
    ...
```

And here we're calling it from the kv file when the second button is pressed:

```
#:kivy 1.11.1
# File name: test.kv
...
<TestLayout>:
    CustomButton:
    CustomButton:
        # This will work only on this button.
        on_press: self.handle_counter()
```

If you now run the app, the counter will be reset back to 1 each time its value exceeds 5. Here the method is defined in the **CustomButton** class and it's called on a button, but we could also define it on the root widget or even in the app class. Let's have a look at the former first. Let's now move the method to the root widget, which is **TestLayout**. Here's the Python code:

```
# File name: test.py
...
class CustomButton(Button):
    counter = NumericProperty(1)

class TestLayout(BoxLayout):
    # Now we're defining the method on the level of the root widget. It takes
    # two parameters: instance and value. The former specifies the button on
    # which the method is called and the latter specifies the value after
    # exceeding which the counter on that instance should be reset.
    def handle_counter(self, instance, value):
        instance.counter += 1
```

```
        if instance.counter > value:
            instance.counter = 1

class TestApp(App):
    ...
```

Now the method is in the **TestLayout** class, so we must use the **root** variable instead of **self** in kv:

```
#:kivy 1.11.1
# File name: test.kv

<CustomButton>:
    font_size: 200
    size_hint_x: .5
    text: str(self.counter)

<TestLayout>:
    CustomButton:
    CustomButton:
        # This method takes two parameters, the button instance and the limit
        # value. We want the method to work on this very button, so we pass
        # self as the first argument. And we pass 8 as the second argument
        # because we want the counter to be reset when its value exceeds 5.
        on_press: root.handle_counter(self, 5)
```

If you now run the app, the method will be called each time the second button is pressed and when the counter value is greater than 5, it will be reset to 1.

And now we can modify the code so that the method is called on the first button. So, whenever we press the second button, the method is called on the first button. To do that, we must reference the first button somehow. As we are inside the **TestLayout** rule, we can use ids directly, so let's add an id to the first button and pass the first button by its id as the first argument to the method:

```
#:kivy 1.11.1
# File name: test.kv
...
<TestLayout>:
    CustomButton:
        id: _button1
    CustomButton:
        # Now whenever we press the second button, the method
        # will be called on the first button.
        on_press: root.handle_counter(_button1, 5)
```

Now if you run the app and press the second button (A) several times, the counter will change on the first one (B).

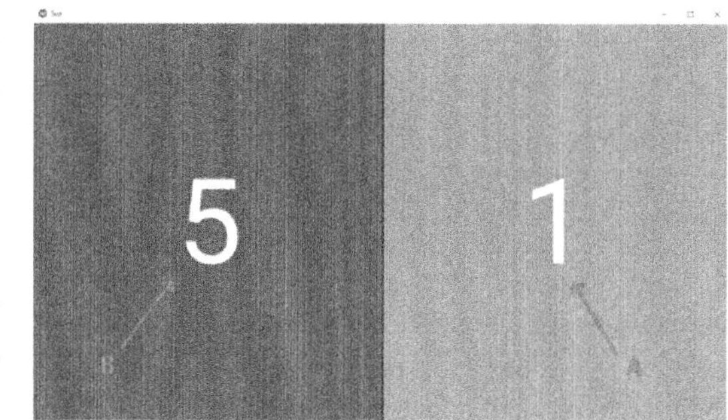


And now let's place the method directly in the app class. This is especially useful if you want to be able to call the method from different locations in your app. Then we can call it from kv using the **app** variable.

Here's the Python code:

```
# File name: test.py
...
class TestLayout(BoxLayout):
    pass

class TestApp(App):
    def build(self):
        return TestLayout()

    # Now the method is defined in the app class.
    def handle_counter(self, instance, value):
        instance.counter += 1

        if instance.counter > value:
            instance.counter = 1

if __name__ == '__main__':
    ...
```

And here's the kv file:

```
#:kivy 1.11.1
# File name: test.kv
...
<TestLayout>:
    CustomButton:
        id: _button1
    CustomButton:
        # Now you can access the method anywhere
        # using the app variable.
        on_press: app.handle_counter(_button1, 5)
```

The program will now work as before.

# Property Events

Finally, you know that if there is a property, you can use the **on_** prefix convention to create events that will be triggered whenever the property changes. Let's modify our example slightly. First, let's remove the **handle_counter** method from the app class. Then let's create the **on_counter** method in the **CustomButton** class.

Here's the Python file:

```
# File name: test.py
...
class CustomButton(Button):
    counter = NumericProperty(1)

    def on_counter(self, instance, value):
        if value % 2:
            self.color = [1, 0, 0, 1] # red
        else:
            self.color = [0, 1, 0, 1] # green

class TestLayout(BoxLayout):
    pass

class TestApp(App):
    def build(self):
        return TestLayout()

if __name__ == '__main__':
    TestApp().run()
```

Here the property is **counter**, so the corresponding event is **on_counter**. It's triggered when the value of **counter** changes. Now the text on the button will be green if the value is an even number and red if it's odd.

Here's the kv file:

```
#:kivy 1.11.1
# File name: test.kv

<CustomButton>:
    font_size: 200
    size_hint_x: .5
    text: str(self.counter)
    on_press: self.counter += 1

<TestLayout>:
    CustomButton:
    CustomButton:
```

As you can see, the **on_press** event is now in the class rule, so it will work for all instances. Each time we press a button, its **counter** value will change and this change will call the **on_counter** method.

We could define the **on_counter** event directly in kv as well. So, remove the method definition from the **CustomButton** class. And here's the kv file that will work just the same:

```
#:kivy 1.11.1
# File name: test.kv

<CustomButton>:
    ...
    on_press: self.counter += 1
    on_counter: self.color = [1, 0, 0, 1] if self.counter % 2 else [0, 1, 0, 1]

<TestLayout>:
    ...
```

As you remember, there's another way of working with events. You can bind them to methods that should be called when a property changes. We'll talk in more detail about binding and unbinding events in a separate chapter, in the next chapter, to be precise.

But before we do, here's a simple exercise for you.

# It's Your Turn Now...

## EXERCISE

In this exercise you will modify the test app a little. First of all remove the **counter** property and all code that is related to it in the kv file. Next add a ListProperty called **enemies** and set its default value to an empty list. Don't forget to import the **ListProperty** class first. You can also remove the **NumericProperty** class from the imports because we're not going to need it.

Now modify the kv file. The font size should be **50** and the text should **'You are safe.'** Now, whenever a button is pressed (any button, so this event should be added in the class rule), a new enemy should be appended to the list. The enemy may be represented by a string object like **'enemy'**.

Then, in the Python file, add a method that will be called whenever the **enemies** property changes. Use the naming convention with the **on_** prefix. The method will need the **instance** and **value** parameters, where the former references the button and the latter the list of enemies. Now, if the number of enemies is greater than 5, the text on the button should change to **'Beware. There are more \nand more enemies!'**(with a newline character in the string!).

## SOLUTION

So, here's the Python file:

```
# File name: test.py
...
from kivy.uix.boxlayout import BoxLayout

# We don't need the NumericProperty anymore,
# but we need the ListProperty.
from kivy.properties import ListProperty

from kivy.uix.button import Button

class CustomButton(Button):
    # Here's the property.
    enemies = ListProperty([])

    # And here's the method that will be called each time
    # the enemies property changes, for example when new
    # elements are appended like in this program.
    def on_enemies(self, instance, value):
        if len(value) > 5:
            self.text = 'Beware. There are more \nand more enemies!'

class TestLayout(BoxLayout):
    ...
```

And here's the kv file:

```
#:kivy 1.11.1
# File name: test.kv

<CustomButton>:
    font_size: 50
    size_hint_x: .5
    text: 'You are safe.'

    # When a button is pressed, a new enemy is appended.
    on_press: self.enemies.append('enemy')

<TestLayout>:
    CustomButton:
    CustomButton:
```

Here's what you should see when you run the app and press the second button more than five times.

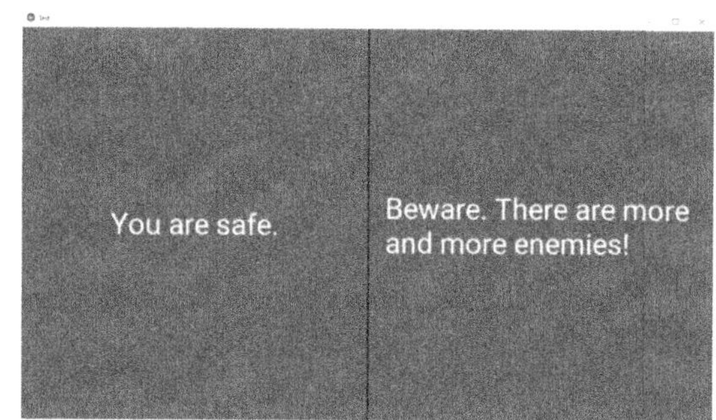

# Chapter 78 - Binding and Unbinding Events

In the previous chapter we were talking about events in Kivy. In this chapter we'll see how to bind and unbind events. In the chapter on observing property changes we talked about the **bind** method, which we used outside the class where the property was defined. Let's have a look at it again. We're going to be working on the test files in this chapter.

## Binding Events

First of all, make sure your **test.py** file looks like this again:

```
# File name: test.py

from kivy.config import Config
Config.set('graphics', 'width', '1200')
Config.set('graphics', 'height', '675')
Config.set('graphics', 'resizable', '1')

import kivy
kivy.require('1.11.1')
from kivy.app import App
from kivy.uix.floatlayout import FloatLayout
from kivy.properties import NumericProperty
from kivy.uix.button import Button

class CustomButton(Button):
    counter = NumericProperty(0)

    def on_press(self):
        self.counter += 1

def make_bigger(instance, value):
    if value < 5:
        instance.font_size += 20

def change_color(instance, value):
    if instance.color == [1, 0, 0, 1]:
        instance.color = [0, 1, 0, 1]
    else:
        instance.color = [1, 0, 0, 1]

class TestLayout(FloatLayout):
    def __init__(self, **kwargs):
        super().__init__(**kwargs)

        self.button1.bind(counter=make_bigger)
        self.button2.bind(counter=make_bigger)
        self.button2.bind(counter=change_color)

class TestApp(App):
    def build(self):
        return TestLayout()

if __name__ == '__main__':
    TestApp().run()
```

Also, make sure your **test.kv** file looks like this:

```
#:kivy 1.11.1
# File name: test.kv

<TestLayout>:
    button1: _button1
    button2: _button2

    CustomButton:
        id: _button1
        text: str(self.counter)
        size_hint_x: .5

    CustomButton:
        id: _button2
        text: str(self.counter)
        size_hint_x: .5
        pos_hint: {'x': .5}
```

Here we have the **CustomButton** class with the **counter** property defined in it. In the **TestLayout** class we use the **bind** method to bind the **counter** property on the particular **CustomButton** instances to the two functions defined in global scope, **make_bigger** and **change_color**. From this point on, the two functions will be called each time the **counter** property changes.

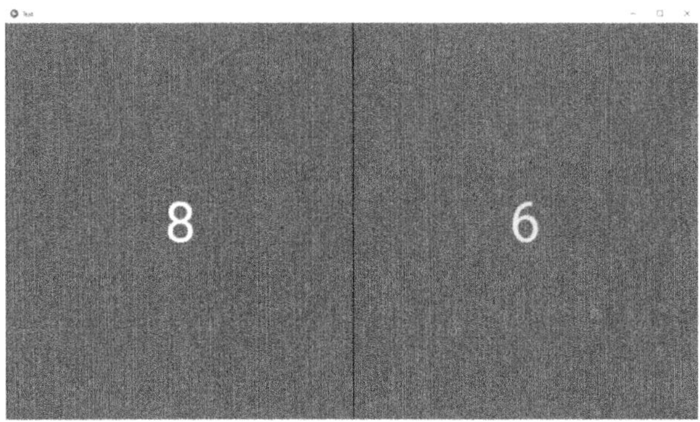


If you now run the app and press the two buttons several times, you will see them in action.

The text on the first button only gets bigger, but doesn't change its color. This is because we bound its **counter** property only to the **make_bigger** function. The second button also changes its color, because here both functions were bound.

In the example above we bound a property to the callbacks. But we can also bind an event to a callback. It works pretty much the same. Suppose we want to bind yet another function to the **on_press** event on the first button. Let's modify our code:

```
# File name: test.py
...
class CustomButton(Button):
    ...
def make_bigger(instance, value):
    ...
def change_color(instance, value):
    ...
# This function will be bound to the on_press event
# on a button.
def paint_red(instance):
    if instance.background_color == [1, 1, 1, 1]: # default
        instance.background_color = [1, 0, 0, 1]
    else:
        instance.background_color = [1, 1, 1, 1]

class TestLayout(FloatLayout):
    def __init__(self, **kwargs):
        super().__init__(**kwargs)

        self.button1.bind(counter=make_bigger)
        self.button2.bind(counter=make_bigger)
        self.button2.bind(counter=change_color)

        # Let's bind the paint_red function to the on_press
        # event on the first button.
        self.button1.bind(on_press=paint_red)

class TestApp(App):
    ...
```

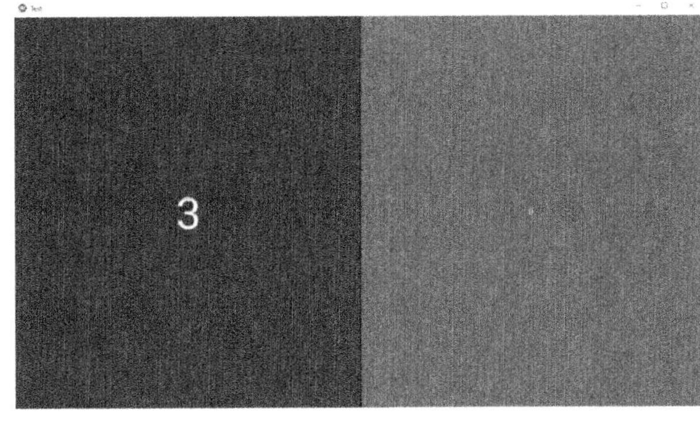


Now if you run the app and press the first button, the color of its background will change to red or back to the default color if it's already red each time you press it.

The two functions will be bound to the **counter** property of either button as long as the app is running. Also, the **paint_red** function will be bound to the **on_press** method of the first button as long as the app is running. But sometimes, for some reason, we may want to unbind a function from an event, so that it's no longer called, especially if we don't need it any more. This is where the **unbind** method comes in handy.

# Unbinding Events

Although this example of unbinding events will be pretty artificial, it still should be enough for you to understand how it works. Don't worry, later in the Slugrace project we'll see more realistic examples of binding and unbinding events.

So, we want to unbind all the three functions from the **on_press** event and the **counter** property as soon as the value of **counter** is greater than 2. This means the moment the value of **counter** is greater than 2 all the callback functions should stop working. We will put the code in the **CustomButton** class, in the **on_press** event for example, but you can put it in any method where it makes sense. The **unbind** method just deactivates the events. Here's the code:

```
# File name: test.py
...
class CustomButton(Button):
    counter = NumericProperty(0)

    def on_press(self):
        self.counter += 1

        if self.counter > 2:
            self.unbind(on_press=paint_red)
            self.unbind(counter=make_bigger)
            self.unbind(counter=change_color)

def make_bigger(instance, value):
    ...
```

If you now run the app, the three methods will be called when the appropriate events are triggered only for a while. As soon the the value of counter is greater than 2, they won't be called anymore.

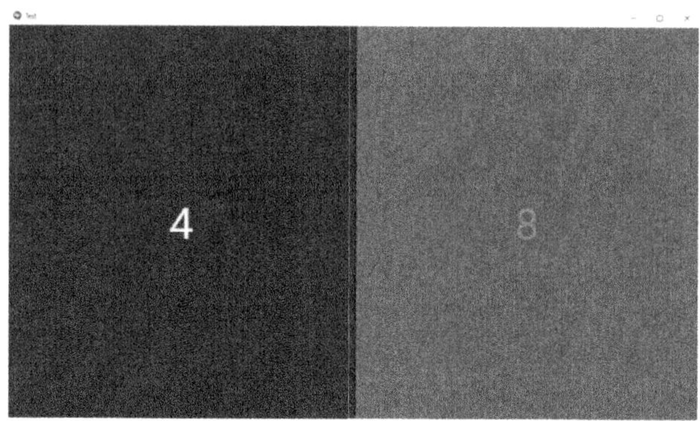


In the image on the left you can see the left button painted red for good because it didn't change back to the default color. The text on the right button didn't change to green either. This is because at this stage the value of **counter** is 4 and 8 respectively on the two buttons, so it's greater than 2 and the callback functions have been turned off, so to speak.

In the next chapter we'll add some events to the Slugrace project, but before that, here's a simple exercise for you.

## It's Your Turn Now...

EXERCISE

In this exercise you'll add a vertical slider to the test app and make it disappear as its value decreases. Follow the steps below:

1. Define the **CustomSlider** class in the **test.py** file that inherits from **Slider**. Don't forget to import the **Slider** class first. For now leave the class implementation empty.

2. Instantiate the **CustomSlider** class in the **test.kv** file. Give the custom slider instance an id (like **_slider**) and set its **min**, **max** and **value** properties to **0**, **1** and **1** respectively. Also, set its **orientation** to vertical. Then add an ObjectProperty to the root widget that will reference the custom slider by id. You can name it **slider**.

3. In the Python file define the **disappear** function in global scope. You will later bind it to the slider's **value** property. The function should take two parameters, **instance** and **value**, and should set the instance's opacity to **value**. To do that use the **opacity** property on the instance (it's available for all widgets). The **opacity** property can be set to any value between 0 and 1, where 0 means fully transparent and 1 means fully opaque. As our slider's **min** and **max** properties are set to **0** and **1** respectively, you can easily use the slider's **value**, which is always somewhere between the two, to set the opacity.

4. In the **__init__** method of the **TestLayout** class bind the **disappear** function to slider's **value** property. When you run the app at this moment, the slider will be fully opaque because its initial value is 1. But as you move it down, it will 'disappear', or rather become transparent.

5. The last thing to do is to unbind the **disappear** function from the **value** property. This should happen when the value of the slider reaches 0. So, the moment the slider becomes fully transparent,

it should be gone for good, there should be no way to make it visible again. To do that, override the **on_value** method in the **CustomSlider** class (it should take the **instance** and **value** parameters). In the function unbind the **disappear** function from the **value** property if **value** equals 0.

## SOLUTION

Here's the Python file:

```
# File name: test.py
...
from kivy.uix.button import Button

# We need to import the Slider class.
from kivy.uix.slider import Slider

class CustomButton(Button):
    ...
class CustomSlider(Slider):
    # Override the on_value method.
    def on_value(self, instance, value):
        if value == 0:
            # The slider is now fully transparent, so unbind the
            # disappear function from the value property.
            self.unbind(value=disappear)

def make_bigger(instance, value):
    ...
def change_color(instance, value):
    ...
def paint_red(instance):
    ...
# Here's the function that we will bind to the value property.
def disappear(instance, value):
    # The value is always between min and max, so between 0 and 1
    # in this case. So is opacity, so they match easily.
    instance.opacity = value

class TestLayout(FloatLayout):
    def __init__(self, **kwargs):
        super().__init__(**kwargs)

        self.button1.bind(counter=make_bigger)
        self.button2.bind(counter=make_bigger)
        self.button2.bind(counter=change_color)
        self.button1.bind(on_press=paint_red)

        # Bind the disappear function to slider's value property.
        self.slider.bind(value=disappear)

class TestApp(App):
    ...
```

And here's the kv file:

```
#:kivy 1.11.1
# File name: test.kv

<TestLayout>:
    button1: _button1
    button2: _button2

    # Here's the ObjectProperty to reference the custom slider.
    slider: _slider

    CustomButton:
        id: _button1
        ...
    CustomButton:
        id: _button2
        ...
        pos_hint: {'x': .5}

    # Here's the custom slider.
    CustomSlider:
        id: _slider
        min: 0
        max: 1
        value: 1
        orientation: 'vertical'
```

Run the app and move the slider more or less halfway down. As you can see, it's semitransparent. You can now slide it up and down to see it gradually disappear and reappear, but remember that once you slide it all the way down, you won't be able to see it again.

# Chapter 79 - Events in the Settings Screen

In the previous two chapters we were talking about events in Kivy and about binding and unbinding events. In this chapter we'll put some of this knowledge into practice. We're not going to bind and unbind events in this chapter just yet, but we will definitely do it later in the book.

There are going to be events everywhere throughout our project. In this chapter we'll concentrate on the Settings screen. We will handle the other screens in the following chapters.

So, let's open the **main.py** file and run the app. This is what we see:

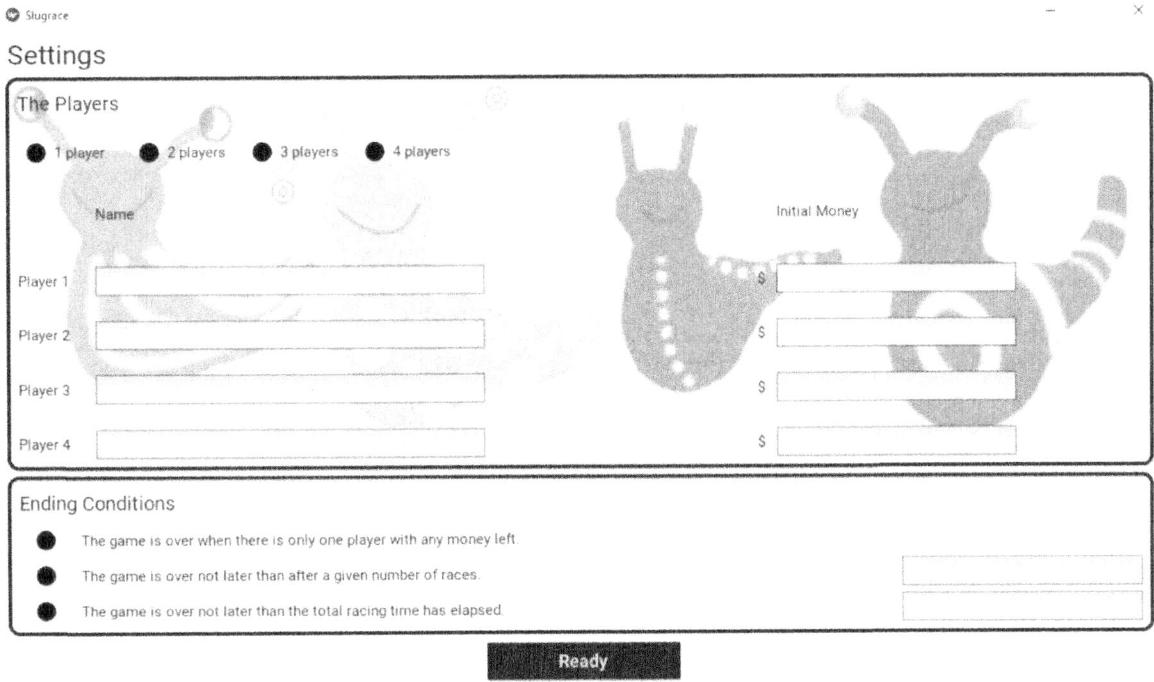


There are lots of places here where events may be triggered. Let's have a look at them:

- First of all there are the four radio buttons where you can choose the number of players. Checking a radio button will trigger an event.

- There are also radio buttons down in the Ending Conditions area. Checking them will also trigger events.

- There are quite a few text inputs here. When we enter text in them, we want the text to be validated, so when the text changes, another event will be triggered. We will handle input validation in a separate chapter, though.

- Finally, when we press the Ready button, another event will be triggered.

In this chapter we're going to handle the Player radio button events and the Ending Conditions radio button events. As far as the latter is concerned, I'll leave it for you as an exercise.

The Ready button's **on_press** event will be handled in the next chapter. So, let's start with the Player radio buttons.

# Player Radio Button Events

First of all, we'll add a NumericProperty to the **Game** class that will hold the number of players. As you remember, there may be up to four players. The default number of players when the game begins will be 2. We will put the two players in a list. If the number of players should be different, there will be a method that will take care of it, which we will add in a minute. Don't forget to import the **NumericProperty** class first. Here's the code:

```
# File name: main.py
...
from player import Player

# We need a NumericProperty for the number of players.
from kivy.properties import NumericProperty

Builder.load_file('settings.kv')
...
class Game(ScreenManager):
    # the players
    player1 = Player()
    player2 = Player()
    player3 = Player()
    player4 = Player()

    # This is the number of players that we set in the Settings screen.
    number_of_players = NumericProperty(2)

    # When you start the game, there are two players by default.
    players = [player1, player2]

class SlugraceApp(App):
    ...
```

Now, in the **settings.kv** file we will add the **on_active** events to the four radio buttons. They are triggered if the state of a radio button changes, so if we check or uncheck it. Here the code is going to be pretty simple. It will just set the **number_of_players** property that we just defined in the **Game** class to an appropriate number.

We also must modify the **PlayerCount** rule so that it has the **active** property. You'll find the explanation in the comments.

As you remember, we now have access to the **Game** class from each screen. In the Settings screen we reference it by the **game** property on the root widget. Here's the **settings.kv** file:

```
#:kivy 1.11.1
# File name: settings.kv
#:import settings settings

<PlayerCount>:
    # The PlayerCount widget is not a check box, but rather a custom widget that
    # consists of other widgets. So, what does it mean for it to be active? Well,
    # when we say the PlayerCount widget is active, we mean by this that the check
    # box it contains (PlayerRadioButton) is active. So, we need to ad an id to the
    # radio button and use it to access the active property on the radio button.
    active: _player_radio_button.active
    PlayerRadioButton:
        id: _player_radio_button

        # The player radio button should be in the same state as the root widget.
        active: root.active
    RegularLabel:
        text: root.count_text

<PlayerSettings>:
    ...
<SettingsScreen>:
    ...
        ### THE PLAYERS ###
        ...
            # Radio Buttons
            BoxLayout:
                ...
                # 1 player
                PlayerCount:
                    count_text: '1 player'

                    # When this radio button is checked (so active), it means
                    # there's going to be just one player in the game, so we want
                    # to set the number_of_players property in the Game class to 1.
                    on_active: root.game.number_of_players = 1

                # 2 players
                PlayerCount:
                    count_text: '2 players'

                    # This is the default number of players, so this radio button
                    # should be active.
                    active: True
```

```
                    # When this radio button is active, the number_of_players
                    # property should be set to 2.
                    on_active: root.game.number_of_players = 2

                # 3 players
                PlayerCount:
                    count_text: '3 players'

                    # Similarly, if this radio button is active, there are going
                    # to be three players.
                    on_active: root.game.number_of_players = 3

                # 4 players
                PlayerCount:
                    count_text: '4 players'

                    # If this radio button is active, there will be 4 players.
                    on_active: root.game.number_of_players = 4

            # Player Name and Initial Money Setup
            ...
```

Now, whenever we check one of the radio buttons, the **number_of_players** property will be changed. But this is not all. We also want the appropriate players to be moved into or out of the **players** list in the **Game** class. Using the naming convention with the **on_** prefix, we will create a method in the **Game** class that will take care of it. The method **on_number_of_players** will be called each time the **number_of_players** property changes and it will handle the **players** list accordingly. Here's the code:

```
# File name: main.py
...
class Game(ScreenManager):
    # the players
    player1 = Player()
    player2 = Player()
    player3 = Player()
    player4 = Player()

    number_of_players = NumericProperty(2)
    players = [player1, player2]

    # This method will be called each time the number_of_players property changes.
    def on_number_of_players(self, instance, value):
        if self.number_of_players == 1:
            self.players = [self.player1]
        elif self.number_of_players == 2:
            self.players = [self.player1, self.player2]
        elif self.number_of_players == 3:
            self.players = [self.player1, self.player2, self.player3]
        elif self.number_of_players == 4:
            self.players = [self.player1, self.player2, self.player3, self.player4]

class SlugraceApp(App):
    def build(self):
```

To make sure it works, let's add just this one line of code at the end of the **on_number_of_players** method:

```
# File name: main.py
...
class Game(ScreenManager):
    ...
    def on_number_of_players(self, instance, value):
        ...
            self.players = [self.player1, self.player2, self.player3, self.player4]

        print(self.number_of_players, self.players)

class SlugraceApp(App):
    ...
```

Now run the app and play with the radio buttons. In the terminal the current number of players should be printed as well as the list of players:

```
1 [<player.Player object at 0x00000276F2E9BBA8>]

3 [<player.Player object at 0x00000276F2E9BBA8>, <player.Player object at 0x00000276F2E9BC18>, <player.Player object at 0x00000276F2E9BC88>]

2 [<player.Player object at 0x00000276F2E9BBA8>, <player.Player object at 0x00000276F2E9BC18>]

4 [<player.Player object at 0x00000276F2E9BBA8>, <player.Player object at 0x00000276F2E9BC18>, <player.Player object at 0x00000276F2E9BC88>, <player.Player object at 0x00000276F2E9BCF8>]

1 [<player.Player object at 0x00000276F2E9BBA8>]
```

Now remove the line you just added, we don't need it anymore. Now it's your turn to implement the Ending Conditions radio button events and then, in the next chapter, we'll take care of the Ready Button's **on_press** event.

# It's Your Turn Now...

### EXERCISE

Follow the steps below to implement the events for the Ending Conditions radio buttons.

1. We'll need three BooleanProperties in the **Game** class, **end_by_money**, **end_by_races** and **end_by_time**. The first one should default to **True**, the other two to **False**. The names of the properties tell us which ending condition we choose. If the game should be over when there's only one player left with any amount of money, the **end_by_money** property should be set to **True**. If the game should end after a given number of races, the **end_by_races** property should be set to **True**.

Finally, if we want to set a time after which the game is over, the **end_by_time** property should be set to **True**. This means that only one of the three properties may be set to **True**. Now, go ahead and add the properties to the **Game** class. Don't forget to import the class that you will need first.

2. As just mentioned, only one of the three properties may be set to **True**. Let's create a method that will take care of it. The method will then be called whenever one of the radio buttons is checked. So, in the **Game** class create the **set_ending_condition** method. It should take a **condition** parameter, which will be a string. In the method we will need some conditional code. If the **condition** parameter is set to **'money'**, the **end_by_money** property should be set to **True** and the other two to **False**. If the **condition** parameter is **'races'**, the **end_by_races** property should be set to **True** and the other two to **False**. Finally, if the **condition** parameter is set to **'time'**, the **end_by_time** property should be set to **True** and the other two to **False**.

3. Now go to the **settings.kv** file and locate the code where the Ending Conditions radio buttons are instantiated. To each of the three ConditionRadioButtons add the **active** property and set it to the same value as the corresponding property in the **Game** class, so for example the **active** property on the first radio button should be the same value as the **end_by_money** property, and so on.

4. Still in the kv file, add the **on_active** event to all three ConditionRadioButtons. This event is triggered whenever the **active** property changes, so both when a radio button is checked and when it's unchecked. But we want it to be triggered only when the button is checked, so we will need a condition. So, as far as the first button is concerned, for example, if the **active** property is **True**, so if the radio button is checked, the **set_ending_condition** method in the **Game** class should be called with the argument **'money'**. Similarly, when the state of the other two radio buttons changes from unchecked to checked, the **set_ending_condition** method should be called, with the argument **'races'** and **'time'** respectively.

HINT: You can write conditional code on a single line, just put a colon after the condition and continue on the same line.

5. Now, this should be working. But to make sure, add a temporary line of code at the end of the **set_ending_condition** method that will print the three variables. So, for example when you select the ending condition by time, it should print **False**, **False**, **True**, where the first and second **False** values refer to the **end_by_money** and **end_by_races** properties and the last **True** value refers to the **end_by_time** property. Then run the app and play with the three radio buttons. See in the terminal if it works as expected. When done with the test, remove the temporary line of code.

## SOLUTION

Now, here's the main.py file:

```
# File name: main.py
...
from player import Player

# We need a BooleanProperty for the ending conditions.
from kivy.properties import NumericProperty, BooleanProperty

Builder.load_file('settings.kv')
...
class Game(ScreenManager):
    # the players
    ...
    players = [player1, player2]

    # We will need these properties for the ending conditions.
    end_by_money = BooleanProperty(True)
    end_by_races = BooleanProperty(False)
    end_by_time = BooleanProperty(False)

    # callback methods
    def on_number_of_players(self, instance, value):
        ...
    # This method will actually set the ending condition.
    def set_ending_condition(self, condition):
        if condition == 'money':
            self.end_by_money = True
            self.end_by_races = False
            self.end_by_time = False
        elif condition == 'races':
            self.end_by_money = False
            self.end_by_races = True
            self.end_by_time = False
        elif condition == 'time':
            self.end_by_money = False
            self.end_by_races = False
            self.end_by_time = True

        #print(self.end_by_money, self.end_by_races, self.end_by_time)

class SlugraceApp(App):
    ...
```

Here's the **settings.kv** file:

```
#:kivy 1.11.1
# File name: settings.kv
#:import settings settings
...
<SettingsScreen>:
    ...
        ### ENDING CONDITIONS ###
        ...
            # radio buttons
            GridLayout:
                rows: 3
                spacing: 10
```

```
# option 1: money
ConditionRadioButton:
    # This radio button should be active if the end_by_money
    # property is set to True.
    active: root.game.end_by_money

    # When this radio button is checked, the set_ending_condition
    # method should be called with the argument 'money'. We want
    # the event to be triggered only when the radio button is
    # checked, not when it's unchecked, hence the conditional
    # code. The same conditional code will be used for the other
    # two radio buttons.
    on_active: if self.active: root.game.set_ending_condition('money')

RegularLabel:
    text: ...

# option 2: races
ConditionRadioButton:
    # This radio button should be active if the end_by_races
    # property is set to True.
    active: root.game.end_by_races

    # When this radio button is checked, the set_ending_condition
    # method should be called with the argument 'races'.
    on_active: if self.active: root.game.set_ending_condition('races')

BoxLayout:
    ...
# option 3: time
ConditionRadioButton:
    # This radio button should be active if the end_by_time
    # property is set to True.
    active: root.game.end_by_time

    # When this radio button is checked, the set_ending_condition
    # method should be called with the argument 'time'.
    on_active: if self.active: root.game.set_ending_condition('time')

BoxLayout:
    ...
```

Here's what you should see in the terminal when you run the app before the additional line of code in the **set_ending_condition** method is removed, provided you check the radio buttons in the following order: time, money, races, time, races, money:

```
False False True

True False False

False True False

False False True

False True False

True False False
```

# Chapter 80 – Player Settings

In the previous chapter we handled the radio button events in the Settings screen. As mentioned before, the text input events will be handled in a separate chapter, so let's now move on to the Ready Button's **on_press** event. At this moment the **on_press** event is implemented like so:

```
#:kivy 1.11.1
# File name: settings.kv
#:import settings settings
...
<SettingsScreen>:
    ...
        ### READY BUTTON ###
        RedButton:
            text: 'Ready'
            on_press:
                root.manager.current = 'racescreen'
```

So, it just switches to another screen. By the way, now **root.manager** and **root.game** reference the same object, the **Game** class instance.

Anyway, besides switching to another screen, we want the Ready button to do much more. We want it to call three methods that will take care of the game's settings. The methods will be defined in the root widget class, which is **SettingsScreen**.

The first method will set the players, so let's name it **set_players**. The second method will set the slugs, so let's name it **set_slugs**. Finally, the third method will set the number of races (if the game should end after a given number of races) or the time of the game (if the game should end after a specified period of time). Let's name it simply **set_game**.

We will add the three callback methods to the **on_press** event on the Ready button and then implement them in the **settings.py** file. We could also implement them directly in the **Game** class in **main.py**, but I just want the methods used for settings to be in the Settings screen.

In this chapter we'll take care of setting the players and in the following chapters we'll set the slugs and the races / time.

## Setting the Players

The **set_players** method will take one argument, the list of players. So we must create the **players** property on the root widget. In the list we'll put the four **PlayerSettings** instances, which we will reference by ids. We could also pass the four players directly as arguments to the method, but this way will be more concise.

Here's the kv file:

```
#:kivy 1.11.1
# File name: settings.kv
#:import settings settings
...
<SettingsScreen>:
    ...
    game: root.manager

    # Here we have the players property set to a list
    # of players. Each player is represented by
    # a PlayerSettings instance. The instances are
    # referenced by ids.
    players: [_player1, _player2, _player3, _player4]

    BoxLayout:
        ...
        ### THE PLAYERS ###
        ...
                # the players rows
                # player 1
                PlayerSettings:
                    id: _player1
                    label_text: 'Player 1'

                # player 2
                PlayerSettings:
                    id: _player2
                    label_text: 'Player 2'

                # player 3
                PlayerSettings:
                    id: _player3
                    label_text: 'Player 3'

                # player 4
                PlayerSettings:
                    id: _player4
                    label_text: 'Player 4'

        ### ENDING CONDITIONS ###
        ...
        ### READY BUTTON ###
        RedButton:
            text: 'Ready'
            on_press:
                # The first method we want to call
                # when this event is triggered is
                # the set_players method. It's
                # defined in the SettingsScreen
                # class, so on the root widget. We
                # pass the list of players (actually
                # PlayerSettings instances) to it.
                root.set_players(root.players)

                # We still want the screen to change.
                root.manager.current = 'racescreen'
```

By setting a player I mean assigning the name and initial money that we enter in the appropriate text inputs to the **name** and **initial_money** properties respectively. To do that, we have to modify the **PlayerSettings** rule. Here's the code with comments:

```
#:kivy 1.11.1
# File name: settings.kv
#:import settings settings
...
<PlayerSettings>:
    # We'll need two properties, one for the name
    # text from the NameInput and one for the
    # intial money text from the NumInput. We'll
    # reference the text inputs by ids.
    name: _player_name.text
    player_initial_money: _player_initial_money.text

    Regular80x30Label:
        text: root.label_text
    NameInput:
        id: _player_name

        # Let's add a hint text for the app user so that
        # they know what kind of input is expected.
        hint_text: "Enter the name of " + root.label_text
    BoxLayout:
        RegularLabel:
            text: ""
            size_hint_x: None
            width: 280
        DollarLabel:
        NumInput:
            id: _player_initial_money

            # Let's add a hint text for the app
            # user with the default amount of
            # initial money. We could use a variable
            # for that in the SlugraceApp class, but
            # this time let's just hard-code it here.
            hint_text: '1000'

<SettingsScreen>:
    ...
```

And now let's implement the method in the **settings.py** file. But before we do that, there's one more thing I'd like to talk about for a while.

# Accessing App Data in Python Code

Each player will have a name and an amount of money at the beginning of the game. These pieces of information will be stored in the **name** and **initial_money** properties that we defined in the **Player** class. We want the name to be no more than 10 characters long. We also want the initial money to be between $10 and $5000. We could naturally hard-code these limitations, but instead I'll use some variables for them on the application level, so in the **SlugraceApp** class. I decided to do it that way not only because hard-coding things doesn't seem good practice in general, but also because I want to use this opportunity to show you how to access data defined on app level in any place in the code. You already know that in the kv files you can simply use the **app** variable, but this time I'll show you how to do it in Python files. So, first let's define the three variables in the **SlugraceApp** class in **main.py**:

```
# File name: main.py
...
class SlugraceApp(App):
    # General Settings
    initial_money_min = 10
    initial_money_max = 5000
    max_name_length = 10

    def build(self):
        return Game()

if __name__ == '__main__':
    ...
```

The names of the variables are pretty self-explanatory, I think.

We will be using the two first variables in this chapter and the third one a bit later, when we add text validation to our code.

# The set_players Method

And now let's go to the **settings.py** file and implement the **set_players** method. In this method we will be using the three variables that we just defined in the **SlugraceApp** class.

To access the class in kv code we use the **app** variable, but in the Python file we have to call the **get_running_app** method defined in the **App** class. This is why we need to import the **App** class, which we can do either in the imports section at the top of the file or directly in the method where we need it.

So, we first import the **App** class and then call the aforementioned method on it. The method returns the running app instance, which we store in the **app** variable (any other name would work too) and then use in a similar way as the **app** variable in kv.

Next, we will use a **for** loop to iterate over the players stored in the **players** list in the **Game** class. As you remember, the list of players may contain 1, 2, 3, or 4 players, depending on which radio button we checked. As we will also need the index of each player inside the list, we're going to use the **enumerate** function, which returns all elements of a list along with their indices.

Inside the **for** loop we'll set the player's names and initial money.

First let's set each player's name. If the text input for the name was left empty, so when the app user did not enter a name for a particular player, the player's name will be set to something generic like **Player 1**, **Player 2**, etc. If a name was entered, the **name** property on the **PlayerSettings** class was set to it and we will use it as the player's name.

Next, let's set the player's initial money. As you remember it may be any value between $10 and $5000. These two extreme values are saved in the two variables we created in the **SlugraceApp** class, **initial_money_min** and **initial_money_max**. Now we can easily access these variables using the **app** variable we just created at the beginning of the method.

So, if no initial money was entered in the appropriate text input for a particular player, the player's initial money will be set to **1000**, which is hard-coded in the code below. If some other amount of initial money was entered, the player's initial money will be set to it, but only if it's between the allowed minimum and maximum values, otherwise to the minimum or maximum value accordingly.

Now, when the game begins, a player's money is the same as their initial money. The **money** property is used to store the amount of money a player currently has. This value will change after each race when each player either wins or loses some money.

And now let's translate it all into Python code:

```
# File name: settings.py
...
class SettingsScreen(Screen):
    # Here's the method used for the players settings.
    def set_players(self, players):
        # Let's import the App class and call the get_running_app method.
        from kivy.app import App
        app = App.get_running_app()

        # Let's iterate over the players.
        for i, player in enumerate(self.game.players):

            # First let's set each player's name.
            player.name = 'Player ' + str(i + 1) if not players[i].name else players[i].name

            # Now let's set the player's initial money.
            player.initial_money = (1000 if not players[i].player_initial_money
                else max(app.initial_money_min,
                    min(int(players[i].player_initial_money), app.initial_money_max)))

            # When the game begins, a player's money is the same as their initial money.
            player.money = player.initial_money
```

In the next chapter we'll take care of slug settings and now, in the exercises below, you will modify the code so that the players' data that was set in the Settings screen is visible in the other screens.

# It's Your Turn Now...

## EXERCISE 1

After we choose some names for the players and assign them some initial money, we want this infomation to be visible in several places throughout the application. The first place is the Players' Stats area in the Race screen. Here we need the players' names and their current money, which is stored in the **money** property. So, go to the **race.kv** file and find the Players' Stats area. It should look like this:

```
#:kivy 1.11.1
# File name: race.kv
#:import race race
...
<RaceScreen>:
    ...
            # Players' Stats
            BoxLayout:
                ...
                BoldLabel:
                    text: "Players' Stats"

                PlayerStats:
                    name: 'Player 1'
                    money: 1000

                PlayerStats:
                    name: 'Player 2'
                    money: 800

                PlayerStats:
                    name: 'Player 3'
                    money: 1300

                PlayerStats:
                    name: 'Player 4'
                    money: 1200

            # Buttons
            ...
```

As you can see, the **name** and **money** properties on the **PlayerStats** instances are set to some hard-coded values. We want them to be set to the values that we set in the Settings screen. So, go ahead and modify the code.

HINT: You need to access the four **Player** objects defined in the **Game** class.

## SOLUTION

So, here's the code:

```
#:kivy 1.11.1
# File name: race.kv
#:import race race
...
<RaceScreen>:
    ...
            # Players' Stats
            BoxLayout:
                ...
                BoldLabel:
                    text: "Players' Stats"

                PlayerStats:
                    # We use the root.game property
                    # to access the Game class.
                    name: root.game.player1.name
                    money: root.game.player1.money
                PlayerStats:
                    name: root.game.player2.name
                    money: root.game.player2.money
                PlayerStats:
                    name: root.game.player3.name
                    money: root.game.player3.money
                PlayerStats:
                    name: root.game.player4.name
                    money: root.game.player4.money

            # Buttons
            ...
```

Now let's check out if it works. Go to the **main.py** file and run the app. The first thing that you will probably notice is the hint text in the text inputs. It'll make it easier for us to understand what type of input the program expects from us. Now, check the 4 players radio button (A) and set the names (B) and initial money values (C) for some of the players:

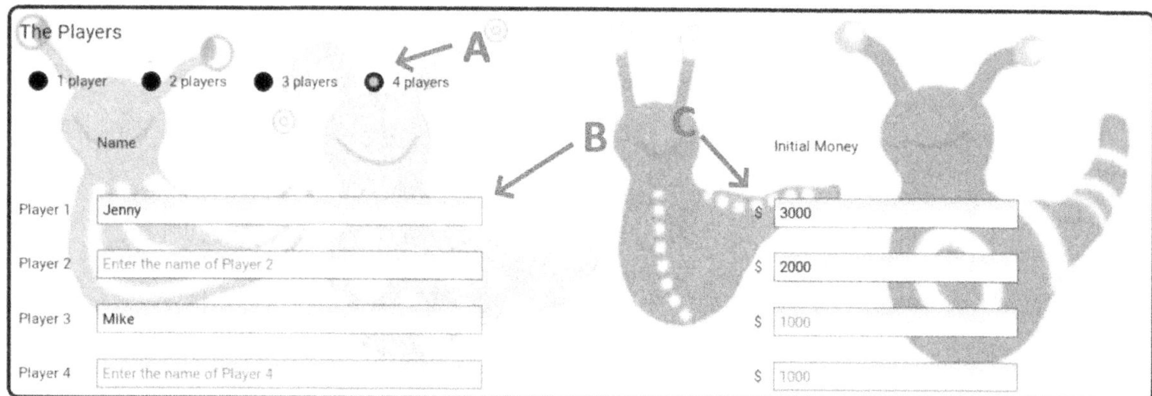


When you hit the Ready button, the names of the players will be set to **`Jenny`**, **`Player 2`**, **`Mike`** and **`Player 4`**. The initial money and money values of the first two players will be set to $3000 and $2000 respectively and to the default $1000 for the other two. These values should be now visible in the Race screen, in the Players' Stats area. Press the Ready button and watch the Players' Stats area in the Race screen.

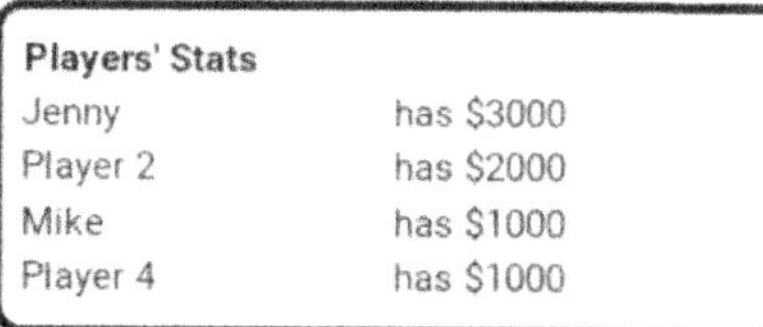


**EXERCISE 2**

The next place where the player data should be visible is the Bets screen. Here's the code we have now:

```
#:kivy 1.11.1
# File name: bets.kv
#:import bets bets
...
<BetsScreen>:
    ...
        ### PLAYER BETS ###
        BoxLayout:
            orientation: 'vertical'
            # player 1
            Bet:
                player_name: 'Player 1'
                bet_amount: 1000
                max_bet_amount: 1000
                player_group: 'player1'
            # player 2
            Bet:
                player_name: 'Player 2'
                bet_amount: 1000
                max_bet_amount: 1000
                player_group: 'player2'
            # player 3
            Bet:
                player_name: 'Player 3'
                bet_amount: 1000
                max_bet_amount: 1000
                player_group: 'player3'
            # player 4
            Bet:
                player_name: 'Player 4'
                bet_amount: 1000
                max_bet_amount: 1000
                player_group: 'player4'

        ### GO BUTTON ###
        ...
```

As you can see, here the names of the players are again set to the generic names which should be used only if no other name is entered. You can change it by accessing the **Player** objects in the **Game** class, just like you did before.

You should also change the values of the **max_bet_amount** property on each **Bet** instance. A player can't bet more than they have, so this value should be set to the player's money amount.

## SOLUTION

So, here's the code:

```
#:kivy 1.11.1
# File name: bets.kv
#:import bets bets
...
<BetsScreen>:
    ...
        ### PLAYER BETS ###
        BoxLayout:
            orientation: 'vertical'

            # player 1
            Bet:
                player_name: root.game.player1.name
                bet_amount: 1000
                max_bet_amount: root.game.player1.money
                player_group: 'player1'

            # player 2
            Bet:
                player_name: root.game.player2.name
                bet_amount: 1000
                max_bet_amount: root.game.player2.money
                player_group: 'player2'

            # player 3
            Bet:
                player_name: root.game.player3.name
                bet_amount: 1000
                max_bet_amount: root.game.player3.money
                player_group: 'player3'

            # player 4
            Bet:
                player_name: root.game.player4.name
                bet_amount: 1000
                max_bet_amount: root.game.player4.money
                player_group: 'player4'

        ### GO BUTTON ###
        ...
```

Let's check it out again. Run the app, check the 4 players radio button and set some players' names and initial money values:

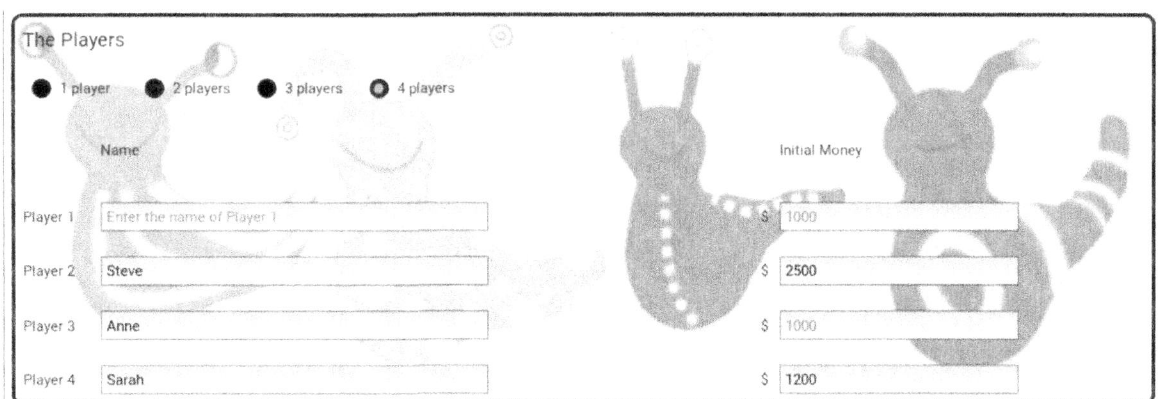


Now when you hit the Ready button, the new settings should be visible in both the Players' Stats (A) and in the Bets screen (B).

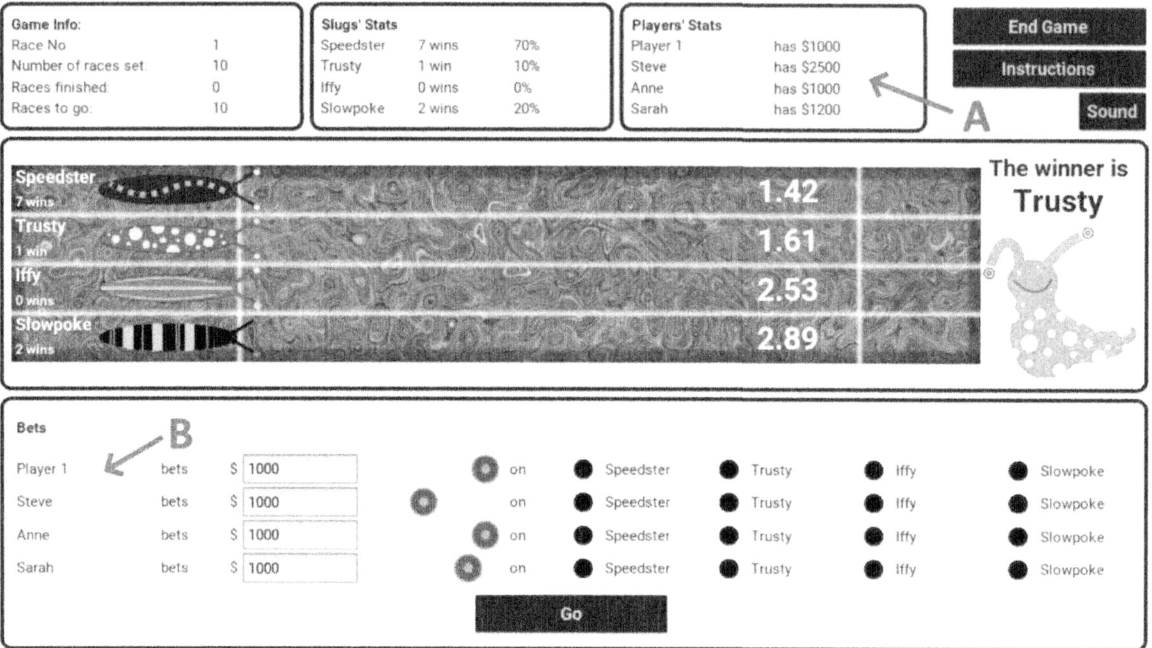


## EXERCISE 3

Another place where the player data should be visible is the Results screen. Here's the code as it is now:

```
#:kivy 1.11.1
# File name: results.kv
#:import results results
...
<ResultsScreen>:
    ...
        ### PLAYER RESULTS ###
        BoxLayout:
            orientation: 'vertical'

            # player 1
            Result:
                player_name: 'Player 1'
                money_before: 1000
                bet_amount: 300
                slug_name: 'Speedster'
                result_info: '- won'
                gain_or_loss: 400
                current_money: 1400
                odds: 2.54

            # player 2
            Result:
                player_name: 'Player 2'
                money_before: 1000
                bet_amount: 300
                slug_name: 'Speedster'
                result_info: '- lost'
                gain_or_loss: 400
                current_money: 600
                odds: 1.59

            # player 3
            Result:
                player_name: 'Player 3'
                money_before: 1000
                bet_amount: 300
                slug_name: 'Trusty'
                result_info: '- won'
                gain_or_loss: 400
                current_money: 1400
                odds: 2.24

            # player 4
            Result:
                player_name: 'Player 4'
                money_before: 1000
                bet_amount: 300
                slug_name: 'Speedster'
                result_info: '- lost'
                gain_or_loss: 400
                current_money: 600
                odds: 1.85

        ### NEXT RACE BUTTON ###
        ...
```

At this moment we can change two things, **player_name** and **current_money**. Just set them to the players' **name** and **money** properties respectively.

**SOLUTION**

OK, here's the code:

```
#:kivy 1.11.1
# File name: results.kv
#:import results results
...
<ResultsScreen>:
    ...
        ### PLAYER RESULTS ###
        BoxLayout:
            orientation: 'vertical'

            # player 1
            Result:
                player_name: root.game.player1.name
                ...
                current_money: root.game.player1.money
                ...
            # player 2
            Result:
                player_name: root.game.player2.name
                ...
                current_money: root.game.player2.money
                ...
            # player 3
            Result:
                player_name: root.game.player3.name
                ...
                current_money: root.game.player3.money
                ...
            # player 4
            Result:
                player_name: root.game.player4.name
                ...
                current_money: root.game.player4.money
                ...
        ### NEXT RACE BUTTON ###
        ...
```

Let's check it out again. Run the app like before, check the 4 players radio button and enter some data in the Settings screen:

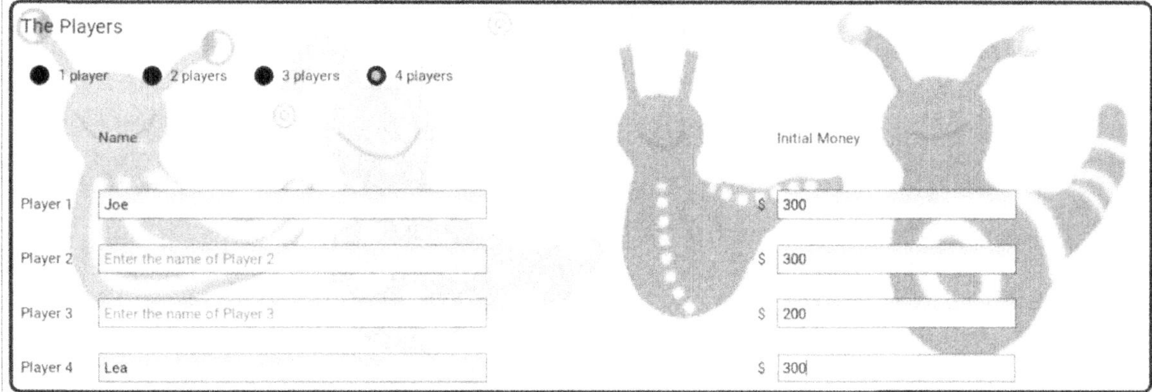


Hit the Ready button. In the Race screen you should see the player data in the Players' Stats area and in the Bets screen. Hit the Go button and you'll see the player data in the Results screen as well.

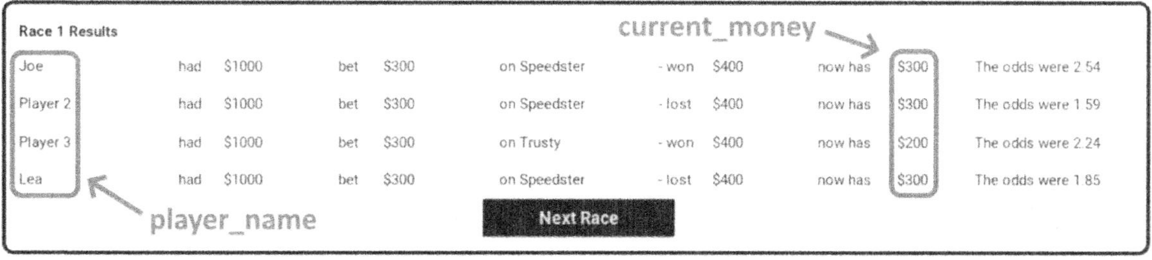

# Chapter 81 – Slug Settings

In the previous chapter we added the **set_players** method to the **on_press** event on the Ready button in the Settings screen. In this chapter we'll add another method, **set_slugs**, which will take no arguments. Let's first add it in the **settings.kv** file and then implement it. Here's the kv file:

```
#:kivy 1.11.1
# File name: settings.kv
#:import settings settings
...
<SettingsScreen>:
    ...
        ### READY BUTTON ###
        RedButton:
            text: 'Ready'
            on_press:
                root.set_players(root.players)
                root.set_slugs()
                root.manager.current = 'racescreen'
```

Setting a slug means setting its properties. If you open the **slug.py** file, you will see that we only defined three properties in the class:

```
# File name: slug.py
...
class Slug(RelativeLayout):
    body_image = StringProperty('')
    eye_image = StringProperty('')
    y_position = NumericProperty(0)
```

We will need some more, so let's add them to the class:

```
# File name: slug.py
...
class Slug(RelativeLayout):
    ...
    y_position = NumericProperty(0)

    # how many times the slug has won so far
    wins = NumericProperty(0)

    # percent of races won by this particular slug
    win_percent = NumericProperty(0)

    # the current odds for the slug - they will change after each race
    odds = NumericProperty(0)
```

And now let's create the **set_slugs** method in the **settings.py** file. We will need the **randint** function from the **random** module to randomize the slugs' odds, so make sure to import it before you use it. And here's the code:

```
# File name: settings.py
...
from kivy.uix.screenmanager import Screen
from random import randint

class PlayerCount(BoxLayout):
    ...
class SettingsScreen(Screen):
    def set_players(self, players):
        ...
    # Here's the method that sets the default values of the slug properties. For each
    # slug the initial wins and win_percent values are zero. The initial odds are
    # randomized and rounded to two decimal places.
    def set_slugs(self):
        self.game.speedster.wins = 0
        self.game.speedster.win_percent = 0.00
        self.game.speedster.odds = round(1.33 + randint(0, 10) / 100, 2)

        self.game.trusty.wins = 0
        self.game.trusty.win_percent = 0.00
        self.game.trusty.odds = round(1.59 + randint(0, 10) / 100, 2)

        self.game.iffy.wins = 0
        self.game.iffy.win_percent = 0.00
        self.game.iffy.odds = round(2.5 + randint(0, 10) / 100, 2)

        self.game.slowpoke.wins = 0
        self.game.slowpoke.win_percent = 0.00
        self.game.slowpoke.odds = round(2.89 + randint(0, 10) / 100, 2)
```

Just like we did with the players, we'll now modify the code in all the screens where we need access to slug data. For now we'll only need it in the Race screen, so we don't have to access it like before. Instead, we can just use the ids. But later we'll need slug data also outside the Race screen, so it's important that it's available in the **Game** class.

I will leave the implementation for you as an exercise. And in the next chapter we'll implement the third method that is called when the Ready button is pressed, the **set_game** method.

# It's Your Turn Now...

## EXERCISE

We will need access to slug data in several places in the Race screen. The first place is the Slugs' Stats area, which at this moment looks like so:

```
#:kivy 1.11.1
# File name: race.kv
#:import race race
...
<RaceScreen>:
    ...
            # Slugs' Stats
            ...
                BoldLabel:
                    text: "Slugs' Stats"

                SlugStats:
                    name: 'Speedster'
                    wins: 7
                    win_percent: 70

                SlugStats:
                    name: 'Trusty'
                    wins: 1
                    win_percent: 10

                SlugStats:
                    name: 'Iffy'
                    wins: 0
                    win_percent: 0

                SlugStats:
                    name: 'Slowpoke'
                    wins: 2
                    win_percent: 20

            # Players' Stats
            ...
```

As you can see, here the values are hard-coded. Use the **wins** and **win_percent** properties instead. As you are in the same rule as the **Slug** instances, you can use the ids to reference the slugs instead of the properties, so, for example, **_speedster** instead of **speedster**.

The next place where we need slug data is in the Track area where we have the white labels with slug info and the labels displaying the odds. Here's the code as it looks now:

```
#:kivy 1.11.1
# File name: race.kv
#:import race race
...
<RaceScreen>:
    ...
        ### THE TRACK ###
        ...
                # white labels with slug info
                # Speedster
                SlugInfo:
                    y_position: .875
                    name: 'Speedster'
                    wins: 7

                # Trusty
                SlugInfo:
                    y_position: .625
                    name: 'Trusty'
                    wins: 1

                # Iffy
                SlugInfo:
                    y_position: .375
                    name: 'Iffy'
                    wins: 0

                # Slowpoke
                SlugInfo:
                    y_position: .125
                    name: 'Slowpoke'
                    wins: 2

                # the odds labels
                # Speedster
                WhiteOddsLabel:
                    text: '1.42'
                    pos_hint: {'x': .77, 'center_y': .875}

                # Trusty
                WhiteOddsLabel:
                    text: '1.61'
                    pos_hint: {'x': .77, 'center_y': .625}

                # Iffy
                WhiteOddsLabel:
                    text: '2.53'
                    pos_hint: {'x': .77, 'center_y': .375}

                # Slowpoke
                WhiteOddsLabel:
                    text: '2.89'
                    pos_hint: {'x': .77, 'center_y': .125}


                # the slugs
                ...
```

Now, modify the code so that we don't have to repeat the literal values of the y positions so many times. Use the **y_position** property defined in the **Slug** class. Also use the **wins** and **odds** properties to replace the literal values in the code. You're still in the same rule, so you can use ids.

## SOLUTION

Here's the code with the modifications:

```
#:kivy 1.11.1
# File name: race.kv
#:import race race
...
<RaceScreen>:
    ...
            # Slugs' Stats
            ...
                SlugStats:
                    name: 'Speedster'
                    wins: _speedster.wins
                    win_percent: _speedster.win_percent
                SlugStats:
                    name: 'Trusty'
                    wins: _trusty.wins
                    win_percent: _trusty.win_percent
                SlugStats:
                    name: 'Iffy'
                    wins: _iffy.wins
                    win_percent: _iffy.win_percent
                SlugStats:
                    name: 'Slowpoke'
                    wins: _slowpoke.wins
                    win_percent: _slowpoke.win_percent

            # Players' Stats
            ...
        ### THE TRACK ###
        ...
                # white labels with slug info
                # Speedster
                SlugInfo:
                    y_position: _speedster.y_position
                    name: 'Speedster'
                    wins: _speedster.wins
                # Trusty
                SlugInfo:
                    y_position: _trusty.y_position
                    name: 'Trusty'
                    wins: _trusty.wins
                # Iffy
                SlugInfo:
                    y_position: _iffy.y_position
                    name: 'Iffy'
                    wins: _iffy.wins
                # Slowpoke
                SlugInfo:
                    y_position: _slowpoke.y_position
                    name: 'Slowpoke'
                    wins: _slowpoke.wins
```

```
# the odds labels
# Speedster
WhiteOddsLabel:
    text: str(_speedster.odds)
    pos_hint: {'x': .77, 'center_y': _speedster.y_position}

# Trusty
WhiteOddsLabel:
    text: str(_trusty.odds)
    pos_hint: {'x': .77, 'center_y': _trusty.y_position}

# Iffy
WhiteOddsLabel:
    text: str(_iffy.odds)
    pos_hint: {'x': .77, 'center_y': _iffy.y_position}

# Slowpoke
WhiteOddsLabel:
    text: str(_slowpoke.odds)
    pos_hint: {'x': .77, 'center_y': _slowpoke.y_position}

# the slugs
...
```

If you now run the app and go to the Race screen, you will see the new values of the properties displayed in the Slugs' Stats area (A), in the left part of the track image (B) and the odds in the right part of the image (C). By the way, you may see different odds on your screen because they are randomized.

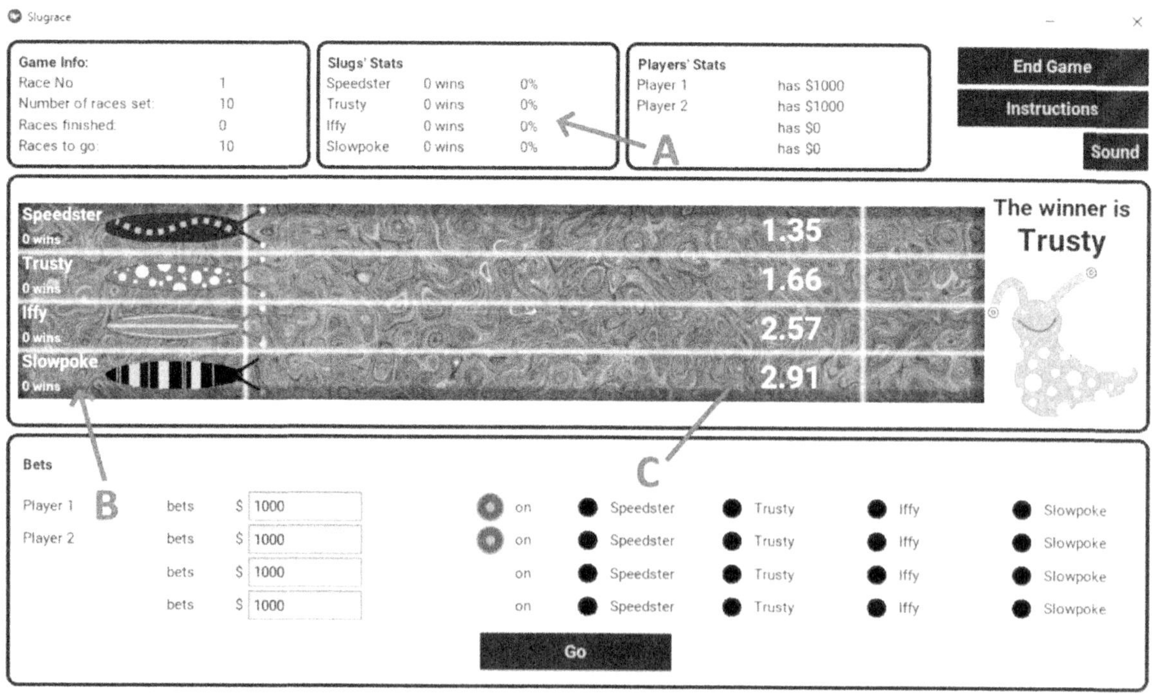

# Chapter 82 – Game Settings

In the previous chapter we handled the slug settings. In this chapter we'll take care of the game settings. By game settings I understand the ending conditions settings, so the number of races and the time of the game. These settings will be implemented in the **set_game** method that will be called, along with the **set_players** and **set_slugs** methods, when the Ready button in the Settings screen is pressed.

The **set_game** method will take two arguments, the value entered in the text input where the number of races is set (A) and the value entered in the text input where we can set the time of the game (B).

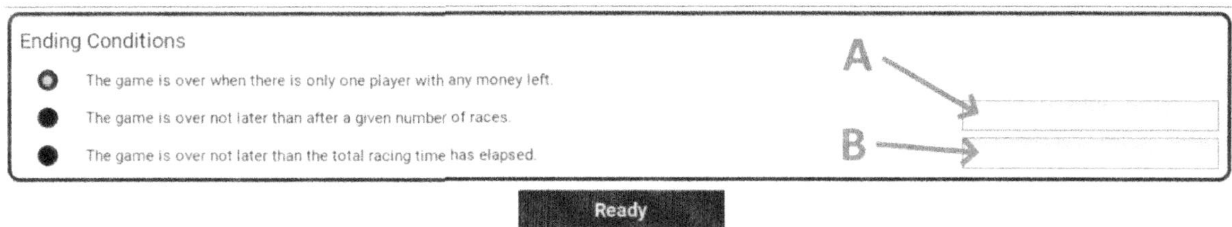


So, we need access to these two text inputs. As the Ready button is in the same rule as the text inputs, we can reference them by ids. Let's add the two ids and the **set_game** method then:

```
#:kivy 1.11.1
# File name: settings.kv
#:import settings settings
...
<SettingsScreen>:
    ...
        ### ENDING CONDITIONS ###
        ...
            # radio buttons
            ...
                # option 2: races
                ...
                BoxLayout:
                    ...
                    NumInput:
                        id: _number_of_races

                # option 3: time
                ...
                BoxLayout:
                    ...
                    NumInput:
                        id: _time_set

        ### READY BUTTON ###
```

```
        RedButton:
            text: 'Ready'
            on_press:
                root.set_players(root.players)
                root.set_slugs()
                root.set_game(_number_of_races.text, _time_set.text)
                root.manager.current = 'racescreen'
```

Before we implement the **set_game** method in the **SettingsScreen** class, we have to add some properties to the **Game** class that the method will need. First of all, we must import the **StringProperty** class because we will need it for the string representations of the game times (set time, elapsed time and remaining time).

We also need to import the **timedelta** function from the **datetime** module. The function is used to calculate differences in time. We will use it to turn the string representations of time in minutes (like for example 120) to time differences (like 2:00:00 for 120 minutes, so 2 hours, 0 minutes, 0 seconds).

Then, in the **Game** class, we'll add three properties to take care of the race count (number of races, finished races and races to go). We'll also add three properties that will handle the times and corresponding time deltas to turn them into time differences.

Here's the **main.py** file:

```
# File name: main.py
...
from player import Player

# We'll need the StringProperty class for the time properties.
from kivy.properties import NumericProperty, BooleanProperty, StringProperty

# We'll need this to calculate durations.
from datetime import timedelta

Builder.load_file('settings.kv')
...
class Game(ScreenManager):
    # the players
    ...
    # ending conditions.
    ...
    # races
    # after how many races the game should end
    number_of_races = NumericProperty(0)

    # how many races are already finished
    races_finished = NumericProperty(0)

    # how many races are left until the game is over
    races_to_go = NumericProperty(0)
```

```
    # time
    # after how much time the game should end
    time_set_delta = timedelta()  # duration
    time_set = StringProperty('') # string representation of duration

    # how much time has already elapsed since the beginning of the game
    time_elapsed_delta = timedelta()   # duration
    time_elapsed = StringProperty('')  # string representation of duration

    # how much time is still left to the end of the game
    time_remaining_delta = timedelta()   # duration
    time_remaining = StringProperty('')  # string representation of duration

    # callback methods
    def on_number_of_players(self, instance, value):
```

And now we're ready to implement the **set_game** method in the Python file. How does it work?

Well, first of all, we enter the number of races only if we choose to end the game after a specific number of races. Otherwise this text input remains empty.

If the input is not empty, then we set the **number_of_races** property that we just added in the **Game** class to that value (converted to an integer). We also set the **races_to_go** property to the same value because at the beginning of the game we haven't finished any race yet.

Similarly, we enter the time of the game only if this ending condition is chosen. Otherwise there's no input. If there is some input, then it's the time in minutes. We first convert the string to an int and use the **timedelta** function to calculate the duration. To do that, we first have to import the **timedelta** function in the imports section at the top of the file.

Let me demonstrate it on an example:

Suppose we enter **85** in the text input, which is understood as 85 minutes. So, **time_set** = **'85'** - it's a string.

Now, the string **'85'** is converted to an int, **85** to be precise, and next the **minutes** argument in the **timedelta** function is set to that integer. The **timedelta** function calculates that 85 minutes is 1 hour and 25 minutes and returns this duration as **1:25:00** (hh:mm:ss). The duration is assigned to the **time_set_delta** property. Then, this timedelta is converted to a string and saved in the **time_set** property as **'1:25:00'**.

The default value of a timedelta is **0:00:00**. We set the value of the **time_elapsed** property to its string representation, so **'0:00:00'**.

At the beginning of the game the remaining time is the same as the total time, so we set the **time_remaining_delta** property to the value of the **time_set_delta** property. Then we assign its string representation to the **time_remaining** property. In our example it's **'1:25:00'**.

And here's the code:

```
# File name: settings.py
...
from random import randint

# We will need this to calculate durations.
from datetime import timedelta

class PlayerCount(BoxLayout):
    ...
class SettingsScreen(Screen):
    def set_players(self, players):
        ...
    def set_slugs(self):
        ...
    # Here's the method to set the ending conditions.
    def set_game(self, number_of_races, time_set):
        # If we choose to end the game after a specific number of races, we set
        # number_of_races and races_to_go to the value entered in the text input.
        if number_of_races != '':
            self.game.number_of_races = int(number_of_races)
            self.game.races_to_go = self.game.number_of_races


        # If the time ending condition is chosen, we set all the time-related
        # properties.
        if time_set != '':
            self.game.time_set_delta = timedelta(minutes = int(time_set))
            self.game.time_set = str(self.game.time_set_delta)
            self.game.time_elapsed = str(self.game.time_elapsed_delta)
            self.game.time_remaining_delta = self.game.time_set_delta
            self.game.time_remaining = str(self.game.time_remaining_delta)
```

This is all we need for now. In the exercise you'll write code that will display the Game Info data in the Race screen. And in the next chapter we'll handle widget visibility. Not all widgets should be visible and enabled at all times. For example we don't want to see the time input if we choose a different ending condition, etc.

# It's Your Turn Now...

### EXERCISE

In this exercise you will write code that will take care of the Game Info area in the Race screen. The race number should be displayed always, so let's just leave it as is for now. If we choose to end the game after a number of races, we want the Game Info area to only contain information about the races (how many we set, how many have finished and how many there are to go). On the other hand, if we choose to end the game after some period of time, we want the Game Info area to show only relevant information, so how much time we set, how much has elapsed and how much is still remaining.

At this point the Game Info area in the **race.kv** file is implemented like this:

```
#:kivy 1.11.1
# File name: race.kv
#:import race race
...
<RaceScreen>:
    ...
            # Game Info
            ...
                BoldLabel:
                    text: 'Game Info:'
                BoxLayout:
                    RegularLabel:
                        size_hint: (2.5, 1)
                        text: 'Race No'
                    RegularLabel:
                        text: '1'
                BoxLayout:

                    RegularLabel:
                        size_hint: (2.5, 1)
                        text: 'Number of races set:'
                    RegularLabel:
                        text: '10'

                BoxLayout:
                    RegularLabel:
                        size_hint: (2.5, 1)
                        text: 'Races finished:'
                    RegularLabel:
                        text: '0'
                BoxLayout:
                    RegularLabel:
                        size_hint: (2.5, 1)
                        text: 'Races to go:'
                    RegularLabel:
                        text: '10'

            # Slugs' Stats
            ...
```

As you can see, we're using some temporary hard-coded values like `'10'` for the number of races set, for example. Actually, now the text `'Number of races set:'` is always displayed, although we only need it if we choose this ending condition. Otherwise it should read `'Time set:'`.

There are two other places like this. The label below reads `'Races finished:'`, but if we chose to end the game after a given period of time, it should read `'Time elapsed:'` instead. And finally the label at the bottom reads `'Races to go:'`. Again, if the time ending condition was chosen, it should read `'Time remaining:'`.

Now, use the ternary `if` statement to set the text properties to only one value in each pair according to which ending condition is chosen. Here are the text pairs again:

| ending condition: END BY RACES | ending condition: END BY TIME |
|---|---|
| `Race No` | `Race No` |
| `Number of races set:` | `Time set:` |
| `Races finished:` | `Time elapsed:` |
| `Races to go:` | `Time remaining:` |

These are just the fixed strings that will never change. But there are also strings that will change. Here they're represented by arbitrary values, but your task is to change it so that the values of the appropriate properties are displayed. Use the ternary `if` statement again. Here are the properties from the **Game** class whose values should be displayed. Some of them must be converted to strings.

| Now there is: | ending condition: END BY RACES | ending condition: END BY TIME |
|---|---|---|
| `'10'` (below `'Number of races set:'`) | `number_of_races` | `time_set` |
| `'0'` (below `'Races finished:'`) | `races_finished` | `time_elapsed` |
| `'10'` (below `'Races to go:'`) | `races_to_go` | `time_remaining` |

### SOLUTION

Here's the code after all the modifications:

```
#:kivy 1.11.1
# File name: race.kv
#:import race race
...
<RaceScreen>:
    ...
            # Game Info
            ...
                BoldLabel:
                    text: 'Game Info:'
                BoxLayout:
                    RegularLabel:
                        size_hint: (2.5, 1)
                        text: 'Race No'
                    RegularLabel:
                        text: '1'
                BoxLayout:
                    RegularLabel:
                        size_hint: (2.5, 1)
                        text: 'Number of races set:' if root.game.end_by_races else 'Time set:'
                    RegularLabel:
                        text: str(root.game.number_of_races) if root.game.end_by_races else root.game.time_set

                BoxLayout:
                    RegularLabel:
                        size_hint: (2.5, 1)
                        text: 'Races finished:' if root.game.end_by_races else 'Time elapsed:'
                    RegularLabel:
                        text: str(root.game.races_finished) if root.game.end_by_races else root.game.time_elapsed

                BoxLayout:
                    RegularLabel:
                        size_hint: (2.5, 1)
                        text: 'Races to go:' if root.game.end_by_races else 'Time remaining:'
                    RegularLabel:
                        text: str(root.game.races_to_go) if root.game.end_by_races else root.game.time_remaining

            # Slugs' Stats
            ...
```

Now, when you run the app and choose the first ending condition (the game should end when there's only one player with some money left), the time properties will be displayed in the Game Info area. This is not what we want, but don't worry about that, we'll fix it in the next chapter.

So, let's check out the other two ending conditions. Run the app, select the second option to end by races (A) and set the number of races to 40 (B).

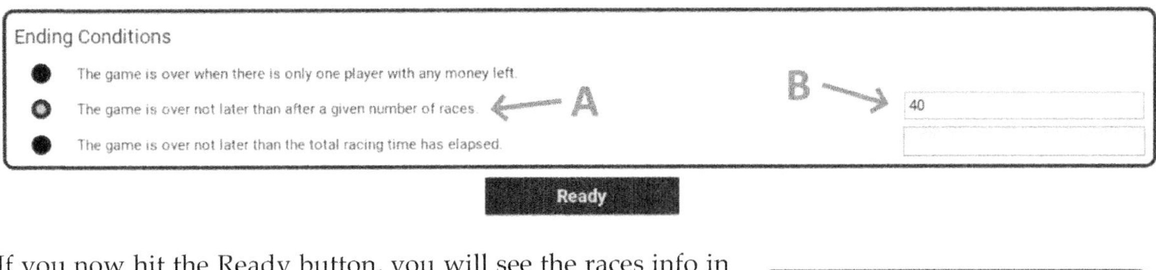


If you now hit the Ready button, you will see the races info in the Game Info area.

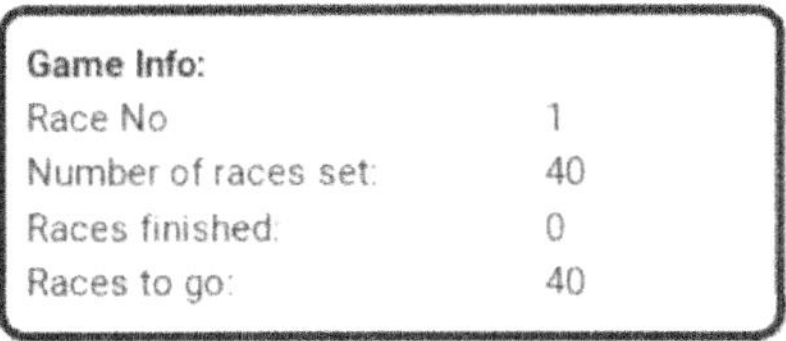


That's fine. And now run the app again and select the end by time ending condition (A). Set the time to 85 minutes (B).

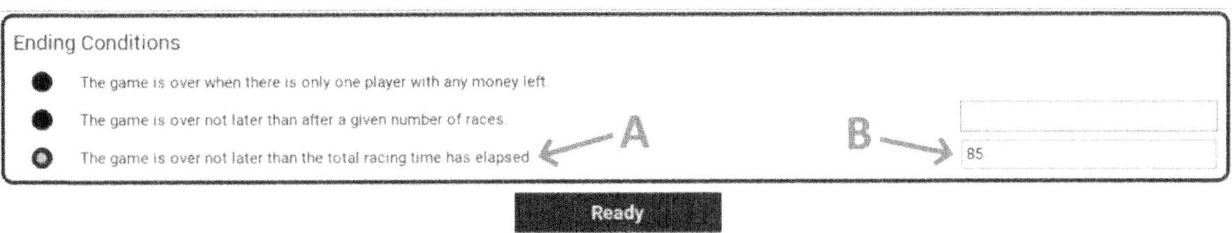


Hit the Ready button and you should see just the time-related info. This is exactly what we want for now.

Game Info:

| | |
|---|---|
| Race No | 1 |
| Time set: | 1:25:00 |
| Time elapsed: | 0:00:00 |
| Time remaining: | 1:25:00 |

# Chapter 83 – Widget Visibility and Functionality

In the previous chapter we implemented the method that sets the game. Before that we implemented methods that set the players and the slugs. But when we run the app, there are quite a few places where we see things that we shouldn't see, at least not always.

Have a look. The default number of players when the game starts is 2, so the appropriate radio button is checked (A). Why do we see the text inputs for Player 3 and Player 4 then (B)?

Or, the default ending condition is the option with money (C). So why do we see the text inputs for the other options (D)?

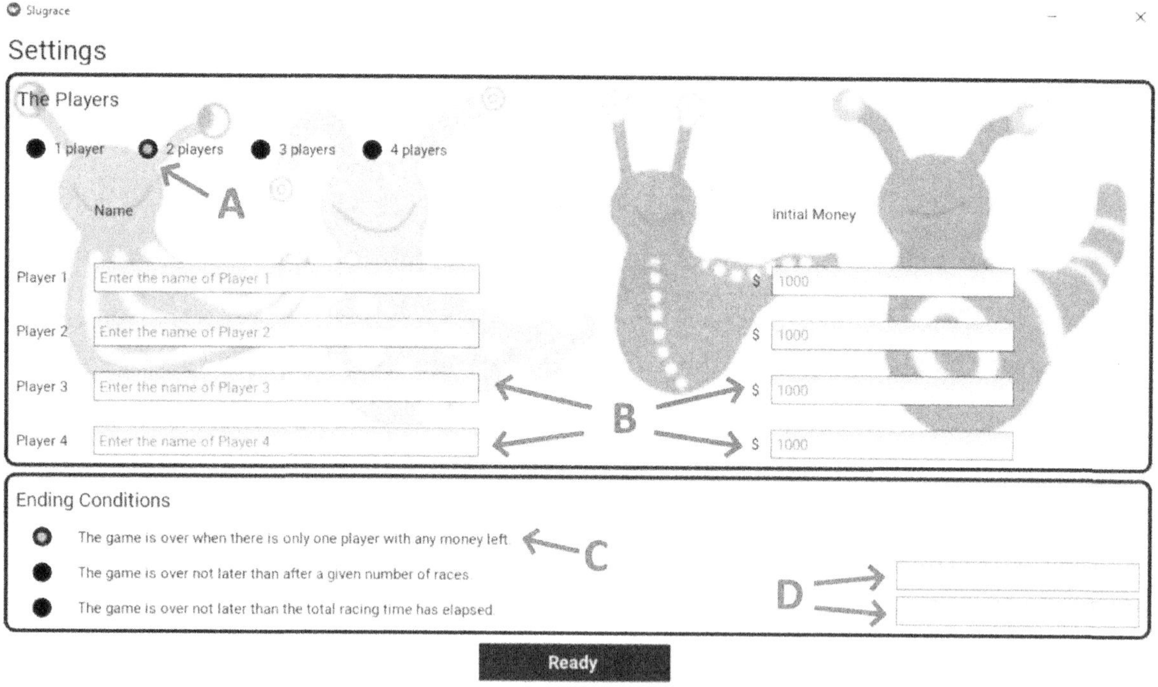


## Disabling Widgets

These are just a few examples of widgets that should be hidden somehow when we don't need them. There are more examples like that in the other screens too. But let's take care of the Settings screen first. In particular, let's focus on the time text input in the Ending Conditions area. There are two things we can do. We can disable the widget or make it fully transparent, so set its opacity to 0. There are some handy properties that we can use. The first one is **disabled**. It's a BooleanProperty, so you can set it to **True** if you want to prevent the user of the app from being able to interact with the widget. Let's disable the text input. Here's the kv file:

```
#:kivy 1.11.1
# File name: settings.kv
#:import settings settings
...
<SettingsScreen>:
    ...
        ### ENDING CONDITIONS ###
        ...
            # radio buttons
            ...
                # option 3: time
                ConditionRadioButton:
                    ...
                BoxLayout:
                    ...
                    NumInput:
                        id: _time_set

                        # Let's temporarily disable the text input.
                        disabled: True

        ### READY BUTTON ###
        ...
```

If you now run the program, you will see that you can't type in any text in the text input.

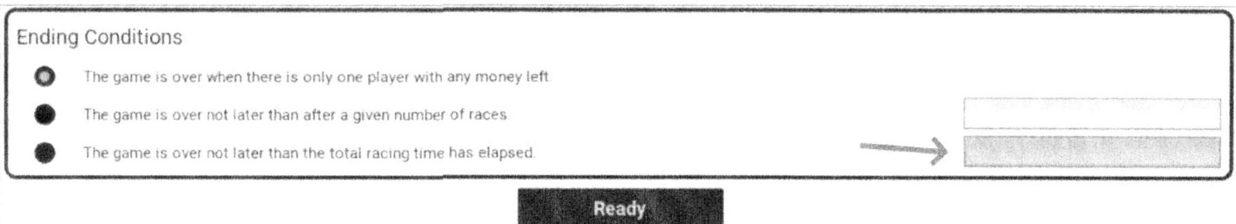


It's grayed out so that you immediately know that this text input is disabled because you are used to similar color changes of disabled widgets from other apps. Well, we can't use the text input, but we can still see it. So how can we make it invisible?

## Widget Opacity

Here another property comes in handy, **opacity**. It's a NumericProperty that defaults to **1.0** (fully opaque). If you set it to 0, the widget will be fully transparent. So, let's remove the code that disables the widget and add the code that makes it transparent:

```
#:kivy 1.11.1
# File name: settings.kv
#:import settings settings
...
<SettingsScreen>:
    ...
        ### ENDING CONDITIONS ###
        ...
            # radio buttons
            ...
                # option 3: time
                ConditionRadioButton:
                    ...
                BoxLayout:
                    ...
                    NumInput:
                        id: _time_set

                        # Let's temporarily make the widget transparent.
                        opacity: 0

        ### READY BUTTON ###
        ...
```

Let's run the app again. Now we don't see the text input anymore.

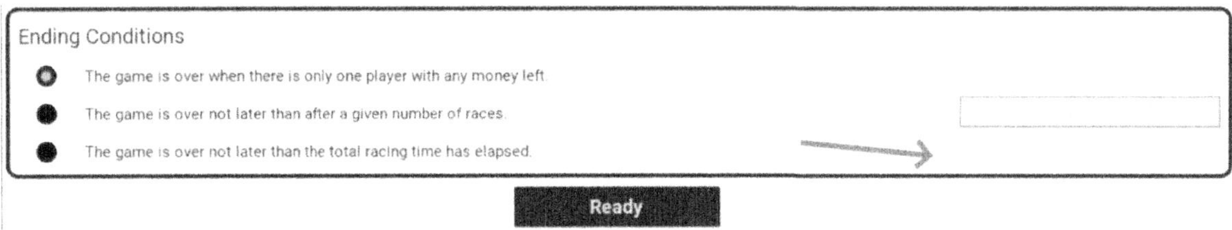


But it turns out that it's still there and we can even type in some text in it. To demonstrate this, let's select the third radio button and then type 45 in the place where we saw the text input before. Naturally, we won't see the characters while we type them in because as part of the widget they are transparent too. But believe me, they are enetered there. To see that it's true, hit the Ready button that will take you to the Race screen. As you can see, the time was set correctly.

| Game Info: | |
|---|---|
| Race No | 1 |
| Time set: | 0:45:00 |
| Time elapsed: | 0:00:00 |
| Time remaining: | 0:45:00 |

So, making a widget transparent even makes things worse because we can enter some text by accident and it may have unpredictable consequences. So, which should we choose: disabling a widget or making it transparent? Fortunately, we don't have to choose. We can do both. So, now the widget will be invisible and we won't be able to interact with it either.

# Disabling and Hiding Widgets in the Settings Screen

As we are now at the text input for the time ending condition, let's handle it first. Let's think: When do we want it to be visible (and enabled) and when do we want it to be invisible (and disabled)? Well, we want to see it and be able to interact with it only if we choose the time ending condition (which we do by checking the third radio button). If any other ending condition is chosen, the text input should be hidden.

As you remember, whenever we check one of the three radio buttons, the **set_ending_condition** method in the **Game** class is called and it sets one of the **end_by_money**, **end_by_races** and **end_by_time** properties to **True** (and the other two to **False**). So, in our case the text input should be visible only if the **end_by_time** property is set to **True**.

Setting the opacity of the text input is simple. It should be the opposite of the **disabled** property's value (which can be understood as 0 when **False** and as 1 when **True**), so whenever the widget is disabled, its opacity should 0, whenever it's enabled, its opacity should be 1. But, as the value of the **opacity** property must be a number, we'll convert it to an int. So, here's the code for our text input:

```
#:kivy 1.11.1
# File name: settings.kv
#:import settings settings
...
<SettingsScreen>:
    ...
        ### ENDING CONDITIONS ###
        ...
            # radio buttons
            ...
                # option 3: time
                ...
                BoxLayout:
                    ...
                    NumInput:
                        id: _time_set

                        # The text input should be only visible and enabled
                        # when the time ending condition is chosen.
                        disabled: not root.game.end_by_time
                        opacity: int(not self.disabled)

        ### READY BUTTON ###
        ...
```

If you now run the app, you won't see the time text input right away (A). It's hidden because the default ending condition is money (B), not time.

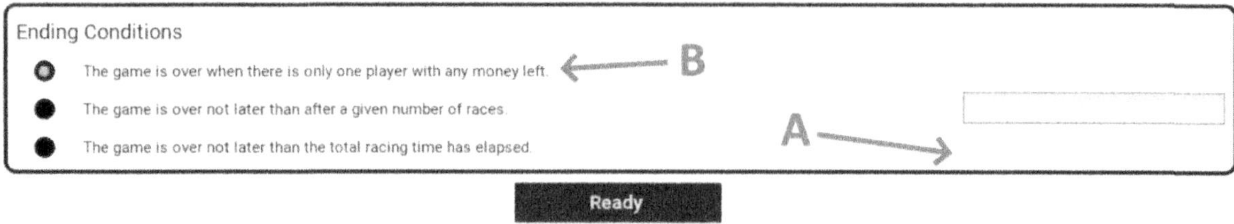


But as soon as you check the third radio button (A), it will be visible again (B), for as long as the third radio button is active.

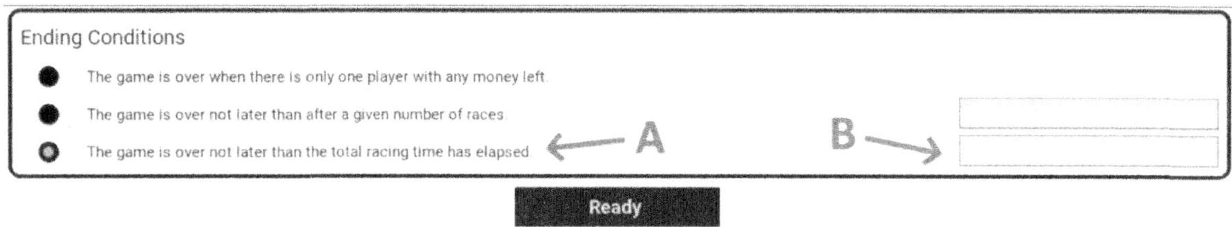


So, now you know how to hide and show widgets in Kivy. We'll be always using the two properties (**disabled** and **opacity**) together. Now, there are lots of other places that need to be handled like this, which I'm leaving for you to implement in the exercises below. And in the next chapter we'll take care of user input validation.

# It's Your Turn Now...

**EXERCISE 1**

We already handled the visibility of the time text input. Now take care of the races text input. It's going to look almost exactly the same, but the condition will be different.

**SOLUTION**

So, here's the implementation:

```
#:kivy 1.11.1
# File name: settings.kv
#:import settings settings
...
<SettingsScreen>:
    ...
        ### ENDING CONDITIONS ###
        ...
            # radio buttons
            ...
                # option 2: races
                ...
                BoxLayout:
```

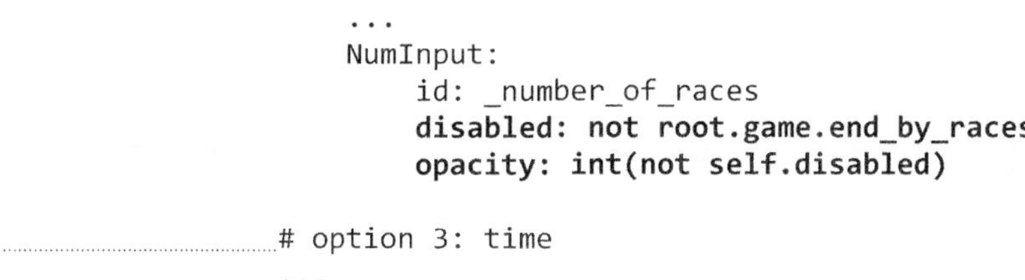

```
        ...
        NumInput:
            id: _number_of_races
            disabled: not root.game.end_by_races
            opacity: int(not self.disabled)

    # option 3: time
    ...
```

Now the races text input won't be visible when you start the game.

It will become visible only when you you check the second radio button.

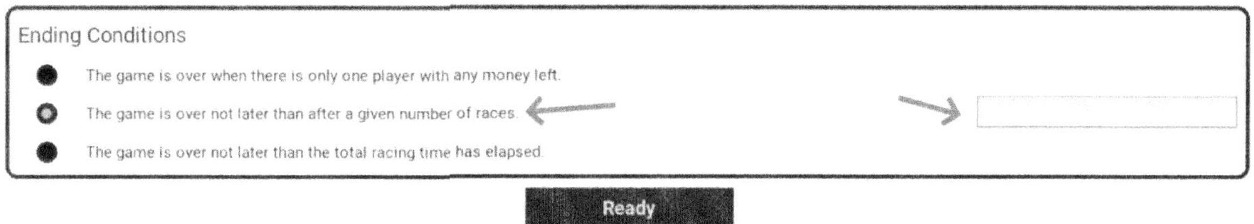


**EXERCISE 2**

Although there is no text input associated with the first ending condition, there is one situation when we don't want to see the radio button and its accompanying label themselves. This is when there is only one player in the game because the condition is that the game should end when there's only one player with any money left. So, if we decide to have only one player in the game, this condition doesn't make sense. That's why we want it to be disabled and invisible whenever the **`number_of_players`** property in the **`Game`** class is set to 1.

You can set the **`disabled`** and **`opacity`** properties on the **`ConditionRadioButton`** and then you can use just the **`opacity`** property on the **`RegularLabel`** instance below (we don't need to disable a label, there's no way to interact with it anyway) and set it to the same value as that of the radio button. In order to be able to reference the radio button, we'll need an id, so set the radio button's **`id`** property to **`_moneyButton`** and then use it in the RegularLabel.

## SOLUTION

So, here's the code:

```
#:kivy 1.11.1
# File name: settings.kv
#:import settings settings
...
<SettingsScreen>:
    ...
        ### ENDING CONDITIONS ###
        ...
            # radio buttons
            ...
                # option 1: money
                ConditionRadioButton:
                    id: _moneyButton
                    active: root.game.end_by_money
                    on_active: if self.active: root.game.set_ending_condition('money')
                    # Here we're taking care of the radio buttons's visibility.
                    disabled: root.game.number_of_players == 1
                    opacity: int(not self.disabled)
                RegularLabel:
                    text: ...
                    # The label should be visible only when the radio button is visible.
                    opacity: _moneyButton.opacity
                # option 2: races
                ...
```

If you check the one player option (A), the end by money option is no longer available (B).

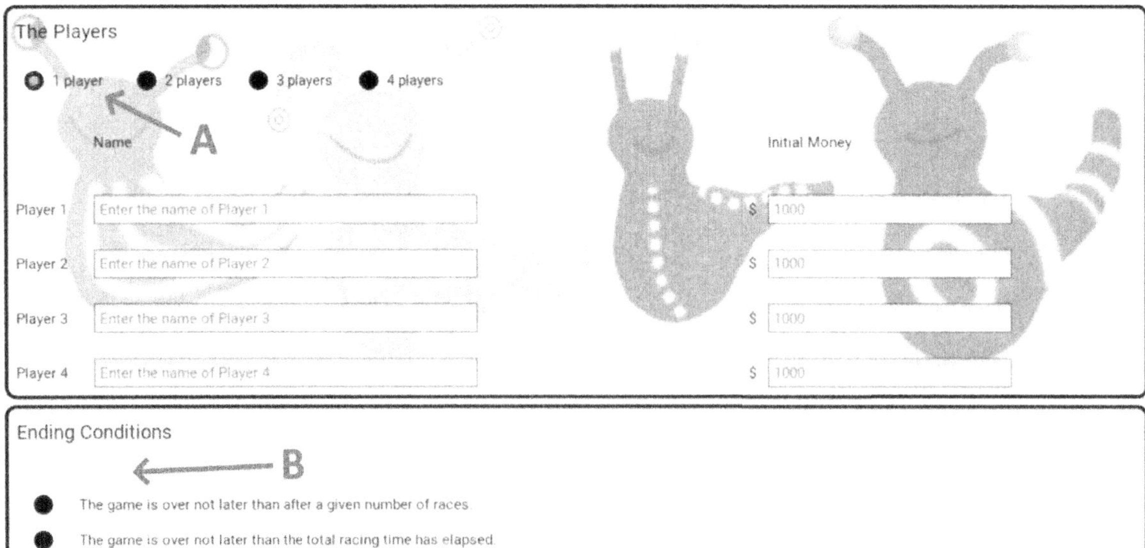

**EXERCISE 3**

Now we must take care of the player settings widgets. At this moment we always see the player settings for four players. But we want to see only as many as many players there are, so for example if we check the two players radio button, we should only see the player settings widgets for the first two players. If we check the one player option, only the first player settings widget should be visible, and so on.

We're going to implement the **disabled** property on each instance individually, but the **opacity** property will be set in the **PlayerSettings** rule. It just should be the opposite of the **disabled** property (just like before, don't forget to convert it to an int).

Now, as far as the **disabled** property is concerned, scroll down your kv code until you find the four **PlayerSettings** instances. The first instance (with the id **_player1**) should be enabled at all times because there always must be at least one player. The second instance should be disabled if the number of players is less than 2, and so on.

**SOLUTION**

So, here's the code:

```
#:kivy 1.11.1
# File name: settings.kv
#:import settings settings
...
<PlayerSettings>:
    name: _player_name.text
    player_initial_money: _player_initial_money.text

    # If the widget is disabled, it should be transparent, and vice versa.
    opacity: int(not self.disabled)

    Regular80x30Label:
        ...
<SettingsScreen>:
    ...
        ### THE PLAYERS ###
        ...
                # the players rows
                # player 1
                PlayerSettings:
                    id: _player1
                    label_text: 'Player 1'

                # player 2
                PlayerSettings:
                    id: _player2
                    label_text: 'Player 2'

                    # This widget should be disabled if the number of
```

```
                # players is less than 2.
                disabled: root.game.number_of_players < 2

            # player 3
            PlayerSettings:
                id: _player3
                label_text: 'Player 3'

                # This widget should be disabled if the number of
                # players is less than 3.
                disabled: root.game.number_of_players < 3

            # player 4
            PlayerSettings:
                id: _player4
                label_text: 'Player 4'

                # This widget should be disabled if the number of
                # players is less than 4.
                disabled: root.game.number_of_players < 4

        ### ENDING CONDITIONS ###
        ...
```

Now when you run the app with the default two players, only the player settings widgets for those two players will be visible.

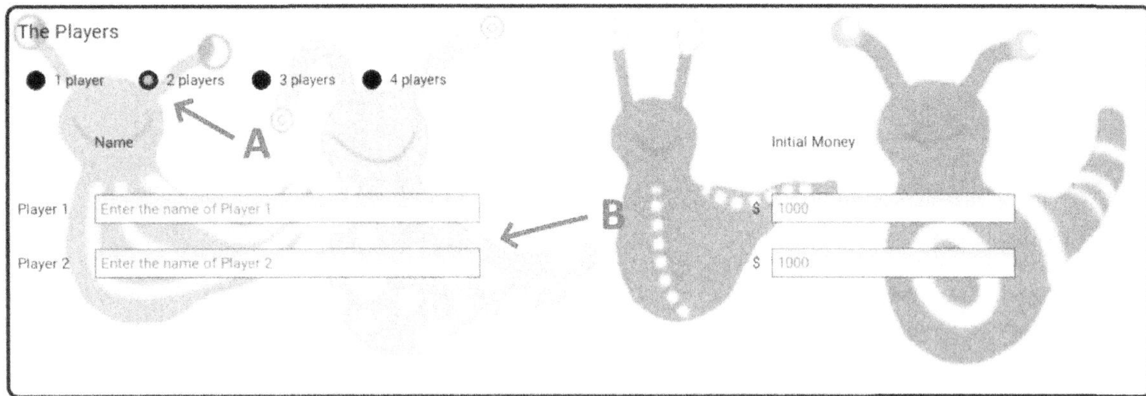


Now check the other radio buttons and watch the player settings widgets show and hide depending on the number of players.

**EXERCISE 4**

There is one more widget in the Settings screen we must take care of. It's the Ready button. Actually, we want the button to be visible all the time, but we don't want it to be enabled all the time.

So, add the **disabled** property to the button and set its value. The button should be disabled if quite a few conditions are met simultaneously, so the conditional expression should be pretty long. Before you write the expression, though, we must set the three ending conditions radio buttons' ids because we'll have to reference the radio buttons. We already set the first button's id to **_moneyButton**, set the other two to **_racesButton** and **_timeButton**.

Now, here are the pairs of conditions that, if met simultaneously, will disable the Ready button. The button will be disabled if both conditions in any pair of conditions are met. Use the **and** and **or** operators to join them accordingly:

- the **_racesButton** is active and the races text input's text is an empty string,

- the **_timeButton** is active and the time text input's text is an empty string,

- the **_moneyButton** is active and also disabled (this happens when there's only one player and we didn't check any other ending condition before).

## SOLUTION

Now, here's the code:

```
#:kivy 1.11.1
# File name: settings.kv
#:import settings settings
...
<SettingsScreen>:
    ...
        ### ENDING CONDITIONS ###
        ...
            # radio buttons
            GridLayout:
                rows: 3
                spacing: 10

                # option 1: money
                ...
                # option 2: races
                ConditionRadioButton:
                    # We'll need to reference the button, hence the id.
                    id: _racesButton

                    active: root.game.end_by_races
                    ...
                # option 3: time
                ConditionRadioButton:
                    # We'll need to reference the button, hence the id.
                    id: _timeButton
```

```
                    active: root.game.end_by_time
                    ...
        ### READY BUTTON ###
        RedButton:
            text: 'Ready'

            # Here are the situations when the button should be disabled.
            disabled: ((_racesButton.active and _number_of_races.text == '') or (_timeBut
ton.active and _time_set.text == '') or (_moneyButton.active and _moneyButton.disabled))

            on_press:
                ...
```

If you now run the app and, for example, select the second ending condition (A), but do not enter the number of races (B), the button will be disabled (C).

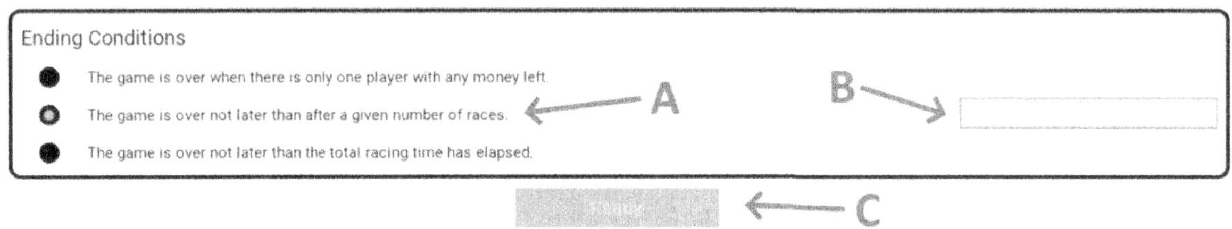


This is because the races radio button is active and the text input is empty, so both conditions in the first pair of conditions are met. If you now type something in (A), the button will be enabled (B).

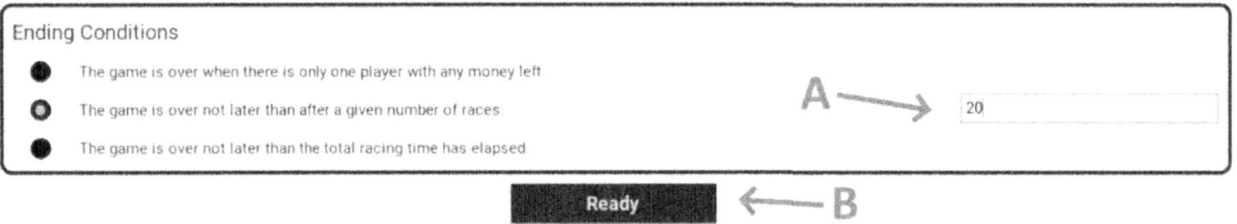


Let's test the second pair of conditions. This time let's select the time radio button (A) and leave the text input empty (B). The button is disabled (C).

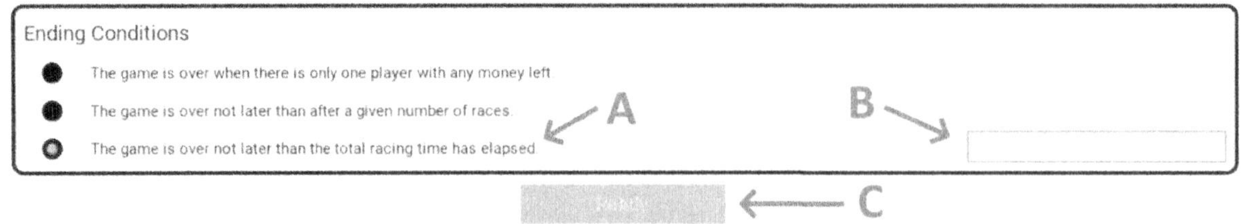


Again, the button will be enabled (B) when you enter some text (A).

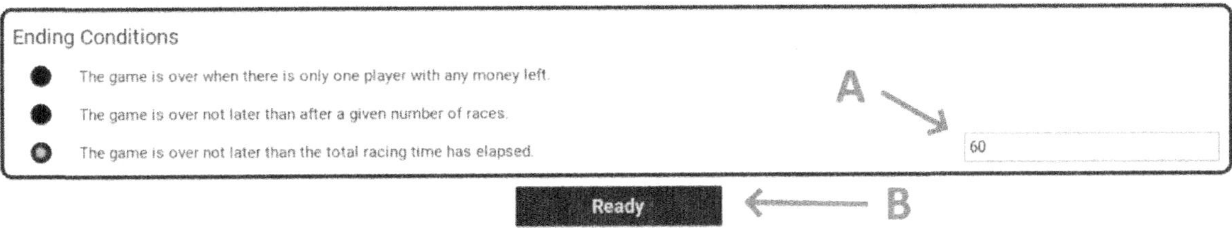


Finally, let's see what happens if the two conditions in the last pair of conditions are met. This time let's select the one player option (A). Now the money button becomes invisible (B) and the Ready button is disabled (C).

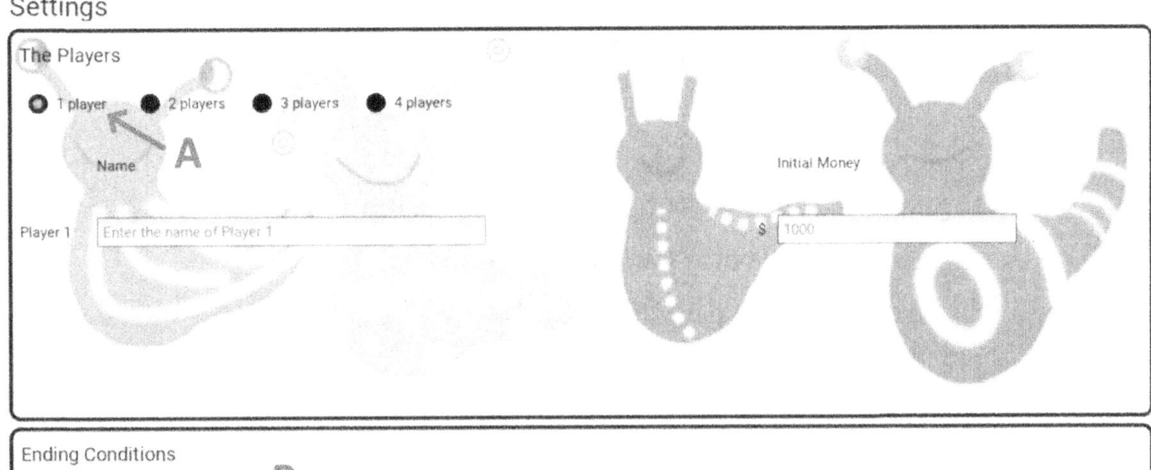

**EXERCISE 5**

That's it as far as the Settings screen is concerned. Now let's move on to the Race screen. There are two places we must take care of, the Game Info area and the Players' Stats area. Let's start with the former. As you remember, the time info is displayed if the game should end by money or by time. We only want it to be visible in the latter case. So, open the **race.kv** file and scroll down until you see the Game Info section.

The Game Info area contains four BoxLayouts. The first one contains the race number info and should be visible at all times. The following three BoxLayouts contain info about the races or the time of the game, depending on which ending condition was chosen. Add the **`opacity`** property to the three BoxLayouts. Set its value so that it's 1 only if the ending condition is not the end by money option. You can use the **`end_by_money`** property defined in the **`Game`** class and convert it to an int. So, the **`opacity`** property must be placed on all three BoxLayouts.

## SOLUTION

Now, here's the code:

```
#:kivy 1.11.1
# File name: race.kv
#:import race race
...
<RaceScreen>:
    ...
            # Game Info
            ...
                BoxLayout:
                    RegularLabel:
                        size_hint: (2.5, 1)
                        text: 'Race No'
                    RegularLabel:
                        text: '1'

                # This and the following two BoxLayouts should be only visible
                # if the ending condition is not end_by_money.
                BoxLayout:
                    opacity: int(not root.game.end_by_money)
                    RegularLabel:
                        ...
                BoxLayout:
                    opacity: int(not root.game.end_by_money)
                    RegularLabel:
                        ...
                BoxLayout:
                    opacity: int(not root.game.end_by_money)
                    RegularLabel:
                        ...
            # Slugs' Stats
            ...
```

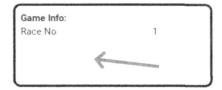

If you now run the app and leave the end by money ending condition on, you won't see the time info when you press the Ready button and move to the Race screen.

Now try out the other two ending conditions. You should now only see relevant information. So, let's run the app again and set the end by races condition and set the number of races to 50. You will see the races set in the Game Info panel.

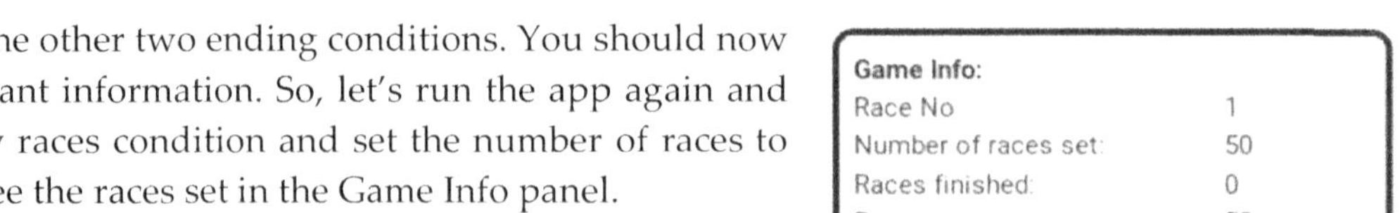

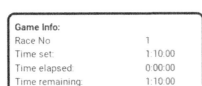


And now let's run the app one more time and choose the time ending condition. Let's set the time of the game to 70 minutes. You will now see just the time-related data.

**EXERCISE 6**

The second area in the Race screen that we must take care of is the Players' Stats area. This area contains just labels, like the Game Info area, so again, we don't have to disable anything, but we have to set the opacity of the strings to 1 or 0, depending on how many players there are. So, the first PlayerStats widget should be always visible because there's always at least one player. The second PlayerStats widget should be only visible if the number of players is greater than or equal to 2. The other two PlayerStats widgets should be set accordingly.

**SOLUTION**

So, here's the code:

```
#:kivy 1.11.1
# File name: race.kv
#:import race race
...
<RaceScreen>:
    ...
            # Players' Stats
            ...
                PlayerStats:
                    name: root.game.player1.name
                    money: root.game.player1.money

                PlayerStats:
                    name: root.game.player2.name
                    money: root.game.player2.money

                    # This widget should be only visible if
                    # there are at least two players.
                    opacity: int(root.game.number_of_players >= 2)

                PlayerStats:
                    name: root.game.player3.name
                    money: root.game.player3.money

                    # This widget should be only visible if
                    # there are at least three players.
                    opacity: int(root.game.number_of_players >= 3)

                PlayerStats:
                    name: root.game.player4.name
                    money: root.game.player4.money

                    # This widget should be only visible if
                    # there are four players.
                    opacity: int(root.game.number_of_players == 4)

            # Buttons
            ...
```

If you now run the app and set the number of players to, say, 3, you should only see three players in the Players' Stats area in the Race screen as well.

| Players' Stats | |
|---|---|
| Player 1 | has $1000 |
| Player 2 | has $1000 |
| Player 3 | has $1000 |

**EXERCISE 7**

We're done with the Race screen. Let's move on to the Bets screen. Here we have four Bet widgets. Again, the first one should be always visible. The other three not necessarily, it should depend on how many players there are. So, set each **`Bet`** instance's (except the first one) **`disabled`** property accordingly and then set the **`opacity`** property in the **`Bet`** class rule to the opposite of **`disabled`** (don't forget to convert it to an int).

**SOLUTION**

So, here's the code:

```
#:kivy 1.11.1
# File name: bets.kv
#:import bets bets

<Bet>:
    spacing: 10

    # If the widget is disabled, it should be transparent, and vice versa.
    opacity: int(not self.disabled)

    RegularLabel:
        ...
<BetsScreen>:
    ...
        ### PLAYER BETS ###
        ...
            # player 1
            ...
            # player 2
            Bet:
                ...
                player_group: 'player2'

                # This widget should be disabled if there
                # are less than two players.
                disabled: root.game.number_of_players < 2

            # player 3
            Bet:
                ...
                player_group: 'player3'

                # This widget should be disabled if there
                # are less than three players.
                disabled: root.game.number_of_players < 3
```

```
            # player 4
            Bet:
                ...
                player_group: 'player4'

                # This widget should be disabled if there
                # are less than four players.
                disabled: root.game.number_of_players < 4

        ### GO BUTTON ###
        ...
```

Now if you run the app, the correct number of **Bet** widgets will be visible. Here we can see only one because in the Settings screen we set the number of players to one.

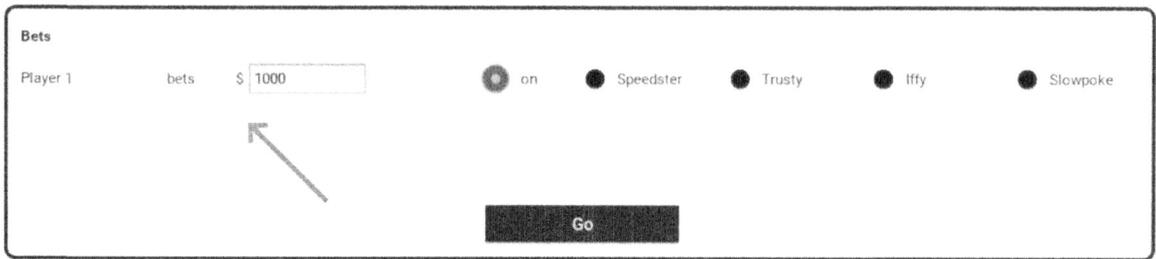


### EXERCISE 8

Finally, the Results screen. Here you should do exactly the same as in the Bets screen. Set the **disabled** property individually on each **Result** instance and then set the **opacity** property to its opposite in the **Result** class rule.

### SOLUTION

Here's the code:

```
#:kivy 1.11.1
# File name: results.kv
#:import results results

<Result>:
    # If the widget is disabled, it should be transparent, and vice versa.
    opacity: int(not self.disabled)

    RegularLabel:
        ...
<ResultsScreen>:
    ...
        ### PLAYER RESULTS ###
        BoxLayout:
            orientation: 'vertical'
```

```
                # player 1
                ...
                # player 2
                Result:
                    ...
                    odds: 1.59

                    # This widget should be disabled if there
                    # are less than two players.
                    disabled: root.game.number_of_players < 2

                # player 3
                Result:
                    ...
                    odds: 2.24

                    # This widget should be disabled if there
                    # are less than three players.
                    disabled: root.game.number_of_players < 3

                # player 4
                Result:
                    ...
                    odds: 1.85

                    # This widget should be disabled if there
                    # are less than four players.
                    disabled: root.game.number_of_players < 4

            ### NEXT RACE BUTTON ###
            ...
```

And now let's run the app and set the number of players to three. Now only three **Result** instances will be visible in the Results screen.

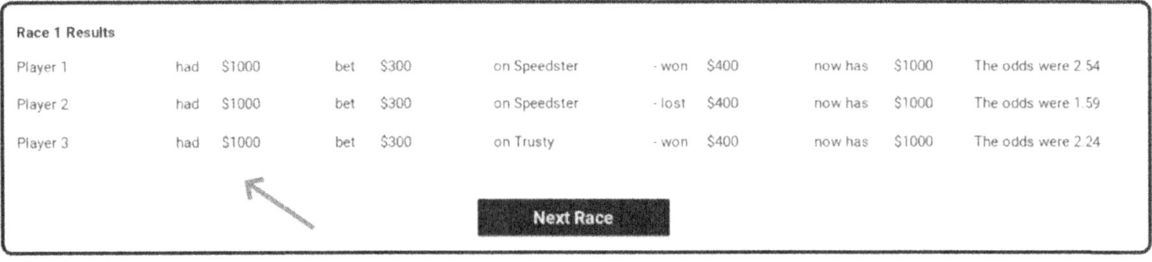

# Chapter 84 – User Input Validation

In the previous chapter we handled the visibility and functionality (whether they are enabled or disabled) of the widgets. In this chapter we'll be talking about user input validation. Now the problem is that there is no validation at all. This means the user can enter a text in the text input that should contain the initial money of a player. Or, a player can bet more money on a slug than they have. Why not? There are no restrictions after all.

So, as you can see, we must take care of input validation as soon as possible. In particular, we want to make sure that:

- the name of a player may contain up to 10 characters,

- only digits may be entered in the initial money text inputs,

- the initial money must be between $10 and $5000,

- if the game should end after a given number of races, the number of races must be between 1 and 100,

- if the game should end after a given amount of time, the time must be between 1 and 120 minutes,

- a player can bet no more on a slug than they have and no less than $1.

So, these are the issues that we're going to fix in this chapter, some of which I'm leaving for you to handle as an exercise. Let's start with the names of the players.

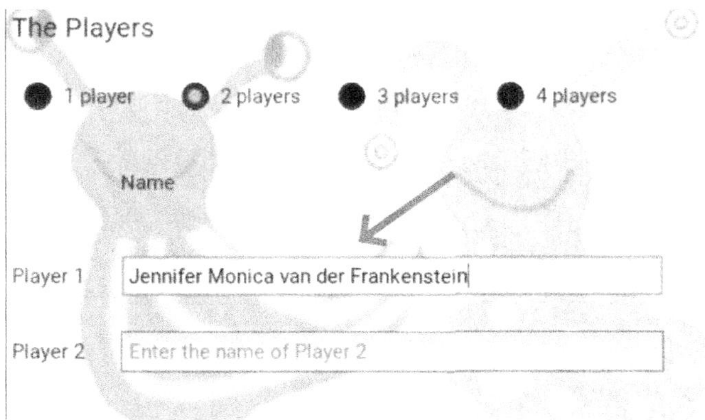


## Maximum String Length for Players' Names

If you now run the application, you can set the players' name to whatever you like. Let's enter a long name.

In the Settings screen it looks OK, but in the Race screen it needs two lines to be printed.

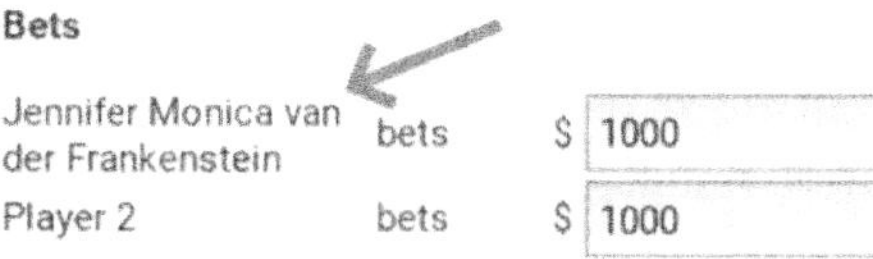

Let's make sure that each name is on one line. This will be the case if we limit its length, like for example to ten characters. Before we actually do it, let's give the user a hint about it. As we already have a hint text with general information about what kind of data is expected, we can just add the information to the label that now reads **'Name'**. So, modify the label text like so:

```
#:kivy 1.11.1
# File name: settings.kv
#:import settings settings
...
<SettingsScreen>:
    ...
        ### THE PLAYERS ###
        ...
            # Player Name and Initial Money Setup
            ...
                    # name header
                    RegularLabel:
                        text: "Name (max. 10 characters)"
                        size_hint_x: None
                        ...
```

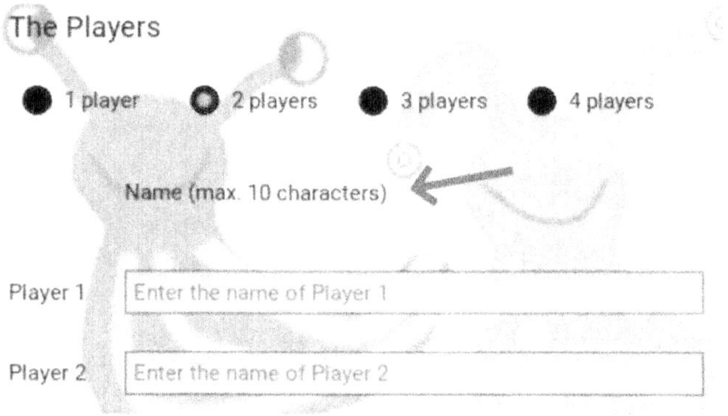

Now when you run the program, you will immediately know how long the name should be.

Naturally, this is just text. And now let's implement the limitation in code. We can implement it in the widget class itself. The **NameInput** class is defined in the **widgets.kv** file:

```
#:kivy 1.11.1
# File name: widgets.kv
...
### TEXTINPUTS ###
<NameInput@TextInput>:
    multiline: False
    size_hint: None, None
    size: 400, 30

<NumInput@TextInput>:
    ...
```

The best place to add some logic is the corresponding Python file. We already created the **widgets.py** file, but it's empty now.

So, let's add the **NameInput** class there and let's move the inheritance from the kv file to the Python file. Now the **widgets.py** file looks like so:

```
# File name: widgets.py

# NameInput inherits from TextInput, so we need this class.
from kivy.uix.textinput import TextInput

class NameInput(TextInput):
    pass
```

This requires two changes in the kv file, though. First, we have to import the **widgets.py** file to the kv file. Second, we must remove the inheritance code from the kv file. Now the kv file looks like so:

```
#:kivy 1.11.1
# File name: widgets.kv
#:import widgets widgets

### LABELS ###
...
### TEXTINPUTS ###
<NameInput>:
    multiline: False
    ...
```

And now, finally, let's add the string length limitation.

We already set the **max_name_length** variable in app scope, so in the **SlugraceApp** class:

```
# File name: main.py
...
class SlugraceApp(App):
    # General Settings
    initial_money_min = 10
    initial_money_max = 5000
    max_name_length = 10

    def build(self):
        ...
```

We're going to need access to it now. As you remember, you can easily access stuff defined in the **SlugraceApp** class using the **app** variable, but it only works in kv code. But you also know that we can get the access from a Python file, which we already did in the **SettingsScreen** class when we needed access to the other two variables defined here, **initial_money_min** and **initial_money_max**. We then imported the **App** class and used its **get_running_app** method. This is exactly what we are going to do now in the **widgets.py** file:

```
# File name: widgets.py

from kivy.uix.textinput import TextInput

# We need the App class.
from kivy.app import App

class NameInput(TextInput):
    # In the __init__ method we'll get access to the running
    # app and assign it to the app variable.
    def __init__(self, **kwargs):
        super().__init__(**kwargs)
        self.app = App.get_running_app()
```

To validate the text as it's being entered, we'll override the **insert_text** method defined in the

**TextInput** class. This method is used to filter text anytime you enter something into a text input. So, this is the right place to control the text that's being entered. Here the overridden version of the method will compare the length of the string with the value of the **max_name_length** variable defined in the app class:

```
# File name: widgets.py

from kivy.uix.textinput import TextInput
from kivy.app import App

class NameInput(TextInput):
    def __init__(self, **kwargs):
        super().__init__(**kwargs)
        self.app = App.get_running_app()

    # Here's the method that will filter the text entered into the text input.
    def insert_text(self, substring, from_undo=False):
        if len(self.text + substring) <= self.app.max_name_length:
            return super(NameInput, self).insert_text(substring, from_undo = from_undo)
```

Now, if you run the app, you won't be able to enter a name that is longer than 10 characters. Try it out with the same long name that we used before. Only the first ten characters (including the space character) will fit in.

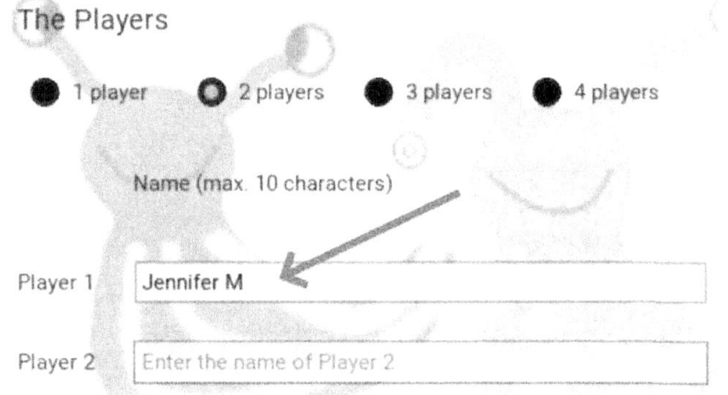


## Only Digits in the Initial Money Text Inputs

Now have a look at the initial money text inputs in the Settings screen. Here I'm entering some text that can by no means be interpreted as a number.

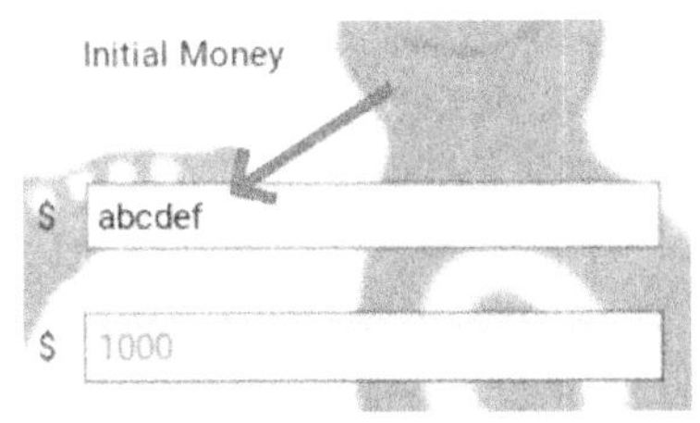


If you now hit the Ready button, the program will crash. So, this shouldn't be possible. Only digits should be allowed.

And one more thing, we want the values to be only from a certain range.

Actually, there are more issues here than just the two I just mentioned, but let's address them one by one. Let's start by modifying the label text (now reading **'Initial Money'**) above the text inputs, though:

```
#:kivy 1.11.1
# File name: settings.kv
#:import settings settings
...
<SettingsScreen>:
    ...
        ### THE PLAYERS ###
        ...
            # Player Name and Initial Money Setup
            ...
                    # money header
                    RegularLabel:
                        text: "Initial Money ($10 - $5000)"

                # the players rows
                ...
```

Now the user will know right away what values are allowed. And how do we make sure that only digits are entered?

This is pretty simple. Actually, we want it to work for both the **NumInput** and **BetInput** classes.

As the latter inherits from the former, let's put the validation code in the **NumInput** class. So, in the **widgets.kv** file scroll down until you find the **NumInput** rule.

We're going to add some logic to the class in Python code, so we'll move the inheritance there in a minute. You could also leave it here, but make sure it's only in one place.

```
#:kivy 1.11.1
# File name: widgets.kv
#:import widgets widgets
...
<NumInput@TextInput>:
    multiline: False
    size_hint: None, None
    size: 250, 30

<BetInput@NumInput>:
    ...
```

But first we'll add the **input_filter** property. It's an ObjectProperty defined in the **TextInput** class. It can be set to a couple values like **'int'** or **'float'**, for example. The former is what interests us here, because it means that only digits will be accepted. If we set it to **'float'**, we could also add a single decimal point, which is not what we want. We want the money be in integer numbers only. So, let's add the property and set it to **'int'**:

```
#:kivy 1.11.1
# File name: widgets.kv
#:import widgets widgets
...
<NumInput@TextInput>:
    multiline: False
    size_hint: None, None
    size: 250, 30
    input_filter: 'int'  # only digits accepted

<BetInput@NumInput>:
    ...
```

Let's run the app and try entering digits and letters. You will no longer be able to enter the latter.

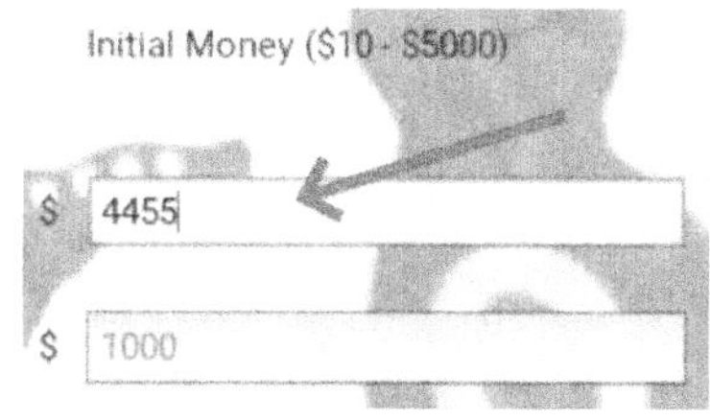

So, now only digits can be entered. But there is another problem. You can also enter the minus sign. We want the initial money to be a positive number, so let's use the **insert_text** method that we used to limit the length of a player's name again. This time it will pass any character except the minus sign. We will implement this in Python, so we have to add this class in the **widgets.py** file. This is the moment, too, to move the inheritance to the Python file. Now the kv file looks like this:

```
#:kivy 1.11.1
# File name: widgets.kv
#:import widgets widgets
...
<NumInput>:
    multiline: False
    size_hint: None, None
    size: 250, 30
    input_filter: 'int'  # only digits accepted

<BetInput@NumInput>:
    ...
```

And here's the Python file:

```
# File name: widgets.py
...
class NameInput(TextInput):
    ...
    def insert_text(self, substring, from_undo=False):
        ...
class NumInput(TextInput):
    def insert_text(self, substring, from_undo=False):
        return (super().insert_text(substring, from_undo=from_undo) if substring != '-'
                else super().insert_text('', from_undo=from_undo))
```

Now you won't be able to type in the minus sign. So, at this moment we can only enter digits. But we can enter any number, which is not what we want. The initial money should be in the range between $10 and $5000. Let's take care of this next.

# Limited Value Range for the Initial Money Text Inputs

Let's start by adding two NumericProperties to the **NumInput** class with the self-explanatory names **min_value** and **max_value**. Then we'll add the **on_text_validate** event defined in the **TextInput** class, which is triggered whenever you hit Enter in a single-line text input. It also defocuses the widget.

The **on_text_validate** event will set the **text** property of the text input to the lower or upper limit of the range if the number you entered is outside the range.

So, there are three possible scenarios:

- if the number you entered is within the range, nothing will happen,

- if the number is less than **min_value**, the latter will replace the former,

- if the number is greater than **max_value**, the latter will replace the former.

Here's the Python file with all necessary changes:

```
# File name: widgets.py

from kivy.uix.textinput import TextInput
from kivy.app import App

# We need the NumericProperty class.
from kivy.properties import NumericProperty
...
class NumInput(TextInput):
    # Here are the two NumericProperties.
    min_value = NumericProperty()
    max_value = NumericProperty()

    def insert_text(self, substring, from_undo=False):
        return (super().insert_text(substring, from_undo=from_undo) if substring != '-'
                else super().insert_text('', from_undo=from_undo))

    # Here's the method that will ensure the number is between min_value and max_value.
    def on_text_validate(self):
        if self.text:
            self.text = str(max(self.min_value, min(int(self.text), self.max_value)))
```

As you can see, both **min_value** and **max_value** now default to 0. I didn't use 10 and 5000 as the default values because we're going to use **NumInput** instances in more than one location in our project and the limits will be different each time. So, let's go to the **settings.kv** file and set the **min_value** and **max_value** properties there. In the **PlayerSettings** rule add the following code:

```
#:kivy 1.11.1
# File name: settings.kv
#:import settings settings
...
<PlayerSettings>:
    ...
    BoxLayout:
        ...
        DollarLabel:
        NumInput:
            id: _player_initial_money
            hint_text: '1000'

            min_value: app.initial_money_min
            max_value: app.initial_money_max

<SettingsScreen>:
    ...
```

Now if you run the app and enter a number between 10 and 5000, it will stay after you hit Enter. If you enter 3, for example, which is less than the minimum value of 10, the text will change to 10. If you enter 6000, for example, which in turn is greater than the maximum value of 5000, the text will change to 5000. This is great. But there is another problem. Suppose you enter a number from outside the range, like 6000 (A), and do not hit Enter, but click in the next NumInput (B) instead.

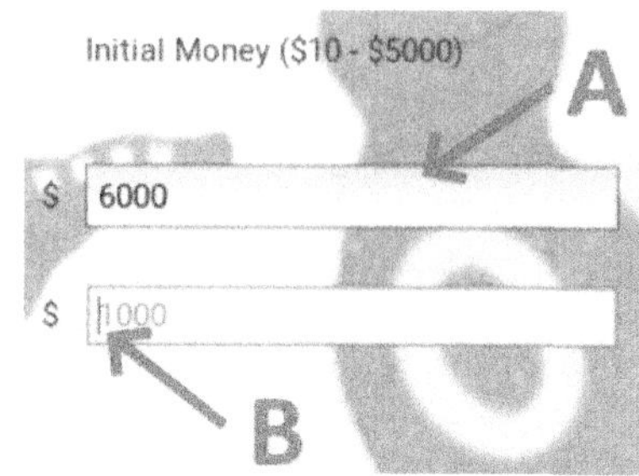


This suggests the first player will start the game with $6000. But if you now hit the Ready button, you will see that this is not the case. The first player's initial money was validated after all, but this is counter-intuitive. It would be more intuitive if the value in the text input changed not only when you hit Enter, but each time the text input loses focus. We can achieve that by means of the **on_focus** event that is triggered whenever focus changes, so whenever a text input gets into or out of focus. All we want the method to do is call the **on_text_validate** method each time a text input loses focus:

```
# File name: widgets.py
...
class NumInput(TextInput):
    min_value = NumericProperty()
    max_value = NumericProperty()

    def insert_text(self, substring, from_undo=False):
        ...
    def on_text_validate(self):
        ...
    # This method is called whenever focus changes.
    def on_focus(self, instance, value):
        # So, if the widget loses focus...
        if not value:
            # ... it should validate its text.
            self.on_text_validate()
```

Let's run the app again, enter 6000 for the first player and then click on the initial money input for the second player. Now the text in the former will immediately change to 5000.

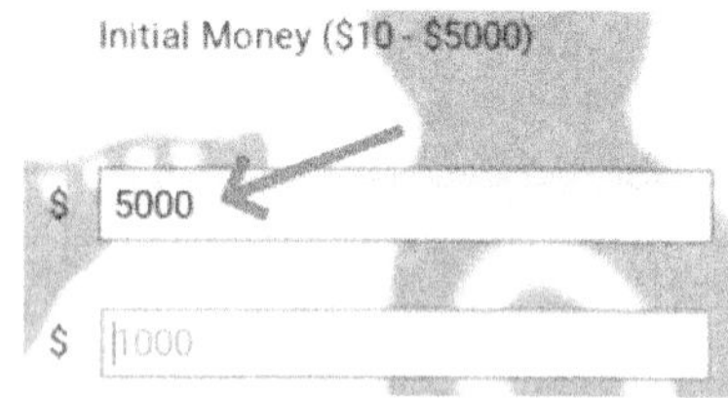


That's almost it. Almost, because we handled only some of the text inputs. I'll leave the rest for you. And in the next chapter we'll handle the bet sliders.

## It's Your Turn Now...

At the beginning of this chapter you could see a TO DO list with all the stuff we're going to handle as far as user input validation is concerned.

If we now remove those which we already handled, we'll be left with the following:

- if the game should end after a given number of races, the number of races must be between 1 and 100,

- if the game should end after a given amount of time, the time must be between 1 and 120 minutes,

- a player can bet no more on a slug than they have and no less than $1.

Now you know what the three exercises below will be all about. Your task will be to implement user input validation so that the requirements are met.

### EXERCISE 1

Let's start with the number of races that you can set in the Settings screen. This is what you enter in the NumInput that becomes visible if you check the end by races radio button. The value should be in the range from 1 to 100. Also, to make life easier for the user of the app, add the following hint text to the text input:

```
"Set number of races (1-100)"
```

There is one more problem you must address. Look at the **on_press** event on the Ready button, and, in particular, at the **set_game** method:

```
#:kivy 1.11.1
# File name: settings.kv
#:import settings settings
...
<SettingsScreen>:
    ...
        ### READY BUTTON ###
        RedButton:
            ...
            on_press:
                root.set_players(root.players)
                root.set_slugs()
                root.set_game(_number_of_races.text, _time_set.text)
                root.manager.current = 'racescreen'
```

It takes two arguments. The first one is the text entered in the races NumInput, the second is the text entered in the time NumInput. Although we're at the former right now, let's handle them both right away. The problem is that if you enter for example 200 races, which is more than allowed, and hit the Ready button, the first argument passed to the **set_game** method will be 200 and in the Race screen, in the Game Info area you will see that the number of races is 200. This happens because the text is read from the text input before the text input loses focus.

As you remember, we have defined the **on_focus** method so that it validates the input. So, all you have to do is defocus the two widgets before the text is read from them.

To this end, add a method in the **SettingsScreen** class that will do just that. Name it **defocus**. It should take an arbitrary number of parameters (use the * notation) and then, in a loop, set each widget's **focus** property to **False**. Then, in the kv file, just before the **set_game** method is called, call the **defocus** method and pass the two NumInputs (races and time) as arguments. After this is done, the text inputs will lose focus, the text will be validated and the correct number of races will be set.

## SOLUTION

So, looks like pretty much to do. Here's the **settings.py** file where you should have added the **defocus** method:

```
# File name: settings.py
...
class SettingsScreen(Screen):
    ...
    def set_game(self, number_of_races, time_set):
        ...

    # The method will make the widgets passed as arguments lose focus.
    def defocus(self, *widgets):
        for widget in widgets:
            widget.focus = False
```

And now the settings.kv file:

```
#:kivy 1.11.1
# File name: settings.kv
#:import settings settings
...
<SettingsScreen>:
    ...
        ### ENDING CONDITIONS ###
        ...
            # radio buttons
            ...
                # option 2: races
                ...
                    NumInput:
                        ...
                        opacity: int(not self.disabled)

                        # Here's the hint text.
                        hint_text: "Set number of races (1-100)"

                        # There can be between 1 and 100 races.
                        min_value: 1
```

```
                    max_value: 100

            # option 3: time
            ...
    ### READY BUTTON ###
    RedButton:
        ...
        on_press:
            root.set_players(root.players)
            root.set_slugs()

            # Here we're calling the defocus method. It should defocus the races
            # NumInput and the time NumInput.
            root.defocus(_number_of_races, _time_set)

            root.set_game(_number_of_races.text, _time_set.text)
            root.manager.current = 'racescreen'
```

If you now run the app, check the end by races radio button, enter a number of races greater than 100, like for example 200, and hit the Ready button, it will be reset to 100 anyway.

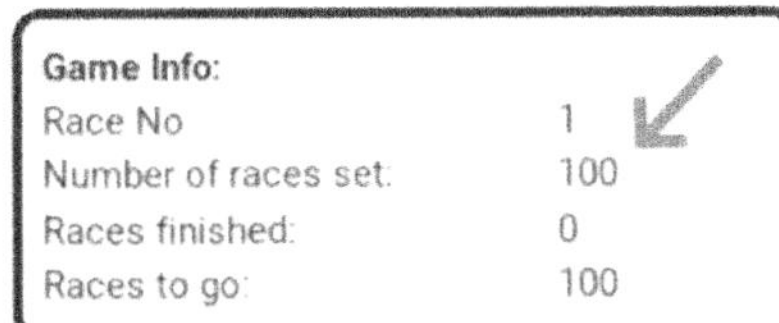

Game Info:
Race No
1
Number of races set:
100
Races finished:
0
Races to go:
100


**EXERCISE2**

With all the code that we added in the previous exercise, this exercise should be a piece of cake. This time make sure the time entered in the time NumInput is between 1 and 120 minutes. Also, add the following hint text:

```
"Set max. game time (1-120 min)"
```

**SOLUTION**

So, here's the kv file:

```
#:kivy 1.11.1
# File name: settings.kv
#:import settings settings
...
<SettingsScreen>:
    ...
        ### ENDING CONDITIONS ###
        ...
            # radio buttons
            ...
                # option 3: time
                ...
                    NumInput:
                        ...
                        opacity: int(not self.disabled)
                        hint_text: "Set max. game time (1-120 min)"
```

```
                                min_value: 1
                                max_value: 120

        ### READY BUTTON ###
        ...
```

If you now run the app, check the end by time radio button and enter a number greater than 120, like for example 180, the time of the game will be reset to 120 minutes (= 2 hours) anyway.

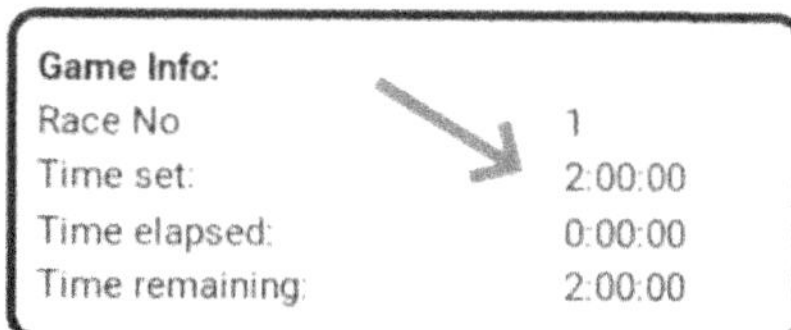


**EXERCISE 3**

Finally, we must take care of the BetInputs, which are closely related with the sliders next to them. This means you can set the amount of money you want to bet either using the slider or typing in the exact number in the text input.

Here we must make sure that each player can bet minimum $1 and no more than they have. We'll handle the sliders in the next chapter, and now let's concentrate on the BetInputs.

You will find the BetInput in the **Bet** rule in the Bets screen:

```
#:kivy 1.11.1
# File name: bets.kv
#:import bets bets

<Bet>:
    ...
    BoxLayout:
        spacing: 5

        RegularLabel:
            text: '$'
            halign: 'right'

        BetInput:
            text: str(root.bet_amount)
    Slider:
        ...
```

In the Python file there's the **max_bet_amount** property in the **Bet** class:

```
# File name: bets.py
...
class Bet(BoxLayout):
    player_name = StringProperty('')
    bet_amount = NumericProperty(0)
    max_bet_amount = NumericProperty(0)
    player_group = StringProperty('')

class BetsScreen(Screen):
    ...
```

In the kv file we set it for each player to their **money** value. Here you can see how we did it for the first player:

```
#:kivy 1.11.1
# File name: bets.kv
#:import bets bets
...
<BetsScreen>:
    ...
        ### PLAYER BETS ###
        BoxLayout:
            orientation: 'vertical'

            # player 1
            Bet:
                player_name: root.game.player1.name
                bet_amount: 1000
                max_bet_amount: root.game.player1.money
                player_group: 'player1'

            # player 2
            ...
```

It works the same with the other players. So now, when a player's money changes after each race, so does the value of the **max_bet_amount** property.

Now, the first thing you should do is add a hint text property to the BetInput in the **Bet** rule. It should read something along the lines:

```
'(1 - {})'
```

where the curly braces is a placeholder for the value of **max_bet_amount**. You can use the **format** method to format the string.

With that in place, set the two properties that are used as the limits of the numbers that can be entered. Set the minimum value to 1 and the maximum value to **max_bet_amount**.

Now each **Bet** instance's **bet_amount** property is set to **1000**. We want it to be set to the value of the **bet** property of each particular **Player** instance. The **bet** property is defined in the **Player** class and defaults to 1. So, make sure **bet_amount** is set to it instead of the hard-coded number.

There's one last thing I want you to take care of. Whenever a bet amount is entered in a BetInput, the corresponding player's **bet** property should be set to it. Have a look at the **bet_amount** property again. As you remember, you can easily add an event that is triggered when a property changes, using the naming convention with the prefix **on_**, so in this case you should add the **on_bet_amount** event to each **Bet** instance that will call a method which will change the corresponding player's **bet** property.

First, you must create the method in the **Bet** class in the Python file. Name it **update_player_bet**. It should take one parameter, let's call it **player**. In the method body, the **bet** property on the player passed as an argument, should be set to the value of the Bet's **bet_amount** property.

With the method defined, add a call to it to each **Bet** instance's **on_bet_amount** event, passing the corresponding player instance as an argument. As you remember, the players are defined in the **Game** class.

## SOLUTION

So, here's the Python file with the **update_player_bet** method:

```
# File name: bets.py
...
class Bet(BoxLayout):
    player_name = StringProperty('')
    bet_amount = NumericProperty(0)
    max_bet_amount = NumericProperty(0)
    player_group = StringProperty('')

    # Here's the method that will update the player's bet property
    # whenever the bet_amount property changes.
    def update_player_bet(self, player):
        player.bet = self.bet_amount

class BetsScreen(Screen):
    ...
```

And here's the kv file with all the modifications:

```
#:kivy 1.11.1
# File name: bets.kv
#:import bets bets

<Bet>:
    ...
    BoxLayout:
        ...
        BetInput:
            text: str(root.bet_amount)

            # Here's the hint text.
            hint_text: '(1 - {})'.format(root.max_bet_amount)

            # Here are the limits.
            min_value: 1
            max_value: root.max_bet_amount

    Slider:
        ...
<BetsScreen>:
    ...
        ### PLAYER BETS ###
        BoxLayout:
            orientation: 'vertical'

            # player 1
            Bet:
                player_name: root.game.player1.name
                bet_amount: root.game.player1.bet
```

```
            max_bet_amount: root.game.player1.money
            player_group: 'player1'

            # Here's the event that will be triggered whenever the bet_amount
            # property changes. Then the method will be called that we just defined.

            # In this instance of Bet we'll pass player1 as the argument, for the
            # other instances we'll pass the other corresponding player objects.
            on_bet_amount: self.update_player_bet(root.game.player1)

        # player 2
        Bet:
            player_name: root.game.player2.name
            bet_amount: root.game.player2.bet
            max_bet_amount: root.game.player2.money
            player_group: 'player2'
            disabled: root.game.number_of_players < 2
            on_bet_amount: self.update_player_bet(root.game.player2)

        # player 3
        Bet:
            player_name: root.game.player3.name
            bet_amount: root.game.player3.bet
            max_bet_amount: root.game.player3.money
            player_group: 'player3'
            disabled: root.game.number_of_players < 3
            on_bet_amount: self.update_player_bet(root.game.player3)

        # player 4
        Bet:
            player_name: root.game.player4.name
            bet_amount: root.game.player4.bet
            max_bet_amount: root.game.player4.money
            player_group: 'player4'
            disabled: root.game.number_of_players < 4
            on_bet_amount: self.update_player_bet(root.game.player4)

    ### GO BUTTON ###
    ...
```

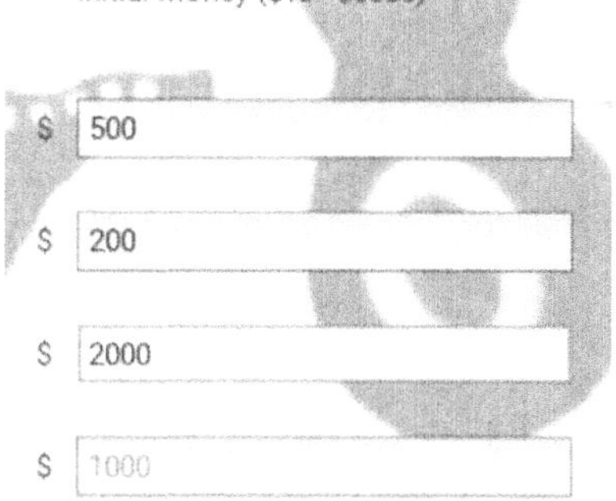


Now let's check it out. Let's run the app, set the number of players to 4 and enter the following values of initial money: 500, 200 and 2000 for players 1-3. Let's leave the default value of 1000 for player 4. Hit the Ready button.

Bets
Player 1 bets $ 1
Player 2 bets $ 1
Player 3 bets $ 1
Player 4 bets $ 1

In the Bets screen you will see the default bet value of 1 in each BetInput.

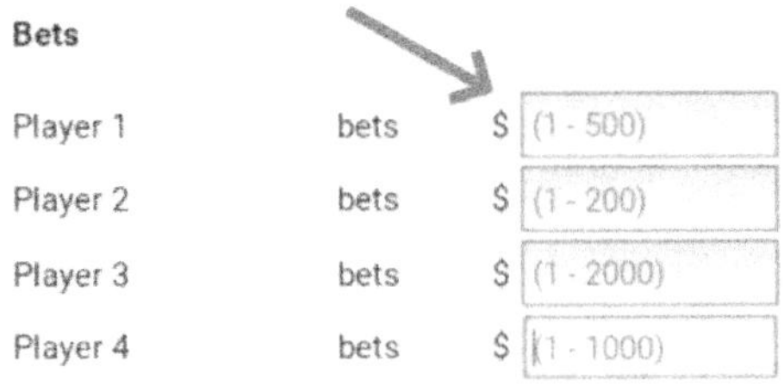

**Bets**

| | | | |
|---|---|---|---|
| Player 1 | bets | $ | (1 - 500) |
| Player 2 | bets | $ | (1 - 200) |
| Player 3 | bets | $ | (1 - 2000) |
| Player 4 | bets | $ | (1 - 1000) |

Now, delete all the text in the BetInputs. Now you should see the hint text with the maximum values set to the amount of money we set for each player.

If you try to enter a number greater than the maximum value, it will be reset to the maximum value anyway.

# Chapter 85 – Using the Sliders

In the previous chapter we handled user input validation. I mentioned that the BetInputs in the Bets screen are closely connected with the sliders. This means that you can place your bet in two ways, either by entering an exact value in the BetInput or by moving the slider. With the slider it's usually more difficult to get an exact number, but still, you can use it if that doesn't matter to you that much.

Now, what we want to achieve is a cooperation between the BetInput and the slider. This means they should react to each other's changes. If we enter a number in the BetInput, the slider should move accordingly. If we set the value using the slider, the value in the BetInput should adjust itself.

So, how does it work now? If you run the app, hit the Ready button and enter a number in one of the BetInputs, the slider next to it won't budge. Similarly, if you move the slider all the way to the right (this position of the slider corresponds to the maximum bet amount that can be placed), the value in the BetInput won't change. The problem is that the BetInput and the slider don't realize they are so closely connected with each other.

Let's now have a look at the code where the text inputs and sliders are defined. It's in the **Bet** class:

```
#:kivy 1.11.1
# File name: bets.kv
#:import bets bets

<Bet>:
    ...
    BoxLayout:
        ...
        BetInput:
            text: str(root.bet_amount)
            hint_text: '(1 - {})'.format(root.max_bet_amount)
            min_value: 1
            max_value: root.max_bet_amount
    Slider:
        min: 1
        max: root.max_bet_amount
        value: root.bet_amount
        step: 1
    RegularLabel:
        ...
```

So, what can we do about it? Well, we'll need to modify both the BetInput and the slider. We'll do the latter here and I'll leave the former for you as an exercise.

All we have to do as far as the slider is concerned is override its **on_value** event. This event is triggered each time the value changes, so each time we move the slider. When this happens, the **bet_amount** property should be set to the new value. That's it.

When you now run the program and move the slider (A), the change will be also visible in the BetInput (B).

But it doesn't work the other way around. If I enter, for example, 500 in the BetInput, the slider won't budge. This must be taken care of in the BetInput itself. So, feel free to do the exercise below where this functionality will be added. And in the next chapter we'll handle the betting logic.

Here's the code:

```
#:kivy 1.11.1
# File name: bets.kv
#:import bets bets

<Bet>:
    ...
    BoxLayout:
        ...
        BetInput:
            ...
    Slider:
        ...
        step: 1

        # Whenever the slider is moved and its
        # value changes, the bet amount should
        # be set to the new value.
        on_value: root.bet_amount = self.value

    RegularLabel:
        ...
```

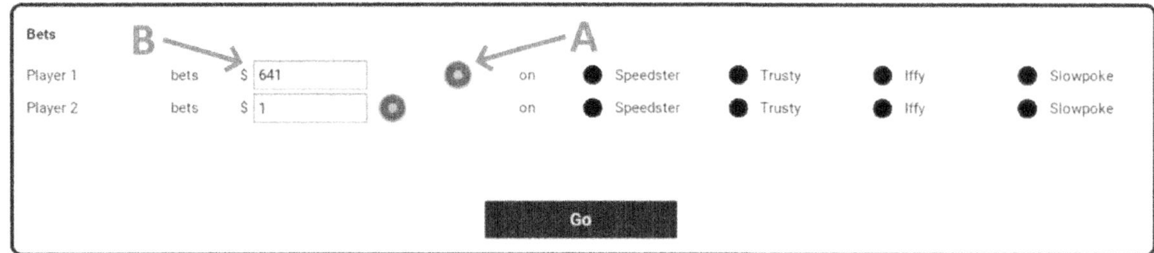


# It's Your Turn Now...

## EXERCISE

Let's take care of the BetInput now. Whenever the text in the BetInput changes, the slider's value should be set to the number entered in the BetInput, but only if it's less than the maximum bet amount. Otherwise it should be set to the maximum value. Besides, if there is no text at all in the BetInput, the slider's value should be set to the minimum value, which is 1. Remember to add an id to the slider (like **_slider**) in order to be able to reference it.

HINT: Use the **on_text** event that is triggered when the text in the text input changes.

## SOLUTION

Here's the code:

```
#:kivy 1.11.1
# File name: bets.kv
#:import bets bets

<Bet>:
    ...
    BoxLayout:
        ...
        BetInput:
            text: str(root.bet_amount)
            hint_text: '(1 - {})'.format(root.max_bet_amount)
            min_value: 1
            max_value: root.max_bet_amount
            on_text: _slider.value = min(int(self.text), root.max_bet_amount) if self.text else self.min_value

    Slider:
        id: _slider
        min: 1
        ...
```

Now if you run the app and set the bet amount in the BetInput (A), the slider will adjust its value (B).

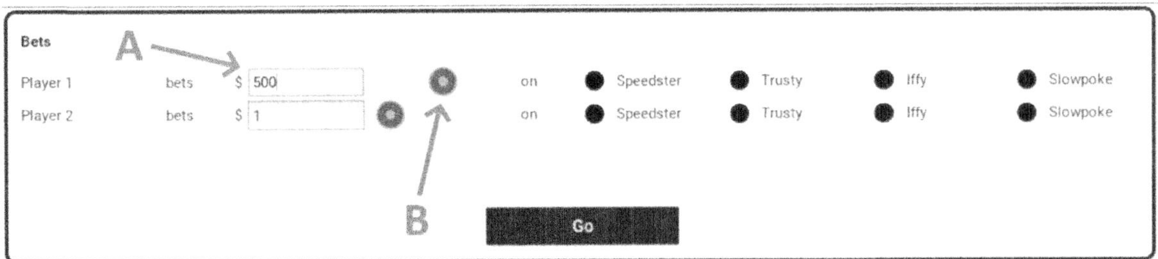

# Chapter 86 – Betting Logic

In the previous chapter we handled the sliders in the Bets screen. Before that we took care of the BetInputs. Now each player can place a bet using either the BetInput or the slider. But how do we know which slug they want to bet on? Well, as you probably guessed, the radio buttons that follow are just for that. Have a look at the Bets screen again. Here Player 1 wants to bet $500 on Trusty and Player 2 wants to bet $350 on Slowpoke:

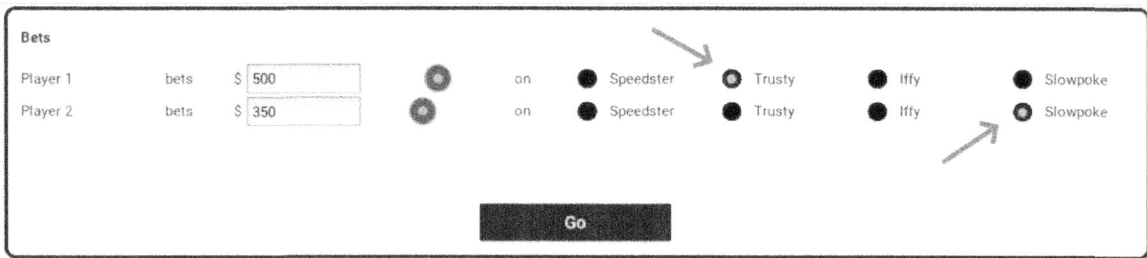


Naturally, at this point it won't work because we didn't implement the betting logic yet. This is what we are going to do in this chapter. And one more thing. The Go button is enabled all the time. We want it to be enabled only if each player has put a bet on a slug. Otherwise the button should be disabled. So, this is something we're going to look to in this chapter too.

## Choosing a Slug

Let's start with choosing a slug. When the game begins and the players are set, none of them has selected a slug to bet on in the first race, so all the radio buttons are unchecked. But, before the first race starts, each of the players should bet on one of the slugs. This chosen slug must be saved somewhere, so let's add an ObjectProperty to the **Player** class that will store it:

```
# File name: player.py

from kivy.properties import StringProperty, NumericProperty, ObjectProperty
from kivy.event import EventDispatcher

class Player(EventDispatcher):
    ...
    bet = NumericProperty(1)

    # the slug the player bets on
    chosen_slug = ObjectProperty(None)
```

As you can see, no slug is selected by default. Next, we have to add a property to the **Bet** class in the Bets screen, which will be used to store the slug selected for a particular player. As you know, there are four **Bet** instances in the Bets screen, which may be all visible or not, depending on how many players there are. The **Slug** instances are defined in the **Game** class (in the **slugrace.kv** file). We could modify our code in order to get access to the **Game** class from within the **Bet** class, but this time I decided to keep things really simple. First of all, I'll put all the slugs into a list in the **Game** class:

```
#:kivy 1.11.1
# File name: slugrace.kv

<Game>:
    ...
    slowpoke: _racescreen.slowpoke

    # list of slugs
    slugs: [self.speedster, self.trusty, self.iffy, self.slowpoke]

    SettingsScreen:
        ...
```

And now I'll add a NumericProperty named **selected_slug** to the **Bet** class. Its default value is going to be 0, which means no slug is selected:

```
# File name: bets.py
...
class Bet(BoxLayout):
    ...
    player_group = StringProperty('')

    # By default no slug is selected,
    # hence the default value 0.
    selected_slug = NumericProperty(0)

    def update_player_bet(self, player):
        ...
```

We don't need access to the **slugs** list inside the **Bet** class. Instead we're going to use numbers that will be stored in the **selected_slug** property. They are generally indices; 0 means no slug selected, 1-4 correspond to the four slugs. Here's the kv code:

```
#:kivy 1.11.1
# File name: bets.kv
#:import bets bets

<Bet>:
    ...
    BoxLayout:
        PlayerSlugButton:
            group: root.player_group
```

```
                # This slug is assigned the number 1.
                # If the radio button is checked, Speedster becomes the selected slug.
                # The other radio buttons behave accordingly.
                on_active: if self.active: root.selected_slug = 1

            RegularLabel:
                text: 'Speedster'
        BoxLayout:
            PlayerSlugButton:
                group: root.player_group
                on_active: if self.active: root.selected_slug = 2
            RegularLabel:
                text: 'Trusty'
        BoxLayout:
            PlayerSlugButton:
                group: root.player_group
                on_active: if self.active: root.selected_slug = 3
            RegularLabel:
                text: 'Iffy'
        BoxLayout:
            PlayerSlugButton:
                group: root.player_group
                on_active: if self.active: root.selected_slug = 4
            RegularLabel:
                ...
```

Now we can use the number saved in **selected_slug** to actually assign the appropriate slugs to the players. Here's the code:

```
#:kivy 1.11.1
# File name: bets.kv
#:import bets bets
...
<BetsScreen>:
    ...
        ### PLAYER BETS ###
        BoxLayout:
            orientation: 'vertical'

            # player 1
            Bet:
                ...
                on_bet_amount: self.update_player_bet(root.game.player1)

                # When a slug is selected, the on_selected_slug event is triggered.
                # Then the number of the slug which is saved in the selected_slug
                # property on the Bet object (1-4, decremented by 1) is used as the
                # index to assign the appropriate slug from the game's slugs list
                # to Player 1. The code for the other players is very similar.
                on_selected_slug: root.game.player1.chosen_slug = root.game.slugs[self.selected_slug - 1]

            # player 2
            Bet:
                ...
                on_bet_amount: self.update_player_bet(root.game.player2)
                on_selected_slug: root.game.player2.chosen_slug = root.game.slugs[self.selected_slug - 1]
```

```
        # player 3
        Bet:
            ...
            on_bet_amount: self.update_player_bet(root.game.player3)
            on_selected_slug: root.game.player3.chosen_slug = root.game.slugs[self.selected_slug - 1]

        # player 4
        Bet:
            ...
            on_bet_amount: self.update_player_bet(root.game.player4)
            on_selected_slug: root.game.player4.chosen_slug = root.game.slugs[self.selected_slug - 1]

    ### GO BUTTON ###
    ...
```

Now, if you run the app, the players will be able to put their bets on particular slugs. We're not going to see any change, though, at least not just yet. But don't worry, in the next chapter we'll start a basic game simulation and then deciding which slug to bet on will have its consequences. And now, in the exercises below, you will handle the Go button. It should be enabled only if all players have chosen their slugs.

# It's Your Turn Now...

### EXERCISE 1

In this exercise we'll handle the functionality of the Go button in the Bets screen. Now it's enabled all the time, so even if some of the players don't select the slug they want to bet on, the Go button will work. And this is not the behavior we expect. When the Go button is pressed, a race will begin. And the race should only begin when all players have placed their bets. This is how we want the game to work. Players will not be allowed to skip races. They can bet even the minimum amount of money on a slug, which is $1, but they can't skip any race.

Here are the steps to follow:

1. Now when you check a radio button, you can't select any other radio button in the same group at the same time. But you can uncheck a radio button so that no radio button is checked. Now, we want to change this. If a radio button is checked, you should only be able to uncheck it by checking another radio button in the group. In order to do that, find the definition of **PlayerSlugButton** in the **widgets.kv** file, add the **allow_no_selection** property to it and set it to **False**.

2. In the **bets.py** add a BooleanProperty to the **BetsScreen** class. Name it **all_slugs_selected** and set its default value to **False**.

3. In each of the four **Bet** instances in the kv file there's the **on_selected_slug** event that will assign the selected slug to the player. But there's one more thing that must happen when a slug is selected. We must check whether all players have selected their slugs. Only if that's the case will

the Go button be enabled. As you know, the **all_slugs_selected** property you just created is a BooleanProperty, so here it should be set to the result of a comparison. What we are going to compare is the number of players who have chosen a slug and the number of players in the game. If these two numbers are equal, it means all the players have chosen a slug. It's easy to check the number of players in the game because we have the list of players in the **Game** class, so it's enough to check the length of the list. As far as the number of players who have chosen a slug is concerned, I suggest you use a list comprehension to create a list that will contain those players whose **chosen_slug** property is not **None**. Then you can just compare the lengths of the two lists and assign the result of this comparison to the **all_slugs_selected** property.

4. Now that the **all_slugs_selected** property is set, use it in the Go button to disable the button until all slugs are selected.

## SOLUTION

So, here's the **widget.kv** file:

```
#:kivy 1.11.1
# File name: widgets.kv
#:import widgets widgets
...
<PlayerSlugButton@CheckBox>:
    ...
    size_hint: (.5, 1)

    # There should always be one radio button selected.
    allow_no_selection: False
```

Here's the **bets.py** file:

```
# File name: bets.py

from kivy.uix.boxlayout import BoxLayout
from kivy.properties import NumericProperty, StringProperty, BooleanProperty
from kivy.uix.screenmanager import Screen
...
class BetsScreen(Screen):
    # This is to make sure all players selected their slugs.
    all_slugs_selected = BooleanProperty(False)
```

Here's the **bets.kv** file:

```
#:kivy 1.11.1
# File name: bets.kv
#:import bets bets
...
<BetsScreen>:
    ...
        ### PLAYER BETS ###
        BoxLayout:
            orientation: 'vertical'

            # player 1
            Bet:
                ...
                on_selected_slug:
                    root.game.player1.chosen_slug = root.game.slugs[self.selected_slug - 1]

                    # Also, whenever a slug is selected, we must check whether all players
                    # have chosen the slugs they want to bet on. It works in the same way
                    # with the other players.
                    root.all_slugs_selected = len([player for player in root.game.players if player.
chosen_slug]) == len(root.game.players)

            # player 2
            Bet:
                ...
                on_selected_slug:
                    root.game.player2.chosen_slug = root.game.slugs[self.selected_slug - 1]
                    root.all_slugs_selected = len([player for player in root.game.players if player.
chosen_slug]) == len(root.game.players)

            # player 3
            Bet:
                ...
                on_selected_slug:
                    root.game.player3.chosen_slug = root.game.slugs[self.selected_slug - 1]
                    root.all_slugs_selected = len([player for player in root.game.players if player.
chosen_slug]) == len(root.game.players)

            # player 4
            Bet:
                ...
                on_selected_slug:
                    root.game.player4.chosen_slug = root.game.slugs[self.selected_slug - 1]
                    root.all_slugs_selected = len([player for player in root.game.players if player.
chosen_slug]) == len(root.game.players)

        ### GO BUTTON ###
        RedButton:
            text: 'Go'

            # The button should be disabled until all players have chosen their slugs.
            disabled: not root.all_slugs_selected

            on_press:
                ...
```

If you now run the app, the Go button will be disabled if some of the players haven't chosen their slugs yet. For example here Player 2 hasn't decided yet:

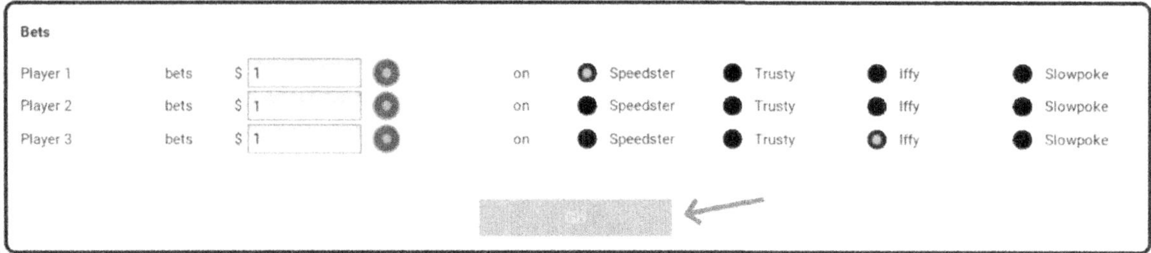


As soon as all players have chosen their slugs, the button gets enabled.

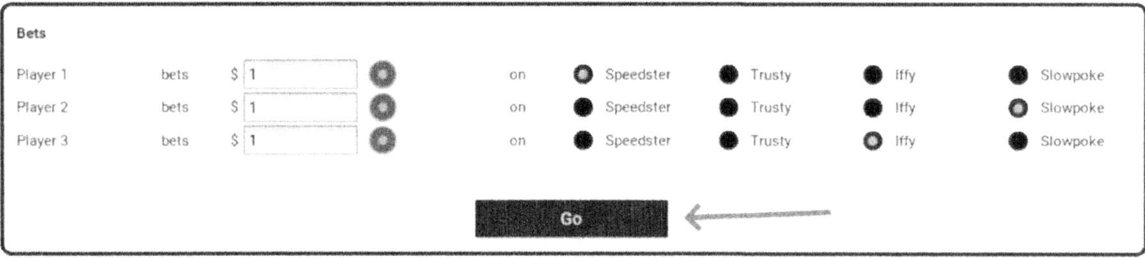


### EXERCISE 2

The code in the **bets.kv** file that is executed when a slug is selected is pretty lengthy and repetitive. In this exercise your task is to refactor it a bit. Follow the steps below:

1. In the **bets.py** file add a method to the **BetsScreen** class. Name it **select_slug**. It should take a **player** parameter and a **slug_index** parameter. In the method set the **chosen_slug** property of the player passed through the **player** parameter to the slug with the index (in the **slugs** list that we defined earlier in the **Game** class) passed through the **slug_index** parameter.

Then use a list comprehension (just like you did in the kv file) to create a list of players who have chosen their slugs. You can name the list **players_with_slugs**, for example. Finally compare the list of players with slugs with the list of all players in the game and assign the result of this comparison to the BooleanProperty **all_slugs_selected**.

2. In the kv file replace the code that is executed when the **on_selected_slug** event is triggered with a call to the **select_slug** method you just created. Pass the appropriate player and slug index for each instance of **Bet** as arguments to the method. Don't forget that the slug index should be one less than the value of the **selected_slug** property, just like before.

**SOLUTION**

So, here's the Python file:

```
# File name: bets.py
...
class BetsScreen(Screen):
    all_slugs_selected = BooleanProperty(False)

    def select_slug(self, player, slug_index):
        # Set the player's chosen_slug to the slug with the index passed as an argument.
        player.chosen_slug = self.game.slugs[slug_index]

        # Create a list of players who have chosen a slug.
        players_with_slugs = [player for player in self.game.players
                              if player.chosen_slug]

        # Compare the list of players with slugs with that of all players and assign the
        # result of this comparison to the all_slugs_selected BooleanProperty.
        self.all_slugs_selected = len(players_with_slugs) == len(self.game.players)
```

And here's the kv file:

```
#:kivy 1.11.1
# File name: bets.kv
#:import bets bets
...
<BetsScreen>:
    ...
        ### PLAYER BETS ###
        BoxLayout:
            orientation: 'vertical'

            # player 1
            Bet:
                ...
                on_selected_slug: root.select_slug(root.game.player1, self.selected_slug - 1)
            # player 2
            Bet:
                ...
                on_selected_slug: root.select_slug(root.game.player2, self.selected_slug - 1)
            # player 3
            Bet:
                ...
                on_selected_slug: root.select_slug(root.game.player3, self.selected_slug - 1)
            # player 4
            Bet:
                ...
                on_selected_slug: root.select_slug(root.game.player4, self.selected_slug - 1)
        ### GO BUTTON ###
        ...
```

If you now run the app, it will work just like before.

# Chapter 87 – Start of the Game

In the previous chapter we implemented the betting logic. In this chapter we'll start simulating the whole game, from beginning to end. This is going to be just a simulation, though, not the final version, so I will keep it simple for now. In this chapter, in particular, we'll handle the start of the game. But first, let's have a look at the general flow of the game.

So, when you launch the app, you can see the Settings screen (after the Splash screen naturally) where you can set the number of players, set their names and initial money, or leave the default generic names Player 1, Player 2, etc. and the default initial money of $1000. You can also choose an ending condition. For our simulation we'll assume that the first ending condition is selected, so the game should end as soon as there is only one player left with any money. We'll also assume that there must be at least two players for now, because, as you remember, the first ending condition is not available when there's only one player. We'll implement the other ending conditions later in the project.

Anyway, the moment you press the Ready button, the game should begin. Later, when we implement the clock, this will be the moment when the time of the game starts running if you select the time ending condition. The Race screen now appears and the players can place their bets. This is the first race. When the bets are all placed and you press the Go button, the actual race begins and after a while one of the slugs reaches the finish line. For the time being, as the slugs are not yet animated, we'll just randomly pick one of the slugs to be the winner. The name and image of the winning slug appear to the right of the track and the players' money values as well as the slugs' odds are updated. The Bets screen is replaced with the Results screen. In the Results screen you can see all the players, their bets and results.

Then you can press the Next Race button and the Bets screen will appear again. In the Game Info panel you can see that now the number of the race is one more than before. The players can place their bets for the second race, and so on. After each race the program must check how many of the players still have some money. Players that no longer have any money should be removed. If there's only one player with any money left, the player becomes the winner of the game. If there isn't any player with any money left, there is no winner at all. In either case, the Game Over screen should appear with relevant information.

If you decide to play again in the Game Over screen, all the settings must be reset to the original state and you will be taken back to the Settings screen.

So, let's now walk through the game flow described above step by step. It will take us some chapters to cover them all. Let's start with the, no pun intended, start of the game.

## Starting the Game

The game should start when the Ready button in the Settings screen is pressed. So, let's create a method in the **Game** class that will be called when the game starts. For now, we'll put some placeholder code that only prints a message when the game starts. We'll replace it with real code later on. Actually, I think you could do it yourself. It's really very simple. Here's the exercise for you and in the next chapter there's going to be much more to do. We'll be simulating a single race.

## It's Your Turn Now...

### EXERCISE

Add the **start_game** method without any parameters (except for **self**, naturally) to the **Game** class. For now it should only print the message **'Game started'** in the terminal. We'll take care of its implementation a bit later. Then, in the **settings.kv** file, make sure the method is called when the Ready button is pressed.

### SOLUTION

So, here's the **Game** class with the new method:

```
# File name: main.py
...
class Game(ScreenManager):
    ...
    def on_number_of_players(self, instance, value):
        ...
    def set_ending_condition(self, condition):
        ...

    # The method will be called when the game starts.
    def start_game(self):
        # just some placeholder code
        print('Game started')

class SlugraceApp(App):
    ...
```

And we need to call the method when the Ready button is pressed:

```
#:kivy 1.11.1
# File name: settings.kv
#:import settings settings
...
<SettingsScreen>:
    ...
        ### READY BUTTON ###
```

```
    RedButton:
        ...
        on_press:
            ...
            root.manager.current = 'racescreen'

            # The game should start now.
            root.game.start_game()
```

If you now run the app and hit the Ready button, you will see the **'Game started'** message printed in the terminal.

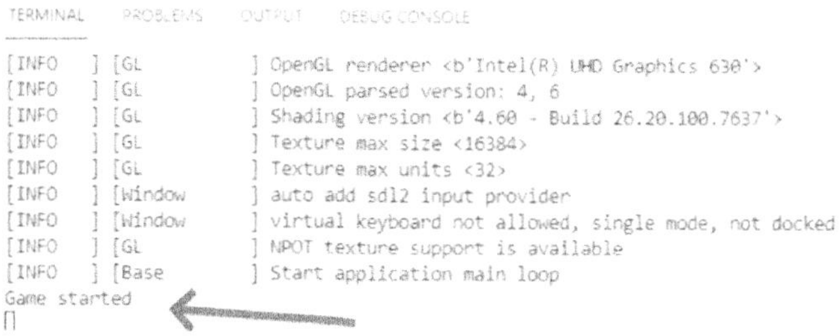

```
TERMINAL    PROBLEMS    OUTPUT    DEBUG CONSOLE

[INFO   ] [GL          ] OpenGL renderer <b'Intel(R) UHD Graphics 630'>
[INFO   ] [GL          ] OpenGL parsed version: 4, 6
[INFO   ] [GL          ] Shading version <b'4.60 - Build 26.20.100.7637'>
[INFO   ] [GL          ] Texture max size <16384>
[INFO   ] [GL          ] Texture max units <32>
[INFO   ] [Window      ] auto add sdl2 input provider
[INFO   ] [Window      ] virtual keyboard not allowed, single mode, not docked
[INFO   ] [GL          ] NPOT texture support is available
[INFO   ] [Base        ] Start application main loop
Game started
```

# Chapter 88 – Race Simulation

In the previous chapter we started implementing the method that is called when the game starts. When this happens, we switch to the Race screen, place the bets and start the first race. Sounds simple, but it involves a couple interesting things we have to take care of. In this chapter we'll implement the logic that is needed to simulate a single race. This includes updating the Results screen, the winner image, the slugs' stats and the odds.

## Simulation of a Race

The race should start as soon as the Go button in the Bets screen is pressed. So, we'll create a method in the **Game** class that will be called when this happens. Let's name it **go**. We're going to implement it in a minute, but first let's add the code to the **on_press** event that will call it:

```
#:kivy 1.11.1
# File name: bets.kv
#:import bets bets
...
<BetsScreen>:
    ...
        ### GO BUTTON ###
        RedButton:
            ...
            on_press:
                root.manager.current = 'resultsscreen'
                root.manager.transition.direction = 'left'

                # Start the race.
                root.game.go()
```

Before we define the **go** method, we have to add an ObjectProperty to the **Game** class, which we will need in the method. We need the ObjectProperty to store the slug that wins a race, so let's name it **race_winner**. Besides, we'll have to check all the players if the slug they chose is the one that wins and update their money values accordingly. We'll add the **update** method in the **Player** class that will take care of it. Here's the **main.py** file:

```
# File name: main.py
...
from player import Player

# We'll need the ObjectProperty to store the
# slug that wins a race.
from kivy.properties import (NumericProperty, BooleanProperty,
                             StringProperty,  ObjectProperty)
```

```
from datetime import timedelta
...
class Game(ScreenManager):
    ...
    # races
    ...
    races_to_go = NumericProperty(0)

    # We need a property to store the slug that wins a race.
    race_winner = ObjectProperty(None)

    # time
    ...
```

Now, how are the money values calculated? Let's have a look at an example. Suppose there are two players, Player 1 and Player 2, both having $1000 in their accounts. They bet $100 each. Player 1 bets on Speedster (odds 1.68) and Player 2 on Iffy (odds 1.82). Iffy wins the race. Here's how the money is calculated:

| Player 1: | Player 2: |
|---|---|
| - had $1000, | - had $1000, |
| - bet $100 on a slug that lost, | - bet $100 on a slug that won, |
| so Player 1 wins -$100 (negative $100, so actually loses) and now has $1000 - $100 = $900. | - the winning slug's odds were 1.82, |
| | so Player 2 wins 1.82 x $100 which is $182, but this includes the $100 wager, so the actual profit is $182 - $100 = $82. |

In the example above Player 2 placed a $100 wager on Iffy, so $900 was left in their account. After winning $182, there's $900 + $182 = $1082 in the account. In our game the wager will be subtracted from the amount won by a player, so in our example Player 2 wins $82 because this is the actual profit.

So, here's the **update** method in the **Player** class:

```
# File name: player.py
...
class Player(EventDispatcher):
    ...
    chosen_slug = ObjectProperty(None)

    def update(self, winning_slug):
        # Let's save the current value of money so that we still have access to it
        # in the Results screen after it has changed.
        self.money_before_race = self.money
```

```
        # The money that the player wins is:
        # a) the product of the bet amount and the slug's odds minus the bet amount,
        #    so self.bet * winning_slug.odds - self.bet, which can be more concisely
        #    written as self.bet * (winning_slug.odds - 1); it's rounded to an integer,
        # b) or the negative of the bet amount if the player loses.
        self.money_won = (int(self.bet * (winning_slug.odds - 1))
                         if self.chosen_slug == winning_slug
                         else -self.bet)

        # The money won by the player is added to their money. If the player loses,
        # a negative number is added.
        self.money += self.money_won
```

There is one thing we must keep in mind, though. This way of calculating the odds may lead to a situation where the actual profit is less than one. If, in the example above, Player 2 had placed a $1 bet wager (instead of a $100 one), the actual profit would be:

$1 x (1.82 – 1) = $0.82

As this is less than one, it'll be rounded down to 0 when passed to the int function:

```
int(0.82) = 0
```

So, this may happen if the odds are less than 2 and the wagers are low. But this is OK because it's how we wanted the odds to be calculated in our app. So, now you won't be surprised to see that a player bet $1 on a slug and won $0. It's perfectly fine. It just means the player won less than $1. However, in order to avoid a message telling us that the player won $0, we'll use another message instead that will inform us that the player won less than $1. We'll take care of it in the Results screen in a minute.

Now we're ready to implement the **go** method:

```
# File name: main.py
...
from datetime import timedelta

# We'll need the choice function to randomly select a slug.
from random import choice

Builder.load_file('settings.kv')
...
class Game(ScreenManager):
    ...
    def start_game(self):
        ...

    # This method will be called when a race begins.
    def go(self):
        # For now the winning slug will be chosen randomly.
```

```
        self.race_winner = choice(self.slugs)

        # We must check all the players to know if they win or lose money.
        # They win if they bet on the race winner, otherwise they lose.
        for player in self.players:
            player.update(self.race_winner)

class SlugraceApp(App):
    ...
```

## The Results Screen

Now that we know the results of the race, we want to update the information displayed in the Results screen, which appears in place of the Bets screen. We have the **Result** class with some properties that are used to display that sort of information. Then we have a **Result** instance for each of the players. Here's how it's currently implemented for the second player, with the other players it's very similar.

```
#:kivy 1.11.1
# File name: results.kv
#:import results results
...
<ResultsScreen>:
    ...
        ### PLAYER RESULTS ###
        BoxLayout:
            ...
            # player 2
            Result:
                player_name: root.game.player2.name
                money_before: 1000
                bet_amount: 300
                slug_name: 'Speedster'
                result_info: '- lost'
                gain_or_loss: 400
                current_money: root.game.player2.money
                odds: 1.59
                disabled: root.game.number_of_players < 2

            # player 3
            ...
```

As you can see, there's a lot of hard-coded data in the code above. Now let's raplace it with actual information from the **Player** objects.

One thing that we want to display is the name of the slug that was chosen by a player, so first let's add the **name** StringProperty to the **Slug** class:

```
# File name: slug.py

from kivy.uix.relativelayout import RelativeLayout
from kivy.properties import StringProperty, NumericProperty

class Slug(RelativeLayout):
    # We'll need the name of the slug
    # in the Results screen.
    name = StringProperty('')

    body_image = StringProperty('')
    ...
```

And now let's set the names in the **race.kv** file where the slugs are instantiated:

```
#:kivy 1.11.1
# File name: race.kv
#:import race race
...
<RaceScreen>:
    ...
        ### THE TRACK ###
        BoxLayout:
            ...
                # the slugs
                # Speedster
                Slug:
                    id: _speedster
                    name: 'Speedster'
                    body_image: 'speedsterBody'
                    ...
                # Trusty
                Slug:
                    id: _trusty
                    name: 'Trusty'
                    body_image: 'trustyBody'
                    ...
                # Iffy
                Slug:
                    id: _iffy
                    name: 'Iffy'
                    body_image: 'iffyBody'
                    ...
                # Slowpoke
                Slug:
                    id: _slowpoke
                    name: 'Slowpoke'
                    body_image: 'slowpokeBody'
                    ...
```

Now we can use the slugs' names in the Results screen. We can also use the other properties that we mentioned before instead of the hard-coded values. Here's the modified code:

```
#:kivy 1.11.1
# File name: results.kv
#:import results results

<Result>:
    ...
        RegularLabel:
            text: root.result_info
            size_hint: (.5, 1)
        RegularLabel:
            # The minimum amount of money a player can win is $1.
            # If it's less, the player wins nothing and there's
            # a short message.
            text: '$' + str(root.gain_or_loss) if root.gain_or_loss >= 1 else 'less than $1'
    BoxLayout:
        RegularLabel:
            text: 'now has'
        ...
<ResultsScreen>:
    ...
        ### PLAYER RESULTS ###
```

```
BoxLayout:
    orientation: 'vertical'

    # player 1
    Result:
        player_name: root.game.player1.name
        money_before: root.game.player1.money_before_race
        bet_amount: root.game.player1.bet
        slug_name: root.game.player1.chosen_slug.name if root.game.player1.chosen_slug else ''
        result_info: '- won' if root.game.player1.money_won >= 0 else '- lost'
        gain_or_loss: abs(root.game.player1.money_won)
        current_money: root.game.player1.money
        odds: root.game.player1.chosen_slug.odds if root.game.player1.chosen_slug else 1

    # player 2
    Result:
        player_name: root.game.player2.name
        money_before: root.game.player2.money_before_race
        bet_amount: root.game.player2.bet
        slug_name: root.game.player2.chosen_slug.name if root.game.player2.chosen_slug else ''
        result_info: '- won' if root.game.player2.money_won >= 0 else '- lost'
        gain_or_loss: abs(root.game.player2.money_won)
        current_money: root.game.player2.money
        odds: root.game.player2.chosen_slug.odds if root.game.player2.chosen_slug else 1
        disabled: root.game.number_of_players < 2

    # player 3
    Result:
        player_name: root.game.player3.name
        money_before: root.game.player3.money_before_race
        bet_amount: root.game.player3.bet
        slug_name: root.game.player3.chosen_slug.name if root.game.player3.chosen_slug else ''
        result_info: '- won' if root.game.player3.money_won >= 0 else '- lost'
        gain_or_loss: abs(root.game.player3.money_won)
        current_money: root.game.player3.money
        odds: root.game.player3.chosen_slug.odds if root.game.player3.chosen_slug else 1
        disabled: root.game.number_of_players < 3

    # player 4
    Result:
        player_name: root.game.player4.name
        money_before: root.game.player4.money_before_race
        bet_amount: root.game.player4.bet
        slug_name: root.game.player4.chosen_slug.name if root.game.player4.chosen_slug else ''
        result_info: '- won' if root.game.player4.money_won >= 0 else '- lost'
        gain_or_loss: abs(root.game.player4.money_won)
        current_money: root.game.player4.money
        odds: root.game.player4.chosen_slug.odds if root.game.player4.chosen_slug else 1
        disabled: root.game.number_of_players < 4

### NEXT RACE BUTTON ###
...
```

Now, have a look at the slugs' names and odds in the code above. When the Results screen is first created there are no chosen slugs yet, so we have to use this conditional code to avoid an error when the app is launched. But don't worry, at the time when the Results screen is shown for the first time, the chosen slugs are already set, so you will see correct data.

Now, the next two things we should take care of are updating the winner image and updating the slugs' stats. But I'll leave that for you as an exercise. Now, let's have a look at updating the odds.

## Updating the Odds

The odds should be updated after each race. If a slug is doing fine in the race, his odds should be lower. If a slug is not doing fine, the odds should be higher. At this moment the odds are not updated. Here you can see them on the track.

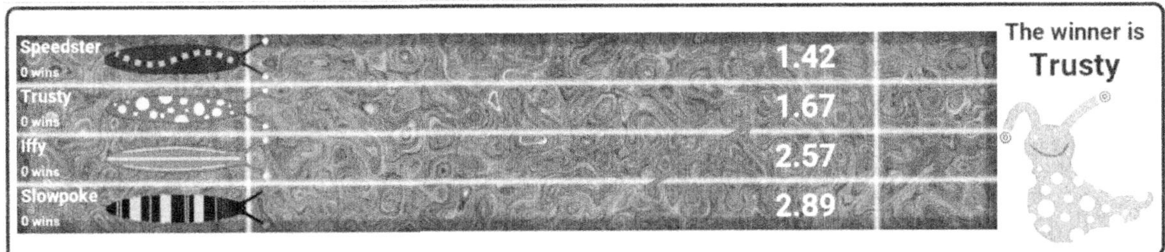


And here's how they are implemented right now:

```
#:kivy 1.11.1
# File name: race.kv
#:import race race
...
<RaceScreen>:
    ...
        ### THE TRACK ###
        ...
                # the odds labels
                # Speedster
                WhiteOddsLabel:
                    text: str(_speedster.odds)
                    ...
```

Now, how should the odds be calculated after each slug? You can do it in lots of different ways. I'm going now to describe my implementation, if you don't like it, feel free to modify it.

Anyway, we'll add an **update** method to the **Slug** class that will update the odds. We added a similar method to the **Player** class before. Later we'll also add code to it that will update the slugs' stats (actually you will do it as an exercise).

So, here's the method:

```
# File name: slug.py
...
class Slug(RelativeLayout):
    ...
    odds = NumericProperty(0)

    # We need this method to update the slug's odds.
    def update(self, winning_slug):
        # Here's how the odds are calculated.
        if self == winning_slug:
            self.odds = round(max(1.01, min(self.odds * .96, 20)), 2)
        else:
            self.odds = round(max(1.01, min(self.odds * 1.03, 20)), 2)
```

So, generally we want the odds to be in a range between 1.01 and 20. If the slug wins the race, the odds should decrease, so we multiply the current odds by an arbitrary number 0.96. If the slug doesn't win, the odds should increase, so we multiply the current odds by an arbitrary number 1.03. In either case we ensure that the odds are no more than 20 and no less than 1.01. We use the built-in Python functions **min** and **max**. We also use the **round** function to make sure the result is rounded to two decimal places.

Now, with the method in place, we must call it for each slug. We'll do it in the **go** method:

```
# File name: main.py
...
class Game(ScreenManager):
    ...
    def go(self):
        ...
        for player in self.players:
            player.update(self.race_winner)

        # The odds of the slugs should be updated.
        for slug in self.slugs:
            slug.update(self.race_winner)

class SlugraceApp(App):
    ...
```

Now let's run the app and see whether it works. Here's what we can see before the race. There are four players, each betting $100 (A) on a different slug (B). Watch the odds (C).

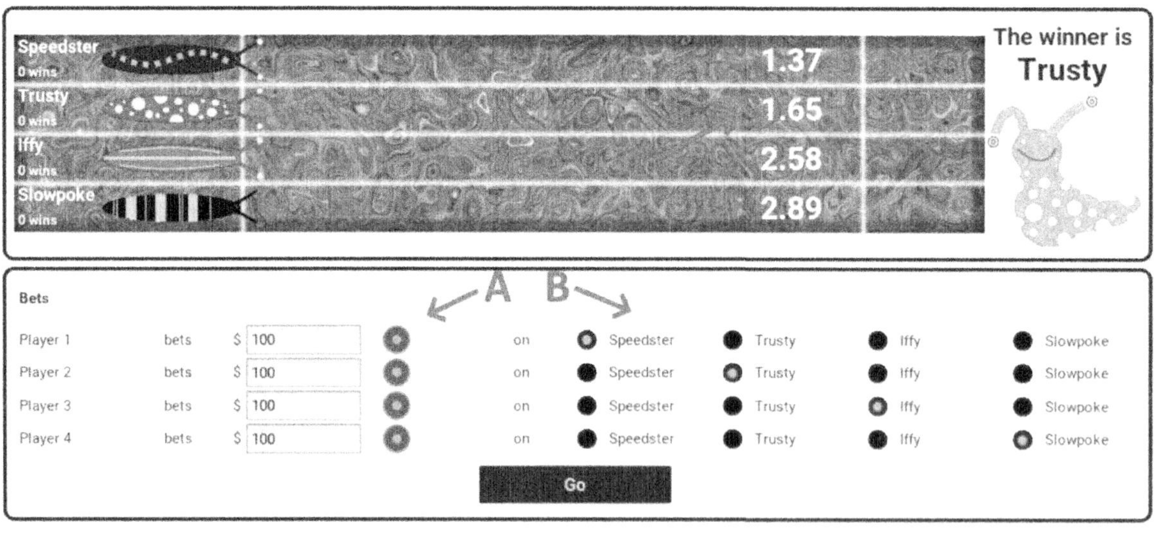

And here's what we can see after the race.

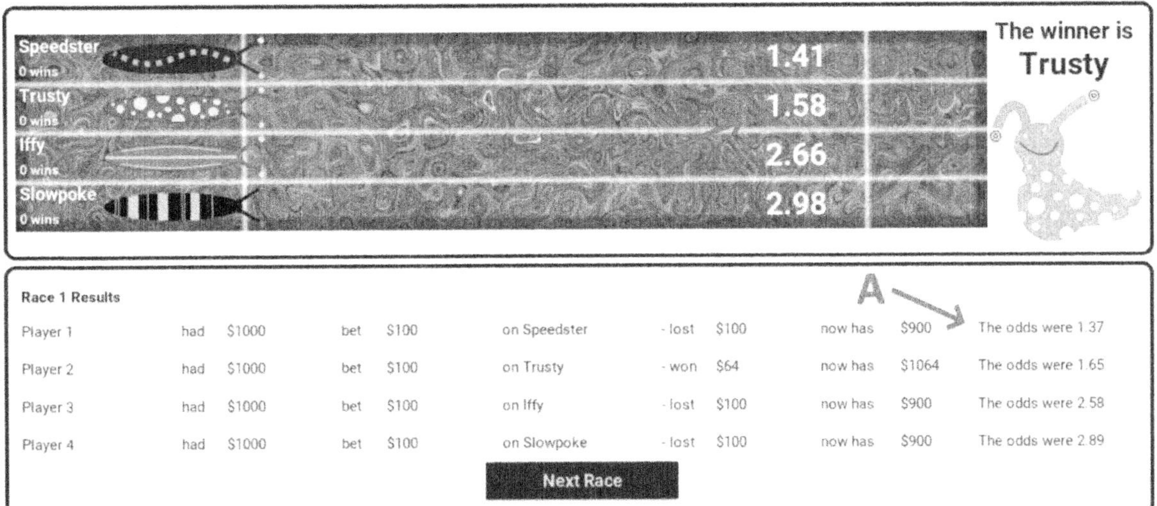


As you can see, Player 2 bet on Trusty and this is the slug that won. The other slugs lost. In the Results screen you can see the odds before the race (A). On the track you can see the new updated odds (B). Trusty's odds were 1.65, now they are 1.58. This is correct because if a slug is good, it's more probable that he will win. The odds of the other slugs are now higher than before. So, it works as expected.

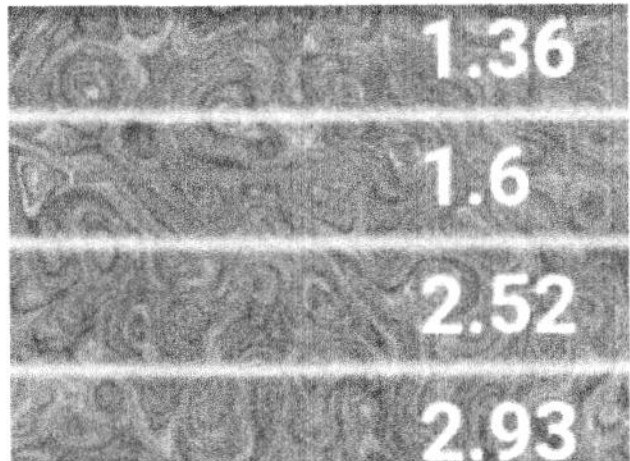


Now, sometimes it may happen that the odds end in 0 after the decimal point. As this is a zero after the decimal point, it's not displayed. Here in the example we can see that the odds 1.60 are displayed as 1.6.

It's not a big issue, but if you want to keep the length of the odds strings equal, you can format the string so that is always displays two digits after the decimal point. To do it, you can use the Python **format** method:

```
#:kivy 1.11.1
# File name: race.kv
#:import race race
...
<RaceScreen>:
    ...
        ### THE TRACK ###
        ...
                # the odds labels
                # Speedster
                WhiteOddsLabel:
                    text: '{:.2f}'.format(_speedster.odds)
                    pos_hint: {'x': .77, 'center_y': _speedster.y_position}
```

```
# Trusty
WhiteOddsLabel:
    text: '{:.2f}'.format(_trusty.odds)
    pos_hint: {'x': .77, 'center_y': _trusty.y_position}

# Iffy
WhiteOddsLabel:
    text: '{:.2f}'.format(_iffy.odds)
    pos_hint: {'x': .77, 'center_y': _iffy.y_position}

# Slowpoke
WhiteOddsLabel:
    text: '{:.2f}'.format(_slowpoke.odds)
    pos_hint: {'x': .77, 'center_y': _slowpoke.y_position}

# the slugs
...
```

Now you will always see two decimal places, even if there's a zero at the end.

And here's what you'll see if the money won by a player is less than $1.

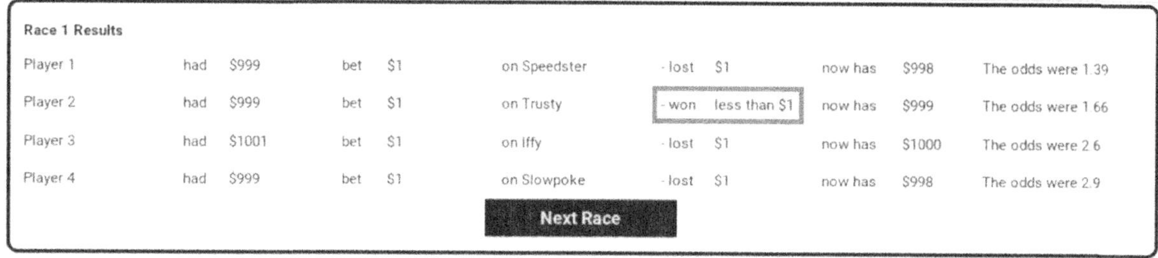


OK, the odds are now updated after each race. But, as you can see, no matter which slug wins, we always see Trusty in the Winner area to the right of the track. Besides, the Slugs' Stats panel isn't updated at all. So, make sure to do the exercises below where you will address these two issues. Additionally, in the third exercise you will handle the odds in the Results screen so that they are displayed correctly and there are always two decimal places displayed, just like on the track. And in the next chapter we'll see how to get ready for the next race.

## It's Your Turn Now...

### EXERCISE 1 - Updating the Winner Image

The next thing that we want to update is the image and name of the winning slug. You can see it all the time to the right of the track, even before the first race starts. And it always shows the same slug, Trusty, no matter which slug actually wins. Follow the steps below to fix this:

1. So, let's take care of the visibility of the winner info first. Here's what we now have:

```
#:kivy 1.11.1
# File name: race.kv
#:import race race
...
<RaceScreen>:
    ...
        ### THE TRACK ###
        ...
            # Winner
            BoxLayout:
                ...
                Label:
                    color: .2, .1, 0, 1
                    text: "The winner is"
                    ...
                Label:
                    color: .2, .1, 0, 1
                    text: "Trusty"
                    ...
                Image:
                    source: 'atlas://assets/silhouettes/silhouettes/Trusty'

        ### THE BETS ###
        ...
```

So, there are three elements displayed: the text **'The winner is'**, the name of the slug and the image of the slug. We'll take care of it in a minute, but so that you know, the two texts should be set to an empty string and the image's opacity to 0 if the **race_winner** ObjectProperty in the **Game** class is set to **None**, which is the case at the beginning of the game and also will be the case before each race eventually. And after each race, when there is a winner, the texts should be set to **'The winner is'** and the name of the winning slug respectively, and the image's opacity to 1.

Also, if there is no winner, the **source** property of the image should be set to an empty string. Otherwise, it should be set to the winning slug's **front_image** property. But, yes, there is no **front_image** property in the **Slug** class. So, add it first. Use a StringProperty to this end.

2. Next, set the **front_image** properties of the four **Slug** instances in the **race.kv** file to the paths to the silhoutte images that we have in the atlas we created.

3. And now you can actually set the name and front image of the winning slug. Read the description in step 1 again where I explain when the two texts and the image in the Winner area should be visible and when they shouldn't.

## SOLUTION

Here's the **Slug** class with the **front_image** property:

```
# File name: slug.py
...
class Slug(RelativeLayout):
    ...
    eye_image = StringProperty('')

    # the front image (silhouette) of the slug
    front_image = StringProperty('')

    y_position = NumericProperty(0)
    ...
```

Here are the four **Slug** instances in the **race.kv** file with the front images set:

```
#:kivy 1.11.1
# File name: race.kv
#:import race race
...
<RaceScreen>:
    ...
        ### THE TRACK ###
        ...
                # the slugs
                # Speedster
                Slug:
                    ...
                    y_position: .875
                    front_image: 'atlas://assets/silhouettes/silhouettes/Speedster'
                # Trusty
                Slug:
                    ...
                    y_position: .625
                    front_image: 'atlas://assets/silhouettes/silhouettes/Trusty'
                # Iffy
                Slug:
                    ...
                    y_position: .375
                    front_image: 'atlas://assets/silhouettes/silhouettes/Iffy'
                # Slowpoke
                Slug:
                    ...
                    y_position: .125
                    front_image: 'atlas://assets/silhouettes/silhouettes/Slowpoke'

            # Winner
            ...
```

And here's the modified Winner subarea after taking into consideration all the remarks above:

```
#:kivy 1.11.1
# File name: race.kv
#:import race race
...
<RaceScreen>:
    ...
        ### THE TRACK ###
        ...
            # Winner
            BoxLayout:
                ...
                Label:
                    color: .2, .1, 0, 1
                    text: '' if not root.game.race_winner else "The winner is"
                    font_size: 24
                    size_hint: 1, .2
                    bold: True

                Label:
                    color: .2, .1, 0, 1
                    text: '' if not root.game.race_winner else root.game.race_winner.name
                    font_size: 32
                    size_hint: 1, .2
                    bold: True

                Image:
                    opacity: 1 if root.game.race_winner else 0
                    source: '' if not root.game.race_winner else root.game.race_winner.front_image

        ### THE BETS ###
        ...
```

If you now run the app, you won't see any winner if there isn't one.

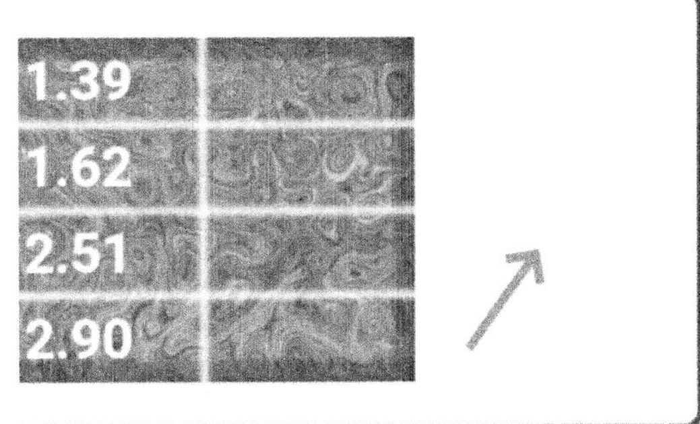


But after the first race, when there is a winner, you will see him.

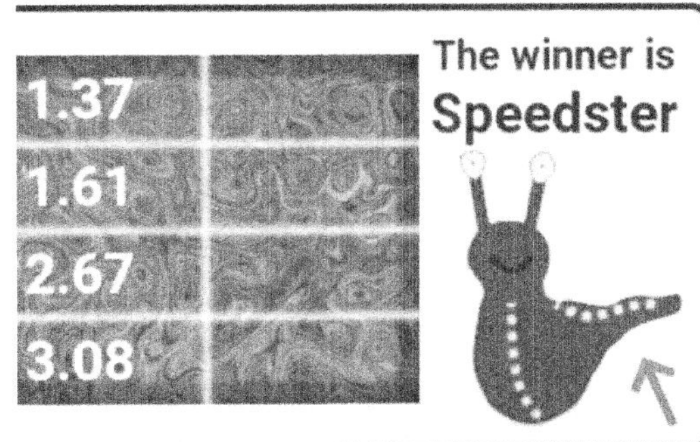

### EXERCISE 2 - Updating the Slugs' Stats

After each race the slugs' statistics must be updated, so the **wins** and **win_percent** properties must be updated. We already have the code we need in the **race.kv** file:

```
#:kivy 1.11.1
# File name: race.kv
#:import race race
...
<RaceScreen>:
    ...
        ### INFO, STATS AND BUTTONS ###
        ...
            # Slugs' Stats
            BoxLayout:
                ...
                BoldLabel:
                    text: "Slugs' Stats"

                SlugStats:
                    name: 'Speedster'
                    wins: _speedster.wins
                    win_percent: _speedster.win_percent

                SlugStats:
                    name: 'Trusty'
                    wins: _trusty.wins
                    win_percent: _trusty.win_percent

                SlugStats:
                    name: 'Iffy'
                    wins: _iffy.wins
                    win_percent: _iffy.win_percent

                SlugStats:
                    name: 'Slowpoke'
                    wins: _slowpoke.wins
                    win_percent: _slowpoke.win_percent

            # Players' Stats
            ...
```

The stats should be updated immediately when the race finishes and there's a winner. And we mustn't forget that we must update all the slugs' stats, not just the winner's. Otherwise the value of the **win_percent** property would be incorrect most of the time.

At this moment the winner is just a randomly picked slug. The slug is picked in the **go** method, so we'll add the code that updates the slugs' statistics in this method. But first things first. Follow the steps below:

1. Just like we did with the **Player** class, we also created an **update** method in the **Slug** class where the odds are updated after each race. It now has one parameter, **winning_slug**. Now you're going to add some code to the method that will update the slug's **wins** and **win_percent** properties. To this end, we'll need another parameter, so add the **race_number** parameter to the method. Now you can add the code that you need below the code that updates the odds.

If the slug is the winner, his **wins** property should be incremented by 1. The win percent, on the other hand, should be calculated regardless of whether or not the slug has won. The value of the **win_percent** property should be calculated as the number of wins divided by the number of races multiplied by 100. Additionally, it should be rounded to two decimal places.

2. Next, we have to modify the call of the **update** method in the **go** method. Now it needs two arguments, the second of which is **race_number**. Actually, we havent created this property yet, so let's start by doing this before we use it in the method call. Add the NumericProperty **race_number** to the **Game** class (preferably in the races section of the code) with the default value of 1.

3. With the **race_number** property defined, you can modify the call to the **update** method for each slug in the **go** method.

### SOLUTION

Let's start by modifying the **update** method in the **Slug** class:

```
# File name: slug.py
...
class Slug(RelativeLayout):
    ...
    odds = NumericProperty(0)

    # We need the race_number parameter to calculate the win percent.
    def update(self, winning_slug, race_number):
        # update odds
        if self == winning_slug:
            self.odds = round(max(1.01, min(self.odds * .96, 20)), 2)
        else:
            self.odds = round(max(1.01, min(self.odds * 1.03, 20)), 2)

        # update wins and win_percent
        # The number of wins should be incremented only for the winner.
        if self == winning_slug:
            self.wins += 1

        # The win percent should be calculated regardless of whether the slug has won.
        self.win_percent = round(self.wins / race_number * 100, 2)
```

Let's now add the NumericProperty **race_number** to the **Game** class:

```
# File name: main.py
...
class Game(ScreenManager):
    ...
    # races
    ...
    races_to_go = NumericProperty(0)

    ### We need a property to store the current race number.
    race_number = NumericProperty(1)

    race_winner = ObjectProperty(None)
    ...
```

And now let's modify the **go** method:

```
# File name: main.py
...
class Game(ScreenManager):
    ...
    def go(self):
        ...
        for slug in self.slugs:
            slug.update(self.race_winner, self.race_number)

class SlugraceApp(App):
    ...
```

Run the app and after a couple races you can see how many times (expressed both as a number and as a percentage) each slug has won so far. In the image on the right you can see what I got after 10 races.

| Slugs' Stats | | |
|---|---|---|
| Speedster | 1 win | 100.0% |
| Trusty | 3 wins | 300.0% |
| Iffy | 4 wins | 400.0% |
| Slowpoke | 2 wins | 200.0% |

The percentages should sum up to 100%. As you can see, they don't. This is because the race number is not updated yet and so the wins are always divided by 1. This will start working correctly in the next chapter when we code race resetting and the race number is incremented after each race. So, don't worry about these strange percentages too much.

**EXERCISE 3 - The Odds in the Results Screen**

We already handled the odds on the track so that they are always displayed with two decimal places. But we haven't handled the odds in the Results screen yet, so you can sometimes see only one decimal place (or even none if the odds have only zeros after the decimal point). Here's an example:

Besides, the odds displayed in the Results screen may be incorrect. Don't worry about that. It's temporary and will change after we make some changes. Now, let's concentrate on the trailing zeros that are missing.

So, modify the code in the Results screen so that two decimal places are always displayed. Before you do that, change the **odds** property in the **Result** class to a **StringProperty**. This also means you no longer have to cast it to a string in the **Result** rule in the kv file. Use similar formatting as on the track.

### SOLUTION

So, here's the **Result** class:

```
# File name: results.py
...
class Result(BoxLayout):
    ...
    current_money = NumericProperty(0)
    odds = StringProperty('')

class ResultsScreen(Screen):
    pass
```

And here's the code that is responsible for displaying the odds:

```
#:kivy 1.11.1
# File name: results.kv
#:import results results

<Result>:
    ...
    RegularLabel:
        # Now odds is a StringProperty, so there's no need to cast.
        text: 'The odds were ' + root.odds

<ResultsScreen>:
    ...
        ### PLAYER RESULTS ###
        BoxLayout:
            orientation: 'vertical'
```

```
            # player 1
            Result:
                ...
                odds: '{:.2f}'.format(root.game.player1.chosen_slug.odds) if root.game.player1
.chosen_slug else '1.00'

            # player 2
            Result:
                ...
                odds: '{:.2f}'.format(root.game.player2.chosen_slug.odds) if root.game.player2
.chosen_slug else '1.00'
                disabled: root.game.number_of_players < 2

            # player 3
            Result:
                ...
                odds: '{:.2f}'.format(root.game.player3.chosen_slug.odds) if root.game.player3
.chosen_slug else '1.00'
                disabled: root.game.number_of_players < 3

            # player 4
            Result:
                ...
                odds: '{:.2f}'.format(root.game.player4.chosen_slug.odds) if root.game.player4
.chosen_slug else '1.00'
                disabled: root.game.number_of_players < 4

        ### NEXT RACE BUTTON ###
        ...
```

And now you can always see two decimal places.

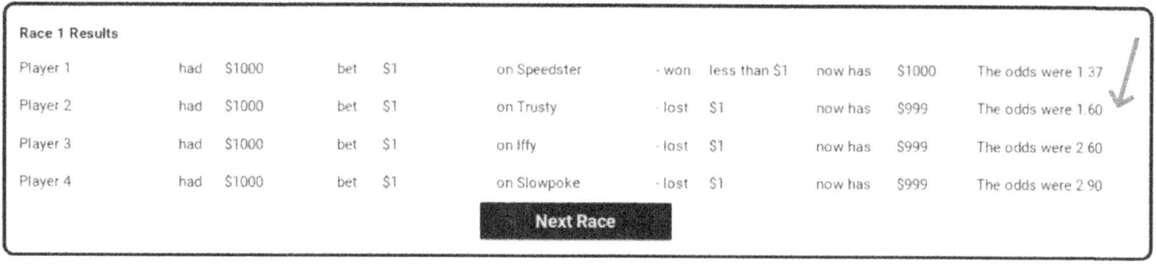

# Chapter 89 – Resetting the Race

In the previous chapter we simulated a single race. When a race finishes, a couple of things happen. There is a winner and the players know whether they have won or lost money on their bets. The winner info is updated and the slugs' statistics are updated. We covered all of that in the previous chapter. But then, before the next race begins, we have to do some cleanup. In this chapter we'll take care of resetting the race, by which I mean getting ready for the next race.

In particular, what does the cleanup involve? First of all, the race number must be incremented. Second, the **chosen_slug** property of the slugs must be set to **None** because we don't want the players to have the same slugs assigned as in the previous race. Third, the race winner must be reset and the Winner area must be updated, so the winner info should disappear. This is what we are going to handle in this chapter.

## Updating the Race Number

After each race the race number must be updated.

We already have the NumericProperty that will store the current race number. We added it in the previous chapter to the **Game** class and named it **race_number**.

We set its default value to 1. Here you can see it again:

```
# File name: main.py
...
class Game(ScreenManager):
    ...
    # races
    number_of_races = NumericProperty(0)
    races_finished = NumericProperty(0)
    races_to_go = NumericProperty(0)
    race_number = NumericProperty(1)
    race_winner = ObjectProperty(None)

    # time
    ...
```

Now, in the Race screen, we want the actual race number to be displayed, not just 1 all the time. So, let's modify the code:

```
#:kivy 1.11.1
# File name: race.kv
#:import race race
...
<RaceScreen>:
    ...
            # Game Info
            ...
                BoldLabel:
                    text: 'Game Info:'
                BoxLayout:
                    RegularLabel:
                        size_hint: (2.5, 1)
                        text: 'Race No'
                    RegularLabel:
                        text: str(root.game.race_number)

                BoxLayout:
                    ...
```

There's one more place where the actual race number should be displayed. It's in the Results screen, so let's modify the code like so:

```
#:kivy 1.11.1
# File name: results.kv
#:import results results
...
<ResultsScreen>:
    ...
        ### TITLE LABEL ###
        BoldLabel:
            text: 'Race {} Results'.format(root.game.race_number)
            size_hint: (1, None)
            ...
```

Now, when do we want the race number to be incremented? Well, when the Next Race button in the Results screen is pressed. So, let's add a method to the **Game** class that will take care of this. This method is going to handle more stuff, as you're about to see, so let's name it **reset_race**. Here's the code:

```
# File name: main.py
...
class Game(ScreenManager):
    ...
    def go(self):
        ...

    # This method will be called to reset the state after each race.
    # For now it's only going to increment the race number.
    def reset_race(self):
        self.race_number += 1

class SlugraceApp(App):
    ...
```

And now all we have to do is call this method in the Results screen:

```
#:kivy 1.11.1
# File name: results.kv
#:import results results
...
<ResultsScreen>:
    ...
        ### NEXT RACE BUTTON ###
        RedButton:
            text: 'Next Race'
            on_press:
                # Let's call the method that will, among other things,
                # increment the race number.
                root.game.reset_race()

                root.manager.current = 'betsscreen'
                root.manager.transition.direction = 'right'
```

If you now run the app you will see the number of races update after each race. So, the race number is now updated in the Game Info area (A) and in the Results screen (B). What's more, the slugs' win percent values are now calculated and displayed correctly because the number of wins is divided by the correct number of races. The percentages should sum up to 100%. Naturally, we have to take the rounding into consideration. The wins should sum up to the race number. Check it out.

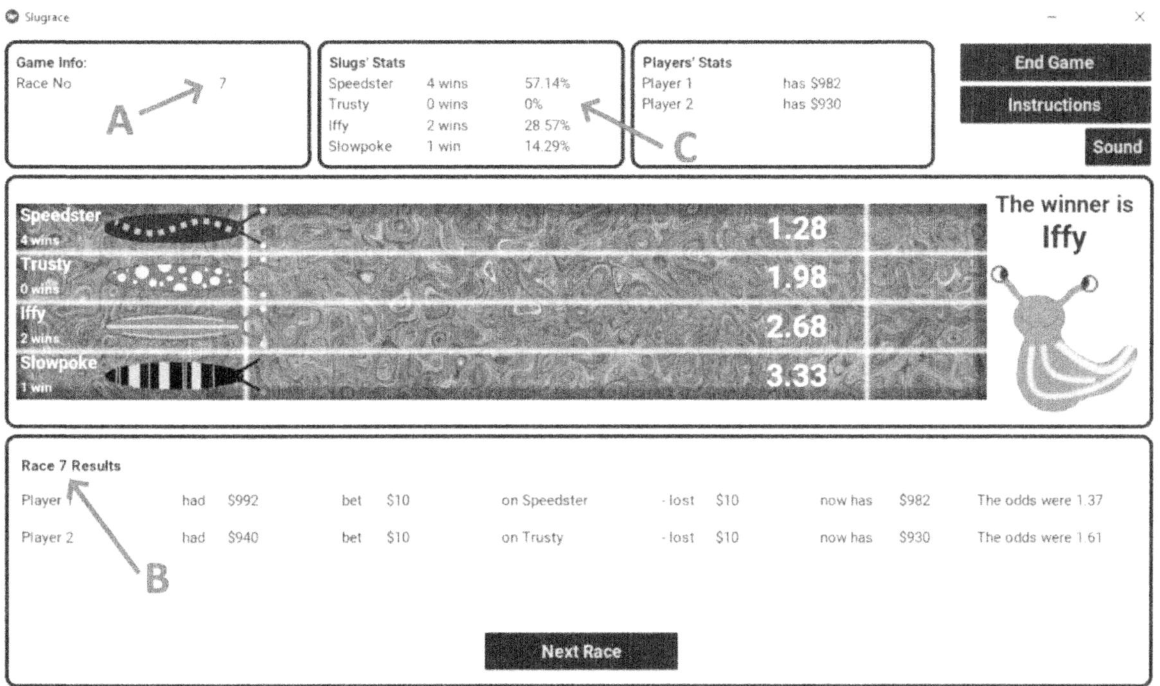


# Resetting the Players' Chosen Slugs and Bets

The next thing we must take care of is resetting the players' slugs and bets. Now when you play the game, the slugs selected by the players are still selected after the first race. When the Results screen switches back to the Bets screen after you press the Next Race button, the radio buttons are still selected and if the players want to bet on the same slugs as before, they don't have to do anything, just press the Go button (provided they want to bet the same amounts of money).

This solution isn't bad because it could save the players some time if they want to bet on the same slugs over and over again. On the other hand, they may hit the Go button by accident and lose the chance to bet on different slugs. This is why I decided to make the players explicitly choose the slugs they want to bet on after each race. So, when the Results screen switches back to the Bets screen, the players should have no chosen slugs assigned and all the radio buttons should be unchecked.

Similarly, the players' bets are set to the same value as in the previous race. We want to set them back to 1, which is the default value.

Well, this requires some work on our part. The general idea is that when the Next Race button in the Results screen is pressed, the players' chosen slugs should be all set to **None**. We already have a method that is called when the Next Race button is pressed, it's the **reset_race** method in the **Game** class that currently only increments the race number. It looks like a good place to add the code that will reset the chosen slugs to **None** and the bets to 1. So, let's go to the **Game** class and add the code we need to the **reset_race** method:

```
# File name: main.py
...
class Game(ScreenManager):
    ...
    def reset_race(self):
        self.race_number += 1

        # The players should be assigned no slugs after a race until they
        # bet again and their bets should be reset to 1.
        for player in self.players:
            player.chosen_slug = None
            player.bet = 1

class SlugraceApp(App):
    ...
```

We're done with the bets, it was the easy part. What about the chosen slugs? When you now run the app, everything works fine until you hit the Next Race button after the first race. Then the app crashes and you can read the following error message in the terminal:

```
ValueError: None is not allowed for Player.chosen_slug
```

The problem is that **chosen_slug** is an ObjectProperty and one feature of Kivy properties we havent's discussed yet is that a property can be set to **None** only at the very beginning to assign it **None** as the default value. But once you set it to anything else, you can't set it back to **None**, hence the error. But there's a very easy way to fix it, you just have to declare the property with the **allownone** parameter set to **True**. So, go to the **Player** class and modify the code like so:

```
# File name: player.py
...
class Player(EventDispatcher):
    ...
    bet = NumericProperty(1)
    chosen_slug = ObjectProperty(None, allownone=True)

    def update(self, winning_slug):
        ...
```

Now you can set the **chosen_slug** property to **None** and you won't get the error anymore. So, let's run the app and set the number of players to 3. Let the players bet on Speedster, Iffy and Trusty respectively. Hit Go and after the race is finished, hit Next Race. This is what you should see:

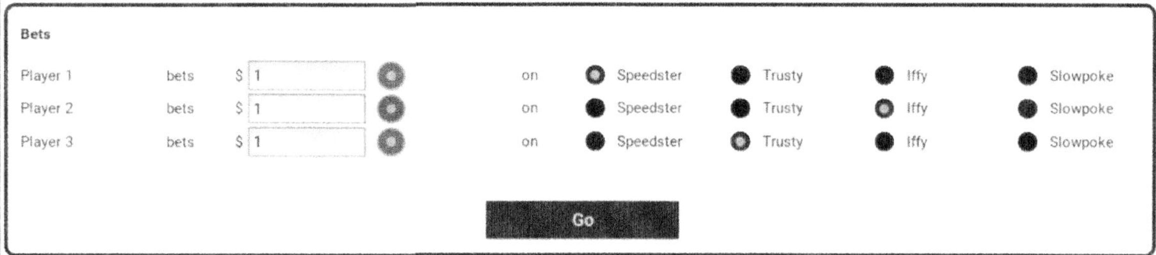


So, the good news is the error is gone. But the three radio buttons are still selected. As you remember, we reset the chosen slugs to **None**, so are the three slugs really still selected? Let's hit the Go button again:

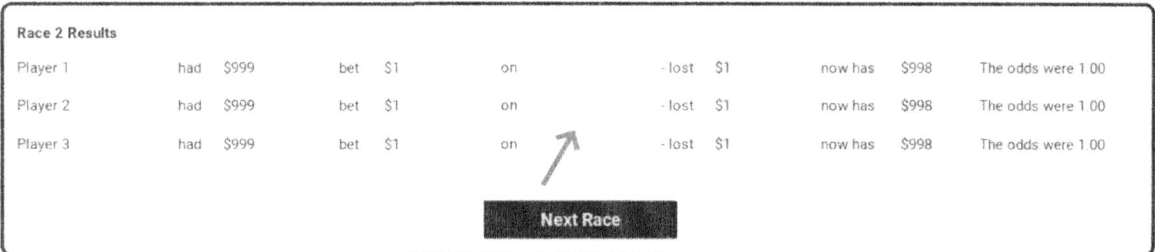


As you can see, there are no slugs selected anymore, so the radio buttons are very misleading and counterintuitive. Let's take care of them then.

We'll create a method that will be called when the Go button is pressed. The method will be defined in the **BetScreen** class and its task will be to uncheck all the radio buttons as soon as the Bets screen is replaced by the Results screen. Let's name the method **clear_bets**. But before we do that, let's add ids to the four bets and to the four radio buttons in the class rule. We'll need them in the **clear_bets** method to reference all the radio buttons. We'll also put the radio buttons and the bets in lists so that it's easier to reference all of them at once. Here's the modified **bets.kv** file:

```
#:kivy 1.11.1
# File name: bets.kv
#:import bets bets

<Bet>:
    spacing: 10
    opacity: int(not self.disabled)

    # the four radio buttons in a bet
    slug_buttons: [_speedsterButton, _trustyButton, _iffyButton, _slowpokeButton]

    RegularLabel:
```

```
        text: root.player_name
    ...
    RegularLabel:
        text: 'on'
        size_hint: (.3, 1)
    BoxLayout:
        PlayerSlugButton:
            id: _speedsterButton
            group: root.player_group
            on_active: if self.active: root.selected_slug = 1
        RegularLabel:
            text: 'Speedster'
    BoxLayout:
        PlayerSlugButton:
            id: _trustyButton
            group: root.player_group
            on_active: if self.active: root.selected_slug = 2
        RegularLabel:
            text: 'Trusty'
    BoxLayout:
        PlayerSlugButton:
            id: _iffyButton
            group: root.player_group
            on_active: if self.active: root.selected_slug = 3
        RegularLabel:
            text: 'Iffy'
    BoxLayout:
        PlayerSlugButton:
            id: _slowpokeButton
            group: root.player_group
            on_active: if self.active: root.selected_slug = 4
        RegularLabel:
            text: 'Slowpoke'

<BetsScreen>:
    ...
    game: root.manager.parent.parent.parent.manager

    # the four bets
    bets: [_bet1, _bet2, _bet3, _bet4]

    BoxLayout:
        ...
        ### PLAYER BETS ###
        ...
            # player 1
            Bet:
                id: _bet1
                player_name: root.game.player1.name
                ...
            # player 2
            Bet:
                id: _bet2
                player_name: root.game.player2.name
```

```
            ...
        # player 3
        Bet:
            id: _bet3
            player_name: root.game.player3.name
            ...
        # player 4
        Bet:
            id: _bet4
            player_name: root.game.player4.name
            ...
    ### GO BUTTON ###
    ...
```

Now we can implement the **clear_bets** method:

```
# File name: bets.py
...
class BetsScreen(Screen):
    ...
    def select_slug(self, player, slug_index):
        ...

    # method used to uncheck all radio buttons
    def clear_bets(self):
        # In each bet uncheck each radio button.
        for bet in self.bets:
            for slug_button in bet.slug_buttons:
                if slug_button.active:
                    slug_button.active = False
```

Next, we have to call the method:

```
#:kivy 1.11.1
# File name: bets.kv
#:import bets bets
...
<BetsScreen>:
    ...
        ### GO BUTTON ###
        RedButton:
            ...
            on_press:
                ...
                root.game.go()

                # Let's clear all the
                # bets by unchecking
                # the radio buttons.
                root.clear_bets()
```

Let's run the app. This time let's set the number of players to 4 and let the players bet on all the slugs in order:

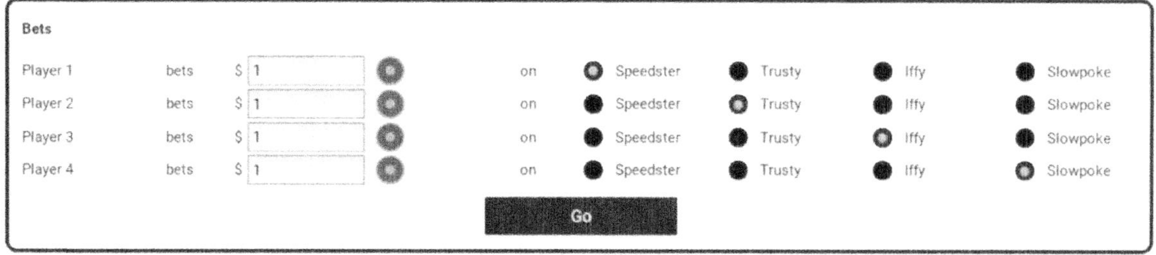


Now hit the Go button and then the Next Race button. Now, all the radio buttons are unchecked (A). But the Go button is enabled (B). As you remember, it should be only enabled if all players have chosen their slugs. So, we'll have to address this issue in a moment.

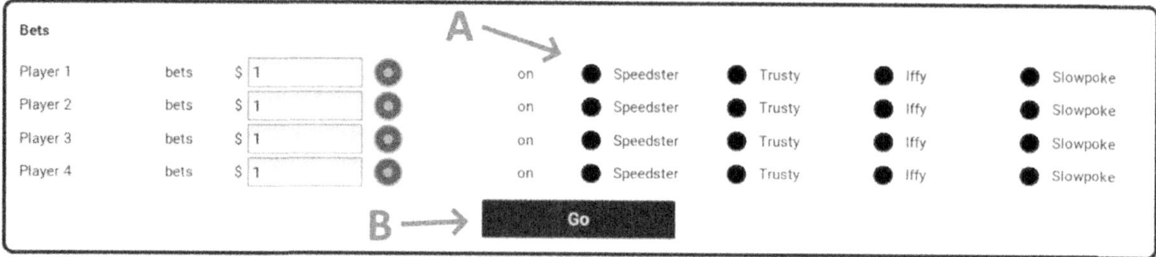


And now let the players select the exact same slugs, so Player 1 should select Speedster, Player 2 should select Trusty, and so on. Hit the Go button and you will see that the players actually didn't choose the slugs. So, this is another issue we must address.

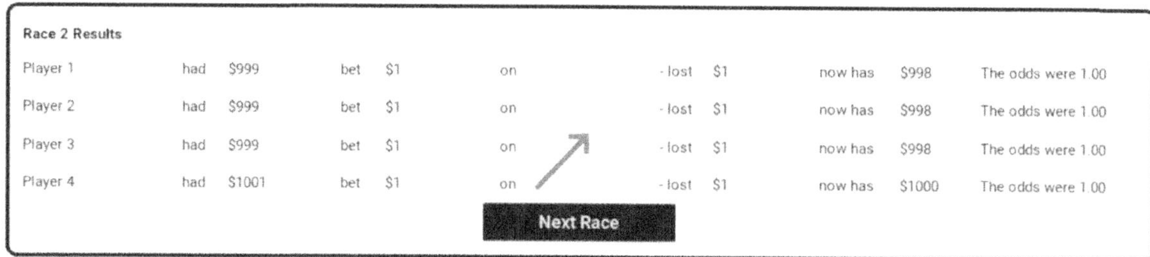


To make things even more interesting, let's hit Next Race and in the Bets screen let just one player select a different slug than before. For example, let Player 1 select Trusty instead of Speedster (A). Now suddenly the Go button becomes disabled (B):

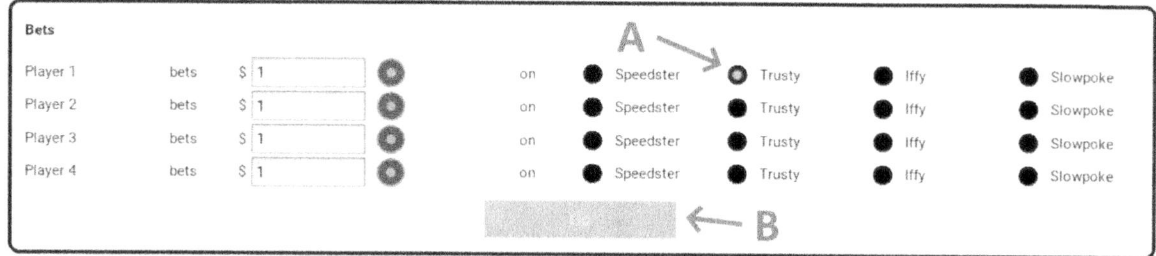


If the other players all select different slugs than before, the Go button will be enabled again.

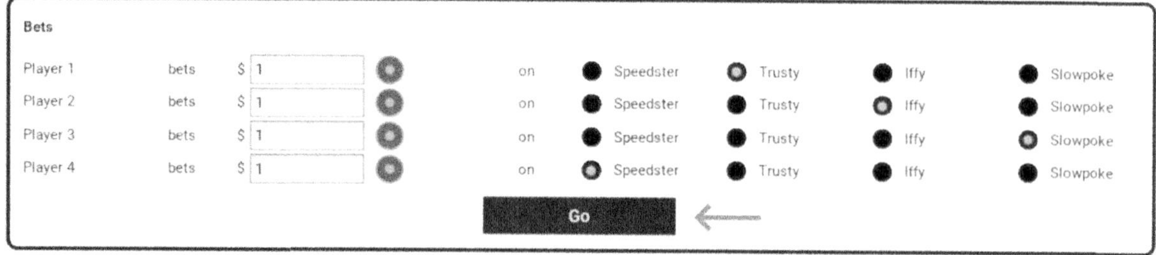


And now if you hit the Go button, the slugs will be selected correctly.

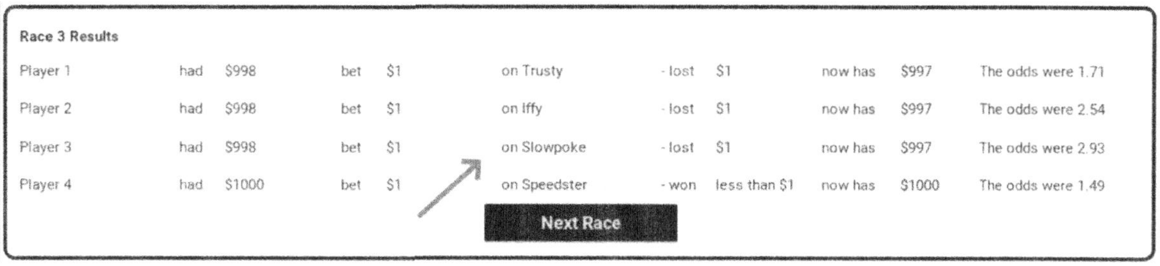

**Race 3 Results**

| | | | | | | | | | | |
|---|---|---|---|---|---|---|---|---|---|---|
| Player 1 | had | $998 | bet | $1 | on Trusty | - lost | $1 | now has | $997 | The odds were 1.71 |
| Player 2 | had | $998 | bet | $1 | on Iffy | - lost | $1 | now has | $997 | The odds were 2.54 |
| Player 3 | had | $998 | bet | $1 | on Slowpoke | - lost | $1 | now has | $997 | The odds were 2.93 |
| Player 4 | had | $1000 | bet | $1 | on Speedster | - won | less than $1 | now has | $1000 | The odds were 1.49 |

Next Race

So, everything works fine, but there is one condition. None of the players can choose the same slug as in the previous race. Naturally, this isn't an ideal solution. So, what's the problem and how to fix it? Let's analyze the code to find out.

Have a look at the following lines of code:

```
#:kivy 1.11.1
# File name: bets.kv
#:import bets bets

<Bet>:
    ...
    BoxLayout:
        PlayerSlugButton:
            ...
            on_active: if self.active: root.selected_slug = 1
        RegularLabel:
            text: 'Speedster'
    BoxLayout:
        PlayerSlugButton:
            ...
            on_active: if self.active: root.selected_slug = 2
        RegularLabel:
            text: 'Trusty'
    BoxLayout:
        PlayerSlugButton:
            ...
            on_active: if self.active: root.selected_slug = 3
        RegularLabel:
            text: 'Iffy'
    BoxLayout:
        PlayerSlugButton:
            ...
            on_active: if self.active: root.selected_slug = 4
        RegularLabel:
            text: 'Slowpoke'

<BetsScreen>:
    ...
        ### PLAYER BETS ###
        ...
            # player 1
            Bet:
                ...
                on_selected_slug: root.select_slug(root.game.player1, self.selected_slug - 1)
```

```
            # player 2
            Bet:
                ...
                on_selected_slug: root.select_slug(root.game.player2, self.selected_slug - 1)
            # player 3
            Bet:
                ...
                on_selected_slug: root.select_slug(root.game.player3, self.selected_slug - 1)
            # player 4
            Bet:
                ...
                on_selected_slug: root.select_slug(root.game.player4, self.selected_slug - 1)

        ### GO BUTTON ###
        ...
```

So, in the **Bet** instances the method **select_slug** is called whenever the **selected_slug** property changes. In the **Bet** rule above you can see that this property changes when a radio button's **active** property changes, but not always. Have a look:

```
on_active: if self.active: root.selected_slug = 1
```

There's a condition. So, the **selected_slug** property only changes if we check the button, but not when we uncheck it. So, when the **active** property of each radio button is set to **False** in the **clear_bets** method, the **selected_slug** property isn't changed because the condition isn't met. This means that if a player then selects the same slug again, the **selected_slug** property is still set to the same value and the **select_slug** method isn't called. And this means, the player doesn't select any slug, because this is what the **select_slug** method should take care of. This is why there were no slugs selected in the second race.

So, let's modify the code so that the **selected_slug** property changes always when the **active** property of the radio button changes, even if the radio button is unchecked. If it's unchecked, the **selected_slug** property should be set to 0:

```
#:kivy 1.11.1
# File name: bets.kv
#:import bets bets

<Bet>:
    ...
    BoxLayout:
        PlayerSlugButton:
            ...
            on_active: root.selected_slug = 1 if self.active else 0
        RegularLabel:
            text: 'Speedster'
    BoxLayout:
        PlayerSlugButton:
            ...
```

```
            on_active: root.selected_slug = 2 if self.active else 0
        RegularLabel:
            text: 'Trusty'
    BoxLayout:
        PlayerSlugButton:
            ...
            on_active: root.selected_slug = 3 if self.active else 0
        RegularLabel:
            text: 'Iffy'
    BoxLayout:
        PlayerSlugButton:
            ...
            on_active: root.selected_slug = 4 if self.active else 0
        RegularLabel:
            text: 'Slowpoke'

<BetsScreen>:
    ...
```

Now the **selected_slug** property changes each time the state of the radio button changes. But what if it's set to 0? This is the case when a radio button is unchecked. We need a small modification in the **select_slug** method to handle this. The code that we already have will now become a conditional block of code that will be executed only if **slug_index** is greater than or equal to zero:

```
# File name: bets.py
...
class BetsScreen(Screen):
    ...
    def select_slug(self, player, slug_index):
        if slug_index >= 0:
            player.chosen_slug = self.game.slugs[slug_index]
            players_with_slugs = [player for player in self.game.players
                                  if player.chosen_slug]
            self.all_slugs_selected = len(players_with_slugs) == len(self.game.players)

    def clear_bets(self):
        ...
```

So now the slug is assigned to a player only if the index that we passed is greater than or equal to 0. As you remember, the slugs were numbered from 1 to 4, but then they were passed as arguments like so:

```
on_selected_slug: root.select_slug(root.game.player4, self.selected_slug - 1)
```

so the actual indices of the slugs are from 0 to 3.

If you now run the app, the radio buttons will be unchecked after the first race and each player will be able to select the same slugs again. But the problem is that the Go button is now enabled, although no radio buttons are checked and the players have no chosen slugs.

Let's have a look at the button again:

```
#:kivy 1.11.1
# File name: bets.kv
#:import bets bets
...
<BetsScreen>:
    ...
        ### GO BUTTON ###
        RedButton:
            text: 'Go'
            disabled: not root.all_slugs_selected
            on_press:
                ...
```

So, when is the button disabled? Only if the **all_slugs_selected** property is set to **False**. So, let's set it back to **False** in the **clear_bets** method:

```
# File name: bets.py
...
class BetsScreen(Screen):
    ...
    def clear_bets(self):
        self.all_slugs_selected = False

        for bet in self.bets:
            ...
```

Now everything should work as expected. Let's try it out. This time we'll set the number of players to 3 and they will select the first three slugs in the first race.

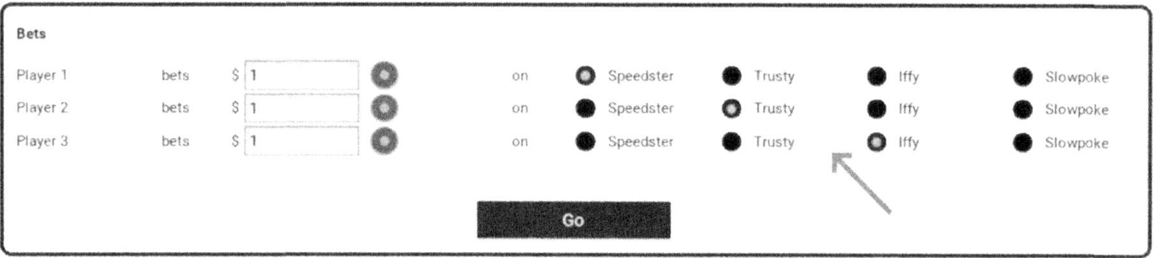


Let's hit Go and see the results:

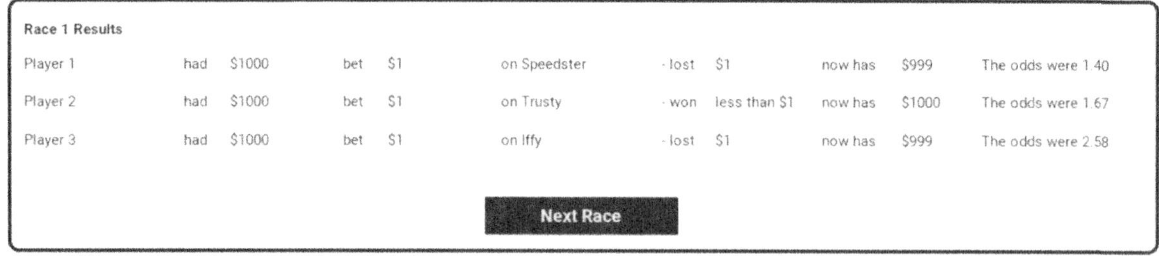


And if we now hit the Next Race button, all the radio buttons will be unchecked and the Go button will be disabled, as it should.

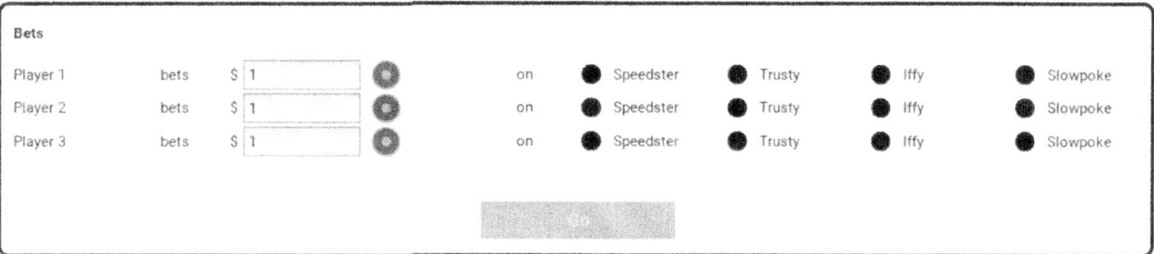


And now let's select the same slugs as before. When the last slug is selected, the Go button becomes enabled.

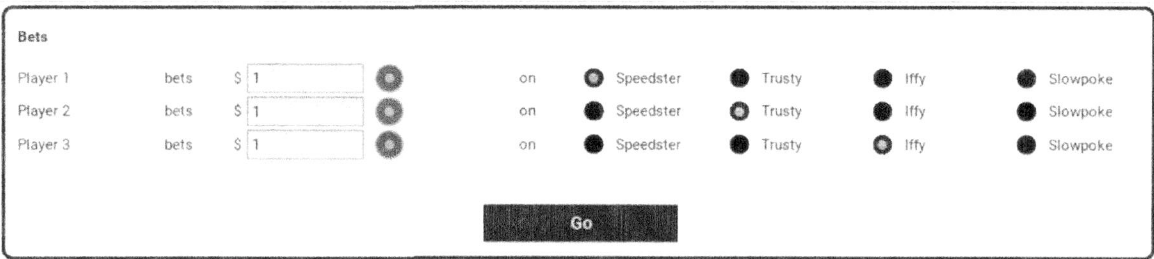


Let's hit the Go button.

As you can see, the slugs are selected correctly. And you can go on like that and select any slugs you like each time, even the same ones all the time if this is your strategy.

There are some more things to do when the race is reset. In particular, the **race_winner** property should be set to **None** and the Winner panel should be taken care of. But I'll leave this for you as an exercise. And in the next chapter we'll implement logic that will check whether a player still has any money left afer a race. If not, the player will be removed from the game.

# It's Your Turn Now...

## EXERCISE

When you now run the app, place some bets and then hit the Next Race button, the winner slug info is still visible. But this is not how we want it to behave. The race winner slug should be reset so that the Winner area is empty at the beginning of the next race. So, make sure the **race_winner** property is reset to **None**. Remember that it's a Kivy property, so it can't be set to **None** just like that. We already had a similar problem when we were trying to reset the chosen slugs to **None**, so check it out. When the **race_winner** property is reset to **None**, the Winner area will be handled automatically because the code that hides the two texts and the winner slug image is already there.

## SOLUTION

So, first of all let's add the code that will set **race_winner** to **None**. This should be done in the **reset_race** method. You also must remember to use **allownone** in the **race_winner** ObjectProperty in order to be able to set it to **None**. Here's the code:

```
# File name: main.py
...
class Game(ScreenManager):
    ...
    # races
    ...
    race_number = NumericProperty(1)
    # The race winner will sometimes have to be set to None,
    # so we must use allownone.
    race_winner = ObjectProperty(None, allownone=True)

    # time
    ...
    def reset_race(self):
        self.race_number += 1
        for player in self.players:
            player.chosen_slug = None
            player.bet = 1

        # The race winner should be reset.
        self.race_winner = None

class SlugraceApp(App):
    ...
```

If you now run the app, the winner info will disappear after each race.

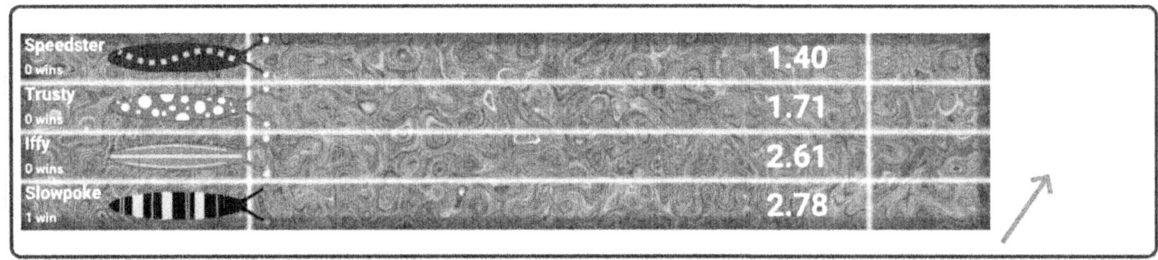

# Chapter 90 – Handling the Players

In the previous chapter we handled the races so that the original state is restored after each race. In particular, it meant detaching the chosen slugs from the players, setting their bets to 1 and cleaning up the Winner area. This reset must be done after each race.

In this chapter we'll be talking about other code that must be run after each race. We need to check whether the players still have money and to remove the players who don't. Later, we'll also add a game over check to the code so that the game is over when there is only one player with any money left (unless there's only one player in the game).

Let's start with some cleanup, though. At this moment the code that resets the players is in the **Game** class:

```
# File name: main.py
...
class Game(ScreenManager):
    ...
    def reset_race(self):
        self.race_number += 1

        for player in self.players:
            player.chosen_slug = None
            player.bet = 1

        self.race_winner = None

class SlugraceApp(App):
    ...
```

As this is all about the players, let's create a **reset** method in the **Player** class and call it in the **reset_race** method then. So, here's the method:

```
# File name: player.py
...
class Player(EventDispatcher):
    ...
    def update(self, winning_slug):
        ...

    def reset(self):
        self.chosen_slug = None
        self.bet = 1
```

And here's how we call it in the **Game** class:

```
# File name: main.py
...
class Game(ScreenManager):
    ...
    def reset_race(self):
        self.race_number += 1

        for player in self.players:
            player.reset()

        self.race_winner = None

class SlugraceApp(App):
    ...
```

Now everything works as before, but the code that handles the player is in the **Player** class now.

# Bankrupt Players

And now let's focus on the players' money. After each race we need to check whether each player still has any money left. All players that are bankrupt must be removed from the **players** list. But they are not going to be removed from the game, just from the **players** list, which basically means they will not be taken into consideration in the game from now on, but we will still have access to them. This is important, because the way they will be represented in the GUI after they go bankrupt will differ. There are going to be three differences actually:

1. In the Bets screen the bets associated with bankrupt players will be disabled and a message (with the text color set to red) will appear at their location informing us that a particular player is bankrupt.

2. The same will happen in the Results screen. A bankrupt player's results will be replaced by the same message.

3. The text color in the Players' Stats area in the Race screen will turn to red as soon as a player is bankrupt.

We're going to take care of all that in a minute. Partially it's going to be your job actually. But now let's modify the code so that the players' money is checked after each race and if there's nothing in their account, the players go bankrupt.

We'll start by adding a new BooleanProperty to the **Player** class. Let's name it **bankrupt** and set to **False**. Then, in the **update** method, if the player's money is zero, it should be set to **True**. Here's the code:

```
# File name: player.py

# We'll need a BooleanProperty for the bankrupt property.
from kivy.properties import (StringProperty, NumericProperty,
                             ObjectProperty, BooleanProperty)
...
class Player(EventDispatcher):
    ...
    chosen_slug = ObjectProperty(None, allownone=True)

    # Here's the bankrupt property. By default it's set to False.
    bankrupt = BooleanProperty(False)

    def update(self, winning_slug):
        ...
        self.money += self.money_won

        # If the player loses all money, the bankrupt property is set to True.
        if self.money == 0:
            self.bankrupt = True

    def reset(self):
        ...
```

Now, the players are updated in the **go** method of the **Game** class. So, we must add code that will remove bankrupt players somewhere below the code that updates the players. Let's define a method that will take care of it, name it **remove_bankrupt_players**, and call it in the **go** method:

```
# File name: main.py
...
class Game(ScreenManager):
    ...
    def go(self):
        ...
        for slug in self.slugs:
            slug.update(self.race_winner, self.race_number)

        # Bankrupt players should be removed
        # from the players list.
        self.remove_bankrupt_players()

    # Here's the method that removes bankrupt players from the players list.
    def remove_bankrupt_players(self):
        # Technically, the method creates a new list that contains just the players
        # who are not bankrupt. We're using a list comprehension to do that.
        # Then the new list is assigned to the players list.
        self.players = [player for player in self.players if not player.bankrupt]

    def reset_race(self):
        ...
```

Good, and now we can take care of the Bets screen, the Results screen and the Players' Stats area inside Race screen. We'll start with the Bets screen and I'll leave the other two for you as an exercise.

## Bankrupt Players in the Bets Screen

So, when a player goes bankrupt, their corresponding bet in the Bets screen should become disabled and invisible. In its place a label with red text should appear that will inform us that the player is bankrupt. As this label will be used in more than one screen, let's define it in the **widgets.kv** file:

```
#:kivy 1.11.1
# File name: widgets.kv
#:import widgets widgets

### LABELS ###
...
<WhiteWinsLabel@BoldLabel>:
    font_size: 14
    color: 1, 1, 1, 1

# This is the label that will be displayed in the Bets and Results
```

```
# screen when a player is bankrupt. The text will be in red.
<BankruptLabel@RegularLabel>:
    # Here's a property where we store the part of the text
    # that is supposed to follow a player's name.
    bankrupt_text:' is bankrupt.'
    size_hint: None, None
    color: 1, 0, 0, 1

### BUTTONS ###
...
```

Now we'll add the BankruptLabels to the Bets screen. So, let's create a FloatLayout with four BankruptLabels. Each BankruptLabel will be visible only when the corresponding player is bankrupt. The text on the label will consist of the player's name and the **`bankrupt_text`** defined in the **`BankruptLabel`** class rule in **widgets.kv**.

We'll also set each label's position and size to be the same as those of the corresponding bet. Finally, we'll set opacity to 1 or 0, depending on whether a player is bankrupt or not.

Next, we'll make the bets disabled when their corresponding players go bankrupt.

Here's the code:

```
#:kivy 1.11.1
# File name: bets.kv
#:import bets bets
...
<BetsScreen>:
    ...
    bets: [_bet1, _bet2, _bet3, _bet4]

    # Here's the FloatLayout with four BankruptLabels.
    FloatLayout:
        BankruptLabel:
            text: root.game.player1.name + self.bankrupt_text
            pos: _bet1.pos
            size: _bet1.size
            opacity: int(root.game.player1.bankrupt)

        BankruptLabel:
            text: root.game.player2.name + self.bankrupt_text
            pos: _bet2.pos
            size: _bet2.size
            opacity: int(root.game.player2.bankrupt)

        BankruptLabel:
            text: root.game.player3.name + self.bankrupt_text
            pos: _bet3.pos
            size: _bet3.size
            opacity: int(root.game.player3.bankrupt)
```

```
        BankruptLabel:
            text: root.game.player4.name + self.bankrupt_text
            pos: _bet4.pos
            size: _bet4.size
            opacity: int(root.game.player4.bankrupt)

    BoxLayout:
        orientation: 'vertical'
        ...
        ### PLAYER BETS ###
        ...
            # player 1
            Bet:
                ...
                player_group: 'player1'

                # This bet will be disabled if Player 1 goes bankrupt.
                disabled: root.game.player1.bankrupt


                ...
            # player 2
            Bet:
                ...
                player_group: 'player2'

                # also disabled if Player 2 goes bankrupt
                disabled: root.game.number_of_players < 2 or root.game.player2.bankrupt
                ...
            # player 3
            Bet:
                ...
                player_group: 'player3'

                # also disabled if Player 3 goes bankrupt
                disabled: root.game.number_of_players < 3 or root.game.player3.bankrupt
                ...
            # player 4
            Bet:
                ...
                player_group: 'player4'

                # also disabled if Player 4 goes bankrupt
                disabled: root.game.number_of_players < 4 or root.game.player4.bankrupt
                ...
        ### GO BUTTON ###
        ...
```

Now let's run the game and make one of the players bet all their money on one of the slugs, as many times as necessary until the player goes bankrupt. When the player loses all the money and you press the Next Race button, you won't see the bet corresponding to the player in the Bets screen anymore. Instead the BankruptLabel with the appropriate message will be displayed.

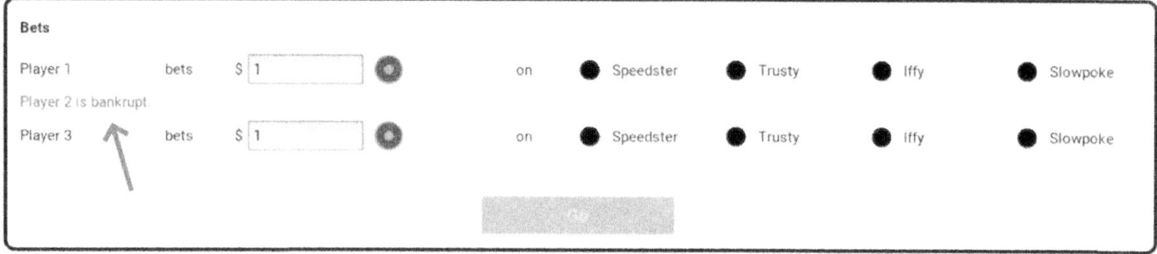


If the remaining players now place their bets and hit the Go button, in the Results screen the previous results of Player 2 will still be visible:

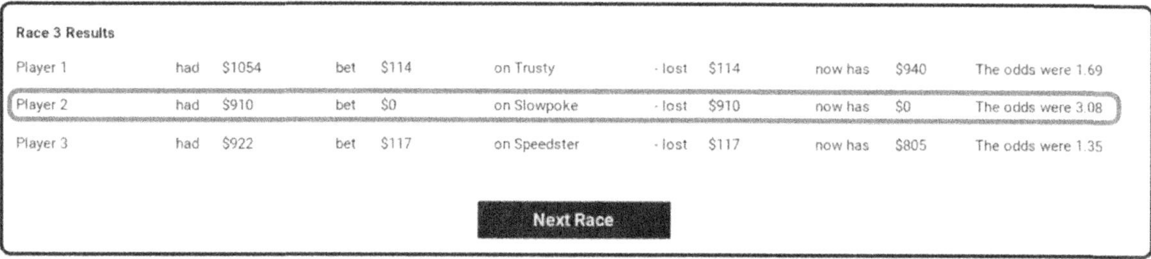


This is not the behavior we expect. The result should be invisible and the same message should be displayed as in the Bets screen. So, it's your turn. You'll fix this in the first exercise below. And in the second exercise you'll handle the Players' Stats area. As far as the next chapter is concerned, we're going to add the Game Over check to the game.

# It's Your Turn Now…

### EXERCISE 1

In this exercise you're going to handle the Results screen in a similar way as we handled the Bets screen. So, follow the steps below:

1. We're going to add a FloatLayout with four labels to the Results screen, just like we did with the Bets screen. In the BankruptLabels we'll need access to the positions and sizes of the four Result instances so that we can place the labels exactly at their location. To this end, add ids to the Result instances. You can use the following ids: **`_result1`**, **`_result2`**, **`_result3`**, **`_result4`**.

2. Add a FloatLayout directly in the ResultsScreen widget above the BoxLayout that holds all the Result-related code. In the FloatLayout add four BankruptLabels and set their properties to the following:

- **`text`** to the name of the corresponding slug + the **`bankrupt_text`** defined in the **`BankruptLabel`** class,

- **pos** and **size** to the corresponding **Result** instance's **pos** and **size** respectively,

- **opacity** to the corresponding player's **bankrupt** property, naturally cast to an integer.

3. In each of the four **Result** instances modify the **disabled** property so that it also takes into account whether the corresponding player is bankrupt or not. Don't forget to set this property on the first **Result** instance because we didn't set it there before.

## SOLUTION

Here's the modified code:

```
#:kivy 1.11.1
# File name: results.kv
#:import results results
...
<ResultsScreen>:
    ...
    game: root.manager.parent.parent.parent.manager

    # Here's the FloatLayout with four BankruptLabels.
    FloatLayout:
        BankruptLabel:
            text: root.game.player1.name + self.bankrupt_text
            pos: _result1.pos
            size: _result1.size
            opacity: int(root.game.player1.bankrupt)

        BankruptLabel:
            text: root.game.player2.name + self.bankrupt_text
            pos: _result2.pos
            size: _result2.size
            opacity: int(root.game.player2.bankrupt)

        BankruptLabel:
            text: root.game.player3.name + self.bankrupt_text
            pos: _result3.pos
            size: _result3.size
            opacity: int(root.game.player3.bankrupt)

        BankruptLabel:
            text: root.game.player4.name + self.bankrupt_text
            pos: _result4.pos
            size: _result4.size
            opacity: int(root.game.player4.bankrupt)

    BoxLayout:
        ...
        ### PLAYER RESULTS ###
        ...
            # player 1
            Result:
```

```
            id: _result1
            player_name: root.game.player1.name
            ...
            odds: ...
            disabled: root.game.player1.bankrupt

        # player 2
        Result:
            id: _result2
            player_name: root.game.player2.name
            ...
            disabled: root.game.number_of_players < 2 or root.game.player2.bankrupt

        # player 3
        Result:
            id: _result3
            player_name: root.game.player3.name
            ...
            disabled: root.game.number_of_players < 3 or root.game.player3.bankrupt

        # player 4
        Result:
            id: _result4
            player_name: root.game.player4.name
            ...
            disabled: root.game.number_of_players < 4 or root.game.player4.bankrupt

    ### NEXT RACE BUTTON ###
    ...
```

Now, as soos as a player goes bankrupt, we'll see the message displayed in the Results screen.

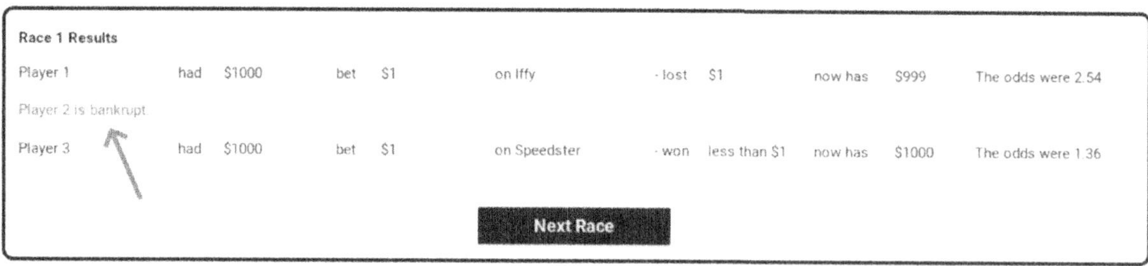


**EXERCISE 2**

In this exercise you're going to take care of the Players' Stats area in the Race screen. The text displayed on the two RegularLabels corresponding to each player should be red if the player's gone bankrupt and the default color otherwise. To avoid repetitive code, first add the **`text_color`** property to the **`PlayerStats`** class and set it to red (**`[1, 0, 0, 1]`** or the default text color (**`[.2, .1, 0, 1]`**) depending on whether the corresponding player still has some money or not. Then set each RegularLabel's **`color`** property to **`text_color`**.

### SOLUTION

Here's the code:

```
#:kivy 1.11.1
# File name: race.kv
#:import race race
...
<PlayerStats>:
    text_color: [1, 0, 0, 1] if root.money == 0 else [.2, .1, 0, 1]
    RegularLabel:
        text: root.name
        color: root.text_color
    RegularLabel:
        text: 'has $' + str(root.money)
        color: root.text_color

<SlugInfo>:
    ...
```

If you now run the app and a player goes bankrupt, the text in the Players' Stats area will be in red.

# Chapter 91 – Game Over Check

In the previous chapter we handled the players. In particular, we now check all the players for money after each race. Players who have gone bankrupt are removed. In this chapter we'll go one step further. We'll check whether the ending condition is met. If so, the Game Over screen should appear with information about the winner. As for now, we will assume that the only ending condition is the first one, so the game is over when there's only one player with any money left. This also entails another assumption: there must be at least two players in the game because otherwise the first ending condition is unavailable. As far as the other two ending conditions are concerned, we'll handle them in separate chapters.

Anyway, there may be three situations after each race:

1. There are still at least two players in the game and the game just goes on – we already handled this (the players who went bankrupt are removed).

2. There's only one player left in the game – this is the winner.

3. All players who are still in the game go bankrupt simultaneously – there is no winner.

As mentioned above, the first case is already handled. The game just goes on. But cases 2 and 3 end the game and the Game Over screen appears. Let's have a look at them one by one.

## One Player Left – the Winner

The first question is: Where in the code should we check for game over? The code should be executed after each race, so a good place for it is the **go** method in the **Game** class. So, we're going to create a method, **gameover_check**, and call it from the **go** method. But first things first. Here are the steps to take:

1. In the **Game** class under the time section we'll add a game over section and define three variables in it:

- **winners** – the list where the winner or winners will be stored (it should be empty for now),

- **game_over_reason** – a StringProperty with the default value of an empty string where the info about the reason why the game is over will be saved,

- **winner_text** - a StringProperty with the default value of an empty string where the info about the game winner will be saved.

We're going to store the winner in a list although there's only one winner now if any, but later, when we handle the other ending conditions, there may be more.

2. We'll create the **game_over_check** method in the **Game** class with no parameters (except **self**). If there's only one player in the players list, it'll be the winner. So, we must append it to the **winners** list. The **game_over_reason** text should be set accordingly and the **winner_text** property should be set to a string containing information about the winner's name, initial money and the money at the end of the game. Also, we want to switch to the Game Over screen.

3. With the **game_over_check** method in place, let's call it in the **go** method.

Here's the **main.py** file after you complete the three steps above:

```
# File name: main.py
...
class Game(ScreenManager):
    ...
    # time
    ...
    time_remaining = StringProperty('')  # string representation of duration

    # game over
    # list of winners - There may be no winners, 1 winner or multiple winners.
    winners = []

    # info about the reason why the game is over
    game_over_reason = StringProperty('')

    # info about the winner
    winner_text = StringProperty('')

    # callback methods
    ...
    def go(self):
        self.race_winner = choice(self.slugs)

        for player in self.players:
            player.update(self.race_winner)

        for slug in self.slugs:
            slug.update(self.race_winner, self.race_number)

        self.remove_bankrupt_players()

        # Let's check whether the game should be over now.
        self.gameover_check()

    def remove_bankrupt_players(self):
        ...

    # Here's the method to check whether the game should be over.
    def gameover_check(self):
        # Clear the winners list.
```

```
            self.winners = []

        # If there is only one player with any money left...
        if len(self.players) == 1:
            # ... the player is appended to the list of winners,
            self.winners.append(self.players[0])

            # ... the reason why the game is over is given,
            self.game_over_reason = "There's only one player with any money left."

            # ... for simplicity's sake the winner is assigned to a variable,
            winner = self.winners[0]

            # ... the message about the winner is created,
            self.winner_text = (f'The winner is {winner.name}, ' +
                                f'having started at ${winner.initial_money}, ' +
                                f'winning at ${winner.money}.')
            # ... we switch to Game Over screen.
            # As our Game class is a subclass of ScreenManager, it has the
            # current property that we can use to set the current screen.
            self.current = 'gameoverscreen'

    def reset_race(self):
        ...
```

4. Now let's have a look at the **gameover.kv** file. Let's use the **game_over_reason** and **winner_text** properties here to replace the hard-coded values:

```
#:kivy 1.11.1
# File name: gameover.kv
#:import gameover gameover

<GameoverScreen>:
    ...
        BoldLabel:
            font_size: 100
            text: 'Game Over'
            halign: 'center'
        BoldLabel:
            font_size: 40
            # We're going to use the game_over_reason property of the Game class
            # to display the reason why the game is over.
            text: root.game.game_over_reason
            halign: 'center'
        BoldLabel:
            font_size: 30
            # Now we can display the actual info about the winner.
            text: root.game.winner_text
            halign: 'center'
        # the buttons
        BoxLayout:
            ...
```

Now let's run the app, set the number of players to, say, three, and let two of them bet all their money on the same slug. The third player should bet on a different slug. If the slug the two players bet on accidentally wins, you'll have to repeat it until there is only one player who isn't bankrupt. Then the Game Over screen will appear with information about the winner.

In the example above we can see that Player 3 is the winner. Although the amount of money at the end of the game is less than at the beginning, it's the only player who isn't bankrupt, thus winning the game.

## All Players Go Bankrupt – No Winner

It may also happen that all players lose all their money in one race. This is the case if all players bet all their money on slugs that don't win. In this situation there is no winner. Now, I think I'll leave this for you as an exercise and in the next chapter we'll have a look at the second ending condition, so game over after a given number of races.

## It's Your Turn Now...

### EXERCISE

Your task in this exercise is to handle the situation when all players who are still in the game go bankrupt simultaneously and there is no winner. Let's keep it simple. Just add another conditional **`elif`** block under the **`if`** block in the **`game_over_check`** method. If there are no players left in the game, there won't be any winners in the **`winners`** list. The **`game_over_reason`** property should be set to **`'All players are bankrupt.'`** and the **`winner_text`** property should be set to **`'There is no winner!'`** And just like before, add the line of code to switch to the Game Over screen.

**SOLUTION**

Here's the code:

```
# File name: main.py
...
class Game(ScreenManager):
    ...
    def gameover_check(self):
        # Clear the winners list.
        self.winners = []

        # one winner
        if len(self.players) == 1:
            self.winners.append(self.players[0])
            self.game_over_reason = "There's only one player with any money left."
            winner = self.winners[0]
            self.winner_text = (f'The winner is {winner.name}, ' +
                                f'having started at ${winner.initial_money}, ' +
                                f'winning at ${winner.money}.')
            self.current = 'gameoverscreen'

        # no winner
        # There's no winner if all players lose all their money simultaneously.
        elif len(self.players) == 0:
            self.game_over_reason = 'All players are bankrupt.'
            self.winner_text = 'There is no winner!'
            self.current = 'gameoverscreen'

    def reset_race(self):
        ...
```

Here's what you will see if all players lose.

# Chapter 92 – Game Over After a Set Number of Races

In the previous chapter we handled the scenario where the game is over because there's only one player with any money left. This ending condition assumes that there are at least two players in the game. In this chapter we'll handle the second game over scenario, which is related to the number of races. As you remember, one of the ending conditions is that we can specify how many races the game should consist of and the game is over as soon as the last race is over.

Here's how we set the number of races in the Settings screen. First we have to check the second radio button (A) and then type in the number of races in the text input that appears (B).

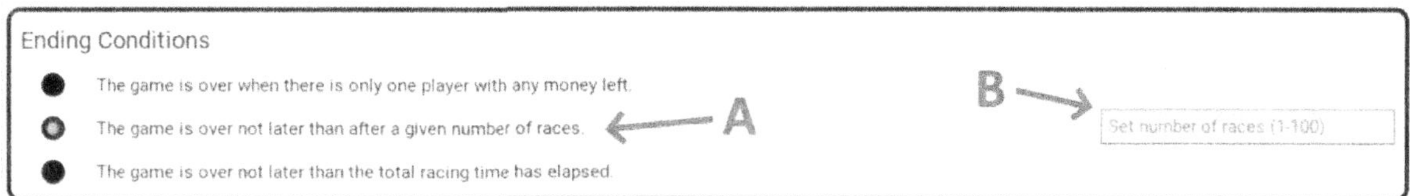


There may be from 1 to 100 races. If you enter a number greater than 100, it will be set to 100 anyway. We already handled this. Now, after you type in the number, the Ready button will be enabled and you move on to the Race screen, where you can see the number of races in the Game Info area.

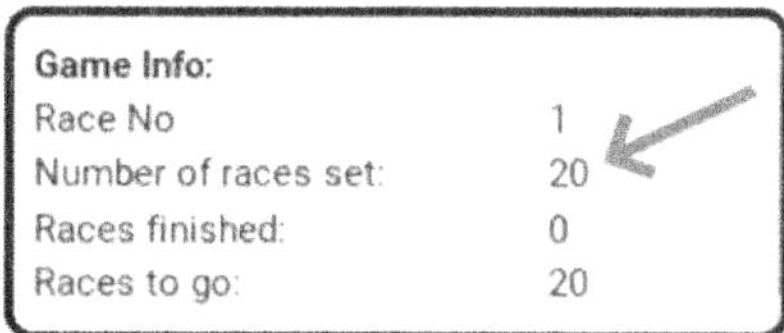


You can also see how many races are already finished and how many there are still to go. At least this is what we want to see. But if you now simulate a couple races, you'll see that it doesn't work yet.

| Game Info: | |
|---|---|
| Race No | 5 |
| Number of races set: | 20 |
| Races finished: | 0 |
| Races to go: | 20 |

## Updating Races Info

We're going to implement this functionality right now. Actually, we already have the properties we need. They are all defined in the **Game** class:

```
# File name: main.py
...
class Game(ScreenManager):
    ...
    # races
    number_of_races = NumericProperty(0)
    races_finished = NumericProperty(0)
    races_to_go = NumericProperty(0)
```

```
    race_number = NumericProperty(1)
    race_winner = ObjectProperty(None, allownone=True)

    # time
    ...
```

Here's how we use them in the **race.kv** file:

```
#:kivy 1.11.1
# File name: race.kv
#:import race race
...
<RaceScreen>:
    ...
        ### INFO, STATS AND BUTTONS ###
        ...
            # Game Info
            ...
                BoxLayout:
                    opacity: int(not root.game.end_by_money)
                    RegularLabel:
                        size_hint: (2.5, 1)
                        text: 'Number of races set:' if root.game.end_by_races else 'Time set:'
                    RegularLabel:
                        text: str(root.game.number_of_races) if root.game.end_by_races else root.game.time_set

                BoxLayout:
                    opacity: int(not root.game.end_by_money)
                    RegularLabel:
                        size_hint: (2.5, 1)
                        text: 'Races finished:' if root.game.end_by_races else 'Time elapsed:'
                    RegularLabel:
                        text: str(root.game.races_finished) if root.game.end_by_races else root.game.time_elapsed

                BoxLayout:
                    opacity: int(not root.game.end_by_money)
                    RegularLabel:
                        size_hint: (2.5, 1)
                        text: 'Races to go:' if root.game.end_by_races else 'Time remaining:'
                    RegularLabel:
                        text: str(root.game.races_to_go) if root.game.end_by_races else root.game.time_remaining

            # Slugs' Stats
            ...
```

In the **SettingsScreen** class the number of races to go is set to the number of races:

```
# File name: settings.py
...
class SettingsScreen(Screen):
    ...
    def set_game(self, number_of_races, time_set):
        if number_of_races != '':
            self.game.number_of_races = int(number_of_races)
            self.game.races_to_go = self.game.number_of_races

        if time_set != '':
            ...
```

Now all we have to do is make the properties change after each race. This is as simple as adding two lines of code in the **reset_race** method in the **Game** class. After each race the number of races that are finished should increment by one and the number of races to go should decrement by one:

```
# File name: main.py
...
class Game(ScreenManager):
    ...
    def reset_race(self):
        self.race_number += 1
        self.races_finished += 1
        self.races_to_go -= 1

        for player in self.players:
            ...
```

Now the values change as expected.

| Game Info: | |
|---|---|
| Race No | 5 |
| Number of races set: | 20 |
| Races finished: | 4 |
| Races to go: | 16 |

# Game Over Check

With this functionality in place, we're ready to modify the game over check so that it takes into account the races ending condition. So, at this point there are two situations when the game should be over:

1. If the first ending condition is selected, the game is supposed to end when there's only one player left with any money or if all players go bankrupt at the same time.

2. If the second ending condition is selected, the game should end after a given number of races, like after 20 races in the example above. But not only. If you read carefully the label next to the second radio button, you'll see the following:

The game is over not later than after a given number of races.

So, what does it mean? It simply means that even though there might still be multiple players with money in the game, the game will be over after a specified number of races and the player with the most money will win. But it also means that if there's only one player left with money or if all players go bankrupt before the last race, the game will be over earlier. So, if you set the number of races to 20, but there's only one player left after race number 8, for example, the game will be over after race 8. It will also happen if all players go bankrupt before the last race.

There's one exception, though. It's when we set the number of players to 1 in the Settings screen. As you remember, this is possible with the races and time ending conditions. So, we must take this situation into account too. We'll be referring to this situation here as 1-player mode, as opposed to multi-player mode, which we'll be using for the case when there is more than one player.

And there's one more thing. It may happen that after the last race there are multiple winners. This is the case when there are more players with the same maximum amount of money. Then we have a tie, but we're prepared for that because we have a list of winners.

So, to recap, here are the possible scenarios:

1. If the first ending condition is selected, the game is over when there's only one player left with money. The player is the winner. If all players go bankrupt at the same time, there is no winner. We handled this case in the previous chapter.

2. If the second ending condition is selected, there are two possible scenarios:

a) If the number of players is set to more than 1, the game is over when there's only one player left with any money but not later than after a given number of races. If there are more players with the same maximum amount of money at the end of the game, there's a tie. If all players go bankrupt in the last race, there is no winner.

b) If there's only one player from the beginning, the game is over when the player goes bankrupt or when the last race finishes. In this scenario there is no winner. In the Game Over screen you can only read how much money the player had at the beginning of the game and how much they ended up with.

# Handling Game Over

And here's how we're going to implement the game over functionality:

1. At first we'll check if the number of players after the race is zero. If so, the game is over regardless of which ending condition was set. But there will be different messages for the 1-player mode and the multi-player mode.

2. If the number of players is not zero, the next condition will be checked. This time the program will check whether there is just one player and whether we are in multi-player mode (so if the **number_of_players** property in the **Game** class was set to a number greater than 1 when we started the game). If these two conditions are met simultaneously, we append the only remaining player to the **winners** list and set the game over reason and winner text messages accordingly.

3. If the two conditions above are not met simultaneously, we test the next condition. This time we check whether the ending condition was **end_by_races** and whether the race number of the current race is the same as the number of races we set the **number_of_races** property to. If so, we check whether we are in 1-player or multi-player mode. In the latter case there may be a single winner or there may be joint winners if there's a tie.

As you can see, things are becoming pretty complex here. But don't worry, I added lots of comments to the code so that you know why things are how they are.

Before we look at the code, there's one more thing. I simplified the **gameover_check** method to just check whether the game should be over and I put the actual code that handles the game over situation into a new method, **gameover**. Here's the **main.py** file:

```
# File name: main.py
...
class Game(ScreenManager):
    ...
    def remove_bankrupt_players(self):
        ...

    # Let's simplify the gameover_check method so that it only checks whether the game
    # should be over and calls the gameover method if so. The actual handling of ending
    # the game is moved to the gameover method.
    def gameover_check(self):
        # The game should be over if:
        # - there are no more players in the game,
        # - there's only one player with money and we're in multi-player mode,
        # - the game should end after a specific number of races and this number
        #   has just been reached.
        if (len(self.players) == 0
            or (len(self.players) == 1 and self.number_of_players > 1)
            or (self.end_by_races and self.race_number == self.number_of_races)):
            self.gameover()

    # This is the method that handles the end of the game.
    def gameover(self):
        # Clear the winners list.
        self.winners = []

        # The game is over regardless of the ending condition as soon as all players
        # go bankrupt. Depending on whether there was only one player or more at the
        # beginning of the game, the messages in the Game Over screen will be different.
        if len(self.players) == 0:

            # 1-player mode
            if self.number_of_players == 1:
                self.game_over_reason = 'You just went bankrupt.'
                self.winner_text = 'There are no winners in 1-player mode.'

            # multi-player mode
            else:
                self.game_over_reason = 'All players are bankrupt.'
                self.winner_text = 'There is no winner!'

        # If there are multiple players, the game should be over always when there's
        # only one player with any money left, regardless of the ending condition. Then
        # this one player is appended to the winners list and is the only winner.
        elif len(self.players) == 1 and self.number_of_players > 1:
            self.winners.append(self.players[0])
            self.game_over_reason = "There's only one player with any money left."
            winner = self.winners[0]
            self.winner_text = (f'The winner is {winner.name}, ' +
                                f'having started at ${winner.initial_money}, ' +
                                f'winning at ${winner.money}.')

        # If none of the conditions above is met, so if there is more than one player
        # still in the game or if we're in 1-player mode, the next condition to check
```

```
# is whether the ending condition is end_by_races. If so, we must check whether
# the number of the last race is equal to the number of races we set. If it is,
# the game should be over.
elif self.end_by_races and self.race_number == self.number_of_races:

    # The game over reason text should be the same regardless of the number of
    # players. One exception is when there's only one player left because then
    # the condition above will be checked before the condition over here, which
    # means the message "There's only one player with any money left." will be
    # displayed. In other cases, so if more than one player is still in the game
    # or if we're in 1-player mode, the message below will be shown.
    self.game_over_reason = 'The number of races you set has been reached.'

    # There is no winner in 1-player mode, so we just see some general info text
    # about how the player did in the game.
    if self.number_of_players == 1:
        you = self.players[0]
        self.winner_text = (f"You were playing in 1-player mode." +
                            f"\nYou started at ${you.initial_money} " +
                            f"and you're ending at ${you.money}.")

    # If there is more than one player with money left, the result depends on
    # how much money the players have. If there is one player with more money
    # than any other player, he or she is the winner. But if there are two or
    # more players with the same maximum amount of money, we have a tie and all
    # these players are joint winners.
    else:

        # First we must find the winner or winners. Let's start by figuring out
        # what is the maximum amount of money that any player has. We can use
        # the Python built-in max function to do that. Besides the unpacked
        # (hence the star operator) list of players, we pass the key argument to
        # tell the function by which criterion to search for the maximum value.
        # Here we're using a simple lambda function to tell the function to
        # search through the players list by money. So, the max function finds
        # the player with the maximum amount of money (or the first such player
        # if there are more). Then the money of the player found by max is
        # assigned to max_money.
        max_money = (max(*self.players, key=lambda player: player.money)).money

        # Now we know what the maximum amount of money is. We can now re-create
        # the list of winners using a list comprehension where all players are
        # placed who have the maximum amount of money. This list may contain
        # just one player, or more if there is more than one player with the
        # maximum amount of money.
        self.winners = [player for player in self.players
                        if player.money == max_money]

        # Now we must display a different message depending on whether there is
        # one winner or more.

        # one winner
        if len(self.winners) == 1:
            winner = self.winners[0]
            self.winner_text = (f'The winner is {winner.name}, ' +
                                f'having started at ${winner.initial_money}, ' +
                                f'winning at ${winner.money}.')
```

```
            # joint winners
            else:
                self.winner_text = "There's a tie. The joint winners are:\n\n"
                for winner in self.winners:
                    self.winner_text += (f'{winner.name}, ' +
                                        f'having started at ${winner.initial_money}, ' +
                                        f'winning at ${winner.money}.\n')

        # Switch to Gameover screen.
        self.current = 'gameoverscreen'

    def reset_race(self):
        ...
```

And now let's test all the different scenarios to make sure everything works.

**Scenario 1:**
**ending condition: money**
**mode: multi-player**
**number of players in game: 1**

First we'll play the game in multi-player mode (which just means there's more than one player at the beginning of the game) and set the ending condition to money, or rather leave the default selection on.

This means the game should be over when there's only one player with any money left. Then let's play the game in such a way that all players lose their money except one.

You can easily do it by settings the players' bets to their maximum values and starting the race. Sooner or later (rather sooner) they will all lose their money. Just remember to leave one player with some money. Here's my setup:

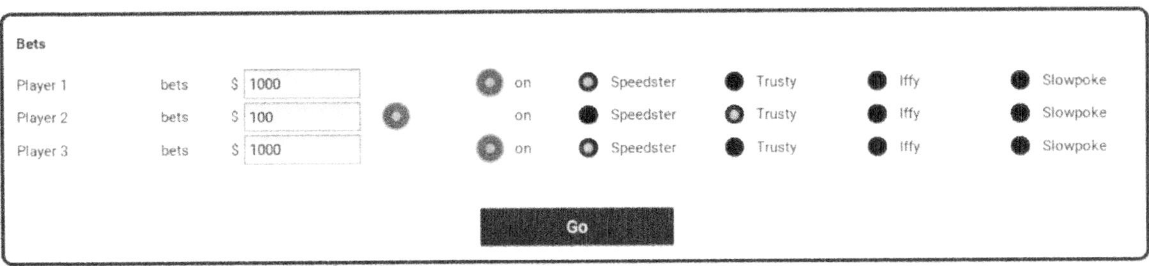


So, Player 1 and Player 3 bet all their money on Speedster and Player 2 bets $100 on Trusty. If Speedster doesn't win the race, Player 1 and Player 3 will go bankrupt, will be removed from the game and there will be only one player, Player 2, with any money left. This is going to be the winner. The Game Over screen should appear. By the way, if Speedster wins the race, try again. On the right you can see what the messages in the Game Over screen should look like.

**There's only one player with any money left.**

**The winner is Player 2, having started at $1000, winning at $900.**

**Scenario 2:**
**ending condition: money**
**mode: multi-player**
**number of players in game: 0**

This scenario is very much like the previous one. The difference is that this time all players go bankrupt. So, let's set all players' bets to maximum values and if all the players bet on the same slug, there's a chance that the slug won't win. If he does, try again. Here's my setup:

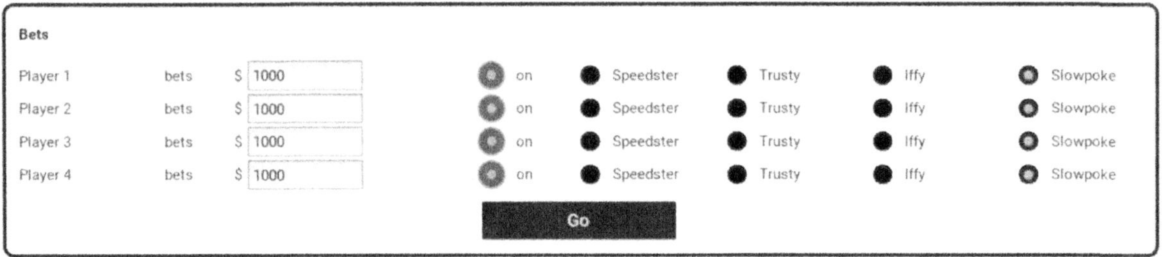


So, all four players are betting all their money on Slowpoke. Unless Slopoke wins, all players will go bankrupt and you will see a message informing you about it in the Game Over screen.

**All players are bankrupt.**

**There is no winner!**

We now have the money ending condition covered. Let's move on to the races ending condition.

**Scenario 3:**
**ending condition: races**
**races finished: not yet all**
**mode: multi-player**
**number of players in game: 0**

In this scenario we'll set the number of races to 5, but the game should be over after an earlier race because all players go bankrupt. We'll be playing in multi-player mode. Here's my setup for the second race:

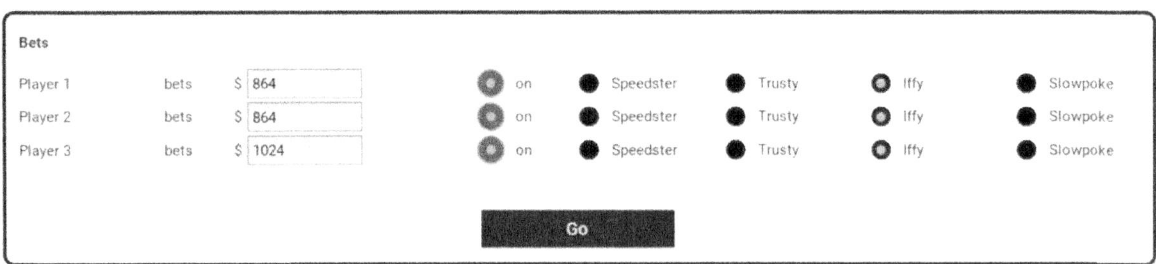


So, here we have three players, each of them won or lost something in the first race. Now, in the second race, they all bet all their money on Iffy. If Iffy is not the winner, all players will lose and the game will be over. Naturally, if Iffy does win, try again and the game will be over after the third or fourth race. In my case Iffy didn't win and I got the Game Over screen with the same message as in the previous scenario.

**All players are bankrupt.**

**There is no winner!**

**Scenario 4:**
**ending condition: races**
**races finished: not yet all**
**mode: multi-player**
**number of players in game: 1**

This scenario is very much like the previous one, but this time the game is going to be over earlier than expected because there will be only one player with any money left. We're still in multi-player mode. I set the number of races to 5 again. Here's my 2-player setup before the second race:

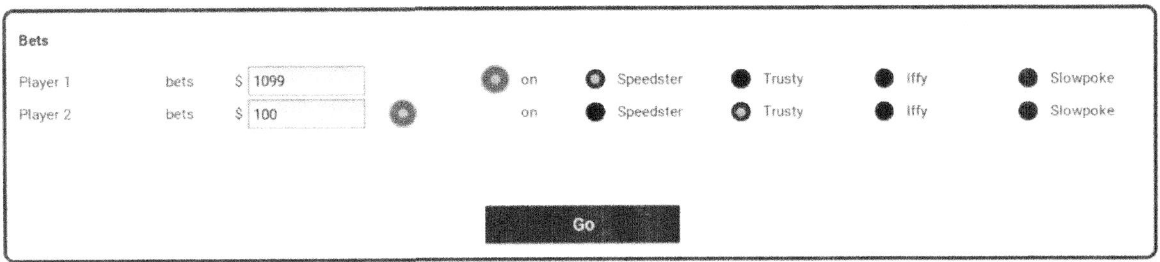


Here Player 1 bets all the money on Speedster. If Speedster doesn't win, Player 2 will be the only one with any money left and will automatically become the winner.

**There's only one player with any money left.**

**The winner is Player 2, having started at $1000, winning at $745.**

**Scenario 5:**
**ending condition: races**
**races finished: not yet all**
**mode: 1-player**
**number of players in game: 0**

In the next scenario we'll be playing in 1-player mode. Let's set the number of races to 5, but then let's finish the game before the fifth race by losing all the money. Here's my setup after the first race:

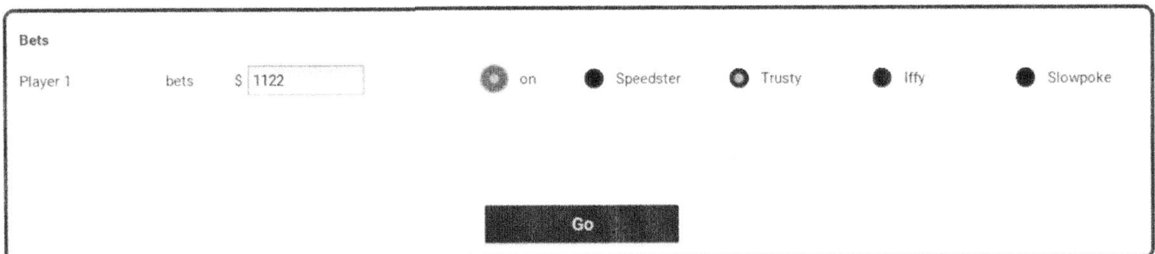


Now the only player is betting all the money on Trusty. If Trusty doesn't win, Player 1 will go bankrupt and the game will be over.

**You just went bankrupt.**

**There are no winners in 1-player mode.**

**Scenario 6:**
**ending condition: races**
**races finished: all**
**mode: multi-player**
**number of players in game: 4**
**number of winners: 1**

In this scenario we won't be losing any money on purpose. Instead we'll set the number of races to three and let the players place differentiated bets so that all players are still in game after the last race and have different amounts of money. This way one of them will have more money than the others and will win. Here's my setup after the second race, so before the final race:

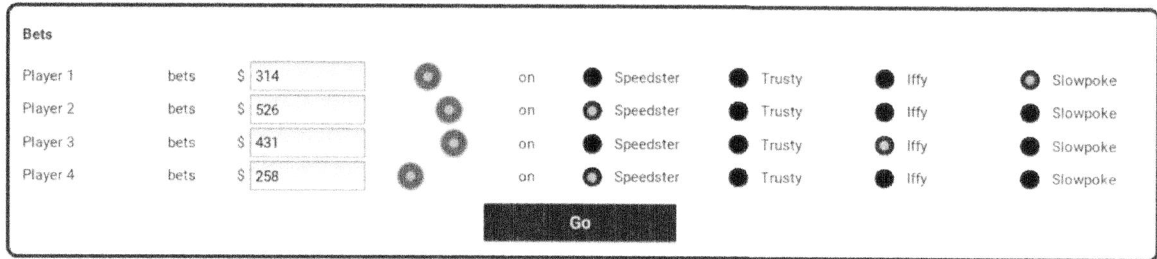


And now, after the third race the game will be over and there will be just one winner.

**The number of races you set has been reached.**

**The winner is Player 1, having started at $1000, winning at $1478.**

**Scenario 7:**
**ending condition: races**
**races finished: all**
**mode: multi-player**
**number of players in game: 4**
**number of winners: 3**

In this scenario we'll set the number of races to two and we'll let three out of the four players win the game. To do this, we'll make three players bet the same amounts of money on the same slugs and one player will bet more in the first race, so hopefully this player will lose and we'll see what happens if there's a tie after the last race. If the fourth player wins instead of the three others, we'll have to play again. Here's my setup after the first race:

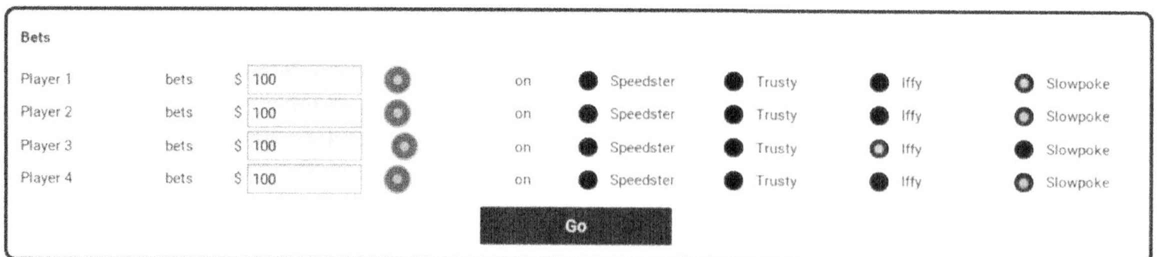


So, it worked for me. Player 3 bet on Trusty in the first race and lost. So now we have three players with the same amount of money. In the last race all players will bet $100, the three ones with the same amount of money on Slowpoke. This way, regardless of whether Slowpoke wins or loses, they will all have the same amount of money again.

**The number of races you set has been reached.**

**Player 1, having started at $1000, winning at $940.**
**Player 2, having started at $1000, winning at $940.**
**Player 4, having started at $1000, winning at $940.**

After the second race is over, the game will be over and we will see the appropriate message in the Game Over screen.

Well, generally it works as expected, but there's a little problem. We don't see the first part of the winner text. The problem here is that the font size is too big for the whole text to fit in if it's so long. It works fine for shorter texts, like if there's one or two winners. Now, to see the whole text, you would have to resize the app window (after enabling resizing in the configuration code before).

Naturally, this must be fixed and you will do it as an exercise in a minute. But before that let's move on to the last scenario for now.

**Scenario 8:**
**ending condition: races**
**races finished: all**
**mode: 1-player**
**number of players in game: 1**

In this last scenario we'll be playing in 1-player mode, with the number of races set to 3. The player will bet small amounts of money on the slugs and will still have some money (more or less than at the beginning) after the third race when the game is over. Here's my setup after the second race:

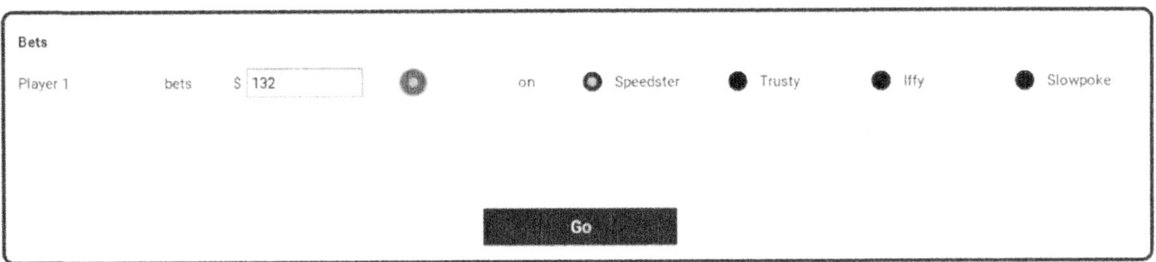


In the image on the right you can see the message in the Game Over screen after the last race.

**The number of races you set has been reached.**

**You were playing in 1-player mode.**
**You started at $1000 and you're ending at $418.**

Fine, this was our last scenario. There's still one ending condition we have to take into account, the time ending condition. If you set the time of the game, the game will be finished after this time has elapsed. But before we add this ending condition to the lot and make the `gameover` method even more complex, we have to talk about the `Clock` class, which we'll be using in the project. I'll introduce the class in the next chapter.

# It’s Your Turn Now...

### EXERCISE

In this exercise we’ll take care of the label that displays the winner text in the Game Over screen. Have a look at the code and in particular at the line where the font size is set:

```
#:kivy 1.11.1
# File name: gameover.kv
#:import gameover gameover

<GameoverScreen>:
    ...
        BoldLabel:
            font_size: 100
            text: 'Game Over'
            halign: 'center'
```

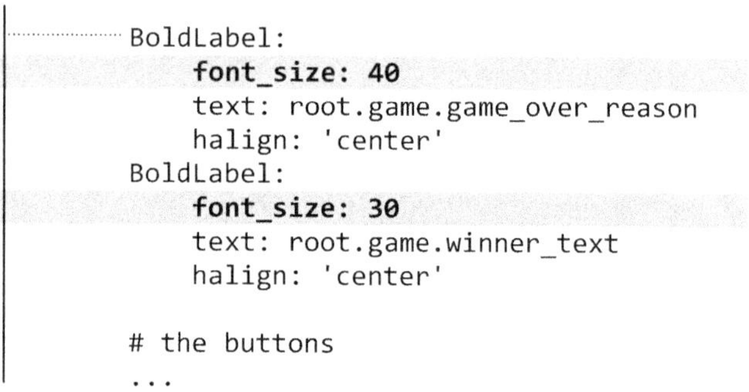

```
        BoldLabel:
            font_size: 40
            text: root.game.game_over_reason
            halign: 'center'
        BoldLabel:
            font_size: 30
            text: root.game.winner_text
            halign: 'center'

        # the buttons
        ...
```

Now let’s run the app with two players and make them place the same bets on the same slugs. This game should end after the first race, so set the number of races to 1. After the first race the game is over and the whole winner text is visible in the Game Over screen.

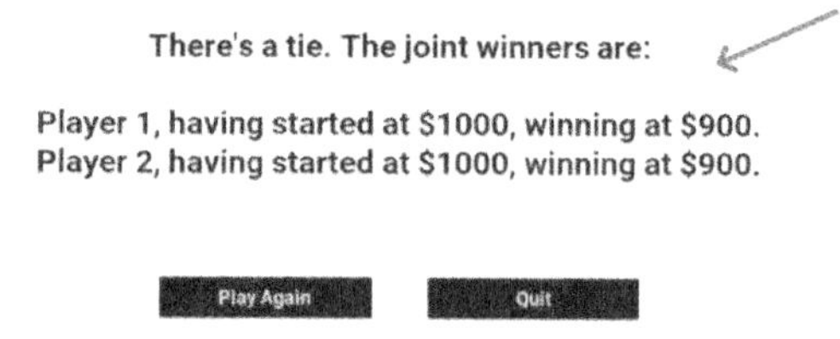


But what if we run the app again, but this time with four players who all win?

Let’s try it out. But first let’s temporarily enable window resizing in the configuration code. Go to the **main.py** file and change the value of **`resizable`** from **`0`** to **`1`**:

```
# File name: main.py
...
Config.set('graphics', 'resizable', '1')
...
```

Now run the app, set the number of players to 4, the number of races to 1 and make all the players bet $100 on Iffy:

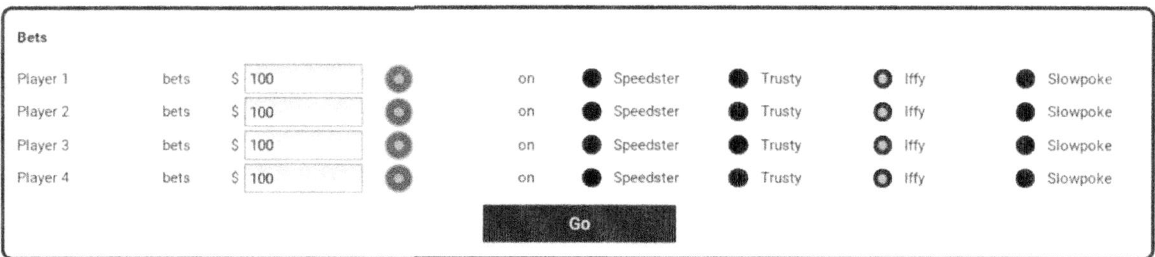


After the first race the game will be over and you will see the Game Over screen with an incomplete message. Now you don't see the first line of the text (A) and the information about the fourth player (B).

But the whole text is there. Just resize the window to see it like in the image below on the right.

Close the app window and set **resizable** back to **0** in the configuration code.

We didn't see the two lines of text before resizing the window because the font size is too big for such a long text and it doesn't fit in its container. So, let's change the font size of the winner text label from 30 to 20:

```
#:kivy 1.11.1
# File name: gameover.kv
#:import gameover gameover

<GameoverScreen>:
    ...
        BoldLabel:
            font_size: 20
            text: root.game.winner_text
            halign: 'center'

        # the buttons
        ...
```

Game Over

The number of races you set has been reached.

A

Player 1, having started at $1000, winning at $900.
Player 2, having started at $1000, winning at $900.
Player 3, having started at $1000, winning at $900.

B

Play Again Quit

Game Over

The number of races you set has been reached.

There's a tie. The joint winners are:

Player 1, having started at $1000, winning at $900.
Player 2, having started at $1000, winning at $900.
Player 3, having started at $1000, winning at $900.
Player 4, having started at $1000, winning at $900.

Play Again Quit

Now you should be able to see the whole text even if there are four joint winners.

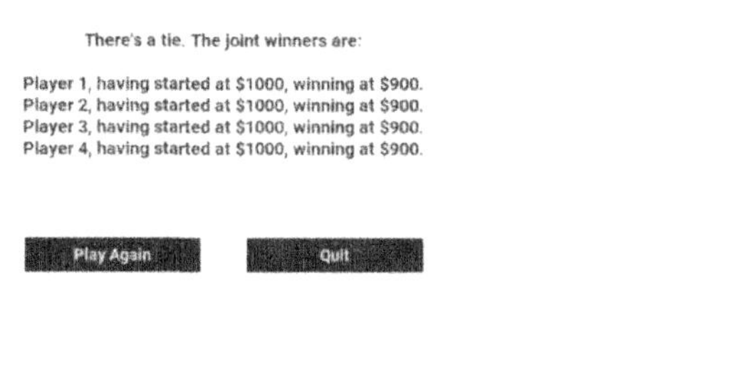


But the small text doesn't look good if there's just one winner, as you can see in the image below on the right.



We could leave it as is because it's not so important. But why not adjust the font size to the length of the text? Try to modify the text in the winner text label so that the font size depends on the length of the winner text.

Here are some guidelines:

- The maximum font size should be 30, so if the text is longer, we'll be subtracting from 30.

- The number that we subtract from 30 is calculated in the following way:

We subtract 150 from the length of the winner text (the length of a text is the number of characters it consists of) and divide the result by 10 using floor division. If you don't remember what floor division is, here's a short reminder.

****************************************************************************************************

There are two division operators in Python:

| **/** - for true division | **//** - for floor division |
|---|---|
| The result of true division is a float number, for example: | In floor division, the result is trimmed down to the nearest integer number, so: |
| **5 / 2** results in **2.5**. | **5 // 2** results in **2**. |

****************************************************************************************************

If we calculate the number like this, its value will be between 0 and 10, which means that the font size that we obtain after subtracting it may range from 20 ( = 30 – 10) to 30 ( = 30 – 0). This is all you need to modify, just one line of code in the Game Over screen.

**SOLUTION**

And here's the code:

```
#:kivy 1.11.1
# File name: gameover.kv
#:import gameover gameover

<GameoverScreen>:
    ...
        BoldLabel:
            # The font size depends on the length of the text. It's between 20 (if there are 4
            # joint winners, so the text is pretty long) and 30 (if there's just one winner).
            font_size: 30 - ((len(root.game.winner_text) - 150) // 10)
            text: root.game.winner_text
            halign: 'center'
        # the buttons
        ...
```

And now compare the font sizes for 1, 2, 3 and 4 winners:

one winner:

Game Over

The number of races you set has been reached.

The winner is Player 4, having started at $1000, winning at $826.

two winners:

Game Over

The number of races you set has been reached.

There's a tie. The joint winners are:

Player 1, having started at $1000, winning at $900.
Player 2, having started at $1000, winning at $900.

Play Again Quit

three winners:

Game Over

The number of races you set has been reached.

There's a tie. The joint winners are:

Player 1, having started at $1000, winning at $1038.
Player 2, having started at $1000, winning at $1038.
Player 4, having started at $1000, winning at $1038.

Play Again Quit

four winners:

Game Over

The number of races you set has been reached.

There's a tie. The joint winners are:

Player 1, having started at $1000, winning at $900.
Player 2, having started at $1000, winning at $900.
Player 3, having started at $1000, winning at $900.
Player 4, having started at $1000, winning at $900.

Play Again Quit

# Chapter 93 – Using the Clock

In the previous chapter we handled the races ending condition, so the one according to which the game should be over after a given number of races. There's still one ending condition left, time. If we choose this ending condition, the game will be over not later than after the time set in the Settings screen has elapsed. Again, if there's only one player with any money left in multi-player mode or if all players go bankrupt, the game will be over earlier.

Anyway, to work with time, we'll need the **Clock** class. This class is used to set the time when a method should be called or to set an interval between continuous calls of a method. In this chapter we'll have a closer look at the **Clock** class and then, in the next chapter we'll make use of it in our project. So, just like we've been doing every now and then in the book, we're going to practice the new stuff using our two test files, **test.py** and **test.kv**.

So, open the test files, remove all the code from them and make sure they contain the following code.

Here's the Python file:

```
# File name: test.py

import kivy
kivy.require('1.11.1')
from kivy.app import App
from kivy.uix.floatlayout import FloatLayout

class TestLayout(FloatLayout):
    def print_star(self):
        self.label.text += ' *'

    def increase_font(self):
        self.label.font_size = 80

class TestApp(App):
    def build(self):
        return TestLayout()

if __name__ == '__main__':
    TestApp().run()
```

And here's the kv file:

```
#:kivy 1.11.1
# File name: test.kv

<Button>:
    font_size: 40
    size_hint: .3, .2

<TestLayout>:
    label: _label

    Button:
        text: 'Button 1'
        pos_hint: {'x': .1, 'top': .9}
        on_press: root.print_star()

    Button:
        text: 'Button 2'
        pos_hint: {'right': .9, 'top': .9}
        on_press: root.increase_font()

    Label:
        id: _label
        text: 'Label'
        font_size: 40
        pos_hint: {'x': .1, 'y': .2}
        size_hint: .8, .2
```

Very simple and straightforward. If you run the test app, you will see two buttons and a label.

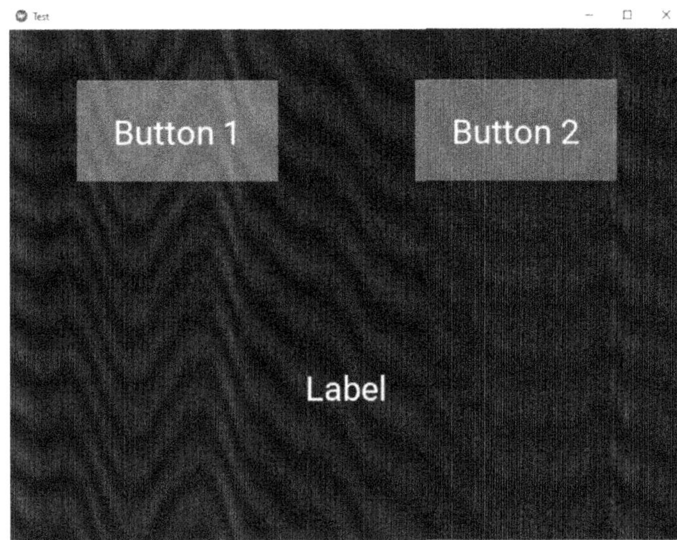


If you press the first button, a star will be added to the label text. If you press the second button, the font size of the label will be changed.

All this happens as soon as you press the appropriate button and only once. But suppose we want the program to behave in a different way. Here's how we want it to work:

1) The font size of the label text should change, but only after three seconds. And then, after another three seconds it should change back to 40.

2) When the first button is pressed, a new star should be printed every second until there are five stars altogether.

To achieve that, we'll need the **Clock** class, which we're going to have a look at right now.

# The Clock Class

The **Clock** class is used to schedule a method call in the future, either just once or multiple times. In the former case we specify the time that must elapse before the method is called. In the latter case we specify the interval between repeated calls of the method. We use the **dt** argument (which stands for delta-time) to get the time elapsed between the scheduling and the calling.

The two main methods that we use on the **Clock** object are **schedule_once** and **schedule_interval**. We're going to use the former to schedule the font size change to happen three seconds after the second button is pressed and the latter to schedule a one second interval between consecutive calls of the **print_star** method. So, let's jump right into the code.

# Scheduling Delay

Let's start by scheduling a delay. We'll use the **schedule_once** method and pass two arguments to it: the name of the method that we want to call and the delay in seconds. In our case, we want the method **increase_font** to be called after a three-second delay. Then we'll create a new method, **decrease_font**, that will change the font size back to 40 and inside the **increase_font** method we'll schedule the new method to be called after another three seconds. We'll also add another method, **handle_font**, that will be called directly when the button is pressed. Its only task will be to schedule the **increase_font** method. Here's the kv file:

```
#:kivy 1.11.1
# File name: test.kv
...
<TestLayout>:
    ...
    Button:
        text: 'Button 2'
        pos_hint: {'right': .9, 'top': .9}

        # Now this method will be called
        # when the button is pressed.
        on_press: root.handle_font()

    Label:
        ...
```

And here's the Python file:

```
# File name: test.py
...
from kivy.uix.floatlayout import FloatLayout

# We need the Clock class.
from kivy.clock import Clock

class TestLayout(FloatLayout):
    def print_star(self):
        self.label.text += ' *'

    # This method's only task is to schedule the increase_font method to be
    # called after three seconds (which is the second argument passed to the
    # schedule_once method.)
    def handle_font(self):
        Clock.schedule_once(self.increase_font, 3)

    # This method is scheduled to be called after a delay, so we use the dt
    # (delta-time) argument to pass the time. The method first changes the
    # font size and then schedules the decrease_font method to be called after
    # another three seconds.
    def increase_font(self, dt):
        self.label.font_size = 80
        Clock.schedule_once(self.decrease_font, 3)

    # This method also needs to know when it should be called, so we also pass
    # the dt argument.
    def decrease_font(self, dt):
        self.label.font_size = 40

class TestApp(App):
    ...
```

If you now run the app and press the second button, the font size of the label text will be increased only after three seconds and then decreased after another three seconds.

# Scheduling Interval

Now, for the first button we'll use the **schedule_interval** method with two arguments, the name of the method to call and the interval in seconds. Here's the kv file:

```
#:kivy 1.11.1
# File name: test.kv
...
<TestLayout>:
    label: _label

    Button:
        text: 'Button 1'
        pos_hint: {'x': .1, 'top': .9}

        # We'll call the handle_star method here.
        on_press: root.handle_star()

    Button:
        ...
```

And here's the Python file:

```
# File name: test.py
...
class TestLayout(FloatLayout):
    # This method is used to schedule the print_star method.
    # The latter should be called repeatedly every second.
    def handle_star(self):
        Clock.schedule_interval(self.print_star, 1)

    # We need to pass the dt argument to the method now.
    def print_star(self, dt):
        # We want no more than five stars, hence the limitation.
        if self.label.text.count('*') < 5:
            self.label.text += ' *'

        # Although the method doesn't print any more stars, it's still called every
        # second. You can check it out using the print function that will print
        # a simple message in the terminal each time the method is called.
        print('print_star method called')

    def handle_font(self):
        ...
```

If you now run the app and press the first button, you will see a star added to the label text every second until there are five (A). You will also see a message printed in the terminal every second (B), even if the stars are no longer added, which means the method is still called every second.

So, what if we don't want the method to be called anymore? We have to unschedule it.

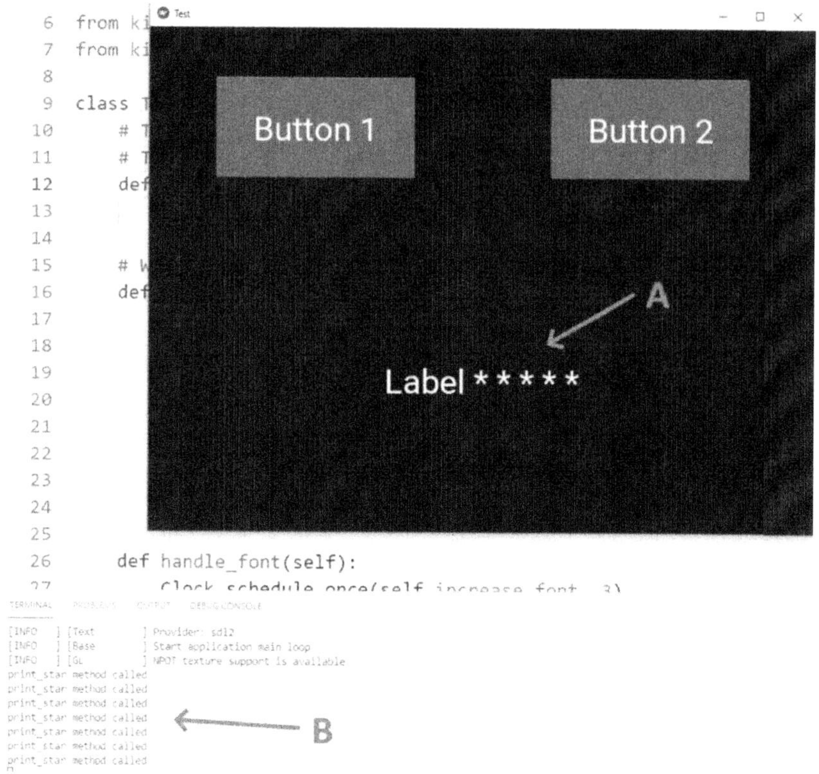

## Unscheduling a Method

If you don't want a method scheduled with one of the **Clock** methods (**schedule_once** or **schedule_interval**) to be scheduled anymore, you can pass its name to the **unschedule** method. Suppose we want to unschedule the **print_star** method in our example after the fifth star is printed:

```
# File name: test.py
...
class TestLayout(FloatLayout):
    def handle_star(self):
        ...

    def print_star(self, dt):
        self.label.text += ' *'
        if self.label.text.count('*') == 5:
            Clock.unschedule(self.print_star)

        print('print_star method called')

    def handle_font(self):
        ...
```

If you now run the app and press the first button, the **print_star** method will be called five times and then unscheduled. This time the message in the terminal will be printed also only five times.

The downside of this approach is that if we schedule a method more than once, all instances of the callback will be unscheduled. Instead, you can bind the **Clock** methods to so-called **triggered events** and then use these events for unscheduling. You can either pass the event to the **unschedule** method or call the **cancel** method on it. Here's how it works with the **unschedule** method:

```
# File name: test.py
...
class TestLayout(FloatLayout):
    def handle_star(self):
        # We schedule the method here to be called multiple times
        # and bind it to print_event.
        self.print_event = Clock.schedule_interval(self.print_star, 1)

    def print_star(self, dt):
        self.label.text += ' *'
        if self.label.text.count('*') == 5:
            # Now we can unschedule the method by passing the event
            # to the unschedule method.
            Clock.unschedule(self.print_event)

        print('print_star method called')

    def handle_font(self):
        ...
```

If you now run the app, it will work like before. And one more way to unschedule a method. This time we'll call the **cancel** method directly on the event:

```
# File name: test.py
...
class TestLayout(FloatLayout):
    def handle_star(self):
        self.print_event = Clock.schedule_interval(self.print_star, 1)

    def print_star(self, dt):
        self.label.text += ' *'
        if self.label.text.count('*') == 5:
            # Now we unschedule the method by calling the cancel method on the event.
            self.print_event.cancel()

        print('print_star method called')

    def handle_font(self):
        ...
```

Again, the app runs like before.

## Scheduling a Method with Arguments

It's also possible to schedule a method that takes arguments. To do that, you need to use the **partial** method from the **functools** module. Suppose we want to pass any symbol, not just a star, to the **print_star** method as an argument and also pass another argument that will tell the program how many times the symbol should be printed before the method is unscheduled. Let's change the name of the method to **print_symbol**, which seems more relevant and modify the code:

```
# File name: test.py

import kivy
kivy.require('1.11.1')
from kivy.app import App
from kivy.uix.floatlayout import FloatLayout
from kivy.clock import Clock

# We need the partial function.
from functools import partial

class TestLayout(FloatLayout):
    def handle_star(self):
        # Here we schedule the print_symbol method to be called every second.
        # We pass the arguments '$' and 7 respectively for the symbol to be
        # printed and the number of the symbols before the method is unscheduled.
        # The method name along with the two arguments is passed as the first
        # argument to the partial function. The second argument is the delta-time.
        self.print_event = Clock.schedule_interval(partial(self.print_symbol, '$', 7), 1)

    # This used to be the print_star method. The new method takes some arguments.
    def print_symbol(self, symbol, reps, dt):
        self.label.text += f' {symbol}'
        if self.label.text.count(symbol) == reps:
            self.print_event.cancel()

        print('print_symbol method called')

    def handle_font(self):
        ...
```

Now when you run the app and press the first button, a dollar sign will be printed every second as long as there are no more than seven of them.

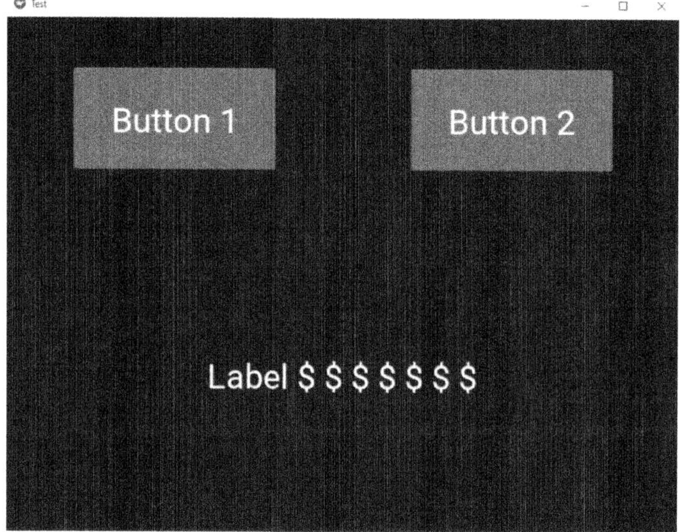


In the next chapter we'll implement a clock in our project so that we can measure the time of the game. But before you move on to the next chapter, here's a short exercise for you.

# It's Your Turn Now...

### EXERCISE

In this exercise you'll create a running button. Remove the **Button** rule, the two buttons and the label from **TestLayout** in the kv file, then add a button with the id **_button** and add an ObjectProperty **button** referencing it at the top of the root widget so that you can later reference the button in Python code.

The text on the button should just read **'button'**. Set its **x** and **y** properties to **20** and **100** respectively and **size_hint** to **(.2, .2)**. When the button is pressed, the **handle_move** method on the root widget should be called. You're going to implement the method in a minute.

Now, go to the Python file and remove all the code from the **TestLayout** class. We don't need to import the **partial** function from the **functools** module either, so go ahead and remove it. Then, in the **TestLayout** class define the **handle_move** method and another method called **move**. The **move** method should change the **x** property of the button by 20 (so 20 is added to the current value) but only if the button's **right** property is less than the TestLayout's **right** property. Otherwise it should set the **x** property of the button back to 20.

Then, in the **handle_move** method, schedule the **move** method to be called repeatedly ten times every second.

### SOLUTION

Here's the kv code:

```
# File name: test.kv

<TestLayout>:
    button: _button

    Button:
        id: _button
        text: 'button'
        x: 20
        y: 100
        size_hint: .2, .2

        on_press: root.handle_move()
```

And here's the Python code:

```
# File name: test.py
...
class TestLayout(FloatLayout):
    def handle_move(self):
        Clock.schedule_interval(self.move, .1)

    def move(self, dt):
        if self.button.right < self.right:
            self.button.x += 20
        else:
            self.button.x = 20

class TestApp(App):
    ...
```

Now if you run the app and press the button, it should jump in 20-pixel steps from left to right until it reaches the right border of the container. Then it should go back to its initial position and continue moving. Check it out.

# Chapter 94 – Using the Clock Class in the Slugrace Project

In the previous chapter we were talking about the **Clock** class. In this chapter we'll use it in our project. As you remember, in one of the previous chapters we added the game over logic to the game. We didn't take the time ending condition into consideration, though. We're going to fix this now. Also, part of the game over logic is switching to the Game Over screen. At this point the screen appears immediately when the game is over so that you don't even have time to look at the results of the last race. We'll add some delay before we switch to the Game Over screen, or rather you will because this is going to be an exercise for you.

## Starting the Game Clock

If you select the time ending condition, the game should be over no later than after a specific amount of time has elapsed. If the time is up during a race, the game will be over immediately after this race. But how do we know how much time has elapsed? Well, we need a clock. And the clock should start ticking the moment the game starts, so when the Ready button in the Settings screen is pressed.

Here's the method that is called (along with some others) when the Ready button is pressed:

```
#:kivy 1.11.1
# File name: settings.kv
#:import settings settings
...
<SettingsScreen>:
    ...
        ### READY BUTTON ###
        RedButton:
            ...
            on_press:
                ...
                root.game.start_game()
```

The method is implemented in the **Game** class. At this moment it just prints the message **'Game started'**.

```
# File name: main.py
...
class Game(ScreenManager):
    ...
    def start_game(self):
        print('Game started')

    def go(self):
        ...
```

So, as you can see, it doesn't do anything useful. We can remove the **print** method now and add some code that will start the game clock. In order to be able to use the clock, we need to import the **Clock** class just like we did in the previous chapter.

We will create a method, **update_time**, that will be scheduled in the **start_game** method to be called repeatedly every second, but only if the ending condition is **end_by_time**.

The **update_time** method will just add one second to the elapsed time and subtract one second from the remaining time. If the time has elapsed, the method will be unscheduled so that we don't run into the time from the day before, because after reaching zero seconds, the next value of the remaining time would be -1 day, 23:59:59. Here's the code:

```
# File name: main.py
...
from random import choice

# We will need the Clock class.
from kivy.clock import Clock

Builder.load_file('settings.kv')
...
class Game(ScreenManager):
    ...
    def start_game(self):
        # If the game is supposed to end by time, the update_time method
        # is scheduled to be called every second.
        if self.end_by_time:
            self.time_event = Clock.schedule_interval(self.update_time, 1)

    # Here's the method that will update the time every second. It takes
    # the dt (delta-time) argument.
    def update_time(self, dt):
        # Add one second to elapsed time.
        self.time_elapsed_delta += timedelta(seconds=1)
        self.time_elapsed = str(self.time_elapsed_delta)

        # Subtract one second from remaining time.
        self.time_remaining_delta -= timedelta(seconds=1)
        self.time_remaining = str(self.time_remaining_delta)

        # Unschedule the update_time method if the time has elepased.
        if self.time_remaining_delta.seconds == 0:
            self.time_event.cancel()

    def go(self):
        ...
```

If you now run the app, the clock should work. So, select the time ending condition (A) and set the time to the minimum time of one second (B).

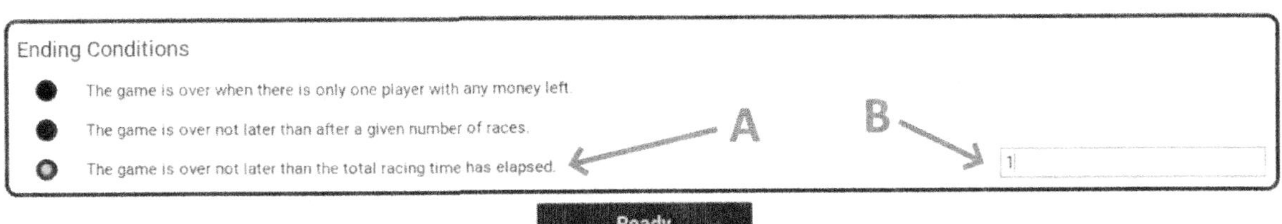

Now hit the Ready button and watch the elapsed and remaining time labels change in the Game Info area.

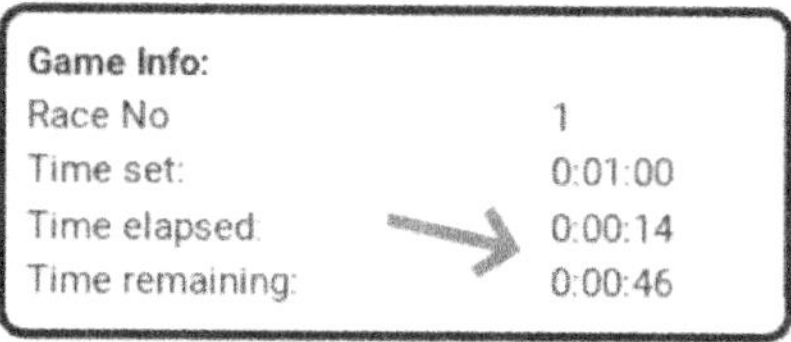


The clock will stop when the time has elapsed.

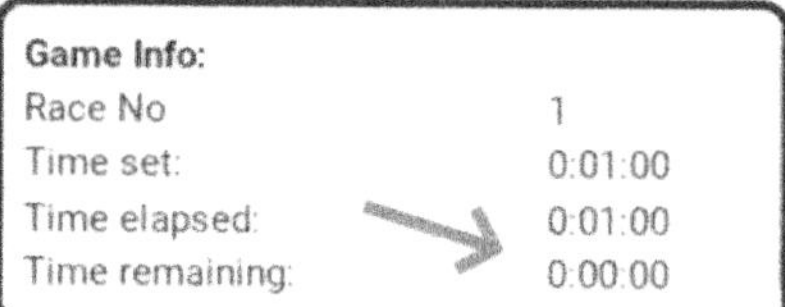


# Game Over Check

So, if we select the time ending condition, the game clock starts ticking the moment we press the Ready button and stops the moment the time has elapsed. But we still haven't handled the game over scenario with the time ending condition enabled. Let's do it now.

Our game over code is in the **Game** class, in four places:

- First, we have the Game Over section with the **winners** list, the **game_over_reason** property and the **winner_text** property.

- Then we have the **go** method where the **gameover_check** method is called.

- Next, we have the **gameover_check** method itself that checks whether the conditions are met to end the game and if so, it calls the **gameover** method.

- And finally we have the **gameover** method that actually handles all the possible game over scenarios.

We have to modify the **gameover_check** and **gamover** methods so that the time ending condition is also taken into consideration. Also, we'll add code to the **update_time** method that will call the **gameover** method when the time is up. We need this because it may happen that the players will not put their bets for a long time even though the time of the game has elapsed. In such a case the game wouldn't be over until the next race where we have the game over check. But we want the game to be over also if the players are idle but the game time has elapsed.

The code that I present below will have to be modified later on. Now the game is supposed to be over the moment the time has elapsed, but later we will make sure it's not over while the slugs are running, but rather only after they finish the race. For now it's not so important because the race practically takes no time, we have the winner slug just after we press the Go button. But this will change when we animate the slugs.

So, here's the code:

```
# File name: main.py
...
class Game(ScreenManager):
    ...
    def update_time(self, dt):
        ...
        if self.time_remaining_delta.seconds == 0:
            self.time_event.cancel()

            # Also call the gameover method when the time is up.
            self.gameover()

    def go(self):
        ...
    def gameover_check(self):
        if (len(self.players) == 0
            or (len(self.players) == 1 and self.number_of_players > 1)
            or (self.end_by_races and self.race_number == self.number_of_races)

            # time ending condition checked
            or (self.end_by_time and self.time_remaining_delta.seconds == 0)):
            self.gameover()

    def gameover(self):
        ...
        elif len(self.players) == 1 and self.number_of_players > 1:
            ...
            self.winner_text = (f'The winner is {winner.name}, ' +
                                f'having started at ${winner.initial_money}, ' +
                                f'winning at ${winner.money}.')

        # after a given number of races or after the game time has elapsed
        elif ((self.end_by_races and self.race_number == self.number_of_races)
              or (self.end_by_time and self.time_remaining_delta.seconds == 0)):

            # The game over reason depends on the ending condition, races or time.
            self.game_over_reason = ('The number of races you set has been reached.'
                if self.end_by_races else 'The game time you set is up.')

            if self.number_of_players == 1:
                ...
```

Now the game will be over when the time you set elapses, regardless whether there have been any races or not. Let's run the app, set the time to 1 minute and wait. If we just wait and do nothing, there are no races and all players end the game with their initial amounts of money.

Here's what it might look like:

As mentioned above, we'll revisit the game over functionality later in the book, for now it works fine, so let's move on.

In the next chapter we'll take care of resetting the game after you decide to play again. And now don't forget to do the exercises below.

# It's Your Turn Now...

In these three exercises we'll take care of the Game Over screen. The problem with this screen is that it appears immediately when the game is over, which means we can't see the results of the last race. Let's add some delay. I think four seconds is enough to have a look at the results before we switch to the Game Over screen. There are also some other minor changes we must not forget. So, do the exercises below to implement the delay.

**EXERCISE 1**

As we want to switch to the Game Over screen after a delay of four seconds, we can use the **Clock** class. We will move the code that switches to the Game Over screen to a new method and we'll schedule the method to be called once. So, add a new method below the **gameover** method and name it **gameover_screen**. Don't forget to pass delta-time to it as an argument. Move the code that we use to switch to the Game Over screen from the former to the latter. In the **gameover** method create a triggered event, name it **gameover_event** and use it to schedule the **gameover_screen** method to be called once after four seconds. Then, in the **gameover_screen** method add another line of code to unschedule the **gameover_screen** method.

**SOLUTION**

Here's the code:

```
# File name: main.py
...
class Game(ScreenManager):
    ...
    def gameover(self):
        ...
                # joint winners
                else:
                    self.winner_text = "There's a tie. The joint winners are:\n\n"
```

```
                for winner in self.winners:
                    self.winner_text += (f'{winner.name}, ' +
                                         f'having started at ${winner.initial_money}, ' +
                                         f'winning at ${winner.money}.\n')

        # Schedule the method that we will use to switch to the Gameover screen.
        self.gameover_event = Clock.schedule_once(self.gameover_screen, 4)

    # Here's the extracted new method that takes care of switching screens.
    def gameover_screen(self, dt):
        # Now we can switch to the Game Over screen.
        self.current = 'gameoverscreen'

        # Let's unschedule the gameover_screen method.
        self.gameover_event.cancel()

    def reset_race(self):
        ...
```

If you now run the app and select any ending condition you like, you will be able to see the results of the last race for four seconds before the Game Over screen shows up. In the image on the right you can see the results of the last race where all players go bankrupt.

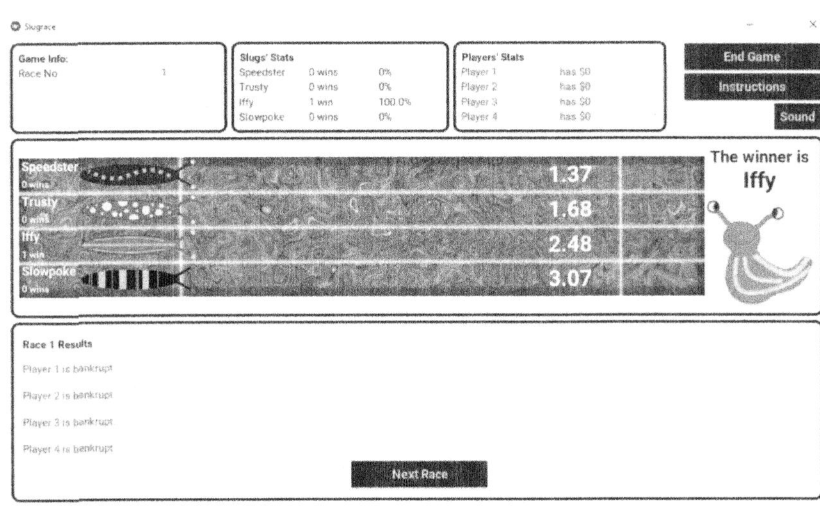


And after four seconds the Game Over screen shows up.

Game Over

All players are bankrupt.

There is no winner!

## EXERCISE 2

Now we have the delay and everthing works, but there's a little problem. During the delay the Next Race button is still enabled. As the game is already over, we shouldn't be able to press it. To address this issue, go to the Game Over section above the callback methods in the **Game** class and add a new BooleanProperty. Name it **game_is_over** and set its default value to **False**. Then, in the **gameover** method, just before you schedule the **gameover_screen** method, set it to **True**. This way the property will be **False** during the whole game and **True** only when the game is over.

Next, use the **game_is_over** property you just created in the Results screen to disable the Next Race button when the game is over.

## SOLUTION

Here's the **main.py** file:

```
# File name: main.py
...
class Game(ScreenManager):
    ...
    # game over
    ...
    winner_text = StringProperty('')

    # We'll use this property to handle the functionality of the Next Race
    # button in the Results screen.
    game_is_over = BooleanProperty(False)

    # callback methods
    ...
    def gameover(self):
        ...
                # joint winners
                else:
                    self.winner_text = "There's a tie. The joint winners are:\n\n"
                    for winner in self.winners:
                        self.winner_text += (f'{winner.name}, ' +
                                             f'having started at ${winner.initial_money}, ' +
                                             f'winning at ${winner.money}.\n')

        # Now the game is over, so let's set the game_is_over BooleanProperty to True.
        self.game_is_over = True

        self.gameover_event = Clock.schedule_once(self.gameover_screen, 4)

    def gameover_screen(self, dt):
        ...
```

And here's the **results.kv** file where we handle the functionality of the Next Race button:

```
#:kivy 1.11.1
# File name: results.kv
#:import results results
...
<ResultsScreen>:
    ...
        ### NEXT RACE BUTTON ###
        RedButton:
            text: 'Next Race'

            # The button is disabled when the game is over.
            disabled: root.game.game_is_over

            on_press:
                root.game.reset_race()
                ...
```

If you now run the app again, the Next Race button will be disabled when the game is over.

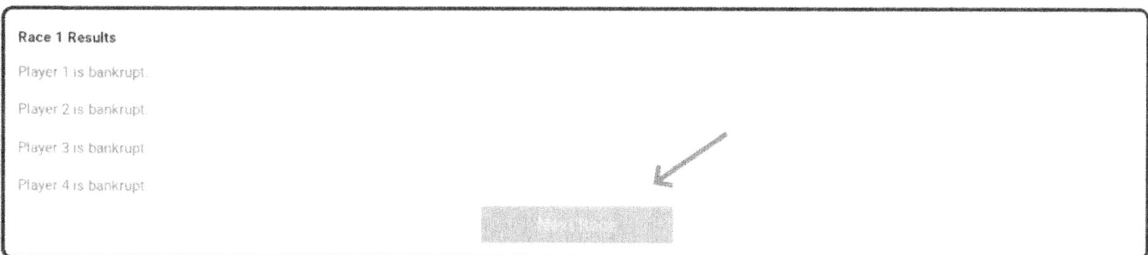


**EXERCISE 3**

There's a similar situation with the Go button in the Bets screen if the ending condition is set to **end_by_time**. When the time elapses, the game is over, but as the Game Over screen is delayed, there's still some time to press the Go button. This should not be possible when the game is over, so modify the code in the Bets screen so that the Go button is disabled when the game is over. Use the **game_is_over** Boolean property just like before.

**SOLUTION**

So, here's the code:

```
#:kivy 1.11.1
# File name: bets.kv
#:import bets bets
...
<BetsScreen>:
    ...
        ### GO BUTTON ###
```

```
        RedButton:
            text: 'Go'

            # The button should be disabled not only if not all of the players
            # have selected their slugs, but also when the game is over.
            disabled: not root.all_slugs_selected or root.game.game_is_over

            on_press:
                ...
```

Now if you play the game and set the time to, say, 1 minute, the Go button will be disabled as soon as the time is up. To watch this you can just hit the Ready button in the Settings screen, select a slug for each player so that the Go button is enabled and then do nothing, just wait for one minute to see how the Go button becomes disabled again.

# Chapter 95 – Restarting the Game

In the couple preceding chapters we handled the Game Over scenarios. Now, when the game is over, we have two options to choose from, represented by the two buttons in the Game Over screen. We can either play again or quit the game. We'll discuss the former in this chapter and the latter in one of the following chapters.

So, what happens if you hit the Play Again button? Let's see. Here's the initial game setup:

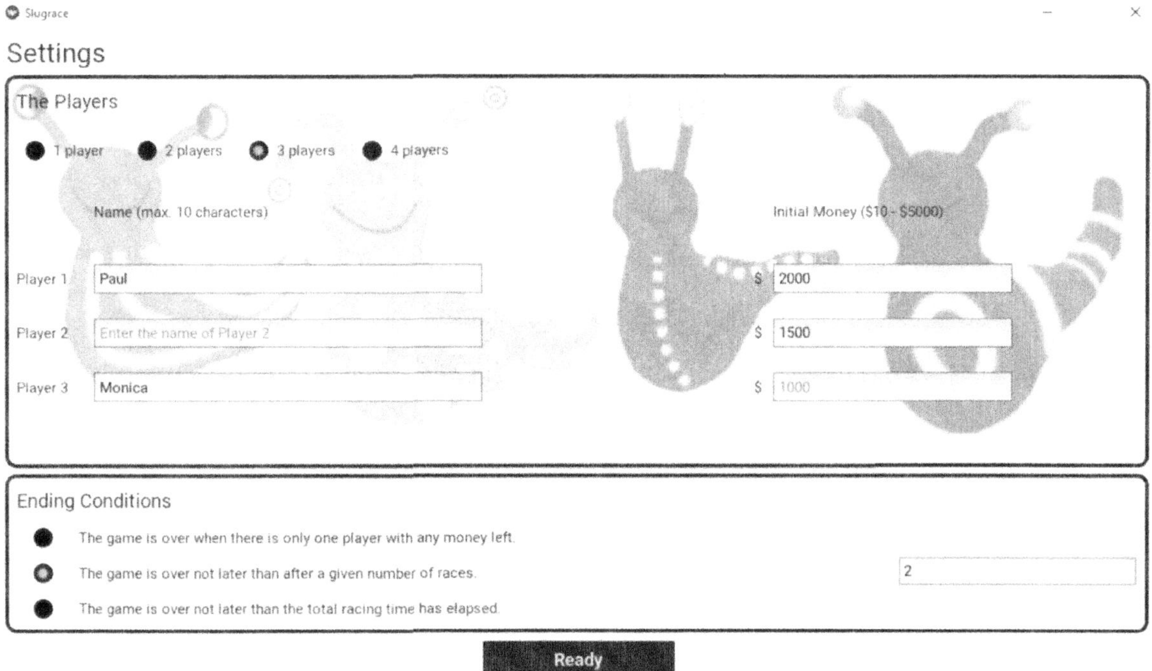


So, as you can see, there are three players with different initial money amounts. Two of them were given names, the middle one will have the generic name Player 2. The ending condition is set to races and the number of races to 2.

Now, let's play the game and after two races it'll be over. Never mind who the winner is. Suppose we want to play again. If we hit the Play Again button,

Game Over

The number of races you set has been reached.

The winner is Paul, having started at $2000, winning at $1102.

Play Again Quit

we'll be taken back to the Settings screen. Everything will look exactly the same as when we started the game. But this isn't the same Settings screen, although all the previous settings here are maintained, so the names of the players, their initial money amounts, the ending condition and the number of races.

What's worse, the race number is still 2, so when we hit the Ready button, we won't be able to play because the game is set just to 2 races. So, there are a couple things we need to take care of.

# Restarting the Game

When we speak about restarting a game, in most cases we don't actually mean closing the app window and starting the app again. What we rather mean is restoring the app to its original state.

There are two approaches that we can take:

1. We can just reset all the values to the original ones, so for example the ending condition to money (by setting the **end_by_money** property to **True**), the number of players to 2, the **players** list to a list containing the first two players, the race number to 1, all players' **bankrupt** properties to **False**, and so on.

2. We can remove the **Game** widget altogether and create it again. Then it will be reset to the original values, so this would work just as if we started the app again.

We could choose either approach, but we're going to opt for the simpler solution. We're going to remove the **Game** widget and add it again. The problem, though, is that **Game** is the root widget and there isn't any widget above it in the hierarchy it could be removed from. This is why we have to create a new root widget and add **Game** to it. We can use just a FloatLayout. Here's the modified code of the **build** method in the **SlugraceApp** class:

```
# File name: main.py
...
from kivy.clock import Clock

# We will need the FloatLayout class for the root widget.
from kivy.uix.floatlayout import FloatLayout

Builder.load_file('settings.kv')
...
class SlugraceApp(App):
    ...
    def build(self):
        # We need a new root widget so that we can add and remove
        # the Game widget from it. Let it be a FloatLayout.
        self.root = FloatLayout()

        # Now we add the Game widget to the FloatLayout and return
        # the latter with the former as its only child.
```

```
        self.root.add_widget(Game())
        return self.root

if __name__ == '__main__':
    ...
```

Now the app works as before, but we have a new root widget. So, let's add the **restart** method in the **SlugraceApp** class that will remove all widgets from the root widget (which in our case just means removing the **Game** widget from the root FloatLayout) and then add the **Game** widget again.

Here it is:

```
# File name: main.py
...
class SlugraceApp(App):
    ...
    max_name_length = 10

    # The method that will be called
    # when the game is over and we
    # decide to play again.
    def restart(self):
        # It first removes all widgets
        # from the root (so the Game
        # widget only in this case)...
        self.root.clear_widgets()

        # ... and then adds the Game
        # widget again.
        self.root.add_widget(Game())

    def build(self):
        ...
```

Now all we have to do is call this method when the Play Again button in the Game Over screen is pressed. As you remember, we use the **app** variable to access the attributes and methods defined in the class that inherits from **App**. Here's the modified code:

```
#:kivy 1.11.1
# File name: gameover.kv
#:import gameover gameover

<GameoverScreen>:
    ...
        # the buttons
        BoxLayout:
            ...
            RedButton:
                text: 'Play Again'
                pos_hint: {'x': 0, 'center_y': .5}
                on_press: app.restart()
            RedButton:
                ...
```

Now let's run the app and use the same setup as before, so three players (Paul with $2000 to start the game, Player 2 with $1500 and Monica with the default $1000) and the ending condition set to 2 races.

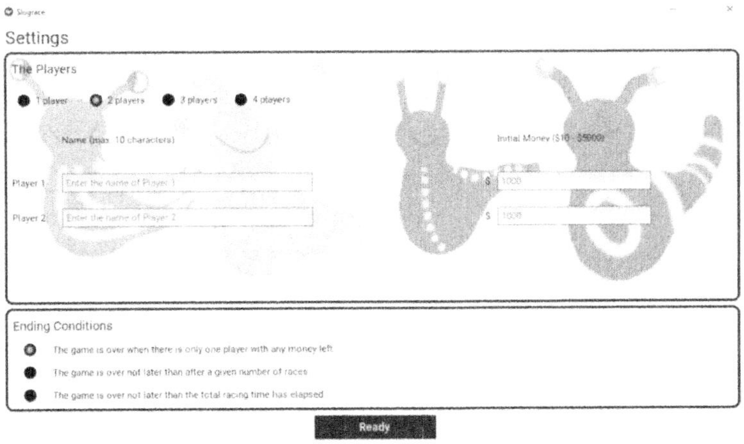

After two races the game is over. When we press the Play Again button, the Settings screen will appear. As you can see, now it looks exactly like when the app was launched for the first time. So, we have all the default settings here – two players, end by money ending condition selected, no explicit names given to the players and their initial money reset to the default $1000.

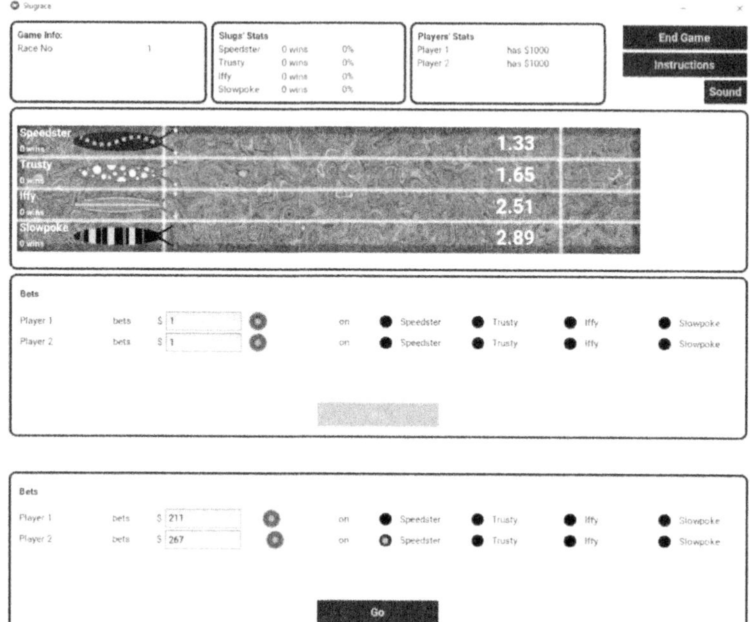


Now, let's hit the Ready button without changing anything. In the image on the left you can see the Race screen of the new game.

As you can see, the race number has been reset to 1. The slugs' and players' stats have been reset too. Everything looks fine, until you select a slug for one of the players.

As soon as you do, the Go button will be enabled, which is wrong. As you remember, it shouldn't be enabled until all players have selected their slugs. So, what's the problem here?

The problem is that the player's **bankrupt** property is still the same as in the old game. To address this issue, let's create a method in the **Game** class that will reset the **bankrupt** property to **False** for each player. In the method we'll loop over all the players and call the **reset** method on each. But we're not going to loop over just the players in the **players** list, but all four potential players.

As you know there are four **Player** instances in the **Game** class, **player1**, **player2**, **player3** and **player4**. These are the four players that can play, but the actual number of players in the game is between one and four. So, let's create another list that will contain all four players and name it **potential_players** because it will contain all players that can potentially play. Then, in the **reset_players** method we'll iterate over this list and call the **reset** method on each potential player.

We already defined the **reset** method in the **Player** class. It's called after each race to reset the players' chosen slugs and bets. Now, we'll modify it slightly by adding some code that will be executed only when the game is over and we want to play again.

To differentiate the two cases, so resetting the players after each race and resetting them before a new game, we'll add a **gameover** parameter to it with the default value set to **False**. However here, before a new game, we'll set it to **True** so that the extra code in the **reset** method is executed and the **bankrupt** property on each player is reset. Now the **reset** method in the **Player** class should look like this:

```
# File name: player.py
...
class Player(EventDispatcher):
    ...
    def update(self, winning_slug):
        ...

    # Now there's the gameover parameter, which will be set to True only
    # before a new game begins.
    def reset(self, gameover=False):
        self.chosen_slug = None
        self.bet = 1

        # This code is only executed when we want to play again after the game
        # is over, not after each race.
        if gameover:
            self.bankrupt = False
```

And here are the modifications in the **main.py** file:

```
# File name: main.py
...
class Game(ScreenManager):
    # the players
    ...
    players = [player1, player2]

    # Here's the list of all four potential players, out of which
    # one, two, three or all four may be the actual players in the game.
    potential_players = [player1, player2, player3, player4]

    # ending conditions
    ...
    def reset_race(self):
        ...

    # Here's the method that will restore all four potential players
    # to their original states.
    def reset_players(self):
        for player in self.potential_players:

            # We pass the gameover keyword argument set to True to the
            # reset method in the Player class to differentiate it from
            # the case when it's called after each race.
            player.reset(gameover = True)

class SlugraceApp(App):
    ...
```

With the **reset_players** method in place, we can call it. We'll do it in the Game Over screen just before restarting the app:

```
#:kivy 1.11.1
# File name: gameover.kv
#:import gameover gameover

<GameoverScreen>:
    ...
        # the buttons
        BoxLayout:
            ...
            RedButton:
                text: 'Play Again'
                pos_hint: {'x': 0, 'center_y': .5}
                on_press:
                    # We first reset the players and then restart the app.
                    root.game.reset_players()
                    app.restart()
            RedButton:
                ...
```

## Some Issues After Restarting the Game

Now if you play again, everything should work as expected. There are just two little details I'd like to talk about. We'll handle the first one together and I'll leave the other one for you as an exercise.

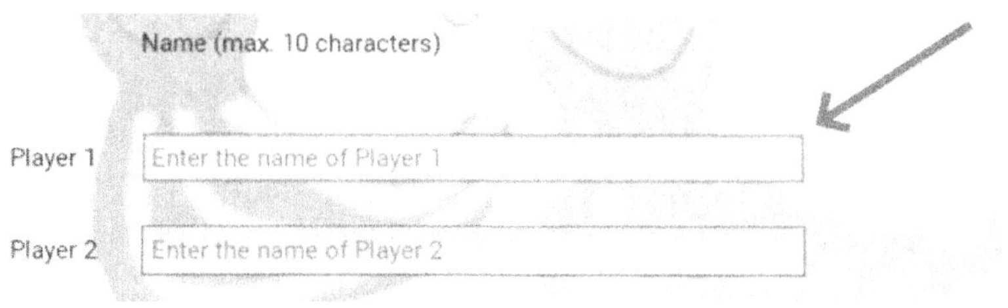


So, when you restart the app and click on one of the text inputs to enter some text, like the names of the players, their initial money, the number of races or the time after which the game should be over, it may happen that there is no mouse cursor in the text input. It's not a big deal because you can still enter text, but it's slightly less intuitive than if the cursor were there. For example here, in the image above, the first text input has focus and we can enter text, but we don't see the cursor.

The cursor will appear when you start typing text and will remain afterward, but you can't see it before you start typing. If this is the case, and it bothers you, there are a couple solutions. One of them is setting the text input's text to anything like a whitespace or **`'0'`** and then setting it to an empty string. This way the cursor will appear and remain and there won't be any text anyway.

We're going to do it in a different way. We'll override the **`on_focus`** method in the **`NameInput`** and **`NumInput`** classes in the **widgets.py** file. It actually already was overridden in the latter class, so we'll have to modify the code slightly. The trick that will do the job is to set the width of the cursor to something more than 1, like for example 1.01. You won't see the difference anyway and it will work. There's even a handy property, **`cursor_width`**, in the **`TextInput`** class that we can use. Here's the code:

```
# File name: widgets.py
...
class NameInput(TextInput):
    ...
    def insert_text(...):
        ...

    # This method will set the cursor
    # width to 1.01 when the text input
    # gets focus and there is no text
    # in it.
    def on_focus(self, instance, value):
        if value and self.text == '':
            self.cursor_width = 1.01
```

```
class NumInput(TextInput):
    ...
    def on_text_validate(self):
        ...

    # Here we already have the code used to
    # validate the text, which we must keep.
    # The validation code is executed when
    # the widget loses focus, so we can add
    # an else block for the code that sets
    # the cursor width.
    def on_focus(self, instance, value):
        if not value:
            self.on_text_validate()
        else:
            if self.text == '':
                self.cursor_width = 1.01
```

Now the cursor will be visible as soon as you click on any text input in the new game.

Now, the second issue I wanted to talk about is the transition between the Game Over screen of the old game and the Settings screen of the new game when you hit the Play Again button. Well, actually there is no transition because we're not switching screens but rather restarting the app completely. But I think it wouldn't look bad if we could mimic such a transition so that the Settings screen fades in. This is what you are going to do in the exercise below.

And in the next chapter we'll handle the End Game button in the Race screen that will let us end the game manually at any time.

## It's Your Turn Now...

### EXERCISE

In this exercise you're going to mimic the transition effect between two screens. We have such transitions between all existing screens, like between the Settings screen and the Race screen, between the Bets screen and the Results screen, as well as between the Race screen and the Game Over screen. But these are all situations where we actually switch between screens. This isn't the case when we hit the Play Again button. Here we just start a new game and the first screen, the Settings screen, appears immediately. Let's change that. We could animate the **opacity** property of the **Game** widget, but we didn't talk about animations yet, so let's do it in a different way, using the **Clock** class. Here are the steps for you to follow:

1. Find the **restart** method in the **SlugraceApp** class. At this point it just removes the **Game** widget from the root widget and adds it again. The first line of code should remain unchanged, the **Game** widget should be removed. But then, before we add it again, we must set its opacity to 0, which

will make it invisible. In order to do it, we'll need access to the **Game** widget, so instead of instantiating it directly in the **add_widget** method further down, let's first create it and assign to a variable. You can name the variable **game**. Then set the **opacity** property on the game object to **0**.

2. Now that we have a **Game** instance with opacity set to 0, we can add it to the root widget. Just pass the object to the **add_widget** method below the code that sets its opacity.

3. Now the **Game** widget is added, but it's invisible. We need another method that will be called multiple times, each time increasing the opacity by a little amount until it reaches the value of 1. So, below the **restart** method add a new method and name it **show**. It will be scheduled to be called every 0.01 seconds in a moment. Don't forget to pass the delta-time argument to it. In the method we first want to increase the opacity by 0.01 and then check whether the value of opacity is greater than or equal to 1. If so, the value of **opacity** should be set to 1 (just in case its value is slightly above 1 due to how float numbers are handled) and the method should be unscheduled. We'll use a triggered event for scheduling and unscheduling the method.

4. So, add a triggered event named **show_event** and use the **Clock** object to schedule the **show** method to be called every 0.01 seconds. That's it. Now we should have a nice transition effect.

**SOLUTION**

Here's the code:

```
# File name: main.py
...
class SlugraceApp(App):
    ...
    def restart(self):
        self.root.clear_widgets()

        # Let's create a Game instance and assign it to a variable.
        self.game = Game()

        # Let's make the Game widget fully transparent.
        self.game.opacity = 0

        # Let's add the Game instance to the root widget.
        self.root.add_widget(self.game)

        # Let's schedule the show method to be called every 0.01 seconds.
        self.show_event = Clock.schedule_interval(self.show, .01)

    # Here's the show method.
    def show(self, dt):
        # It increases the opacity by 0.01.
        self.game.opacity += .01

        # If the opacity is 1 or more...
        if self.game.opacity >= 1:
```

```
            # ...it's set to exactly 1 and...
            self.game.opacity = 1

            # ... the method is unscheduled.
            self.show_event.cancel()

    def build(self):
        ...
```

If you now run the app, you will see the Settings screen fade in after you hit the Play Again button.

# Chapter 96 – Ending the Game Manually

In the previous chapter we handled the first of the two buttons that you can see in the Game Over screen. Its role is to restart the game. In the next chapter we'll handle the other button, which is supposed to close the app window. And in this chapter let's go back to the Race screen and handle the End Game button over there which will be used to manually end the game at any time.

## Ending the Game Manually

Why do we even need the End Game button to end the game manually? Well, there are lots of situations where this functionality might come in handy. For example if you set the number of races to a large number but then decide that you don't feel like playing twenty more races or if you set the game time to an hour but then don't have time to play so long. Whatever the reason, you may just want to end the game before it would normally end.

At this point the End Game button only does one thing. When you press it, you switch to the Game Over screen. Here's the code as it is right now:

```
#:kivy 1.11.1
# File name: race.kv
#:import race race
...
<RaceScreen>:
    ...
            # Buttons
            BoxLayout:
                ...
                RedButton:
                    text: 'End Game'
                    pos_hint: {'right': 1}
                    on_press: root.manager.current = 'gameoverscreen'

                RedButton:
                    text: 'Instructions'
                    ...
```

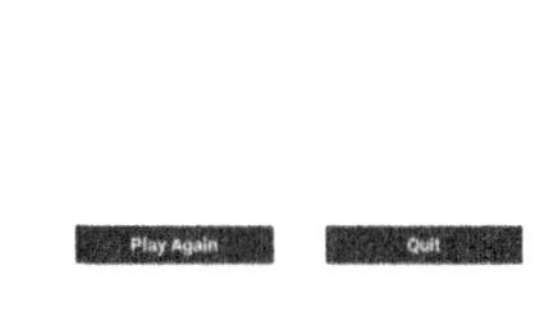


If you run the app and press the button at any time, you will see this the Game Over screen, but without any useful information.

So, you know that the game is over, but you don't see the winner. This is because we just switched to the Game Over screen and the

**gameover** method wasn't called. Let's fix this then:

```
#:kivy 1.11.1
# File name: race.kv
#:import race race
...
<RaceScreen>:
    ...
            # Buttons
            BoxLayout:
                ...
                RedButton:
                    text: 'End Game'
                    pos_hint: {'right': 1}
                    on_press: root.game.gameover()

                RedButton:
                    text: 'Instructions'
                    ...
```

If you run the app now, the gameover method will be called, but will it change anything? Let's have a look at the **gameover** method one more time. Well, the method covers the following cases:

- all players go bankrupt,

- only one player with money is left in multi-player mode,

- the number of races you set has been reached,

- the game time you set has elapsed.

In all the cases described above the game ends automatically, but the method doesn't cover the case we're interested in, which is game over at any time. We have to add this case to the method. To do that, we'll add a parameter to the method definition, named **manual**, and set its default value to **False**. If it's **False**, it means the game was ended automatically and nothing will change. However, when the End Game button is pressed in the Race screen, the value of **manual** will be set to **True** and the method will behave slightly differently. In particular, the game over reason will be different.

OK, here's the modified code:

```
# File name: main.py
...
class Game(ScreenManager):
    ...
    def gameover_check(self):
        ...

    # Now the method will have the parameter manual, which by default is set to False.
    def gameover(self, manual=False):
        self.winners = []
```

```
        # all players go bankrupt
        if len(self.players) == 0:
            ...
        # one player left in multi-player mode
        elif len(self.players) == 1 and self.number_of_players > 1:
            ...

        # after a given number of races, after the game time has elapsed
        # or if the game was ended manually
        elif ((self.end_by_races and self.race_number == self.number_of_races)
              or (self.end_by_time and self.time_remaining_delta.seconds == 0)
              or manual):

            # The game over reason depends on why the game ends. There's now one
            # more option, manual ending of the game.
            if manual:
                self.game_over_reason = 'You ended the game manually.'
            elif self.end_by_races:
                self.game_over_reason = 'The number of races you set has been reached.'
            else:
                self.game_over_reason = 'The game time you set is up.'

            if self.number_of_players == 1:
                ...
```

Don't forget to set the **manual** argument to **True** in the kv file:

```
#:kivy 1.11.1
# File name: race.kv
#:import race race
...
<RaceScreen>:
    ...
            # Buttons
            BoxLayout:
                ...
                RedButton:
                    text: 'End Game'
                    pos_hint: {'right': 1}
                    on_press: root.game.gameover(manual=True)

                RedButton:
                    text: 'Instructions'
                    ...
```

Game Over

You ended the game manually.

The winner is Player 2, having started at $1000, winning at $877.

Play Again Quit

Now if you run the app and end it manually, you will see the Game Over screen four seconds after you hit the End Game button (this is the time after which the transition to the Game Over screen begins). You should now see a meaningful message. There is just one more improvement I think will make our experience better. The four-second delay after we hit the End Game button is not very intuitive. On the contrary, the user of the app may think the button doesn't work because nothing is happening for four seconds. So, in the exercise below you will modify the code so that there is a four-second delay only if the game ends automatically, but not if it's ended manually. And in the next chapter we'll make the Quit button work. This is the other button in the Game Over screen.

# It's Your Turn Now...

### EXERCISE

As you remember, the Game Over screen normally appears 4 seconds after the game is ended. We don't want this delay when we end the game manually, so this is also something the code must take care of. Let's keep it simple. Instead of passing the literal value of 4 seconds as the second argument to the **Clock.schedule_once** method inside the **gameover** method, define a variable named **delay** and set it to **4** or **0** depending on whether the game is ended automatically or manually. In the latter case there should be no delay, so the value should be set to **0**. How do we know if the game was ended manually? Well, there's the **manual** argument in the **gameover** method, so make use of it. Finally pass the **delay** variable to the **Clock.schedule_once** method.

### SOLUTION

Here's the code:

```
# File name: main.py
...
class Game(ScreenManager):
    ...
    def gameover(self, manual=False):
        ...
        self.game_is_over = True

        # The delay is 4 seconds if the game ends automatically, but there isn't
        # any delay if it ends manually.
        delay = 0 if manual else 4

        # We now use delay in the schedule_once method.
        self.gameover_event = Clock.schedule_once(self.gameover_screen, delay)

    def gameover_screen(self, dt):
        ...
```

If you now run the app and end the game manually by pressing the End Game button, you will immediately switch to the Game Over screen, without any delay.

# Chapter 97 – Quitting the Game

In one of the previous chapters we handled the first of the two buttons that you can see in the Game Over screen, the Play Again button, which we use to restart the game. In this chapter we'll handle the other button, which we will use to quit the game.

So, let's handle the Quit button in the Game Over screen. To close the application we can call the **stop** method that is defined in the **App** class. But this would be too easy. Instead, when the Quit button is pressed a popup window should appear and ask us to confirm whether we really want to quit the game. A **popup window** is a special kind of widget. It's a modal widget, so when it appears, you must first close it in order to continue work in the main window. Normally it will disappear if you click anywhere outside its borders, but this behavior can be changed. By default it fills the whole app window, so in order to be able to click outside it, you first have to change its size.

Anyway, there should be three widgets in the popup window:

- a label with the question **'Are you sure you want to quit?'**,

- a button with the text **'No, I was wrong. Cancel.'** that will just dismiss the window and take you back to the Game Over screen,

- a button with the text **"Yes, I'm sure. Quit."** that will actually close the game window.

We will define a method in the **SlugraceApp** class and call it in the Game Over screen when the Quit button is pressed. Let's name the method **quit**. Here's how we call it in the kv file:

```
#:kivy 1.11.1
# File name: gameover.kv
#:import gameover gameover

<GameoverScreen>:
    ...
        # the buttons
        ...
            RedButton:
                text: 'Quit'
                pos_hint: {'right': 1, 'center_y': .5}

                # Let's call the quit method in the SlugraceApp class.
                on_press: app.quit()
```

Yes, I know, we haven't defined the method yet. Let's do it now. Go to the **SlugraceApp** class in the **main.py** file and add the method there. But before you do that, we'll need some imports. As I just said above, we're going to need the **Popup** class, as well as **Label** and **Button**. Besides, we're going to organize the widgets in the popup window using BoxLayouts, so we need to import the **BoxLayout** class too.

Now we are ready to add the **quit** method in the **SlugraceApp** class. In the method we create the popup window, add the widgets to it and open it. We also add code that will be executed when either of the two buttons is pressed. Here's the code with detailed explanations in the comments:

```
# File name: main.py
...
from kivy.uix.floatlayout import FloatLayout

# Here are the classes we'll need for the popup window.
from kivy.uix.boxlayout import BoxLayout
from kivy.uix.popup import Popup
from kivy.uix.button import Button
from kivy.uix.label import Label

Builder.load_file('settings.kv')
...
class SlugraceApp(App):
    ...
    def build(self):
        ...

    # Here's the quit method that will display a popup window and then either quit the
    # game or just dismiss the popup window.
    def quit(self):
        # Let's create a basic popup window.
        confirm_popup = Popup()

        # The content of the popup window will be in a vertical BoxLayout with a label
        # in the upper part and two buttons below.
        content = BoxLayout(orientation='vertical')

        # Here's the label that will appear in the upper part of the popup window.
        confirm_label = Label(text='Are you sure you want to quit?')

        # Here's the first button. When it's pressed, the window should be dismissed. As
        # this is very simple code that does just one thing, we'll use a lambda function
        # instead of defining a separate method. The dismiss method in the Popup class is
        # used to dismiss the popup window.
        cancel_button = Button(text='No, I was wrong. Cancel.')
        cancel_button.bind(on_press=lambda x: confirm_popup.dismiss())

        # Here's the second button. When this button is pressed, the app window should
        # close. To do this, we use the stop method defined in the App class, so we can
        # use self.stop, because here self is the instance of SlugraceApp.
        confirm_button=Button(text="Yes, I'm sure. Quit.")
        confirm_button.bind(on_press=lambda x: self.stop())

        # Here we create a horizontal BoxLayout and add the two buttons to it.
        buttons = BoxLayout()
```

```
        buttons.add_widget(cancel_button)
        buttons.add_widget(confirm_button)

        # Now we add the label and the BoxLayout with the two buttons to the bigger
        # vertical BoxLayout.
        content.add_widget(confirm_label)
        content.add_widget(buttons)

        # Here we set the popup's content property to the content BoxLayout that contains

        # the label and the buttons.
        confirm_popup.content = content

        # Finally we open the popup window so that we can see it.
        confirm_popup.open()

if __name__ == '__main__':
    ...
```

Now let's play the game and lose quickly so that the Game Over screen appears or just press the End Game button in the Race screen to make it happen. And when the Game Over screen appears, let's press the Quit button. You should now see the popup window.

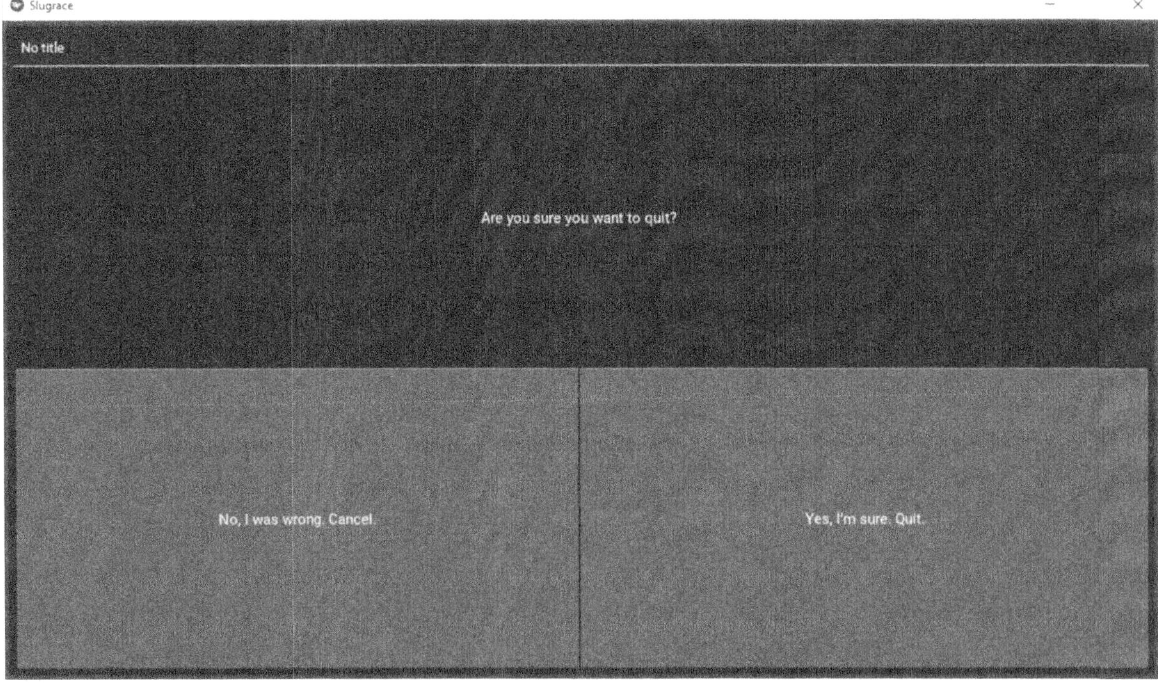


Here the popup window covers the whole app window. It's too big for our purposes. And there are some other improvements we could make. But this is going to be an exercise for you.

Anyway, if you now hit the first button, you will go back to the Game Over screen. If you hit the second button, you will quit the game and the app window will close. Try out both scenarios.

This is the last chapter in this part on game logic. In the next part we'll make the slugs actually move along the track and rotate their tentacles, among other things. We'll also add some audio. The topic of the next part of the book is animation and sound in Kivy. But before we do that, don't forget to do the exercise below that will make your popup window shine, figuratively speaking.

# It's Your Turn Now...

### EXERCISE

In this exercise you will modify the popup window so that it doesn't cover the whole app window. You will also modify its appearance a bit. You can set all the properties in the popup's constructor. Here are the properties you should set:

- **`title`** — This is the message written at the very top of the popup window. By default it reads **`'No title'`** as you just saw above. Set the property to **`'Confirmation Required'`**.

- **`title_color`** — This is the color of the title string you just set. Let's make it red, so set it to **`[1, 0, 0, 1]`**.

- **`size_hint`** and **`size`** — You know these two properties very well. We want the window to be much smaller. Set its size to 400 by 200. Remember to set the **`size_hint`** property to **`(None, None)`** because you're inside a layout.

- **`pos_hint`** — You also know this property very well. Use it to set the popup's position to be in the center of the app window.

- **`background_color`** — This is not the background color of the popup window itself, but rather the tint of the app window. We'll use a light reddish semitransparent tint to make it clear that the main window is sort of disabled until we dismiss the popup. So, set the property to **`[1, 0, 0, .3]`**.

- **`auto_dismiss`** — This property is by default set to **`True`**, which means the popup is dismissed if you click anywhere outside it. But we don't want this behavior, so set it to **`False`**. This way clicking outside the popup will have no effect and you won't be able to interact with the main app window until you dismiss the popup by hitting the first button. This is how modal windows work. Naturally, if you hit the second button, the main app window will close.

**SOLUTION**

Here's the code:

```
# File name: main.py
...
class SlugraceApp(App):
    ...
    def quit(self):
        # Set the properties of the popup in the constructor.
        confirm_popup = Popup(title='Confirmation Required',
                              title_color=[1, 0, 0, 1],
                              size_hint=(None, None),
                              size=(400, 200),
                              pos_hint={'center_x': .5, 'center_y:': .5},
                              background_color=[1, 0, 0, .3],
                              auto_dismiss=False)

        content = BoxLayout(orientation='vertical')
        ...
```

If you now hit the Quit button in the Game Over screen, you will see a much smaller popup window. You will also see how the main app window is now tinted.

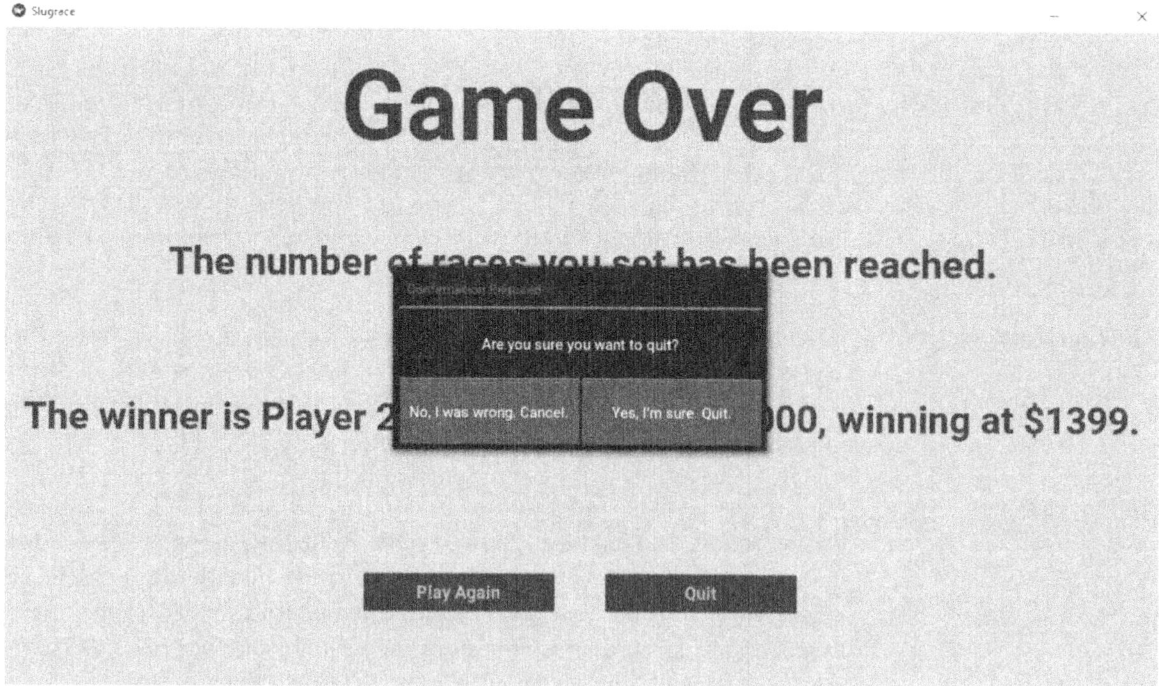


Now the only thing you can do is press one of the popup's buttons. They work like before.

# Part X

# Animation and Sound

In this part of the book everything will get moving. We'll be talking about animations in Kivy and we'll add quite a few to our project. We'll also discuss sounds in Kivy and we'll add background music and some funny sound effects. We'll also add accidents that will from time to time happen to the slugs.

# Chapter 98 – Introduction to Animation in Kivy

We now have a pretty functional game. In the previous part of the book we implemented the game logic. But we still don't see the slugs racing along the track. We don't hear any sounds either. In this part we're going to implement animations and sounds in our project. The slugs will not only move along the track, but they will also move their eyes (or rather the whole tentacles on top of which the eyes sit).

Additionally, from time to time some accidents will happen to the slugs, which we are also going to enrich with simple animations. But before we do that, let's talk about animations in Kivy in general. In this introductory chapter we'll be using our two test files, **test.py** and **test.kv**.

As you remember, in one of the previous chapters, the one where we were talking about the **Clock** class, to be precise, we created a button and a method that moved the button in horizontal direction by 20 pixels every 0.1 seconds. Here we were calling a scheduled method repeatedly, which created an effect of an animation. This is one way of doing this, but there's a better way, which we are going to discuss now.

Let's clean up the code in the test files so that there is just a simple button.

Here's the Python code:

```
# File name: test.py

import kivy
kivy.require('1.11.1')
from kivy.app import App
from kivy.uix.floatlayout import FloatLayout

class TestLayout(FloatLayout):
    pass

class TestApp(App):
    def build(self):
        return TestLayout()

if __name__ == '__main__':
    TestApp().run()
```

And here's the kv file:

```
#:kivy 1.11.1
# File name: test.kv

<TestLayout>:
    button: _button

    Button:
        id: _button
        text: 'button'
        font_size: 40
        pos: 20, 100
        size_hint: None, None
        size: 200, 50
```

If you run the app, you will see the button.

Now, let's make the button move to the right in a similar way as before.

## A Simple Animation

In Kivy we use the **Animation** class to animate widget properties. As we want the button to move horizontally, the property that we want to animate is **x**. In a basic scenario we first have to create an **Animation** object and pass to it as an argument the property that we want to animate and its target value. Then we have to call the **start** method on the **Animation** object and pass to it the widget that is to be animated. In our example the animation will be created and started when the button is pressed. So, let's add the **on_press** event in the kv file:

```
#:kivy 1.11.1
# File name: test.kv

<TestLayout>:
    ...
    Button:
        ...
        size: 200, 50
        on_press: root.animate()
```

And now we have to implement the **animate** method in the Python file:

```
# File name: test.py
...
from kivy.uix.floatlayout import FloatLayout

# We need the Animation class.
from kivy.animation import Animation

class TestLayout(FloatLayout):
    # the method that will be called when the button is pressed
    def animate(self):

        # the Animation object
        # The value of the x property should change continuously until it's 500.
        # The animation will take 1 second to complete.
        anim = Animation(x=500)

        # Here we start the animation on the button.
        anim.start(self.button)

class TestApp(App):
    ...
```

As you can see, here we created an **Animation** object and assigned it to the **anim** variable. We passed the target value of **x** as the argument to the contructor. If we create an **Animation** object like this, the animation takes 1 second to complete. So, when we start the animation using the **start** method, the value of **x** will change continuously from 20 (to which it's set now) to 500 in one second. We pass the button to the **start** method as the widget that we want to animate.

If you now run the app and click the button, the button will move to the right.

If you want the animation to take more or less time than one second, all you have to do is set the **duration** argument, or **d** for short. The duration of the animation is in seconds, so let's modify the code so that this time the width of the button is animated and the animation takes four seconds. Here's the code:

```
# File name: test.py
...
class TestLayout(FloatLayout):
    def animate(self):

        # Let's animate the button's width so that
        # it stretches from its current 200 px to
        # 500 px. The animation will take 4 seconds
        # to complete.
        anim = Animation(width=500, duration=4)

        # Here we start the animation
        # on the button.

        anim.start(self.button)

class TestApp(App):
    ...
```

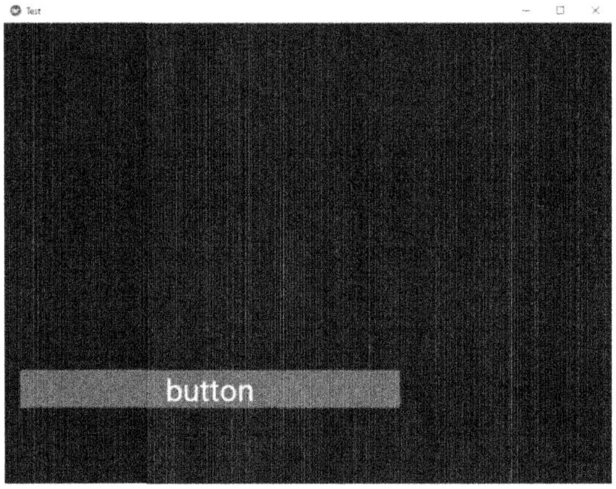

If you now run the app and press the button, it will stretch.

## Animating Multiple Properties

If you want, you can animate multiple properties at the same time. You just have to pass them all one by one to the **Animation** class constructor.

For example, let's animate the button's size, backround color and font size. Remember that you should use the target values of each property in the constructor.

Here's the code:

```
# File name: test.py
...
class TestLayout(FloatLayout):
    def animate(self):

        # Let's animate the button's size, backround color and font size.
        anim = Animation(size=(400, 400),
                         background_color=[0, 1, 0, 1],
                         font_size=100, duration=4)
        anim.start(self.button)

class TestApp(App):
    ...
```

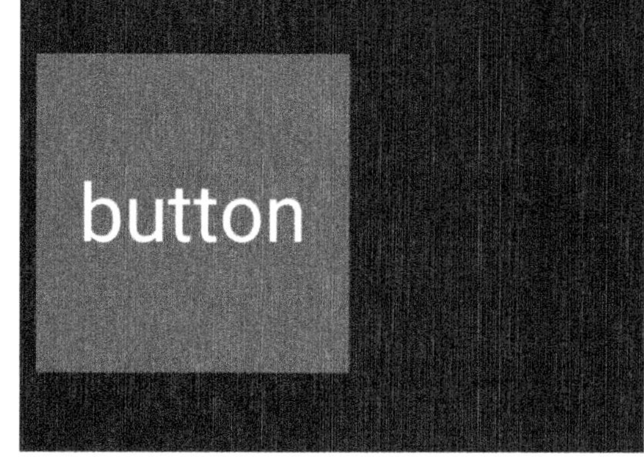


When the animation is over, you should see a big green button.

## Transitions

You can use one of the built-in transitions in your animations or even create custom ones. To do that, you just have to set the **transition** argument, or **t** for short. Transitions are easing functions that tell the animation how it should behave at the beginning, in the middle and at the end, when it should accelerate or decelerate, etc. We're going to see some transitions in action, but first let's simplify the code a bit so that only the size of the button is animated:

```
# File name: test.py
...
class TestLayout(FloatLayout):
    def animate(self):

        # Let's animate the button's size.
        # The duration (d) of the animation is 4 seconds.
        anim = Animation(size=(400, 400), d=4)
        anim.start(self.button)

class TestApp(App):
    ...
```

Run the app and watch the animation. You can see that the button is expanding at a constant rate. This is because the default transition is linear. But you can change it. There are lots of transitions available, so if you want to learn more about them, just check out the documentation. Here let's just have a look at a couple examples.

Let's start with the **in_quad** transition. Here's the code:

```
# File name: test.py
...
class TestLayout(FloatLayout):
    def animate(self):
        anim = Animation(size=(400, 400), d=4, t='in_quad')
        anim.start(self.button)

class TestApp(App):
    ...
```

Now the animation starts slower and then accelerates toward the end. If you want it to start faster and then decelerate instead, you can use the **out_quad** transition. Try it out.

If you use the **in_out_quad** transition, the animation first eases in and then out, so it first accelerates and then decelerates toward the end. Go ahead and test it.

There are lots of pretty fancy transitions as well. Try the **in_bounce** transition for example. This will add a bouncing effect to the animation.

Feel free to experiment with the other transitions, I'm sure you will find something that will meet your expectations. And if not, you can create your own animation functions, but this is outside the scope of this course.

## Step

By default the animation is updated every frame. If you want it to be updated less frequently, you can set the **step** argument, or **s** for short. It should be a float number that tells the animation how often the animation should be updated. The default value of **step** is 0, which is why the animation is updated every frame, as I just mentioned.

Let's remove the transition from the previous example and set the step to 1/10, which means the animation should update at 10 FPS (frames per second):

```
# File name: test.py

...

class TestLayout(FloatLayout):
    def animate(self):
        # update at 10 FPS
        anim = Animation(size=(400, 400), d=4, step=1/10)

        # Here we start the animation.
        anim.start(self.button)

class TestApp(App):
    ...
```

As our animations takes 4 seconds to complete and the step is 1/10, it means it will update 40 times during this time. The choppiness of this animation should be visible with the naked eye.

The animation will be even choppier if you set the step to 1/2. This time it will be updated every half second, so only 8 times during the whole animation. If you set **step** to 1, the animation will be updated only once per second, so four times altogether. And if you set it to the same value as **duration**, so 4 in our case, the whole animation will be reduced to just one step. In our case it means you will see the button change its size instantly after 4 seconds. Give it a shot.

# Stopping and Canceling Animations

You know that you use the **start** method to start an animation. Similarly, there are two other methods, **stop** and **cancel**, that you can use to respectively stop or cancel the animation. The difference between stopping and canceling an animation is that in the former case the **on_complete** event (which we are going to talk about in one of the following chapters) is triggered, but it isn't if you cancel the animation. So, if you don't need to implement the **on_complete** event (that's the event that is triggered when the animation completes), it doesn't really matter which of the two methods you use.

Let's have a look at some examples. This time we'll have two buttons. The first button will be the one that we want to animate and the second one will enable us to cancel the animation at any time. If you want to cancel or stop the animation on a widget, you just pass the widget as the argument to the respective method. Here's the kv file:

```
#:kivy 1.11.1
# File name: test.kv

# We'll be using a custom
# button this time.
<CustomButton@Button>:
    size_hint: None, None
    size: 200, 50
    font_size: 40

<TestLayout>:
    button1: _button1
    CustomButton:
        id: _button1
        text: 'button 1'
        font_size: 40
        pos: 20, 100
        on_press: root.animate()

    CustomButton:
        text: 'button 2'
        pos: 300, 100

        # When this button is pressed,
        # the cancel_animation method
        # is called that cancels the
        # animation on button 1.
        on_press: root.cancel_animation()
```

In the Python file we'll now create the animation on the **TestLayout** instance (so using the **self** variable) so that we have access to it in all the methods.

Here's the Python file:

```
# File name: test.py
...
class TestLayout(FloatLayout):
    def animate(self):
        # Animate height in 5 seconds on button1.
        self.anim = Animation(height=400, d=5)
        self.anim.start(self.button1)

    # Cancel the animation on button 1.
    def cancel_animation(self):
        self.anim.cancel(self.button1)

class TestApp(App):
    ...
```

If you now run the app and press the first button, it will grow in height until, after 5 seconds, it reaches the target height of 400 px. But if you press the second button during the animation, the animation will be canceled and the first button will not reach its target height.

If you used the **stop** method instead of **cancel**, it would work just the same.

There are a couple more methods you can use to stop or cancel an animation. You will use some of them in the exercise below. And in the next chapter we'll be talking about sequential, parallel and repeated animations.

# It's Your Turn Now...

## EXERCISE

In this exercise we'll be using two methods that we use to stop animations, **stop_all** and **stop_property**. They also have their counterparts, **cancel_all** and **cancel_property**, which, in our example would work the same. But before we do, let's rewrite the kv file so that there are four buttons and a label.

As far as the label is concerned, it will have four properties that we will animate. You already know two of them, **font_size** and **color**. The other two are **outline_width** and **outline_color**. We use them to add an outline around the text. At first the outline width will be 0, so there won't be any outline, then it will be animated to reach the target width of 20 pixels. Here's the kv file:

```
#:kivy 1.11.1
# File name: test.kv

<CustomButton@Button>:
    size_hint: None, None
    size: 250, 50

<TestLayout>:
    label: _label

    CustomButton:
        text: 'start animations'
        pos: 20, 100
```

```
        on_press: root.start_animations()

    CustomButton:
        text: 'stop all animations'
        pos: 400, 100
        on_press: root.stop_all_animations()

    CustomButton:
        text: 'stop color animations'
        pos: 20, 20
        on_press: root.stop_color_animations()

    CustomButton:
        text: 'stop outline width animation'
        pos: 400, 20
        on_press: root.stop_outline_animation()

    Label:
        id: _label
        pos_hint: {'center_x:': .5, 'center_y': .5}
        text: 'L a b e l'
        bold: True

        # properties to animate
        font_size: 50
        outline_width: 0
        color: [1, 0, 0, 1]
        outline_color: [0, 1, 0, 1]
```

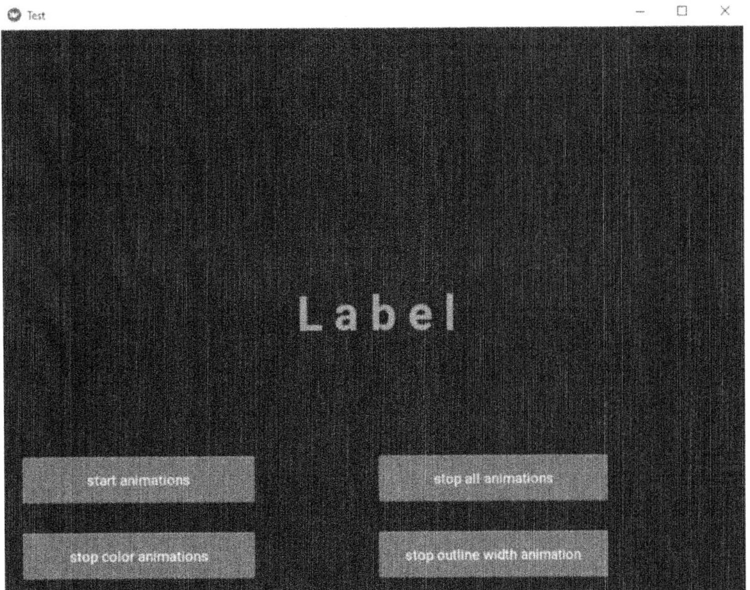


As you can see, there are four buttons and each of them does something. Each button, when pressed, calls a method in the root widget class. Your task is to implement those four methods.

But before you start, let's have a look at our application window as it looks when you launch the app. You can see a red label sitting in the app window.

And now follow the steps below to implement the four methods in the Python file:

1. Let's start with the **start_animations** method. This method will be called when the first button is pressed. As its name might suggest, it's going to start more than one animation, and to be precise, there are going to be two animations. Name them **anim1** and **anim2** respectively. The

durations of both animations should be 5 seconds.

Now, in the first animation, **anim1**, we want to animate only one property, **font_size**. It is supposed to change from the initial value of 50 to the target value of 200.

In the second animation, **anim2**, we want to animate three properties:

- **color** (from red to green) – you can use the colors **[1, 0, 0, 1]** and **[0, 1, 0, 1]** for red and green respectively,

- **outline_width** (from 0 to 20),

- **outline_color** (from green to red) – use the same values as with **color**.

After you create the two animations, don't forget to start them.

2. The next method you're going to implement is **stop_all_animations**. This one will be called when the second button is pressed. Now, in this method we'll make use of the **stop_all** method defined in the **Animation** class. This is a static method so you have to call it like so:

```
Animation.stop_all(...)
```

This method can take one or more arguments. In our case, it will take just one argument, which is the widget on which the animations should be stopped. Naturally, the widget here is the label. This will stop all the animations on the label, so, in our case, **anim1** and **anim2**.

3. The next method to implement is **stop_color_animations**. It will be called when the third button is pressed. In this method we'll also make use of the **stop_all** method. We're going to use it like before, but it would also work if you called it on just the second animation, so using the following syntax:

```
anim2.stop_all(...)
```

Another difference is that this time the method will take three arguments. The first argument is, just like before, the widget on which we want to stop the animations. And then we can pass as many arguments as we want. These arguments are the properties that you want to stop animating. In our case, the method is supposed to stop the two color animations (technically this is one animation, but multiple properties are animated), so the properties **color** and **outline_color** should be passed. Make sure to pass the two property names as strings.

With this method in place, whenever the third button is pressed during an animation, the two color properties will stop being animated, but the other properties will continue being animated.

4. Finally, the **stop_outline_animation** method. It will be called when the fourth button is

pressed. In this method we're going to use another method defined in the **Animation** class, **stop_property**. Make sure to call it on the second animation only. The **stop_property** method takes two arguments, the widget on which the animation is set and the property that you want to stop animating. In our case the widget is the label and the property that we want to stop animating is **outline_width**.

## SOLUTION

Here's the code:

```
# File name: test.py
...
class TestLayout(FloatLayout):

    # create and start two animations
    def start_animations(self):
        self.anim1 = Animation(font_size=200, d=5)
        self.anim2 = Animation(color=[0, 1, 0, 1],
                               outline_width=20,
                               outline_color=[1, 0, 0, 1],
                               d=5)
        self.anim1.start(self.label)
        self.anim2.start(self.label)

    # stop both animations
    def stop_all_animations(self):
        Animation.stop_all(self.label)

    # stop animating just the two color properties from the second animation
    def stop_color_animations(self):
        Animation.stop_all(self.label, 'color', 'outline_color')

    # stop animating the outline_width property from the second animation
    def stop_outline_animation(self):
        self.anim2.stop_property(self.label, 'outline_width')

class TestApp(App):
    ...
```

Now let's test the app. The first time we launch it, let's just press the first button and let the animation complete. In the image on the right is what you should see after the animation completes.

Let's close the app window and launch the app again. Now let's hit the first button to start the animations. Then, let's press the second button to stop all the animations.

You should see something like in the image on the right. This may, of course, differ depending on how far into the animation you were when you stopped it. Now, before you close the app window, click the first button again. This will create and start the two animations again. The initial values of the four animated properties will be the same as at the moment when we stopped the animation and the target values will be the same as before, so the visual effect of this will be as if the animations were just paused and then resumed. But it won't work exactly like that. This is because when you stop the animation and then start it again, a new animation will be created that also needs five seconds to complete, from the values you left off at to the target ones, so the visual effect will be that the animation will be slower.

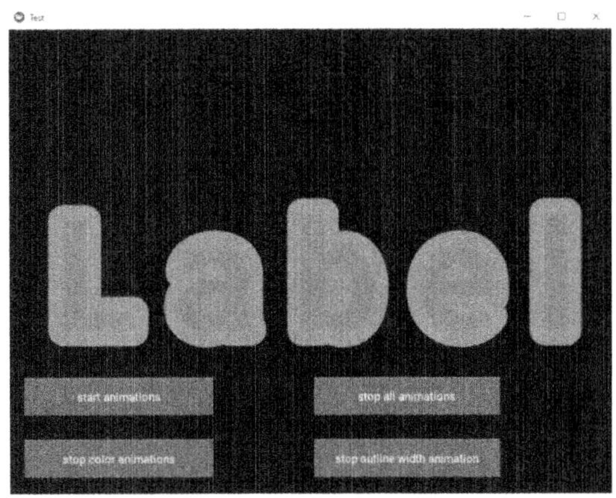
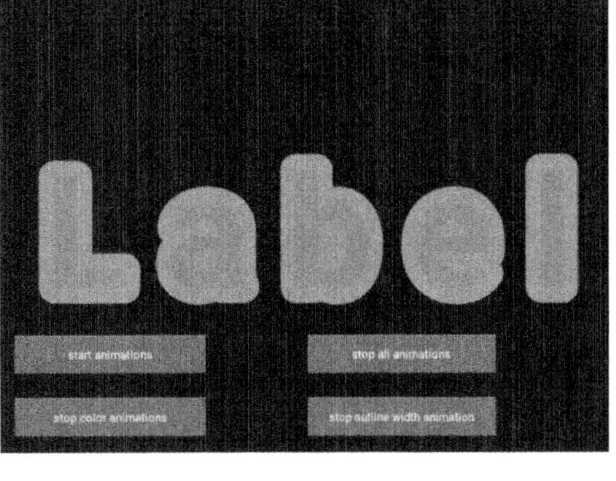


Anyway, close the app window now and launch the app again. Start the animations again and then press the third button to stop the color animations. This time the two color animations (the color of the text and that of the outline) will stop, but not the others. This is why the colors will remain the same till the end of the animation as at the time when you pressed the button. In the image on the left is what I got at the end of the animation after hitting the third button somewhere in the middle of the animation.

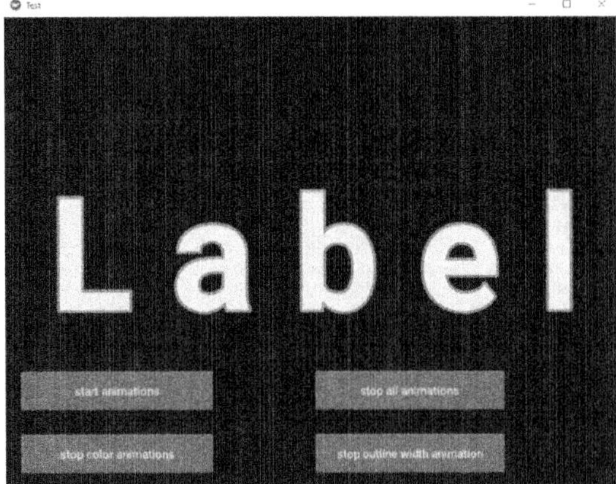


Finally, let's launch the app one more time and start the animations. Then let's press the last button. The moment we press the button, the **`outline_width`** property will stop being animated, but not the other properties. This is why the outline may be pretty thin if you hit the button early in the animation (look at the image on the left).

Now, one warning. If you hit the fourth button before you start the animations, the program will crash. This is because the **`anim2`** animation doesn't exist before we press the first button.

And one more thing. Let's press the third button and then immediately the fourth one. This time both methods will be called one after the other and both the color animation and the outline width animation will be stopped:

# Chapter 99 – Sequential, Parallel and Repeated Animations

In the previous chapter we were talking about animations in general. So, you know that in order to make an animation, you need to create an **Animation** object and specify the property that you want to animate. You can also specify the duration of the animation, which by default is 1 second, as well as the transition and step. Then you just start the animation on a widget.

But sometimes you may want to join or repeat animations. As far as the former is concerned, animations may be joined in a sequential way or in a parallel way, which means they can respectively run one after another or at the same time.

Let's have a look at sequential animations first.

## Sequential Animations

To join operations sequentially, we use the **+** operator. Let's create a simple GUI with just one button. First we'll animate the button's x position, then its y position. In this chapter, just like in the previous one, we're going to use our test files.

Here's the kv file:

```
#:kivy 1.11.1
# File name: test.kv

<TestLayout>:
    button: _button

    Button:
        id: _button
        text: 'button'
        font_size: 40
        size_hint: .2, .1
        pos: 20, 100

        # The animations will be created and
        # started when the button is pressed.
        on_press: root.start_animations()
```

And here's the Python file. Only the **TestLayout** class has changed. All the rest is the same as in the previous chapter.

```
# File name: test.py
...
class TestLayout(FloatLayout):

    # create and start two animations sequentially
    def start_animations(self):
        anim1 = Animation(x=400, d=3)
        anim2 = Animation(y=300, d=1)

        # join the animations sequentially
        anim = anim1 + anim2

        # start the combined animation
        anim.start(self.button)

class TestApp(App):
    ...
```

Now, when you start the app, you will see a button. When you press the button, it will first be moving horizontally for three seconds and then immediately up for one second.

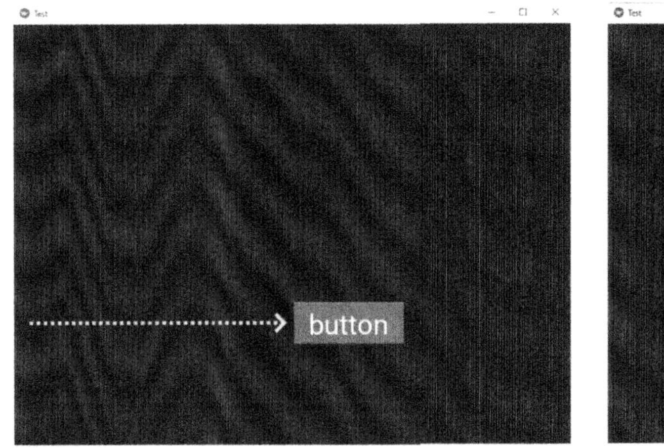


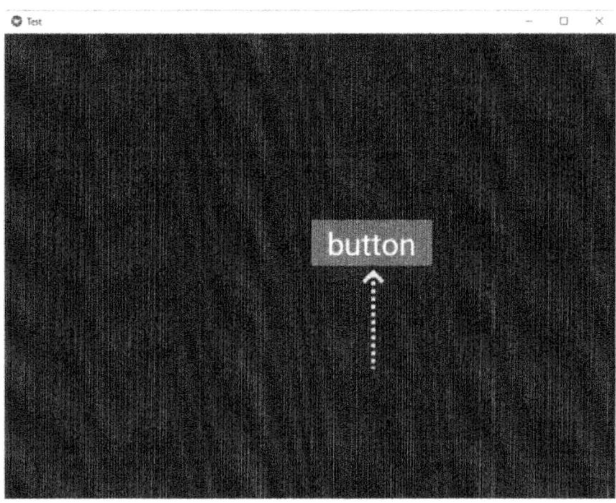


And now let's add one more animation to the lot, this time we'll animate the **size_hint** property. You can use the **+=** augmented operator to add an animation:

```
# File name: test.py
...
class TestLayout(FloatLayout):

    # create and start three animations sequentially
    def start_animations(self):
        anim1 = Animation(x=400, d=3)
        anim2 = Animation(y=300, d=1)

        # join the animations sequentially
        anim = anim1 + anim2

        # add one more animation sequentially
        anim += Animation(size_hint=(.3, .2), d=2)

        # start the combined animation
        anim.start(self.button)

class TestApp(App):
    ...
```

Now, after first moving horizontally and then vertically, the button will also expand. Here we have three animations altogether, but there may be any number of them.

# Parallel Animations

You can also use two or more animations at the same time. You just shouldn't make parallel animations on the same property, though, because this may have unexpected results. Anyway, we join animations in parallel using the & operator. Let's modify our previous example so that this time the two animations that move the button horizontally and vertically run at the same time. If we set the duration to the same value for both animations, this will make the button move diagonally. Have a look:

```
# File name: test.py
...
class TestLayout(FloatLayout):
    def start_animations(self):
        anim1 = Animation(x=400, d=3)
        anim2 = Animation(y=300, d=3)

        # join the animations in parallel
        anim = anim1 & anim2

        # start the combined animation
        anim.start(self.button)

class TestApp(App):
    ...
```

Now if you run the app and press the button, it will move diagonally. Let's add one more animation in parallel. This time we'll animate the button's background color. You can use the augmented **&=** operator. Here's the code:

```
# File name: test.py
...
class TestLayout(FloatLayout):
    def start_animations(self):
        anim1 = Animation(x=400, d=3)
        anim2 = Animation(y=300, d=3)

        # join the animations in parallel
        anim = anim1 & anim2

        # add one more animation in parallel to animate the color
        anim &= Animation(background_color=[1, 0, 0, 1], d=3)

        # start the combined animation
        anim.start(self.button)

class TestApp(App):
    ...
```

Now if you press the button, not only will it move, but it will also change its color over a period of three seconds. At the end of the animation the button will be red.

Naturally, you can combine sequential and parallel animations if it makes sense. Let's add another animation sequentially to the three parallel ones.

We'll add the same **size_hint** animation that we used before:

```
# File name: test.py
...
class TestLayout(FloatLayout):
    def start_animations(self):
        anim1 = Animation(x=400, d=3)
        anim2 = Animation(y=300, d=3)

        # join the animations in parallel
        anim = anim1 & anim2

        # add the color animation in parallel
        anim &= Animation(background_color=[1, 0, 0, 1], d=3)

        # add the size_hint animation sequentially
        anim += Animation(size_hint=(.3, .2), d=2)

        # start the combined animation
        anim.start(self.button)

class TestApp(App):
    ...
```

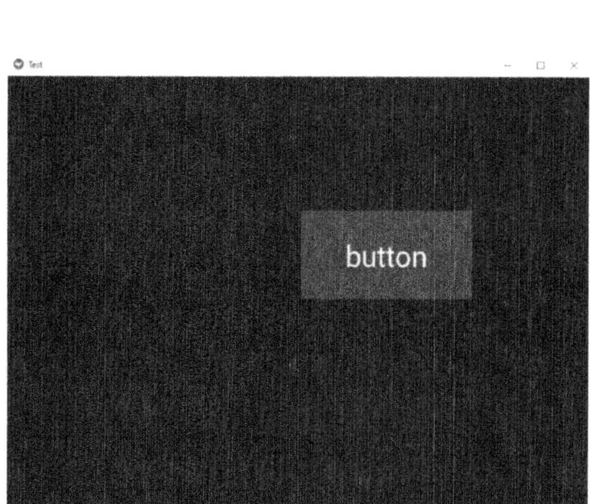


If you now run the app and press the button, it will first simultaneously move horizontally and vertically and change its background color and when it's done doing this, it will grow.

In the exercise below you will create a repeated animation. And in the next chapter, we'll be talking about animation events.

# It's Your Turn Now...

## EXERCISE

Sequential animations may be repeated. In this exercise you will create two repeated animations, each of which will consist of two animations joined sequentially. The first animation will animate the x position of the button and the second one its background color. These two repeated animations will then be joined in parallel so that you can see the button move forth and back and change its color (in a pulsating way) at the same time. You can leave the kv file as is. You only have to modify the **start_animations** method in the **TestLayout** class in the Python file. So, start by removing all the code from the method and then follow the steps below:

1. The button is supposed to be moving in horizontal direction, so its **x** property will change between its initial value (which, by the way, is 20, as you can see in the kv file) and 400. It's also supposed to change its color from its current value to red and back. So, start by saving the current x position and background color in variables for future reference. You can name the two variables **start_x** and **button_color** respectively.

2. Create the **pos_anim** animation. It should consist of two animations joined sequentially. You don't have to create the two animations beforehand. Just create them on the fly using the following syntax:

```
pos_anim = Animation(...) + Animation(...)
```

The two animations should animate the **x** property. The target value for the first animation is **400** and the target value for the second animation is the value you saved in the **start_x** variable. The durations of the animations should be 3 seconds and 0.5 seconds respectively.

3. Create the **color_anim** animation. It should also consist of two animations joined sequentially. Use the same syntax as before.

The two animations should animate the **background_color** property. The target value for the first animation is **[1, 0, 0, 1]**, which is red, and the target value for the second animation is the value you saved in the **button_color** variable. The durations of the animations should be 0.2 seconds and 0.1 seconds respectively.

4. Now, we want the **pos_anim** and **color_anim** animations to repeat. This is very easy to do. Just set the **repeat** property on each of them to **True**.

5. The two combined animations, **pos_anim** and **color_anim**, should run in parallel, so create an **anim** animation where these two animations are joined in parallel.

6. Start the **anim** animation on the button widget.

**SOLUTION**

Here's the code:

```
# File name: test.py
...
class TestLayout(FloatLayout):
    def start_animations(self):
        # save the button's initial x position for future use
        start_x = self.button.x

        # save the button's background color for future use
        button_color = self.button.background_color

        # Let's create an animation consisting of two animations joined
        # sequentially to animate the x position of the button. It will
        # move to the right in three seconds and then back to the left
        # in half a second.
        pos_anim = Animation(x=400, d=3) + Animation(x=start_x, d=.5)

        # Let's create another animation consisting of two animations
        # joined sequentially to animate the background color of the button.
        # It will change to red in 0.2 seconds and then back to its original
        # color in 0.1 seconds. This will make the button pulsate.
        color_anim = (Animation(background_color=[1, 0, 0, 1], d=.2)
                      + Animation(background_color=button_color, d=.1))

        # set the animations to repeat
        pos_anim.repeat = True
        color_anim.repeat = True

        # Let's make the two combined animations run in parallel.
        anim = pos_anim & color_anim

        # start the combined animation
        anim.start(self.button)

class TestApp(App):
    ...
```

Now, if you run the app and press the button, it will move right and left and pulsate at the same time. Make sure to check it out.

# Chapter 100 – Animation Events

In the previous two chapters we were discussing the basics of animation in Kivy. In this chapter we'll be talking about animation events, which is going to be the last theoretical topic for the time being. In the following chapters we'll be implementing animations in the Slugrace project.

Anyway, there are three animation events:

**on_start** – triggered when the animation starts,

**on_complete** – triggered when the animation is completed or stopped (but not canceled),

**on_progress** – triggered when the progression of the animation is changing.

To demonstrate how these events work, let's create a simple app using the test files. Here's the kv file:

```
#:kivy 1.11.1
# File name: test.kv

<TestLayout>:
    button: _button
    label: _label

    Button:
        id: _button
        text: 'button'
        font_size: 40
        size_hint: .2, .1
        pos: 20, 100
        on_press: root.start_animation()
    Label:
        id: _label
        pos_hint: {'center_x': .5, 'center_y': .5}
        font_size: 60
        bold: True
        text: 'start animation'
```

As you can see, there's a button and a label. The button will be animated and the label will display information about the animation. The animation will be created and started when the button is pressed.

In the Python code we implement the **start_animation** method. It creates a 10-second animation of the **x** property. Then we bind three custom methods to the three events. Finally, we start the animation.

The three custom methods defined below just change the label text. Again, only the **TestLayout** class has changed, the remaining part of the code is just like in the preceding two chapters.

Here's the Python code with comments:

```
# File name: test.py
...
class TestLayout(FloatLayout):
    def start_animation(self):
        # Let's create a simple animation on the x property that will take 10 seconds
        # to complete.
        self.anim = Animation(x=500, d=10)

        # Let's bind custom methods to the three events.
        self.anim.bind(on_start=self.on_start)
        self.anim.bind(on_progress=self.on_progress)
        self.anim.bind(on_complete=self.on_complete)

        # Let's start the animation.
        self.anim.start(self.button)

    # Here are the custom methods.

    # This method will be called when the animation starts. It will change the text on
    # the label.
    def on_start(self, instance, value):
        self.label.text = 'animation started'

    # This method will be called multiple times while the animation is in progress. The
    # last parameter, progression, is used to indicate how far it is in its progress. The
    # values of progression range from 0 to 1, so in order to have the value represented
    # as an integer between 0 and 100, we multiply it by 100 and cast to an integer.
    # We want the label text to change only after 25% of the animation is completed.
    # This is because we need some time to read the label after it's changed in the
    # on_start method.
    def on_progress(self, instance, value, progression):
        if progression > .25:
            self.label.text = f'animation in progress... {int(progression * 100)}%'

    # This method will be called when the animation is completed. It will just change the

    # label text again.
    def on_complete(self, instance, value):
        self.label.text = 'animation completed'

class TestApp(App):
    ...
```

When you run the app, you will see a button and a label. Then, when the animation is started and before 25% of it is completed, you will see the 'animation started' message. After reaching 25% of its progression, you will see the continuously updated message regarding the progression. Finally, after the animation is completed, you will see the 'animation completed' message:

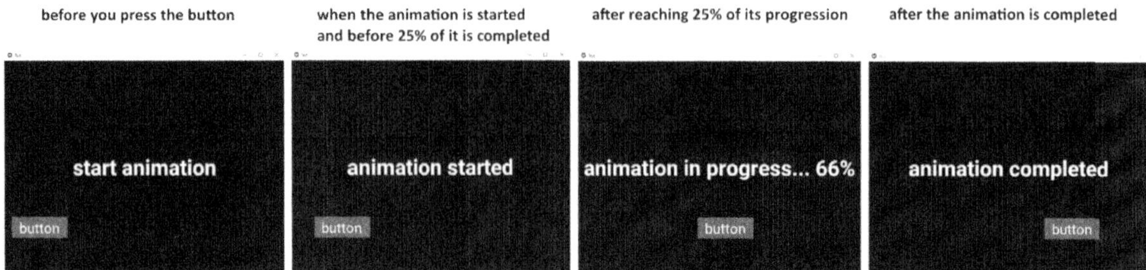


# Stopping vs Canceling the Animation

As I mentioned before, stopping and canceling an animation usually have the same effect. The difference is, though, that in case of the former, the **on_complete** method is called, whereas it's not called when you cancel an animation. To see the difference in action, let's modify the code so that the animation is stopped when its progression is greater than 50%:

```
# File name: test.py
...
class TestLayout(FloatLayout):
    def start_animation(self):
        ...

    def on_start(self, instance, value):
        ...

    def on_progress(self, instance, value, progression):
        if progression > .25:
            self.label.text = f'animation in progress... {int(progression * 100)}%'
        if progression > .50:
            self.anim.stop(self.button)

    def on_complete(self, instance, value):
        ...
```

Now if you run the app and hit the button, the animation will run and then stop when its progression reaches 50%. So, as you can see, the **on_complete** method was called. This means that if you stop an animation, it's treated as completed.

But what if we replace the **stop** method with the **cancel** method? Let's check it out:

```
# File name: test.py
...
class TestLayout(FloatLayout):
    ...
    def on_progress(self, instance, value, progression):
        if progression > .25:
            self.label.text = f'animation in progress... {int(progression * 100)}%'
        if progression > .50:
            self.anim.cancel(self.button)

    def on_complete(self, instance, value):
        ...
```

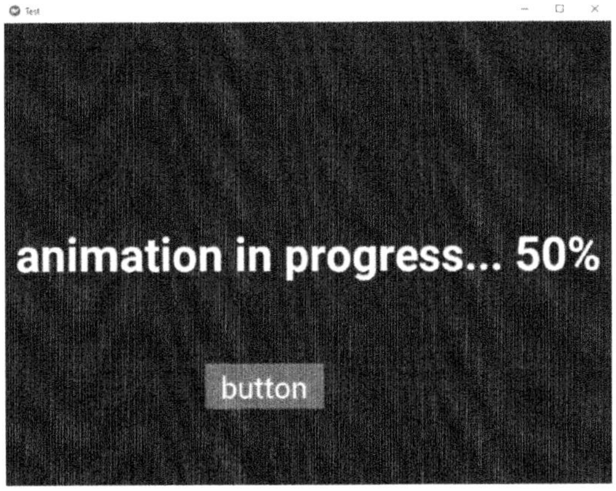

This time, the **on_complete** method is not called. The message just stops updating.

In the exercise below you'll have an opportunity to practice the animation methods a bit.

And in the next chapter we'll implement the first animation in the Slugrace project. In particular, we'll make the slugs change their positions from the start line to the finish line.

# It's Your Turn Now...

## EXERCISE

In this exercise we'll implement the animation methods directly on the widget. We'll use the **Button** widget to demonstrate it. Let's start by creating a simple GUI with three custom buttons. **CustomButton** inherits from the **Button** class, but we'll handle the inheritance in the Python file. Here's the kv file you can start with:

```
#:kivy 1.11.1
# File name: test.kv

<CustomButton>:
    size_hint: .2, .1
    font_size: 60
    text: '*'
    bold: True
    color: [1, 0, 0, 1] # red
```

```
<TestLayout>:
    CustomButton:
        pos_hint: {'center_x': .2, 'center_y': .2}

    CustomButton:
        pos_hint: {'center_x': .5, 'center_y': .2}

    CustomButton:
        pos_hint: {'center_x': .8, 'center_y': .2}
```

Now, your task is to implement the animation events in the Python file. Follow the steps below to do that:

1. The **TestLayout** class, which inherits from **FloatLayout**, is now fully implemented in the kv file, so remove all the code from it in the Python file, or rather use a **pass** statement in its place.

2. Create a **CustomButton** class that inherits from **Button**. Don't forget to import the **Button** class first. In the class definition you should start by creating the **animate** method that will take care of animating the button. This method should take a **time** argument and set the animation duration to it. Inside the **animate** method first create an animation. We want to animate two properties:

- **pos_hint** – the target value is **{'center_y': .8}**

- **backgound_color** – the target value is **[0, 1, 0, 1]**

Then bind three custom methods (**on_start**, **on_progress** and **on_complete**) to the **on_start**, **on_progress** and **on_complete** events respectively. Finally, start the animation on the button itself.

3. The **animate** method should be called when the button is pressed, so override the **on_press** method so that it calls it. Now, we want the duration of each button's animation to be somewhat randomized, so in the **on_press** method let's call the **animate** method with the **time** argument set to a random integer between 1 and 5, thus making the animation last between 1 and 5 seconds. To do that, we'll need the **randint** method from the **random** module, so make sure to import it first. The **randint** method takes two arguments, which correspond to the minimum and maximum integer value we want to use, so in our case 1 and 5 respectively.

4. Now we must create the three custom methods we bound the three animation events to. Let's start with the **on_start** method. This method should set the color of the button text (so its **color** property) to white (which is **[1, 1, 1, 1]**).

5. Next, add the **on_progress** method. During the first half of the animation (so when the **progression** argument is less than 0.5), the font size of the button text should be decreased by 0.4 in each frame. Then, in the second half of the animation, it should be increased by the same number.

6. Finally, in the **on_complete** method the button should become fully transparent, so just set its **opacity** property accordingly.

**SOLUTION**

Now, here's the Python code with comments:

```
# File name: test.py
...
from kivy.animation import Animation

# We'll need the Button class and the randint function.
from kivy.uix.button import Button
from random import randint
```

```
class CustomButton(Button):
    # When the button is pressed, the animation should be created and started.
    # We pass a random integer number between 1 and 5 to the animate method.
    def on_press(self):
        self.animate(randint(1, 5))

    # The animate method takes the time argument which it uses to set the duration
    # of the animation.
    def animate(self, time):
        # We're going to animate two properties of the button: pos_hint
        # and background_color.
        self.anim = Animation(pos_hint={'center_y': .8},
                              background_color=[0, 1, 0, 1],
                              d=time)

        # Here are the bindings to the custom methods.
        self.anim.bind(on_start=self.on_start)
        self.anim.bind(on_progress=self.on_progress)
        self.anim.bind(on_complete=self.on_complete)

        # Here we start the animation on the button itself.
        self.anim.start(self)

    # When the animation starts, the text color on the button changes to white.
    def on_start(self, instance, value):
        self.color = [1, 1, 1, 1] # white

    # During the first half of the animation the font size of the button text
    # decreases, during the second half it increases again.
    def on_progress(self, instance, value, progression):
        if progression < .5:
            self.font_size -= .4
        else:
            self.font_size += .4

    # When the animation finishes, the button becomes fully transparent.
    def on_complete(self, instance, value):
        self.opacity = 0

class TestLayout(FloatLayout):
    pass

class TestApp(App):
    ...
```

If you now run the app, you should see the three buttons near the bottom of the window. When you press the buttons one by one, the animation is started on each of them. The time of the animation is different for each button, between 1 and 5 seconds. Then, when the animation is completed, the buttons just turn invisible.

So, you can expect something like this during the animation:

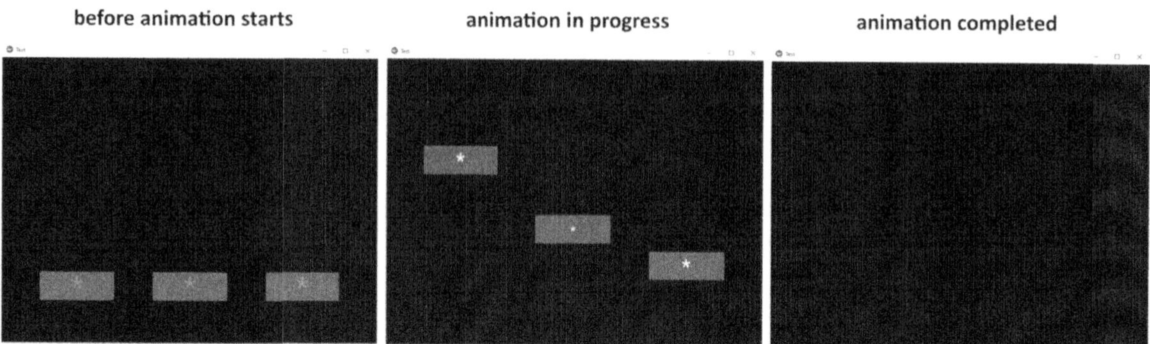

# Chapter 101 – Animating the Slugs on the Track

In the previous chapters we were talking about animation in Kivy. We were working on the test files to demonstrate how animation and animation events are implemented. In this chapter we'll start adding animations to the Slugrace project. In particular, we'll start by animating the slugs. Now when the race begins, a random winner is picked and that's it. But in the final version of the game the slugs should race against one another along the track. This is what we're going to implement in this chapter.

## Adding the Running Animation to the Slug Class

So, let's get the slugs moving. We're going to implement the running animation in the **Slug** class, so open the **slug.py** and **slug.kv** files in order to modify them. Before we create the animation, though, let's quickly make one small change. The property that we are going to animate is **pos_hint**, and in particular we'll change the **x** property in the **pos_hint** dictionary. As you can see, this property is now set to **0.09**:

```
#:kivy 1.11.1
# File name: slug.kv
#:import slug slug

<Slug>:
    pos_hint: {'x': .09, 'center_y': root.y_position}
    ...
```

Instead of hard-coding this value, let's create a **start_position** NumericProperty with the default value of **0.09**. We're also going to create a **finish_position** NumericProperty with the default value of **0.83**. I figured this value out by experimenting with multiple values between 0.8 and 0.9 and it seems right. If the **x** property in the **pos_hint** dictionary is 0.83, the slug's eyes will be just a little bit before the end of the track. So, here are the two properties in Python code:

```
# File name: slug.py
...
class Slug(RelativeLayout):
    ...
    odds = NumericProperty(0)

    # Here are the two properties that we'll be using in the running animation.
    # The slug will move along the track from start_position to finish_position.
```

```
    start_position = NumericProperty(.09)
    finish_position = NumericProperty(.83)

    def update(self, winning_slug, race_number):
        ...
```

Now we can use the **start_position** property in kv:

```
#:kivy 1.11.1
# File name: slug.kv
#:import slug slug

<Slug>:
    pos_hint: {'x': self.start_position, 'center_y': root.y_position}
    ...
```

And now, let's finally create the animation. Let's start with a simplified version. For now all the slugs will run exactly for three seconds. The code will sit in a new **run** method. Have a look:

```
# File name: slug.py
...
from kivy.properties import StringProperty, NumericProperty

# We need the Animation class.
from kivy.animation import Animation

class Slug(RelativeLayout):
    ...
    def update(self, winning_slug, race_number):
        ...
    # Here's the method that will take care of creating and starting the animation.
    def run(self):
        # Let's create the animation first. It should take three seconds to complete.
        # The target value of the x property inside pos_hint is finish_position.
        self.run_animation = Animation(pos_hint={'x': self.finish_position}, d=3)

        # And now let's start the animation on the slug itself.
        self.run_animation.start(self)
```

And now, where should this method be called? As we want the slugs to start running when the Go button is pressed, we should put the code that calls the **run** method on each slug in the **go** method in the **Game** class:

```
# File name: main.py
...
class Game(ScreenManager):
    ...
    def go(self):
        # Let's animate all four slugs.
        for slug in self.slugs:
            slug.run()

        self.race_winner = choice(self.slugs)
        ...
```

If you now run the app and press the Go button, the slugs will start moving to the right.

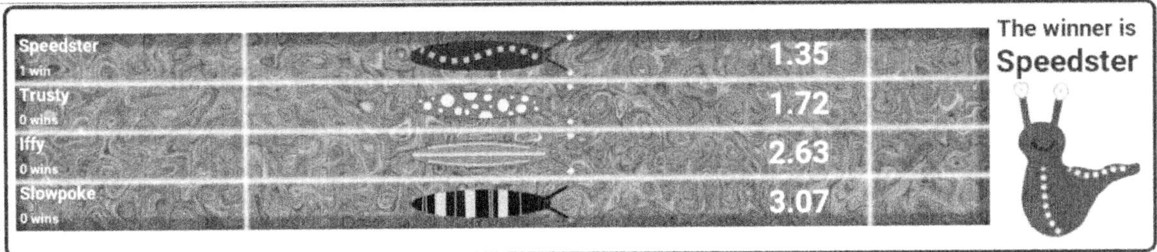


After three seconds they finish the race, all at the same time.

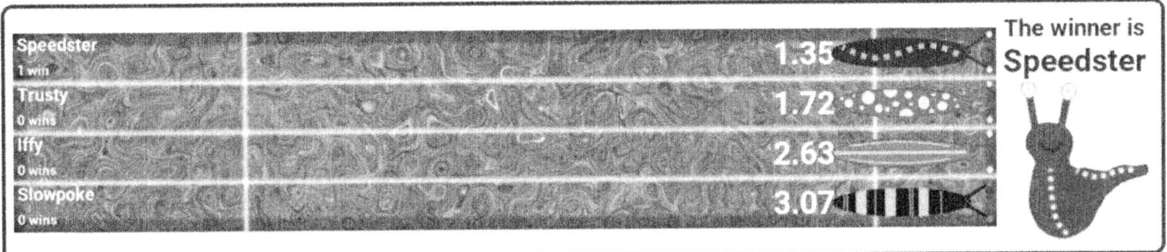


There are a couple problems, though. For example, if you hit the Next Race button, the slugs will stay at the end of the track. Or another problem, the winner, it's still randomly picked like before and there is no correspondence between how the slugs are doing in the race and which of them wins, although it's hard to tell right now because they all run at the same speed.

And these are still not all the problems we have to address before moving on. You'll handle repositioning the slugs to the start line of the track after each race as an exercise at the end of this chapter. And now let's take care of differentiating the speeds of the individual slugs. They shouldn't all run at the same speed and they should have a different speed in each race, so some randomization will be necessary. There are multiple ways to do it. I've just picked one of the many possible solutions.

## Differentiating the Speeds of the Slugs

Let's start by adding a ListProperty to the **Slug** class and set its default value to an empty list. We can name the property **speeds**. We must also remember to import the **ListProperty** class in the imports section of the file. Here's the code:

```
# File name: slug.py

from kivy.uix.relativelayout import RelativeLayout

# We must also import the ListProperty.
from kivy.properties import StringProperty, NumericProperty, ListProperty
```

```
from kivy.animation import Animation

class Slug(RelativeLayout):
    ...
    finish_position = NumericProperty(.83)

    # Here's the speeds ListProperty.
    speeds = ListProperty([])

    def update(self, winning_slug, race_number):
        ...
```

We will set the property for each slug in the **race.kv** file where the slugs are created. You will better understand how this property is used later when we use it in the **run** method in the **Slug** class, but generally speaking, the list contains two integers between 1 and 10. The more probable it is that a slug will be rather fast than slow, the lower the two integers should be. Here's a short description of the four slugs with respect to their expected performance:

**Speedster**, as his name suggests is pretty fast. He's probable to win the race pretty often, but occasionally he may be pretty slow and even finish the race as last. We will set Speedster's **speeds** property to **[1, 6]**.

**Trusty** can be trusted, so he will be fast pretty often too. Actually it will be fast less frequently than Speedster, but he will also be slow less often than Speedster. So, in most cases his speed will be somewhere in the middle of the range. We will set Trusty's **speeds** property to **[2, 8]**.

**Iffy** is, as his name suggests, iffy, so not certain. He may be equally often fast and slow. We will set Iffy's **speeds** property to **[4, 6]**.

**Slowpoke**, also as his name suggests, is rather slow. But occasionally he will surprise you and beat all the other slugs in the race. We will set Slowpoke's **speeds** property to **[4, 9]**.

Here's the code:

```
#:kivy 1.11.1
# File name: race.kv
#:import race race
...
<RaceScreen>:
    ...
            # the slugs
            # Speedster
            Slug:
                ...
                front_image: ...
                speeds: [1, 6]

            # Trusty
            Slug:
                ...
                front_image: ...
                speeds: [2, 8]

            # Iffy
            Slug:
                ...
                front_image: ...
                speeds: [4, 6]

            # Slowpoke
            Slug:
                ...
                front_image: ...
                speeds: [4, 9]

        # Winner
        ...
```

And now we can use the **speeds** property in the **run** method to differentiate the speeds of the slugs. As we want the speeds to be randomized, we'll need two functions from the **random** module, **randint** for random integer numbers and **uniform** for random float numbers.

First, we'll use the **randint** function to pick a random integer number between 1 and 10. Then we'll compare the number with the first value in the **speeds** list. If it's less than or equal to this value, the slug will be moving slowly. So, now you understand what the first value is for. If it's a small number, like 1 in case of Speedster or 2 in case of Trusty, it's less probable than the random integer will be less than or equal to it. If it's a higher number, like 4 in case of the other two slugs, it's more probable.

If the random number is not less than or equal to the first value in the **speeds** list, it's next compared with the second value from the list. Again, if it's less than or equal to this value, the slug's speed will be in the medium range.

Otherwise, so if the random integer is greater than both the first and the second value in the **speeds** list, the slug will run fast. So, the lower the second value is, the more probable it is that the slug will be fast.

OK, now we know when the slug will be slow or fast, but how exactly do we set his speed? Well, technically speaking, we set his running time to a float value using the **uniform** function. There are three possible ranges:

- between 8 and 10 seconds – this is the running time of a slow slug,

- between 6 and 8 seconds – a medium running time,

- between 4 and 6 seconds – this is the running time of a fast slug.

So, as you can see, the running time will be between 4 and 10 seconds. This is the value we will set the animation duration to.

Here's the code:

```
# File name: slug.py
...
from kivy.animation import Animation

# We'll need two functions from the random module.
from random import randint, uniform

class Slug(RelativeLayout):
    ...
    def update(self, winning_slug, race_number):
        ...
    def run(self):
        # Let's pick a random integer between 1 and 10.
        move_base = randint(1, 10)
```

```
        # The random integer is compared with the value in the speeds
        # list and the running time is set accordingly.
        if move_base < self.speeds[0]:
            running_time = uniform(8, 10)  # slow
        elif move_base <= self.speeds[1]:
            running_time = uniform(6, 8)  # medium
        else:
            running_time = uniform(4, 6)  # fast

        # The animation duration will be set to running_time.
        self.run_animation = Animation(pos_hint={'x': self.finish_position},
                                       d=running_time)
        self.run_animation.start(self)
```

Run the app again. Now the slugs will be running at different speeds.

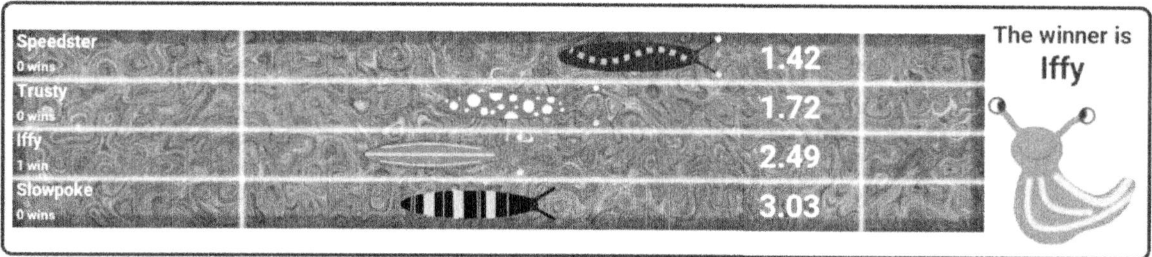


# It's Your Turn Now...

## EXERCISE

The slugs should be reset to their original positions when the Next Race button in the Results screen is pressed. As pressing this button calls the **reset_race** method on the **Game** object, this is the right place to put our code. We'll just call the **reset** method on each of the slugs. But as we didn't define the **reset** method yet, add it to the **Slug** class first. The method should set the slug's **pos_hint** property so that the **x** property is set to the start position we defined before.

Then call the method for each slug in the **reset_race** method in the **Game** class.

## SOLUTION

Here's the **reset** method:

```
# File name: slug.py
...
class Slug(RelativeLayout):
    ...
    def run(self):
        ...

    # This method will just reset the slug to his
    # start position.
    def reset(self):
        self.pos_hint = {'x': self.start_position}
```

And here's the **reset_race** method in the **Game** class where we call the **reset** method for each slug:

```
# File name: main.py
...
class Game(ScreenManager):
    ...
    def reset_race(self):
        ...
        self.race_winner = None

        # Reset all slugs to their start positions.
        for slug in self.slugs:
            slug.reset()

    def reset_players(self):
        ...
```

Now if you press the Next Race button after a race, the slugs will be reset to their start positions.

# Chapter 102 – Animating the Eyes

In the previous chapter we got the slugs moving along the track. They move at randomized speeds and each of them has different chances of winning. We didn't change the game logic yet, though, so now there is no correspondence between what you see on the track and what you see in the Winner subarea. So, you may see something like this for example:

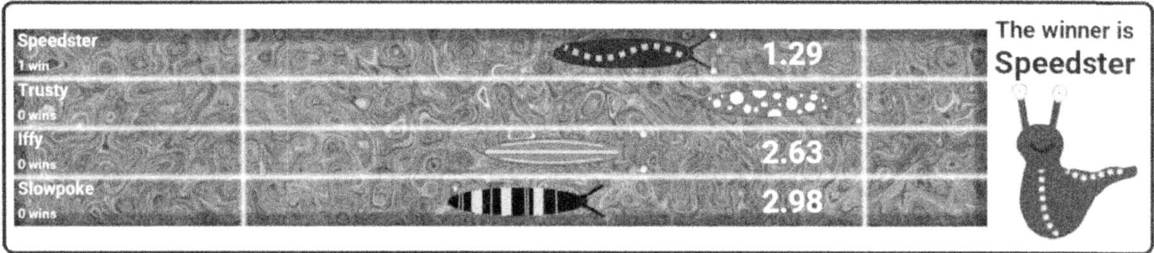


Here Trusty is the winner as he crosses the finish line first, but in the Winner subarea you can see that the winner is Speedster. This is because the winning slug is still randomly picked when you press the Go button so that you can see the winner before the race even finishes. Naturally, this isn't the behavior that we want and we're going to change it, but let's leave it for the next chapter. In this chapter I'd like to do something else. We'll add one more animation to the slugs. They will move their eyes. Each eye will rotate 30 degrees in one direction or the other.

As you can see in the kv file, the eyes are now rotated 30 degrees in both directions:

```
#:kivy 1.11.1
# File name: slug.kv
#:import slug slug

<Slug>:
    ...
    # the left eye image
    Image:
        canvas.before:
            PushMatrix
            Rotate:
                angle: 30
                axis: 0, 0, 1
                ...
    # the right eye image
    Image:
        canvas.before:
            PushMatrix
            Rotate:
                angle: -30
                axis: 0, 0, 1
                ...
```

This is fine except that this is a fixed value and we want it to change. The 30 and -30 degrees values should be the maximum values for each respective eye to rotate. The minimum value for each eye should be 0 degrees, which is the case when the eyes are not rotated at all and they are positioned horizontally. Let's change the angles to 0 degrees to see what it should look like:

```
#:kivy 1.11.1
# File name: slug.kv
#:import slug slug

<Slug>:
    ...
    # the left eye image
    ...
                angle: 0
                ...
    # the right eye image
    ...
                angle: 0
                ...
```

Now the eyes will be pointing out to the finish line.

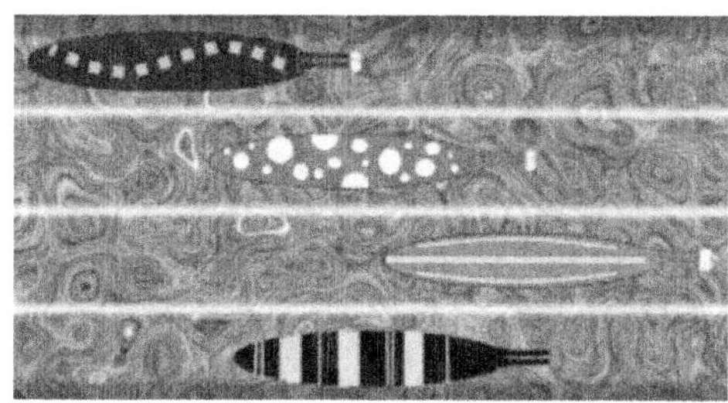

Now that you can visualize the minimum and maximum angles the eyes should rotate to, let's create a property that we can animate. This is going to be a NumericProperty with the default value of 0. Let's name it **rot_angle**.

Here's the **Slug** class:

```
# File name: slug.py
...
class Slug(RelativeLayout):
    ...
    speeds = ListProperty([])

    # This is the property we're going to
    # use to animate the eye rotation.
    rot_angle = NumericProperty(0)

    def update(self, winning_slug, race_number):
        ...
```

And now let's use this property in the kv file instead of the fixed values:

```
#:kivy 1.11.1
# File name: slug.kv
#:import slug slug

<Slug>:
    ...
    # the left eye image
    ...
                angle: root.rot_angle
                ...
    # the right eye image
    ...
                angle: -root.rot_angle
                ...
```

As you can see, we're using a positive value for the left eye and a negative value for the right eye. This is because we want the eyes to rotate in opposite directions. And now let's create the animation.

# Creating the Eye Rotation Animation

Just like with the running animation, we'll create a method in the **Slug** class that will create the eye rotation animation and start it. Let's name the method **rotate_eyes**. It will take two parameters (apart from **self**, naturally), **max_angle** and **duration**. The former will be used to set the maximum angle of the rotation.

As far as the animation is concerned, we're actually going to join two simple animations sequentially. The first one will rotate the eye from its initial horizontal orientation to the maximum angle and the other one back to horizontal. The duration will be the same for both animations. As you remember, we use the **+** operator to join animations sequentially. Let's name the resulting animation **eye_animation**. We don't need names for the two simple animations it consists of.

The property we're going to animate is **rot_angle** that we just added. We also want the animation to be infinitely repeated so that the slugs are waving at us with their tentacles all the time. When the animation is created, we can start it. Here's the code:

```
# File name: slug.py
...
class Slug(RelativeLayout):
    ...
    def reset(self):
        ...

    # This method will be used to create and start the eye rotation animation.
    # It takes two parameters: the maximum angle of the rotation and duration.
    def rotate_eyes(self, max_angle, duration):
        # The animation is going to consist of two sequential animations.
        # First each eye will be rotated from the horizontal orientation
        # to the maximum angle and then back to horizontal.
        self.eye_animation = (Animation(rot_angle=max_angle, d=duration) +
                              Animation(rot_angle=0, d=duration))

        # This animation should be infinitely repeated.
        self.eye_animation.repeat = True

        # And now we're ready to start it on the Slug instance.
        self.eye_animation.start(self)
```

And now, the last piece of the puzzle is to call the method that will start the animation. We want the slugs to move their tentacles all the time during the game (except when an accident happens, which we are going to discuss later in the course). So, the animation should be started right away when we create the slugs. A good place to do it is the **__init__** method, which is the constructor that actually constructs the objects of a class. So, let's override the **__init__** method in the **Slug** class:

```
# File name: slug.py
...
class Slug(RelativeLayout):
    ...
    rot_angle = NumericProperty(0)

    # Here's the constructor method
    # where the eye rotation method
    # will be called and the eye
    # rotation animation will be
    # created and started.
    def __init__(self, **kwargs):
        super().__init__(**kwargs)

        # Let's set the maximum angle
        # to 30 degrees and the duration
        # to 1 second.
        self.rotate_eyes(30, 1)

    def update(self, winning_slug, race_number):
        ...
```

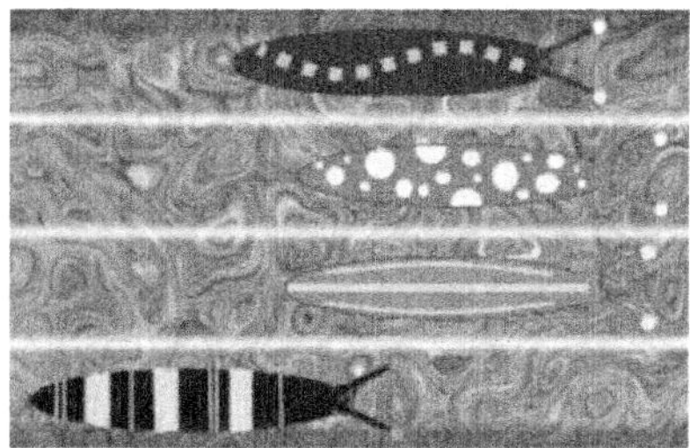

If you now run the app again, the slugs will be moving their tentacles. As you can see, they are all moving their tentacles in unison. In the exercise below you will add some variation to it, so that each slug moves his tentacles at a different speed.

And in the next chapter we're going to adjust the game logic to the new situation with these two animations in place.

## It's Your Turn Now...

### EXERCISE

This exercise is going to be really quick and easy. All I want you to do is randomize the speed of the eye movement, so, technically speaking, the duration of the animation. Use the **uniform** function from the **random** module that we used in the previous chapter. Make sure the duration of the animation is between 0.3 and 1.5 seconds.

### SOLUTION

Here's the code:

```
# File name: slug.py
...
class Slug(RelativeLayout):
    ...
    def __init__(self, **kwargs):
        super().__init__(**kwargs)
        self.rotate_eyes(30, uniform(.3, 1.5))

    def update(self, winning_slug, race_number):
        ...
```

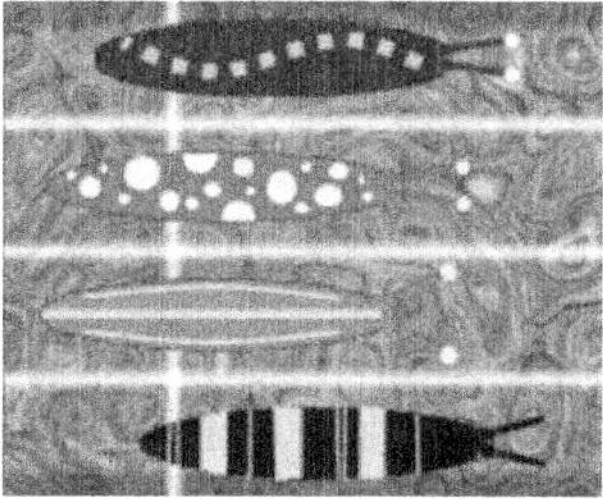

Now if you run the app, each slug will move his tentancles at a different speed.

The problem is, though, that this speed is only determined once, in the constructor, which means each slug will move its eyes at the same speed in each race. And we want the speeds to change in each race. This is something we must address too.

# Chapter 103 – Game Logic Revisited

In the previous chapters we animated the slugs and their eyes. But there is still no correlation between the animations and game logic. In particular, the winning slug is picked randomly, independent of which slug actually crosses the finish line first. Besides, the slugs are rotating their tentacles at random speeds that are determined at the beginning of the game, which means the speed of the animation is constant for each slug throughout the game. We want it to change in each race, though. So, let's address these issues now.

## The Race and the Winning Slug

So, what do we have now? The moment you hit the Go button in the Bets screen, the next race begins. In particular, the **go** method in the **Game** class is called. In the method, the slug animations are started and then, before the slugs even start running, the winning slug is picked randomly from the **slugs** list.

This means the race has a winner while the slugs are still running and it actually doesn't matter how fast they run, evertything has already been decided. Then, also while the slugs are still running, the players and slugs are updated using the **update** method on each respective class, bankrupt players are removed and the program checks for game over. So, why are the slugs running in the first place if the result is practically known before they start moving? Naturally, this must be fixed.

We actually want the Go button to just start the slug animations and bind some custom methods to the animation events. Actually, there are going to be two such methods, let's name them **while_running** and **finish_race**. They will be defined in the **Game** class and will be bound to the **on_progress** and **on_complete** animation events respectively.

The actual logic that will handle picking the winning slug, the game over check and the transition to the Results screen will be moved to these methods so that it's fired when needed. So, let's modify the code by simplifying the **go** method and implementing the two aforementioned methods.

But before we do that, there's one more thing to take care of. We will need access to each slug's **Animation** object, so let's first modify the **run** method in the **Slug** class so that it returns the animation object.

We're not going to start the animation directly in the method anymore. Instead, we'll start it in the **go** method in the **Game** class after getting access to it, so let's remove the line of code where the animation is started. Here's the modified **run** method:

```
# File name: slug.py
...
class Slug(RelativeLayout):
    ...
    def run(self):
        ...
        self.run_animation = Animation(pos_hint={'x': self.finish_position},
                                       d=running_time)
        # Return the animation instead of starting it.
        return self.run_animation

    def reset(self):
        ...
```

Now we can access each slug's animation object and start the animation in the **go** method. We'll also need to know whether a slug has finished the race, which happens when the finish line is crossed. But we haven't defined the finish line yet.

As you look at the image of the racetrack, you can see that the whole track is 1000 pixels wide. The finish line is at the x position 850, so we will use this value to define the finish line.

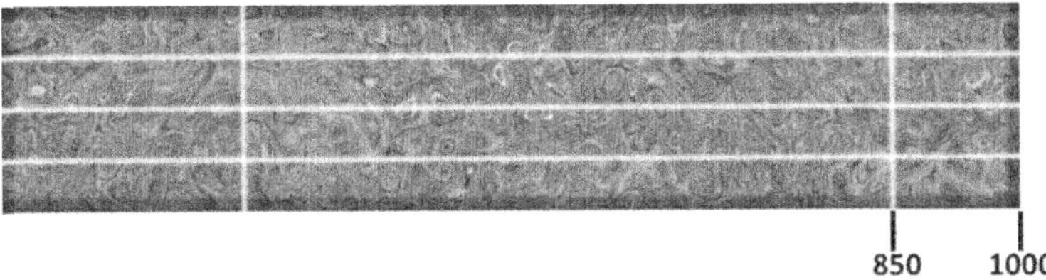


Here's the modified code of the **go** method along with the two methods bound to the animation events:

```
# File name: main.py
...
class Game(ScreenManager):
    ...
    # races
    ...
    race_winner = ObjectProperty(None, allownone=True)

    # The finish line is at the x position 850 from the left of the racetrack image.
    finish_line = 850

    # time
    ...
    def go(self):
        for slug in self.slugs:
            # Let's create a running animation on each slug and save it in the
            # anim variable. At this point the animations are not started yet.
            anim = slug.run()

            # Let's bind the while_running and finish_race methods to the
            # on_progress and on_complete animation events.
            anim.bind(on_progress=self.while_running)
```

```
            anim.bind(on_complete=self.finish_race)

            # Let's actually start the animations.
            anim.start(slug)

    # Here's the method that will be called when the animation is in progress.
    # Let's give the parameters meaningful names.
    # This method will be called for each slug. It will check whether the slug
    # has crossed the finish line. If so, the slug will be the winner, but only
    # if none of the other slugs crossed the finish line before.
    # This method will also update the players and the slugs when the winner is
    # known, remove bankrupt players and check for game over.
    # So, it contains most of the functionality that was in the go method before.
    def while_running(self, animation, slug, progression):
        # To check if a slug has crossed the finish line, we need a finish line.
        # Scroll up to the races section and you'll see that we added the
        # finish_line attribute there. Let's now check whether the right border
        # of the slug widget is greater than 850.
        if slug.right > self.finish_line:
            # If it is, the slug has finished the race. But is he the winner?
            # It depends on whether he was the first to cross the finish line.
            # If this is the case, the race_winner property should be set to None
            # because this is what the reset_race method takes care of.
            # So, if the race_winner property is None, the slug is the winner.
            if not self.race_winner:
                self.race_winner = slug

                # Now that we have the winner, let's update the players and the
                # slugs. Let's also remove bankrupt players and check for game over.
                for player in self.players:
                    player.update(self.race_winner)

                for slug in self.slugs:
                    slug.update(self.race_winner, self.race_number)

                self.remove_bankrupt_players()
                self.gameover_check()

    # Here's the method that will be called when the animation is completed. It will just
    # change the screen from Bets to Results. We're going to implement it in a moment.
    def finish_race(self, animation, slug):
        pass

    def remove_bankrupt_players(self):
        ...
```

As you can see, we're not yet done with the implementation of the race logic, but there is considerable improvement. Let's run the program to see how it works.

So, first of all, when you press the Go button and the slugs begin running, the Winner area is empty, which is good because there is no winner before the race finishes. As soon as the first slug crosses the finish line, we have the winner.

**still running, no winner yet**

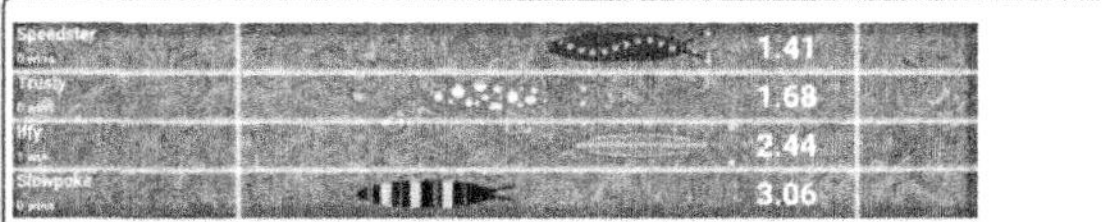

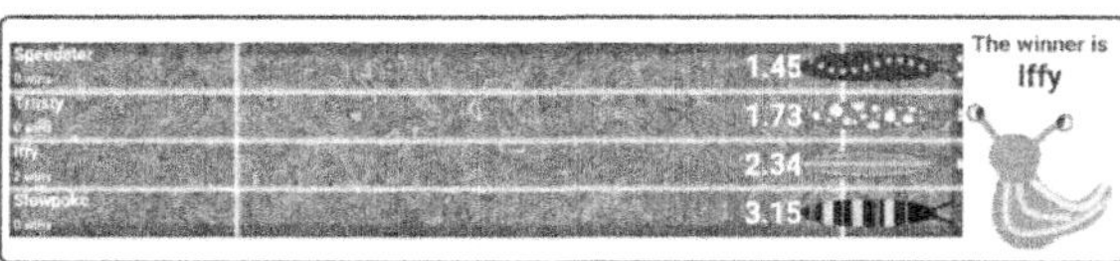


But there's another problem. We can see the Results screen as soon as the slugs start running. This is because the screen is switched when the Go button is pressed.

We want the Results screen to be visible only when the race is finished, so we'll move the code that is responsible for switching screens to the **finish_race** method in the **Game** class. But when exactly should the Results screen appear?

We could make it appear as soon as there's the winner. But then the other slugs would still be running, so it would be advisable to disable the Next Race button until all slugs have finished the race. Or, we can wait until all the slugs have finished the race and the Results screen will appear only then. In our project we'll opt for the second solution.

So, first of all, there must be a way to tell whether all slugs have finished the race. Let's add a BooleanProperty to the **Slug** class that will hold the information about whether the particular slug has finished the race. Let's name it **finished** and set its default value to **True**. Make sure to import the **BooleanProperty** class first. Here's the code:

```
# File name: slug.py

from kivy.uix.relativelayout import RelativeLayout
from kivy.properties import (StringProperty,
                             NumericProperty,
                             ListProperty,
                             BooleanProperty)
from kivy.animation import Animation
...
class Slug(RelativeLayout):
    ...
    rot_angle = NumericProperty(0)

    # This property that will be set to True
    # when the slug has finished the race.
    # It'll be also set to True by default.
    finished = BooleanProperty(True)

    def __init__(self, **kwargs):
        ...
```

We'll reset the property to **False** when a new race begins, so let's add the following line of code at the top of the **run** method:

```
# File name: slug.py
...
class Slug(RelativeLayout):
    ...
    def run(self):
        # When the race begins, the slug, naturally,
        # hasn't finished it yet.
        self.finished = False

        move_base = randint(1, 10)
        ...
```

And there is one more problem. It was easy to switch to the Results screen from the Bets screen using the RaceScreenManager defined in the Race screen.

Here it is again:

```
#:kivy 1.11.1
# File name: race.kv
#:import race race

<RaceScreenManager>:
    BetsScreen:
        name: 'betsscreen'
    ResultsScreen:
        name: 'resultsscreen'

<SlugStats>:
    ...
```

As you can see, the screen manager is the parent of both the BetsScreen and ResultsScreen. But now we have to be able to access the RaceScreenManager in the **Game** class as well in order to switch screens.

So, let's pass the screen manager as an argument to the **go** method. First, we need to modify the **go** method so that it can take the additional parameter and then we're good to go.

As the screen will be now switched in the **finish_race** method, let's remove the code that takes care of it from the Bets screen. This code is now in the Go button area, just delete it. Here's the modified Go button code where the **go** method is called:

```
#:kivy 1.11.1
# File name: bets.kv
#:import bets bets
...
<BetsScreen>:
    ...
        ### GO BUTTON ###
        RedButton:
            text: 'Go'
            disabled: not root.all_slugs_selected or root.game.game_is_over

            on_press:
                # Pass the RaceScreenManager as an argument to the go method so
                # that we can later access the screen manager in the Game class.
                root.game.go(root.parent)
                root.clear_bets()
```

And here's the **go** method with the new parameter. In the method we set the **race_manager** attribute on the **Game** class to the screen manager passed as the argument:

```
# File name: main.py
...
class Game(ScreenManager):
    ...
    def update_time(self, dt):
        ...

    # Now the go method will take the screen_manager parameter to gain access to the
    # RaceScreenManager, which we can use to switch to the Results screen later in
    # the finish_race method.
    def go(self, screen_manager):
        for slug in self.slugs:
            ...
            anim.start(slug)

        # Here we assign the RaceScreenManager to the race_manager attribute.
        self.race_manager = screen_manager

    def while_running(self, animation, slug, progression):
        ...
```

With this in place, we can implement the **finish_race** method that will be called when the running animation is completed. In the method the slug's **finished** property will be set to **True** and then, provided all slugs have finished the race, the Results screen will appear. Here's the code:

```
# File name: main.py
...
class Game(ScreenManager):
    ...
    def finish_race(self, animation, slug):
        # This slug just finished the race.
        slug.finished = True

        # If all slugs finished the race,
        # let's switch to the Results screen.
        if (self.speedster.finished
            and self.trusty.finished
            and self.iffy.finished
            and self.slowpoke.finished):
            self.race_manager.current = 'resultsscreen'
            self.race_manager.transition.direction = 'left'

    def remove_bankrupt_players(self):
        ...
```

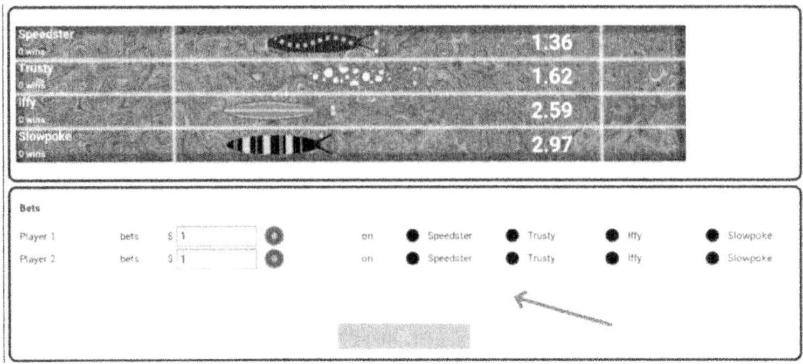


If you now run the app, you will see that the Results screen is not visible while the slugs are running. Instead we can see the Bets screen.

As soon as the last slug finishes the race, the Results screen will replace the Bets screen.

So, we can see the Bets screen while the slugs are running. The widgets of the Bets screen are not disabled, so theoretically we could play with the sliders or radio buttons, for example, during the race, which is not what we want. So, we could just disable the widgets for the duration of the race, but we're going to address this issue in a different way, because disabling them alone wouldn't look so good. Actually, you're going to do it as one of the exercises. In the other exercise you'll take care of the eye rotation animation. And in the next chapter we'll be talking about sound in Kivy.

# It's Your Turn Now...

**EXERCISE 1 - Race Started Animation**

In this exercise we'll take care of the Bets screen. Now, when a race starts, you can still see the Bets screen, with the radio buttons being unchecked. The Bets screen is not disabled so you could possibly mess with it during the race, which should be avoided. Instead of just disabling the whole screen, we'll disable and hide it behind an animated label.

As this exercise is pretty lengthy, let's do it step by step. This is why I'm going to show you the solution for each step. And here are the steps to follow:

1. At this point we can say that the Bets screen contains two layers that overlap. Go to the Bets screen to see how the code is organized. The first layer, which is the main layer, is the BoxLayout we see most of the time. It contains the Title Label, the Player Bets and the Go button areas. The second layer is the FloatLayout with the bankrupt labels. The bankrupt labels are only visible if a player goes bankrupt.

Now, we'll add one more layer which will sit on top of the main layer and hide it completely. This layer will be visible only when a race starts. We'll need access to the main layer, so set the BoxLayout's id to **`_main_layer`** and add the **`main_layer`** property to the **`BetsScreen`** class rule that references the BoxLayout by id.

**SOLUTION - Step 1**

Here's the code:

```
#:kivy 1.11.1
# File name: bets.kv
#:import bets bets
...
<BetsScreen>:
    ...
    bets: [_bet1, _bet2, _bet3, _bet4]

    # We need access to the main layer of the Bets screen.
    main_layer: _main_layer

    # bankrupt labels
    FloatLayout:
        ...
        BankruptLabel:
            ...
            opacity: int(root.game.player4.bankrupt)

    # main layer
    BoxLayout:
        # Let's set the id.
        id: _main_layer

        orientation: 'vertical'
        ...
```

2. Now it's time to add the third layer. We can place it between the bankrupt labels FloatLayout and the main layer BoxLayout. So, find this location and add a FloatLayout with a BoldLabel in it. Set the BoldLabel's **`id`** to **`_race_label`** and add the **`race_label`** property to the **`BetsScreen`** rule like you did with the **`main_layer`** property in the previous step. This way we'll have easy access to the label. Now, there are a couple settings you should take care of as far as the race label is concerned. Here they are:

- the label text should be **`'RACE STARTED'`**,

- the font size should be 70,

- the position and size should be the same as the root widget's,

- the text size should be the size of the label,

- the text should be centered both horizontally and vertically.

**SOLUTION - Step 2**

Here's the code:

```
#:kivy 1.11.1
# File name: bets.kv
#:import bets bets
...
<BetsScreen>:
    ...
    main_layer: _main_layer

    # Here's the property that will give
    # us access to the race label.
    race_label: _race_label

    # bankrupt labels
    FloatLayout:
        ...

    # race label layer
    FloatLayout:
        BoldLabel:
            id: _race_label
            text: 'RACE STARTED'
            font_size: 70
            pos: root.pos
            size: root.size
            text_size: self.size
            halign: 'center'
            valign: 'center'

    # main layer
    BoxLayout:
        ...
```

If you run the program now, you will see the race label under the main layer.

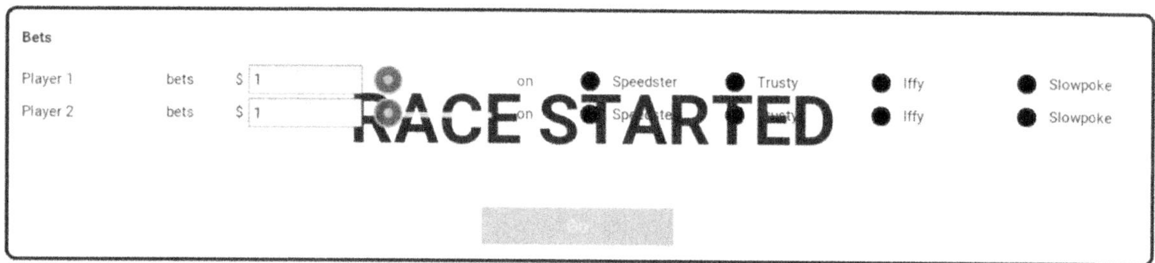


The label is visible all the time, which looks ugly and shouldn't be the case at all. We want it to be only visible during a race. So, in the following steps we must take care of the label's visibility.

3. So, before a race starts we should only be able to see the main layer. After it starts, the main layer should be disabled and the race label should turn visible. The race starts when we press the Go button, so this is where the main layer should be disabled. Just add the line of code that will take care of it in the Go button section.

**SOLUTION - Step 3**

Here's the code:

```
#:kivy 1.11.1
# File name: bets.kv
#:import bets bets
...
```

```
<BetsScreen>:
    ...
        ### GO BUTTON ###
        RedButton:
            ...
            on_press:
                root.game.go(root.parent)
                root.clear_bets()

                # Disable the main layer.
                root.main_layer.disabled = True
```

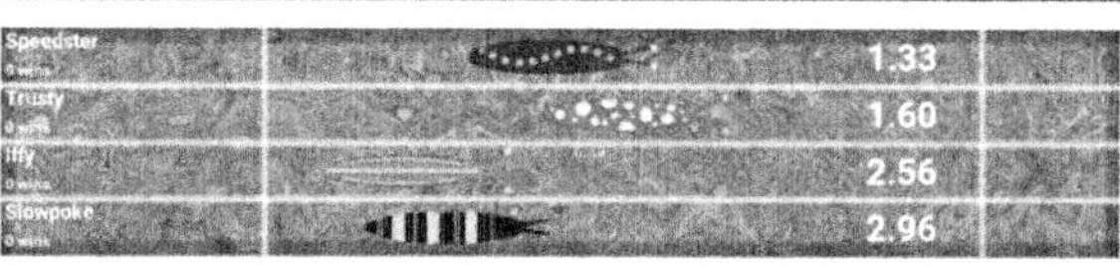


If you run the app now, you will still see both the main layer and the race label at the same time, but when you press the Go button, the former will be disabled and you won't see it anymore, just the label.

4. We want the race label to be visible only when the main layer is disabled. This way we won't see it at the beginning because by default the main layer is enabled when the game starts. So, go to the race label code in the **bets.kv** file and set its **opacity** property accordingly.

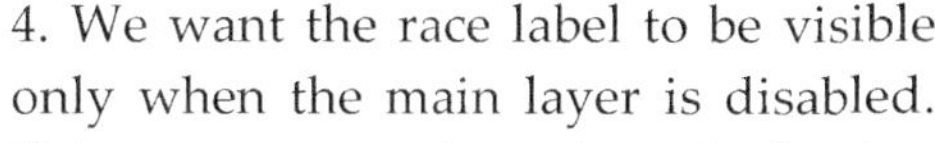

**SOLUTION - Step 4**

Here's the code:

```
#:kivy 1.11.1
# File name: bets.kv
#:import bets bets
...
<BetsScreen>:
    ..
    # race label layer
    FloatLayout:
        BoldLabel:
            ...
            valign: 'center'

            # The race label should be visible if
            # the main layer is disabled.
            opacity: int(root.main_layer.disabled)

    # main layer
    ...
```

5. If you now run the code you won't see the race label until the first race starts. When it does, the race label will appear and the main layer will disappear (or, to be correct, will be disabled). But when you press the Next Race button and the Bets screen replaces the Results screen, you will still see just the race label. This is because the main layer of the Bets screen is still disabled.

To address this issue, we'll override the **on_leave** method in the **BetsScreen** class. This method is called when you leave a screen, so if you switch from one screen to another. In our case we'll be switching from the Bets screen to the Results screen.

This is a good time to set the main layer's **disabled** property back to **False**. This is also a good time to uncheck all the radio buttons in the main layer. At this moment the radio buttons are cleared when the Go button is pressed, so remove the code that calls the **clear_bets** method from the Go button section and add it to the **on_leave** method.

So, let's recap. What I want you to do in this step after removing the **clear_bets** method call from the Go button section is add the **on_leave** method in the Python file and add code to it that will call the **clear_bets** method and then set the main layer's **disabled** property to **False**.

**SOLUTION - Step 5**

Here's the **bets.kv** file:

```
#:kivy 1.11.1
# File name: bets.kv
#:import bets bets
...
<BetsScreen>:
    ...
        ### GO BUTTON ###
        RedButton:
            text: 'Go'
            disabled: not root.all_slugs_selected or root.game.game_is_over

            # Let's move the clear_bets method
            # call to Python code.
            on_press:
                root.game.go(root.parent)
                root.main_layer.disabled = True
```

And here's the **BetsScreen** class with the **on_leave** method:

```
# File name: bets.py
...
class BetsScreen(Screen):
    ...
    def clear_bets(self):
        ...

    # This method will be called when you change from Bets screen to any other
    # screen. In our case it's the Results screen, of course.
    def on_leave(self):
        # Here's the method call moved from the Go button section.
        self.clear_bets()

        # Time to enable the main layer of the Bets screen again so that we
        # can see it in the next race.
        self.main_layer.disabled = False
```

Now when you run the app, the label will be visible only during the race. As soon as you hit the Next Race button and the Bets screen appears, you will see just the main layer of the latter.

6. Finally, let's add a simple animation to the race label, so make sure to import the **Animation** class. We'll be animating the label's **color** property, but the color change is going to be rather subtle. In the **BetsScreen** class add the **animate_race_label** method. In this method create a sequential animation and assign it to a variable, which you can name **race_label_animation**. The animation should consist of two simple animations joined sequentially so that the second one follows the first one. You don't need to name the two simple animations because you can define them inline when creating them. Anyway, the first simple animation should animate the **color** property so that the target color is **[.2, .1, 0, 1]**. The target color in the second simple animation should be **[.5, .1, 0, 1]**. The duration of each simple animation should be 1 second.

Make sure the joined animation is repeated. And then start the animation on the race label. Now, we must call the **animate_race_label** method somewhere in order to create and start the animation. The best way to do it is when the Go button is pressed, so add the appropriate line of code there.

And one more thing. The animation is repeated and never stops. But we don't need it when we can't see the label. So, cancel the animation in the **on_leave** method because this is where the main layer is enabled and thus the race label becomes invisible.

**SOLUTION - Step 6**

Here's the Python code:

```
# File name: bets.py
...
from kivy.uix.screenmanager import Screen

# We'll need the animation class.
from kivy.animation import Animation

class Bet(BoxLayout):
    ...
class BetsScreen(Screen):
    ...
    def on_leave(self):
        self.clear_bets()
        self.main_layer.disabled = False

        # Let's cancel the animation here.
        self.race_label_animation.cancel(self.race_label)

    # Here's the method where we create and start the race label animation.
    def animate_race_label(self):
        # The animation should consist of two simple animations joined sequentially.
        self.race_label_animation = (Animation(color=[.2, .1, 0, 1], d=1) +
                                     Animation(color=[.5, .1, 0, 1], d=1))
```

```
        # The animation should be repeated.
        self.race_label_animation.repeat = True

        # Let's start the animation.
        self.race_label_animation.start(self.race_label)
```

And here's the Go button section where we call the **animate_race_label** method:

```
#:kivy 1.11.1
# File name: bets.kv
#:import bets bets
...
<BetsScreen>:
    ...
        ### GO BUTTON ###
        RedButton:
            ...
            on_press:
                root.game.go(root.parent)
                root.main_layer.disabled = True

                # Let's call the method that will
                # create and start the race label
                # animation.
                root.animate_race_label()
```

Now if you run the app, you will see the animation in action. The race label color pulsates between two different shades.

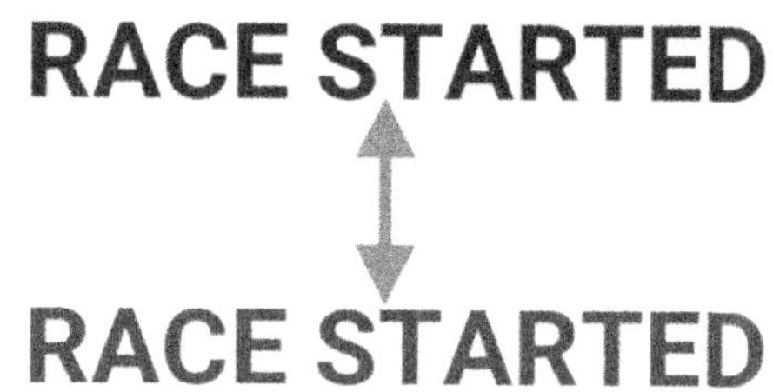


**EXERCISE 2 - Eye Animation Speed**

In this exercise you will change the eye rotation speed in each race. At this point the speed is picked randomly for each slug only once, in the **__init__** method of the **Slug** class and remains the same throughout the game. We will leave the code in the constructor so that the slugs can move their eyes when the game starts. But then we'll add some code that will cancel the eye animation when the slugs' running times are determined and start it again so that its speed matches that of the slug. We don't need any spectacular changes in the code to achieve that. Here's what you should do:

In the **run** method, just below the conditional code where the running time is set add code that cancels the eye animation. Then call the **rotate_eyes** method with the maximum angle of 30 degrees, so just like in the constructor. But the duration should be different. In the **__init__** method the duration was a random number between 0.3 and 1.5. Here, let it be a value depending on the running time so that the slugs move their eyes faster when they run faster and the other way around. If you divide the running time (which is a value between 4 and 10) by 6, you will get a value between 0.66 and 1.66. I think this will do.

The last thing you can do is change the duration range in the **__init__** method from **(0.3, 1.5)** to **(0.6, 1.6)** to better match the range that is possible to obtain in the **run** method. The rest of the **run** method should remain unchanged.

**SOLUTION**

Here's the code:

```
# File name: slug.py
...
class Slug(RelativeLayout):
    ...
    def __init__(self, **kwargs):
        super().__init__(**kwargs)

        # Let's change the duration range from (0.3, 1.5) to (0.6 to 1.6).
        self.rotate_eyes(30, uniform(.6, 1.6))

    def update(self, winning_slug, race_number):
        ...

    def run(self):
        ...
        else:
            running_time = uniform(4, 6)  # fast

        # Cancel the eye animation.
        self.eye_animation.cancel(self)

        # Call the rotate_eyes method again so that a new eye animation is created
        # with the same maximum angle, but with duration depending on the running time.
        self.rotate_eyes(30, running_time/6)

        self.run_animation = Animation(pos_hint={'x': self.finish_position},
                                       d=running_time)
        ...
```

Now if you run the app, the speed of the eye animation will be different each time you press the Go button.

# Chapter 104 – Sound in Kivy

In the previous chapters we were discussing and implementing animations in our project. But a game without sound seems incomplete. There may be background music and sound effects. In this chapter we'll learn how to implement sound in Kivy. We'll be working on the test files. In the next chapter we'll add sounds to the Slugrace project.

In Kivy there are two classes that we use to work with sound, **Sound** and **SoundLoader**, both defined in the **kivy.core.audio** module. We shouldn't use the **Sound** class directly, though. Instead we should use the **load** method on the **SoundLoader** class, which will return a class that will be the optimal sound provider for our particular file type.

## Loading, Playing and Stopping Sound

OK, let's then add some sounds to our GUI. First, we have to create a simple GUI. We'll have just a toggle button, which we will use to toggle the background music on and off. As the background music I will use a file that I downloaded from Zapsplat, which is an online resource where you can get free music and sound effects. The particular file we're going to use is called **music_zapsplat_game_music_kids_warm_soft_slow_chilled_piano_bass_warm_pads_vocal_ahs_022.mp3**, but to keep things simple, I renamed it **'Background Music.mp3'**. By the way, this is the exact same file we're going to use for background music in the project. It's included in the **assets** folder.

Here's the kv file:

```
# File name: test.py

import kivy
kivy.require('1.11.1')
from kivy.app import App
from kivy.uix.boxlayout import BoxLayout

# We'll need this class to load audio files.
from kivy.core.audio import SoundLoader

class TestLayout(BoxLayout):
    def __init__(self, **kwargs):
        super().__init__(**kwargs)

        # Here we load the audio file.
        self.music = SoundLoader.load('assets/sounds/Game/Background Music.mp3')

    def toggle_music(self):
        if self.music.state == 'play':
            self.music.stop()
        else:
```

```
                self.music.play()

class TestApp(App):
    def build(self):
        return TestLayout()

if __name__ == '__main__':
    TestApp().run()
```

In this example we load the file in the **_init_** method of the root widget and save it in a variable. Then we have the **toggle_music** method that is called when you press the toggle button. We can use the **state** property to check whether or not the music is currently playing. Then we use the **stop** and **play** methods to stop and play the music respectively.

Run the app and press the toggle button. You should hear the background music. As soon as you press the toggle button again, the music will stop. If you press the button one more time, the music will play from the beginning.

# Playing vs Looping

You can play an audio file just once or loop it. To do either of the two, you need the **play** method. If you want to loop the file, you should set the **loop** property to **True**. Let's load another file in the constructor and add two buttons. If the first button is pressed, the sound effect will be played once. If the second button is pressed, it will loop.

This time I will use the **zapsplat_horror_gore_bone_arm_leg_break_crunch_57125.mp3** file downloaded from Zapsplat. This file will be used in the project for one of the accidents, and in particular if a slug breaks his leg. Again, for simplicity's sake I renamed the file **'Broken Leg.mp3'**.

Here's the kv file with the two buttons:

```
#:kivy 1.11.1
# File name: test.kv

<Button>:
    # These settings will also be
    # used by the toggle button.
    size_hint: None, None
    size: 250, 100
    font_size: 28

<TestLayout>:
    ToggleButton:
        text: 'Background Music'
        on_state: root.toggle_music()

    Button:
        text: 'Play Once'
        on_press: root.play_once()

    Button:
        text: 'Loop'
        on_press: root.loop()
```

If the buttons are pressed, the **play_once** and **loop** methods are called on the root widget. We are going to define them next. Here's the Python file:

```
# File name: test.py
...
class TestLayout(BoxLayout):
    def __init__(self, **kwargs):
        super().__init__(**kwargs)

        # background music
        self.music = SoundLoader.load('assets/sounds/Game/Background Music.mp3')

        # Let's load the sound effect file.
        self.sound_effect = SoundLoader.load('assets/sounds/Accidents/Broken Leg.mp3')

    def toggle_music(self):
        ...

    def play_once(self):
        # Let's play the sound effect only once.
        self.sound_effect.play()

    def loop(self):
        # Let's play the sound effect in a loop.
        self.sound_effect.loop = True
        self.sound_effect.play()

class TestApp(App):
    ...
```

If you now run the app, you will see three buttons.

| Background Music | Play Once | Loop |
|---|---|---|

If you press the Play Once button, you will hear the sound effect once. If you press the Loop button, you will hear it play in a loop until you close the app window because we didn't write any code to stop it earlier.

# Sound Events

There are two events associated with sounds that may come in handy: **on_play** and **on_stop**, which are triggered when the sound is played or stopped respectively. Let's see how we can use them. In this example we don't change anything in the kv file. And here's the Python code:

```
# File name: test.py
...
class TestLayout(BoxLayout):
    def __init__(self, **kwargs):
        ...
```

```
        self.sound_effect = SoundLoader.load('assets/sounds/Accidents/Broken Leg.mp3')

        # Let's bind custom methods to the sound events.
        self.sound_effect.bind(on_play=self.start_playing)
        self.sound_effect.bind(on_stop=self.stop_playing)

    def toggle_music(self):
        ...
    def play_once(self):
        ...
    def loop(self):
        ...
        self.sound_effect.play()

    # Here are the two custom methods
    # that we bound to the sound events.
    # They just print simple messages.
    def start_playing(self, instance):
        print('Started playing')

    def stop_playing(self, instance):
        print('Stopped playing')

class TestApp(App):
    ...
```

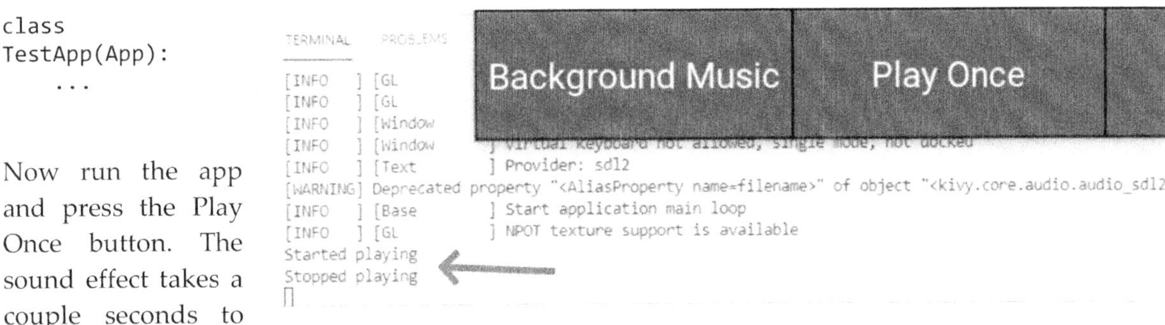


Now run the app and press the Play Once button. The sound effect takes a couple seconds to play. You will see the first message appear in the terminal as soon as the sound starts playing and then the second one as soon as it stops playing.

```
TERMINAL    PROBLEMS

Stopped playing
Started playing
Stopped playing
Started playing
Stopped playing
Started playing
Stopped playing
Started playing
Stopped playing
Started playing
```

And now watch what happens if you press the Loop button. As you can see, the sound starts and stops playing over and over again.

## Unloading Audio File from Memory

If you don't need a sound anymore, you can unload it from memory. To do that you should use the **unload** method. Let's add another button that will do just that.

Here's the kv file:

```
#:kivy 1.11.1
# File name: test.kv
...
<TestLayout>:
    ...
    Button:
        text: 'Loop'
        on_press: root.loop()

    Button:
        text: 'Unload Sounds'
        on_press: root.unload_sounds()
```

And here's the Python file:

```
# File name: test.py
...
class TestLayout(BoxLayout):
    ...
    def stop_playing(self, instance):
        ...

    # Here's the method to unload both
    # sounds from memory.
    def unload_sounds(self):
        self.music.unload()
        self.sound_effect.unload()

class TestApp(App):
    ...
```

Run the app and resize the window slightly (because we didn't configure its size). You can now see the four buttons.

| Background Music | Play Once | Loop | Unload Sounds |
|---|---|---|---|

The toggle button and the first two buttons still work as before until you press the Unload Sounds button. If you do that and then press any of the other buttons, you won't hear anything because the sounds have been unloaded. If you press the Unload Sounds button while the sound effect is looping, it will stop looping and playing.

In the exercise below you'll have an opportunity to play with the **volume** property and in the next chapter we'll add some sounds to the Slugrace project.

# It's Your Turn Now...

### EXERCISE

You can use the **volume** property to adjust the volume of the sound. The **volume** property is a **NumericProperty** with values between 0 for mute and 1 for full volume. Let's simplify the kv and Python files a bit. Here's the kv file:

```
#:kivy 1.11.1
# File name: test.kv

<TestLayout>:
    ToggleButton:
        size_hint: None, None
```

```
        size: 250, 100
        pos_hint: {'center_y': .5}
        font_size: 28
        text: 'Background Music'
        on_state: root.toggle_music()
```

As you can see, there's only the toggle button now. I also centered it vertically. And here's the simplified Python file:

```
# File name: test.py
...
class TestLayout(BoxLayout):
    def __init__(self, **kwargs):
        super().__init__(**kwargs)

        # background music
        self.music = SoundLoader.load('assets/sounds/Game/Background Music.mp3')

    def toggle_music(self):
        if self.music.state == 'play':
            self.music.stop()
        else:
            self.music.play()

class TestApp(App):
    ...
```

Now, your task is to add a horizontal slider to the root widget that will be used to change the volume. The minimum and maximum values on the slider should match the range of the **volume** property and the current value should match full volume. Add an event to the slider that, when triggered, will call the **change_volume** method that you are going to define in the root widget class in a minute. The method should take the slider's value as an argument.

Now, in the Python file define the **change_volume** method in the **TestLayout** class. It should take a **value** argument and set the volume of the sound to this value.

### SOLUTION

Here's the kv file:

```
#:kivy 1.11.1
# File name: test.kv

<TestLayout>:
    ToggleButton:
        ...
    Slider:
        min: 0
        max: 1
        value: 1
        on_value: root.change_volume(self.value)
```

And here's the Python file:

```
# File name: test.py
...
class TestLayout(BoxLayout):
    ...
    def toggle_music(self):
        ...

    # Here's the method called when
    # the value of the slider changes.
    def change_volume(self, value):
        self.music.volume = value

class TestApp(App):
    ...
```

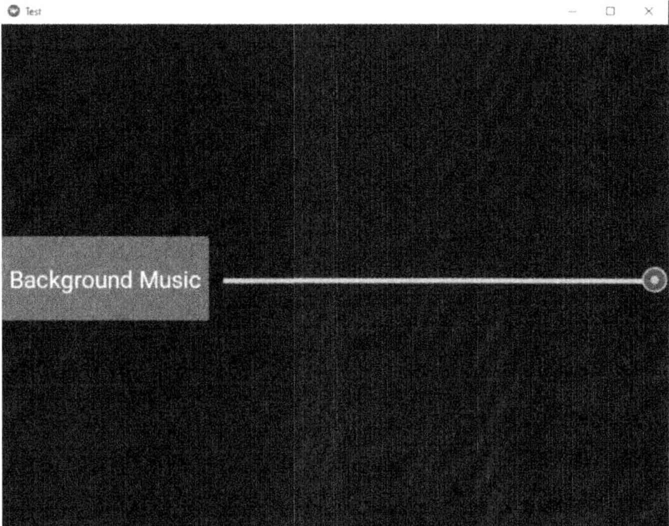


If you now run the app, you will see the toggle button and the slider.

When you press the toggle button, you will here the music at full volume. Move the slider and watch how the volume changes. If you slide it all the way to the left, you will mute the music.

# Chapter 105 – Adding Sounds to the Slugrace Project

In the previous chapter we were talking about sound in Kivy. We already know how to add and play sounds, be it just once or in a loop. In this chapter we're going to add sound to the Slugrace project.

## Sound Assets Overview

You will find the audio files in the **sounds** folder inside the **assets** folder. They are divided into three groups, each represented by a subfolder: **Accidents**, **Game** and **Slugs Winning**.

Accidents
Game
Slugs Winning

We're not going to discuss the sounds in the **Accidents** folder in this chapter, because we didn't implement the accidents yet, but for the sake of completeness, I'll briefly discuss the files from this folder that we are going to use as well.

Anyway, all sounds that I'm using for the project were downloaded from Zapsplat. I renamed them so that you can easily see what each file is going to be used for. In the table below you can see both the names that we are going to use in the project and the original ones.

So, in the **Game** folder we have the following sounds:

| File Name in Slugrace | Original Zapsplat File Name |
|---|---|
| Background Music.mp3 | music_zapsplat_game_music_kids_warm_soft_slow_chilled_piano_bass_warm_pads_vocal_ahs_022.mp3 |
| Slugs Running.mp3 | zapsplat_animals_leach_or_worm_slimy_movement_squelch_003_10795.mp3 |
| Game Over.mp3 | cartoon_success_fanfair.mp3 |
| Go.mp3 | esm_8bit_explosion_medium_with_voice_bomb_boom_blast_cannon_retro_old_school_classic_cartoon.mp3 |

The **Background Music.mp3** file is going to be used for the background music. It's the one we used in the previous chapter too. It will start playing as soon as you launch the app and loop until the game is over or until you press the Sound button in the Race screen to mute all sounds.

The **Slugs Running.mp3** file will start playing when a race begins and loop until all slugs have finished the race.

The **Game Over.mp3** file will play just once when the Game Over screen appears.

The **Go.mp3** file will be played just once the moment a race starts.

In the **Slugs Winning** folder we have the following files:

| File Name in Slugrace | Original Zapsplat File Name |
|---|---|
| Speedster Win.mp3 | human-toddler-18-months-boy-single-laugh.mp3 |
| Trusty Win.mp3 | human_baby_3_months_short_laugh.mp3 |
| Iffy Win.mp3 | jessey_drake_vox_10month_baby_SMOOCH_really_excited_laugh_build_HEX_JD.mp3 |
| Slowpoke Win.mp3 | zapsplat_human_boy_3_years_old_british_laugh_001.mp3 |

Each of these sounds will be played just once when the corresponding slug wins a race, so you will hear just one of them in each race.

Finally, in the **Accidents** folder we have the following files:

| File Name in Slugrace | Original Zapsplat File Name |
|---|---|
| Asleep.mp3 | zapsplat_human_man_elderly_snore_20087.mp3 |
| Blind.mp3 | horror_eyes_gouged_out_001.mp3 |
| Broken Leg.mp3 | zapsplat_horror_gore_bone_arm_leg_break_crunch_57125.mp3 |
| Devoured.mp3 | fork_media_horror_monster_roar_growl_reverberant.mp3 |
| Drown.mp3 | zapsplat_nature_water_bubble_rise_underwater_002_20093.mp3 |
| Electroshock.mp3 | sound_design_effect_electricity_electric_arc.mp3 |
| Grass.mp3 | zapsplat_animals_slug_eat_designed_001_42438.mp3 |
| Heart Attack.mp3 | zapsplat_human_child_heartbeat_fast_26491.mp3 |
| Overheat.mp3 | Blastwave_FX_AcidBurnSizzle_S011SF.3.mp3 |
| Rubberizer.mp3 | zapsplat_foley_latext_glove_pull_stretch_squeak_006_12113.mp3 |
| Shooting Eyes.mp3 | warfare_gunshot_rifle_exterior_001.mp3 |
| Turning Back.mp3 | zapsplat_cartoon_voice_funny_gibberish_worried_scared_19920.mp3 |

Each of these sounds will be associated with one of the accidents. The names of the files are pretty self-explanatory. But, as mentioned above, we're not going to use these sounds for now.

OK, so now that we know all the sounds that we're going to use, let's start implementing them.

# Loading the Sounds

Just like we did in the test app, let's start by loading all the sounds that we're going to need. To this end, let's add a constructor method to the **Game** class that will take care of it:

```
# File name: main.py
...
from kivy.uix.label import Label

# We need to import the SoundLoader class.
from kivy.core.audio import SoundLoader

Builder.load_file('settings.kv')
...
class Game(ScreenManager):
    ...
    # game over
    ...
    game_is_over = BooleanProperty(False)

    # Here's the constructor method where we load all the sounds.
    def __init__(self, **kwargs):
        super().__init__(**kwargs)

        game_sounds = 'assets/sounds/Game/'
        slug_sounds = 'assets/Sounds/Slugs Winning/'

        self.background_music = SoundLoader.load(game_sounds + 'Background Music.mp3')
        self.slugs_running_sound = SoundLoader.load(game_sounds + 'Slugs Running.mp3')
        self.gameover_sound = SoundLoader.load(game_sounds + 'Game Over.mp3')
        self.go_sound = SoundLoader.load(game_sounds + 'Go.mp3')

        # These sounds are assigned to particular slugs.
        self.speedster.win_sound = SoundLoader.load(slug_sounds + 'Speedster Win.mp3')
        self.trusty.win_sound = SoundLoader.load(slug_sounds + 'Trusty Win.mp3')
        self.iffy.win_sound = SoundLoader.load(slug_sounds + 'Iffy Win.mp3')
        self.slowpoke.win_sound = SoundLoader.load(slug_sounds + 'Slowpoke Win.mp3')

    # callback methods
    ...
```

# Background Music

Let's handle the background music first. We want to hear it throughout the whole game, so from beginning to end. In particular, it should start as soon as we launch the app and stop when the game is over. So, we'll put the code that plays the music in the constructor of the **Game** class. The code that stops the music and unloads it from memory will be in the **gameover_screen** method:

```
# File name: main.py
...
class Game(ScreenManager):
    ...
    def __init__(self, **kwargs):
        ...
        self.slowpoke.win_sound = SoundLoader.load(slug_sounds + 'Slowpoke Win.mp3')

        # Here's the code that plays the background music.
        # Let's set the volume to 10% its full value.
        self.background_music.volume = .1

        # We make it loop.
        self.background_music.loop = True

        # And now let the music play.
        self.background_music.play()

    # callback methods
    ...
    def gameover_screen(self, dt):
        # We'll stop and unload the background music here.
        self.background_music.stop()
        self.background_music.unload()

        self.current = 'gameoverscreen'
        self.gameover_event.cancel()

    def reset_race(self):
        ...
```

Now if you run the app, you will hear the background music, pretty calm, from the very beginning of the game. When the game is over and the Game Over screen appears, the music will stop playing. It will also be unloaded from memory.

# The Slugs Running Sound

Next we're going to implement the sound that we will hear while the slugs are running. This sound should start playing in the **go** method and stop playing in the **finish_race** method when all slugs are done running:

```
# File name: main.py
...
class Game(ScreenManager):
    ...
    def go(self, screen_manager):
        # Let's play the slugs running sound
        # in a loop at 20% of its full volume.
        self.slugs_running_sound.volume = .2
        self.slugs_running_sound.loop = True
        self.slugs_running_sound.play()

        for slug in self.slugs:
            ...
    def finish_race(self, animation, slug):
        ...
            self.race_manager.transition.direction = 'left'

            # Now all slugs are done running so we can stop
            # the slugs running sound.
            self.slugs_running_sound.stop()

    def remove_bankrupt_players(self):
        ...
```

Run the app and start a race to hear the sound of the running slugs.

# The Go Sound

The next sound we're going to implement is the sound that we want to hear just once when a race begins. So, the best place to implement this sound is in the **go** method again:

```
# File name: main.py
...
class Game(ScreenManager):
    ...
    def go(self, screen_manager):
        # Let's play this sound once when a race starts. This sound is
        # pretty loud, so let's turn down the volume.
        self.go_sound.volume = .1
        self.go_sound.play()

        # slugs running sound
        self.slugs_running_sound.volume = .2
        ...
```

Run the app now and check out the sound you just implemented.

# The Game Over Sound

As you know, the background music stops playing when the game is over. Let's play the game over sound when this happens. A good place to implement this seems the **`gameover_screen`** method:

```
# File name: main.py
...
class Game(ScreenManager):
    ...
    def gameover_screen(self, dt):
        self.background_music.stop()
        self.background_music.unload()

        # Let's play the game over sound here.
        self.gameover_sound.volume = .1
        self.gameover_sound.play()

        self.current = 'gameoverscreen'
        ...
```

Run the app now and check out the game over sound.

Now, the last sounds we want to add at this moment are the sounds produced by each slug when he wins a race. Each slug will produce his own individual sound, so after a while you'll get used to them and you'll be able to recognize the winner by the sound. But I'll leave the implementation of the slugs' sounds for you as an exercise.

In the second exercise you'll take care of the Sound button in the Race screen. And in the next chapter we'll start talking about accidents in Slugrace. To implement the accidents, we'll make use of both animations and sounds.

# It's Your Turn Now...

**EXERCISE 1 - Slugs Winning Sounds**

Each slug should produce his individual sound when he wins. We assigned the sounds to the slugs in the **`__init__`** method, so now all we have to do is play the winning slug's win sound. So, find the location in the code where the race winner is known after each race and write the code that will play the race winner's sound. The sound should be played just once and you don't have to change its volume.

**SOLUTION**

So, the location where the race winner is known is the **`while_running`** method. This is where the win sound should be played.

Here's the code:

```
# File name: main.py
...
class Game(ScreenManager):
    ...
    def while_running(self, animation, slug, progression):
        if slug.right > self.finish_line:
            if not self.race_winner:
                self.race_winner = slug

                # We have the winner, so let's hear him
                # enjoy his victory.
                slug.win_sound.play()

                for player in self.players:
                    ...
```

Run the app a couple times and listen to the slugs' victory sounds.

**EXERCISE 2 - The Sound Button**

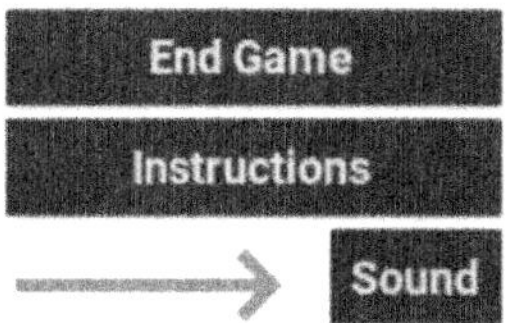


In this exercise you will take care of the Sound button. It will be used to mute and unmute the sound. If you now run the app, you will see the button under the other two buttons in the Info, Stats and Buttons area of the Race screen.

The button now displays the string **'Sound'**. But we want to use an icon instead. Actually, there are going to be two icons, one when the sound is unmuted and another one when it's muted. So, follow the steps below to handle the Sound button:

1. In the **Game** class, under the game over section, add another section, sound, and in it define a **sound_on** BooleanProperty with the default value set to **True**.

2. In the **race.kv** file find the location where the Sound button is defined. It looks like this:

```
#:kivy 1.11.1
# File name: race.kv
#:import race race
...
<RaceScreen>:
    ...
        ### INFO, STATS AND BUTTONS ###
        ...
            # Buttons
            ...
                RedButton:
                    text: 'Sound'
                    pos_hint: {'right': 1}
                    size: 70, 40

        ### THE TRACK ###
        ...
```

As you can see, it's a regular button. Let's rewrite it as a toggle button. This will require some work on your part.

Let's define the **SoundButton** class in the **widgets.py** and **widgets.kv** files. First, in the **widgets.py** file define the **SoundButton** class that inherits from **ToggleButton** and contains the **image_source** StringProperty set to an empty string. Don't forget to import the **StringProperty** and **ToggleButton** classes before.

In the **widgets.kv** file add the **SoundButton** class rule in the Buttons section, right below the **RedButton** rule. Set its background color to the same value as the **RedButton**'s, so **(.8, 0, 0, 1)**. Use the **pos_hint** property to position the toggle button on the right. The size of the button should be 70 by 40 (don't forget to set **size_hint** accordingly). And, the most important element to add is an image, so add an instance of the **Image** class to the **SoundButton** and set its **source** property to the **image_source** StringProperty you just defined in the **widgets.py** file. Also, set the image's **pos** and **size** properties to the SoundButton's **pos** and **size** values.

Now in the **race.kv** file replace the sound RedButton by SoundButton and set its **image_source** property so that the **sound_on.png** image (that you can find directly in the **assets** folder) is shown if the **sound_on** property that you defined in the **Game** class is **True** and the **sound_off.png** image is shown otherwise. Use a ternary **if** statement to do it.

3. Now let's add some functionality to the SoundButton. Actually, it should be quite simple. If you press the button, it will mute all the sounds in the game. When the button is pressed again and returns to its normal state, the sounds will be unmuted.

But, first of all, we have to make it possible to manage all the sounds in a comfortable way. The easiest way to do it is by putting all the sounds in a list in the constructor of the **Game** class where they are loaded in the first place. So, in the **__init__** method of the **Game** class, below the code that loads all the sounds, add a **sounds** list that contains all the sounds.

Next, in the callback methods section let's add the **mute_unmute** method that will be called when the SoundButton is pressed. The method should take three arguments: **self**, **instance** and **value**. The last one of the three refers to the state of the toggle button. If the state of the toggle button is **'down'**, the method should do the following:

- set the **sound_on** property to **False** so that the right icon is displayed on the Sound button,

- set all sounds' volumes to 0, but first save their default volumes so that we can restore them later (you can name the variable to store the default volume **default_volume** to keep things simple).

Otherwise, so if the toggle button is no longer pressed, the method should do the following:

- set the **sound_on** property to **True** so that the right icon is displayed on the Sound button,

- restore all sounds' volumes

Finally, with the **mute_unmute** method in place, add an **on_state** event to the SoundButton in the **race.kv** file that just calls the **mute_unmute** method whenever the state of the toggle button changes. Don't forget to pass ***args** to the method call because the method takes a couple arguments.

4. There's still one problem. Although you mute the sounds, you will still hear some of them, like the start signal and the sound of the running slugs. This is because their volumes are set directly before the sounds are played, so even if they're set to 0 in the **mute_unmute** method, they will be

reset to other values anyway, like in the **go** and **gameover_screen** methods.

This can be solved in a couple ways. You can just move the code that sets the volumes of all the sounds to the constructor of the **Game** class where they are loaded. So, below the code that loads the sounds set the volumes of the following sounds:

- **slugs_running_sound** to **.2**

- **go_sound** to **.1**

- **gameover_sound** to **.1**

Then remove the code that sets the volume from the **go** and **gameover_screen** methods accordingly.

## SOLUTION

So, in this exercise we modified quite a few files. Here's the **main.py** file with all the modifications:

```
# File name: main.py
...
class Game(ScreenManager):
    ...
    # game over
    ...
    game_is_over = BooleanProperty(False)

    # Sound
    sound_on = BooleanProperty(True)

    def __init__(self, **kwargs):
        ...
        self.slowpoke.win_sound = SoundLoader.load(slug_sounds + 'Slowpoke Win.mp3')

        # Here are the default volumes (if different than 1)
        self.slugs_running_sound.volume = .2
        self.go_sound.volume = .1
        self.gameover_sound.volume = .1

        # Here's the list of all the sounds in the app.
        self.sounds = [self.background_music,
                       self.slugs_running_sound,
                       self.gameover_sound,
                       self.go_sound,
                       self.speedster.win_sound,
                       self.trusty.win_sound,
                       self.iffy.win_sound,
                       self.slowpoke.win_sound]
```

```
        # background music
        self.background_music.volume = .1
        ...
    # callback methods
    ...
    def go(self, screen_manager):
        # go sound (without setting the volume)
        self.go_sound.play()

        # slugs running sound (without setting the volume)
        self.slugs_running_sound.loop = True
        self.slugs_running_sound.play()

        for slug in self.slugs:
            ...
    def gameover_screen(self, dt):
        self.background_music.stop()
        self.background_music.unload()

        # Let's play the game over sound (without setting the volume).
        self.gameover_sound.play()

        self.current = 'gameoverscreen'
        self.gameover_event.cancel()

    def reset_race(self):
        ...
    def reset_players(self):
        ...
    # This method is used to mute and unmute sounds.
    def mute_unmute(self, instance, value):
        # If the toggle button is pressed...
        if value == 'down':
            # 1. Set the sound_on property to False so that the right
            # icon is displayed on the Sound button.
            self.sound_on = False
            # 2. Set all sounds' volumes to 0, but first save their
            # default volumes so that we can restore them later.
            for sound in self.sounds:
                sound.default_volume = sound.volume
                sound.volume = 0

        # If the toggle button is back in normal state...
        else:
            # 1. Set the sound_on property to True so that the right
            # icon is displayed on the Sound button.
            self.sound_on = True

            # 2. Restore all sounds' volumes.
            for sound in self.sounds:
                sound.volume = sound.default_volume

class SlugraceApp(App):
    ...
```

Here's the **widgets.py** file:

```
# File name: widgets.py

from kivy.uix.textinput import TextInput
from kivy.app import App

# We'll need the StringProperty class as well.
from kivy.properties import NumericProperty, StringProperty

# We'll need the ToggleButton class to inherit from.
from kivy.uix.togglebutton import ToggleButton

class NameInput(TextInput):
    ...

class NumInput(TextInput):
    ...

# Here's the SoundButton class that inherits from ToggleButton.
# It contains the image_source StringProperty.
class SoundButton(ToggleButton):
    image_source = StringProperty('')
```

Here's the **widgets.kv** file:

```
#:kivy 1.11.1
# File name: widgets.kv
#:import widgets widgets
...
### BUTTONS ###
<RedButton@Button>:
    ...

# Here's the SoundButton class rule.
<SoundButton>:
    background_color: .8, 0, 0, 1
    pos_hint: {'right': 1}
    size_hint: (None, None)
    size: 70, 40
    Image:
        source: root.image_source
        pos: root.pos
        size: root.size

### TEXTINPUTS ###
...
```

Here's the **race.kv** file:

```
#:kivy 1.11.1
# File name: race.kv
#:import race race
...
<RaceScreen>:
    ...
        ### INFO, STATS AND BUTTONS ###
        ...
            # Buttons
            BoxLayout:
                ...
                RedButton:
                    text: 'Instructions'
                    pos_hint: {'right': 1}

                # Here's the SoundButton toggle button.
                SoundButton:
                    # It will show one of the two icons (for sound on and sound off)
                    # depending on the value of the sound_on property.
                    image_source: 'assets/sound_on.png' if root.game.sound_on else 'assets/sound_off.png'

                    # If the state of the toggle button changes, the mute_unmute method
                    # should be called.
                    on_state: root.game.mute_unmute(*args)

        ### THE TRACK ###
        ...
```

That's it. If you now run the app, you should be able to mute and unmute the sounds at any time. You will also see the icon on the Sound button change.

Here's the button when the sound is unmuted.

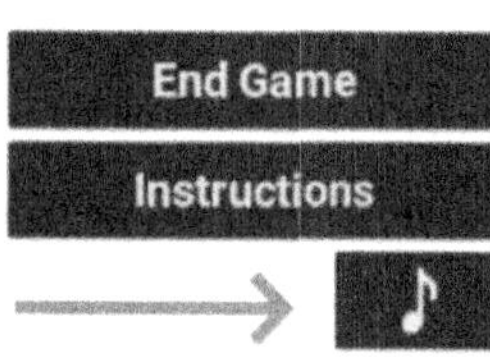


And here it is when the sound is muted.

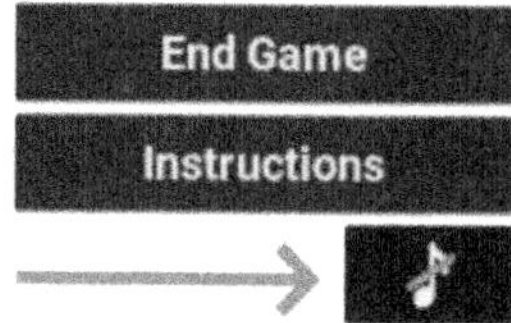


**EXERCISE 3 - Unload All Sounds**

Let's unload all the sounds that we no longer need. In the **gameover_screen** method remove the line of code that unloads the background music. Below the code that stops the background music add code that will unload all the sounds except the gameover sound (because otherwise we wouldn't be able to hear the latter).

Then, in the **gameover.kv** file add code to both buttons' **on_press** events that will unload the gameover sound.

**SOLUTION**

Here's the **main.py** file:

```
# File name: main.py
...
class Game(ScreenManager):
    ...
    def gameover_screen(self, dt):
        self.background_music.stop()

        # Unload all sounds except gameover_sound.
        for sound in self.sounds:
            if sound != self.gameover_sound:
                sound.unload()

        self.gameover_sound.play()
        ...
```

And here's the **gameover.kv** file:

```
#:kivy 1.11.1
# File name: gameover.kv
#:import gameover gameover

<GameoverScreen>:
    ...
        # the buttons
        BoxLayout:
            ...
            RedButton:
                text: 'Play Again'
                pos_hint: {'x': 0, 'center_y': .5}
                on_press:
                    root.game.reset_players()

                    # unload the gamover sound
                    root.game.gameover_sound.unload()

                    app.restart()
            RedButton:
                text: 'Quit'
                pos_hint: {'right': 1, 'center_y': .5}
                on_press:
                    # unload the gamover sound
                    root.game.gameover_sound.unload()

                    app.quit()
```

Now all sounds will be unloaded before you restart or quit the game.

# Chapter 106 – Accidents in the Slugrace App

In the preceding chapters we were talking about animations and sounds in Kivy. Now that we know how to use them, let's add some pizzazz to our project. Accidents happen, also to slugs. During a race an accident may happen to one of the slugs. It's not going to be very frequent, but still, it may influence the result of the race when it happens. I'm using the name 'accident' here to keep things simple, but some of them may be convenient for a slug and even help him win.

Anyway, whatever happens, it will only have consequences in the race in which it happens. In the next race the affected slug will be up and running again.

In this chapter we'll have a look at all the accidents that may happen and in the following chapters we'll be implementing them one by one. Each accident will have a graphical representation, which you can see below. So, here are the accidents that may happen to the slugs:

## Broken Leg

If this accident happens, the slug stops moving and doesn't even make it to the finish line. This race is lost.

## Overheating

Overheating means stopping and not being able to continue the race either.

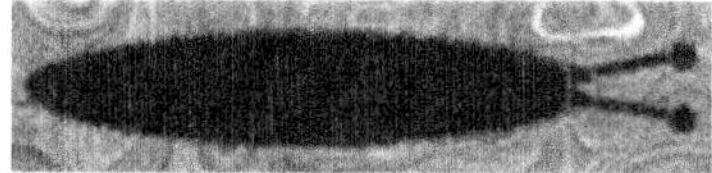

## Heart Attack

If a slug suffers from a heart attack, it's definitely not convenient either. The race is over for that slug. He needs a rest. His heart is beating like crazy, which you can see and hear. You will see a small heart image on top of the affected slug.

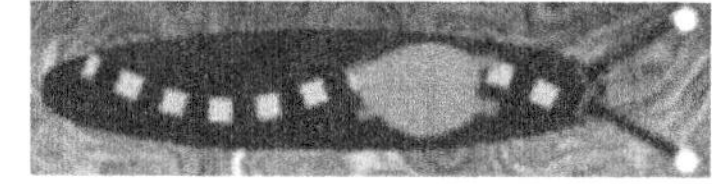

## Power Grass

This is the first accident that may be very convenient actually. First, some magic grass appears on the racetrack, just in front of the slug, and he stops to eat it, which takes a while. But the grass powers him up and then he starts racing much faster than before.

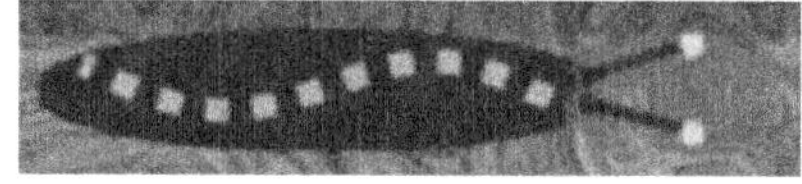

## Falling Asleep

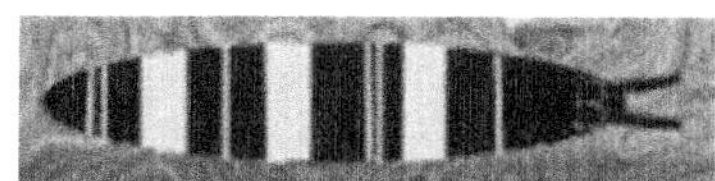

Falling asleep during a race is never a good idea. The slug stops and starts breathing slowly. You can hear him snore and see some changes in his size when the sleeping animation is played.

## Going Blind

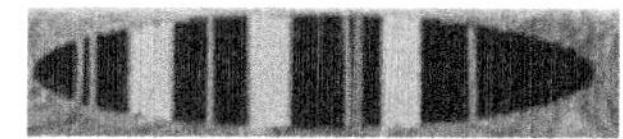

If a slug goes blind, he doesn't stop running, but without his eyes he starts staggering, so winning the race becomes pretty difficult.

## Drowning in a Puddle

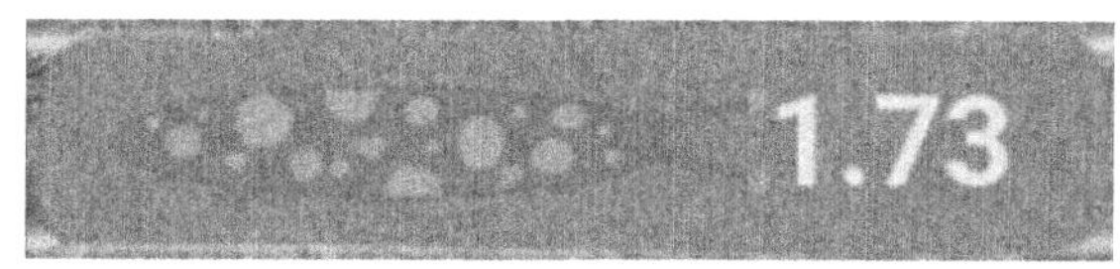


Drowning sucks. When this accident happens, a puddle of water appears on the racetrack and when the slug enters it, he drown. The slug becomes less and less visible under the water until he disappears completely.

## Electroshock

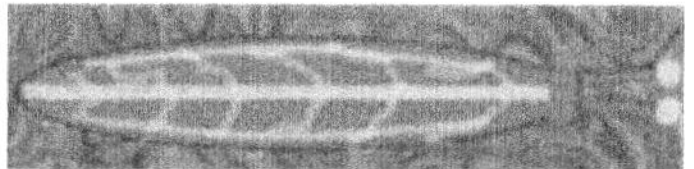

An electroshock is good, at least for a slug. Not only doesn't it kill him, but it even speeds him up considerably, which often results in a vistory. You'll see a pulsating bolt on the slug's back.

## Turning Back

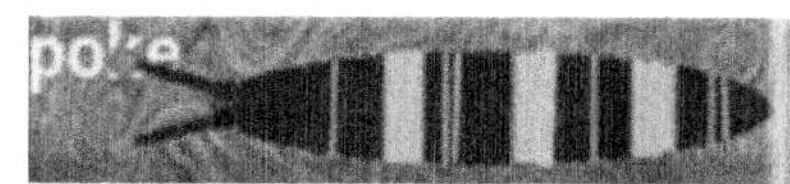

Sometimes a slug forgets something and turns back. By doing so he looses his chances of winning.

## Shooting Eyes

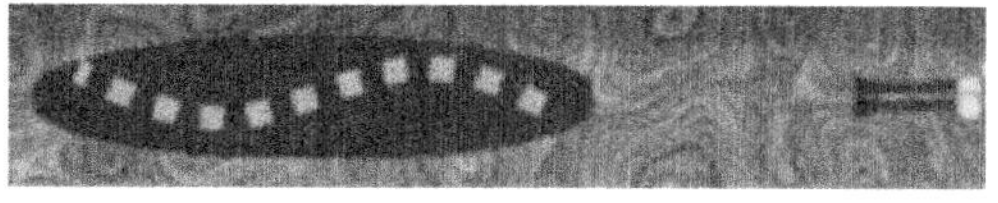

Our slugs are smart and sometimes they cheat. They can shoot their eyes. When this happens, the eyes start moving much faster than the rest of the body, helping the slug to win.

## Stretching Like Rubber

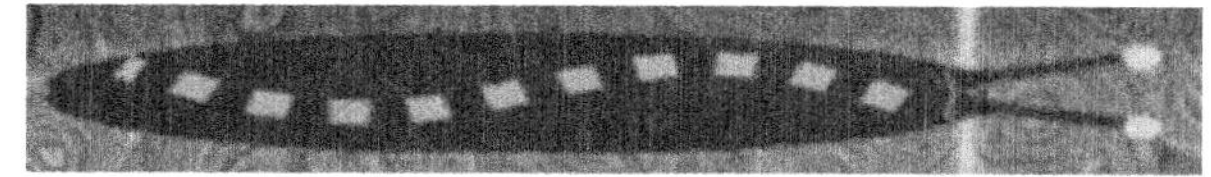

Slugs may also cheat in a different way. They can strech like rubber, which also helps them win.

## Slug Monster

Finally, a slug may be eaten by the horrifying slug monster. Being devoured is never good.

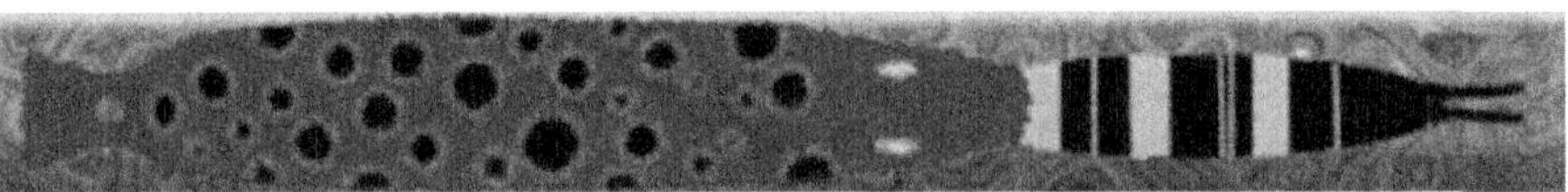

So, these are all the accidents that may happen in the game. In the next chapter we'll implement some classes that we will need for the accidents. And there's no exercise for you this time.

# Chapter 107 – Accident Classes

In the previous chapter we were talking about the accidents that may occasionally happen to our slugs. But we didn't implement them yet. This is what we are going to do in this chapter.

## The **Accident** Abstract Class

We're going to implement a bunch of classes that will be used for our accidents, one class for each accident, to be precise. But as there's a lot of functionality that is common and may be shared by all the accident classes, let's first create one base class and then make subclasses of it.

So, to keep things clear and organized, let's add the accident-related code in a separate file. We already created the **accident.py** file, but for now it's empty. In the file let's create a new class, **Accident**. Here's the code:

```
# File name: accident.py

class Accident:
    pass
```

The point is that we actually don't want to be able to create objects of that class. We want to be able to create objects of its subclasses, like **BrokenLegAccident** or **HeartAttackAccident**, but not **Accident** itself.

In order to prevent a class from being instantiated, we should define it as an abstract class. To do that, our class should inherit from the **ABC** class defined in the **abc** module and contain abstract methods.

So, let's make our class inherit from **ABC**:

```
# File name: accident.py

# We need to import the ABC class
# for our class to inherit from.
from abc import ABC

# Now the class inherits from ABC.
class Accident(ABC):
    pass
```

As mentioned above, we also need abstract methods. Without abstract methods it's still possible to instantiate an abstract class. Try this code out:

```
# File name: accident.py

from abc import ABC

class Accident(ABC):
    pass

accident = Accident()
print(accident)
```

Here we're instantiating the class and printing it out. If you run the **accident.py** file, you should see something like this in the terminal:

```
<__main__.Accident object at 0x00000228269C8948>
```

So, we have an object of the abstract class. In order to no longer be able to instantiate an abstract class, let's add abstract methods to it.

Abstract methods are methods that must be implemented in the subclasses. In the base class they may be either not implemented at all or implemented partially. But the real implementation, which is going to be different for each subclass, will be in the subclasses. To mark a method as abstract, you should use the **@abstractmethod** decorator.

Our **Accident** class is going to contain two abstract methods, **happen** and **reset**. These two methods will be implemented by each subclass differently, but the general idea behind the former is to run code that takes care of the accident itself, like stopping a slug, playing an animation, a sound, adding some visuals and so on.

The **reset** method will take care of bringing the slug who suffered from an accident to his original state after each race.

This is because, as I mentioned before, even if an accident happens to a slug, as soon as the race is over everything goes back to normal and the slug is up and running again, ready to take part in the next race.

Here are our two abstract methods:

```
# File name: accident.py

# We need to import the abstractmethod
# decorator as well.
from abc import ABC, abstractmethod

class Accident(ABC):
    # Here are the two abstract
    # methods.They do nothing for now.
    @abstractmethod
    def happen(self):
        pass

    @abstractmethod
    def reset(self):
        pass

accident = Accident()
print(accident)
```

If you now run this code, you will get an error because you can't instantiate the class anymore. This is what you should see in the terminal:

```
TypeError: Can't instantiate abstract class Accident with abstract methods happen, reset
```

You can't instantiate a class if it contains at least one abstract method. So, let's remove the last two lines of code where we're trying to instantiate the class and print it out.

# The __init__ Method

Each accident will contain some properties to store data, in particular:

- **name** – a simple name like **'Electroshock'** or **'Overheat'**,

- **headlines** – a list of messages that are associated with the accident and displayed for the app user to see what happened,

- **sound** – the sound that you can hear when the accident happens,

- **position** – the position along the track at which the accident happens,

- **slug** – the slug to which the accident happens,

- **image** – the image associated with the accident.

Let's set it all up in the constructor. By default **position** will be set to **0**, **slug** and **image** to **None**.

We'll also set the **intro** attribute on the **Accident** class that will be shared by all objects of the **Accident** subclasses.

It's going to be a simple string that will be displayed in a popup window that will appear when an accident happens.

So, having said that, let's jump into the code.

Here it is:

```
# File name: accident.py

from abc import ABC, abstractmethod

# We need SoundLoader to load sounds.
from kivy.core.audio import SoundLoader

class Accident(ABC):
    # This string will be displayed if
    # any accident happens.
    intro = 'BREAKING NEWS: '

    # the constructor
    def __init__(self, name,
                 headlines,
                 sound,
                 position = 0,
                 slug = None,
                 image = None):
        self.name = name
        self.headlines = headlines
        self.sound = SoundLoader.load(sound)
        self.position = position
        self.slug = slug
        self.image = image

    @abstractmethod
    def happen(self):
        ...
```

# The Subclasses

With the base class in place, let's create the subclasses. We need one subclass for each accident type. As for now, we're not going to implement the **happen** and **reset** methods just yet, but we know they must be implemented, so we'll put them there.

We will define the headlines for each class. This is a list of strings, one of which will be randomly picked and displayed in the popup window when an accident happens.

We will also define the **name** and **sound** properties for each accident, and, for some of the classes, also the **image** property.

Here's the code:

```
# File name: accident.py
...
class Accident(ABC):
    ...
```

```
### BROKEN LEG ###
class BrokenLegAccident(Accident):
    name = 'Broken Leg'

    headlines = [
        "just broke his leg and is grounded!",
        "broke his leg, which is practically all he consists of!",
        "suffered from an open fracture. All he can do now is watch the others win!",
        "broke his only leg and now looks pretty helpless!",
        "tripped over a root and broke his leg!"]

    sound = 'assets/sounds/Accidents/Broken Leg.mp3'

    def __init__(self, **kwargs):
        super().__init__(name=self.name, headlines=self.headlines,
                         sound=self.sound, **kwargs)

    def happen(self):
        pass

    def reset(self):
        pass

### OVERHEAT ###
class OverheatAccident(Accident):
    name = 'Overheat'

    headlines = [
        "has been running faster than he should have. He burned of overheat!",
        "burned by friction. Needs to cool down a bit before the next race!",
        "roasted on the track from overheat. He's been running way too fast!",
        "looks like he has been running faster than his body cooling system can handle!",
        "shouldn't have been speeding like that. Overheating can be dangerous!"]

    sound = 'assets/sounds/Accidents/Overheat.mp3'

    def __init__(self, **kwargs):
        super().__init__(name=self.name, headlines=self.headlines,
                         sound=self.sound, **kwargs)

    def happen(self):
        pass

    def reset(self):
        pass

### HEART ATTACK ###
class HeartAttackAccident(Accident):
    name = 'Heart Attack'

    headlines = [
        "had a heart attack. Definitely needs a rest!",
        "has a poor heart condition. Hadn't he stopped now, it could have killed him!",
```

```
        "beaten by cardiac infarction. He'd better go to hospital asap!",
        "almost killed by heart attack. He had a really narrow escape!",
        "beaten by his weak heart. He'd better get some rest!"]

    sound = 'assets/sounds/Accidents/Heart Attack.mp3'
    image = 'atlas://assets/accidents/accidents/heart attack'

    def __init__(self, **kwargs):
        super().__init__(name=self.name, headlines=self.headlines,
                         sound=self.sound, image=self.image, **kwargs)

    def happen(self):
        pass

    def reset(self):
        pass

### GRASS ###
class GrassAccident(Accident):
    name = 'Grass'

    headlines = [
        "just found magic grass. It's famous for powering slugs up!",
        "just about to speed up after eating magic grass!",
        "powered up by magic grass found unexpectedly on the track!",
        "seems to be full of beans after having eaten the magic grass on his way!",
        "heading perhaps even for victory after his magic grass meal!"]

    sound = 'assets/sounds/Accidents/Grass.mp3'
    image = 'atlas://assets/accidents/accidents/grass'

    def __init__(self, **kwargs):
        super().__init__(name=self.name, headlines=self.headlines,
                         sound=self.sound, image=self.image, **kwargs)

    def happen(self):
        pass

    def reset(self):
        pass

### ASLEEP ###
class AsleepAccident(Accident):
    name = 'Asleep'

    headlines = [
        "just fell asleep for a while after the long and wearisome running!",
        "having a nap. He again has chosen just the perfect time for that!",
        "sleeping instead of running. It's getting one of his bad habits!",
        "always takes a short nap at this time of the day, no matter what he's doing!",
        "knows how important sleep is. Even if it's not the best time for that!"]

    sound = 'assets/sounds/Accidents/Asleep.mp3'
```

```
    def __init__(self, **kwargs):
        super().__init__(name=self.name, headlines=self.headlines,
                         sound=self.sound, **kwargs)

    def happen(self):
        pass

    def reset(self):
        pass

### BLIND ###
class BlindAccident(Accident):
    name = 'Blind'

    headlines = [
        "gone blind. Now staggering to find his way!",
        "shouldn't have been reading in dark. Now it's hard to find the way!",
        "temporarily lost his eyesight. Now it's difficult for him to follow the track!",
        "trying hard to find his way after going blind on track!",
        "staggering to finish the race after going blind because of an infection!"]

    sound = 'assets/sounds/Accidents/Blind.mp3'

    def __init__(self, **kwargs):
        super().__init__(name=self.name, headlines=self.headlines,
                         sound=self.sound, **kwargs)

    def happen(self):
        pass

    def reset(self):
        pass

### PUDDLE ###
class PuddleAccident(Accident):
    name = 'Puddle'

    headlines = [
        "drowning in a puddle of water!",
        "beaten by yesterday's heavy rainfalls. Just drowning in a puddle!",
        "shouldn't have skipped his swimming lessons. Drowning in a puddle now!",
        "has always neglected his swimming lessons. How wrong he’s been!",
        "disappearing in a puddle of water formed afted heavy rainfall!"]

    sound = 'assets/sounds/Accidents/Drown.mp3'
    image = 'atlas://assets/accidents/accidents/puddle'

    def __init__(self, **kwargs):
        super().__init__(name=self.name, headlines=self.headlines,
                         sound=self.sound, image=self.image, **kwargs)

    def happen(self):
        pass
```

```
    def reset(self):
        pass

### ELECTROSHOCK ###
class ElectroshockAccident(Accident):
    name = 'Electroshock'

    headlines = [
        "speeding up after being struck by lightning!",
        "powered up by lightning. Now running really fast!",
        "hit by electric discharge. Seems to have been powered up by it!",
        "accelerated by a series of electric discharges!",
        "now running much faster after being struck by lightning!"]

    sound = 'assets/sounds/Accidents/Electroshock.mp3'
    image = 'atlas://assets/accidents/accidents/electroshock'

    def __init__(self, **kwargs):
        super().__init__(name=self.name, headlines=self.headlines,
                         sound=self.sound, image=self.image, **kwargs)

    def happen(self):
        pass

    def reset(self):
        pass

### TURNING BACK ###
class TurningBackAccident(Accident):
    name = 'Turning Back'

    headlines = [
        "has forgotten to turn off the gas. Must hurry home before it's too late!",
        "just received a phone call. His house is on fire. No time to lose!",
        "seems to have more interesting stuff to do than racing.",
        "seems to have lost orientation. Well, how these little brains work!",
        "has left his snack in the kitchen. He won't race when he's hungry!"]

    sound = 'assets/sounds/Accidents/Turning Back.mp3'

    def __init__(self, **kwargs):
        super().__init__(name=self.name, headlines=self.headlines,
                         sound=self.sound, **kwargs)

    def happen(self):
        pass

    def reset(self):
        pass

### SHOOTING EYES ###
class ShootingEyesAccident(Accident):
    name = 'Shooting Eyes'
```

```
    headlines = [
        "shooting his eyes. Is he ever going to stop cheating?",
        "just shot his eyes. It seems he would do anything to win!",
        "sacrificing his eyes for victory's sake!",
        "shooting his eyes for victory and hoping for quick regeneration!",
        "too slow to win? Maybe him, but who knows, possibly not his eyes!"]

    sound = 'assets/sounds/Accidents/Shooting Eyes.mp3'

    def __init__(self, **kwargs):
        super().__init__(name=self.name, headlines=self.headlines,
                         sound=self.sound, **kwargs)

    def happen(self):
        pass

    def reset(self):
        pass

### RUBBERIZED ###
class RubberizedAccident(Accident):
    name = 'Rubberized'

    headlines = [
        "stretching like rubber. This can help!",
        "stretching for victory. Seems to be approaching finish line faster!",
        "has never forgotten he was an eraser as a kid.",
        "cheating again. This time pretending to be a piece of rubber!",
        "just discovered his ability to stretch like rubber. Why not use it right now?"]

    sound = 'assets/sounds/Accidents/Rubberizer.mp3'

    def __init__(self, **kwargs):
        super().__init__(name=self.name, headlines=self.headlines,
                         sound=self.sound, **kwargs)

    def happen(self):
        pass

    def reset(self):
        pass

### DEVOURED ###
class DevouredAccident(Accident):
    name = 'Devoured'

    headlines = [
        "devoured by the infamous slug monster. Bad luck!",
        "just swallowed by the terrible slug monster!",
        "next on the long list of the slug monster's victims!",
        "has never suspected he's gonna end up as a snack!",
        "devoured by the legendary slug monster from the nearby swamps!"]

    sound = 'assets/sounds/Accidents/Devoured.mp3'
```

```
    image = 'atlas://assets/accidents/accidents/slug monster'

    def __init__(self, **kwargs):
        super().__init__(name=self.name, headlines=self.headlines,
                         sound=self.sound, image=self.image, **kwargs)

    def happen(self):
        pass

    def reset(self):
        pass
```

In the next chapter we'll add some code in the **main.py** file that will handle accidents. After that we'll be able to implement the accidents one by one.

# Chapter 108 – Accident Logic

In the previous chapter we created the abstract **Accident** class and a bunch of its subclasses. We'll need all these classes in the **main.py** file, so let's start by importing them there:

```
# File name: main.py
...
from kivy.core.audio import SoundLoader

# Let's import the accident classes.
from accident import *

Builder.load_file('settings.kv')
...
```

## Instantiating Accident Classes

In this chapter we're going to add some accident-related logic into the game. We'll need instances of the accident classes, so let's instantiate them now. Let's also create a list of all the accidents. We can put all the instantiation code in the constructor of the **Game** class:

```
# File name: main.py
...
class Game(ScreenManager):
    ...
    def __init__(self, **kwargs):
        ...
        self.background_music.play()

        # accidents
        self.acc_broken_leg = BrokenLegAccident()
        self.acc_overheat = OverheatAccident()
        self.acc_heart_attack = HeartAttackAccident()
        self.acc_grass = GrassAccident()
        self.acc_asleep = AsleepAccident()
        self.acc_blind = BlindAccident()
        self.acc_puddle = PuddleAccident()
        self.acc_electroshock = ElectroshockAccident()
        self.acc_turning_back = TurningBackAccident()
        self.acc_shooting_eyes = ShootingEyesAccident()
        self.acc_rubberized = RubberizedAccident()
        self.acc_devoured = DevouredAccident()

        self.accidents = [self.acc_broken_leg,
                          self.acc_overheat,
                          self.acc_heart_attack,
                          self.acc_grass,
                          self.acc_asleep,
```

```
                                          self.acc_blind,
                                          self.acc_puddle,
                                          self.acc_electroshock,
                                          self.acc_turning_back,
                                          self.acc_shooting_eyes,
                                          self.acc_rubberized,
                                          self.acc_devoured]

    # callback methods
    ...
```

## When Should an Accident Happen?

And now it's time to ask a couple simple questions (and answer them):

1) How often should an accident happen?

Well, we definitely don't want an accident to happen in each and every race. First of all, we don't want it to happen in the first 5 races at all. Starting from race 6 there should be an accident every couple races. To achieve that we'll use the **randint** function from the **random** module to randomly pick an integer between 0 and 3. As both 0 and 3 are included, there are four possibilities, so the accident has a 25% chance of happening.

2) Which accident should happen?

The accident should be picked by chance from the accident list. To do that we'll use the **choice** function from the **random** module.

3) Where should the accident happen?

Let's say we don't want the accident to happen too early, like immediately after a race starts, or too late, like just before the finish line. A good position for an accident to happen seems like between 290 and 500, which is the distance along the X axis from the left border of the racetrack and is to be understood as the value of the slug's **x** property. Again, we're going to use the **randint** function to pick an integer between 290 and 500.

4) Which slug should the accident happen to?

The accident may happen to any slug. We'll use the **choice** function to pick one of the slugs. But, as Trusty's name suggests that we should trust him more than the other slugs, if this slug is picked by the function, the function is called again, so Trusty is the least probable slug to be picked.

And one more question, now about the code. Where exactly should the program decide whether or not there should be an accident and if so, which one it should be, where it should happen and to which slug? This decision must be taken at the beginning of each race, so the **go** method seems the right place. Let's add the lines of code that will take care of all this:

```
# File name: main.py
...
from datetime import timedelta

# We also need the randint function.
from random import choice, randint

from kivy.clock import Clock
...
class Game(ScreenManager):
    ...
    def go(self, screen_manager):
        ...
        self.race_manager = screen_manager

        # Accident
        # Should there be an accident? Yes, but only if the randomly picked number is 0.
        # There should be no accident in the first five races.
        self.accident_expected = (randint(0, 3) == 0
                                  if self.race_number > 5
                                  else False)

        # If there is going to be an accident...
        if self.accident_expected:
            # ... which exactly is it going to be?
            self.accident = choice(self.accidents)

            # ... what position should it happen at?
            self.accident.position = randint(290, 500)

            # ... which slug should it happen to?
            self.accident.slug = choice(self.slugs)
            # If it's Trusty, let's try again.
            if self.accident.slug == self.trusty:
                self.accident.slug = choice(self.slugs)

    def while_running(self, animation, slug, progression):
        ...
```

In the **go** method the program decides if an accident should happen, and if so, which one, where and to which slug. But the accident doesn't happen just yet. For and accident to happen, its **happen** method must be called, so let's take care of it next.

# Let the Accident Happen

As you know, there's the **while_running** method that is repeatedly called while a slug's running animation is in progress. This method checks whether the slug is the winner of the race and whether the game should be over. It also updates the players and slugs and removes bankrupt players. So, this function does a lot of things. Let's make it also responsible for calling the **happen** method if there should be an accident.

So, first the method should check whether **accident_expected** is set to **True** and whether this particular slug is the one to which the accident should happen. Only if these two conditions are met, should it call the **happen** method. But before it does, the method checks whether the slug is at the position at which the accident should happen. If this condition is also met, the **happen** method is called.

Just one remark about the accident position. We don't want to miss the position, which may happen if we compare the exact position of the slug with the accident position. That's why the accident should happen if the slug is within a certain range around the accident position. To make sure it's called only once, the **accident_expected** attribute is reset to **False**. Let's see the code:

```
# File name: main.py
...
class Game(ScreenManager):
    ...
    def while_running(self, animation, slug, progression):
        if slug.right > self.finish_line:
            ...
                self.gameover_check()

        # Accident
        # If an accident is supposed to happen and the slug is the one to which
        # it should happen...
        if self.accident_expected and slug == self.accident.slug:
            # ... and if the slug is near the position at which it should happen...
            if self.accident.position < slug.x < self.accident.position + 10:
            # ... let it actually happen.
                self.accident.happen()
                # To prevent the accident from happening again while the slug is
                # still in the range around the accident position, let's set
                # the accident_expected attribute to False.
                self.accident_expected = False

    def finish_race(self, animation, slug):
        ...
```

# Testing the Accidents

With the logic in place, let's test our accidents. But to do it painlessly, let's temporarily modify the code in the **go** method so that the **accident_expected** attribute is always **True**. This way an accident will happen in each race.

You can just comment out the part of the code that we want to temporarily disable and set the attribute to **True**:

```
# File name: main.py
...
class Game(ScreenManager):
    ...
    def go(self, screen_manager):
        ...
        # Accident
        # self.accident_expected = (randint(0, 3) == 0
        #                           if self.race_number > 5
        #                           else False)
        self.accident_expected = True

        if self.accident_expected:
            ...
```

Now, to keep things simple, we'll just print out a message to the terminal with the name and position of the accident and the name of the slug to which the accident happens.

As you know, we have the abstract method **happen** defined in the abstract class **Accident**. An abstract method in an abstract class doesn't have to be empty. It may have some basic implementation, which can be used and expanded or overridden by the implementations in the subclasses. In our case we'll put the code that should be executed whenever any of the accidents happens and more specific implementation for each particular accident type will be placed inside the appropriate subclasses.

So, let's now put some code in the abstract class that should be executed for any accident. For now it's going to print a message to the terminal, as mentioned above. Here's the code:

```
# File name: accident.py
...
class Accident(ABC):
    ...
    @abstractmethod
    def happen(self):
        info = f'accident: {self.name} | position: {self.position} | slug: {self.slug.name}'
        print(info)

    @abstractmethod
    def reset(self):
        ...
```

Naturally, the message won't be printed now because the **happen** methods of the particular subclasses haven't been implemented yet. For now we want all the subclasses to implement them in exactly the same way as the base class. This is very easy to do. You just have to use the **super** keyword to refer to the base class and call its **happen** method. So, in each of the subclasses add the following line of code in the **happen** method:

```
super().happen()
```

So, the line of code should be added 12 times altogether. Here's what it should look like in the first accident subclass, but in the other subclasses it should look exactly the same.

```
# File name: accident.py
...
### BROKEN LEG ###
class BrokenLegAccident(Accident):
    ...
    def happen(self):
        super().happen()

    def reset(self):
        ...
```

So, let's run the app and watch the terminal. Here are the accidents that happened in the first five races when I ran the app:

```
accident: Rubberized | position: 425 | slug: Iffy
accident: Turning Back | position: 312 | slug: Iffy
accident: Devoured | position: 482 | slug: Trusty
accident: Overheat | position: 465 | slug: Speedster
accident: Blind | position: 312 | slug: Speedster
```

Naturally, the output will be different each time you run your app. Now that we have our accidents tested and see that they work, it's time to implement them one by one. In the next chapter we'll be implementing the Broken Leg accident. But before we do that, there's an exercise for you. Instead of the message we just saw printed in the terminal, we want a popup window to show up. This popup window should contain information about the accident. We already created a popup window that appears when the game is over and you hit the Quit button, so you may want to have a look at it again before you start creating the window.

# It's Your Turn Now...

### EXERCISE

In this exercise you're going to create a popup window with information about the accident. It should appear whenever any of the accidents happens, so the code should go to the abstract **happen** method in the base class. The window is going to contain a headline informing us what happened and the silhouette image of the slug to which the accident happened. Follow the steps below to create the popup window.

1) To create the popup we're going to need some classes, so import them in the **accident.py** file. In particular, we're going to need the following classes: **Popup**, **Label**, **Image**, **BoxLayout**. You can read the documentation to check which modules they sit in, but we already used all of them before, so you can just browse through the code to find them.

2) Remove the code in the abstract **happen** method that prints the message to the terminal that we just added. Make sure NOT to remove the calls to the base class's **happen** method in the subclasses.

3) We can now start creating the popup. This code should go in the abstract **happen** method inside the **Accident** class.

In the popup a headline will be displayed. As you look at the subclasses, you can see that each of them has its own list of five possible headlines. We need only one each time an accident happens, so use the **choice** function (which you must import first) to randomly pick a headline. Assign the headline returned by the **choice** function to the **headline** variable.

4) As you look at the headlines, you can see that these are sentences without subjects. This is because the subject is going to be the name of the slug to which the accident happened. So, the whole headline should consist of the name of the slug followed by the rest of the text. But we want the headline to be formatted using markup text. We talked about markup text in Kivy in one of the first chapters of the course, so you can have a look at it again if you need a refresher.

Anyway, we're going to create a label with the headline text. As we want to use markup, we must set the **markup** property of the label to **True**. Now, as far as the **text** property is concerned, it should be set to an f-string (so a string preceded by the prefix **f**). Inside the f-string the name of the slug should be followed by the text saved in the **headline** attribute. And now the markup. It should also be contained in the f-string, so inside the quotes and it should enclose the actual text, with the opening tags preceding the slug's name and the closing tags following the headline text. Use the markup to make the text bold and set its color to the hex value **ff3333**.

So, now the label has two properties set, **markup** and **text**. The other properties that should be set include **text_size**, which should be set to **(400, 100)** and the two alignment properties: **halign** and **valign**. The text should be left-aligned horizontally and centered vertically.

Assign the label to a variable, which you may name **label**.

5) Another element of the popup window is going to be the silhouette of the affected slug. The path to this image is saved in the slug's **front_image** property. Now, create an instance of the **Image** class and set its **source** property to the slug's silhouette image and its **size_hint** property to **(.2, 1)**. Assign the image to a **popup_image** variable.

6) Our popup window is going to display the image of the slug on the left and the headline text on the right, so we can pack the two in a horizontal BoxLayout. Assign the BoxLayout to a **content** variable and add the two widgets to it.

7) Now we are ready to create the popup itself. To do that, you have to create an instance of the **Popup** class with some arguments that set the window's properties. Set the properties as follows:

- The **title** property should be set to the class attribute intro.

- The **title_color** property should be set to **[.9, .2, 0, .2]**, which will give us a shade of red.

- The **content** property should be set to the **content** variable that stores the BoxLayout you just created.

- The **size_hint** property should be set to **(None, None)** because we want to use a fixed size.

- The **size** property should be set to **(600, 150)**.

- The **pos_hint** property should be set to **center_x** = **0.5** and **top** = **1**, so that the window is at the top-center.

- The **background_color** property should be set to **[0, 0, 0, .2]**, which will make the background darker, but almost fully transparent.

Assign the popup to a **popup** variable.

8) Finally, to show the popup window, call the **open** method on it.

## SOLUTION

Here's the code:

```
# File name: accident.py
...
from kivy.core.audio import SoundLoader

# the classes we need for the popup window
from kivy.uix.popup import Popup
from kivy.uix.label import Label
from kivy.uix.image import Image
from kivy.uix.boxlayout import BoxLayout

# We'll need the choice function to randomly pick a headline.
from random import choice

class Accident(ABC):
    ...
    @abstractmethod
    def happen(self):
        # Let's randomly pick a headline and assign it to a variable.
        headline = choice(self.headlines)

        # Let's create the label that will display the headline.
        label = Label(markup = True,
                      text = f'[b][color=ff3333]{self.slug.name} {headline}[/color][/b]',
                      text_size = (400, 100),
                      halign = 'left',
                      valign = 'center')

        # the slug's image
        popup_image = Image(source = self.slug.front_image, size_hint = (.2, 1))

        # the content
        content = BoxLayout()
        content.add_widget(popup_image)
        content.add_widget(label)
```

```
        # the popup
        popup = Popup(title = self.intro,
                      title_color = [.9, .2, 0, 1],  # red
                      content = content,
                      size_hint = (None, None),
                      size = (600, 150),
                      pos_hint = {'center_x': .5, 'top': 1},
                      background_color = [0, 0, 0, .2])

        # Open the popup window.
        popup.open()

    @abstractmethod
    def reset(self):
        ...
```

If you now run the app and you start a race, an accident will happen and you will see a popup window.

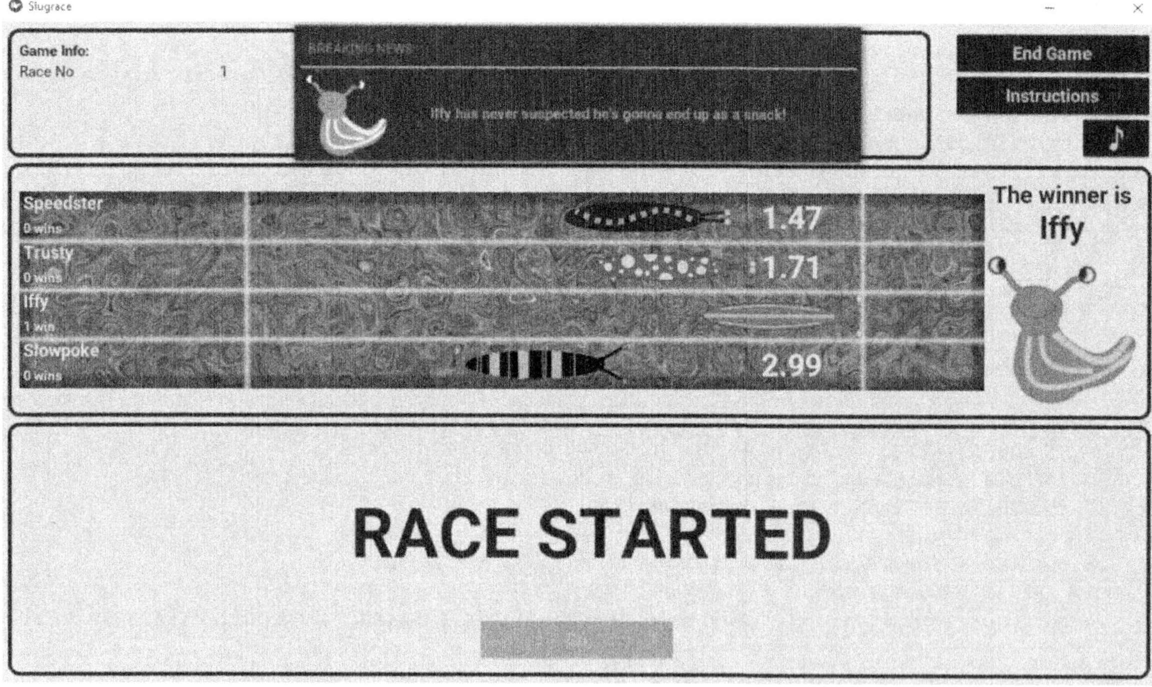


As you can see, here the Devoured accident happened to Iffy. Naturally, we didn't implement it yet, so nothing special happens for now (except for the popup window showing up). To dismiss the popup window, just click anywhere outside it.

# Chapter 109 – The Broken Leg Accident

In the previous chapter we implemented logic that will be shared by all accidents. In this and the following chapters we'll have a look at all the accidents one by one and implement them. Let's start with the Broken Leg accident.

First, let's find the code where the accident is chosen:

```
# File name: main.py
...
class Game(ScreenManager):
    ...
    def go(self, screen_manager):
        ...
        if self.accident_expected:
            self.accident = choice(self.accidents)
            self.accident.position = randint(290, 500)
            ...
```

So, the program picks a random accident. In order to be able to smoothly test particular accidents without having to count on the right one being randomly picked, we'll be modifying this piece of code so that the accident that is picked is the one we want to test.

So, let's ensure that the Broken Leg accident is picked in this chapter:

```
# File name: main.py
...
class Game(ScreenManager):
    ...
    def go(self, screen_manager):
        ...
        if self.accident_expected:
            # self.accident = choice(self.accidents)
            self.accident = self.acc_broken_leg
            self.accident.position = randint(290, 500)
            ...
```

If you now run the app, you may be sure one of the slugs will break his leg.

In the image below you can see that when I ran the app Speedster was the unlucky one.

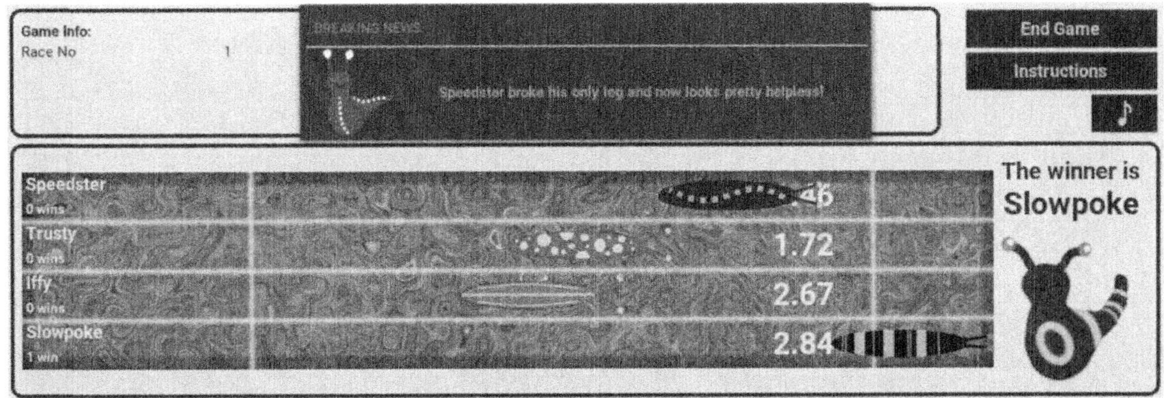

The accident happened because the **happen** method was called in the **while_running** method. As you remember, this method is an abstract method, implemented in the base class **Accident**. The **BrokenLegAccident** class as of now doesn't deliver any other implementation. It just calls the base class's version. This is why you can see the popup window, just like with any other accident. But we want to add some accident-specific code to the **BrokenLegAccident** class.

# The BrokenLegAccident Class's happen Method

So, what exactly do we want to happen when a slug breaks his leg? Well, a couple things:

1) We should hear the sound of a breaking leg.

2) The slug should stop running.

3) The image of the slug should change to the one with a broken leg.

We still want the **happen** method to call the base class's **happen** method, so this code should stay intact. But let's implement the three things we just mentioned.

So, we already have the sound associated with the accident loaded, so all we have to do is play it.

Next, if we want the slug to stop running, all we have to do is cancel his **run_animation**. This is the animation that is started when a race begins.

Now, about the last thing. In the atlas with the accident images we have four separate images for the broken leg accident, one for each slug, so **'broken leg speedster'**, **'broken leg trusty'** and so on. So we can use these images to replace the regular body images of the slugs.

To reference the body image, let's add a **body** ObjectProperty in the **Slug** class. Here's the modified kv file:

```
#:kivy 1.11.1
# File name: slug.kv
#:import slug slug

<Slug>:
    ...
    size: 143, 30

    # reference to the body image
    body: _body

    # the body image
    Image:
        id: _body
        source: ...

    # the left eye image
    ...
```

With that said, here's the implementation of the **happen** method in the **BrokenLegAccident** class:

```
# File name: accident.py
...
### BROKEN LEG ###
class BrokenLegAccident(Accident):
    ...
    def happen(self):
        super().happen()

        # Play the sound.
        self.sound.play()

        # Stop the running animation.
        self.slug.run_animation.stop(self.slug)

        # Change the body image.
        self.slug.body.source = ('atlas://assets/accidents/accidents/broken leg '
                                 + self.slug.name.lower())

    def reset(self):
        ...
```

If we now run the program, we will see something like this:

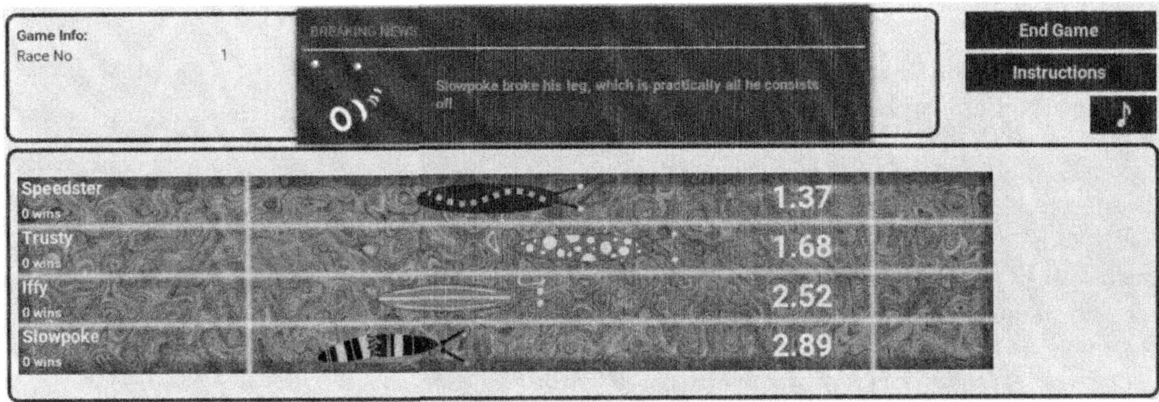


We can also hear the sound of a breaking leg. Naturally, in your case it may be a different slug.

So now we can see the broken leg image, but there is one issue. The eyes of the slug are now detached from the body. This is because of the size difference between the regular and the broken leg body image. We can easily handle this by moving the body image ten pixels to the right:

```
# File name: accident.py
...
### BROKEN LEG ###
class BrokenLegAccident(Accident):
    ...
    def happen(self):
        ...
        self.slug.body.source = ('atlas://assets/accidents/accidents/broken leg '
```

```
                                  + self.slug.name.lower())
        # Move the body image ten pixels to the right.
        self.slug.body.x += 10

    def reset(self):
        ...
```

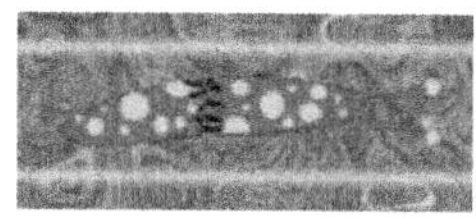

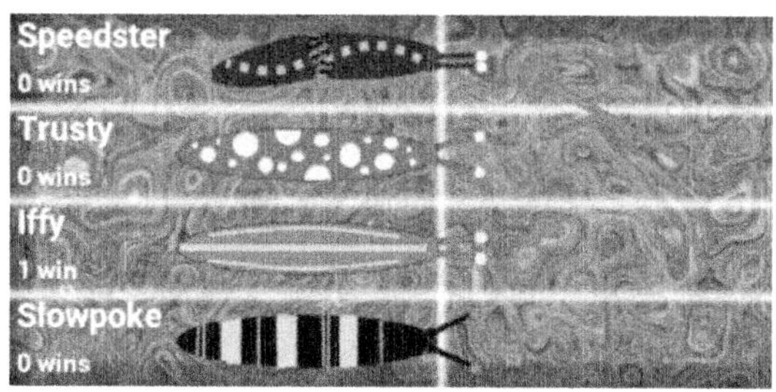


And now wait until the race finishes and hit the Next Race button.

As you can see, the body image is still the one of a slug with a broken leg. This is what the **reset** method is going to take care of. You'll implement it as an exercise. And in the next chapter we'll be implementing the Overheat accident.

## It's Your Turn Now...

### EXERCISE

In this exercise you'll be implementing some functionality related to resetting accidents in general, and resetting the Broken Leg accident in particular. You will be shown the solution for each particular step below. Speaking of which... Follow the steps below:

1. After each race where an accident happened, we want to restore the state from before it happened. In case of the Broken Leg accident, we want the body image to be the regular one, so the one we had before the accident. This will be the same with the other accidents, so let's create a method in the **Game** class that will take care of it. Let's name it **reset_accidents**. Now, implement the method like so: If there is an accident, the **reset** method on the **Accident** object should be called and the accident should be set to **None**.

### SOLUTION - Step 1

Here's the implementation:

```
# File name: main.py
...
class Game(ScreenManager):
    ...
    def mute_unmute(self, instance, value):
        ...

    # Resetting the accident.
    def reset_accidents(self):
        if self.accident:
            self.accident.reset()
            self.accident = None

class SlugraceApp(App):
    ...
```

2. So, we have the method, but when do we call it? A good place to call it seems when the Next Race button is pressed. When this happens, the **reset_race** method is called, so just call the **reset_accidents** method from within the **reset_race** method.

**SOLUTION - Step 2**

Here's the code:

```
# File name: main.py
...
class Game(ScreenManager):
    ...
    def reset_race(self):
        ...
        for slug in self.slugs:
            slug.reset()

        # Reset the accidents.
        self.reset_accidents()

    def reset_players(self):
        ...
```

3. Finally, we have to implement the **reset** method in the **BrokenLegAccident** class. The code is very simple. It should do two things:

- change the body image to the normal body image,

- move the body image back ten pixels to the left.

However, to make it easier for us, let's save the normal body image in a **normal_image** attribute on the **slug** object in the **happen** method before changing it to the broken leg image.

This way it will be easier for us to quickly restore it to the normal image in the **reset** method.

So, to sum it up, here's what you should do:

- In the **happen** method assign the source of the body image to the **slug.normal_image** attribute before you change it.

- In the **reset** method assign the saved normal image back to the body image's source.

- Also in the **reset** method move the body image ten pixels to the left.

**SOLUTION - Step 3**

Here's the modified code:

```
# File name: accident.py
...
### BROKEN LEG ###
class BrokenLegAccident(Accident):
    ...
    def happen(self):
        ...
        self.slug.run_animation.stop(self.slug)

        # Let's save the body image source in an attribute.
        self.slug.normal_image = self.slug.body.source

        # Now let's change the image.
        self.slug.body.source = ('atlas://assets/accidents/accidents/broken leg '
                                 + self.slug.name.lower())
```

```
        self.slug.body.x += 10

    def reset(self):
        # Restore the body image.
        self.slug.body.source = self.slug.normal_image

        # Move the image back to the left.
        self.slug.body.x -= 10

### OVERHEAT ###
...
```

If you now run the app, the body image will be restored to normal when a new race begins.

# Chapter 110 – The Overheat Accident

In the previous chapter we implemented the Broken Leg accident. In this chapter we're going to implement the Overheat accident.

So, what is going to happen if a slug overheats? This is generally pretty much like with the Broken Leg accident, so the slug should stop running. Additionally, his eyes should stop moving. Also, the image of the slug's body should change, as should the eye images. And, last but not least, we want to hear the sizzling sound of the burning slug.

So, as far as the running and eye animations are concerned, things are pretty easy. We just have to stop or cancel them. We can cancel the eye animation, but we will stop the running animation because an animation is considered complete when it's stopped, but not when canceled. And we need it to be complete so that the slug can finish the race.

As to the eye images, we have to reference them somehow. We can do it just like we did with the body image, so let's add two object properties in the **Slug** class that will reference the images:

```
#:kivy 1.11.1
# File name: slug.kv
#:import slug slug

<Slug>:
    ...
    body: _body

    # properties to reference
    # the eye images
    left_eye: _left_eye
    right_eye: _right_eye

    # the body image
    ...
```

```
    # the left eye image
    Image:
        ...
            PopMatrix

        id: _left_eye
        source: ...
        ...
    # the right eye image
    Image:
        ...
            PopMatrix

        id: _right_eye
        source: ...
        ...
```

In the **happen** method of the **OverheatAccident** class we'll save the body and eye images in attributes so that we can then quickly restore them in the **reset** method.

We have to set the sources of the body and eye images to the overheat body and overheat eye images in the **accidents** atlas.

Here's the **happen** method:

```
# File name: accident.py
...
### OVERHEAT ###
class OverheatAccident(Accident):
    ...
    def happen(self):
        super().happen()

        # Let's play the sound.
        self.sound.play()

        # Let's stop the running animations and
        # cancel the eye animation.
        self.slug.run_animation.stop(self.slug)
        self.slug.eye_animation.cancel(self.slug)

        # Let's save the normal body and eye images in attributes.
        self.slug.normal_body_image = self.slug.body.source
        self.slug.normal_eye_image = self.slug.left_eye.source

        # Let's change the images.
        self.slug.body.source = 'atlas://assets/accidents/accidents/overheat body'
        self.slug.left_eye.source = 'atlas://assets/accidents/accidents/overheat eye'
        self.slug.right_eye.source = 'atlas://assets/accidents/accidents/overheat eye'

    def reset(self):
        ...
```

Before we run the app, let's make sure the Overheat accident is the one that happens.

All you have to do to ensure that is change the line of code where the accident is set in the **go** method of the **Game** class:

```
# File name: main.py
...
class Game(ScreenManager):
    ...
    def go(self, screen_manager):
        ...
        if self.accident_expected:
            # self.accident = choice(self.accidents)
            self.accident = self.acc_overheat
            ...
```

Now run the app and one of the slugs will definitely overheat, which you will both see and hear.

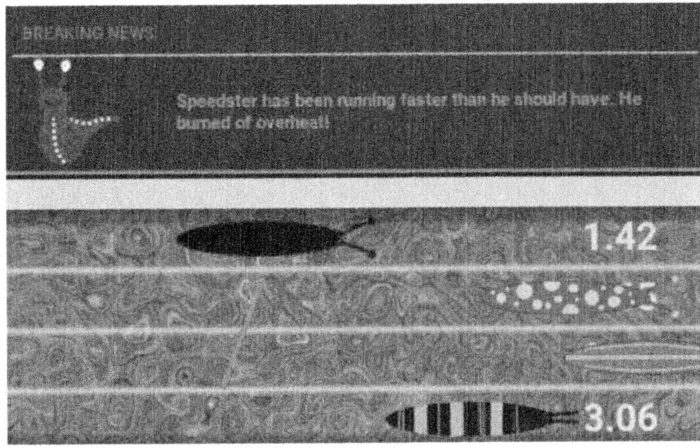


Naturally, when you hit the Next Race button, the body and eye images won't change back automatically.

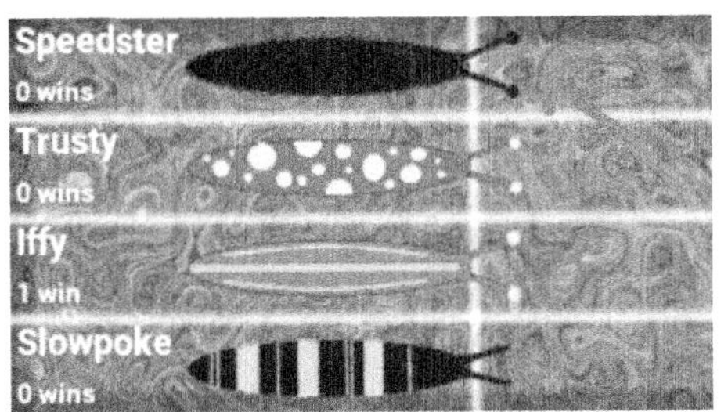


This is the task of the **reset** method, which you are going to implement as an exercise. But before you do that, there's one more thing. It's about the sound. We have very similar code that plays the sound in the **BrokenLegAccident** class and in the **OverheatAccident** class. This is also going to be the case in some of the other **Accident** subclasses, but not all of them. This is why, in order to make the code less repetitive, we're going to move the code to the base class. We'll add an optional parameter to the **happen** method, let's name it **autoplay**, and set it to **True**. The sound will play if **autoplay** is set to **True**. This means that by default the sounds will play automatically when an accident happens. We can naturally remove the code that plays the sound from the two subclasses.

So, here are the modified **Accident**, **BrokenLegAccident** and **OverheatAccident** classes:

```
# File name: accident.py
...
class Accident(ABC):
    ...
    @abstractmethod
    # If autoplay is set to True, the sound will play automatically.
    def happen(self, autoplay=True):

        # Here's the code to play the sound.
        if autoplay:
            self.sound.play()

        headline = choice(self.headlines)
        ...
### BROKEN LEG ###
class BrokenLegAccident(Accident):
    ...
    def happen(self):
        super().happen()
        # We don't need the code that plays the sound here, so I removed it.
        self.slug.run_animation.stop(self.slug)
        ...
```

```
### OVERHEAT ###
class OverheatAccident(Accident):
    ...
    def happen(self):
        super().happen()
        # We don't need the code that plays the sound here, so I removed it.
        self.slug.run_animation.stop(self.slug)
        ...
```

If you now run the app, everything will work just like before. After making sure it does, you can do the exercise and implement the **reset** method. And in the next chapter we'll implement the Heart Attack accident.

# It's Your Turn Now...

### EXERCISE

In this exercise your task is to implement the **reset** method of the **OverheatAccident** class. This is what the method should do:

- restore the normal body image

- restore the normal eye images

- restart the eye animation

### SOLUTION

Here's the code:

```
# File name: accident.py
...
### OVERHEAT ###
class OverheatAccident(Accident):
    ...
    def reset(self):
        # restore the normal body image
        self.slug.body.source = self.slug.normal_body_image

        # restore the normal eye images
        self.slug.left_eye.source = self.slug.normal_eye_image
        self.slug.right_eye.source = self.slug.normal_eye_image

        # restart the eye animation
        self.slug.eye_animation.start(self.slug)

### HEART ATTACK ###
...
```

Now if you run the app, one of the slugs will overheat. But in the next race, he will be up and running again.

# Chapter 111 – The Heart Attack Accident

In the previous chapter we implemented the Overheat accident. In this chapter we're going to implement the Heart Attack accident. Let's start by setting the accident in the **go** method of the **Game** class so that this is the accident that happens:

```
# File name: main.py
...
class Game(ScreenManager):
    ...
    def go(self, screen_manager):
        ...
        if self.accident_expected:
            # self.accident = choice(self.accidents)
            self.accident = self.acc_heart_attack
            self.accident.position = randint(290, 500)
            ...
```

Now, this accident is slightly different than the Broken Leg and Overheat accidents we saw before in that the images of the slug's body and his eyes do not change. Instead, another image is displayed on top of the slug's body image. This is an animated image of a beating heart.

But let's take it slowly, step by step. What should happen when a slug has a heart attack? Here's what:

- The slug should stop running.

- The heart image should be created, scaled and placed on the slug. Its size should be animated so that it looks as if it was beating. The path to the image is already stored in the **image** attribute inside the **HeartAttackAccident** class.

The heart animation should start and be repeated until the race is over. We have to import the **Animation** class first.

So, let's write the code that will handle that:

```
# File name: accident.py
...
from random import choice

# We'll need the Animation class for the heart
# attack animation (and some other animations too).
from kivy.animation import Animation

class Accident(ABC):
    ...

...
### HEART ATTACK ###
class HeartAttackAccident(Accident):
    ...
```

```
    def happen(self):
        super().happen()

        # The running animation should stop.
        self.slug.run_animation.stop(self.slug)

        # Let's create an image from the source saved in image.
        self.heart = Image(source = self.image)

        # Let's scale the heart image down.
        self.heart.size_hint = .8, .8

        # Let's position the heart image on top of the slug's body image.
        self.heart.x = self.slug.body.x + 40
        self.heart.y = self.slug.body.y + 3

        # Let's add the heart image as a widget to the slug image.
        self.slug.add_widget(self.heart)

        # Let's create an animation for the heart image. It will consist of
        # two consecutive animations. First the image will shrink during 0.2
        # seconds, then it will expand to its original size during a period
        # of 0.62 seconds. We'll also add some transitions.
        self.heart_animation = (Animation(size_hint = (.6, .6),
                                 duration = .2, t = 'out_back')
                                + Animation(size_hint = (.8, .8),
                                 duration = .62, t = 'out_back'))

        # The animation should be repeated.
        self.heart_animation.repeat = True

        # Let's start the animation.
        self.heart_animation.start(self.heart)

    def reset(self):
        ...
```

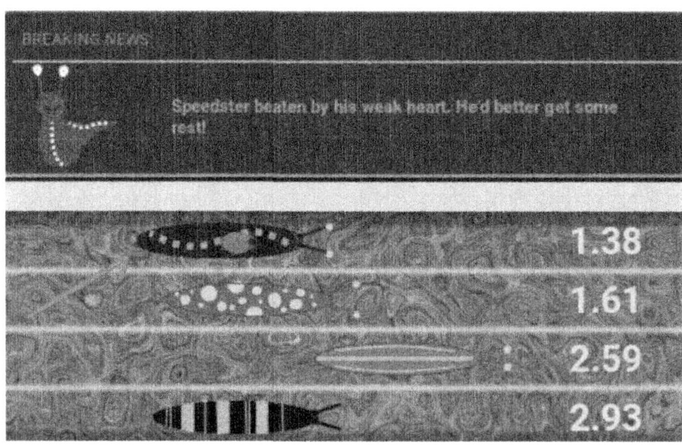


If you now run the app, one of the slugs will suffer from a heart attack. As you can see in the image on the right, in my case it's Speedster.

The problem now is that you can hear the heart beat a couple of times and then the sound stops. This is because the sound file contains several beats of the heart and it's played only once. To fix this and make it loop, you will modify the code in the base class. But this is going to be the first exercise for you. In the second exercise you will implement the **reset** method. And in the next chapter we'll implement the Grass accident.

# It's Your Turn Now...

## EXERCISE 1 - Looping Sound

In some accidents we'll need looping sound, like in the Heart Attack accident. In others, like the Broken Leg or Overheat accidents, the sound should play only once. So, modify the code in the base class's **happen** method by adding an optional parameter **loop** and setting it by default to **False**. You should do it just like we did with the **autoplay** parameter in the previous chapter. Then, in the function body make the sound loop if the **loop** parameter is set to **True**.

Finally, in the **HeartAttackAccident** class's **happen** method set the **loop** parameter to **True** in the super class's call so that the heart beat sound loops.

## SOLUTION

Here's the code:

```
# File name: accident.py
...
class Accident(ABC):
    ...
    @abstractmethod
    # Add the loop parameter and set it to False.
    def happen(self, autoplay=True, loop=False):
        # Make the sound loop if the loop parameter is set to True.
        if loop:
            self.sound.loop = True

        if autoplay:
            ...
### HEART ATTACK ###
class HeartAttackAccident(Accident):
    ...
    def happen(self):
        # Call the base class's happen method with the loop parameter set to True.
        super().happen(loop=True)
        self.slug.run_animation.stop(self.slug)
        ...
```

If you now run the app, the heart beat sound will loop.

## EXERCISE 2 - The reset Method

In the **reset** method you should take care of restoring the original state. In particular, write code that will do the following:

- stop the heart beat sound,

- cancel the heart animation,

- remove the heart image widget.

## SOLUTION

Here's the code:

```
# File name: accident.py
...
### HEART ATTACK ###
class HeartAttackAccident(Accident):
    ...
    def reset(self):
        self.sound.stop()
        self.heart_animation.cancel(self.heart)
        self.slug.remove_widget(self.heart)

### GRASS ###
class GrassAccident(Accident):
    ...
```

If you now run the app and hit the Next Race button after there's an accident, you will see the slug just like it was before.

# Chapter 112 – The Grass Accident

In the previous chapter we implemented the Heart Attack accident.

In this chapter we're going to implement the Grass accident.

As usual, let's start by setting the accident that is supposed to happen to the Grass accident:

```
# File name: main.py
...
class Game(ScreenManager):
    ...
    def go(self, screen_manager):
        ...
        if self.accident_expected:
            # self.accident = choice(self.accidents)
            self.accident = self.acc_grass
            self.accident.position = randint(290, 500)
            ...
```

And now let's think about the grass accident for a while. What does it entail? Here's what:

- The slug should stop running.

- An image of grass should appear on the racetrack in front of the slug.

- The slug should be eating the grass for a while and then the grass image should disappear and the slug should continue the race with more power than before.

This time the code is going to be slightly more complicated than with the other accidents so far, so let's take it piece by piece.

So, we already know how to stop the running animation. We also know how to add an image widget to the slug image because we already added the heart image when we were talking about the Heart Attack accident. So, here's the code that will take care of it:

```
# File name: accident.py
...
### GRASS ###
class GrassAccident(Accident):
    ...
    def happen(self):
        super().happen()

        # The running animation should stop.
        self.slug.run_animation.stop(self.slug)

        # Let's create the grass image from the source saved in image.
        self.grass = Image(source = self.image)

        # Let's position the grass image in front of the slug. A distance of 90 pixels
        # seems fine.
```

```
        self.grass.x = self.slug.body.x + 90

        # Let's add the grass image as a widget to the slug image. Unlike with the heart
        # image, we want the grass image to be under the slug image, not on top of it,
        # so we have to set index to -1.
        self.slug.add_widget(self.grass, index=-1)

    def reset(self):
        ...
```

If you now run the app, you will see the grass appear in front of the slug.

The slug is still moving his eyes, which looks as if he was eating the grass.

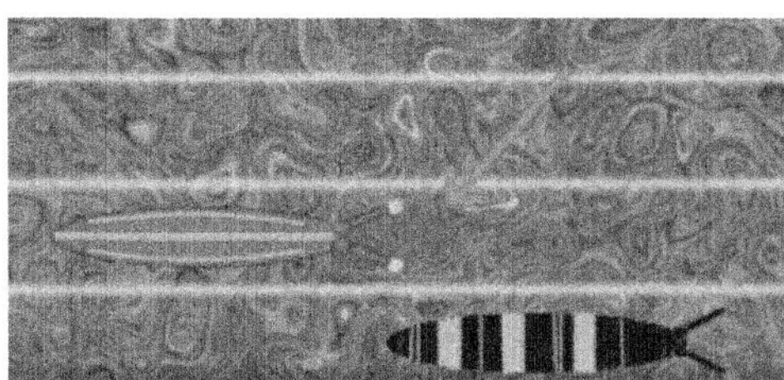

# Race Continuation

So, while the slug is eating the grass, he's wasting time. But he still has a chance of winning the race because the grass gives power and accelerates him. Anyway, he should spend two seconds eating the grass and then start running again.

So, we need the **Clock** class to schedule the race continuation after two seconds. The race continuation will consist in calling a method, let's name it **continue_race**, that will remove the grass image, stop the sound associated with this accident and call the slug's **run** method to access the running animation and then start the animation. Here's the code:

```
# File name: accident.py
...
from kivy.animation import Animation

# We'll need the Clock class.
from kivy.clock import Clock

class Accident(ABC):
    ...
### GRASS ###
class GrassAccident(Accident):
    ...
    def happen(self):
        ...
        self.slug.add_widget(self.grass, index=-1)

        # We have to schedule the continue_race method to be called after two seconds.
        Clock.schedule_once(self.continue_race, 2)

    # And now we have to define the method.
    def continue_race(self, dt):
```

```
        # Remove the grass image widget.
        self.slug.remove_widget(self.grass)

        # Stop the accident sound.
        self.sound.stop()

        # Start the running animation. As you remember, the run method returns
        # the running animation, but then we have to start it on the slug.
        self.slug.run().start(self.slug)

    def reset(self):
        ...
```

If you now run the app, the grass image will disappear after two seconds and you won't hear the sound of the slug eating the grass. But the slug's running time will be recalculated in the **run** method and it's very probable that the slug will run slower than before. This is not what we want. The magic grass should have given him power and he should now be running much faster than before. So, let's take care of this now. Actually, it's your task. This is what you are supposed to do in the first exercise and in the second exercise you'll take care of one more issue that has to do with finishing the race, but you will find the exact description of the problem down in the exercise below.

This time you don't have to do anything with the reset method, because we don't need any special implementation here. In the next chapter we'll handle the Asleep accident.

# It's Your Turn Now...

### EXERCISE 1 - Accelerating the Slug

As you know, the magic grass powers up the slug and he should accelerate. But look at how the **run** method in the **Slug** class is now implemented:

```
# File name: slug.py
...
class Slug(RelativeLayout):
    ...
    def run(self):
        self.finished = False
        move_base = randint(1, 10)
        if move_base < self.speeds[0]:
            running_time = uniform(8, 10)  # slow
        elif move_base <= self.speeds[1]:
            running_time = uniform(6, 8)  # medium
        else:
            running_time = uniform(4, 6)  # fast

        self.eye_animation.cancel(self)
        ...
```

We're interested in the part that contains the conditional statements where the running time is determined.

If the slug is supposed to run faster, the running time must be shorter. So, why not divide it by a value?

That's how we're going to do it. So, add a keyword parameter to the **run** method, name it **acceleration**, and set its default value to **1**.

Then, in the three conditional blocks where the running time is set using the **uniform** function, divide it by **acceleration**. This way the running time won't change most of the time, because we're dividing by the default value of 1, but it will be possible to use a different value if necessary.

Now, go back to the **GrassAccident** class and in the **continue_race** method set acceleration to **10** in the **run** method call. This will make the slug run much faster, try it out.

## SOLUTION

So, here's the modified **Slug** class:

```
# File name: slug.py
...
class Slug(RelativeLayout):
    ...
    def update(self, winning_slug, race_number):
        ...

    # We add the acceleration parameter with the default value of 1.
    def run(self, acceleration=1):
        self.finished = False

        move_base = randint(1, 10)
        if move_base < self.speeds[0]:
            running_time = uniform(8, 10) / acceleration  # slow
        elif move_base <= self.speeds[1]:
            running_time = uniform(6, 8)  / acceleration # medium
        else:
            running_time = uniform(4, 6) / acceleration # fast

        self.eye_animation.cancel(self)
        ...
```

And here's the **GrassAccident** class with **acceleration** set to 10:

```
# File name: accident.py
...
### GRASS ###
class GrassAccident(Accident):
    ...
    def continue_race(self, dt):
        self.slug.remove_widget(self.grass)
        self.sound.stop()

        # If we now set acceleration to 10, the random
        # running time will be divided by 10 and the
        # slug will be way faster.
        self.slug.run(acceleration=10).start(self.slug)

    def reset(self):
        ...
```

Run the app and you'll see a slug stop to eat the grass and then start running again, this time much faster. There's one problem, though. You can't finish the race. Although all slugs have finished it, you still don't see the Results screen. What's even worse, even if the slug accelerates and is the first one to cross the finish line, he still doesn't win. Being the fastest is useless if you can't win. You will address this issue in the second exercise.

**EXERCISE 2 - Finishing the Race**

As you just saw, the race isn't finished even after all slugs cross the finish line. Besides, the accelerated slug never wins a race, even if he is the first one to cross the finish line. The reason for this can be found in the **go** method in the **Game** class. Have a look at these lines of code:

```
# File name: main.py
...
class Game(ScreenManager):
    ...
    def go(self, screen_manager):
        ...
        for slug in self.slugs:
            anim = slug.run()
            anim.bind(on_progress=self.while_running)
            anim.bind(on_complete=self.finish_race)
            anim.start(slug)
        ...
    def while_running(self, animation, slug, progression):
        ...
    def finish_race(self, animation, slug):
        ...
```

So, we bind the **while_running** and **finish_race** methods to the running animation's **on_progress** and **on_complete** events respectively. Now, what do these two methods do? Let's have a look:

```
# File name: main.py
...
class Game(ScreenManager):
    ...
    def while_running(self, animation, slug, progression):
        if slug.right > self.finish_line:
            if not self.race_winner:
                self.race_winner = slug
                slug.win_sound.play()
                ...
    def finish_race(self, animation, slug):
        slug.finished = True
        if (self.speedster.finished
            and self.trusty.finished
            and self.iffy.finished
            and self.slowpoke.finished):
            self.race_manager.current = 'resultsscreen'
            ...
```

So, in the **while_running** method the position of the slug is continuously checked and if a slug crosses the finish line, he wins the race. In the **finish_race** method, on the other hand, the slug's **finished** property is set to **True** and if all slugs have finished the race, the Results screen appears.

Now, after the running animation stops when the slug eats the grass, the binding is gone until the **go** method is executed again. So, what we have to do is bind the two methods to the running animation's **on_progress** and **on_complete** events in the **continue_race** method. But this will require some code modification because we need to access the **Game** class, where the two methods are defined, inside the **Slug** class. So, follow the steps below:

1. In the **Accident** class (the base class) add the **game** keyword parameter to the constructor and set its default value to **None**. In the body of the **__init__** method set **self.game** to **game**.

2. In the **Game** class, in the **go** method, find the section of code where the accident's attributes are set (like **position** and **slug**). Add one more line of code where you set the accident's **game** attribute to the **Game** object.

HINT: The **go** method is inside the **Game** class, so you can use the **self** variable to reference the **Game** object.

3. Now you have access to the **Game** object in the **Accident** class, and also, through inheritance, in all the **Accident** subclasses. So, in the **continue_race** method in the **GrassAccident** class bind the **Game** object's **while_running** and **finish_race** methods to the running animation's **on_progress** and **on_complete** events respectively.

## SOLUTION

So, here's the modified code. Let's start with the **main.py** file:

```
# File name: main.py
...
class Game(ScreenManager):
    ...
    def go(self, screen_manager):
        ...
        # Accident
        ...
        if self.accident_expected:
            ...
            if self.accident.slug == self.trusty:
                self.accident.slug = choice(self.slugs)

            # Set the accident's game attribute to the Game object. We are now inside
            # the Game class, so we can refer to it by self.
            self.accident.game = self

    def while_running(self, animation, slug, progression):
        ...
```

And now the **accident.py** file:

```
# File name: accident.py
...
class Accident(ABC):
    intro = 'BREAKING NEWS: '

    # Let's add the game keyword parameter to the constructor.
    def __init__(self, name,
                 headlines,
                 sound,
                 position = 0,
                 slug = None,
                 image = None,
                 game=None):
        self.name = name
        self.headlines = headlines
        self.sound = SoundLoader.load(sound)
        self.position = position
        self.slug = slug
        self.image = image

        # We'll need to access the Game object.
        self.game = game

    @abstractmethod
    def happen(self, autoplay=True, loop=False):
        ...
### GRASS ###
class GrassAccident(Accident):
    ...
    def continue_race(self, dt):
        self.slug.remove_widget(self.grass)
        self.sound.stop()
        self.slug.run(acceleration=10).start(self.slug)

        # We now have access to the Game object, so let's bind its
        # two methods to the animation's events.
        self.slug.run_animation.bind(on_progress=self.game.while_running)
        self.slug.run_animation.bind(on_complete=self.game.finish_race)

    def reset(self):
        ...
```

If you now run the app, the slugs will be able to finish the race and win.

# Chapter 113 – The Asleep Accident

In the previous chapter we implemented the Grass accident.

In this chapter we're going to implement the Asleep accident.

As usual, let's start by setting the accident that is supposed to happen to the Asleep accident:

```
# File name: main.py
...
class Game(ScreenManager):
    ...
    def go(self, screen_manager):
        ...
        if self.accident_expected:
            # self.accident = choice(self.accidents)
            self.accident = self.acc_asleep
            self.accident.position = randint(290, 500)
            ...
```

And here's what should happen when a slug falls asleep:

- The slug animations (both the running and eye animation) should stop.

- A new animation should be created and started. The property to animate is the **size_hint** of the body image. This will imitate the peaceful breathing of the slug and will be accompanied by a sound of snoring.

So, now that we know what to do, let's actually do it. Just like with the Overheat accident, we'll stop the running animation and cancel the eye animation. By stopping the former we'll make sure it's completed and the slug's **finished** property is set to **True**.

As for the new animation, let's name it **asleep_animation**. It's going to consist of two simple animations:

- first the **size_hint** property will change to **(1.05, 1.05)** in 2.6 seconds,

- then it will change back to **(1, 1)** in 3 seconds.

I just found that these two durations work fine with the snoring sound as far as synchronization is concerned.

Anyway, the animation should be repeated and we will start it on the body image.

Here's the code:

```
# File name: accident.py
...
### ASLEEP ###
class AsleepAccident(Accident):
    ...
    def happen(self):
        super().happen()

        # Let's stop the running animation and cancel the eye animation.
        self.slug.run_animation.stop(self.slug)
        self.slug.eye_animation.cancel(self.slug)

        # Here's the animation that will imitate the slug's breathing.
        self.asleep_animation = (Animation(size_hint = (1.05, 1.05), duration = 2.6)
                                + Animation(size_hint = (1, 1), duration = 3))
        self.asleep_animation.repeat = True
        self.asleep_animation.start(self.slug.body)

    def reset(self):
        ...
```

If you now run the app, one of the slugs will fall asleep and you will see him breathing. You will also hear him snoring. The problem, though, is that the snoring sound will be played only once. The sound is a series of breaths, not just a single breath, but if you wait for a couple seconds, the snoring sound will be over, although the breathing animation will still be in progress. So, we want to loop the sound too. We already had a similar situation with the heart beat sound. We then added the **loop** parameter to the **happen** method in the base class. Now all we have to do is set it to **True**:

```
# File name: accident.py
...
### ASLEEP ###
class AsleepAccident(Accident):
    ...
    def happen(self):
        # Let's set loop to True so that the sound loops.
        super().happen(loop=True)
        ...
```

That's all as far as the **happen** method is concerned. In the exercise below you will implement the **reset** method and in the next chapter we'll handle the Blind accident.

# It's Your Turn Now...

## EXERCISE

After a slug falls asleep, he must wake up before the next race. This is what the **reset** method should take care of. So, implement the **reset** method so that it does the following:

- The sound should stop playing.

- The asleep animation should be canceled.

- The eye animation should be started again.

## SOLUTION

Here's the code:

```
# File name: accident.py
...
### ASLEEP ###
class AsleepAccident(Accident):
    ...
    def reset(self):
        # Stop the sound.
        self.sound.stop()

        # Cancel the asleep animation on the body image.
        self.asleep_animation.cancel(self.slug.body)

        # Start the eye animation on the slug.
        self.slug.eye_animation.start(self.slug)

### BLIND ###
...
```

# Chapter 114 – The Blind Accident

In the previous chapter we implemented the Asleep accident.

In this chapter we're going to implement the Blind accident. As usual, let's start by setting the accident that is supposed to happen to the Blind accident:

```
# File name: main.py
...
class Game(ScreenManager):
    ...
    def go(self, screen_manager):
        ...
        if self.accident_expected:
            # self.accident = choice(self.accidents)
            self.accident = self.acc_blind
            self.accident.position = randint(290, 500)
            ...
```

Now, what is going to happen if a slug goes blind? A couple things:

- The eyes should disappear – the slug is blind after all.

- Without his eyes the slug can't run so fast anymore, so, yes, he continues the race, but at a slower pace.

- The slug can't see the track ahead of him, so he begins to stagger.

Now, let's implement it all in the **happen** method. Let's start with the running animation. We want the slug to slow down. To do that, we can just stop the running animation and start it again with an acceleration less than 1.

I'm sure you remember the **acceleration** parameter we introduced when we were talking about the Grass accident. There we used it to make the slug move faster, now we need it for the contrary. Also, just like before, we have to bind the **while_running** and **finish_race** methods from the **Game** class to the **on_progress** and **on_complete** events of the new animation.

Now, as for the eyes. They should disappear, so we can set their opacity to 0. We don't need the eye animation either, because we wouldn't see it anyway, so let's cancel it.

Finally, we have to create the staggering animation and start it. In this animation we'll change the vertical position of the body image so that it moves up and down on the track. This animation should be repeated and started on the body image. Before the animation is even created, though, we'll save the current Y position of the body image so that we can quickly restore it later in the **reset** method.

So, with that said, let's implement the **happen** method:

```
# File name: accident.py
...
### BLIND ###
class BlindAccident(Accident):
    ...
    def happen(self):
        super().happen()

        # Let's stop the running animation.
        self.slug.run_animation.stop(self.slug)

        # Let's create and start a new running animation with an acceleration
        # of 0.7. This will make the slug slower.
        self.slug.run(acceleration=.7).start(self.slug)

        # Let's handle the bindings.
        self.slug.run_animation.bind(on_progress=self.game.while_running)
        self.slug.run_animation.bind(on_complete=self.game.finish_race)

        # Let's cancel the eye animation and make the eyes disappear. We'll use
        # the left_eye and right_eye properties to access the eye images.
        self.slug.eye_animation.cancel(self.slug)
        self.slug.left_eye.opacity = 0
        self.slug.right_eye.opacity = 0

        # Let's save the Y position of the body image so that we can easily restore
        # it in the reset method.
        self.slug_y = self.slug.body.y

        # Let's create the staggering animation. The property we want to animate is
        # y, which represents the Y position of the body image. The animation shoud
        # be repeated and started on the body image.
        self.stagger_animation = (Animation(y = self.slug.body.y + 10, duration = 1)
                                + Animation(y = self.slug.body.y - 10, duration = 1))


        self.stagger_animation.repeat = True
        self.stagger_animation.start(self.slug.body)

    def reset(self):
        ...
```

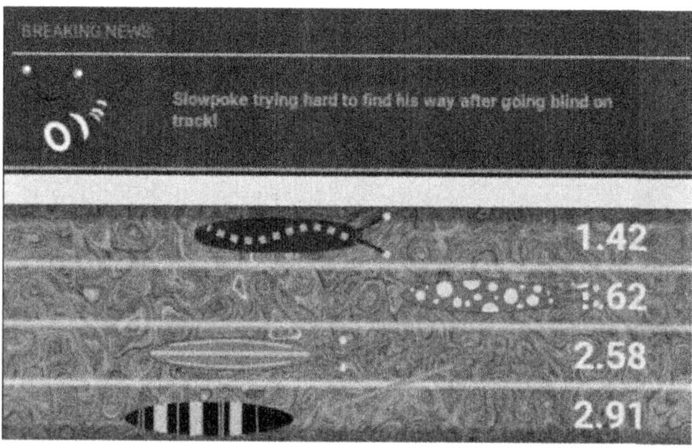


Run the app and watch one of the slugs go blind and stagger.

Now, when the race is finished and you press the Next Race button, the slug will still be staggering and he will still be blind. So, in the exercise below you will fix this. And in the next chapter we'll be talking about the Puddle accident.

# It's Your Turn Now...

## EXERCISE

In this exercise you are supposed to implement the **reset** method of the **BlindAccident** class. The method should do the following:

- Make the eyes visible again.

- Cancel the staggering animation.

- Restore the original Y position of the body image.

## SOLUTION

Here's the code:

```
# File name: accident.py
...
### BLIND ###
class BlindAccident(Accident):
    ...
    def reset(self):
        # Let's make the eyes visible again.
        self.slug.left_eye.opacity = 1
        self.slug.right_eye.opacity = 1

        # Let's cancel the staggering animation.
        self.stagger_animation.cancel(self.slug.body)

        # Let's restore the Y position of the body image. To this end we'll
        # use the slug_y attribute that we defined in the happen method.
        self.slug.body.y = self.slug_y

### PUDDLE ###
...
```

# Chapter 115 – The Puddle Accident

In the previous chapter we implemented the Blind accident.

In this chapter we're going to implement the Puddle accident. As usual, let's start by setting the accident that is supposed to happen to the Puddle accident:

```
# File name: main.py
...
class Game(ScreenManager):
    ...
    def go(self, screen_manager):
        ...
        if self.accident_expected:
            # self.accident = choice(self.accidents)
            self.accident = self.acc_puddle
            self.accident.position = randint(290, 500)
            ...
```

Let's have a closer look at what the Puddle accident entails. Here's what's going to happen:

- A puddle image will appear on the racetrack in front of the slug.

- The slug will fall into the puddle and drown.

This accident is in a way similar to the Grass accident in that there's an image that appears in front of the slug, but there's a difference, though. In case of the Grass accident the image was added as a widget to the slug widget. Here the puddle image is going to be added as a widget to the racetrack. This means we'll need access to the racetrack.

## Accessing the Racetrack

By accessing the racetrack we actually mean accessing the RelativeLayout with the racetrack image on it. The RelativeLayout is defined in the **race.kv** file, so let's add an id to it and create an object property to access it:

```
#:kivy 1.11.1
# File name: race.kv
#:import race race
...
<RaceScreen>:
    ...
    slowpoke: _slowpoke

    # Here's the track property to access the
    # RelativeLayout with the racetrack image.
    track: _track

    BoxLayout:
        orientation: 'vertical'
        spacing: 10
        padding: 10
        ### INFO, STATS AND BUTTONS ###
        ...
        ### THE TRACK ###
        ...
            # Track Image
            RelativeLayout:
                id: _track
                size_hint: None, None
                size: 1000, 200
                pos_hint: {'center_y': .5}
                Image:
                    source: 'assets/racetrack.png'

                # white labels with slug info
                ...
```

We don't have direct access to the Race screen from our **Accident** class, but we do have access to the **Game** class. And the **Game** class has access to the Race screen and indirectly to the track. So, let's just implement this connection:

```
#:kivy 1.11.1
# File name: slugrace.kv

<Game>:
    ...
    slugs: [self.speedster, self.trusty, self.iffy, self.slowpoke]

    # the racetrack
    track: _racescreen.track

    SettingsScreen:
        ...
```

With that in place, we can start implementing the **happen** method in the **PuddleAccident** class. So, first we'll create an image from the source that we already defined in the class. Then we have to position the image. Let's say the X position should be 220. The Y position depends on which slug is affected. The puddle should appear on that slug's lane. To do that, we'll use the following formula:

```
75 - self.game.slugs.index(self.slug) * 50
```

So, we get the index of the slug in the **slugs** list in the **Game** object and multiply it by 50.

Then we subtract the result from 75. This way we get the following Y positions for the particular slugs:

Speedster: 75 – 0 * 50 = 75

Trusty: 75 – 1 * 50 = 25

Iffy: 75 – 2 * 50 = -25

Slowpoke: 75 – 3 * 50 = -75

Then we have to get access to the racetrack and add the image to it so that it sits below the slug image. To do that we have to set its index to -1.

Next, we have to make the slug drown in the puddle. To do that, we'll bind a **drown** method to the running animation's **on_progress** event.

In the **drown** method we'll stop the running animation and create a drowning animation. This will actually consist of two simple animations played one after the other:

- First we'll animate the **x** property on the slug widget so that the slug moves to a specific position.

- Then we'll animate the slug's **opacity** property. This way the slug will be becoming more and more transparent over a period of three seconds, which will look as if he was drowning in the puddle.

We then have to start the animation on the slug and play the drowning sound. This is why we have to set the **autoplay** parameter in the **happen** method to **False**. Otherwise the sound would play right away when the accident happened and we would hear the slug drown while it still was just approaching the puddle.

Here are the **happen** and **drown** methods:

```
# File name: accident.py
...
### PUDDLE ###
class PuddleAccident(Accident):
    ...
    def __init__(self, **kwargs):
        ...

    # We don't want the drowning sound to be played right away, so we must
    # set autoplay to False.
    def happen(self, autoplay=False):
        super().happen()

        # Let's create the puddle image.
        self.puddle = Image(source = self.image)

        # Let's position the image.
        self.puddle.pos = 220, 75 - self.game.slugs.index(self.slug) * 50

        # Let's get access to the racetrack.
        self.track = self.game.track

        # Let's add the puddle image to the track. We want it to be under
        # the slug, not on top of it, so let's set index to -1.
        self.track.add_widget(self.puddle, index=-1)

        # Let's bind the drown method to the running animation's
        # on_progress event.
        self.slug.run_animation.bind(on_progress=self.drown)

    # And here's the drown method.
    def drown(self, animation, slug, progression):
        # If the slug's position is greater than or equal to 600...
        if slug.x >= 600:
            # ...stop the running animation,...
            animation.stop(slug)

            # ... and create a new one. First we want to animate the x property
            # on the slug widget so that it moves to a specific position. This
            # should take 2 seconds and we're using the out_quad transition.
            # Then we want to animate the slug's opacity so that the slug becomes
            # fully transparent after three seconds.
            self.drowning_animation = (Animation(x = 680, duration = 2, t ='out_quad')
                                  + Animation(opacity = 0, duration = 3))

            # Let's start the drowning animation on the slug.
            self.drowning_animation.start(slug)
```

```
        # We want the sound to play only now.
        self.sound.play()

    def reset(self):
        ...
```

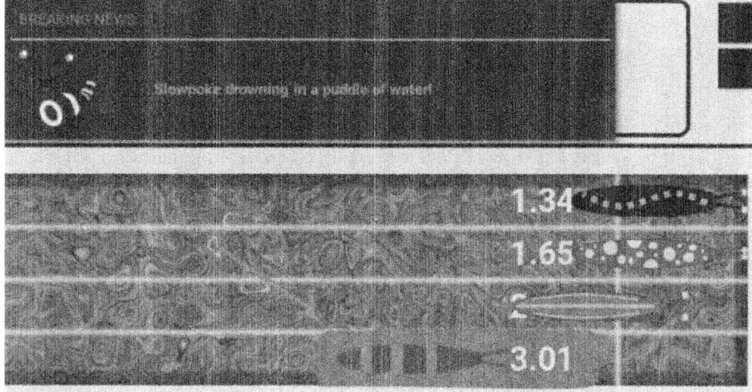


If you now run the app, one of the slugs will drown.

Here Slowpoke turned out to be the unlucky one. You can see him slowly disappear in the puddle.

Now, in the exercise below you will implement the **reset** method and in the next chapter we'll implement the Electroshock accident.

# It's Your Turn Now...

## EXERCISE

Your task is to implement the **reset** method in the **PuddleAccident** class. You need to take care of a couple things:

1. It may happen that you hit the Next Race button before the drowning animation is complete. Then you will not see the slug again. In order to prevent it, just stop the animation at the top of the **reset** method.

2. If you hit the Nect Race button too soon, the sound may be still playing in the next race. In order to prevent it, stop the sound if it's still in the **'play'** state.

3. The slug should become visible again.

4. The puddle image should disappear.

## SOLUTION

Here's the code:

```
# File name: accident.py
...
### PUDDLE ###
class PuddleAccident(Accident):
    ...
    def reset(self):
        # Just in case the animation is not yet complete, stop it.
        self.drowning_animation.stop(self.slug)
```

```
        # If the sound is still playing, stop it.
        if self.sound.state == 'play':
            self.sound.stop()

        # The slug should be visible again:
        self.slug.opacity = 1

        # We don't need the puddle anymore.
        self.track.remove_widget(self.puddle)

### ELECTROSHOCK ###
...
```

# Chapter 116 – The Electroshock Accident

In the previous chapter we handled the Puddle accident.

In this chapter we're going to handle the Electroshock accident. Let's go to the **go** method in the **Game** class and set the accident to Electroshock:

```
# File name: main.py
...
class Game(ScreenManager):
    ...
    def go(self, screen_manager):
        ...
        if self.accident_expected:
            # self.accident = choice(self.accidents)
            self.accident = self.acc_electroshock
            self.accident.position = randint(290, 500)
            ...
```

So, how does the Electroshock accident work? Well, it's definitely convenient for the slug. Here's what will happen:

- An animated bolt image will appear on top of the slug's body image.

- The slug will be powered up by the bolt and will accelerate.

Let's start implementing the **happen** method then. Both the sound and the bolt animation will be repeated. To loop the sound we'll set the **loop** keyword argument to **True**. We'll create an image of a bolt and position it on the slug's body.

The running animation should be stopped, but we won't see it because a new running animation with the **acceleration** parameter set to **5** will be created and started right away.

Next, the repeated bolt animation will be created and started on the bolt image. In the animation we'll be animatig the image's **opacity** property a couple times. This will produce the effect of flickering. OK, let's do it. Here's the **happen** method:

```
# File name: accident.py
...
### ELECTROSHOCK ###
class ElectroshockAccident(Accident):
    ...
    def happen(self):
        # The sound should be looping.
        super().happen(loop=True)

        # Let's create the bolt image and position it on the slug's body.
        self.bolt = Image(source = self.image)
        self.bolt.x = self.slug.body.x
        self.slug.add_widget(self.bolt)

        # Let's stop the running animation and start a new one with
```

```
        # acceleration set to 5.
        self.slug.run_animation.cancel(self.slug)
        self.slug.run(acceleration=5).start(self.slug)

        # We must remember to bind the two methods from the Game class
        # to the animations' events so that the slugs can finish the race.
        self.slug.run_animation.bind(on_progress=self.game.while_running)
        self.slug.run_animation.bind(on_complete=self.game.finish_race)

        # Here's the bolt animation. It consists of four simple animations.
        self.bolt_animation = (Animation(opacity = 0, duration = .2)
                             + Animation(opacity = 1, duration = .1)
                             + Animation(opacity = .2, duration = .05)
                             + Animation(opacity = 1, duration = .05))

        self.bolt_animation.repeat = True
        self.bolt_animation.start(self.bolt)

    def reset(self):
        ...
```

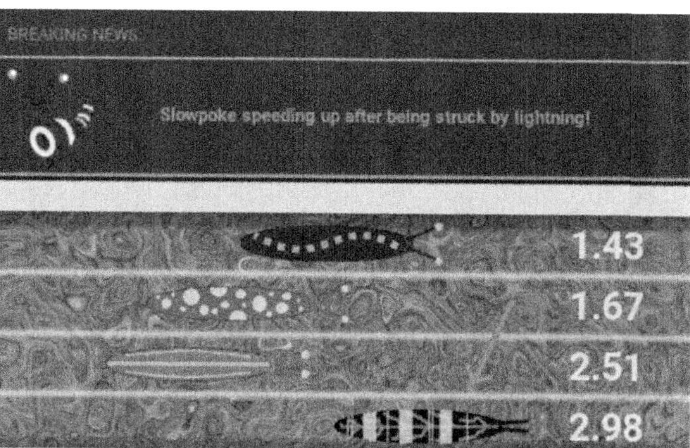


If you now run the app, one of the slugs will be struck by lightning, which may help him win.

In the exercise below you will implement the **reset** method, and in the next chapter we'll be talking about the Turning Back accident.

# It's Your Turn Now...

## EXERCISE

In this exercise your task is to implement the **reset** method. This method should take care of the following:

- cancel the bolt animation,

- remove the bolt image,

- stop that annoying sizzling sound of the bolt.

## SOLUTION

Here's the code:

```
# File name: accident.py
...
### ELECTROSHOCK ###
class ElectroshockAccident(Accident):
    ...
    def reset(self):
        # Cancel the bolt animation.
        self.bolt_animation.cancel(self.bolt)
        # Remove the bolt image.
        self.slug.remove_widget(self.bolt)
        # Stop the sound.
        self.sound.stop()
### TURNING BACK ###
...
```

# Chapter 117 – The Turning Back Accident

In the previous chapter we implemented the Electroshock accident.

In this chapter we're going to implement the Turning Back accident. As usual, let's start by setting the accident that is supposed to happen to the Turning Back accident:

```
# File name: main.py
...
class Game(ScreenManager):
    ...
    def go(self, screen_manager):
        ...
        if self.accident_expected:
            # self.accident = choice(self.accidents)
            self.accident = self.acc_turning_back
            self.accident.position = randint(290, 500)
            ...
```

So, what is this accident all about? Well, it's slightly different than the others. Here the slug stops, turns around and goes in backward direction. So, first the running animation should stop. Then we want the slug to turn around, which can be done in several ways. One is rotation, but the slug is pretty long and he could hit the slugs on the neighboring lanes of the racetrack. So, let's do it in a different way, by animating the slug's scale on the X axis. We have to add a property to the **Slug** class that we can animate. Let'sname it **x_scale**. This is going to be a NumericProperty with the default value of 1. If we set it to -1, the widget is flipped horizontally. So, here's the property:

```
# File name: slug.py
...
class Slug(RelativeLayout):
    ...
    finished = BooleanProperty(True)

    # We'll need this property in the Turning Back accident.
    x_scale = NumericProperty(1)

    def __init__(self, **kwargs):
        ...
```

We now need to add a canvas instruction in the kv file so that we can use the **x_scale** property to set the scale of the slug widget:

```
#:kivy 1.11.1
# File name: slug.kv
#:import slug slug

<Slug>:
    # Here's how we can set the scale of the slug widget on the X axis.
```

```
        canvas:
            Scale:
                x: root.x_scale

    pos_hint: {'x': self.start_position, 'center_y': root.y_position}
    ...
```

We're also going to create a **continue_race** method and bind it to the animation's **on_complete** event. In this method we're going to start another running animation, but this time the slug should be running in the opposite direction, so toward the start line and even farther beyond. In order to do it, we have to modify the **run** method in the **Slug** class.

Let's add another keyword parameter to the method, **backward**, and set its default value to **False**. Then we can use it in a conditional block to decide which direction the slug should be running in. Most of the time the **backward** parameter will be set to **False**, so the slug will be running toward the finish line, just like now. But if it's set to **True**, which will be the case when the Turning Back accident happens, the slug will be running in the opposite direction until he leaves the screen completely. So, here's our modified **run** method:

```
# File name: slug.py
...
class Slug(RelativeLayout):
    ...
    def update(self, winning_slug, race_number):
        ...

    # Here's the new backward parameter.
    def run(self, acceleration=1, backward=False):
        ...
        self.rotate_eyes(30, running_time/6)

        # If the slug should be running toward the finish line...
        if not backward:
            # ... nothing changes...
            self.run_animation = Animation(pos_hint={'x': self.finish_position},
                                           d=running_time)
        # ... but otherwise he should be running to the left and leave the screen.
        else:
            self.run_animation = Animation(pos_hint={'x': -.1}, d=1)

        return self.run_animation

    def reset(self):
        ...
```

Now, with the **run** method modified, we can implement the **happen** method. Actually, you're going to do it in the first exercise. And in the second exercise you'll implement the **reset** method. As for the next chapter, we'll be implementing the Shooting Eyes accident in it.

# It's Your Turn Now...

### EXERCISE 1 - The happen and continue_race methods

So, here's how we are going to implement the **happen** and **continue_race** methods. Just follow the steps below:

1. In the **happen** method stop the running animation.

2. Also in the **happen** method create a new animation. Name it **turn_animation**. The property to animate is **x_scale** and the target value is **-1**. The animation should take 2 seconds. Start the animation on the slug.

3. Create the **continue_race** method. In the method create and start the running animation on the slug again. This time the slug should run in the opposite direction. The **continue_race** method must have the **animation** and **slug** parameters.

4. There is one more line of code you must add in the **continue_race** method. We must bind the **finish_race** method in the **Game** class so that the slug is able to finish the race. Otherwise we wouldn't be able to finish the race because it's only possible when all four slugs have finished the race. So, add the binding to the backward running animation.

### SOLUTION

Here's the code:

```
# File name: accident.py
...
### TURNING BACK ###
class TurningBackAccident(Accident):
    ...
    def happen(self):
        super().happen()

        # Stop the running animation.
        self.slug.run_animation.stop(self.slug)

        # Create the turn animation and start it on the slug.
        self.turn_animation = Animation(x_scale = -1, duration = 2)
        self.turn_animation.start(self.slug)

        # Bind the continue_race method to the on_complete event
        # of the turn animation.
        self.turn_animation.bind(on_complete=self.continue_race)

    # The slug should continue the race in the opposite direction.
    def continue_race(self, animation, slug):
        self.slug.run(backward=True).start(self.slug)
```

```
        # The slug must be able to finish the race.
        self.slug.run_animation.bind(on_complete=self.game.finish_race)

    def reset(self):
        ...
```

### EXERCISE 2 - The **reset** method

The **reset** method is going to be very simple. Just reset the **x_scale** property back to **1**.

### SOLUTION

Here's the code:

```
# File name: accident.py
...
### TURNING BACK ###
class TurningBackAccident(Accident):
    ...
    def reset(self):
        self.slug.x_scale = 1

### SHOOTING EYES ###
...
```

And now if you run the app, you can see one of the slugs turn back.

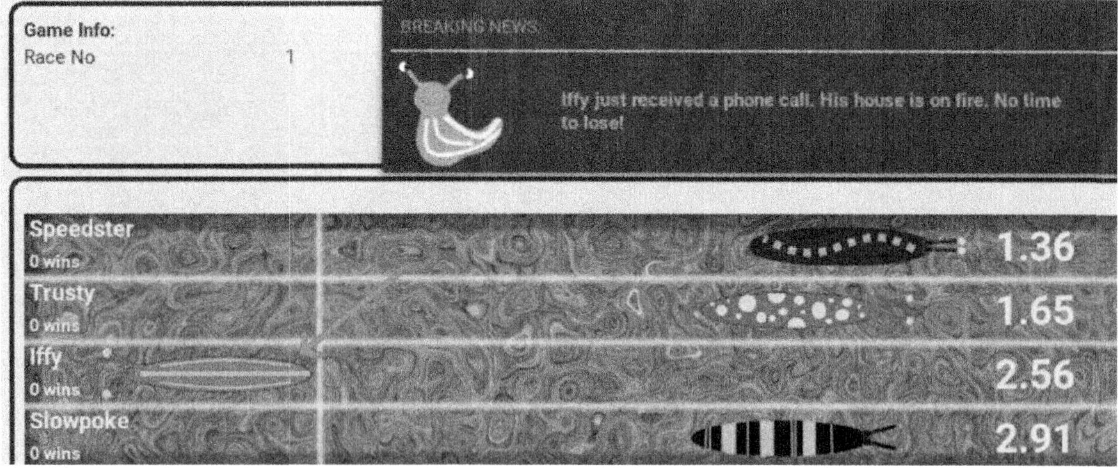

# Chapter 118 – The Shooting Eyes Accident

In the previous chapter we implemented the Turning Back accident.

In this chapter we're going to implement the Shooting Eyes accident. As usual, let's start by setting the accident that is supposed to happen to the Shooting Eyes accident:

```
# File name: main.py
...
class Game(ScreenManager):
    ...
    def go(self, screen_manager):
        ...
        if self.accident_expected:
            # self.accident = choice(self.accidents)
            self.accident = self.acc_shooting_eyes
            self.accident.position = randint(290, 500)
            ...
```

This is one of the most drastic accidents. A slug can shoot his eyes to make his chances of winning bigger. This is because the race is won by the slug who first crosses the finish line, so the first part of the body that crosses the line counts. Fortunately, the eyes regenerate after the race.

Anyway, let's start with the **happen** method, as usual. Here's what should happen:

- The slug should stop moving his eyes.

- The eyes should be directed straight forward.

- They eyes should be shot and start moving toward the finish line at a greater speed.

So, how are we going to implement this? First of all, we're going to use translation to control the movement of the eyes. As you remember, this is a canvas instruction. We have to import the **Translate** class then.

Now, to stop the eye animation, we'll just use the **cancel** method. Then we have to rotate the eyes so that they both point toward the finish line. To do that we will set the **rot_angle** property to **0**. This will rotate the eyes instantaneously.

Next, to move the eyes, we'll define two attributes on the slug: **translation_left** for the left eye and **translation_right** for the right eye. These are going to be instances of the **Translate** class. The default **x** translation will be 0. We'll use a context manager (which is the **with** block that we use for canvas instructions in Python code) to do it.

And now the most important part – we'll need a method that will actually take care of moving the eyes. The method, let's name it **move_eyes**, should be called 60 times per second (so every 1/60 seconds) and check the value of **x**. If it's not greater than 500 (it's a safe distance so that the eyes are beyond the screen and we don't see them anymore), the eyes will be moved by 3 pixels to the right. Naturally, we have to schedule this method to be called every 1/60 seconds, which we'll do in the **happen** method.

Here's the code:

```
# File name: accident.py
...
from kivy.clock import Clock

# We'll need the Translate class to move the eyes.
from kivy.graphics import Translate

class Accident(ABC):
    ...
### SHOOTING EYES ###
class ShootingEyesAccident(Accident):
    ...
    def happen(self):
        super().happen()

        # The eyes should stop moving...
        self.slug.eye_animation.cancel(self.slug)

        # ...and they should be directed forward.
        self.slug.rot_angle = 0

        # We define a Translate object for each eye so that we can control
        # the distance it has traveled.
        with self.slug.left_eye.canvas.before:
            self.slug.translation_left = Translate(x = 0)

        with self.slug.right_eye.canvas.before:
            self.slug.translation_right = Translate(x = 0)

        # We schedule the move_eyes method to be called every 1/60 seconds,
        # so 60 times per second.
        self.shoot_event = Clock.schedule_interval(self.move_eyes, 1/60)

    # Here's the method that will actually push the eyes forward until the
    # distance from the original position is 500 pixels.
    def move_eyes(self, dt):
        if self.slug.translation_left.x < 500:
            self.slug.translation_left.x += 3
            self.slug.translation_right.x += 3

    def reset(self):
        ...
```

If you now run the app, you will see the eyes rotate so as to point to the finish line, you will hear a shot and the eyes will start moving.

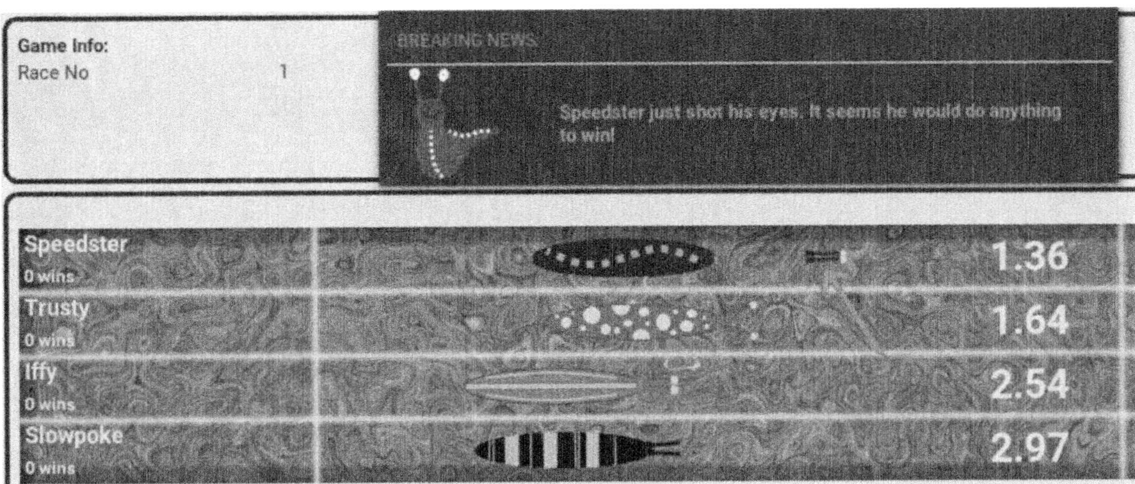


There is a problem, though. Even if the eyes cross the finish line first, the slug doesn't win. This is what we are going to take care of next.

So, where in the code is it decided which slug wins the race? Have a look at the **while_running** method in the **Game** class. Now, the problem is that if the eyes move away from the body, we mess up with the **right** property on the slug instance and it doesn't work as we might expect. So, let's distinguish two situations:

1) The slug is not shooting his eyes, so everything should work fine.

2) The slug is shooting his eyes and we have to redefine the condition when he wins.

In order to distinguish these two situations in code, let's add a BooleanProperty to the **Slug** class.

We can name it **shooting** and set its default value to **False** because most of the time the slug won't be shooting his eyes:

```
# File name: slug.py
...
class Slug(RelativeLayout):
    ...
    x_scale = NumericProperty(1)

    # This property will tell us if
    # the slug is shooting his eyes.
    shooting = BooleanProperty(False)

    def __init__(self, **kwargs):
        ...
```

Now, we have to set the **shooting** property to **True** in the **happen** method of the **ShootingEyesAccident** class:

```
# File name: accident.py
...
### SHOOTING EYES ###
class ShootingEyesAccident(Accident):
    ...
    def happen(self):
        super().happen()

        # Now we know the slug is shooting his eyes,
        # so let's set the shooting property to True.
        self.slug.shooting = True

        self.slug.eye_animation.cancel(self.slug)
        ...
```

And now we can modify the **while_running** method in the **Game** class. Here we have to decide which part of the slug is the one that makes him win when it crosses the finish line. We'll create a **front** attribute on the slug and set it accordingly. There should be two scenarios:

1) If the slug is not shooting, **front** should be the same as **right**, just like up to now.

2) If the slug is shooting his eyes, we'll have to add the **x** translation of either eye to **right** (let's use the left eye for example, but either would do), as well as the eye's width. Then it will be the tip of the eye that will make the slug win when it crosses the finish line.

So, with that said, let's implement it in code:

```
# File name: main.py
...
class Game(ScreenManager):
    ...
    def while_running(self, animation, slug, progression):
        # Now we have to decide which part of the slug is the front. When this part
        # crosses the finish line, the slug will win.

        # If the slug is shooting his eyes, the eye's translation and width must be
        # taken into consideration.
        if slug.shooting:
            slug.front = slug.right + slug.translation_left.x + slug.left_eye.width
        # Otherwise we can still use the right property.
        else:
            slug.front = slug.right

        # Now we should check whether the slug's front has crossed the finish line.
        if slug.front > self.finish_line:
            if not self.race_winner:
                ...
```

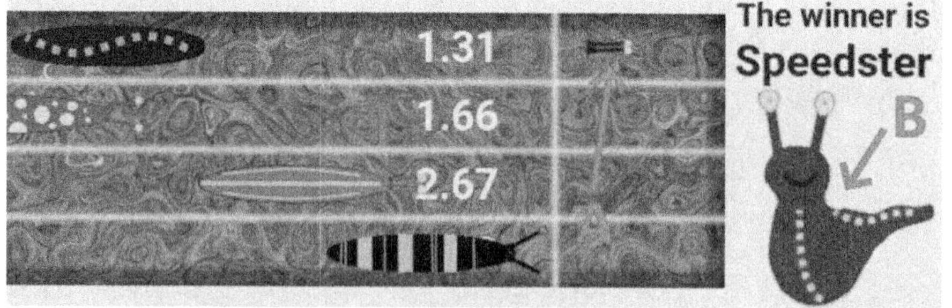


Now if you run the app and a slug's eyes cross the finish line as first (A), the slug will win (B).

In the exercise below you will implement the **reset** method.

And in the next chapter we'll handle the Rubberized accident.

# It's Your Turn Now...

## EXERCISE

In the **reset** method of the **ShootingEyesAccident** class we have to take care of a couple things for our program to work. So, here's what you should do:

1. The slug's **shooting** BooleanProperty should be set to **False**.

2. **shoot_event** should be unscheduled, we don't want the eyes to move forward anymore.

3. The **translation_left_x** and **translation_right_x** properties should be reset to **0** so that the eyes are attached to the body again.

4. The eyes should start rotating again. Set the rotation angle to **30** and time to **1**.

## SOLUTION

Here's the code:

```
# File name: accident.py
...
### SHOOTING EYES ###
class ShootingEyesAccident(Accident):
    ...
    def reset(self):
        # The slug is no longer shooting, so let's reset the shooting property.
        self.slug.shooting = False

        # We don't want the eyes to move anymore, so let's unschedule shoot_event.
        Clock.unschedule(self.shoot_event)

        # The eyes should be attached to the body again.
        self.slug.translation_left.x = 0
        self.slug.translation_right.x = 0

        # The eyes should start rotating again.
        self.slug.rotate_eyes(30, 1)

### RUBBERIZED ###
...
```

Now if you run the app and one of the slugs shoots his eyes, everything will go back to normal when you hit the Next Race button.

# Chapter 119 – The Rubberized Accident

In the previous chapter we implemented the Shooting Eyes accident.

In this chapter we're going to implement the Rubberized accident. So, let's set the accident that is supposed to happen to the Rubberized accident:

```
# File name: main.py
...
class Game(ScreenManager):
    ...
    def go(self, screen_manager):
        ...
        if self.accident_expected:
            # self.accident = choice(self.accidents)
            self.accident = self.acc_rubberized
            self.accident.position = randint(290, 500)
            ...
```

The Rubberized accident is an accident in which the shape of the slug's body changes. The slug stretches in horizontal direction, which makes it easier for him to win. After crossing the finish line, he takes again his original shape.

So, here's how we are going to implement the accident:

First we're going to schedule a method to be called every 1/60 seconds, so 60 times per minute, just like with the Shooting Eyes accident. We can name the method **stretch**, because just like we translated the eyes in the Shooting Eyes accident, here we're going to stretch the body. We can make use of the **x_scale** property to do that. As you remember, we defined this property in the **Slug** class when we were implementing the Turning Back accident.

About the **stretch** method... In the method we'll check whether the value of **x_scale** is less than or equal to 3. So, the maximum stretching factor should be 3. If it is, and if the slug hasn't finished the race yet, the value of the property will be increased by 0.01. This should continue until the slug finishes the race.

Then the scale is decreased by 0.03 for as long as **x_scale** is greater than 1. So, regaining the original size is going to take less time than stretching. The moment **x_scale** is less than 1.1, the sound should stop playing if it hasn't yet (we set it to loop in the **happen** method).

Here's the code:

```
# File name: accident.py
...
### RUBBERIZED ###
class RubberizedAccident(Accident):
    ...
    def happen(self):
        super().happen(loop=True)

        # Let's schedule the stretch method to be called 60 times per second.
```

```
        self.stretch_event = Clock.schedule_interval(self.stretch, 1/60)

    # Here's the method that actually  takes care of  stretching the slug.
    def stretch(self, dt):
        if self.slug.x_scale <= 3 and not self.slug.finished:
            self.slug.x_scale += 0.01
        elif self.slug.x_scale > 1 and self.slug.finished:
            self.slug.x_scale -= 0.03
            if self.slug.x_scale < 1.1 and self.sound.state == 'play':
                    self.sound.stop()

    def reset(self):
        pass
```

If you now run the app, one of the slugs will stretch.

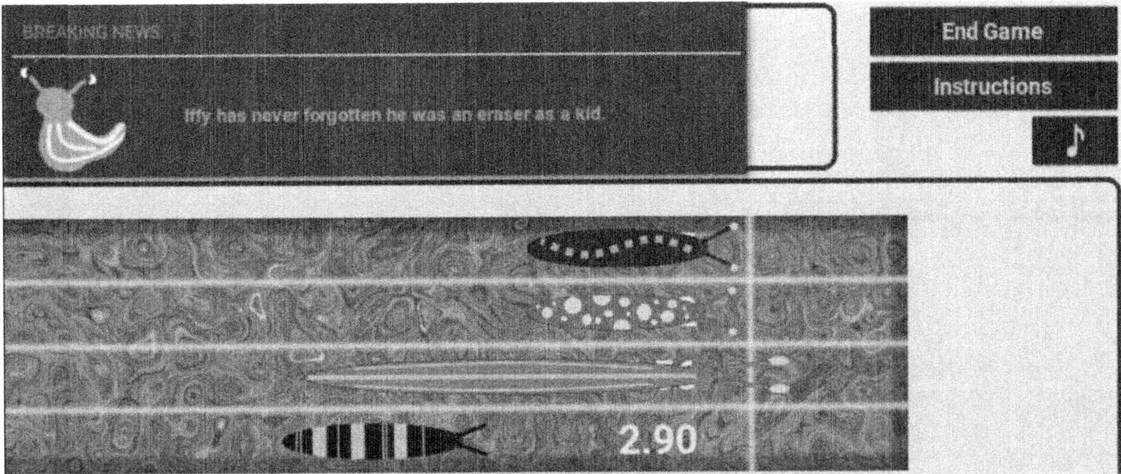


The problem, though, is that, just like with the Shooting Eyes accident, the slug doesn't win when he crosses the finish line. So, let's handle it in a similar way.

Let's start by adding the **rubberized** BooleanProperty to the **Slug** class:

```
# File name: slug.py
...
class Slug(RelativeLayout):
    ...
    shooting = BooleanProperty(False)

    # True if the accident happened.
    rubberized = BooleanProperty(False)

    def __init__(self, **kwargs):
        ...
```

Now we're going to modify the **while_running** method in the **Game** class again so that it takes into account whether the slug should be rubberized or not. We're just going to add one more condition in the conditional block so that the slug's front is calculated correctly.

So, if the slug is rubberized, we calculate his front by adding to his **x** position the product of the sum of his body and eye widths and **x_scale**. Complicated as it sounds, it's not that scary.

Have a look:

```
# File name: main.py
...
class Game(ScreenManager):
    ...
    def while_running(self, animation, slug, progression):
        if slug.shooting:
            slug.front = slug.right + slug.translation_left.x + slug.left_eye.width
        # We calculate the slug's front differently if he's rubberized.
        elif slug.rubberized:
            slug.front = slug.x + (slug.body.width + slug.left_eye.width) * slug.x_scale
        else:
            slug.front = slug.right

        if slug.front > self.finish_line:
            ...
```

Naturally, for this to work, we must set the **rubberized** property to **True** in the **happen** method first:

```
# File name: accident.py
...
### RUBBERIZED ###
class RubberizedAccident(Accident):
    ...
    def happen(self):
        super().happen(loop=True)
        self.slug.rubberized = True
        self.stretch_event = Clock.schedule_interval(self.stretch, 1/60)

    def stretch(self, dt):
        ...
```

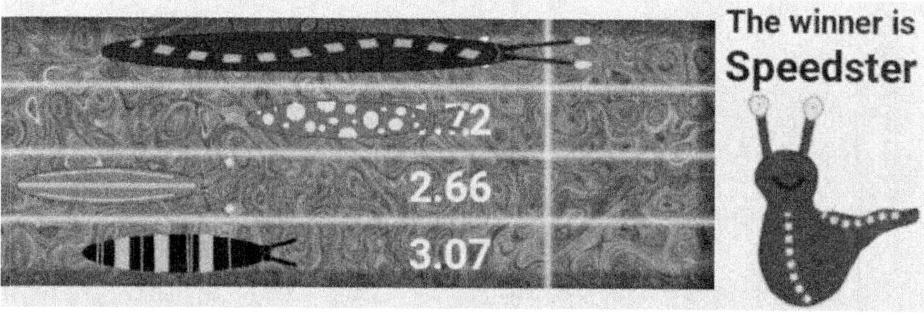


Now the slug can win the race also if he's stretched.

If you hit the Next Race button and the next race begins, you will notice that one of the slugs will start stretching right away. This is because the **stretch** method is still called every 1/60 seconds. This issue must be handled in the **reset** method, which you are going to implement as an exercise. And in the next chapter we're going to implement the last accident, the Devoured accident.

# It's Your Turn Now...

## EXERCISE

Implement the **reset** method in the **RuberrizedAccident** class. It should do the following:

- set the **rubberized** property on the slug to **False**,

- unschedule **strech_event** so that the **stretch** method is no longer called every 1/60 seconds,

- set the slug's **x_scale** property back to **1**.

## SOLUTION

Here's the code:

```
# File name: accident.py
...
### RUBBERIZED ###
class RubberizedAccident(Accident):
    ...
    def reset(self):
        # Set the rubberized property to False.
        self.slug.rubberized = False

        # Unschedule strech_event.
        Clock.unschedule(self.stretch_event)

        # Set the x_scale property back to 1.
        self.slug.x_scale = 1

### DEVOURED ###
...
```

# Chapter 120 – The Devoured Accident

In the previous chapter we implemented the Rubberized accident.

In this chapter we're going to implement the Devoured accident, which is the last accident in our game. So, let's set the accident that is supposed to happen to the Devoured accident:

```
# File name: main.py
...
class Game(ScreenManager):
    ...
    def go(self, screen_manager):
        ...
        if self.accident_expected:
            # self.accident = choice(self.accidents)
            self.accident = self.acc_devoured
            self.accident.position = randint(290, 500)
            ...
```

Well, what is this accident all about? When it happens, a slug monster appears (which is an **Image** widget) at a position outside the visible app window. The position is relative to the position of the affected slug. The monster widget should be added to the slug widget.

Then an animation is created and started on the monster widget. It's an animation on the **x** property and the target value is 500. The duration of the animation will depend on the slug's speed, which, in turn, is determined by his **running_time**. So, we need access to the slug's running time. To this end let's modify the code of the **run** method in the **Slug** class by defining the **running_time** attribute on the object, so using **self**:

```
# File name: slug.py
...
class Slug(RelativeLayout):
    ...
    def run(self, acceleration=1, backward=False):
        ...
        if move_base < self.speeds[0]:
            self.running_time = uniform(8, 10) / acceleration  # slow
        elif move_base <= self.speeds[1]:
            self.running_time = uniform(6, 8)  / acceleration # medium
        else:
            self.running_time = uniform(4, 6) / acceleration # fast
        ...
        if not backward:
            self.run_animation = Animation(pos_hint={'x': self.finish_position},
                                           d=self.running_time)
        ...
        return self.run_animation

    def reset(self):
        ...
```

The monster will chase the slug and try to devour it. So, we'll bind a **chase** method to the **on_progress** event of the monster's animation. Anyway, here's the **happen** method and the not yet implemented **chase** method:

```
# File name: accident.py
...
### DEVOURED ###
class DevouredAccident(Accident):
    ...
    def happen(self):
        super().happen()

        # Let's create and add a monster Image widget.
        self.monster = Image(source = self.image)
        self.monster.size_hint = (2, 2)
        self.monster.x = self.slug.body.x - 800
        self.monster.y = self.slug.body.y - 15
        self.slug.add_widget(self.monster)

        # Here's the monster animation. The monster is moving six times
        # faster than the slug.
        self.monster_animation = Animation(x=500, d=self.slug.running_time / 6)

        # Let's bind the chase method to the on_progress event.
        self.monster_animation.bind(on_progress=self.chase)

        # Let's start the animation on the monster widget.
        self.monster_animation.start(self.monster)

    # We're going to implement the method in a minute.
    def chase(self, animation, monster, progression):
        pass

    def reset(self):
        ...
```

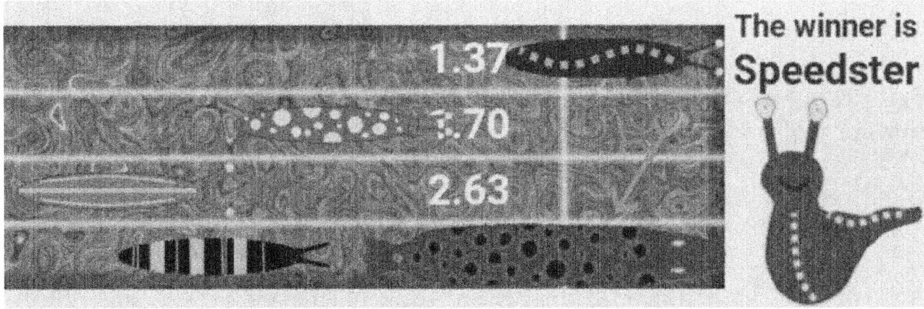


If you now run the app, you'll see the monster appear, run all the way along the racetrack and to the right.

But the monster doesn't do any harm to the slug. He doesn't even catch him, let alone devour. This is what the **chase** method is for.

In the **chase** method we compare the **x** position of the monster with that of the slug. If the former is greater than or equal to the latter, the slug is caught and devoured. But as this all happens while the monster animation is in progress, we must make sure the slug is caught and devoured only once. So, let's add a **devoured** BooleanProperty flag to the **Slug** class:

```
# File name: slug.py
...
class Slug(RelativeLayout):
    ...
    rubberized = BooleanProperty(False)

    # This will change to True the moment the slug is devoured by the slug monster.
    devoured = BooleanProperty(False)

    def __init__(self, **kwargs):
        ...
```

Let's go back to the **chase** method. So, the slug will be devoured when the monster passes him, but only if he hasn't been devoured before. Then, the value of the **devoured** BooleanProperty will be set to **True**, the slug's running animation will be stopped and the monster animation will be canceled:

```
# File name: accident.py
...
### DEVOURED ###
class DevouredAccident(Accident):
    ...
    def chase(self, animation, monster, progression):
        if monster.x >= self.slug.body.x - 20 and not self.slug.devoured:
            self.slug.devoured = True
            self.slug.run_animation.stop(self.slug)
            self.monster_animation.cancel(self.monster)

    def reset(self):
        ...
```

Now if you run the application, the monster will catch the slug. Both the slug and the monster will stop moving.

In the exercise below you will implement the **reset** method.

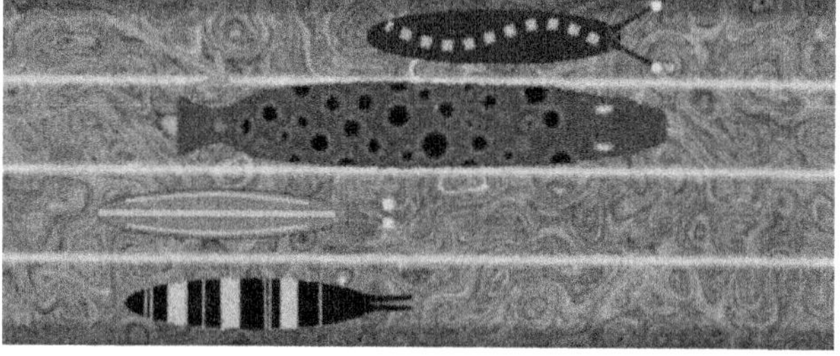

This was the last accident. In the next chapter we'll clean up the code a little so that the accidents happen only occasionally and not in each race. We'll also test the app because now we have all the functionality in place.

# It's Your Turn Now...

## EXERCISE

Your task is to implement the **reset** method in the **DevouredAccident** class. It should take care of the following:

- resetting the value of the slug's **devoured** property to **False**,

- stopping the sound if it's still playing (HINT: check the sound's state),

- removing the monster widget from the slug.

## SOLUTION

Here's the code:

```
# File name: accident.py
...
### DEVOURED ###
class DevouredAccident(Accident):
    ...
    def reset(self):
        # Set the devoured property of the slug to False.
        self.slug.devoured = False

        # Check if the sound is still playing and if it is, stop it.
        if self.sound.state == 'play':
            self.sound.stop()

        # Remove the monster widget.
        self.slug.remove_widget(self.monster)
```

# Chapter 121 – Accident Setup

In the preceding chapters we implemented all the accidents one by one. Now our app is almost complete. As far as accidents are concerned, we need to clean up the code slightly so that the accidents only happen from time to time.

In the chapter on accident logic we already implemented all the functionality that we need. There isn't going to be anything new in this chapter, we'll just uncomment some of the code so that it all works as expected.

Just a quick reminder. Here are the guidelines for the accidents again:

1. There should be no accidents at all in the first five races.

2. The accidents should happen with random frequency.

3. The accidents should be picked randomly from the list of accidents.

4. The accidents should happen on a particular stretch of the racetrack, between X position 290 and 500.

5. The accidents may happen to any slug with equal probability, with one exception: Trusty is less prone to accidents than the other slugs.

All the code we need is already there, in the **go** method of the **Game** class. At this point an accident is expected in every race and it's always the Devoured accident. Let's restore the original code that we created before:

```
# File name: main.py
...
class Game(ScreenManager):
    ...
    def go(self, screen_manager):
        ...
        # Accident
        #There's a 25% probability that an accident will happen,
        # starting from race 6.
        self.accident_expected = (randint(0, 3) == 0
                                  if self.race_number > 5
                                  else False)
        if self.accident_expected:
            # The accident is picked randomly.
            self.accident = choice(self.accidents)
            self.accident.position = randint(290, 500)
            ...
```

Now, there is one more problem. When we were implementing the accidents, there always was an accident expected to happen. This is no longer the case. The problem is in the **reset_race** method.

The method calls the **reset_accidents** method and if there is no accident, we get an error because the **accident** attribute of the **Game** object doesn't exist:

```
# File name: main.py
...
class Game(ScreenManager):
    ...
    def reset_race(self):
        ...
        self.reset_accidents()
    ...
    def reset_accidents(self):
        if self.accident:
            self.accident.reset()
            self.accident = None

class SlugraceApp(App):
    ...
```

So, let's add this attribute in the constructor of the **Game** class:

```
# File name: main.py
...
class Game(ScreenManager):
    ...
    def __init__(self, **kwargs):
        ...
        # accidents
        ...
        self.accidents = [self.acc_broken_leg,
                          ...
                          self.acc_devoured]

        self.accident = None

    # callback methods
    ...
```

And now let's run the app and see if any accidents happen and if so, which ones and how often. I'm going to select the races ending condition so that the game is over after 20 races. Naturally, there won't be any accidents in the first five races.

Even if you simulate the game with the same settings, your results are going to be different because of the randomness of the accidents. Anyway, here's what I got:

<ins>Race 6</ins>: Iffy gets struck by lightning.

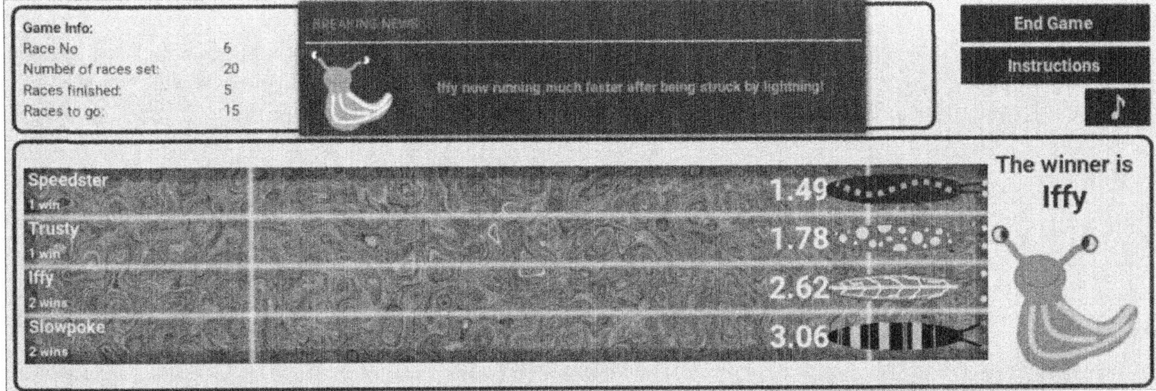

Race 11: Iffy is devoured by slug monster.

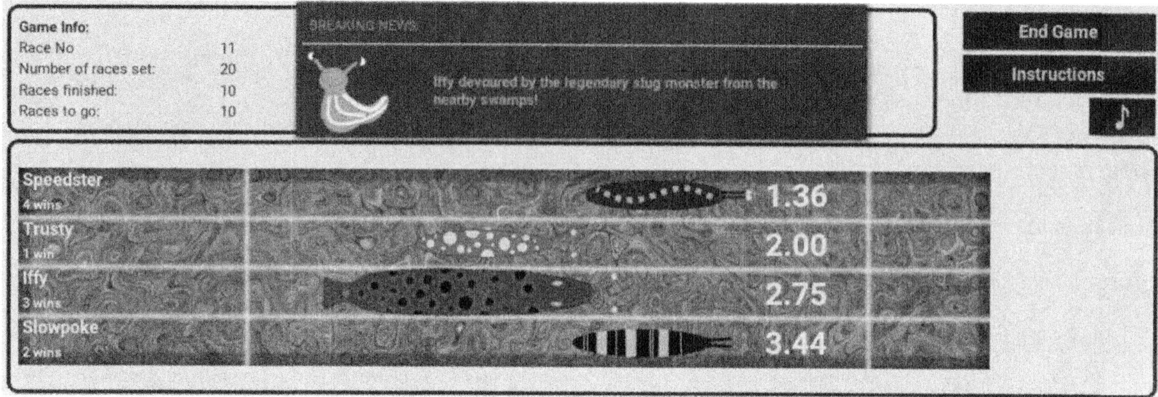


Race 13: Speedster is rubberized.

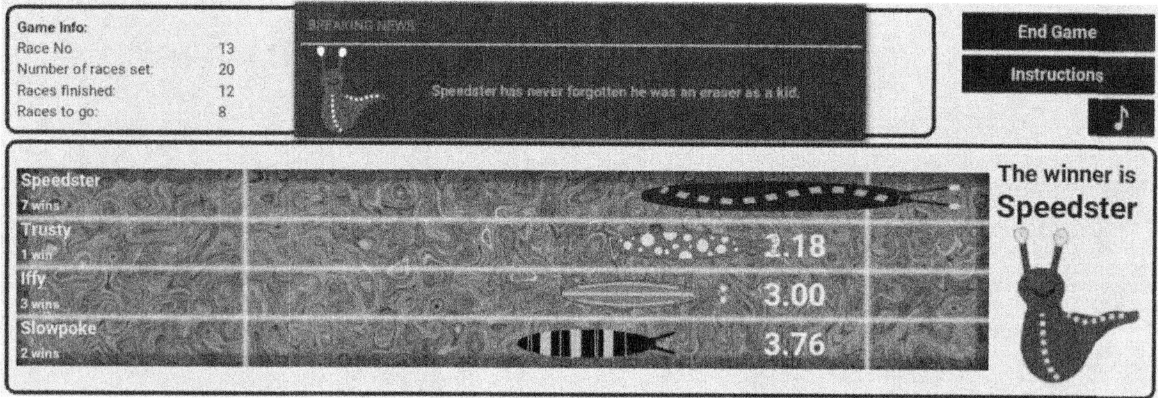


So, this time there were three accidents altogether in the 20 races. You may have had more or less, naturally.

We're done with the game logic. It's time for some final touches, which we are going to take care of in the next, final part of the book.

# Part XI

# Final Touches and Deployment

In this part of the book we'll add some final touches to the project, like the Instructions and Splash screens. We'll also deploy the application to Windows.

# Chapter 122 – Game Instructions

In the previous part of the book we completed our Slugrace game. There is still one button that does nothing, though. This is the Instructions button in the Race screen. We're going to implement it in this chapter.

Although our game seems easy and straightforward to use, it's mainly because we've spent so many hours on it. But to someone who launches it for the first time, it may seem confusing. So, even with simple games, it's always a good idea to add instructions that will tell new users how to play.

The Instructions button will take us to the Instructions screen, a screen we're going to build from scratch. The button will be only enabled between races and disabled when a race begins.

So, let's start by creating the screen.

## Screenshots

We're going to create step-by-step instructions that guide the user through all the screens and parts of screens. To this end we'll need some screenshots. Open the assets folder in your project folder, and create a **screenshots** folder.

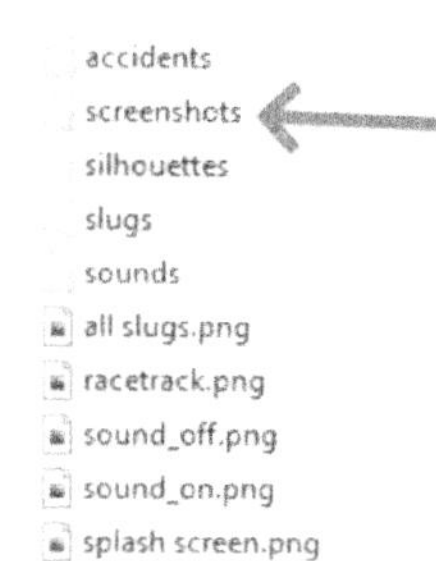


This is where the screenshots will go. I made the screenshots in the Paint.Net graphics editor, but you can use any program you like. The screenshots are 1200 x 675 px PNG images, so the same size as our app window, which we configured in the **main.py** file.

To keep things simple, I put the numbered instructions directly on the images so that it's easier for the user to quickly identify the part of the GUI we're talking about.

Here are the screenshots:

**Settings screen:**

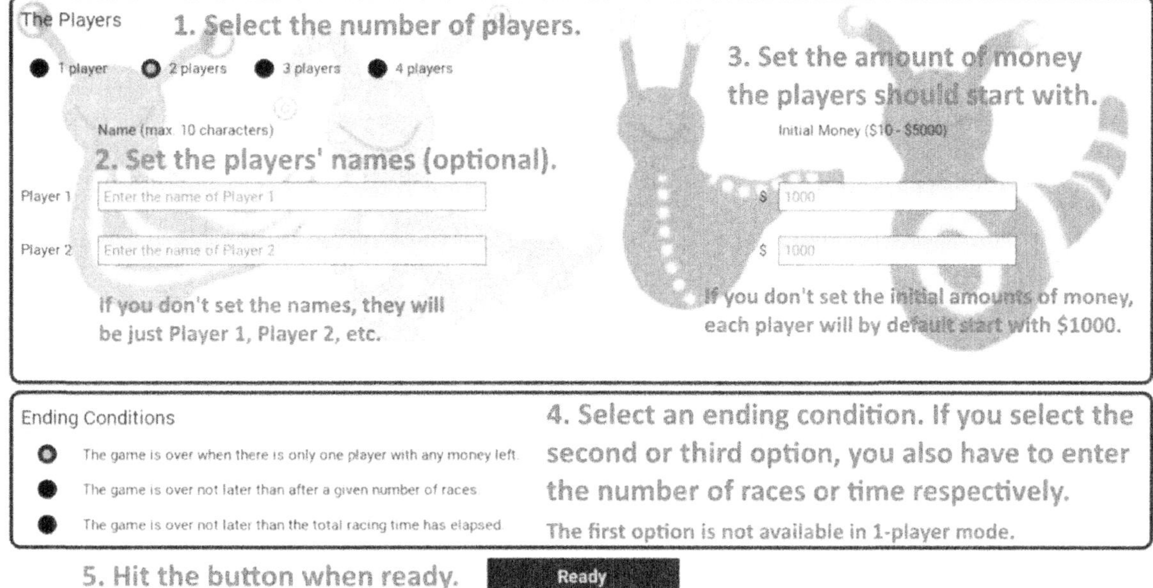


**Race screen with Bets screen:**

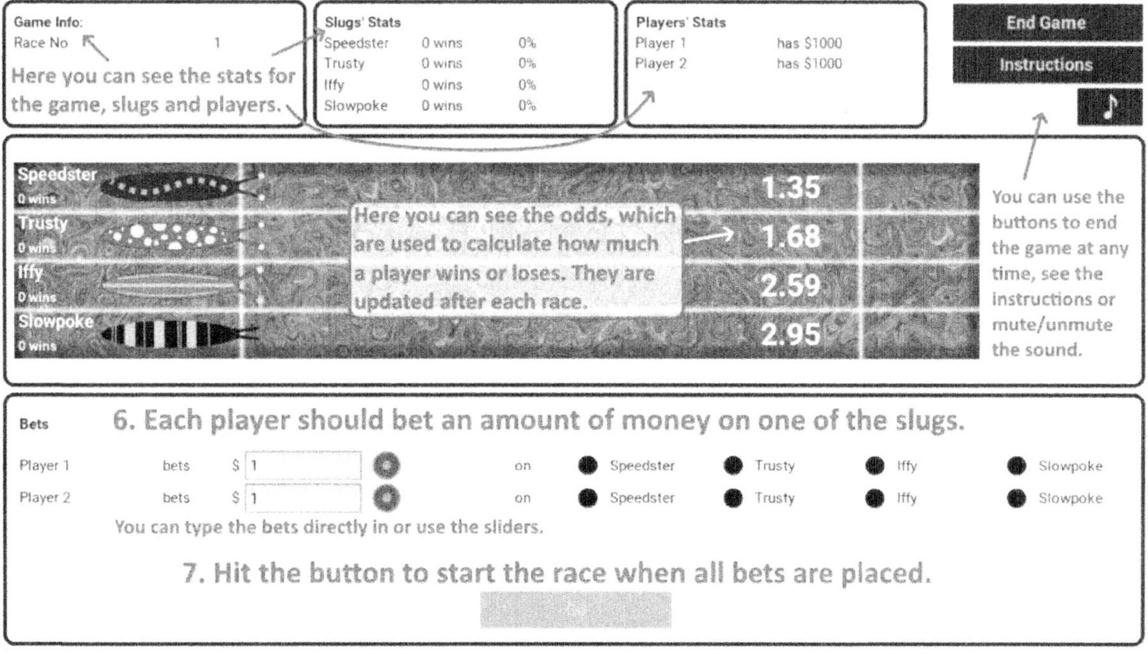

Race screen with Results screen:

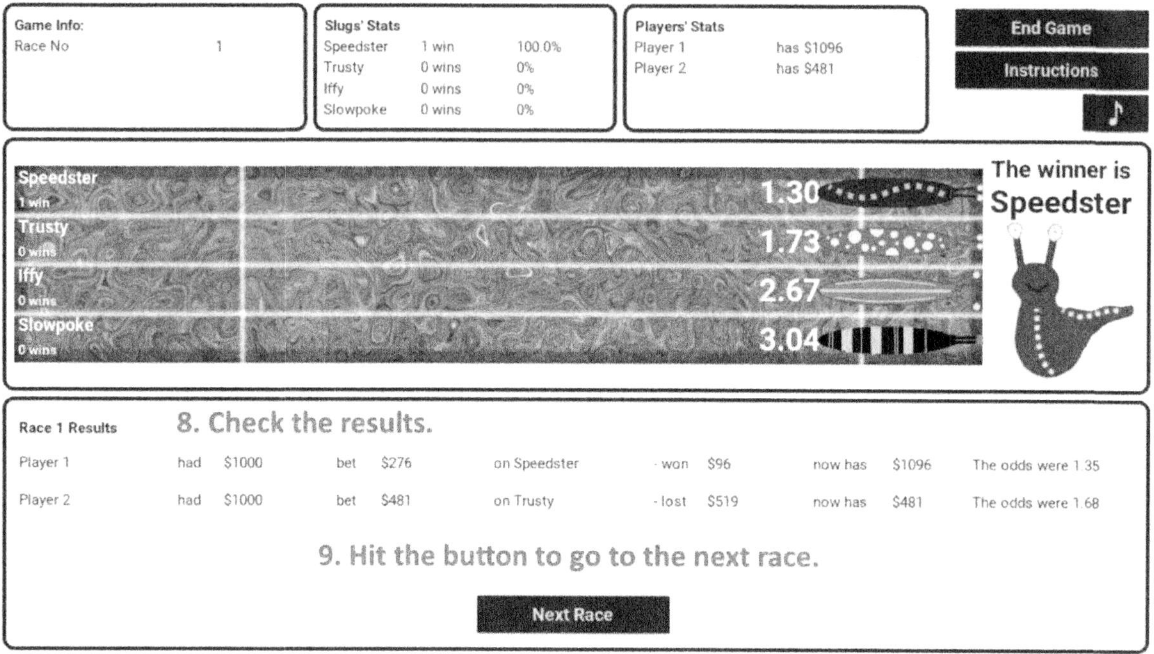


Game Over screen:

# Game Over

Here's the reason why the game ended.

**You ended the game manually.**

Here's the winner information.

**The winner is Player 1, having started at $1000, winning at $1096.**

10. Hit one of the buttons to either play again or quit.

Make sure to put the four images in the **screenshots** folder. Rename them respectively **settings.png**, **race_bets.png**, **race_results.png** and **gameover.png**.

# The Instructions Screen

We're ready to create the Instructions screen. We already have the **instructions.py** and **instructions.kv** files, but they are empty for now.

The Instructions screen is going to be simple. It's going to contain two widgets inside a vertical BoxLayout, a carousel and a button. The carousel is a Kivy widget that enables us to swipe between slides. The slides will be the aforementioned screenshots.

Let's start with the Python file. It's very much like that of the other screens:

```
# File name: instructions.py

from kivy.uix.screenmanager import Screen

class InstructionsScreen(Screen):
    pass
```

So, the root widget inherits from `Screen`, which is necessary if we want to use it with a screen manager. And here's the kv file:

```
#:kivy 1.11.1
# File name: instructions.kv
#:import instructions instructions

<InstructionsScreen>:
    canvas.before:
        # black background
        Color:
            rgba: 0, 0, 0, 1
        Rectangle:
            pos: self.pos
            size: self.size

    BoxLayout:
        orientation: 'vertical'
        spacing: 10
        padding: 10

        Carousel:
            # the four slides
            Image:
                source: 'assets/screenshots/settings.png'
            Image:
                source: 'assets/screenshots/race_bets.png'
```

```
            Image:
                source: 'assets/screenshots/race_results.png'
            Image:
                source: 'assets/screenshots/gameover.png'

        RedButton:
            text: 'Back'
```

There's nothing new about this code. For the screen to work, though, some further modifications are necessary.

First of all, we have to add the screen to the screen manager, which is, as you know, the **Game** object:

```
#:kivy 1.11.1
# File name: slugrace.kv

<Game>:
    ...
    GameoverScreen:
        name: 'gameoverscreen'

    # Let's add the Instructions
    # screen to the screen manager.
    InstructionsScreen:
        name: 'instructionsscreen'
```

Next, we have to load the kv file in the **main.py** file:

```
# File name: main.py
...
Builder.load_file('slug.kv')

# Let's load the Instructions kv file.
Builder.load_file('instructions.kv')

class Game(ScreenManager):
    ...
```

Finally, we have to add some code to the Instructions button in the Race screen so that we can switch to the Instructions screen:

```
#:kivy 1.11.1
# File name: race.kv
#:import race race
...
<RaceScreen>:
    ...
            # Buttons
            BoxLayout:
                ...
                RedButton:
                    text: 'Instructions'
                    pos_hint: {'right': 1}

                    # Switch to Instructions screen.
                    on_press: root.manager.current = 'instructionsscreen'

                SoundButton:
                    ...
```

You can now run the app and hit the Instructions button. This will take you to the Instructions screen.

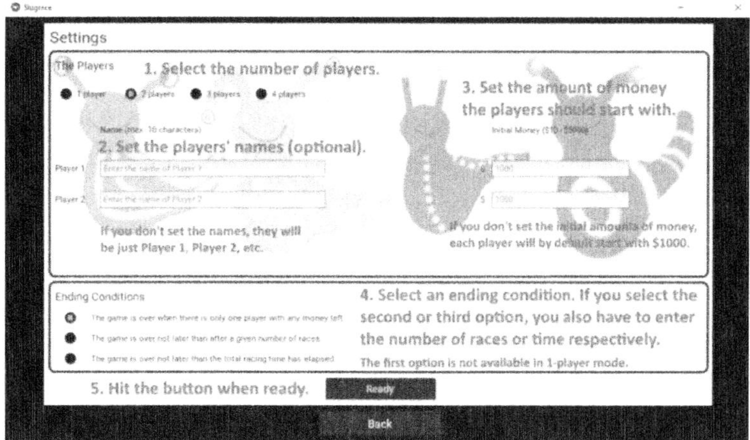


Go ahead and swipe between the screenshots both left and right.

As for now there is no way to go back to the Race screen, though. This is what the Back button is for.

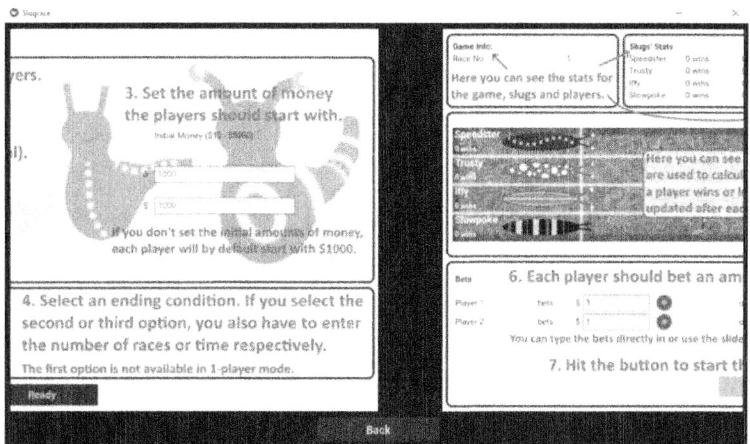


## Navigation Between Instructions Screen and Race Screen

If there is a way to go to the Instructions screen from the Race screen, there must be a way to go back. The Instructions button in the Race screen is enabled all the time, so you can see the instructions whenever you want. Let's implement the Back button's **on_press** event then:

```
#:kivy 1.11.1
# File name: instructions.kv
#:import instructions instructions

<InstructionsScreen>:
    ...
        RedButton:
            text: 'Back'

            # Let's go back to the Race screen.
            on_press: root.manager.current = 'racescreen'
```

# Chapter 123 – Splash Screen

In the previous chapter we implemented the Instructions screen. There's one more thing we want to do. When you launch the app, you go straight to the Settings screen. Let's add a splash image at the beginning so that we first see the image for a couple seconds and only then the Settings screen. The splash image should also contain the title of the game.

There are several ways we could do that. The one we're going to choose is by creating another screen that will only contain the splash image. You won't be able to interact with it and after a while it will switch to the Settings screen.

## Splash Image

Let's start with the image. Here's the image that we are going to use. It contains the title of the game and the silhouettes of the four slugs.

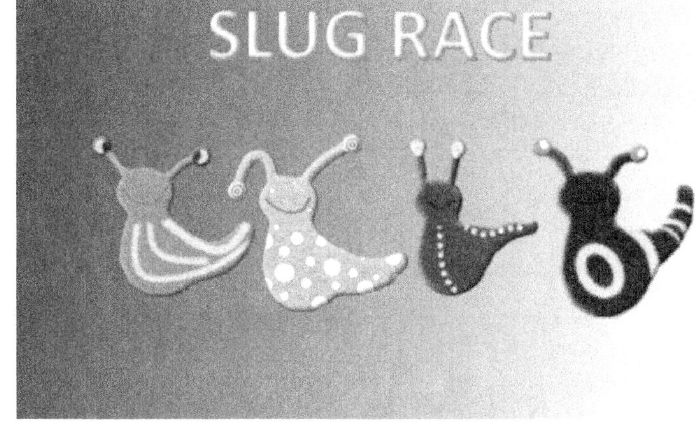


It's a 1200 x 675 image and you already have it in the assets folder.

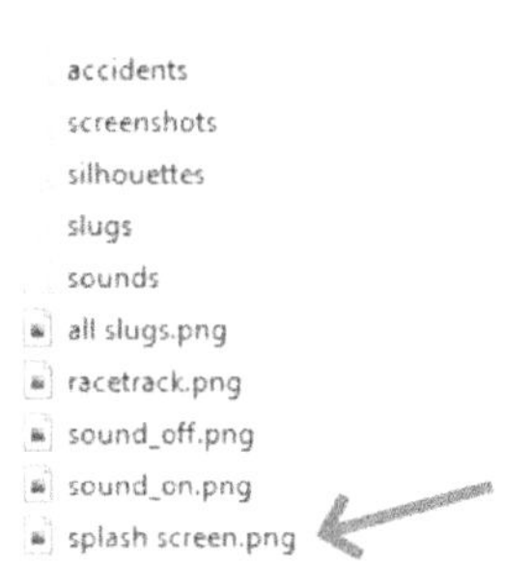


## Splash Screen

The Splash screen is going to be very simple. The root widget is going to be a screen and this is the only widget we need.

Instead of embedding an Image widget in it, we'll add the image to the canvas instructions just like we did with the background image of all the slugs in the Settings screen before.

We already have the **splash.py** and **splash.kv** files in our project folder, but they are empty for now. Open the kv file and type in the following code:

```
#:kivy 1.11.1
# File name: splash.kv
#:import splash splash

<SplashScreen>:
    canvas:
        # The splash screen image will be drawn in the background of the root widget.
        Rectangle:
            pos: self.pos
            size: self.size
            source: 'assets/splash screen.png'

    game: root.manager
```

We will need the **game** property to switch to the Settings screen in the Python file. Speaking of which, here it is:

```
# File name: splash.py

from kivy.uix.screenmanager import Screen, FadeTransition, SlideTransition
from kivy.clock import Clock

class SplashScreen(Screen):
    def on_enter(self):
        # Call the move_on method in 5 seconds.
        Clock.schedule_once(self.move_on, 5)

    def move_on(self, dt):
        # Change transition type to FadeTransition and switch to Settings screen.
        self.game.transition = FadeTransition()
        self.game.current = 'settingsscreen'

    def on_leave(self):
        # On leaving the Splash screen change the transition type back to
        # SlideTransition so that we don't have the FadeTransition everywhere.
        self.game.transition = SlideTransition()
```

Here we're using the **Screen**'s **on_enter** and **on_leave** methods. The former is called when the screen is displayed, the latter when the screen is removed.

In the **on_enter** method we schedule the **move_on** method to be called after 5 seconds.

In the **move_on** method we change the transition type because for this particular transition we want the screen to fade out. We also switch to the Settings screen.

In the **on_leave** method we set the transition type back to **SlideTransition**. Otherwise, the **FadeTransition** would be used everywhere.

Naturally, for this to work, we need to add the Splash screen as the first screen, so the one that is displayed when the application is launched.

Here's the code:

```
#:kivy 1.11.1
# File name: slugrace.kv

<Game>:
    ...
    track: _racescreen.track

    # This should be the first screen,
    # displayed right after the app
    # is launched.
    SplashScreen:
        name: 'splashscreen'

    SettingsScreen:
        ...
```

And we have to load the kv file in the **main.py** file:

```
# File name: main.py
...
Builder.load_file('instructions.kv')

# We have to load the Splash screen.
Builder.load_file('splash.kv')

class Game(ScreenManager):
    ...
```

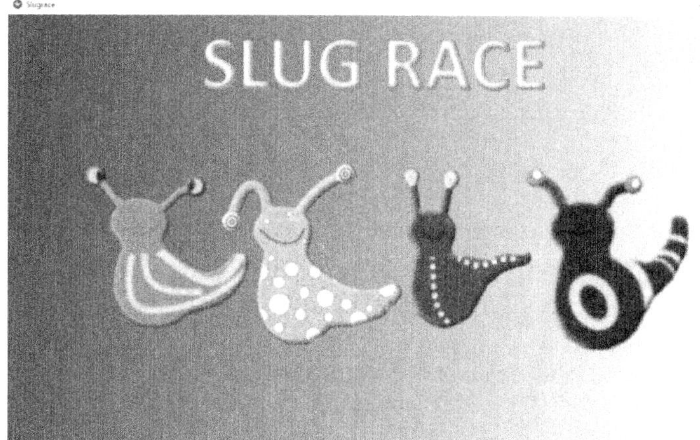


Now when you run the app, you will see the Splash screen for a while, which will then fade out into the Settings screen.

You will also see the Splash screen when you restart the game. In the next chapter we'll polish some configurations.

# Chapter 124 – Final Configuration

In the previous chapter we created the Splash screen. We're almost done with our game. The last thing to do is make the final configurations for our game.

You will find the current configurations in the **main.py** file:

```
# File name: main.py

from kivy.config import Config
Config.set('graphics', 'width', '1200')
Config.set('graphics', 'height', '675')
Config.set('graphics', 'resizable', '0')

import kivy
...
```

As you can see, here we set the width and height of the app window.

We also set **resizable** to **0**, so if you run the app, you can't resize the window. Let's leave these settings as is.

## Window Frame

Now, if you want, you can get rid of the window frame. It contains the title (A) and the two buttons used to minimize the window (B) and close it (C). The maximize button is disabled anyway.



If you don't need these, you can just set the value of **borderless** in the configuration to **1**:

```
# File name: main.py
Config.set('graphics', 'resizable', '0')

# Let's get rid of the window border.
Config.set('graphics', 'borderless', '1')

import kivy
...
```

If you now run the app, you won't see the window frame anymore. It's up to you whether or not to leave the window frame. I will leave mine so that I can easily manipulate the window. If you want to keep the frame too, just set the value of **borderless** to **0** or just remove this piece of code altogether as 0 is the default value. I'm going to do the latter.

So, that's it. In the next chapter we'll deploy our app to Windows.

# Chapter 125 – Deployment

In the previous chapter we wrapped up our Slugrace app. It's time to deploy it. In this course we're only going to deploy it to the Windows platform, for which it was meant. You can package the app for Windows only inside the Windows operating system.

## PyInstaller

First of all, we'll need the PyInstaller, version 3.1 or greater. So, open your terminal and install it using pip:

```
pip install pyinstaller
```

If you already have it, you may want to upgrade it:

```
pip install --upgrade pyinstaller
```

## Getting Ready to Package the App

Now we're ready to package our app. To make things clear, I created a new folder on my desktop, named it **Slugrace** (A) and copied the latest version of the app there, which is **slugrace125**. As you remember, I've been using a naming convention throughout the book according to which the number of the chapter is included in the name of the folder. I renamed the folder **slugraceFinal** (B), which, in my opinion, looks better that **slugrace125**, but this isn't necessary.

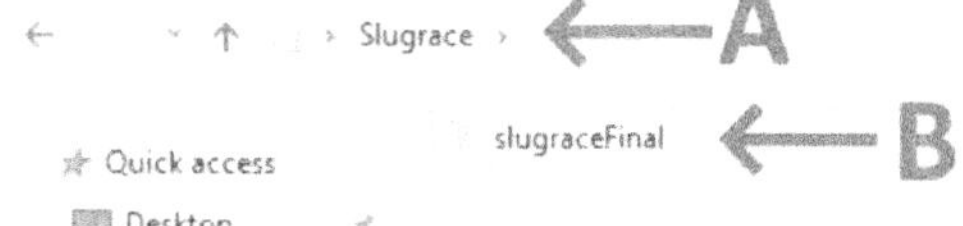


The **slugraceFinal** folder contains all the files, including the assets, that are necessary to run the app.

Let's now create a new subfolder in the same **Slugrace** folder, but outside the **slugraceFinal** folder, and name it **SlugraceApp**. This is the folder where the packaged app will be placed.

# Creating an App Icon

We can use an icon that will represent our app. This should be an ico file. If you don't have an icon, you can create one using the web app ConvertICO. Here's the link: https://www.convertico.com.

I'm going to use the 400 x 400 px **icon.png** image that you can see on the left as the icon.

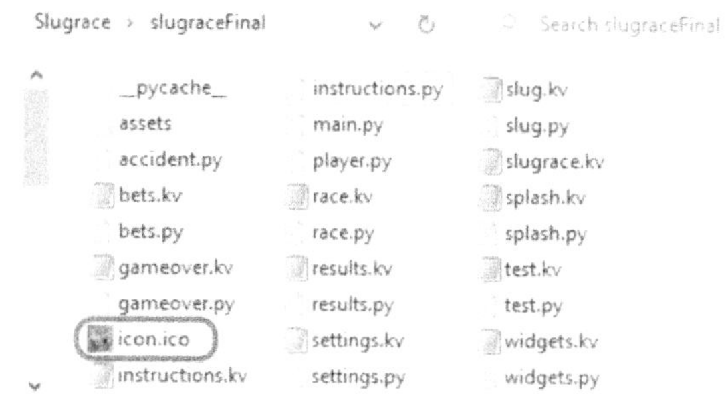


After the conversion we have an **icon.ico** file. Put it inside the **slugraceFinal** folder.

# Packaging the App

Now go to the terminal and navigate to the **SlugraceApp** folder.

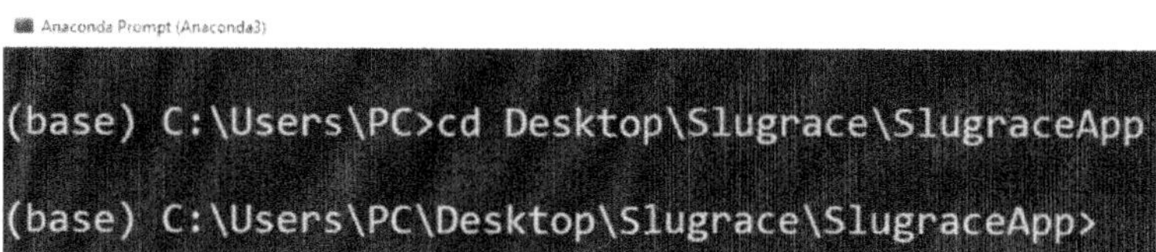


Next, type the following in the terminal:

```
python -m PyInstaller --name slugraceFinal --icon C:\Users\PC\Desktop\Slugrace\slugraceFinal\icon.ico
C:\Users\PC\Desktop\Slugrace\slugraceFinal\main.py
```

Let's break it down so that you can see what it does. Here's the syntax:

```
python -m PyInstaller --name A --icon B C
```

So, **A** is the name of the folder where your files are. **B** is the path to the icon image file and **C** is the path to the **main.py** file. In our example we have:

A = `slugraceFinal`

B = `C:\Users\PC\Desktop\Slugrace\slugraceFinal\icon.ico`

C = `C:\Users\PC\Desktop\Slugrace\slugraceFinal\main.py`

When you execute the command in your terminal, two folders (**build** and **dist**) and a **spec** file will be created in the **SlugraceApp** folder.

› Slugrace › SlugraceApp ›

build

dist

slugraceFinal.spec

Go ahead and open the **slugraceFinal.spec** file in a text editor. It should look something like this:

```
# -*- mode: python ; coding: utf-8 -*-
block_cipher = None

a = Analysis(['C:\\Users\\PC\\Desktop\\Slugrace\\slugraceFinal\\main.py'],
             pathex=[],
             binaries=[],
             datas=[],
             hiddenimports=[],
             hookspath=[],
             hooksconfig={},
             runtime_hooks=[],
             excludes=[],
             win_no_prefer_redirects=False,
             win_private_assemblies=False,
             cipher=block_cipher,
             noarchive=False)
pyz = PYZ(a.pure, a.zipped_data,
             cipher=block_cipher)

exe = EXE(pyz,
          a.scripts,
          [],
          exclude_binaries=True,
          name='slugraceFinal',
          debug=False,
          bootloader_ignore_signals=False,
          strip=False,
          upx=True,
          console=True,
          disable_windowed_traceback=False,
          target_arch=None,
          codesign_identity=None,
          entitlements_file=None ,
icon='C:\\Users\\PC\\Desktop\\Slugrace\\slugraceFinal\\icon.ico')
coll = COLLECT(exe,
               a.binaries,
               a.zipfiles,
               a.datas,
               strip=False,
               upx=True,
               upx_exclude=[],
               name='slugraceFinal')
```

Now, in order to be able to correctly build the **exe** file, we have to add some dependencies hooks to the file. Add the following line of code at the top of the file:

```
# -*- mode: python ; coding: utf-8 -*-
from kivy_deps import sdl2, glew
block_cipher = None
...
```

Next, we have to make some changes in the **COLLECT** part of the code, which is here:

```
# -*- mode: python ; coding: utf-8 -*-
...
coll = COLLECT(exe,
               a.binaries,
               a.zipfiles,
               a.datas,
               strip=False,
               upx=True,
               upx_exclude=[],
               name='slugraceFinal')
```

We must add all the files that should be collected, so all the Python files, kv files, PNG images and so on. As this would be rather tedious, we can use a **Tree** object that will do it for us. The **Tree** object will search all the folder hierarchy and add all the files to the final package.

You should pass the path to the app folder as an argument to the **Tree** object:

```
# -*- mode: python ; coding: utf-8 -*-
...
coll = COLLECT(exe, Tree('C:\\Users\\PC\\Desktop\\Slugrace\\slugraceFinal\\'),
               a.binaries,
               ...
```

Next we need to add the dependencies. We need a **Tree** object for every path of the dependencies, so it's convenient to use a list comprehension. This code should go before the first keyword argument:

```
# -*- mode: python ; coding: utf-8 -*-
...
coll = COLLECT(exe, Tree('C:\\Users\\PC\\Desktop\\Slugrace\\slugraceFinal\\'),
               a.binaries,
               a.zipfiles,
               a.datas,
               *[Tree(p) for p in (sdl2.dep_bins + glew.dep_bins)],
               strip=False,
               ...
```

Save the **spec** file and close it. Now we can build the **spec** file. Just execute the following command in the terminal:

```
python -m PyInstaller slugraceFinal.spec
```

You will get the following warning after a while:

```
WARNING: The output directory "C:\Users\PC\Desktop\Slugrace\SlugraceApp\dist\slugraceFinal" and ALL ITS CONTENTS will be REMOVED! Continue? (y/N)
```

This is fine, so just type **y** and hit Enter. You should soon see a success message.

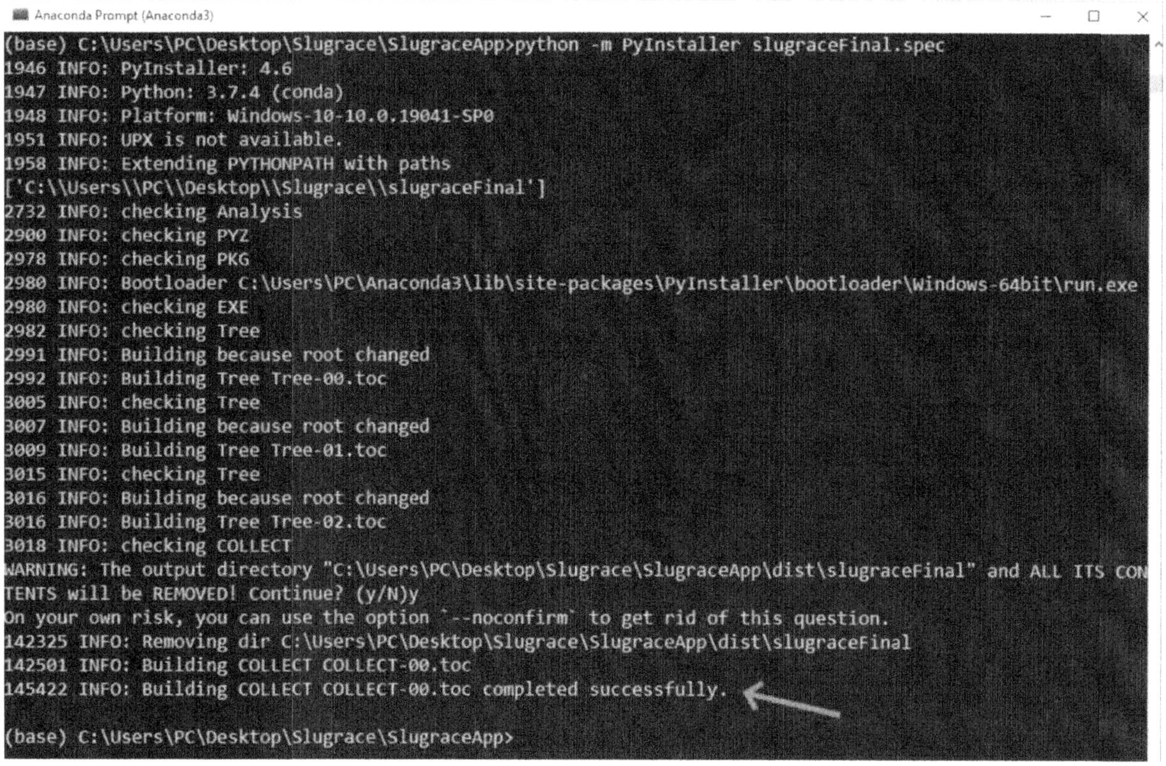

```
(base) C:\Users\PC\Desktop\Slugrace\SlugraceApp>python -m PyInstaller slugraceFinal.spec
1946 INFO: PyInstaller: 4.6
1947 INFO: Python: 3.7.4 (conda)
1948 INFO: Platform: Windows-10-10.0.19041-SP0
1951 INFO: UPX is not available.
1958 INFO: Extending PYTHONPATH with paths
['C:\\Users\\PC\\Desktop\\Slugrace\\slugraceFinal']
2732 INFO: checking Analysis
2900 INFO: checking PYZ
2978 INFO: checking PKG
2980 INFO: Bootloader C:\Users\PC\Anaconda3\lib\site-packages\PyInstaller\bootloader\Windows-64bit\run.exe
2980 INFO: checking EXE
2982 INFO: checking Tree
2991 INFO: Building because root changed
2992 INFO: Building Tree Tree-00.toc
3005 INFO: checking Tree
3007 INFO: Building because root changed
3009 INFO: Building Tree Tree-01.toc
3015 INFO: checking Tree
3016 INFO: Building because root changed
3016 INFO: Building Tree Tree-02.toc
3018 INFO: checking COLLECT
WARNING: The output directory "C:\Users\PC\Desktop\Slugrace\SlugraceApp\dist\slugraceFinal" and ALL ITS CON
TENTS will be REMOVED! Continue? (y/N)y
On your own risk, you can use the option `--noconfirm` to get rid of this question.
142325 INFO: Removing dir C:\Users\PC\Desktop\Slugrace\SlugraceApp\dist\slugraceFinal
142501 INFO: Building COLLECT COLLECT-00.toc
145422 INFO: Building COLLECT COLLECT-00.toc completed successfully.

(base) C:\Users\PC\Desktop\Slugrace\SlugraceApp>
```

Now you will find the **exe** file in the **SlugraceApp -> dist -> slugraceFinal** folder.

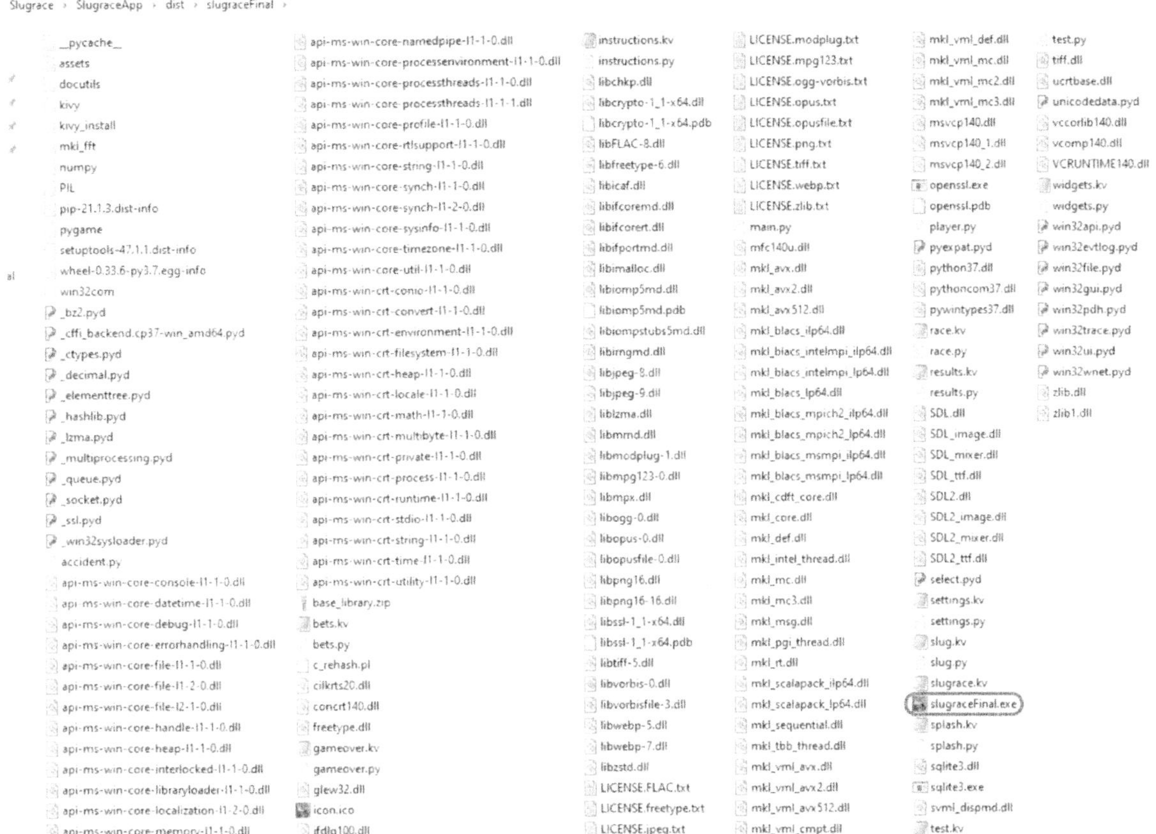

Go ahead and double-click it to run the app. It should work fine. You just finished your first Kivy application. Now have fun playing the game and good luck.

# Chapter 126 – Conclusion

Throughout this book we were building a GUI application from scratch. Each part of the book started with a theoretical introduction of a topic or idea that you then implemented in the project.

We built a fully functional game using many tools that Kivy has to offer. I'm sure you took to the library and are going to use it a lot in your own GUI projects of any kind, not just games. I wish you good luck with it.

# Index

# ABOUT THE AUTHOR

My name is Kamil Pakula. In 2011 I graduated from the Warsaw University of Technology where I had studied computer science. Since then I've worked on many C++, C#, Java and Python programming projects.
I specialize in GUI programming and game development. Now my focus of interest is programming GUI applications with Kivy and programming games using the Panda3D game engine. I also use Python for science and data science and 3D visualizations with Blender.